Achim Bachem · Ulrich Derigs
Michael Jünger · Rainer Schrader (Eds.)

Operations Research '93

Extended Abstracts of the 18th Symposium
on Operations Research
held at the University of Cologne
September 1-3, 1993

With 61 Figures

Physica-Verlag
A Springer-Verlag Company

Professor Dr. Achim Bachem
Mathematisches Institut
Universität zu Köln
Weyertal 80
D-50931 Köln, FRG

Professor Dr. Dr. Ulrich Derigs
Lehrstuhl für Wirtschaftsinformatik
Universität zu Köln
Pohligstraße 1
D-50969 Köln, FRG

Professor Dr. Michael Jünger
Institut für Informatik
Universität zu Köln
Pohligstraße 1
D-50969 Köln, FRG

Professor Dr. Rainer Schrader
Institut für Informatik
Universität zu Köln
Pohligstraße 1
D-50969 Köln, FRG

ISBN 978-3-7908-0794-3 ISBN 978-3-642-46955-8 (eBook)
DOI 10.1007/978-3-642-46955-8

88/2202-5 4 3 2 1 0 - Printed on acid-free paper

Preface

This proceedings volume contains extended abstracts of talks presented at the 18th Symposium on Operations Research held at the University of Cologne, September 1-3, 1993.

The Symposia on Operations Research are the annual meetings of the Gesellschaft für Mathematik, Ökonometrie und Operations Research (GMÖOR), a scientific society providing a link between research and applications in the areas of applied mathematics, economics and operations research. The broad range of interests and scientific activities covered by GMÖOR and its members was demonstrated by about 250 talks presented at the 18th Symposium. As in recent years, emphasis was placed on optimization and stochastics, this year with a special focus on combinatorial optimization and discrete mathematics. We appreciate that with sections on parallel and distributed computing and on scientific computing also new fields could be integrated into the scope of the GMÖOR.

This book contains extended abstracts of most of the papers presented at the conference. Long versions and full papers of the talks are expected to appear elsewhere in refereed periodicals.

The contributions were divided into sixteen sections: (1) Theory of Optimization, (2) Computational Methods of Optimization, (3) Combinatorial Optimization and Discrete Mathematics, (4) Scientific Computing, (5) Decision Theory, (6) Mathematical Economics and Game Theory, (7) Banking, Finance and Insurance, (8) Econometrics, (9) Macroeconomics and Economic Theory, (10) Stochastics, (11) Production and Logistics, (12) System and Control Theory, (13) Routing and Scheduling, (14) Knowledge Based Systems, (15) Information Systems and (16) Parallel and Distributed Computing.

The conference was opened by the Vice Rector of the University, Professor Speth. Further opening addresses were given by the Vice Mayor of Cologne, Mrs. Canisius, and the chairman of the GMÖOR, Professor Bachem. This year, also the GMÖOR Senior Scientist Prize was awarded during the opening ceremony. The awardee was Professor Krelle, one of the founders of the predecessor organizations of GMÖOR.

The scientific program consisted of semi-plenary lectures, invited and contributed talks. In the semi-plenary lectures, twelve leading experts gave a one-hour survey on recent developments and most interesting results in their fields. Egon Balas and Joel L. Horowitz started this series with talks on the prize collection TSP and bootstrap methods in applied econometrics. They were followed by Michael Ball who spoke about the design and analysis of reliable networks and by Denis Boyssou with a talk on preference modelling. Rainer Burkard and Bernard Cornet gave talks on the Monge property and exchange economies. Bezalel Gavish surveyed recent results in the area of telecommunication and Jonathan Borwein discussed trends in convex programming. Jan Karel Lenstra spoke about local search methods in job shop scheduling and Robert A. Becker dealt with Ramsey equilibria. The series of semi-plenary talks was closed by David Shmoys and Luk van Wassenhove with talks on the role of linear programming for solving scheduling problems and on recent results in logistics.

With over 370 participants, about 250 presentations, software demonstrations, press conferences and a lot of other designated actions we were able to show that our field remains active, vital and open for new topics. We would like to thank the authors for presenting their papers and the chairmen of the sections, who helped us in attracting so many distinguished speakers from all over the world. We also thank Dr. Müller of Physica-Verlag for his continuous support and cooperation in publishing this proceedings volume and Mrs. Krupp for her patience and perseverance in preparing its final version.

The conference was generously sponsored by the Ministerium für Wissenschaft und Forschung des Landes Nordrhein-Westfalen and the Deutsche Forschungsgemeinschaft (DFG), which allowed us to support people from abroad and which made it possible that so many authors from Eastern Europe could attend the Symposium. We are deeply indebted to both institutions.

Finally we would like to thank our university and the members of our organizational staff without whose enthusiastic and unselfish support this symposium would not have been possible.

Köln, December 1993

Achim Bachem
Ulrich Derigs
Michael Jünger
Rainer Schrader

Organizing Staff

Jürgen Antes, Oliver Bastert, Petra Bauer, Jens Behrendt, Andre Blumberg, Irina Brüggemann, Norbert Büchen, Nicole Cochems, Jens Cords, Frank Damm, Thorsten Demmer, Martin Diehl, Stefan Ditzen, Kristof Doffing, Klaus Dresbach, Stefan Eßer, Thomas Fabian, Martin Fabini, Sandor Fekete, Stefan Fischer, Gregor Grabenbauer, Conchita Graf, Marc Gürtler, Thomas Harth, Udo Heinrichs, Rainer Heesen, Winfried Hochstättler, Martin Kabath, Jutta Kaibel, Kerstin Kalisch, Antje Kerwer, Thomas Klöcker, Rainer Kowallik, Martina Kramer, Stefan Kromberg, Claudia Krupp, Thomas Lange, Sebastian Leipert, Susanne Lummerich, Martin Malich, Harald Mika, Christoph Moll, Thomas Müller, Sabine Muffert, Petra Mutzel, Stephan Noy, Martin Olschewski, Thomas Pfenning, Christian Platter, Ilona Ratensperger, Hans Rhenius, Marcus Rickert, Lothar Schickhoff, Peter Stangier, Andreas Steffens, Judith Steinmann, Peter Störmer, Stefan Thienel, Georg Wambach, Thomas Wieczorek, Imke Windmöller, Katja Wolf, Michael Wottawa.

List of Sections and Chairpersons

Section 1:	Theory of Optimization	J. Jahn
Section 2:	Computational Methods of Optimization	U. Suhl
Section 3:	Combinatorial Optimization and Discrete Mathematics	H. Hamacher
Section 4:	Scientific Computing	H.G. Bock
Section 5:	Decision Theory	W. Gaul
Section 6:	Mathematical Economics and Game Theory	E. Dierker
Section 7:	Banking, Finance and Insurance	W. Bühler
Section 8:	Econometrics	W. Härdle
Section 9:	Macroeconomics and Economic Theory	A. Karmann/G. Uebe
Section 10:	Stochastics	P. Kall
Section 11:	Production and Logistics	B. Fleischmann
Section 12:	System and Control Theory	R.F. Hartl
Section 13:	Routing and Scheduling	R.H. Möhring
Section 14:	Knowledge Based Systems	M. Richter/W. Mellis
Section 15:	Information Systems	M. Jarke
Section 16:	Parallel and Distributed Computing	B. Monien

Invited Semiplenary Talks

The Prize Collecting TSP: Polyhedral Results and Applications
Egon Balas

The Design and Analysis of Reliable Networks
Michael Ball

Ramsey Equilibria
Robert A. Becker

Convex Programming and Entropy Type Functionals
Jonathan M. Borwein

Preference Modelling: A Survey of Recent Advances
Denis Bouyssou

Monge Properties and their Role in Linear and Discrete Optimization
Rainer E. Burkard

Linear Exchange Economies and Dynamics of Exchange
Bernard Cornet

Telecommunications - Huge Capacity and Mobility, New Modelling Challenges
Bezalel Gavish

The Bootstrap as a Tool of Applied Econometrics
Joel L. Horowitz

Job Shop Scheduling and Local Search
Jan Karel Lenstra

Performance Guarantees for Scheduling Algorithms via Linear Programming
David Shmoys

Third Party Logistics and Reverse Logistics
Luk van Wassenhove

Contents Alphabetically by Authors

The Scheduling Problem in High-Level Synthesis: Extended 0/1 LP Model and Solution Methods
H. Achatz 1

An Application of an Interior Point Method for Problems with Uncertainty
A. Altmann 5

Spline Approximation of the Mathematical Programming Task
T.A. Arakelian, I.E. Danielian 8

Decision Making Concerning Product Line Design Based on Conjoint Analysis
E. Aust, W. Gaul 12

The Simulated Trading Heuristic for Solving Vehicle Routing Problems
A. Bachem, M. Malich 16

Expert System for Handling Dangerous Goods
D. Barbucha, W. Filipowicz, P. Jedrzejowicz 20

Linear 0-1 Inequalities and Extended Clauses
P. Barth 24

A Model- and Method Base System for Discrete Optimization Problems
P. Becker 28

A Simple Model of Political Affairs
H. Behnke 32

Groundstates in Ising Spin Lattices by Optimal Matchings
J. Bendisch, U. Derigs, A. Metz 36

Parallel Tabu Search for Irregular Cutting
J. Blazewicz, J. Kaczmarek, R. Walkowiak 40

Optimization of the Spare Parts Storage for the Power Units Equipments
P.P. Bocanete, L. Neamtu 43

Using Strong Cutting Planes in Constraint Logic Programming
A. Bockmayr 47

Efficient Workload-Balancing on Grids, Hypercubes and Trees
M. Böhm, E. Speckenmeyer 50

Outline of a Theory of Risk Under Partial Probability Information
H.W. Brachinger 52

Enhanced Reliability and the Demand Impact of Jointly Normally Distributed Signals
T. Braun 56

Optimal Control of Investment, Level of Employment and Stockkeeping
M.H. Breitner, B. Koslik, O. von Stryk, H.J. Pesch 60

Computational Complexity in Infinite Combinatorial Structures
V.E. Brimkov, R.P. Barneva ... 64

On the 2D Knapsack Problem with Real Coefficients under the Blum-Shub-Smale Computational Model
V.E. Brimkov, S.S. Danchev ... 68

The Job-Shop Problem and Immediate Selection
P. Brucker, B. Jurisch, A. Krämer ... 72

The Advantage of and System Support for Combined Bankassurance Products
H.U. Buhl, K. Sandbiller, A. Will ... 76

Utilization of Integer Programming for the Optimization of Class Timetables
J.V. Caixeta Filho, J.C.V. de Oliveira ... 80

A Sequential Generalized Quadratic Programming Algorithm Using Exact L_1 Penalty Functions
E. Casas, C. Pola ... 84

Eventman - A Business Event Tracking System
D. Cepar, F. Mulec ... 88

Demographer - A New Version
D. Cepar, E. Ursic, R. Zaloznik ... 92

The 1-Part m-Machine Cyclic Scheduling Problem in Robotic Cells
Y. Crama, J. van de Klundert ... 97

Consistent Restricted Shapley Values
J. Derks, H. Peters ... 100

Model of Optimization of Wood Waste Processing in Slovenia
S. Devjak, M. Tratnik, F. Merzelj ... 103

On Uniformization for Continuous-Time Markov Chains
N.M. van Dijk ... 108

Crew Scheduling for an Urban Transit Company
K. Djellab, G. Fleury, M. Gourgand, A. Quilliot ... 115

Some Remarks on Dependence Among the Consistency Tests
C. Domanski, D. Parys ... 119

Is there Room for Convergence in the E.C. ?
R.C. Douven, J.C. Engwerda ... 122

Reduced Game Properties of Egalitarian Division Rules for Cooperative Games
T. Driessen, Y. Funaki ... 126

Decomposition Algorithms Based on Knowledge Based Models
E. Dudek-Dyduch ... 130

On Some Expert Control
T. Dyduch ... 134

Stochastic Solution of Closed Leontief Input-Output Models
K. Egle, S. Fenyi 138

On Connectivity of Efficient Matroid Bases
M. Ehrgott 142

On Stochastic Vector Optimization Problems with General Stochastic Parameters in the Constraints Using Chance-Constrained Approach
A.-Z. H. El-Banna 145

Existence of an Optimal Sampling Frequency for LQ-Controlled Economic Systems
J. Engwerda 149

Approximating the Core of Euclidean TSP Games
U. Faigle, W. Kern, S. Fekete, W. Hochstättler 153

LP-Relaxations for the Edge-Weighted Subclique Problem
U. Faigle, R. Garbe, K. Heerink, B. Spieker 157

On the Equilibrium Dynamics of a Two-Sector Overlapping-Generations Model with Heterogeneous Capital Goods
K. Farmer 161

New Results on a Newton-Type Method for LCP
A. Fischer 165

Routing in Meshes Using Linear Assignment Problem
D. Fortin, A. Tusera 169

On Stochastic Dynamic Optimization in Discrete Time
K. Frauendorfer 172

A Reexamination of Utility Functions Derived from Demand Functions
S. Fuchs-Seliger 176

Exact Matroid Parity and Polynomial Identities
G. Galbiati, F. Maffioli 180

Structural Exchange Rate Relationships in the Foreign Exchange Markets
T. Gerhards 190

Spectral Moments of Graphs and Some Applications
D. Gernert 194

Polymatroids, Bipartite Graphs and the Cone of Boolean Submodular Functions
E. Girlich, M. Höding 198

Expected Waste for a Bin-Packing Algorithm Using Items that are Exponentially Distributed
W. Goessens 200

Algorithms for the Capacitated-Chinese-Postman-Problem in Mixed Graphs
P. Greistorfer 203

Human Capital and International Capital Flows
T. Gries 207

Computer Simulation for Image Reconstruction from a very Limited Number of Projections
N. Gubareny 211

Capacitated Lot-Sizing with Linked Production Quantities of Adjacent Periods
K. Haase, A. Drexl 212

The Equal Gain Splitting Rule for Sequencing Situations and the General Nucleolus
H. Hamers, I. Curiel, J. Potters, S. Tijs 216

Consequentialism, Non-Archimedean Probabilities, and Lexicographic Expected Utility
P.J. Hammond 219

Boltzmann-Like and Force Models for Behavioral Changes
D. Helbing 251

Value Preserving Intertemporal Portfolio Selection
K. Hellwig, T. Wiesemann 255

Generating Convex Polyominoes at Random
W. Hochstättler, C. Moll, M. Loebl 259

A New Linear Time Algorithm for Computing the Convex Hull of a Simple Polygon
W. Hochstättler, S. Kromberg, C. Moll 263

A Production-Transportation Problem with Stochastic Demand and Concave Production Costs
K. Holmberg, H. Tuy 266

Biconvex Quadratic Maximization Subject to Linear Constraints
S. Indihar 270

K-Fold Complementarity Problem and the Order Complementarity Problem
G. Isac 272

A Fault Diagnosis Information System Using Temporary Relations Between Symptoms
S. Jacobs 276

On the Solution of Linear Vector Optimization Problems in the Image Space
J. Jahn 280

Bifurcated Routing with Transition Costs
A. De Jongh 284

Batch Sequencing with Sequence Dependent Setup-Times and -Costs: A Comparison of Logic and Mixed Integer Programming Approaches
C. Jordan, A. Drexl 286

Collective Selforganized Computer Processes in Digital Network Structures
A. Katkov 287

Linear Dependences of Random Variables and Simulation
I. Kavkler, L. Arih 288

Heterogeneity and Multivariate Logistic Distributions
L. Knüppel 292

Competitive Advantages through Flexible Design of Decentralized Information Systems
H.J. König 296

Long Run Simulation of the German Social Security System
G. Köpp, G. Uebe 300

Modelling Simulated Annealing with History Dependent Cooling Schedules
M. Kolonko 304

Intelligent Multiple Criteria Decision Support
E. Konarzewska Gubala 306

Program Allocation Prediction by Neural Networks
A. Krysiak, F. Seredynski 310

An Assessment of Flexibility Concepts and their Practical Usefulness to Decision Modelling
A. Ku 313

Some Results Concerning the Complexity of Interval Edge-Colorings of Graphs
M. Kubale 317

On the Variance of the Number of Pivot Steps Required by the Simplex Algorithm
K.-H. Küfer 321

Inversion Problems in Pyramidal Classification
R. Lasch 324

A Comparison of Heuristic Methods in Scheduling Flexible Assembly Systems
G. List, A. Nußbaumer 331

Sequential Estimation through Estimating Equations
R. Magiera 335

Inflation and Credit Market Shocks: A Signal Extraction Problem
K. Matthews, C. Ioannidis 339

The General Business Optimization Model
I. Mesko, T. Mesko 343

Time-Series Forecasting by Pattern Imitation - Outliers
B. Motnikar, T. Pisanski 347

Periodic Networks and Railway Scheduling
K. Nachtigall 351

A Note on Two Person Full-Information Best Choice Problems with Imperfect Observation
P. Neumann, Z. Porosinski, K. Szajowski 355

Complexity of Optimization on Vectorweighted Bipartite Graphs
P. Neumayer 359

Shortest Path Problem in Parallel Processors
V. Nica, C. Fabian, Z. Kormos 362

Bicriterial and Restrictive Planar 2-Median Problems
S. Nickel 366

Optimal Solutions to Approximate Integer Programming Problems
O. Oguz 370

Analysis of Panel Data by Means of the Gambler-Mover-Stayer Model
M. Overbeck-Larisch 373

Aggregation & Clustering of Preferences: Opinion vs. Action
J. W. Owsinski 377

Inverse Function Theorems for Nonsmooth Mappings in Banach Spaces
Z. Páles 385

Knowledge Acquisition Through Schedule Decomposition
E. Pesch 389

Multilevel Control of Aquatic Ecosystems in Lake
G. Petriczek, Z. Uhrynowski 393

Short Proofs of Some Theorems in Probability and Statistics Based on a Weak Compactness Argument for Tests
D. Plachky 397

Approximation Algorithms for Multi-Index Transportation Problems with Decomposable Costs
M. Queyranne, F.C.R. Spieksma 401

Multicriterial Optimization in Production and Management
M. Rabinovitch 405

Convexity-Concavity: Matrices and Matrix Games
T. Radzik 408

Generalizations of Erlang Formulae and Some of Their 2nd Order Properties
M.F. Ramalhoto, A. Pacheco 412

An Efficient Approach for Down-and-out-Calls in a Binomial Model
M. Reimer, K. Sandmann 418

Horizontal Stretching in the Mapping of Algorithms onto a Data-driven Array
B. Robic 422

An Optimal Marketing Strategy for Heterogeneous Groups of Porkers
J. Roemen 425

A Discrete Min-Max Algorithm for Inequality Contraints
B. Rustem 428

On Two and Three Person Exchange Games
M. Sakaguchi 430

Binomial Term Structure Models and the Forward Probability Measure: Algorithmic Model Specification and Simulation Results
K. Sandmann, E. Schlögl 434

Monte Carlo Simulations and the Pricing of Options in the Discontinuous Case
K. Schäfer 438

Nine Kinds of Monotone and Generalized Monotone Maps
S. Schaible 442

Equivalence of Cutting Stock Problems
G. Scheithauer 445

Numerical Experiments to the Modified Integer Round-Up Property of the One-dimensional Cutting Stock Problem
G. Scheithauer, J. Terno 449

Optimality for a Generalized Stackelberg Problem
H. Schmidt 452

Non-Simple Polymatroids and Corresponding Submodular Functions
G. Schneidereit, A. Zaporoshetc 455

Evaluation Techniques for Disjunctive Logic Programs
D. Seipel, H. Argenton 458

An Algorithm for Finding the Global Minimum of Multiextremal Lipschitz Functions
Y.D. Sergeyev 463

Comparison of Some Classifiers Based on Parametric or Nonparametric Learning Algorithms
F. Shaghaghi, H. Sadeghi 466

General Structures of Primal Scaling Interior Point Methods
D. X. Shaw 470

Scheduling and Allocation in High-Level Synthesis
J. Silc 474

A Modelling of Energy-Economy Interaction under Uncertainty
N.V. Simakov 478

Value Convergence in Generalized Markov Decision Chains
K. Sladky 480

Managerial Attitudes Toward the Valuation of Information Technology
C.A. Snyder, M.D. Miller 483

Convergences for Sequences of Sets and Linear Mappings
Y. Sonntag, C. Zalinescu 487

Solving the "Business System Planning"-Problem Using Specialized Branch & Bound Algorithms
D.M. Spahni 491

A Knowledge-Based Environment for Decision Support
Z. Strezova 495

Optimal On-Line Detection of Multiple Parameter Changes
K. Szajowski 498

Using Uncertain Information from a Telecommunication Network
E. Szmidt 502

Characterizations of Qualitative Data
U. Tüshaus 506

High Order Iterative Methods for Nonlinear Egvations
O. Vaarmann 510

Computer Simulation of Observation Systems under Attainment of Supersolvability by Mathematical Reduction Method
A. Verlan 512

Risk Based Equity Cost Calculation in Banking
M. Wahrenburg, R. De Mello 513

An Alternative Approach to Robust Design Problems
J. Wallacher 515

Workflow Model Verification of Cooperating Agents in Cardiological Intensive Care Units
G. von der Weiden, P. Szczurko, B. Thull 518

Dually-Weighted Cross Decomposition for the Capacitated Facility Location Problem
P. Wentges 522

Preassignments in Chromatic Scheduling
D. de Werra 526

Reconstruction of Public Finance in a Stochastic Differential Game Framework
D.W.K. Yeung 529

Stochastic Forest Management Based on an Interactive Technique
L. Zadnik Stirn 533

Solving Dial-A-Ride Problems in Practice
D. Zepf 537

Robust Mappings and Optimization
D. Zhuang 539

The Profitability of Insurance
H.-J. Zwiesler 542

Author Index 546

Contents by Sections

Section 1: Theory of Optimization

Computational Complexity in Infinite Combinatorial Structures
V.E. Brimkov, R.P. Barneva 64

Optimization of the Spare Parts Storage for the Power Units Equipments
P.P. Bocanete, L. Neamtu 43

On the 2D Knapsack Problem with Real Coefficients under the Blum-Shub-Smale Computational Model
V.E. Brimkov, S. Danchev 68

New Results on a Newton-Type Method for LCP
A. Fischer 165

K-Fold Complementarity Problem and the Order Complementarity Problem
G. Isac 272

On the Solution of Linear Vector Optimization Problems in the Image Space
J. Jahn 280

On the Variance of the Number of Pivot Steps Required by the Simplex Algorithm
K.-H. Küfer 321

Optimal Solutions to Approximate Integer Programming Problems
O. Oguz 370

Inverse Function Theorems for Nonsmooth Mappings in Banach Spaces
Z. Páles 385

Nine Kinds of Monotone and Generalized Monotone Maps
S. Schaible 442

Optimality for a Generalized Stackelberg Problem
H. Schmidt 452

High Order Iterative Methods for Nonlinear Egvations
O. Vaarmann 510

Convergences for Sequences of Sets and Linear Mappings
Y. Sonntag, C. Zalinescu 487

Robust Mappings and Optimization
D. Zhuang 539

Section 2: Computational Methods of Optimization

An Application of an Interior Point Method for Problems with Uncertainty
A. Altman 5

Spline Approximation of the Mathematical Programming Task
T.A. Arakelian, I. E. Danielian 8

Linear 0-1 Inequalities and Extended Clauses
P. Barth 24

Biconvex Quadratic Maximization Subject to Linear Constraints
S. Indihar 270

A Sequential Generalized Quadratic Programming Algorithm Using Exact L_1 Penalty Functions
E. Casas, C. Pola 84

An Algorithm for Finding the Global Minimum of Multiextremal Lipschitz Functions
Y.D. Sergeyev 463

General Structures of Primal Scaling Interior Point Methods
D.X. Shaw 470

A Production-Transportation Problem with Stochastic Demand and Concave Production Costs
K. Holmberg, H. Tuy 266

Section 3: Combinatorial Optimization and Discrete Mathematics

Utilization of Integer Programming for the Optimization of Class Timetables
J.V. Caixeta Filho, J.C.V. de Oliveira 80

On Connectivity of Efficient Matroid Bases
M. Ehrgott 142

Spectral Moments of Graphs and Some Applications
D. Gernert 194

Expected Waste for a Bin-Packing Algorithm Using Items that are Exponentially Distributed
W. Goessens 200

LP-Relaxations for the Edge-Weighted Subclique Problem
U. Faigle, R. Garbe, K. Heerink, B. Spieker 157

Polymatroids, Bipartite Graphs and the Cone of Boolean Submodular Functions
E. Girlich, M. Höding 198

A New Linear Time Algorithm for Computing the Convex Hull of a Simple Polygon
W. Hochstättler, S. Kromberg, C. Moll 263

Some Results Concerning the Complexity of Interval Edge-Colorings of Graphs
M. Kubale 317

Generating Convex Polyominoes at Random
W. Hochstättler, C. Moll, M. Loebl 259

Exact Matroid Parity and Polynomial Identities
G. Galbiati, F. Maffioli 180

Complexity of Optimization on Vectorweighted Bipartite Graphs
P. Neumayer 359

Bicriterial and Restrictive Planar 2-Median Problems
S. Nickel 366

Equivalence of Cutting Stock Problems
G. Scheithauer 445

Non-Simple Polymatroids and Corresponding Submodular Functions
G. Schneidereit, A. Zaporoshetc 455

Approximation Algorithms for Multi-Index Transportation Problems with Decomposable Costs
M. Queyranne, F.C.R. Spieksma 401

Numerical Experiments to the Modified Integer Round-Up Property of the One-dimensional Cutting Stock Problem
G. Scheithauer, J. Terno 449

Dually-Weighted Cross Decomposition for the Capacitated Facility Location Problem
P. Wentges 522

Preassignments in Chromatic Scheduling
D. de Werra 526

Section 4: Scientific Computing

Groundstates in Ising Spin Lattices by Optimal Matchings
J. Bendisch, U. Derigs, A. Metz 36

Demographer - A New Version
D. Cepar, E. Ursic, R. Zaloznik 92

Computer Simulation for Image Reconstruction from a very Limited Number of Projections
N. Gubareny 211

Computer Simulation of Observation Systems under Attainment of Supersolvability by Mathematical Reduction Method
A. Verlan 512

Section 5: Decision Theory

Decision Making Concerning Product Line Design Based on Conjoint Analysis
E. Aust, W. Gaul 12

Outline of a Theory of Risk Under Partial Probability Information
H.W. Brachinger 52

Intelligent Multiple Criteria Decision Support
E. Konarzewska Gubala 306

An Assessment of Flexibility Concepts and their Practical Usefulness to Decision Modelling
A. Ku 313

Inversion Problems in Pyramidal Classification
R. Lasch 324

Aggregation & Clustering of Preferences: Opinion vs. Action
J.W. Owsinski 377

An Optimal Marketing Strategy for Heterogeneous Groups of Porkers
J. Roemen 425

Value Convergence in Generalized Markov Decision Chains
K. Sladky 480

Characterizations of Qualitative Data
U. Tüshaus 506

Section 6: Mathematical Economics and Game Theory

A Simple Model of Political Affairs
H. Behnke 32

Is there Room for Convergence in the E.C. ?
R. Douven, J. Engwerda 122

Reduced Game Properties of Egalitarian Division Rules for Cooperative Games
T. Driessen, Y. Funaki 126

Consequentialism, Non-Archimedean Probabilities, and Lexicographic Expected Utility
P.J. Hammond 219

Boltzmann-Like and Force Models for Behavioral Changes
D. Helbing 251

Approximating the Core of Euclidean TSP Games
U. Faigle, W. Kern, S. Fekete, W. Hochstättler 153

Consistent Restricted Shapley Values
J. Derks, H. Peters 100

Convexity-Concavity: Matrices and Matrix Games
T. Radzik 408

On Two and Three Person Exchange Games
M. Sakaguchi 430

An Efficient Approach for Down-and-out-Calls in a Binomial Model
M. Reimer, K. Sandmann 418

The Equal Gain Splitting Rule for Sequencing Situations and the General Nucleolus
H. Hamers, I. Curiel, J. Potters, S. Tijs 216

Reconstruction of Public Finance in a Stochastic Differential Game Framework
D.W.K. Yeung 529

Section 7: Banking, Finance and Insurance

Enhanced Reliability and the Demand Impact of Jointly Normally Distributed Signals
T. Braun 56

The Advantage of and System Support for Combined Bankassurance Products
H.U. Buhl, K. Sandbiller, A. Will 76

Structural Exchange Rate Relationships in the Foreign Exchange Markets
T. Gerhards 190

Inflation and Credit Market Shocks: A Signal Extraction Problem
K. Matthews, C. Ioannidis 339

Monte Carlo Simulations and the Pricing of Options in the Discontinuous Case
K. Schäfer 438

Binomial Term Structure Models and the Forward Probability Measure: Algorithmic Model Specification and Simulation Results
K. Sandmann, E. Schlögl 434

Risk Based Equity Cost Calculation in Banking
M. Wahrenburg, R. De Mello 513

Value Preserving Intertemporal Portfolio Selection
K. Hellwig, T. Wiesemann 255

The Profitability of Insurance
H.-J. Zwiesler 542

Section 8: Econometrics

A Modelling of Energy-Economy Interaction under Uncertainty
N.V. Simakov 478

Section 9: Macroeconomics and Economic Theory

On the Equilibrium Dynamics of a Two-Sector Overlapping-Generations Model with Heterogeneous Capital Goods
K. Farmer 161

Human Capital and International Capital Flows
T. Gries 207

Long Run Simulation of the German Social Security System
G. Köpp, G. Uebe 300

Section 10: Stochastics

Stochastic Solution of Closed Leontief Input-Output Models
K. Egle, S. Fenyi 138

On Stochastic Vector Optimization Problems with General Stochastic Parameters in the Constraints Using Chance-Constrained Approach
A.-Z. H. El-Banna 145

On Stochastic Dynamic Optimization in Discrete Time
K. Frauendorfer 172

Linear Dependences of Random Variables and Simulation
I. Kavkler, L. Arih 288

Heterogeneity and Multivariate Logistic Distributions
L. Knüppel 292

Modelling Simulated Annealing with History Dependent Cooling Schedules
M. Kolonko 304

Sequential Estimation through Estimating Equations
R. Magiera 335

Time-Series Forecasting by Pattern Imitation - Outliers
B. Motnikar, T. Pisanski 347

Analysis of Panel Data by Means of the Gambler-Mover-Stayer Model
M. Overbeck-Larisch 373

Some Remarks on Dependence Among the Consistency Tests
C. Domanski, D. Parys 119

Short Proofs of Some Theorems in Probability and Statistics Based on a Weak Compactness Argument for Tests
D. Plachky 397

A Note on Two Person Full-Information Best Choice Problems with Imperfect Observation
P. Neumann, Z. Porosinski, K. Szajowski 355

Generalizations of Erlang Formulae and Some of Their 2nd Order Properties
M.F. Ramalhoto, A. Pacheco 412

Optimal On-Line Detection of Multiple Parameter Changes
K. Szajowski 498

An Alternative Approach to Robust Design Problems
J. Wallacher 515

Stochastic Forest Management Based on an Interactive Technique
L. Zadnik Stirn 533

On Uniformization for Continuous-Time Markov Chains
N.M. van Dijk 108

Section 11: Production and Logistics

Model of Optimization of Wood Waste Processing in Slovenia
S. Devjak, M. Tratnik, F. Merzelj 103

Capacitated Lot-Sizing with Linked Production Quantities of Adjacent Periods
K. Haase, A. Drexl 212

Batch Sequencing with Sequence Dependent Setup-Times and -Costs: A Comparison of Logic and Mixed Integer Programming Approaches
C. Jordan, A. Drexl 286

The General Business Optimization Model
I. Mesko, T. Mesko 343

Multicriterial Optimization in Production and Management
M. Rabinovitch 405

Section 12: System and Control Theory

Optimal Control of Investment, Level of Employment and Stockkeeping
M.H. Breitner, B. Koslik, O. von Stryk, H.J. Pesch 60

On Some Expert Control
T. Dyduch 134

Existence of an Optimal Sampling Frequency for LQ-Controlled Economic Systems
J. Engwerda 149

Knowledge Acquisition Through Schedule Decomposition
E. Pesch 389

A Discrete Min-Max Algorithm for Inequality Contraints
B. Rustem 428

Multilevel Control of Aquatic Ecosystems in Lake
G. Petriczek, Z. Uhrynowski 393

Section 13: Routing and Scheduling

The Scheduling Problem in High-Level Synthesis: Extended 0/1 LP Model and Solution Methods
H. Achatz 1

Expert System for Handling Dangerous Goods
D. Barbucha, W. Filipowicz, P. Jedrzejowicz 20

Bifurcated Routing with Transition Costs
A. De Jongh 284

Crew Scheduling for an Urban Transit Company
K. Djellab, G. Fleury, M. Gourgand, A. Quilliot 115

Routing in Meshes Using Linear Assignment Problem
D. Fortin, A. Tusera 169

Algorithms for the Capacitated-Chinese-Postman-Problem in Mixed Graphs
P. Greistorfer 203

The Job-Shop Problem and Immediate Selection
P. Brucker, B. Jurisch, A. Krämer 72

A Comparison of Heuristic Methods in Scheduling Flexible Assembly Systems
G. List, A. Nußbaumer 331

The Simulated Trading Heuristic for Solving Vehicle Routing Problems
A. Bachem, M. Malich 16

Periodic Networks and Railway Scheduling
K. Nachtigall 351

Scheduling and Allocation in High-Level Synthesis
J. Silc 474

Solving Dial-A-Ride Problems in Practice
D. Zepf 537

The 1-Part m-Machine Cyclic Scheduling Problem in Robotic Cells
Y. Crama, J. van de Klundert 97

Section 14: Knowledge Based Systems

Using Strong Cutting Planes in Constraint Logic Programming
A. Bockmayr 47

Decomposition Algorithms Based on Knowledge Based Models
E. Dudek-Dyduch 130

Comparison of Some Classifiers Based on Parametric or Nonparametric Learning Algorithms
F. Shaghaghi, H. Sadeghi 466

Evaluation Techniques for Disjunctive Logic Programs
D. Seipel, H. Argenton 458

A Knowledge-Based Environment for Decision Support
Z. Strezova 495

Using Uncertain Information from a Telecommunication Network
E. Szmidt 502

Section 15: Information Systems

A Model- and Method Base System for Discrete Optimization Problems
P. Becker 28

A Fault Diagnosis Information System Using Temporary Relations Between Symptoms
S. Jacobs 276

Competitive Advantages through Flexible Design of Decentralized Information Systems
H.J. König 296

Eventman - A Business Event Tracking System
D. Cepar, F. Mulec 88

Managerial Attitudes Toward the Valuation of Information Technology
C.A. Snyder, M.D. Miller 483

Solving the "Business System Planning"-Problem Using Specialized Branch & Bound Algorithms
D.M. Spahni 491

Workflow Model Verification of Cooperating Agents in Cardiological Intensive Care Units
G. von der Weiden, P. Szczurko, B. Thull 518

Section 16: Parallel and Distributed Computing

Parallel Tabu Search for Irregular Cutting
J. Blacewicz, J. Kaczmarek, R. Walkowiak 40

Efficient Workload-Balancing on Grids, Hypercubes and Trees
M. Böhm, E. Speckenmeyer 50

A Reexamination of Utility Functions Derived from Demand Functions
S. Fuchs-Seliger 176

Collective Selforganized Computer Processes in Digital Network Structures
A. Katkov 287

Shortest Path Problem in Parallel Processors
V. Nica, C. Fabian, Z. Kormos 362

Horizontal Stretching in the Mapping of Algorithms onto a Data-driven Array
B. Robic 422

Program Allocation Prediction by Neural Networks
A. Krysiak, F. Seredynski 310

The Scheduling Problem in High-Level Synthesis: Extended 0/1 LP Model and Solution Methods

Hans Achatz
Universität Passau
Lehrstuhl Rechnerstrukturen (Prof. W. Grass)
D-94030 Passau, Germany

As demonstrated by the activity in this area high-level synthesis - often referred to as behavioral synthesis - is becoming an increasingly popular research topic. A main part of high-level synthesis is scheduling where each operation from a data flow graph is assigned to a control step besides several constraints. We have formulated the scheduling problem as a 0/1 LP. For the first time we have extended the model to different execution times and multifunctional function units. To decrease the computation time we have developed a method for constructing new lower bounds with the help of LP (!). The results show that computation time is superior to comparable approaches though our model is able to describe a larger set of problems.

1. INTRODUCTION

High-level synthesis tools transform a behavioral description in terms of algorithm into a RT-level structural description observing several constraints. In order to produce the data path part of a digital processor the following subtasks have to be solved: scheduling, resource allocation and resource binding. This paper is concerned with the scheduling problem as a first step in the sequence of subtasks. Scheduling is the task of assigning operations to control steps optimizing a certain objective function. Several different methods for scheduling have been published. Most of them are heuristics.

We have extended the 0/1 formulation of Hwang (1991) and Lee (1989) combined with ideas from Gebotys (1991) to enlarge the set of scheduling problems that can be described in our model. These 0/1 LP approaches are very promising with respect to the set of allowable constraints like chaining, multicycle operations, functional pipelining, mutually exclusive operations and loop folding. They also reported very short computing times to get optimal solutions for benchmark examples. However there are at least two drawbacks of these approaches, which are very important for practical applications. They cannot correctly handle multifunctional function units with different operator combinations and they require assigning operation time to operation instances in the behavior description. In practice operation time is a feature of the function unit

(FU) or even better of an operation performed by a module. In the second case, different operations of a module for example "add" and "and" may be done in different execution times. The algorithm to be described has been implemented as a part of a high-level synthesis system SUSAN (System for Universal Scheduling and Allocation) (see Achatz (1993b)) transforming VHDL behavioral description into composition of formally verified RT-level modules.

2. 0/1 LP MODEL AND EXTENSIONS

We start with the notation of the 0/1 LP formulations introduced by Lee (1989). A short summary of the abbreviations should make this paper more readable. *As soon as possible* (ASAP) and *as last as possible* (ALAP) times are computed for every operation. For simplicity the 0/1 LP model in this introduction is restricted to operations with one cycle propagation delay and function units with only one operation type executable.

Notation:

n	number of operations in the data flow graph
s	number of control steps
o_i	operation i where $1 \leq i \leq n$
$o_i \rightarrow o_j$	precedence relation between o_i and o_j
S_i	start time (ASAP) of operation o_i
L_i	start time (ALAP) of operation o_i
m	number of different function types
t_k	function unit type number k where $1 \leq k \leq m$
FU_{t_k}	function unit of type t_k
c_{t_k}	cost of a function unit of type t_k
$o_i \in FU_{t_k}$	FU_{t_k} is able to execute operation o_i
$d(t_k(o_i))$	propagation delay of o_i on FU-type t_k

Variables used in the formulation:

M_{t_k}	number of function units of type t_k needed
x_{ij}	variable associated with operation o_i $x_{ij}=1$ if o_i is scheduled in control step j; $x_{ij}=0$ otherwise.

The scheduling problem with *time constraints* can be formulated as minimizing

objective function $$\sum_{k=1}^{m} c_{t_k} \cdot M_{t_k} \qquad (1)$$

subject to

resource constraints $$\sum_{o_i \in FU_{t_k}} x_{ij} - M_{t_k} \leq 0 \qquad \forall\ 1 \leq j \leq s,\ 1 \leq k \leq m \qquad (2)$$

execution constraints $$\sum_{j=S_i}^{L_i} x_{ij} = 1 \qquad \forall\ 1 \leq i \leq n \qquad (3)$$

precedence constraints $$\sum_{j=S_i}^{L_i} j \cdot x_{ij} - \sum_{j=S_k}^{L_k} j \cdot x_{kj} \leq -1 \qquad \forall\ o_i \rightarrow o_k \qquad (4)$$

The 0/1 LP formulation for *resource-constrained* scheduling can be modeled in a similar way. For more details see Achatz (1993a).

In the original model every function unit can only compute one type of operation. If there are multifunctional function units with empty intersection of operation types, then the model is also able to describe the problem. These type of function units are only a problem, if the intersection of the sets of executable operations of two function units is not empty and operation sets of the units are not equal.

For example $FU_{t_1} = \{ +,-,* \}$, $FU_{t_2} = \{ + \}$, $FU_{t_3} = \{ +,- \}$, $M_{t_1} = M_{t_2} = M_{t_3} = 1$

It is easy to see that all the constraints are too strong. Instead, we have to construct the powerset Π of the not disjunctive operation types (of course the empty set can be omitted) and to introduce new constraints . Let Π_k denote the k-th set out of Π and $M(\Pi_k)$ denote the number of function units which are able to execute at least one operation out of Π_k. Building the powerset of the not disjunctive operation types seems to be exhaustive, but in real applications the number of these operation types is usally small. Most of the new constraints are redundant and can be omitted.

$$\sum_{o_i \in \Pi_k} x_{ij} - M(\Pi_k) \leq 0 \qquad \forall\, 1 \leq j \leq s, \forall\, \Pi_k \tag{2'}$$

$M(\{+,-\})$ equals 3, because all three function units FU_{t_1}, FU_{t_2} and FU_{t_3} are able to execute the operation +. If a function unit has no operation types in common with other function units, then the original constraint can be taken. A proof that constraint (2') is necessary and sufficient can be found in Achatz (1993a).

If there are function units with different execution times for one operation type, many problems appear. Most of the scheduling algorithms (even the heuristically ones) have the restriction that every operation type has one unique execution time. Suppose $t_{i_1}, t_{i_2}, \ldots, t_{i_p}$ are functional units with different execution times for the operation o_i. We introduce new 0/1 variables $s_{i_1 j}, s_{i_2 j}, \ldots, s_{i_p j}$ instead of x_{ij}. If $s_{i_k j}$ equals 1, then operation o_i is executed on unit t_{i_k} in control step j.

resource constraints $\displaystyle\sum_{o_i \in FU_{t_k}} x_{ij} - M_{t_k} \leq 0 \qquad \forall\, 1 \leq j \leq s,\ 1 \leq k \leq m$ (2)

resource constraints $\displaystyle\sum_{o_i \in FU_{t_{iq}}} s_{iqj} - M_{t_{iq}} \leq 0 \qquad \forall\, 1 \leq j \leq s,\ 1 \leq k \leq m,\ 1 \leq q \leq p$ (2")

execution constraints $\displaystyle\sum_{j=S_i}^{L_i} \sum_{q=1}^{p} s_{iqj} = 1 \qquad \forall\, 1 \leq i \leq n$ (3')

precedence constraints

$$\sum_{j=S_i}^{L_i} (j + D) \cdot s_{i_1 j} - \sum_{j=S_k}^{L_k} (j + D) \cdot x_{kj} \leq -d(t_{i_1}(o_i)) \qquad \forall\, o_i \rightarrow o_k$$

$$\vdots \qquad\qquad \vdots \qquad\qquad \vdots$$

$$\sum_{j=S_i}^{L_i} (j + D) \cdot s_{i_p j} - \sum_{j=S_k}^{L_k} (j + D) \cdot x_{kj} \leq -d(t_{i_p}(o_i)) \qquad \forall\, o_i \rightarrow o_k \tag{4'}$$

$D = \max \{ d(t_{i_q}(o_i)) : 1 \leq q \leq p \}$, the maximal execution time for operation o_i. A proof can also be found in Achatz (1993a).

3. GENERATING LOWER BOUNDS VIA LP

The efficiency of solving the 0/1 LP is extremely dependent on good bounds. In our approach we generate lower bounds via LP. In all applications so far we did not have problems with computing times. For determination of these lower bounds we have to distinguish between time-constrained and resource-constrained scheduling. In the time-constrained model we assume that the number of csteps is given and that we want to minimize the hardware costs. If we know how many units of one type are needed at least the solution space would be reduced. In order to achieve a lower bound for the number of FU-types needed we construct a new objective function

$$\text{minimize} \qquad c_{t_k} \cdot M_{t_k} \tag{1'}$$

Notice that the objective function only depends on one type of function unit. The problem is solved as LP (!). Therefore computing times are no problem. The solution expresses how many FUs of Type t_k are needed at least if all other FU-types do not have any costs. The optimal value of the cost function can be rounded up because the LP solution is always a lower bound for the 0/1 LP solution. This estimation can be made for every FU-type. So we have generated lower bounds for every FU-type and therefore reduced the solution space drastically. For our experiments most of the lower bounds were also the optimal values. If there are multi-functional FUs with non disjunctive operation type sets the bounds are of course weaker, because one FU-type can replace the other. In a similar way we can compute new bounds for resource-constrained scheduling.

4. References

Achatz H. (1993a) Extended 0/1 LP Model for the Scheduling Problem in High-Level Synthesis, EURODAC, Hamburg, to appear.

Achatz H. (1993b) SUSAN: System for Universal Scheduling and Allocation, SASIMI Synthesis And SImulation Meeting and International Interchange, NARA, Japan, to appear.

Gebotys C. H., Elmasry M. I. (1991) Simultaneous Scheduling and Allocation for Cost Constrained Optimal Architectural Synthesis, 28th ACM/IEEE DAC, San Francisco, pp. 2 - 7.

Hwang C.-T., Lee J.-H., Hsu Y.-C. (1991) A Formal Approach to the Scheduling Problem in High Level Synthesis, IEEE Transactions on Computer-Aided Design **10** (4), pp. 464 - 475.

Lee J.-H., Hsu Y.-C., Lin Y.-L. (1989) A New Integer Linear Programming Formulation for the Scheduling Problem in Data Path Synthesis, ICCAD, pp. 20 - 23.

AN APPLICATION OF AN INTERIOR POINT METHOD FOR PROBLEMS WITH UNCERTAINTY

Anna Altman *
Systems Research Institute,
Polish Academy of Sciences
ul. Newelska 6, 01-447 Warszawa,
Poland

Interior point methods (IPM) were first proposed for linear programming (LP) problems. Since 1984, when Karmarkar published his famous paper (Karmarkar (1984)), IPM were rapidly developed and improved. It is now widely accepted that the primal-dual logarithmic barrier method is the most efficient IPM. The idea of IPM was not restricted to linear programming alone. These methods quickly spread to quadratic, nonlinear and integer programming. The developments in quadratic programming (QP) are closely parallel to those in LP. While theoretical worst-case behaviour for LP and QP are the same, QP problems are harder to solve in practice. The derivation of the higher order primal-dual method for QP is analogous to the derivation for the linear case presented in Mehrotra (1991) and implemented by Altman and Gondzio (1992).

Let us consider the QP problem

$$\begin{aligned} \text{minimize } & c^T x + \frac{1}{2} x^T Q x, \\ \text{subject to } & Ax = b, \\ & x + s = u, \\ & x, s \geq 0, \end{aligned} \tag{1}$$

where $c, x, s, u \in \mathcal{R}^n, b \in \mathcal{R}^m$ and $A \in \mathcal{R}^{m*n}$ is assumed to have a full row rank. The dual of (1) is given by

$$\begin{aligned} \text{maximize } & b^T y - u^T w - \frac{1}{2} x^T Q x, \\ \text{subject to } & A^T y + z - w - Qx = c, \\ & x, z, w \geq 0, \end{aligned} \tag{2}$$

where $y \in \mathcal{R}^m$ and $x, z, w \in \mathcal{R}^n$.

Having incorporated inequality-type constraints in a logarithmic term added to the objective function, we obtain the first order necessary conditions for the optimal solution of (1) and (2):

$$Ax = b, \tag{3}$$

*This work was done during the author's stay at the International Institute for Applied Systems Analysis, Laxenburg, Austria

$$x + s = u, \tag{4}$$
$$A^T y + z - w - Qx = c, \tag{5}$$
$$XZe = \mu e, \tag{6}$$
$$SWe = \mu e, \tag{7}$$
$$x, s, z, w > 0,$$

where X, S, Z and W are diagonal matrices with the elements x_j, s_j, z_j and w_j, respectively and $e \in \mathcal{R}^n$ is a vector of ones. There is only one difference between necessary conditions for LP and QP, namely the term Qx in (5).

The basic primal-dual algorithm applies one iteration of Newton's method to find an approximate solution to (3-7) for a current (fixed) parameter μ and terminates when the duality gap is reduced to a predetermined tolerance. It may be viewed as an optimal trajectory from a given starting point to the optimum of (1) and (2). In the Mehrotra method a higher order Taylor approximation of the optimal trajectory is computed. Knowing Taylor terms we can compute the search directions in the primal and dual spaces.

Undoubtedly, the main computational effort in any IPM implementation is expanded in solving for the direction. To obtain the direction we solve the normal equation with matrix $A^T \Theta A$. The difference between linear case and quadratic one is in the matrix Θ, for the quadratic case

$$\Theta = (Q + X^{-1}Z + S^{-1}W)^{-1}. \tag{8}$$

For a linear case $Q = 0$ and other matrices in (8) are diagonal, and computing Θ is very simple. In many practical problems the matrix Q is either diagonal or we can reformulate the problem (1) to obtain a diagonal quadratic matrix, cf. Vanderbei and Carpenter (1993). Therefore computing Θ for separable QP is as easy as for a LP.

The method described above was used for finding cost-effective environmental policy under uncertainty. We considered the problem of reduction of SO_2 emissions in Europe, cf. Amann et al. (1993). We minimize European-wide emission control costs subject to the condition that grid-specific SO_2 deposition targets are attained. The costs of emission control are uncertain. There are many possible scenarios of energy production, consumption, fuel characteristics and installed emission control measures. Having scenarios and their probabilities we construct mean-variance model. In such a method we minimize a weighted sum of expected value of total costs and their variance.

Finally we construct the stochastic optimization problem:

$$\min E\{c(x)\} + \alpha V\{c(x)\} \tag{9}$$
$$\text{s. t. } Tx \leq b,$$
$$l \leq x \leq u,$$

where $c(x)$ is a random function and costs are values of this function, x denotes emissions to be reduced, b is a vector of maximal grid depositions, and depositions y are linear function of emissions ($y = Tx$).

The costs for each country are piecewise linear convex functions. Since variance is a quadratic function, the objective function is quadratic too. The problem is reformulated in such a way that the quadratic part of the objective is separable. All constraints are linear.

To make the model more useful for decision makers we solve the model with different weighting factors for the variance. It enables us to control the value of variance at the solution found; in other words, uncertainty or risk. The method was successfully used at

IIASA in Transboundary Air Pollution Project. We hope that these ideas can be exploited for a wider class of other stochastic optimization problems.

References

[1] N. Karmarkar. A new polynomial-time algorithm for linear programming. *Combinatorica*, 4:373–395, 1984.

[2] S. Mehrotra. Higher order methods and their performance. Technical Report 90-16R1, Department of Industrial Engineering and Management Sciences, Northwestern University, Evanston, 1991.

[3] A. Altman and J. Gondzio. An efficient implementation of a higher order primal-dual interior point method for large sparse linear programs. To appear in *Archiv of Control Sciences*, 1993.

[4] A. Altman and J. Gondzio. HOPDM - a higher order primal-dual method for large scale linear programming. *European J. Oper. Res.*, 66(1):159–160, 1993.

[5] M. Amann, G. Klaassen, and W. Schöpp. Closing the gap between the 1990 deposition and the critical sulfur deposition values. Technical report, International Institute for Applied Systems Analysis, 2361 Laxenburg, Austria, 1993.

[6] R. J. Vanderbei and T. J. Carpenter. Symmetric indefinite systems for interior point methods. *Math. Programming*, 58:1–32, 1993.

Spline Approximation of the Mathematical Programming Task

Tigran A. Arakelian, Irina E. Danielian.
Yerevan State University, Faculty of Mathematics,
1 Alek Manoukian Str.,
375049 Yerevan,
Armenia

This paper is a continuation and development of the methods, considered in [1] and devoted to solving of the mathematical programming task using methods of spline approximation.

TASK: Minimize

(1). $\overline{\mathrm{f}}(x)$

function, when

(2). $\overline{\mathrm{g}_s}(x) \leq 0,\ s = 1,\dots,t$

(3). $x_i \geq 0,\ i = 1,\dots,n$

with $\overline{\mathrm{f}}(x)$, $\overline{\mathrm{g}_s}(x)$ convex functions, which meet the conditions, noted in [2] (Chapter II, Paragraph 5), of existence of approximating splines.

Regard

$$x\|x_i = (x_1,\dots x_{i-1}, x_{i+1},\dots,x_n)$$

$$\mathrm{p}(x) = a_0 + \sum_{i\neq l} a_i x_i + a_l x_l + \sum_{j=1}^{n} a_{lj} x_l x_j + \sum_{i=1}^{n} a_{il} x_i x_l + \sum_{i,j\neq l} a_{ij} x_i x_j$$

$$\mathrm{p_j}(x\|x_i) = a_l^j + \sum_{l\neq k\neq i} a_{lk}^j x_k + 2a_{ll}^j x_l + \sum_{l\neq k\neq i} a_{kl}^j x_k$$

$$\mathrm{p}^s(x) = b_0^s + \sum_{i\neq l} a_i^s x_i + a_l^s x_l + \sum_{j=1}^{n} a_{li}^s x_l x_j + \sum_{i=1}^{n} a_{il}^s x_i x_l + \sum_{i,j\neq l} a_{ij}^s x_i x_j$$

$$\mathrm{p_j^s}(x\|x_i) = b_l^{js} + \sum_{l\neq k} b_{lk}^{js} x_k + 2b_{ll}^{js} x_l + \sum_{l\neq k\neq i} b_{kl}^{js} x_k$$

then,

(4). $$\frac{\partial \mathrm{p}(x)}{\partial x_l} = a_l + \sum_{j=1}^{n} a_{lj} x_j + \sum_{i=1}^{n} a_{il} x_i$$

(5). $$\frac{\partial \mathrm{p}_j(x \| x_i)}{\partial x_l} = 2a_{ll}^{j}$$

(6). $$\frac{\partial \mathrm{p}^s(x)}{\partial x_l} = b_l^s + \sum_{j=1}^{n} b_{lj}^s x_j + \sum_{i=1}^{n} b_{il}^s x_i$$

(7). $$\frac{\partial \mathrm{p}_j^s(x \| x_i)}{\partial x_l} = 2b_{ll}^{js}$$

(8). $$\varphi(x_l) = \frac{\partial}{\partial x_l}(x_l - u_{lj})_+^2 = \begin{cases} 2(x_l - u_{lj}), & \text{if } x_l > u_{lj} \\ 0, & \text{if } x_l \le u_{lj} \end{cases}$$

with $(x-t)_+^m = [\max\ (0, x-t)]^m$.

Let the set $\prod_{i=1}^{n}[a_i, b_i]$ corresponds to the system of inequalities (2) [3] (Chapter II, paragraph 11.3).

Consider the parabolic spline-approximation of the functions $\overline{\mathrm{f}}(x)$ and $\overline{\mathrm{g}}_s(x),\ s = 1, \ldots, t$:

$$\mathrm{f}(x) = \mathrm{p}(x) + \sum_{i=1}^{n} \sum_{j=1}^{m_i} \mathrm{p}_j(x \| x_i)(x_i - u_{ij})_+^2 + \sum_{i_1 \ldots i_n} b_{i_1 \ldots i_n} (x_1 - u_{1,i_1})_+^2 \ldots (x_l - u_{l,i_l})_+^2 \ldots (x_n - u_{n,i_n})_+^2$$

$$\mathrm{g}_s(x) = \mathrm{p}^s(x) + \sum_{i=1}^{n} \sum_{j=1}^{m_i} \mathrm{p}_j^s(x \| x_i)(x_i - u_{ij})_+^2 + \sum_{i_1 \ldots i_n} b_{i_1 \ldots i_n} (x_1 - u_{1,i_1})_+^2 \ldots (x_l - u_{l,i_l})_+^2 \ldots (x_n - u_{n,i_n})_+^2$$

$s = 1, 2, \ldots, t$

Then the task (1)-(3) can be approximated by the
TASK L: minimize

(9). $\mathrm{f}(x)$

when

(10). $\mathrm{g}_s(x) \le 0,\ s = 1, 2, \ldots, t$

(11). $x_i \ge 0,\ i = 1, 2, \ldots, n$

The Lagrange's function of the TASK L have the following form:

$$\mathrm{L}(x, \lambda) = \mathrm{f}(x) + \sum_{s=1}^{t} \lambda_s \mathrm{g}_s(x)$$

So, we get

$$\frac{\partial f}{\partial x_l} = a + \sum_{j=1}^{n} a_{lj} x_j + \sum_{i=1}^{n} a_{il} x_i + 2\sum_{i=1}^{n}\sum_{j=1}^{m} a_{il}^{j} (x_i - u_{ij})_+^2 +$$
$$+ \sum_{j=1}^{m} p_j (x \| x_l) \varphi(x_l) + \sum_{i_1 \ldots i_n} b_{i_1 \ldots i_n} (x_1 - u_{1,i_1})_+^2 \ldots \varphi(x_l) \ldots (x_n - u_{n,i_n})_+^2$$

$$\frac{\partial g_s(x)}{\partial x_l} = b_l^s + \sum_{j=1}^{n} b_{lj}^s x_j + \sum_{i=1}^{n} b_{il}^s x_i + 2\sum_{i=1}^{n}\sum_{j=1}^{m} b_{il}^{j} (x_i - u_{ij})_+^2 +$$
$$+ \sum_{j=1}^{m} p_j^s (x \| x_l) \varphi(x_l) + \sum_{i_1 \ldots i_n} b_{i_1 \ldots i_n}^s (x_1 - u_{1,i_1})_+^2 \ldots \varphi(x_l) \ldots (x_n - u_{n,i_n})_+^2$$

The algorithm for solving (1)-(3) task.

STEP 1. Define the $[a_i^1, b_i^1]$ segments for every x_i, $i = 1,2,\ldots,n$, which correspond to the system of inequalities (3).

STEP 2. We define the system of nodes for $[a_i^1, b_i^1]$, $i = 1,2,\ldots,n$

$$\{u_{i,k}\},\ k = 1,2,\ldots,m_i,\ i = 1,2,\ldots,n$$

with

$$u_{i,k} < u_{i,k+1},\ u_{i,0} = a_i,\ u_{i,m-1} = b_i,\ k = 0,1,\ldots,m-1.$$

STEP 3. Define the spline approximation (9)-(11) of the function (1)-(3).
STEP 4. Solve the following inequality:

(12). $\dfrac{\partial f}{\partial x_l} + \sum_{s=1}^{n} \lambda_s \dfrac{\partial g_s(x)}{\partial x_l} = 0,\ l = 1,2,\ldots,n$

(13). $\lambda_s \geq 0;\ g_s(x) \leq 0$

(14). $\lambda_s g_s(x) = 0$

STEP 5. Let $x^{(1)}$ is a solution of the task (12)-(14).
STEP 6. Define

$$a_i^2 = a_i^1 + \frac{x_i^{(1)} - a_i^1}{2},\ b_i^2 = b_i^1 - \frac{b_i^1 - x_i^{(1)}}{2},\ i = 1,2,\ldots,n$$

Then return to STEP 2 and exchange $[a_i^1, b_i^1]$ to $[a_i^2, b_i^2]$, $i = 1,2,\ldots,n$

Let we have a solution x^k on k-th step. If $\bar{f}(x^k) < \bar{f}(x^{k-1})$ then we define

$$a_i^{k+1} = a_i^k + \frac{x_i^k - a_i^k}{2};\ b_i^{k+1} = b_i^k - \frac{b_i^k - x_i^k}{2},\ i = 1,2,\dots,n$$

and return to STEP 2, exchanging $[a_i^k, b_i^k]$ to $[a_i^{k+1}, b_i^{k+1}]$.
If $\bar{f}(x^k) > \bar{f}(x^{k-1})$, then define

$$a_i^{k+1} = a_i^{k-1} + \frac{x_i^{k-1} - a_i^{k-1}}{2};\ b_i^{k+1} = b_i^k - \frac{b_i^{k-1} - x_i^{k-1}}{2},\ i = 1,2,\dots,n$$

and return to STEP 2, exchanging $[a_i^{k-1}, b_i^{k-1}]$ to $[a_i^{k+1}, b_i^{k+1}]$.
The process of solving of the task (1)-(3) will be continued until the conditions

$$\left\| x^{r+1} - x^r \right\| < \varepsilon;\ \left| \bar{f}(x^{r+1}) - \bar{f}(x^r) \right| < \varepsilon$$

are satisfied on step *r*.
Then we select the vector $x^* = x^{r+1}$ as a solution of the task (1)-(3).

REFERENCES

1. T.Arakelian, *"About the Method of Minimization of a Function"*. Proceedings of the 17th Symposium on Operations Research, Physica Verlag 1992.
2. S.B.Stechkin, Yu.N.Subbotin, *"Splainy v vichislitelnoy matematike"*, Moscow 1986.
3. M.S.Basaraa, C.M.Shetty, *"Non-Linear Programming Theory and Algorithms"*. N.Y., Chichester, Brisbane, Toronto 1979.

Decision Making Concerning Product Line Design Based on Conjoint Analysis

Eberhard Aust, Wolfgang Gaul
Institut für Entscheidungstheorie
und Unternehmensforschung
Universität Karlsruhe
D-76128 Karlsruhe

Introduction

Conjoint analysis has many applications (Cattin, Wittink (1982), Wittink, Cattin (1989)). Frequently, it is used in the context of new product design (Mahajan, Wind (1992)). Practical applications involve the estimation of the importance of selected product attributes (Gaul, Lutz, Aust (1993)) or the assessment of new product candidates where part worth estimates on an individual level and profiles of established products to model competition in the marketplace are taken as inputs (Page, Rosenbaum (1987)).
Recently, analytic approaches within the framework of (mixed) integer programming have been formulated (Dobson, Kalish (1993)) where in the buyers' problem, the share of choices problem, or the seller's problem the objective is to maximize welfare, market share, or profit with respect to product line decisions. Sequential and simultaneous approaches can be distinguished dependent on whether the new products of the line are determined one after the other or at the same time. All simultaneous approaches so far rely on the first choice assumption which postulates that buyers deterministically choose the product with the highest idiosynchratic, i.e. individual, utility. However, stringently deterministic buying behaviour is very seldom in the marketplace and it should also be remembered that product utilities obtained by conjoint analysis will always contain a certain amount of estimation and measurement error (Elrod, Kumar (1989)). Thus, the output of approaches to product line design using the first choice assumption, where new products only need an infinitely small increase in utility over the existing products to draw their complete market shares, should be regarded with due caution. Alternatives to the first choice rule that have proven to be more successful in aggregate market share prediction are, e.g., the LOGIT-model and a generalized formulation of the BTL-model used by Pessemier et al. (1971). The latter features an additional parameter α, exponent to all product utilities, that allows to model anything between equal choice probabilities for all products ($\alpha = 0$) and first choice ($\alpha = \infty$). Hence, given idiosynchratic product utilities for a representative sample of the buyers, the choice model may be calibrated to reproduce as closely as possible given status quo market shares (Silk, Urban (1978)). The generalized BTL-model has been applied successfully in SIMOPT, the in many respects most elaborate conjoint analysis based approach to sequential product line optimization to date (Green, Krieger (1991, 1992)). Concerning model specifications and data input, PROLIN, a new simultaneous approach for probabilistic line optimization – the core of which is introduced in the following – could be seen as natural extension of SIMOPT to the case of multiple products with additional consideration of fixed cost.

Model Formulation

We will focus on the seller's problem as the buyers' and share of choices problems are shown to be special cases of this more general formulation. Denote by $i = 1, \ldots, I$ the buyers under consideration, $k = 1, \ldots, K$ the attributes, and $j = 1, \ldots, J_k$ the attribute levels. Let $l = 1, \ldots, F + E + R$ describe the products where the first F indices are reserved for competitors' products, the ensuing E indices for own products, both already established in the market, and the final indices for the at

most R new products to be introduced. Basic model inputs are idiosynchratic part worths u_{ijk} and idiosynchratic marginal returns d_{ijk}. Denote by w_i idiosynchratic purchasing rates or alternative weights as output from segmentation approaches such as SEQUE (Green, Krieger (1991)). Let f_{jk} be the part fixed cost incurred if a new product with the corresponding attribute level is introduced. (In practice, fixed cost will usually be estimated directly even though a conjoint approach assessing a fractionated factorial orthogonal design on a dollar metric scale is also feasible.) Denote by x_{jkl}, $j = 1,\ldots,J_k$, $k = 1,\ldots,K$, $l = 1,\ldots,F+E$, binary constants describing whether an already established product l features level j in attribute k ($x_{jkl} = 1$) or not ($x_{jkl} = 0$). For x_{jkl}, $j = 1,\ldots,J_k$, $k = 1,\ldots,K$, $l = F+E+1,\ldots,F+E+R$, the x_{jkl} values constitute binary optimization variables similarly defined as the binary constants of the established products. Here, $x_{jkl} = 0$, $\forall j,k$, and $l > F+E$, indicates that product l will not be introduced. The objective of the following SP (seller's problem) formulation with probabilistic choice assumption is to maximize the sum of marginal returns weighted with purchase rates and choice probabilities where summation is taken over buyers, the own products (established ones as well as those to be introduced) of the product line under consideration, attributes and their attribute levels. For new products, additionally, fixed cost for introduction into the market have to be substracted.
With the notations z for the objective function and $X = (x_{jkl})$ for a feasible solution of SP (in terms of the set of optimization variables mentioned before) a formulation of the underlying problem can be given in the following way:

$$\text{max: } z(X) = \sum_{k=1}^{K}\sum_{j=1}^{J_k}\Big(\sum_{l=F+E+1}^{F+E+R} x_{jkl}\Big(\Big(\sum_{i=1}^{I} p_{il}w_i d_{ijk}\Big) - f_{jk}\Big) + \sum_{l=F+1}^{F+E} x_{jkl}\Big(\sum_{i=1}^{I} p_{il}w_i d_{ijk}\Big)\Big) \tag{SP}$$

$$p_{il'} = \frac{\Big(\sum_{k=1}^{K}\sum_{j=1}^{J_k} x_{jkl'}u_{ijk}\Big)^{\alpha}}{\sum_{l=1}^{F+E+R}\Big(\sum_{k=1}^{K}\sum_{j=1}^{J_k} x_{jkl}u_{ijk}\Big)^{\alpha}} \qquad \forall i,l' \quad (1)$$

$$\sum_{j=1}^{J_k} x_{jkl} \leq 1 \qquad \forall k, \text{ and } l = F+E+1,\ldots,F+E+R \quad (2)$$

$$\sum_{j=1}^{J_k} x_{jkl} = \sum_{j=1}^{J_{k+1}} x_{j(k+1)l} \qquad k = 1,\ldots,K-1,\ l = F+E+1,\ldots,F+E+R \quad (3)$$

$$x_{jkl} \in \{0,1\} \qquad \forall j,k, \text{ and } l = F+E+1,\ldots,F+E+R \quad (4)$$

Constraint (1) incorporates the generalized BTL-model. Constraint (2) ensures that for all attributes at most one level is selected. Products offered are completely specified with one level for every attribute by constraint (3). Constraint (4) restricts the optimization variables to binary values.

Note, that the buyers' problem can be mimiced by setting $d_{ijk} := u_{ijk}, \forall i,j,k$, and $f_{jk} := 0$, $\forall j,k$, whereas the share of choices problem can be achieved by $d_{ijk} := \frac{1}{\sum_{i=1}^{I} w_i K}$, $\forall i,j,k$, and $f_{jk} := 0$, $\forall j,k$.

Solution

Due to the discrete nature of the underlying optimization smaller problems with no more than 3 new products described by approximately 5 attributes with an average of 3 attribute levels and up to 400 buyers can be solved within hours on a 486PC. For larger problems or sensitivity

analysis one can use heuristics. In a large scale Monte Carlo Simulation 18 alternative heuristics applied to a total of 480 simulated markets were compared. A modified version of the Kohli, Sukumar (1990) dynamic programming heuristic (with adapted column selection criteria, a new scheme for building partial product profiles, and an additional interchange phase) and a so-called Advanced Greedy Heuristic (AGH) – introduced in the following – outperformed the remaining heuristics. The basic idea of the AGH is that whenever complete enumeration is infeasible the largest possible fraction of promising solutions should be investigated to obtain good results. In contrast to the DESOP/LINEOP methodology (Green, Krieger (1985, 1987a, 1987b)) the AGH is a one step procedure that operates directly on the complete set of products without an intermediate product candidate subset constructed only on the basis of buyers' utilities. A feasible initial starting solution is the empty new product set. In each of the following $R-1$ steps that product is selected from the set of the N best products (Best in the sense of maximal increase in the objective function z if taken on its own.) to enter the solution that – combined with an additional product – leads to the maximal increase in the objective function. For product $F+E+R$ the additional product already determined for the selection of product $F+E+R-1$ is chosen. The current solution can be enhanced in an interchange phase.
We need some additional notation for a formal description of the AGH: For X as feasible solution of SP let $\mathcal{X}(X,l') = (\chi_{jkl})$ denote a set of solutions derived from X by

$$\chi_{jkl} = x_{jkl} \qquad \forall j,k, \text{ and } l \neq l' \qquad (5)$$

$$\chi_{jkl} \in \{0,1\} \qquad \forall j,k, \text{ and } l = l' \qquad (6)$$

Due to the additional constraints (5), (6) a restricted seller's problem, denoted by SP(X,l'), can be created in which optimization is only possible with respect to the l'-th product. Let $\mathcal{X}(X,l',n)$ be the n-best solution of SP(X,l') and $N \in \mathcal{N}$ a large number. The AGH uses the following phases:

Initialization :
$X = (0)$, i.e., $x_{jkl} := 0, \forall j,k,$ and $l > F+E$

Starting Phase :

STEP $r = 1 \ldots R-1$:
  $X := \mathcal{X}(X, E{+}F{+}r, n^*)$ where n^* is calculated according to
  $z(\mathcal{X}(\mathcal{X}(X,E{+}F{+}r,n^*),E{+}F{+}r{+}1,1)) = \max_{n\in\{1..N\}} z(\mathcal{X}(\mathcal{X}(X,E{+}F{+}r,n),E{+}F{+}r{+}1,1))$
$X := \mathcal{X}(X, E{+}F{+}R, 1)$

Interchange Phase :

REPEAT

  $z_{old} := z(X)$

  STEP $r = 1 \ldots R$:
    IF $z(X) < z(\mathcal{X}(X,E{+}F{+}r,1))$
    THEN $X := \mathcal{X}(X,E{+}F{+}r,1)$

UNTIL $z_{old} = z(X)$

$\mathcal{X}(X,l',n)$ can be computed by explicit enumeration except for large problems with $\prod_{k=1}^{K} J_k > T$, where T is a constant determined by answering time restrictions. In this case a divide & conquer heuristic is proposed for the determination of $\mathcal{X}(X,l',n)$.

Outlook

The PROLIN approach has already been used in a number of applications, including the design of package holidays, margarine, public baths and transport services. The results confirm that product lines designed on the basis of the first choice rule may markedly differ from those based on the generalized BTL- or the LOGIT-model. Differences are especially evident with increasing product line sizes in the case of profit maximization, i.e., when idiosynchratic marginal returns and idiosynchratic utilities are not similar.

References

Cattin P, Wittink D R (1982) Commercial Use of Conjoint Analysis: A Survey. Journal of Marketing 46 (Summer): 44-53

Dobson G, Kalish S (1993) Heuristics for Pricing and Positioning a Product-Line Using Conjoint and Cost Data. Management Science 39, 2 (February): 160-175

Elrod T, Kumar S K (1989) Bias in the First Choice Rule for Predicting Share. 1989-Sawtooth Software Conference Proceedings. Sawtooth Software Inc. Ketchum, ID

Gaul W, Lutz U, Aust E (1993) Goodwill Towards Domestic Products as Segmentation Criterion: An Empirical Study Within the Scope of Research on Country-of-Origin Effects. Studies in Classification, Data Analysis, and Knowledge Organization 4 (forthcoming)

Green P E, Krieger A M (1985) Models and Heuristics for Product Line Selection. Marketing Science 1 (Winter): 1-19

Green P E, Krieger A M (1987a) A Simple Heuristic for Selecting "Good" Products in Conjoint Analysis. Applications of Management Science 5: 131-153

Green P E, Krieger A M (1987b) A Consumer-Based Approach to Designing Product Line Extensions. Journal of Product Innovation Management 4: 21-32

Green P E, Krieger A M (1991) Product Design Strategies for Target-Market Positioning. Journal of Marketing Research 55: 28-38

Green P E, Krieger A M (1992) An Application of a Product Positioning Model to Pharmaceutical Products. Marketing Science 11, 2 (Spring): 117-132

Kohli R, Sukumar R (1990) Heuristics for Product-Line Design Using Conjoint Analysis. Management Science 36, 12 (December): 1464-1478

Mahajan V, Wind J (1992) New Product Models: Practice, Shortcomings and Desired Improvements. Journal of Product Innovation Management 9: 128-139

Page A L, Rosenbaum H F (1987) Redesigning Product Lines with Conjoint Analysis: How Sunbeam Does it. Journal of Product Innovation Management 4: 121-137

Pessemier E A, Burger P, Teach R, Tigert T (1971) Using Laboratory Brand Preference Scales to Predict Consumer Purchases. Management Science 17 (February): 371-385

Silk A J, Urban G L (1978) Pre-Test-Market Evaluation of New Product Goods: A Model and Measurement Methodology. Journal of Marketing Research 15: 171-191

Wittink R D, Cattin P (1989) Commercial Use of Conjoint Analysis: An Update. Journal of Marketing 53 (July): 91-96

The Simulated Trading Heuristic for Solving Vehicle Routing Problems

A. Bachem, M. Malich
Department of Mathematics
University of Cologne
Weyertal 86–90, D-50931 Köln, Germany

We present a new heuristic for solving vehicle routing problems. The heuristic uses complex customer interchanges to improve the initial solution. Simulated Trading is a general improvement procedure for a wide class of combinatorial optimization problems, thus it is able to handle many different side constraints like time windows, backhauls and a heterogeneous vehicle fleet. The algorithm is well suited for parallelization. A parallel version of Simulated Trading was implemented on a cluster of workstations using PVM. The results we have obtained with sequential and parallel Simulated Trading show that the quality of our solutions is superior to all heuristics for which solution values were known. Because of the limitation of space we will explain only the basic principle of Simulated Trading with a short example and will give an outline of the algorithm. A formal and detailed description of Simulated Trading can be found in [BHM92].

The Standard Vehicle Routing Problem (SVRP) can be considered as the task to satisfy the demands d_i of a set of customers $\{1, \dots, n\}$ with a number of vehicles under some side constraints and to minimize the total costs. The side constraints include that each customer has to be served by exactly one vehicle which starts and ends at the depot, the total load of a vehicle may not exceed its capacity and the vehicle has to be back at the depot after a certain amount of time. The total costs usually include travel times and fixed costs for each used vehicle. Extensions of the SVRP like time windows, heterogenous vehicle fleet or multiple depots are possible.

1 The Idea of Simulated Trading

Consider the following conversation between four truck drivers:

Joe: "*I would be glad if someone could serve my customer A otherwise I will need an extra hour of driving time."*

Jim answers: *"A is right on my way but my truck is full. I need 20 minutes additional time for customer B. If someone can satisfy these demands I will be able to insert A in my tour with only 10 minutes of extra time."*

Jack says: *"My truck has enough free capacity for B, but if I would insert B in my tour then I would violate the time window of C."*

John says: *"If I serve B then I would arrive at home too late. But if someone delivers my customer D then I would be able to take B and would be back in time."*

Joe finishes the discussion: *"I'm able to serve customer C with costs of 15 minutes and we have an overall improvement of 40 minutes."*

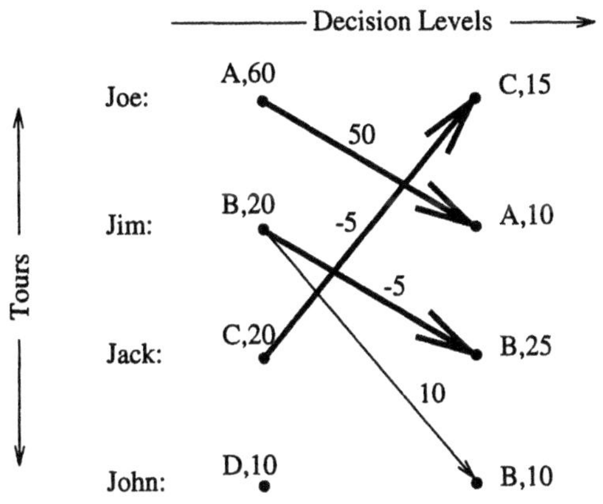

Figure 1: Example Trading Graph

If we take a closer look at the example we can construct a directed graph — we will call it trading graph — in which every node corresponds to an insertion (buy) or deletion (sell) of a customer. The edges which represent the relations between inserted and deleted customers are weighted with the gain that is obtained by the corresponding move of the customer (savings−insertcosts). Figure 1 shows the trading graph for the above example.

Every matching which can be found in the trading graph corresponds to an interchange of customers. If the value of the matching is positive we can improve our current tourplan. Clearly not every matching leads to a *feasible* tourplan. Consider the matching $\{((A,60),(A,10))\}$: if we would realize this move of customer A from Joe to Jim then the load would exceed the capacity of Jim's truck. Thus we have to look for a maximal weighted matching under additional constraints which will be called a trading matching. The bold printed edges in figure 1 show a trading matching with an improvement of 40.

2 The Algorithm Outline

We will now take a short look at the algorithm outline of Simulated Trading:

Let $\mathcal{T} = (T_1, \ldots, T_t)$ be a feasible tourplan
REPEAT
  Sell–And–Buy phase
  Trading–Matching–Search phase
  IF Trading–Matching M is found THEN Update tourplan $\mathcal{T}$ according to M
UNTIL timelimit is reached

During the Sell–And–Buy phase we buy and sell customers using weighted probabilities and build up the trading graph until a certain decision level (3–6) is reached. After that we search for a maximal weighted trading matching. If we have found a positive matching M we can improve the current tourplan. To get out of local minima we allow negativ matchings and infeasibilities.

In addition to the sequential algorithm we have implemented a parallel version of Simulated Trading on a cluster of workstations using PVM. The idea of the parallelization is to distribute the tours of the current tourplan among the workstations and to start a Simulated Trading algorithm on each machine. After a certain time (1–2 seconds) we collect the improved tours and restart with a new clustering. We use a *farthest customer* clustering in order to map only tours on one machine which are closely related.

3 Computational Results

The used test problem set was randomly generated by Solomon [Sol87] and contains vehicle routing problems with time windows, waiting times, capacity constraints and a restriction on the maximal tour time. Each problem contains 100 customers. In the first place the objective is to minimize the number of tours and second to reduce the total route time. The Simulated Trading results were obtained using floating point arithmetic without rounding or truncating any distances. Due to the lack of space we cannot show all results. The following table shows average values for 12 vehicle routing problems and allows a comparison between Simulated Trading and other heuristics. "Tabu Search 2" resp. "Simulated Trading 2" are the best solutions of two runs. "Tabu Search Best" resp. "Simulated Trading Best" are the best results which have been obtained during the experimentation phase. We have to mention that each run of Simulated Trading was done on the entire set of problems R1 without changing any parameter of the heuristic. Because of the different computer machines we give only the computation times for Simulated Trading and Tabu Search which are both obtained on a SUN Sparcstation 10. We can clearly point out that the solutions found by Simulated Trading are superior to the solutions of the other heuristics.

R1: 12 Problems	# Tours	Route Time	Time (min:sec)
Initial Solution	13.5	1697.0	—
Solomon [Sol87]	13.5	1685.4	—
Potvin and Rousseau [PR91]	13.3	—	—
GRASP_Routing [KB92]	13.1	—	—
Tabu Search [PKGR93]	12.92	1417.3	4:33
Tabu Search 2	12.83	1412.5	9:58
Tabu Search best	12.75	1403.9	—
Simulated Trading	12.75	1427.7	5:58
Simulated Trading 2	12.75	1417.0	10:11
Simulated Trading best	**12.58**	**1392.0**	—

References

[BHM92] Achim Bachem, Winfried Hochstättler, and Martin Malich. Simulated trading — a new parallel approach for solving vehicle routing problems. Technical Report 92.125, Mathematisches Institut, Universität zu Köln, Weyertal 86–90, D-50931 Köln, December 1992.

[KB92] Georgios Kontoravdis and Jonothan F. Bard. Improved heuristics for the vehicle routing problem with time windows. Technical report, Operations Research Group, Department of Mechanical Engineering, The University of Texas, Austin, TX78712-1063, September 1992.

[PKGR93] Jean Yves Potvin, Tanguy Kervahut, Bruno Laurent Garcia, and Jean Marc Rousseau. A tabu search heuristic for the vehicle routing problem with time windows. Technical report, Centre de Recherche sur les Transports, Université de Montréal, C.P. 6128, Succ. "A", Montréal (Québec), Canada H3C 3J7, 1993.

[PR91] Jean Yves Potvin and Jean Marc Rousseau. A parallel route building algorithm for the vehicle routing and scheduling problem with time windows. Technical Report 729, Centre de Recherche sur les Transports, Université de Montréal, C.P. 6128, Succ. "A", Montréal (Québec), Canada H3C 3J7, 1991.

[Sol87] Marius M. Solomon. Algorithms for the vehicle routing and scheduling problems with time window constraints. *Operations Research*, 35(2):254–265, March 1987.

EXPERT SYSTEM FOR HANDLING DANGEROUS GOODS

Dariusz Barbucha, Włodzimierz Filipowicz, Piotr Jędrzejowicz
Merchant Marine Academy, Gdynia, Poland

INTRODUCTION

There exist several computer data bases containing information on dangerous goods. As a rule they contain a description of the most of substances which can appear as a part of any consignment transported onboard ship, road vehicle or stored in a warehouse. Highest priority problems which may arise when handling dangerous substances are those related to the environment pollution. Strict, well defined, precautionary measures are to be observed when loading, stowing or storing any dangerous goods. In this field there are also some examples of the computer advisory systems.
Most of the chemical substances, which can bear potential risk, have been classified and described in a unique way in "International Maritime Dangerous Code" |3|. This book and chemistry expert are usually involved when handling dangerous substances. The existing decision support systems /EXIS, DANLOAD/ |2||4||5| do not however, embrace the whole range of problems which may arise when carrying, stowing or storing dangerous goods. Some typical problems involve a reduction of risk when such substances are handled with both, time and cost constraints or efficient use of the transportation means as well as of the storage capacity. In order to obtain practical solutions to these problems knowledge of some related disciplines such as:
- chemistry, especially in terms of dangerous good physical and chemical properties identification,
- computer science, especially data and knowledge based systems,
- applied mathematics to generate optimal decisions is also required.

DATA BASE

Computer systems use data or facts and process them while searching for solutions. Description of dangerous substances are widely available even on CD-Rom units.
For the purpose of this project a data format description from the IMDG Code is used. Data are grouped into fields most of which are common for all substances.
Information contained in each field provides some clues which may come useful when reasoning about properties of the substance, which directly can be found at "properties" field. Reaction with others substances are also stated there. Such information is of the highest importance when appropriate action in case of an incident is to be taken.
With reference to the properties and subsequent potential risks involved, there exist special constraints on segregation of the substances, details

of which are stated at the "stowage" field. This field reflects irregularities in segregation requirements roughly stated in the general segregation table available in any guide to the transport of dangerous materials. Formula field contains encoded data, easily understandable to chemist expert or a computer with sufficient knowledge base, which can supply further information about the substance.
Other fields provide more additional data supplementary to the stated above as well as these used for proper identification of a substance.

DANGEROUS GOODS PROBLEMS

Dangerous goods or substances are those which are inherently dangerous or those which are liable to chemical reaction with others. Product of such reaction is usually risky for environment or can cause damage to the nearest surrounding. Strict precautionary measures are to be observed when handling and allocating any dangerous goods.

SEGREGATION CALCULATIONS

If transportation of different substances is potentially risky and may cause a spontaneous reaction, components involved must be properly separated. In the maritime transportation, four segregation distances have been introduced taking into account potential hazard as well as construction of the vessel.
Nine classes of hazardous goods have been introduced as a guideline for the first and rough assessment of their properties. These classes are further divided into subclasses. The table containing segregation distances between subclasses /classes/ is easily available in every guide to dangerous goods, including the IMDG Code.
In addition to the segregation requirements there might be necessary to segregate a particular substance from others in a different, individual way. Such irregularities may refer to the whole class, particular type of substance or may be expressed in treating a substance as if it were in different class. Properties of some goods may vary with respect to their flushpoint, solution etc. To arrive at a proper segregation one has to select the worst case from all possible distances.
Requirements which refer to the substance type are not always directly available. Sometimes, an expert has to be consulted. Alternatively an expert system with appropriate knowledge should be at hand. Existing DANLOAD system |4||5| is short of this ability. Implementation of the proper knowledge base has already been started with knowledge elicited from chemical experts.
Result of segregation calculations can be thought of as a matrix which rows and columns are marked with substances and intersection element is equal to the segregation distance between each pair of goods.

DANGEROUS SUBSTANCE TYPE IDENTIFICATION - KNOWLEDGE BASE AND KNOWLEDGE REPRESENTATION

Every program or algorithm contains knowledge about some problem. This can be expressed in forms of equations, formulas and some "common sense" restrictions. Knowledge systems are different from traditional programs and include a higher-level form of knowledge, which is usually stored in the form of rules and facts. Furthermore, traditional programs can not explain its way of reasoning. Expert systems are supposed to behave more like intelligent assistant. Whenever it reaches a conclusion, a user should be able to ask about the way it has been arrived at. Knowledge about any subject is constantly growing and changing, an expert system must be flexible enough to accept and modify its base.
In order to recognize properties of substances the presented system requires some chemical knowledge. This knowledge is used for identification of substances types /or type/.
In order to be of use, knowledge must be captured in some manner inside computer. A simple approach is to use some explicit declarative language, which sentences can be considered as more or less direct symbolic encoding of the knowledge. Of course, knowledge must be accessed, used, modified and ammended. The adopted notation should be easy to read and enable generation of explanations.
In our case available knowledge has been encoded in form of conditional sentences.

DANGEROUS SUBSTANCE TYPE IDENTIFICATION - EXPLANATORY MECHANISM

Possibility to get an explanation on how facts and rules were used to reach goals is a useful feature of any expert system. Presented system contains such mechanism, too. It is an integrated part of dangerous substance type identification unit, offering the two kinds of explanations:
1. "How" explanation providing information on which rule was directly used to reach conclusion.
This information show a chain of rules which have led to the final conclusion, therefore available when reasoning process is executed. As a result appropriate rules and related facts are shown on the screen.
2. Type explanation providing information on which rules, included in knowledge base, are related to given dangerous substance type. In this case, all rules for given substance type identification are displayed.

FINDING MINIMAL NUMBER OF SEPARATED COMPARTMENTS

Once segregation matrix has been calculated, dangerous goods are to be allocated in such a way that proper distances are observed and is space available used efficiently. Assuming that the store, ship or another transportation mean is free of any other load of hazardous substances, minimal number of the separated compartments can be generated by the graph coloring procedure |6|. Methods used for graph coloring

have been adopted by assigning goods to nodes and greater that 1 segregation distance to edges between appropriate pairs of nodes. Such an assignment does not distinguish proper segregation from the distances 2, 3 and 4, so further consideration of substances allocation to the compartments appears necessary. Structure of a warehouse or ship as well as capacity of the compartments impose additional constraints which are supposed to be taken into account in real applications.
It should be stressed that worst case running time of graph coloring algorithms is bounded by exponential function on the number of input |7|. Such problems are said to belong to the NP-Complete class and their optimal solution might be unreachable within reasonable time, therefore some suboptimal solutions are proposed and assessed.

REFERENCES

|1| "CHEMADATA" National Chemical Emergency Center, United Kingdom Atomic Energy Authority

|2| "EXIS" Chemical and Hazardous Materials and Transport Regulations Database, Exis Limited, London

|3| "International Maritime Dangerous Goods Code", London 1983 /International Maritime Organization/; United Nations

|4| Belli F., Filipowicz W., Jędrzejowicz P., "Validation of The Expert System DANLOAD", The Second IFAC/IFIP Workshop on Experience with The Management of Software Projects, Sarajewo 1988

|5| Belli F., Filipowicz W., Jędrzejowicz P., "Some Aspects on the Development and Validation of FIREX - a Knowledge-Base System for the Transport of Dangerous Goods and Fire Department Consulting", The Second International Conference on Industrial and Engineering Applications of Artificial Intelligence and Expert Systems IEA/AIE-89, Tennessee USA 1989

|6| Filipowicz W., "Decision Support for Optimal Stowage of Dangerous Goods", Vth IMAEM Congress, Athens 1990

|7| Lawler E., "A Note on The Complexity of the Chromatic Number Problem", Information Processing Letters, Vol 5 no 3 1976

Linear 0-1 Inequalities and Extended Clauses

Peter Barth

Max-Planck-Institut für Informatik
Im Stadtwald
66123 Saarbrücken, Germany

1 Introduction

0-1 constraint satisfaction problems have been investigated for a long time. The idea to instantiate the computational domain $\mathcal{X}$ in the CLP($\mathcal{X}$) scheme [JL87] with 0-1 or pseudo-Boolean constraints was first introduced in [Boc92]. The resulting language CLP($\mathcal{PB}$) aims to be a logic programming environment suitable for various applications where 0-1 problems naturally arise. This is the case for many AI-applications [BB93] and operations research.

The *solved form* of the accumulated constraints should provide an easy check of logical entailment and therefore satisfiability. Recently [Hoo92] has presented a symbolic algorithm, *generalized resolution* working with *extended clauses*, which satisfies the special requirements in the context of constraint logic programming.

Extended clauses are linear 0-1 inequalities $c_1 * L_1 + \ldots c_n * L_n \geq d$ where all the c_i are $1, 0$ or -1. *Classical clauses* of the form $L_1 \vee \ldots \vee L_n$ are disjunctions of literals. They can be written as linear 0-1 inequality $L_1 + \ldots + L_n \geq 1$, where negative literals $\overline{X_i}$ are seen as $1 - X_i$. Extended clauses are therefore a generalization of classical clauses by allowing different values than 1 on the right hand side. The advantage of extended clauses versus classical clauses is the more compact representation while preserving computational handability. The equivalent representation of the extended clause $L_1 + \ldots + L_n \geq d$ using classical clauses without introducing new variables is

$$\bigwedge_{I \subseteq \{1,\ldots,n\}:|I|=n-d+1} (\vee_{i \in I} L_i)$$

which are $\binom{n}{n-d+1}$ clauses.

Because the constraint solver works on extended clauses, we need to transform arbitrary 0-1 constraints into extended clauses. After applying a linearization procedure [BM84] and a normalization process to arbitrary 0-1 constraints the problem is reduced to transform a linear 0-1 inequality of the form $c_1 * L_1 + \ldots c_n * L_n \geq d$ $(c_i \geq 0)$ into a set of equivalent extended clauses. The algorithm presented here produces efficiently the minimal number of extended clauses which are equivalent to a linear 0-1 inequality. This is achieved using cutting plane techniques in combination with specialized redundancy criteria. All theorems used in this extended abstract are proofed in [Bar93].

We use the following notation [Hoo92]. A *linear 0-1 inequality* is of the form $c_1 * X_1 + \ldots + c_n * X_n \geq d$ where $c_i \in \mathcal{Z}$. An inequality is *satisfiable* if $\sum_{i \in N_n} |c_i| \geq d$. Let us say that the *extension* $Ext(I)$ of an inequality I is the set of 0-1 vectors X that satisfy I. The extension $Ext(S)$ of a set of inequalities S is the intersection of the extensions of the inequalities in S. A set S is *feasible* if $Ext(S)$ is nonempty. A set *(strictly) dominates* an inequality if the extension of the set is a *(proper) subset* of the extension of the inequality. Two sets of inequalities are *equivalent* if they are *coextensive* (either dominates the other). A pseudo-Boolean inequality is of the form $c_1 * L_1 + \ldots + c_n * L_n \geq d$. If we replace in a linear 0-1 inequality every product $c_i * X_i$ where $c_i < 0$ by $-c_i * \overline{X_i} + c_i$, then, after bringing the negative c_i on the right side, we obtain a linear pseudo-Boolean inequality having only positive c_i. We represent a vector of variables X_i (resp. literals L_i,resp. constants c_i) as $X(resp.L, resp.c)$. Vectors can also be seen as sets. We abbreviate $c_1 * L_1 + \ldots + c_n * L_n$ by cL.

Definition 1 *A linear pseudo-Boolean inequality* $cL \geq d$ *is in (pseudo-Boolean)* normal form *if*

$$d \geq c_1 \geq \ldots \geq c_n \geq 1 \text{ and } \forall i \neq j : \mathcal{V}(L_i) \neq \mathcal{V}(L_j).$$

We can safely suppose that $d \geq 1$ because otherwise the inequality is a tautology, that is it is valid for every vector $L^* \in \{0,1\}^n$. Every non tautologous linear 0-1 inequality has an equivalent (pseudo-Boolean) normal form [HR68]. From now on we identify with inequalities their pseudo-Boolean normal form.

Let us say that an inequality $I \equiv cL \geq d$ *reduces* to $c'L' \geq d'$ (the *reduction*) if $\forall_i : 0 \leq c'_i \leq c_i$ and $1 \leq d - d' = \sum_i (c_i - c'_i)$. Obviously an inequality dominates all its reductions. We denote with $Red(I)$ the set of all reductions of an inequality I. We say an inequality $cL \geq d$ *strictly reduces* to $c'L' \geq d'$ if $c'L' \geq d'$ is a reduction and for all i either $c'_i = c_i$ or $c'_i = 0$. We denote with $SRed(I)$ the set of all strict reductions of an inequality I.

An *extended clause* is an inequality where all the c_i are 1. An extended clause is written $L_1 + \ldots + L_n \geq d$, abbreviated $L \geq d$. We say d is the *degree* of the extended clause $L \geq d$. Domination between extended clauses can be easily decided.

Lemma 1 *An extended clause* $L \geq d$ *dominates another extended clause* $L' \geq d'$ *iff* $|L \setminus L'| \leq d - d'$.

2 Generating Valid Extended Clauses

Let us look at a pseudo-Boolean inequality in normal form. Obviously the following inequalities are valid

$$\lceil c_1/k \rceil * L_1 + \ldots + \lceil c_n/k \rceil * L_n \geq \lceil d/k \rceil \tag{1}$$

for all integer $k \geq 1$, where $\lceil a \rceil = min(\{b \in \mathcal{Z} : b \geq a\})$. These inequalities are also called *cutting planes*. We restrict our attention to the k making the coefficients of the left side equal to 1 and maximizing the right side, that is $k = c_1$. The resulting inequalities are extended clauses of the form $L_1 + \ldots + L_n \geq \lceil d/c_1 \rceil$. The cutting plane operation gives us a valid extended clause $L \geq d'$ of an inequality $cL \geq d$. We are now interested in the greatest right hand side β such that $L \geq \beta$ is dominated by $cL \geq d$.

Proposition 1 *Given an inequality* $I \equiv cL \geq d$, *then the extended clause*

$$L \geq \beta \tag{2}$$

such that $\sum_{i \in N_{\beta-1}} c_i < d \leq \sum_{i \in N_\beta} c_i$ *is dominated by* I *and* $L \geq \beta + l$ *is not dominated by* I *for all* $l \geq 1$. *Therefore (2) is the strongest extended clause (with respect to I) having L as left hand side.*

For an inequality $I \equiv cL \geq d$ we denote with $SCP(I) \equiv L \geq \beta$, the extended clause (2). For a set of inequalities S we denote with $SCP(S)$ the set of all $SCP(I)$ such that $I \in S$.

We know that all reductions are valid inequalities. Therefore for all strict reductions R, $SCP(R)$ is a valid extended clause. We show that $SCP(SRed(I))$, the set of strongest extended clauses derived from all strict reductions of an inequality I, is equivalent to I.

Theorem 1 *Let* $I \equiv cL \geq d$ *be an arbitrary linear 0-1 inequality, then* $Ext(I) = Ext(SCP(SRed(I)))$.

This leads directly to an algorithm which transforms a linear pseudo-Boolean inequality into a set of equivalent extended clauses. Unfortunately a large number of extended clauses may be produced. Obviously we preserve equivalence if we consider only extended clauses which are not dominated by others.

3 Identifying redundant extended clauses

We derive several redundancy criteria for extended clauses in $SCP(SRed(I))$. We call an extended clause EC in $SCP(SRed(I))$ *redundant* if there is another extended clause in $SCP(SRed(I))$ which dominates EC. Our goal is to minimize the number of domination checks between the generated clauses. We show how to decide redundancy of an extended clause in $SCP(SRed(I))$ by checking domination against *two* other extended clauses.For this purpose we first define a tree view of $SCP(SRed(I))$.

Let $T = T(cL \geq d)$ be a finite tree where the nodes are labeled with the inequalities in $SRed(cL \geq d)$. The root of T is labeled by $cL \geq d$. Let $SRed_1(cL \geq d)$ be the set of all strict reductions $c'L' \geq d'$ of $cL \geq d$ where $|L| - 1 = |L'|$. The subtrees of T are all trees $T(R)$ where $R \in SRed_1(cL \geq d)$. We denote with $\mathcal{T}(T, j)$

the subtree of T with the label $\sum_{1\leq i\neq j\leq n} c_i L_i \geq d - c_j$. We abbreviate $\mathcal{T}(\mathcal{T}(\ldots(\mathcal{T}(T, j_1), j_2), \ldots), j_k)$ by $\mathcal{T}(j_1 \ldots j_k)$. We denote with $T_j = L' \geq \beta$ the strongest extended clause of the root label of $\mathcal{T}(T, j)$. The strongest extended clause of the root label of $\mathcal{T}(j_1 \ldots j_k)$ is referenced with $T_{j_1 \ldots j_k}$. Let $L' \geq \beta$ be $T_{j_1 \ldots j_k}$, then we define the *degree* $d(T_{j_1 \ldots j_k}) = \beta$. Note that $T_{j_1 \ldots j_k}$ has $n-k$ literals, therefore the length of the path determines the number of literals of the label. We say $j_1 \ldots j_k$ is the *path* of the tree $\mathcal{T}(j_1 \ldots j_k)$. Let J_k be the set of indices $\{j_1, \ldots, j_k\}$. Obviously for all permutations P_k, P'_k of J_k we have that $\mathcal{T}(P_k) = \mathcal{T}(P'_k)$. So by identifying all nodes representing the same tree we obtain a directed graph where each element of $SRed(I)$ is represented by exactly one node. In the graph we identify a path with the set of its indices.

Theorem 2 *A strongest extended clause $T_{J_{k+1}}$ is redundant iff*

[a] *$T_{J_{k+2}}$ dominates $T_{J_{k+1}}$ where $c_{j_{k+2}} \leq c_i$ for all c_i, $i \in N_n \setminus J_{k+1}$ or*

[b] *there exists a $J_k = J_{k+1} \setminus \{j_{k+1}\}$ such that T_{J_k} dominates $T_{J_{k+1}}$ and $c_{j_{k+1}} \geq c_{j_l}$ for all c_{j_l} where $j_l \in J_k$.*

So using Theorem 2 we can decide redundancy of a strongest extended clause by investigating exactly 2 other strongest extended clauses. An algorithm based on these results can construct a graph labeled as described earlier and mark all redundant clauses using the efficient decision procedure presented here. The set of the remaining unmarked clauses is then the set of equivalent extended clauses.

4 Application to 0-1 Integer Programming

Preprocessing 0-1 integer programming problems and applying constraint generation techniques have made large scale 0-1 problems solvable in reasonable time [CJP83, JKS85]. The general method is solving the linear programming relaxation repeatedly in combination with a branch and bound method. The main speedup comes from generating valid 0-1 inequalities, so called strong cuts, which better approximate the integral solution of the problem and therefore normally require less branch and bound cycles.

The constraint set of a linear 0-1 integer programming problem consists of a set of inequalities of the form

$$c_1 * X_1 + \ldots + c_n * X_n \leq d \tag{3}$$

which is equivalent to $-c_1 * X_1 - \ldots - c_n * X_n \geq -d$ and can then be brought into pseudo-Boolean normal form. In [NW88] some constraint generation techniques are presented. They are based mainly on the notion of *minimal covers* or *minimal dependent sets.*

Definition 2 *A set $C \subseteq N_n$ is a minimal dependent set of (3) if $\sum_{i\in C\setminus\{j\}} \leq d < \sum_{i\in C} c_i$ for all $j \in C$.*

Proposition 2 *If C is a minimal dependent set for (3) then the* extended cover inequality $\sum_{i\in E(C)} X_i \leq |C| - 1$ *where $E(C) = C \cup \{k \in N_n | \forall j \in C : c_k \geq c_j\}$ is a valid inequality for (3).*

Let us write the extended cover inequality in pseudo-Boolean normal form.

$$\sum_{i\in E(C)} \overline{X_i} \geq |E(C) \setminus C| + 1 \tag{4}$$

We know that $\sum_{i\in E(C)} \overline{X_i} \geq |E(C) \setminus C| + 2$ is not a valid inequality, because otherwise $\sum_{i\in E(C)} X_i \leq |C| - 2$ would be valid which is not the case as C is minimal. Therefore (4) is the strongest extended clause containing exactly the literals $\{X_i | i \in E(C)\}$. We can therefore use our transformation procedure to systematically construct the set S of all strongest non redundant extended cover inequalities. The constraint generation techniques produce extended cover inequalities and add them to the original problem. Because of our equivalence result we can safely replace the original inequality by S. It would be very interesting to preprocess large scale 0-1 integer programming problems with this method and then applying a simple branch and bound method. In comparison to a traditional 0-1 constraint solver with constraint generation techniques the number of branch and bound cycles should decrease, although the number of inequalities surely tends to be very large. If too many constraints are generated one can limit the path length of the graph and so generate a limited set of extended cover inequalities. We finish this section with some examples.

Example 1 [a] *Let I be* $79X_1 + 53X_2 + 53X_3 + 45X_4 + 45X_5 \leq 178$ *[NW88, page 266]. The pseudo-Boolean form of I is* $79\overline{X_1}+53\overline{X_2}+53\overline{X_3}+45\overline{X_4}+45\overline{X_5} \geq 97$. *Applying our transformation procedure we obtain the two extended clauses* $\overline{X_1} + \overline{X_2} + \overline{X_3} + \overline{X_4} + \overline{X_5} \geq 2$ *and* $\overline{X_1} + \overline{X_2} + \overline{X_3} \geq 1$. *Writing them as "≤-inequalities" we obtain the two extended cover inequalities* $X_1 + X_2 + X_3 + X_4 + X_5 \leq 3$ *and* $X_1 + X_2 + X_3 \leq 2$.

[b] *Let I be* $774X_1 + 76X_2 + 22X_3 + 42X_4 + 21X_5 + 760X_6 + 818X_7 + 62X_8 + 785X_9 \leq 1500$ *[NW88, page 460]. Our transformation gives us the single extended cover inequality* $X_1 + X_6 + X_7 + X_9 \leq 1$ *which is equivalent to I.*

[c] *Let I be* $300X_3+300X_4+285X_5+285X_6+265X_8+265X_9+230X_12+230X_13+190X_14+200X_22+400X_23+200X_24+400X_25+200X_26+400X_27+200X_28+400X_29+200X_30+400X_31 \leq 2700$ *[NW88, page465], which is the inequality producing the largest number (4282) of clauses in this problem. They have been calculated with a simple PROLOG-implementation of the algorithm in 17 sec. cpu time on a SPARC 2. The number of non redundant equivalent classical clauses, as needed in [GH71], is 117520.*

References

[Bar93] P. Barth. Linear 0-1 inequalities and extended clauses. In *Logic Programming and Automated Reasoning : international conference LPAR '93; St. Petersburg, Russia; proceedings*, July 1993.

[BB93] P. Barth and A. Bockmayr. Solving 0-1 problems in CLP(PB). In *Proc. 9th Conf. Artificial Intelligence for Applications (CAIA), Orlando*. IEEE, 1993.

[BM84] E. Balas and J. B. Mazzola. Nonlinear 0-1 programming: I. Linearization techniques. *Mathematical Programming*, 30:1–21, 1984.

[Boc92] A. Bockmayr. Logic programming with pseudo-Boolean constraints. In A. Colmerauer and F. Benhamou, editors, *Constraint Logic Programming - Selected Research*. MIT Press, 1992. (to appear).

[CJP83] H. Crowder, E.L. Johnson, and M. Padberg. Solving large-scale zero-one linear programming problems. *Operations Research*, 31(5):803–834, September 1983.

[GH71] F. Granot and P. L. Hammer. On the use of boolean functions in 0-1 programming. *Methods of Operations Research*, 12:154–184, 1971.

[Hoo92] J. N. Hooker. Generalized resolution for 0-1 linear inequalities. *Annals of Mathematics and Artificial Intelligence*, 6:271–286, 1992.

[HR68] P.L. Hammer and S. Rudeanu. *Boolean Methods in Operations Research and Related Areas*. Springer-Verlag, 1968.

[JKS85] E.L. Johnson, M. Kostreva, and U.H. Suhl. Solving 0-1 integer programming problems arising from large scale planning models. *Operations Research*, 33(4):803–819, July 1985.

[JL87] J. Jaffar and J.-L. Lassez. Constraint logic programming. In *Proc. 14th ACM Symp. Principles of Programming Languages*, Munich, 1987.

[NW88] G. L. Nemhauser and L. A. Wolsey. *Integer and Combinatorial Optimization*. Series in Discrete Mathematics and Optimization. Wiley–Interscience, 1988.

A Model- and Method Base System for Discrete Optimization Problems

Peter Becker

Wilhelm-Schickard-Institut für Informatik, Universität Tübingen

1. Introduction

Methods of discrete optimization play an important role in the area of control and optimization of industrial processes. Due to the fact that most discrete optimization problems are NP-complete, a lot of specialized methods have been developed for them, which differ with respect to algorithmic properties, see e.g [5, 7] . For this reason a user is not always able to select the algorithm that fits his needs best.

Because of the above mentioned difficulties I propose a method base approach to support unexperienced users in the solution of discrete optimization problems. Analogous to a data base a *method base* is defined as a software system consisting of a *method base system* and a set of *methods*. The most important tasks of the method base system are: (1) providing an interface to other systems and applications, (2) automatic method selection based on user preferences (3) and data handling. (1) comprises the offering of a data definition and manipulation language to define new problem classes and new problems as well as providing interfaces to various optimization methods and databases. (2) means, that the method base system has to provide adequate representation methods for knowledge about method application and (3) means the persistent storage of models and problems in a database orientied fashion.

In the following the method base system $\mathcal{M}$ is presented, which fullfills the above mentioned requirements. Similar approaches exist for linear programming problems, see [1, 9, 12] .

$\mathcal{M}$ is written in C and C++ and is based on the relational database system TRANSBASE as well as the software library LEDA [8] . The concepts of $\mathcal{M}$ are validated by knapsack problems [2] and precedence constraint hamilton path problems [3] .

2. A short survey of $\mathcal{M}$

$\mathcal{M}$ is an object oriented software tool for the definition of models and the solution of problems in the field of discrete optimization. $\mathcal{M}$ is based on a client-server concept: the server administers all objects of the method base, the client may be one of the generic user interfaces to $\mathcal{M}$ or any program that has connected to the method base by the means of a special library. This approach has the advantage that the method base can easily be embedded in other systems. Interprocess communication between clients and server is done by *remote procedure calls* via networks.

Operations on the method base are performed only by sending messages to objects. An object may be a class, a problem, a method or any other instance of predefined or user defined classes. *Classes* can be seen as factories for instances (resp. objects) and are objects too. For the objects they create, classes possess construction plans that contain information about the attributes an object can have and the methods that are applicable to an object. *Instances* or *objects* are created by sending a constructor message to a class. A *problemclass* or *model* is a factory for *problems*. In this sense a model is the abstract definition of a specific problem and achieves model/data independence. New models are created by sending a constructor message to a special class named *problemclasses*. After doing this, attributes and methods can be defined for the instances of the new model by the means of special messages.

The objects are internally mapped to tuples of a relational database or to special file structures. The latter is especially necessary for dealing with large comlex objects. Operations are embedded in transactions.

3. Extensibility and method integration

To support complex mathematical structures like graphs or networks efficiently the method base system offers an interface for the integration of user defined data types. A user written *type handler* function for a new data type can be installed via a dynamic library. Whenever a message is sent to an object of a user defined type this message is forwarded to the attached type handler. The type handler calls the necessary functions that implement the message. So it is easy to integrate new data types for mathematical structures by using software libraries, e.g. LEDA. $\mathcal{M}$ offers a set of common discrete structures, e.g. arrays, lists, matrices, posets, graphs and others.

A *method* is implemented by a function of a dynamic library, by a function written in the method base language or by an external program. It is represented by objects of the class *methods* or derived subclasses which provide the attributes necessary for the communication between the method and the server. By that, definition of methods by standard software is easy. For example, a method *xshow* for the graphical representation of partial orders has been realized using the public domain graph editor EDGE [10]

4. The Method Base Language

Operations on the method base are formulated in a *method base language (mbl).* This mbl can either be used by an user via one of the interactive user interfaces or by an application via calls to library functions. Here is a simple example of the interactive definition and solution of a knapsack problem in mbl (example 2.2 of [7]). User input is typeset in boldface:

```
M> kp.create_instance(id:"mt2_2")
_744451004_304678
M+> mt2_2.capacity <- 50
(void)
M+> mt2_2.profit <- [70,20,39,37,7,5,10]
(void)
M+> mt2_2.weight <- [31,10,20,19,4,3,6]
(void)
M+> mt2_2.brabo
_744451603_371556
M+> mt2_2.solution_set
[1,4]
M+> mt2_2.solution_val
107
M+> ct
M>
```

First, an instance of the problemclass `kp` is created. This is done by sending the message `create_instance` with the parameter `id` to the object `kp`. The new problem gets the alias `mt2_2` and has the unique *object identifier (oid)* _744451004_304678, which is the result of this statement. In the next three statements its input data is assigned, profits and weights are represented as integer lists. In the fifth statement the method `brabo` is called to solve the knapsack problem. After the method returns successfully we are able to take a look at the solution values: `brabo` decided to take the items 1 and 4 into the knapsack. This results in a profit of 107. The command `ct` commits the transaction and the new defined object is saved to disk.

The right side of an assignment as well as the parameter values may consist of an arbitrary expression. In the following statement the profit list assigned to problem `kp100_1` is created by calling a random generator method:

```
M> kp100_1.profit <- random_uniform_discrete.call(
      samplesize:100,lower:1,upper:1000)
```

The language offers the data types *integer, real, string, constant, list* and *lambda expression*. Lists can be nested and may comprise heterogenous elements. Lambda expressions are not evaluated immediatly, they are useful to define rules, integrity constraints or simple methods. For example the following lines create the model kp and define the attribute capacity as a positive integer. The constraint is represented by an lambda expression. This expression will be evaluated whenever an assignment to capacity is made.

```
M> problemclasses.create_instance(id:"kp")
_738510687_992659
M+> kp.define_attr(
        name:"capacity",
        constraint:'($capacity.type = INTEGER and $capacity > 0))
(void)
```

Besides the data types presented the language offers the usual control structures (if, case, different loop constructs).

5. User support and automatic selection of methods

The strongest user support is achieved by *method plans.* These method plans are an adaption of skeleton plans, which are an usual artificial intelligence technique for the solution of planning or configuration problems, see e.g. [11] . Like skeleton plans, method plans can be viewed as non-recursive and-or-graphs. The sinks of a method plan represent the basic solution methods for the problem e.g. optimization methods, integrity checks or transformation methods. Intermediate nodes of the method plan represent partial problems in the solution process. Such a node depends on other basic or intermediate nodes. We distinguish two types of nodes.

A *planning node* divides the associated problem into subproblems that have to be solved sequentially. For instance, to solve a knapsack problem we have to do the following steps: (1) Check whether the problem has been defined correctly. (2) Sort the items according to decreasing values of the profit per unit weight. This a precondition for all existing solution methods currently available. (3) Reduce the problem by a reduction method to fix the optimal value of as many variables as possible. This results in a smaller problem. (4) Solve the reduced problem with one of the existing optimization methods. (5) Transform the solution back into terms of the original problem. It seems to be adequate to represent this knowledge by an planning node.

The other type of nodes are *fork nodes.* These nodes represent alternative strategies in the solution process. For instance step (4) in the solution of a knapsack problem can be achieved by applying a branch and bound algorithm, an algorithm based on dynamic programming or a polynomial approximation scheme. What to do depends on the users preferences and the input data, e.g the number of items. For this reason rules can be connected to a fork node. These rules control the expansion of the solution process by selecting at least one of the alternatives offered by the node. Selecting more than one node results in different strategies to achieve the desired goal, which may be executed in parallel. This leads to the advantage that a race between different methods (resp. strategies) can be started and we get a solution in the minimum of the running times.

The method plan concept has two advantages: (1) knowledge about the problem domain is structured in small pieces that are independent and reusable. For instance if we want to apply one of the basic operators we go back in a predefined way from the sink to the source. Every planning node on that path gives us the operators we have to apply before resp. after the call of the basic operator. In this manner the necessary tasks for the application of any node can be easily deduced. (2) Every intermediate node represents a powerful and sophisticated operator. Application of the source node results in an automatic solution.

Beside method plans, other concepts for user support exist. It is possible to define a model as a special case of another model. Associated with this relationship are test and transformation methods. Based on this relationship between models classification hierachies can be defined. Using a classification hierarchy, it is possible to classify a problem under the control of the test methods. In this way we get the most specific models to which a problem belongs.

6. Other Features

Beyond the facilities mentioned in the above sections $\mathcal{M}$ offers the following two important features: (1) Interfaces to database systems. At the moment an interface to TRANSBASE exists. For example the statement

```
transbase.query(database:<database name>,sqlquery:<sql-query>)
```

leads to the execution of the specified query against the database named `<database name>`. `<sql-query>` is a string that contains an arbitrary query in SQL. The result table is given as a list of lists and can further be processed. Interfaces to other database systems can be easily realized by the technique of user defined types. (2) A generic graphical interface called *Mint*, see [6] . This tool represents objects by graphical means. For instance buttons are offered for the applicable messages and methods. Moreover the user is supported in the definition of parameters to methods by giving explanations.

7. Summary

In this paper the method base system $\mathcal{M}$ has been presented. Main features of $\mathcal{M}$ are: (1) facilities to define models and solve problems in the area of discrete optimization in an object oriented, persistent and consistent way, (2) efficient support for complex mathematical stuctures and support for reuse of these structures in various models, (3) user support by automatic selection of methods. Due to these aspects $\mathcal{M}$ can be seen as one step towards a model managment system proposed in [4] .

References

1. Daniel R. Dolk, ''A Generalized Model Managment System for Mathematical Programmimg,'' *ACM Transactions on Mathematical Software*, vol. 12, no. 2, pp. 92-126, 1986.
2. Christoph Gauger, ''Implementierung und Bewertung von Verfahren zur Lösung von Rucksackproblemen unter der Berücksichtigung der Integration in eine Methodenbank,'' Studienarbeit, Universität Tübingen, 1993.
3. M. Grötschel, M. Jünger, and G. Reinelt, ''Programmpaket zur Behandlung symmetrischer Hamilton-Wege-Probleme mit Ordnungsbeziehungen,'' Internal Paper, 1991.
4. M. Jarke and F. J. Radermacher, ''The AI Potential of Model Managment and Its Central Role in Decision Support,'' *Decision Support Systems*, vol. 4, no. 4, pp. 387-404, 1988.
5. E. L. Lawler, J. K. Lenstra, A. H. G. Rinnooy Kan, and D. B. Shmoys, *The Traveling Salesman Problem*, Wiley, 1985.
6. Andreas Ludwig, ''Erstellung einer graphischen Benutzerschnittstelle für das Methodenbanksystem $\mathcal{M}$,'' Studienarbeit, Universität Tübingen, 1992.
7. Silvano Martello and Paolo Toth, *Knapsack Problems*, Wiley, Chichester, 1990.
8. Kurt Mehlhorn and Stefan Näher, ''LEDA - A Library of Efficient Data Types and Algorithms,'' in *Proceedings Graph-theoretic Concepts in Computer Science 1990*, pp. 88-106, Springer.
9. F. H. Murphy and E. A. Stohr, ''An Intelligent System for Formulating Linear Programs,'' *Decision Support Systems*, vol. 2, pp. 39-47, 1986.
10. F. N. Paulisch and W. F. Tichy, ''EDGE: An Extendible Graph Editor,'' *Software-Practice and Experience*, vol. 20, no. S1, pp. 63-88, 1990.
11. Frank Puppe, *Problemlösungsmethoden in Expertensystemen*, Springer, Berlin, 1990.
12. Richard G. Ramirez, Chee Ching, and Robert D. St. Louis, ''Model-Data and Model-Solver Mappings: A Basis for an Extended DSS Framework,'' in *ISDSS Conference Proceedings 1990*, pp. 283-312.

A Simple Model of Political Affairs

Horst Behnke

Sozialökonomisches Seminar der Universität Hamburg,
Max Brauer—Allee 60, 22765 Hamburg

During the last two years a sharply increasing number of political affairs with ministers, chiefs of political parties and leading managers of worker unions or combines become known in Germany. A last famous example is VW's manager Jose Lopez.
The horizon of this paper is to cause with game theoretic arguments, that the often seen behaviour of peoples in such affairs is either an immediate resignation of the attacked persons free will or a consequent denying of all accusations. The last one ends either with a seeing the affair through or ends in a situation where the accusation is proved to be true and the person must resignate or have to be discharged by its chief, if there is one.
Fig.1 is showing a simple game in extensive form which is building up the basic structure of political affairs with their courses, uncertainty, and possible decisions.

Fig.1 :

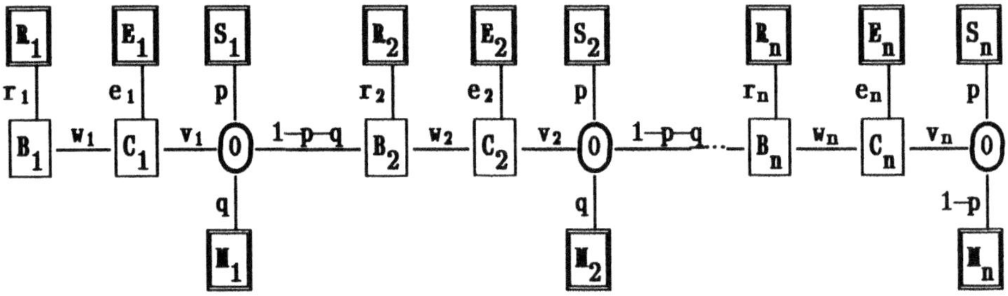

The game starts with an attack against player B by a not proved accusation in magazines and television. He has only two possibilities to react. At first, he could resignate (local strategy r_1) and the game ends at point R_1. Secondly, he could deny all accusations (local strategy w_1). In the second case B's chief, named player C, is knowing B's decision and has also two possible actions. He could discharge B (local strategy e_1) and the game ends at point E_1 or he could proclaim his trust in B (local strategy v_1). If both players choose to remain in the game, three events are possible, which are represented by the random player 0. At first the affair and consequently the game ends with probability q at endpoint M_1, because there are no new facts for progressing the accusation. Secondly new facts become known which prove the accusation and the game ends with probability p at endpoint S_1. This is to interpret as an enforced removing of B.

The third event with remaining probability (1–p–q) is given in new, again not entirely proved, accusations against B (and possible against C by reason of his proclamation of trust in B). If this last event is realised, the game goes on in the same manner as before. In the last stage the game ends either with probability p at endpoint S_n or with probability (1–p) at endpoint M_n (the intermediate death of the affair, because there is no more public interesting).

Assumptions:
At first, there is a strict positive probability for reaching the next stage: $p + q < 1$
Utility pay–offs at each type of endpoint (M,S,R, and E) are equal at each stage, but different for both players. These utility pay–offs are named M_B, S_B, R_B, and E_B (resp. M_C, S_C, R_C, and E_C)
About pay–offs the following realistic assumptions and standardizations are made:

(a1) $$1 = M_B > R_B > E_B > S_B = 0\ ,$$

(a2) $$1 = M_C > E_C > R_C > S_C = 0\ ,$$

and moreover all utility pay–offs are known by both players.
The probabilities p and q are not known for both players, so that each of them acts with his own individual probabilities estimations p_B and q_B resp. p_C and q_C.
In the basic model both players know all individual probabilities and they are risk neutral, so that they are become Bayesian–players and make their decisions by using utility expectation values. This assumption is a realistic simplification, because B and C are familiar with the behaviour of the other.
The game illustrated in Fig.1 is an extensive two person game with incomplete information. Such games should be rewritten as games of types of players like Harsanyi (1967,p.173–175) has shown. ([For an overview see for example Selten (1982), Holler/Illing(1991)).

Fig. 2:

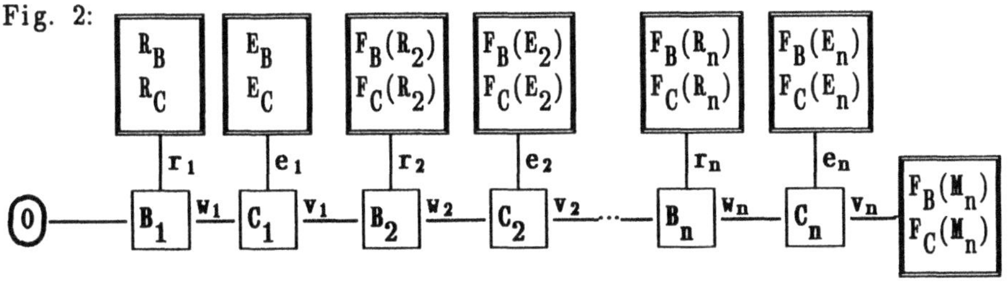

Here, at point 0 a random mechanism chooses two types of players B and C defined by their individual probability estimations (p_B,q_B) and (p_C,q_C).
In Fig. 2 $F_*(.)$ stands for the individual utility pay–off expectation value of player * at the endpoints of the original game in Fig. 1.

The pure strategies in the original and in the Bayes–equivalent game are summarized to behaviour strategies in the following manner:
For player B: $w \approx (w_1,..,w_n)$ and $r_k \approx (w_1,..,w_{k-1},r_k,*)$, $\forall k=1,..,n$.
For player C: $v \approx (v_1,..,v_n)$ and $e_k \approx (v_1,..,v_{k-1},r_k,*)$, $\forall k=1,..,n$.
The following lemmas and propositions characterize equilibrium points

Lemma 1:
Given the game described before, the following relations are true for all $k = 1,..,n$:
a) $F_B(R_k) > F_B(E_k)$
b) $F_C(E_k) > F_C(R_k)$

Lemma 2:
Given the game described before, there follows for all $k=1,..,n$:

a) $F_B(R_k) > F_B(R_{k+1})$ is given if $R_B > \frac{q_B}{q_B+p_B}$.

b) $F_B(R_k) \leq F_B(R_{k+1})$ is given if $R_B \leq \frac{q_B}{q_B+p_B}$.

Now the question of the relation between $F_B(M)$ and the optimum given by Lemma 2 arises. Proposition 1 is shows that only w and r_1 could be the optimal behaviour strategies of B, if C plays v. (And vice versa for C if B plays w).

Propostion 1:
Given the game described before, for all combinations of admissible R_B, p_B, and q_B is fulfiled:

a) If $R_B \leq \frac{q_B}{q_B+p_B}$, then w is the unique optimal behaviour strategy of B.
b) If $R_B > 1-p_B$, then r_1 is the unique optimal behaviour strategy of B.
c) If $\frac{q_B}{q_B+p_B} < R_B < 1-p_B$, then either w or r_1 is the optimal behavior strategy.

The number of stages n, the planning horizon, is of relevance only in case c)
Because of Proposition 1, the game in Fig.2 could be reduced to that in Fig. 3.
Proposition 2 is the result of analysing the game after elimination of dominated behaviour strategies.

Proposition 2:
In the game described before, only (w;v), (r_1;e_1), and (r_1;v) could be equilibrium points in not dominated pure behaviour strategies. Whereby

a) (v;w) is such an equilibrium point if, and only if,

$$F_B(M) = q_B \sum_{j=1}^{n-1} (1-p_B-q_B)^{(j-1)} + (1-p_B-q_B)^{(n-1)} (1-p_B) \geq R_B$$

and

$$F_C(M) = q_C \sum_{j=1}^{n-1} (1-p_C-q_C)^{(j-1)} + (1-p_C-q_C)^{(n-1)} (1-p_C) \geq E_C ,$$

b) (r_1;e_1) is such an equilibrium point, if and only if

$$F_C(M) = q_C \sum_{j=1}^{n-1} (1-p_C-q_C)^{(j-1)} + (1-p_C-q_C)^{(n-1)} (1-p_C) \leq E_C ,$$

c) (r_1;v) is such an equilibrium point if and only if

$$F_B(M) = q_B \sum_{j=1}^{n-1} (1-p_B-q_B)^{(j-1)} + (1-p_B-q_B)^{(n-1)} (1-p_B) \leq R_B$$

and

$$F_C(M) = q_C \sum_{j=1}^{n-1} (1-p_C-q_C)^{(j-1)} + (1-p_C-q_C)^{(n-1)} (1-p_C) \geq E_C .$$

d) (w;e_1) could never be an equilibrium point.

Finally, three slight variations in the assumptions are realistic to discuss: Different expected planning horizons n_B and n_C, a little bit uncertainty about the other player's individual probability estimations, and from stage to stage varying pay–offs. Dealing with these variations and numerical tests show that from a theoretical point of view the discussed modifications are only technical problems by finding of equilibrium points. Of these discussed modifications are only from stage to stage changing pay–offs are interesting for involved peoply choosing their right decisions.

Literature:

Harsyani, J (1967/8): Games with incomplete Information Played by Bayesian Players, Management Science 14, p.159—182, 320—334, 486—502

Holler, M.J. / Illing, G. (1991): Einführung in die Theorie der Spiele

Selten, R. (1982): Einführung in die Theorie der Spiele bei unvollständiger Information, in: Schriften des Vereins für Socialpolitik, Neue Reihe Bd. 126.

GROUNDSTATES IN ISING SPIN LATTICES BY OPTIMAL MATCHINGS

Jürgen Bendisch
Gesellschaft für Mathematik
und Datenverarbeitung GmbH
Postfach 1316, 53731 Sankt Augustin

Ulrich Derigs
Lehrstuhl für Wirtschaftsinformatik
Universität zu Köln
Pohligstraße 1
50969 Köln

Achim Metz
Lehrstuhl für Wirtschaftsinformatik
Universität zu Köln
Pohligstraße 1
50969 Köln

The investigated application refers to simulations of exact *groundstate* energies and magnetizations of two–dimensional random Ising spin models on *square* as well as *regular hexagonal* and *triangular* $L \times L$–lattices as considered in Solid State Physics when trying to determine for $L \to \infty$ the phase transition from ferro– to paramagnetism in magnetic crystal systems at zero temperature, cf. Bieche et al. (1980). In particular this requires to solve a quadratic integer programming problem, equivalent to a matching problem. The latter is efficiently solved by an exact algorithm based on works of Burkard, Derigs, Metz.

PHYSICAL PROBLEM FORMALIZED

Considering, see Fig. 1, $L \times L$ lattices of Ising spins $\sigma_1 = \pm 1$ (in reality generated by atoms in the lattice nodes), for mixed boundary conditions and given pattern J of random couplings $J_{i,j} = \pm 1$ between nearest neighbor (n.n.) spins we have, searching for groundstate spin configurations $(\tilde{\sigma})$, to minimize the energy

$$E_{p,L,J}(\sigma) = -\sum_{n.n.} J_{i,j}\sigma_i\sigma_j \qquad (1)$$

where p is a given probability that a coupling $J_{i,j}$, not on the left or right boundary, is equal to -1 (thus $J = J_p$). With S the number of lattice spins and $x_{p,L,J}$ the number of different groundstates $(\tilde{\sigma})_k = (\tilde{\sigma}_{1,k}, \tilde{\sigma}_{2,k}, \ldots, \tilde{\sigma}_{S,k}), k = 1, 2, \ldots$, we are interested in the $L \to \infty$ behaviour of the expected value $< \cdots >_{J_p}$ of the groundstate magnetization per spin:

$$m_L(p) = \left\langle \sum_{k=1}^{x_{p,L,J}} \left| \sum_{i=1}^{S} \tilde{\sigma}_{i,k} \right| \Big/ (S \cdot x_{p,L,J}) \right\rangle_{J_p} ,$$

see Fig. 2. We have to estimate $m_L(p)$ by empirical magnetization curves from simulation and then to extrapolate to the unknown $p_{c,type}$ (indicating the phase transition with respect to the considered lattice type) by an empirical inflection point curve.

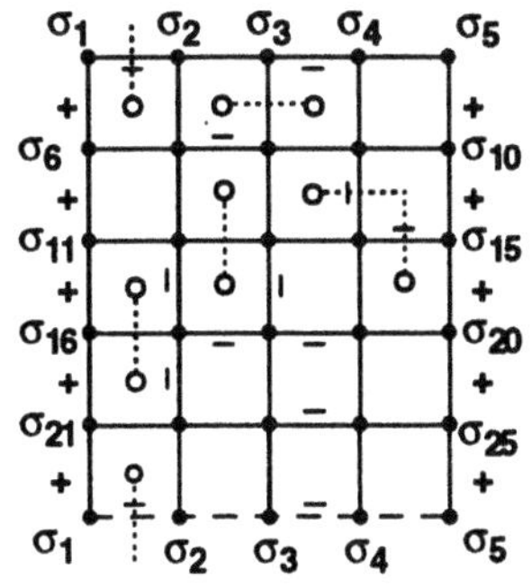

Figure 1: 5 × 5 square lattice with mixed boundary conditions (upper and lower boundary coincide, couplings $J_{i,j}$ on the left and right boundary are $+1$, spins on the left are $+1$). Couplings -1 are marked by minus signs, unsigned couplings are $+1$. Small circles indicate frustrated plaquettes. The set of dotted strings (called a stringing) between the frustrated plaquettes illustrates an optimal matching of length $\Lambda_{\min} = 1+1+1+1+2 = 6$, using a center–to–center–distance 1 for adjacent plaquettes.

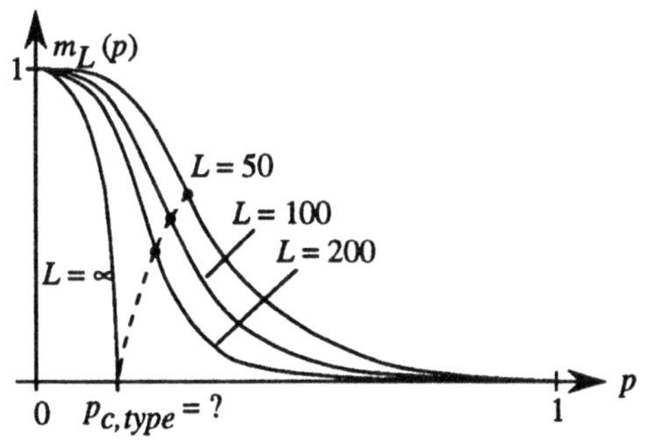

Figure 2: The sequence of $m_L(p)$– inflection points (dark dots) indicates for $L \to \infty$ the critical concentration $p_{c,type}$. $m_\infty(p) = 0$ for $p \geq p_{c,type}$.

Using the concept of frustrated plaquettes (i.e. a mesh with an odd number of couplings -1 on its perimeter) and between adjacent plaquettes a center–to–center distance equal to 1, the minimal energy in (1) is $E^{\min}_{p,L,J} = -B + 2\Lambda_{\min}$, cf. Bieche et al. (1980), where B is the number of lattice edges and $\Lambda_{\min}$ the minimal length of the matchings between the frustrated plaquettes, see Fig. 1. To determine in the simulations, p, L, J given, an optimal matching an efficient algorithm, resulting from works of Burkard et al. (1980), Derigs (1981, 1986), Derigs et al. (1991), has been applied to square, hexagonal and triangular lattices up to a size of 300×300 plaquettes and among these up to 34 000 frustrated ones. As for the square lattice case, cf. Bendisch et al. (1994). A stringing based on an optimal matching, see Fig. 1, crosses just the edges with $\sigma_i J_{i,j} \sigma_j = -1$. By this rule, the known couplings $J_{i,j}$ and $\sigma_1 = +1$ we can recursively construct a groundstate $(\tilde{\sigma})$.

By simulations (on an IBM RS 6000/540) we got estimates $\hat{\mu}_{p,L,n,s}$ for $m_L(p)$ where $\hat{\mu}_{p,L,n,s}$ is the mean magnetization from n patterns of random couplings $J_{i,j}$ and from $s = 15$ random stringings for each of the n optimal matchings ($0.05 \leq p \leq 0.20$, $10 \leq L \leq 300$, $480 \geq n \geq 20$). We got $p_{c,hex} \approx 0.06$, $p_{c,sq} \approx 0.10$, $p_{c,tri} \approx 0.15$. In particular, our estimates for $p_{c,hex}$ and $p_{c,tri}$ improve the known so far estimates considerably. As an example, we add for $p = 0.10$ and $L \times L$ square lattices with F frustrated plaquettes the average CPU–times (in seconds) for an optimal matching and for the magnetization $\mu_{p,L,s}$ of a pattern J (the latter time in brackets):

L (F)	50 (735)	100 (2941)	200 (11781)	300 (26540)
CPU–time	0.8 (1.62)	9.3 (21)	263 (330)	690 (1658)

Fig. 3 illustrates the simulation results in the hexagonal lattice case.

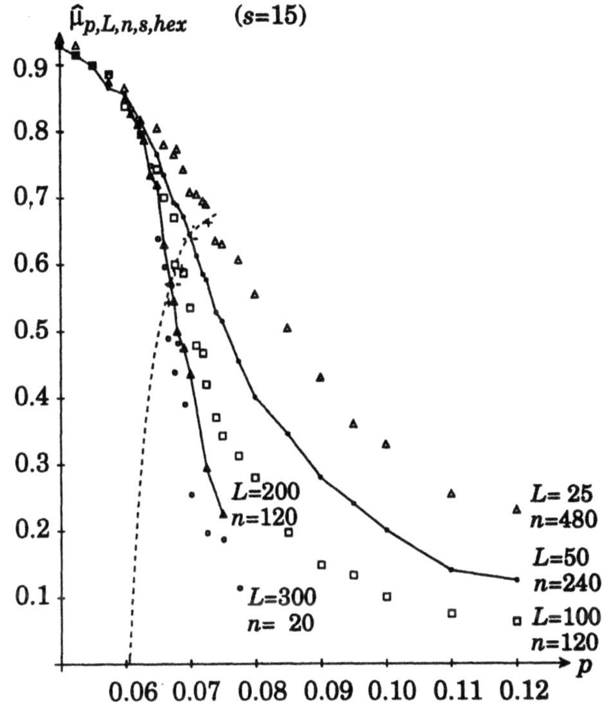

Figure 3: $p_{c,hex} \approx 0.06$ from simulations.

REFERENCES

Bendisch J, Derigs U, Metz A (1994) An efficient matching algorithm applied in Statistical Physics. Discrete Applied Mathematics

Bieche I, Maynard R, Rammal R, Uhry J (1980) On the groundstates of the frustration model of a spin glass. J. Phys A: Math Gen 13: 2553–2576

Burkard R, Derigs U (1980) Assignment and matching problems. Lecture Notes in Economics and Mathematical Systems 184. Springer–Verlag. Berlin NewYork

Derigs U (1981) A shortest augmenting path method for solving minimal perfect matching problems. Networks 11: 379–390

Derigs U (1986) Solving large–scale matching problems efficiently — A new primal approach Networks 16: 1–16

Derigs U, Metz A (1991) Solving large scale matching problems combinatorially. Mathematical Programming 50: 113–121

Parallel Tabu Search for Irregular Cutting

J.Błażewicz, J.Kaczmarek, R.Walkowiak
Institute of Computing Science
Technical University of Poznań
ul.Piotrowo 3a, 60-965 Poznań

The problem of cutting figures of various shapes out from the rectangular area is considered. The paper is devoted to the development of the earlier versions of the original method presented in [2,3]. A new approach is different from the previous one in the following points:

1. the use of an optimal algorithm for polygon placement [1],
2. new elements of tabu search policy,
3. parallelization of the algorithm.

The problem of two-dimensional irregular cutting consists in defining a cutting layout for a rectangular area (a material) and arbitrary given irregular figures. As the width of the material is fixed, the goal is to minimize the length of the material used. The proposed method is based (from the geometrical point of view) on the idea of allocating a polygon (a given shape) in another polygon (a part of material to be cut). The first of the two stages leads to a generation of a feasible (in the sense of geometrical constrains) solution. Elements are arranged from the left to the right starting with the biggest one. The second stage is made according to the tabu search [4] policy. Starting with the initial solution the search through the solution's space is carried out in order to improve quality of the solution. As the geometrical phase of the algorithm (repeatedly executed) is time consuming the parallelization of the original "tabu" method is proposed. The implementation of the algorithm is proposed for message-passing multi computer and the issue of dynamic load balancing is attacked.

Geometrical phase

The geometrical part of the method can be divided into three sub-problems:

- generation of (non-overlapping) placements of two polygons,
- allocating an element in the given point of a layout,
- removing an element from a layout.

While the two last issues are easier, the former one is more complicated in the sense of an algorithm's complexity [1] and implementation difficulties. It has to give all mutual non-overlapping allocations of two polygons. A simpler version of the algorithm with a fixed rotation angle has been implemented. The implementation showed that errors may occur (i.e. some extra erroneous placements are reported) in the case when polygons have equal dimensions in the same direction. Some modifications made led to rejecting the bad solutions and also some proper ones (in the above case). The only possibility to get the full set of proper placements seemed to check overlapping of elements in one freely chosen position of each separated area (polygon, line, point) of the placement found by the original procedure.

Parallel tabu search

Tabu search policy applied here differs from the one which has been used earlier [2,3].New classification and additional moves (insert, exchange and slide moves) have been introduced. The optimum function is based on parameters of solution rather than the type and parameters of a move. Two factors: the length of a layout and density of element's allocation are taken into account. The candidate moves are generated and the optimal move selection is made according to a new solution's quality, a tabu condition and an aspiration level. Possible moves consist in allocation of one or more figures (elements) in selected areas (holes). As the number of possible moves may be quite big, the parallel execution of the moves has been proposed. The sub-processes are created to find new solutions, which are results of element's extraction and reallocation. The geometrical procedures of the types described above has to be executed at least once within the sub-process. Two level hierarchical structure of tasks arises.

This parallelization supplies the computation process with tasks of small granularity. The computations are centralized and highly synchronized. This introduces a limitation on a speed up of computation but makes process management easier.

In this context, it seemed interesting to consider ideas for tabu search parallelization presented by Voß[6]. The proposals differ in a number of various strategies of the search and a number of basic processes (i.e. different starting solutions) created. Multiregional and multistrategical approach is interesting in big multi processor systems or in the case of small neighborhood of tabu search. This kind of approach introduces additional issues of process' synchronization and assurance of search diversification and demands extra processing and exchange of information.

Load balancing

The problem of load balancing of the multi computer system has to be considered in connection with the dynamic nature of the algorithm. The number of tasks, task's costs vary as the application runs. Hence for such a variable workload the dynamic load balancing scheme has to be applied. In a small multicomputer system when granularity of the tasks is rough and the computation process is centralized also centralized approach for load balancing is applicable. This type of a policy (but in fact a potentially distributed one) has been used in our system. The scheme has a feature of an auction algorithm [5], where two sides sellers and buyers shows their intentions.

To activate the subprocess the main process sends the proposal message containing a cost (an estimated time of computation) of the task and a proposed maximal price for its execution. The price for service required by a processor depends on processor's workload. If the price proposed is not lower than the required one the task will run on the processor enquired. If no processor accepts the price, it is increased by the control process above the lowest value proposed by processors in previous inquiry. The proposal message is sent again.

An acceptance of next task influences the workload of a processor and price for service. As the task execution is completed both factors decrease.

Challenging issues of various parallelization schemes and load balancing in large multi computer systems for generated process give directions of further research.

References

[1] F.Avnaim, J.D.Boissonnat: Polygon placement under translation and rotation, *LNCS N.294* Springer Verlag, 1988, pp.322-333.

[2] J.Błażewicz, P.Hawryluk, R.Walkowiak: Using a tabu search approach for solving the two-dimensional irregular cutting problem, Annals of Operations Research 41, 1993, pp.313-325

[3] J.Błażewicz, R.Walkowiak: An improved version of tabu search for irregular cutting problem, in: Operations Research'92, A.Karmann et all (eds.) Physica-Verlag, 1993, pp.102-104

[4] F.Glover, E.Taillard, D. de Werra, A user's guide to tabu search, Annals of Operations Research 41, 1993, pp.3-28

[5] T.C.Hu: Combinatorial and Network Algorithms, in: Operations Research'92, A.Karmann et all (eds.) Physica-Verlag, 1993, pp.128-129

[6] S.Voß: Concepts for parallel tabu search, Symposium on Applied Mathematical Programing and Modeling, Volume of extended Abstracts, Budapest, 1993

OPTIMIZATION OF THE SPARE PARTS STORAGE FOR THE POWER UNITS EQUIPMENTS

Prof. Paul Petre Bocănete, Ph.D.
Assist.prof Laurentiu Neamtu, M.S.
Institutul de Marină Civilă Constanta
Str. Mircea nr. 104, 8700 Constanta
Romania

In order to elaborate an optimization model for the spare parts storage, we use some assumptions, justified by practice :

a) the distribution of the uninterrupted working time and of the uninterrupted reparation time are exponential by respect to the intensity of damages λ and the intensity of the reparations μ ;

b) the substitution time is a random variable, following a certain distribution;

c) while keeping in storage space or while transportation to/from storehouse, spare parts could be defected, being unable to respond under loads;

d) spare part is used only in case that the reparation time is longer than the substitution time;

e) the reparation time is known immediately after the damage;

f) immediately after the damage, the element is going to be repaired, no matter if it is or it isn't substituted;

g) it is neglected the influence of the spare parts storage on the time of the preventive maintenance actions;

h) it's possible the refusal of response from the spare part under load, in case of a null interchange.

The basic term in the optimization model based on such hypotheses we shall call "the recover time" (t_{rt}) and we define it as the time interval between the moment of the refusal state of the system without reserves and the moment of the recovering of the successful state of the system in the same time with the refunctionality of the element. So, t_{rt} and its medium value T_{rt} are random terms with a distribution law that depends on the number of reserves from the stock. Therefore, considering an experimentally confirmed law

$$T_{rt} = a + cb^{-r} \qquad (1)$$

we get the graphic $T_{rt} = f(r)$ as shown in figure 1 (for burned gases fan).

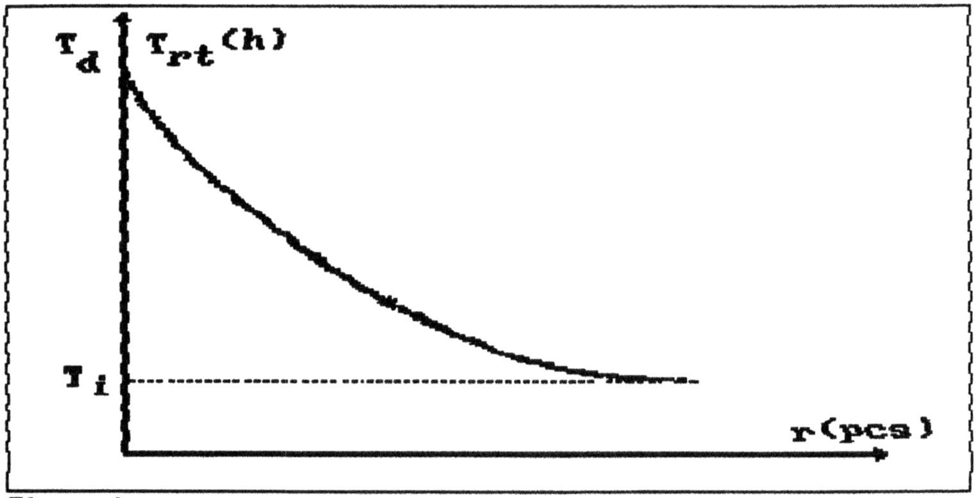

Figure 1

We can see the flat part of the curve and the corresponding value of r we shall call "the critical number of reserves" (r_{crt}). We suggest to consider the limits:

a) in case of $r=r_{crt}-1$ then $\Delta s = \frac{T_{rtcrt}-T_{rt\infty}}{T_d} > 0.0025$ (2)

b) in case of $r \geq r_{crt}$ then $\Delta s = \frac{T_{rtcrt}-T_{rt\infty}}{T_d} \leq 0.0025$ (3)

where T_{rtcrt} and $T_{rt\infty}$ correspond to r_{crt} and $r=\infty$ respectively

and T_d is the medium time for repairing the element. For practical needs, we suggest the use of the expression:

$$T_{rt} = \frac{1}{\mu}[1-e^{-\mu T_i}(1-\frac{\frac{(\frac{me^{-T_i}}{\mu})^r}{r!}}{\frac{(\frac{me^{-T_i}}{\mu})^k}{k!}})] \qquad (4)$$

where m - number of elements with spare parts; r - the total number of reserves; k - the number of reserves used in a certain moment to substitute elements with flaw; λ , μ - damage and repairing equipments; T_i - the medium substitution time.

Considering the idea of a common reserve for all kind of identical equipments, we suggested an algorithm that could be applied on any system with many functional groups ,with a similar role in the equivalent technological scheme, for the calculus of the disposal and maintenance of the power units. We've considered the criterion of the actualised total expenses in which we've taken the case of the minimal value. The steps of the algorithm are :

1. - determination of $r_{crt}(k)$ and recovering values $\mu_r(k,r)$ for each category k from the N_c value, considered with reservation; we used (2),(3),(4);
2. - calculus of the reservation variants R(i,k) for each k and in each variant i;
3. - evaluation of the damage per year due to the missed deliverance of energy in the system;
4. - in each variant we determine the cost of reserved elements I(i), the expenses per year for stocks C1(i), the expenses per year because the missed deliverance of energy Da(i), the remained value of reserves at the end of the studied period Re(i);
5. - calculus of the total actualised expenses in variant i A(i), which by respect to the end of the first year gives us:

$$A(i)=I(i)+Da(i)\sum_{p=1}^{s}(1+a)^{1-p}+C1(i)\sum_{p=1}^{s}(1+a)^{1-p}-Re(i)(1+a) \qquad (5)$$

where a - actualised rate and p - the currently studied year;

6. - comparation between variants and the determination of the optimum by using an auxiliary value Ca to which we give a sufficiently great value initially, that it can be greater than the total actualised expenses value in first variant: A(1) < Ca .

On the base of the shortly presented algorithm we've made an original computational program structured on four parts:
a main programme and three procedures. The procedures are:
RECRIT - calculates the critical value for reserves and the intensities of recovering for each reserved category; RESMIU - gets the intensities of recovering for each reserved variant; TREG - calculates the medium time of unproduced power on a certain flat

zone of the curve in each variant of reservation.
Using the programme at Turceni Power Plant, for 330MW power units and considering two categories of reservation, we've obtained:

Table I

Number of blocks	1	2	4	6
Optimal variant	40	72	162	252
First category	4	5	8	10
Second category	7	11	17	21

We conclude that:
- the optimum number of reserves goes to saturation in the same time with the growth of the functionals groups of the system,so that is recommendable the common spare parts storage;
- the optimum number of reserves is more influenced by the number of damages because of the missed deliverance of energy in the system than the medium time for substitution;
- the optimum number of reserves is not proportional with the number of basic elements from the equivalent scheme of the combination of damaged elements that produce the refusal of the system on a certain flat zone of the power.

References

Paul Bocânete - " Contributions on the optimization of maintenance activity for the power units", Doctorate Thesis,1985.

Using strong cutting planes in constraint logic programming

Alexander Bockmayr
Max-Planck-Institut für Informatik
Im Stadtwald
D-66123 Saarbrücken

1 Constraint logic programming and 0-1 constraints

Constraint logic programming has been one of the major developments in the area of declarative programming during the last years. The idea is to combine a logic programming language similar to Prolog with a constraint solver for a specific domain of computation such as linear arithmetic, Boolean algebra, finite domains or lists [BC93].

In [Boc93] we introduced a new constraint logic programming language CLP($\mathcal{PB}$) for logic programming with pseudo-Boolean constraints. *Pseudo-Boolean constraints* or *0-1 constraints* combine Boolean algebra with arithmetic. A *pseudo-Boolean function* is an integer-valued function $f : \{0,1\}^n \to \mathcal{Z}$ of 0-1 variables. Any such function can be represented as a multilinear polynomial in its variables. A *pseudo-Boolean constraint* is an equation or inequality between pseudo-Boolean functions.

The aim of this paper is to present a constraint solver for *linear* pseudo-Boolean constraints of the form $a_1x_1 + \ldots + a_nx_n \leq b$, with $a_1, \ldots, a_n, b \in \mathcal{Z}$ and 0-1 variables $x_1, \ldots, x_n$. The constraint solver has to provide solutions to the following typical problems in constraint logic programming:

Solvability: Decide whether a constraint set C has a solution.

Simplification: Simplify a constraint set C to a *solved form* $\mathcal{S}(C)$.

Entailment: Decide whether a constraint c is implied by a constraint set C.

In many applications, it is not sufficient to compute an arbitrary solution of the constraint set C but one has to find a solution which is *optimal* with respect to some pseudo-Boolean function f [Boc93, BB93]. Therefore we have also the problem

Optimization: Optimize a pseudo-Boolean function f subject to a constraint set C.

The problem of optimization has recently received considerable attention within the constraint logic programming community.

2 Simplifying 0-1 constraints

When executing a constraint logic program, the main problem is to simplify a given constraint set C and to compute a *solved form* $\mathcal{S}(C)$. What should this solved form look like? There are the following basic requirements:

- $\mathcal{S}(C)$ should be equivalent to C.
- $\mathcal{S}(C)$ should be "simpler" than C.

- $\mathcal{S}(C)$ should be *false* if C is unsolvable.

From a mathematical point of view, a set C of 0-1 constraints is the same as a system $Ax \leq b$ of linear inequalities in 0-1 variables with $A \in \mathcal{Z}^{m \times n}$, $x \in \{0,1\}^n$ and $b \in \mathcal{Z}^m$. Such a system defines a possibly empty set S of 0-1 points in $\mathcal{R}^n$. The same 0-1 set S can be represented in many different ways. Since we are interested in constraint simplification, we have to decide when a representation C_1 of S is "simpler" or "better" than a representation C_2. There are many possibilities to compare linear inequality descriptions $Ax \leq b$ of a 0-1 set S. In particular we may consider

- the size of the system $Ax \leq b$ depending on the number of inequalities and the size of their coefficients.
- the strength of the inequalities in the system $Ax \leq b$.

Given the various possibilities which one should we choose for the solved form? Since we are interested not only in constraint solving but also in constrained optimization we need a solved form that supports optimization. One of the most powerful techniques to obtain provably good solutions of combinatorial optimization problems is *branch-and-cut*, which combines classical branch-and-bound with cutting plane techniques from polyhedral combinatorics.

In order to simplify a constraint set C we propose to compute strong valid inequalities for the convex hull $conv(S)$. Given two constraint sets $C : Ax \leq b$ and $C' : A'x \leq b'$ with the same set of 0-1 solutions S, we say that C is *simpler* than C' iff $\{x \in \mathcal{R}^n \mid Ax \leq b\} \subseteq \{x \in \mathcal{R}^n \mid A'x \leq b'\}$. The *ideal solved form* of C is a constraint set $\bar{C} : \bar{A}x \leq \bar{b}$ with $conv(S) = \{x \in \mathcal{R}^n \mid \bar{A}x \leq \bar{b}\}$ such that there is a 1-1 correspondence between the inequalities in $\bar{A}x \leq \bar{b}$ and the facets of $conv(S)$.

In practice, this ideal solved form cannot be computed, because an exponential number of inequalities may be needed. Nevertheless, constraint solving can be done in a lazy way by approximating the ideal solved form. This is the topic of the next section.

3 Computing the solved form

How can we find strong valid inequalities for a given set of 0-1 constraints? For special problems (knapsack, set covering, traveling salesman etc.) strong valid inequalities have been found by analyzing the specific problem structure. To find strong cutting planes for general 0-1 problems, we propose to use the new *lift-and-project* method for mixed 0-1 optimization due to [BCC93]. It has been applied very successfully to many hard 0-1 optimization problems and is even competitive with a number of special purpose algorithms.

The starting point ot this method is a sequential convexification theorem.
If $P = \{x \in \mathcal{R}^n \mid Ax \geq b, 0 \leq x \leq 1\} \stackrel{\text{def}}{=} \{x \in \mathcal{R}^n \mid \tilde{A}x \geq \tilde{b}\}$ is a polyhedron in $\mathcal{R}^n$ and

$$R_j(P) = conv(P \cap \{x \in \mathcal{R}^n \mid x_j \in \{0,1\}\}), \text{ for } j = 1, \ldots, n,$$

then $R_1(R_2(\ldots R_n(P))) = conv(S)$, where $S = P \cap \{0,1\}^n$. The idea of [BCC93] is to use facets of $R_j(P)$ as strong cutting planes for S. By lifting the problem into a higher-dimensional space they show that $R_j(P) = \{x \in \mathcal{R}^n \mid \alpha x \geq \beta \text{ for all } (\alpha,\beta) \in R_j^*(P)\}$ with

$$\begin{aligned} R_j^*(P) \;=\{\; & (\alpha,\beta) \in \mathcal{R}^{n+1} \mid \exists u, v \in \mathcal{R}^{m+2n}, u_0, v_0 \in \mathcal{R} : \\ & \alpha - u\tilde{A} - u_0 e_j = 0,\ \alpha - v\tilde{A} - v_0 e_j = 0,\ u\tilde{b} = \beta,\ v\tilde{b} + v_0 = \beta,\ u, v \geq 0 \;\}, \end{aligned}$$

where e_j is the j-th unit vector in $\mathcal{R}^n$.

If $P \cap \{x \mid x_j = 0\} \neq \emptyset \neq P \cap \{x \mid x_j = 1\}$, then for any constant $\beta \neq 0$, $\alpha x \geq \beta$ defines a facet of $R_j(P)$ iff (α, β) is an extreme ray of $R_j^*(P)$. To compute such extreme rays one can solve a linear program of the form $max\{a\alpha + b\beta \mid (\alpha,\beta) \in R_j^*(P) \cap T\}$, where $(a,b) \in \mathcal{R}^{n+1}$ is a vector that determines the direction of the cut and T a normalization set that truncates the cone $R_j^*(P)$.

Strong Cutting Plane Algorithm for Solving 0-1 Constraints

1. $t := 1; C^1 := C = \{Ax \geq b, 0 \leq x \leq 1\}$,
2. Let $P^t = \{x \in \mathcal{R}^n \mid x$ is a solution of $C^t\}$.
   If $P^t = \emptyset$, stop, C is unsolvable.
3. Find a vertex x^t of P^t by optimizing a suitable linear function g^t.
   If $x^t_j \in \{0,1\}$, for $j = 1,\ldots,n$, stop, x^t is a feasible 0-1 solution, C^t is the solved form of C.
4. For $j \in \{1,\ldots,n\}$ with $0 < x^t_j < 1$ generate a j-cut $\alpha^j x \geq \beta^j$ by solving

$$max\{\beta - \alpha x^t \mid (\alpha,\beta) \in R^*_j(P^t) \cap T\}.$$

5. Define C^{t+1} by adding the j-cuts $\alpha^j x \geq \beta^j$ to the constraint set C^t (and perhaps removing some cuts added earlier).
6. Let $t := t + 1$ and goto 2.

The same algorithm can also be used for *optimization* and *entailment*.

There are many possibilities to improve this basic algorithm. First of all, we should apply the various preprocessing techniques for 0-1 programs which are described in the literature. Then the generation of strong cutting planes has to be combined with classical branch-and-bound techniques. Cuts generated in one part of the branch-and-bound tree can be made valid for the whole tree by a cut lifting procedure. Finally, various parameters in the cutting plane procedure have to be fixed.

4 Mixed 0-1 constraints

When solving linear 0-1 constraints by cutting plane techniques, we have to use linear arithmetic constraints and linear optimization. A natural extension of this approach would be to use linear arithmetic already from the beginning. This leads to a new kind of constraints, *mixed 0-1 constraints* $\sum_{i\in I} a_i x_i + \sum_{j \in J} b_j y_i \leq c$, with real variables x_i and 0-1 variables y_j.

Mixed 0-1 constraints are particularly interesting because they integrate two of the most important domains in constraint logic programming, Boolean algebra and linear arithmetic. The strong cutting plane method presented in the previous section works also for the mixed 0-1 case. Therefore it provides also the basis for a constraint logic programming language for mixed 0-1 constraints.

References

[BB93] P. Barth and A. Bockmayr. Solving 0-1 problems in CLP($\mathcal{PB}$). In *Proc. 9th Conf. Artificial Intelligence for Applications CAIA, Orlando, Florida.* IEEE, 1993.

[BC93] F. Benhamou and A. Colmerauer, editors. *Constraint Logic Programming - Selected Research.* MIT Press, 1993.

[BCC93] E. Balas, S. Ceria, and G. Cornuéjols. A lift-and-project cutting plane algorithm for mixed 0-1 programs. *Mathematical Programming*, 58:295 – 324, 1993.

[Boc92] A. Bockmayr. Embedding OR techniques into constraint logic programming. In *Operations Research '92. 17th Symposium on Operations Research*, Hamburg, 1992

[Boc93] A. Bockmayr. Logic programming with pseudo-Boolean constraints. In [BC93].

Efficient Workload–Balancing on Grids, Hypercubes and Trees

Max Böhm[1], Ewald Speckenmeyer
Mathematisches Institut / Abteilung für Informatik
Heinrich–Heine–Universität Düsseldorf
D–40225 Düsseldorf

Extended Abstract: We present several algorithms for achieving efficient workload balancing (WLB) on message based MIMD machines. Given a set of n processors $P = \{p_1, \ldots, p_n\}$ and a communication network $N \subset P \times P$. At a fixed point in time every processor $p \in P$ has a workload (WL) $\lambda(p) \in \mathbb{R}^+$, which is an estimation for the time needed to solve the problems placed on p. In the following we assume, that WL is dividible in infinitely small pieces, which can be exchanged between processors. The basic step $move(p, q, l)$ with $p, q \in P$, $(p, q) \in N$, $-\lambda(q) \leq l \leq \lambda(p)$ means that workload l is moved from p to q if $l > 0$ or workload $-l$ is moved from q to p if $l < 0$. WL $\lambda(p)$ changes into $\lambda(p) - l$ and $\lambda(q)$ changes into $\lambda(q) + l$.

The WLB problem consists of exchanging WL between processors resulting in a *uniformly distributed* WL, i. e. $\forall p, q \in P : \lambda(p) = \lambda(q)$. The following algorithm solves the problem for processor–trees $T = (P, N)$ in time $O(h \cdot d_{max})$ with h = *height of* T and d_{max} = *maximal number of sons per processor.*

WLB algorithm for processor–trees

Every processor $p \in P$ performs the following steps:

1. calculate *prefixsum* $\hat{\lambda}(p) := \lambda(p) + \sum_{q \in sons(p)} \hat{\lambda}(q)$
2. the root processor r calculates *optimal* WL $\mu := \frac{\hat{\lambda}(r)}{n}$; distribute μ to all processors
3. calculate $l(p) := \hat{\lambda}(p) - n(p) \cdot \mu$ with $n(p)$ = *number of nodes of subtree rooted at* p
4. $move(p, father(p), l(p))$

In step 1 every processor determines $\hat{\lambda}(p)$ which is the total WL in the subtree rooted at p. This is done in less than $h \cdot d_{max}$ steps from the leaf processors upwards to the root processor. In step 2 the root processor r knows the total WL $\hat{\lambda}(r)$ of all processors. The optimal workload μ is calculated and distributed downwards in the tree also in less than $h \cdot d_{max}$ steps. In step 3 every processor calculates its *optimal prefixsum* $n(p) \cdot \mu$. The difference to the actual prefixsum $\hat{\lambda}(p)$ is the overload or underload $l(p)$ of the subtree rooted at p, which has to be balanced over the edge $(p, father(p))$. Some *move* steps of step 4 need a special sequence of executions, because a processor p, which has to send a WL greater than $\lambda(p)$ may has to wait for receipt of sufficient WL from other processors first. Nevertheless the WLB–algorithm for processor–trees can be shown to achieve a uniform distribution of WL among the processors within $2 \cdot h \cdot d_{max}$ steps of moving WL, which can easily be seen to be optimal. Particularly we want to stress the point that the algorithm achieves a uniform distribution of WL by moving the smallest possible amount of WL among the processors, which is important, in case of WL consisting of huge data–packets.

WLB for linear arrays can be done in $O(n)$ steps using the algorithm for processor–trees with the processor $p_{\lfloor n/2 \rfloor}$ as root processor.

WLB for d–dimensional m–sided grids ($n = m^d$) can be done in time $O(d \cdot m)$ using WLB for linear arrays for each dimension:

for k=1 to d do
  $\forall i_j \in \{1, \ldots, m\}$, $1 \leq j \leq d$, $j \neq k$ do in parallel
    WLB for linear array with processor set $\{p_{i_1,\ldots,i_d} \mid i_k \in \{1, \ldots, m\}\}$

[1]This research was supported by the Federal State of Nordrhein-Westfalen in the *Forschungsverbund Paralleles Rechnen*, Az.: IV A 3 - 107 021 91 -

WLB for the d–dimensional hypercube, which is a d–dimensional 2-sided grid, can be done in time $O(d)$. The algorithm simplifies to:

for k=1 to d do
  $\forall(p,q) \in N(k)$ do in parallel with $N(k)$ = edges of dimension k
    $move(p, q, \frac{\lambda(q)-\lambda(p)}{2})$

Implementation and Experimental Results

We have implemented these algorithms on a T805 transputer system. The NP–complete satisfiability problem (SAT) was chosen as a demonstration problem. The input intance of the SAT problem is a boolean formula F in conjunctive normal form and we have to determine whether or not a truth assignment for the variables exists, which satisfies F. The problem of solving F can be divided into two subproblems $F_{\{x=0\}}$ and $F_{\{x=1\}}$ for any variable x assigning 0 resp. 1 to x. We have used a fast sequential SAT–Solver [1] for solving small subproblems. The WL of a problem with k boolean variables is approximated by α^k with $\alpha \approx 1.04$ which was experimentally determined. A sample of 25 hard unsatisfiable random 3–SAT formulas (clause length = 3) with 400 variables and 2000 clauses was used as test instance. The table shows the the average running time and standard deviation in seconds for the network topologies *linear array*, *2–dimensional grid* and *complete binary tree*. The following figures show average speedup– and efficiency–values with respect to varying numbers of processors.

linear array			2–dimensional grid			complete binary tree		
n	time	std. dev.	n	time	std. dev.	n	time	std. dev.
1	40201.2	13046.3	1	40201.2	13046.3	1	40201.2	13046.3
16	2637.1	851.9	4×4	2558.6	826.7	2^4-1	2712.8	876.5
32	1321.5	426.1	4×8	1280.6	413.1	2^5-1	1316.3	424.3
64	667.2	213.5	8×8	642.3	206.5	2^6-1	651.1	209.1
128	350.3	107.7	8×16	322.8	103.5	2^7-1	338.4	123.1
256	301.9	80.4	16×16	163.5	51.9	2^8-1	183.1	62.2

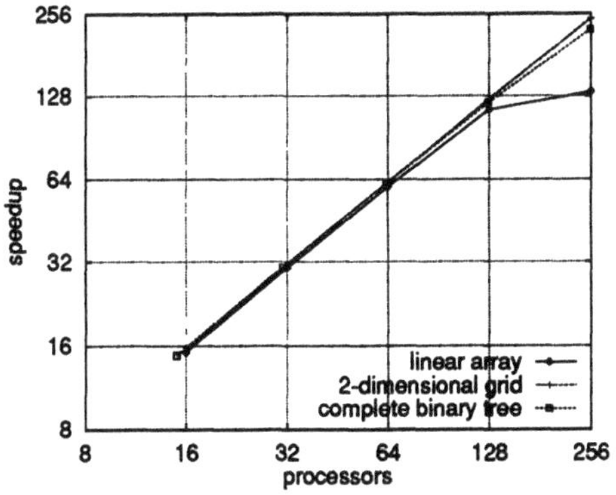

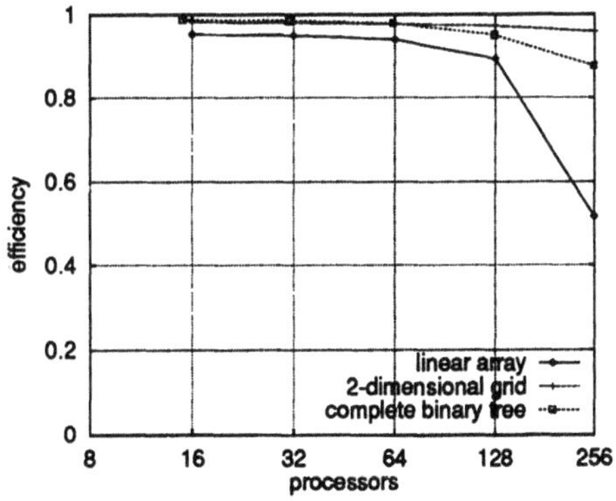

Acknowledgement: We would like to thank Frank Meisgen and Thorsten Rudolph for their implementations of the workload balancing algorithm, the communication framework and for the helpful discussions.

References

[1] Buro, M. and Kleine Büning, H.: *Report on a SAT competition*, EATCS Bulletin, No 49, Feb 1993, 143–151

OUTLINE OF A THEORY OF RISK UNDER PARTIAL PROBABILITY INFORMATION

Hans Wolfgang Brachinger
Seminar of Statistics
University of Fribourg

Introduction

In the decision-theoretic literature, usually, a distinction is made between decisions under risk and decisions under complete ignorance. In practice, however, the case of "partial ignorance" (Luce and Raiffa (1958), p. 299) is prevailing which lies anywhere between the extreme cases of complete ignorance, with no knowledge of probabilities, and the opposite extreme of risk, with well-known quantitative probabilities.

In situations of partial probability information, the question arises of how to decide rationally. There is some empirical evidence that in practical economic situations of partial ignorance, e.g. project apraisal, decision makers use some sort of generalized mean-risk decision rule (cf. Brachinger (1991)). Modeling that kind of decision behavior presupposes a theory of risk under conditions of partial probability information.

Based on previous work on the perceived risk of gambles, the theory outlined in this paper is the first attempt to attack the problem of perceived risk under conditions of partial probability information. For a detailed exposition of that theory see Brachinger (1993).

General Framework

Let $\mathcal{Z}$ be a set of mutually exclusive states of nature, $|\mathcal{Z}| = m \geq 2$, $\mathcal{E}$ a (nonempty) set of consequences, and $\mathcal{A}$ a set of functions $a : \mathcal{Z} \longrightarrow \mathcal{E}$, $|\mathcal{A}| \geq 2$. A probability distribution over $\mathcal{Z}$ is a m-dimensional vector $\underline{p} = (p_1, \ldots, p_m)'$ with $p_i \geq 0$ for every $i = 1, \ldots, m$ and $\sum p_i = 1$. Let $\mathcal{P}_{\mathcal{Z}}$ be the set of all probability distributions over $\mathcal{Z}$. Each nonempty subset $\mathcal{P}$ of the set $\mathcal{P}_{\mathcal{Z}}$ may be called ***probability information***. It may be called ***quantitative*** if $|\mathcal{P}| = 1$, ***partial*** if $|\mathcal{P}| > 1$ and $\mathcal{P} \subsetneq \mathcal{P}_{\mathcal{Z}}$, and ***trivial*** if $\mathcal{P} = \mathcal{P}_{\mathcal{Z}}$. Obviously, the classical decision situation under risk is characterized by quantitative probability information, whereas in decisions under complete ignorance only trivial probability information is available. In most practical cases probability information is partial.

In the context of the finite basic decision-theoretic model, it is presumed that consequences $e \in \mathcal{E}$ as well as "differences" between consequences can be preferentially ordered and assigned numerical values $u(e)$ that preserve these preference orderings. It is assumed further that a "target" consequence $e^* \in \mathcal{E}$ can be identified. The value $u^* := u(e^*) \geq 0$ will be called ***target utility***. Every utility value smaller than u^* as well as the underlying consequence is viewed as ***risky*** and will be called a ***loss***. Every utility value as large as u^* is viewed as nonrisky and will be called a ***gain***.

As a whole, the general framework for treating the problem of perceived risk under partial probability information is given with the triple

$$(\mathcal{A}, (\mathcal{Z}, \mathcal{P}), (u, u^*)) \quad .$$

Pure Risk

First, a theory of pure risk is sketched, where only potential losses are considered: risk increases with probability and amount of loss.

Within the framework $(\mathcal{A},(\mathcal{Z},\mathcal{P}),(u,u^*))$ the quality of an action $a \in \mathcal{A}$ is characterized by its vector $\mathrm{u}(a) = (u(a(z_1)),\ldots,u(a(z_m)))$ of potential utilities. Every utility value $u(a(z_j))$ smaller than u^* is a potential loss whose amount is given with $S_j^a := u^* - u(a(z_j))$. Therefore, the total amount of potential losses of an action is given with the vector whose j-th component equals S_j^a, if z_j leads to a loss, and 0 otherwise. Formally this vector can be described by the vector

$$X^+ := X^+(a) := (\chi^+(S_1^a)\cdot S_1^a,\ldots,\chi^+(S_m^a)\cdot S_m^a)$$

where χ^+ is the characteristic function of the positive reals. Given an action $a \in \mathcal{A}$, for every state z_j, the j-th component $\chi_j^+ := \chi_j^+(a) := \chi^+(S_j^a)\cdot S_j^a$ of X^+ specifies the corresponding amount of loss. The degree of uncertainty over the potential losses of an action is covered by the partial probability information $\mathcal{P}$. I.e., the objects of our theory of risk under partial information will be the set of all pairs $(X^+,\mathcal{P})$, where $X^+ \in \Re^m_{o+}$ is a m-dimensional vector of potential losses and $\mathcal{P} \subset \mathcal{P}_\mathcal{Z}$ a partial probability information. In the sequel, each pair $(X^+,\mathcal{P}) \in \Re^m_{o+} \times \wp(\mathcal{P}_\mathcal{Z})$ will be called *risk vector.*

The axioms for risk measurement under partial information are based on a binary relation $\succeq$, read "is at least as risky as", defined on $\Re^m_{o+} \times \wp(\mathcal{P}_\mathcal{Z})$ which is assumed to be a *quasi-order*. In a first axiom an action is viewed as *riskless* if and only if there are no potential losses. In the second axiom (*"Utility Dominance"*) it is assumed that a potential loss is greater the more the corresponding utility value deviates from the target utility. According to conventional notion, risk also increases as the chance of losses increases. In its intuitive sense, risk is the worst that can happen under given conditions. In the case of a partial probability information $\mathcal{P}$, given a specified loss vector X^+, the "worst that can happen" is that probability distribution p $\in \mathcal{P}$ which maximizes loss expectation. This leads to a *probability dominance* axiom which is essentially a new interpretation of the well-known MaxEmin-criterion (cf. Kofler and Menges (1976)). In a further axiom it is assumed that the risk order is scale-invariant.

Every pair $(\Re^m_{o+} \times \wp(\mathcal{P}_\mathcal{Z}),\succeq)$, where $\succeq$ is a relation on $\Re^m_{o+} \times \wp(\mathcal{P}_\mathcal{Z})$ which meets the axioms mentioned, will be called *risk order (under partial information).*

Risk Measures

Let the intersection of all risk orders be called *risk structure (under partial information)*, denoted by $(\Re^m_{o+} \times \wp(\mathcal{P}_\mathcal{Z}),\succeq^*)$. For each risk order, it is this structure which is, at least, to be numerically represented by a risk measure. The numerical risk value of a risk vector should be nonnegative. Therefore, the numerical relational structure $(\Re^1_{o+},\geq)$ will be used for representing the risk structure.

A risk measure should be a homomorphism of the risk structure and should indicate zero risk if and only if X^+ is riskless, i.e. $X^+ = 0$. Furthermore, it is assumed that rescaling effects multiplicatively on R. Finally, as it is generally accepted in the literature on risk measurement risk measures should have a kind of expectation property.

Then, the following *representation theorem* is easy to show:

The mapping $\Phi : \Re^m_{o+} \times \wp(\mathcal{P}_\mathcal{Z}) \longrightarrow \Re^1_{o+}$ defined by

$$\Phi(X^+, \mathcal{P}) = \sup_{p \in \mathcal{P}} \sum_{j=1}^{m} \chi_j^+ p_j$$

is a risk measure under partial information.

In addition, the following *uniqueness theorem* can be formulated:

A realvalued mapping R of $\Re^m_{o+} \times \wp(\mathcal{P}_\mathcal{Z})$ is a risk measure under partial information if and only if there exist some positive real constants k_1, k_2 such that for all risk vectors $(X^+, \mathcal{P})$

$$R(X^+, \mathcal{P}) = R^{k_2}_{k_1}(X^+, \mathcal{P}) := k_1 \Phi(X^+, \mathcal{P})^{k_2} \quad .$$

This uniqueness theorem shows that risk measurement under partial information is measurement on a log-interval scale.

Speculative Risk

If risk is conceived such that also effects of potential gains are admitted, then this is usually called *"speculative risk"* in the literature (cf., e.g. , Fishburn (1982)). All other things being equal, risk increases as loss probability or amount increases, and greater gains or gain probabilities reduce perceived risk.

Within the framework $(\mathcal{A}, (\mathcal{Z}, \mathcal{P}), (u, u^*))$, for a given action, every utility value $u(a(z_j))$ greater than u^* is a potential gain whose amount is given with $-S^a_j := u(a(z_j)) - u^*$. The total amount of potential gains of an action $a \in \mathcal{A}$ can be described by its gain vector

$$X^- := X^-(a) := (\chi^-(S^a_1) \cdot (-S^a_1), \ldots, \chi^-(S^a_m) \cdot (-S^a_m)) \quad ,$$

where χ^- is the characteristic function of the negative reals. Given an action $a \in \mathcal{A}$, for every state z_j the j-th component $\chi_j^- := \chi_j^-(a) := \chi^-(S^a_j) \cdot (-S^a_j)$ of X^- specifies the corresponding amount of gain. The degree of uncertainty over the potential gains as well as over the potential losses is covered by the partial probability information $\mathcal{P}$. I.e., the objects of our theory of speculative risk under partial information will be the set of all triples $(X^+, X^-, \mathcal{P})$, where X^+, X^- are m-dimensional vectors of potential losses or gains respectively, and $\mathcal{P} \subset \mathcal{P}_\mathcal{Z}$ is a partial probability information. In the sequel, each triple $(X^+, X^-, \mathcal{P}) \in \Re^m_{o+} \times \Re^m_{o+} \times \wp(\mathcal{P}_\mathcal{Z})$ will be called ***generalized risk vector***.

Analogous to the axioms for pure risk measurement, the axioms for speculative risk measurement under partial information are based on a binary relation $\succeq$ defined on $\Re^m_{o+} \times \Re^m_{o+} \times \wp(\mathcal{P}_\mathcal{Z})$, which is assumed to be a quasi-order. In the main axiom (***"Sign"***) of that theory it is admitted that greater gains or gain probabilities not only reduce but even overcompensate perceived risk. Ceteris paribus, generalized risk should increase with increasing loss amount but decrease with increasing gains. This leads to two utility dominance axioms (***Risk Dominance and Chance Dominance***) Furthermore, all other things being equal, generalized risk should increase with increasing loss probability and with decreasing gain probability. Therefore, also some kind of generalized ***Probability Dominance*** is assumed. Finally, as rescaling of risk vectors simultaneously reduces or augments its losses and gains respectively, it seems reasonable to assume that risk-augmenting and risk-reducing effects compensate and speculative risk remains unchanged (***scale invariance***).

Every pair $(\Re^m_{o+} \times \Re^m_{o+} \times \wp(\mathcal{P}), \succsim)$ where $\succsim$ is a relation on $\Re^m_{o+} \times \Re^m_{o+} \times \wp(\mathcal{P})$ meeting the axioms mentioned is called (generalized) risk order (under partial probability information).

Generalized Risk Measures

A generalized risk measure should be a mapping

$$R^* \ : \ \Re^m_{o+} \times \Re^m_{o+} \times \wp(\mathcal{P}) \longrightarrow \Re$$

which can take on positive as well as negative values, because chances may overcompensate risks.

Under certain separability and homogeneity conditions it follows (***representation theorem***) that the mapping

$$\Phi^* : \begin{cases} \Re^m_{o+} \times \Re^m_{o1} \times \wp(\mathcal{P}_Z) & \longrightarrow \quad \Re^1 \\ (X^+, X^-, \mathcal{P}) & \longmapsto \quad \alpha\Phi^2(X^+, \mathcal{P}) - \Phi^2(X^-, \mathcal{P}) \end{cases} .$$

is a generalized risk measure under partial probability information. Thereby, the parameter α characterizes the decision maker's risk attitudes.

Under additional assumptions, it follows that an essential class of generalized risk measures $R^* : \Re^m_{o+} \times \Re^m_{o+} \times \wp(\mathcal{P}_Z) \longrightarrow \Re^1$ is the three-parametric class

$$R^*(X^+, X^-, \mathcal{P}) = R^*_{\alpha,\ell,k}(X^+, X^-, \mathcal{P}) := \ell(\alpha^k \Phi(X^+, \mathcal{P})^k - \Phi(X^-, \mathcal{P})^k) \ ,$$

with $\alpha, \ell, k > 0$ (cf. Brachinger (1994)).

References

Brachinger, H. W. (1991). The Sensitivity Approach to Decision Making under Uncertainty: A Decision Theoretic Foundation. In: Jones, S. B. und Davies, D. G. S. (Eds.), Modelling Under Uncertainty (pp. 219-229). Institute of Physics: Bristol und Boston.

Brachinger, H. W. (1993). Risk Measurement Under Partial Probability Information. Paper presented at the 14th Conference on Subjective Probability, Utility and Decision Making (SPUDM14), Aix-en-Provence, 1993.

Fishburn, P. C. (1982). Foundations of Risk Measurement. II. Effect of Gains on Risk. Journal of Mathematical Psychology, 25, 226-242.

Kofler, E. und Menges, G. (1976): Entscheidungen bei unvollständiger Information. Berlin.

Luce, R. D., & Raiffa, H. (1957). Games and Decisions. New York, London: Wiley.

ENHANCED RELIABILITY AND THE DEMAND IMPACT OF JOINTLY NORMALLY DISTRIBUTED SIGNALS

Thomas Braun
Wirtschaftswissenschaftliches Seminar
Eberhard-Karls-Universität Tübingen
Nauklerstr. 47, D-72074 Tübingen

1. THE PROBLEM

The objective of this paper is to contribute to a better understanding of rational expectations equilibria. These equilibria emerge from demand decisions of investors who try to extract information about future market prices from current ones. Therefore from an economist's perspective it seems crucial to quantify the impact of information on investors' demand decisions in a way that readily allows for economic interpretation. Unfortunately matrix algebra although widely used in normal distribution theory has its shortfalls with respect to this aim. That is why this paper provides a different approach.

2. THE METHOD

Models of capital market equilibrium with risk averse investors having rational expectations are usually based on the so called *hybrid model.* According to this model prices P and signals S driving the economy are jointly normally distributed and investors have an exponential utility function.

If there are only two investment opportunities, one riskless asset earning an interest rate r and one risky asset with current market price P_0, an investor's optimal demand x for the risky asset is

$$x = \frac{t}{\operatorname{var}(P_1 \mid I)} \left(E(P_1 \mid I) - (1+r)\, P_0\right) , \tag{1a}$$

where t relates to his risk tolerance and $I = \{S_1 \ldots S_n\}$ to the information available at the time of decision making.

Although being concise this representation does not allow to trace the demand impact of the signals which determines the existence and quality of not necessarily unique equilibria. Setting

$RP := E(P_1) - (1+r) P_0$ and $\hat{S}_j := S_j - E(S_j)$

and rearranging (1a) to

$$x = \alpha \, RP + \sum_{j=1}^{n} \beta_j \hat{S}_j \tag{1b}$$

clearly appears more promising in this regard.

Usually the derivation of equation (1b) heavily draws on matrix algebra implying what is often referred to as tedious but straightforward calculations challenging readers' patience and imagination. This may be avoided by defining conditional covariances, variances and expectations of jointly normally distributed variables as recursions. Proper orthogonalisation of the original random variables [2] leads to the following expressions

$$\operatorname{cov}(P_1, S_n \mid S_{n-1} \ldots S_1)$$

$$= \operatorname{cov}(P_1, S_n \mid S_{n-2} \ldots S_1) - \frac{\operatorname{cov}(P_1, S_{n-1} \mid S_{n-2} \ldots S_1) \operatorname{cov}(S_n, S_{n-1} \mid S_{n-2} \ldots S_1)}{\operatorname{var}(S_{n-1} \mid S_{n-2} \ldots S_1)}$$

[implying

$$\operatorname{var}(P_1 \mid S_{n-1} \ldots S_1) = \operatorname{var}(P_1 \mid S_{n-2} \ldots S_1) - \frac{\operatorname{cov}(P_1, S_{n-1} \mid S_{n-2} \ldots S_1)^2}{\operatorname{var}(S_{n-1} \mid S_{n-2} \ldots S_1)}$$]

and

$$E(P_1 \mid S_n \ldots S_1) = E(P_1 \mid S_{n-1} \ldots S_1) + \frac{\operatorname{cov}(P_1, S_n \mid S_{n-1} \ldots S_1)}{\operatorname{var}(S_n \mid S_{n-1} \ldots S_1)} (S_n - E(S_n \mid S_{n-1} \ldots S_1))$$

For

$$k_{S_n \to P_1} := \frac{\operatorname{cov}(P_1, S_n \mid S_{n-1} \ldots S_1)}{\operatorname{var}(S_n \mid S_{n-1} \ldots S_1)}$$

$$k_{S_i \to P_1} := \frac{\operatorname{cov}(P_1, S_i \mid S_{i-1} \ldots S_1)}{\operatorname{var}(S_i \mid S_{i-1} \ldots S_1)} - \sum_{j=1}^{n-i} \frac{\operatorname{cov}(S_{i+j}, S_i \mid S_{i-1} \ldots S_1)}{\operatorname{var}(S_i \mid S_{i-1} \ldots S_1)} k_{S_{i+j} \to P_1} \quad (i = 2 \ldots n-1)$$

$$k_{S_1 \to P_1} := \frac{\operatorname{cov}(P_1, S_1)}{\operatorname{var}(S_1)} - \sum_{j=1}^{n-1} \frac{\operatorname{cov}(S_{1+j}, S_1)}{\operatorname{var}(S_1)} k_{S_{1+j} \to P_1}$$

the latter rearranges to

$$E(P_1 \mid S_n \ldots S_1) = E(P_1) + \sum_{j=1}^{n} k_{S_j \rightarrow P_1} \hat{S}_j$$

Assuming risk tolerance normalized to t = 1 for expositional purpose the above expressions yield

$$\alpha := \frac{1}{var(P_1 \mid I)} \text{ and } \beta_j := \frac{k_{S_j \rightarrow P_1}}{var(P_1 \mid I)}$$

In the remaining part of this paper the relative ease and clearness of proceeding as outlined above shall be demonstrated for the two most prominent set-ups to analyse the use of private information in rational expectations models with heterogenously informed investors.

3. TWO EXAMPLES

In both cases the information set is restricted to only one signal and the current market price, i. e.

$$I = \{S, P_0\}$$

In the first set-up [1, 4, 5] an individual investor receives the signal

$$S = P_1 + \omega$$

which resembles the future market price plus noise. It is assumed, however, that the individual forecasting errors cancel out in the aggregate demand decisions of the theoretically infinitely large group of informed investors so that the the current market price

$$P_0 = a\,P_1 + b\,X + c$$

reflects the actual future market price besides some other source of uncertainty X uncorrelated with P_1. Now proceeding as outlined above and making proper use of

$$cov(\omega, P_1) = cov(\omega, P_0) = 0 \Leftrightarrow cov(P_1, S \mid P_0) = cov(P_1, P_1 + \omega \mid P_0) = var(P_1 \mid P_0)$$

simple manipulations lead to

$$\beta_S = \frac{1}{var(P_1 \mid S, P_0)} - \frac{1}{var(P_1 \mid P_0)} = \frac{1}{var(P_1 \mid S)} - \frac{1}{var(P_1)} = \frac{1}{var(\omega)} \qquad (2a)$$

and

$$\beta_{P_0} = \frac{\dfrac{cov(P_0, P_1)}{var(P_0)}}{var(P_1 \mid P_0)} = \frac{1}{a}\left(\frac{1}{var(P_1 \mid P_0)} - \frac{1}{var(P_1)}\right) \qquad (3a)$$

Equation (2a) reveals that the demand impact of signal S can be exclusively attributed to and measured in terms of the enhanced reliability it is providing without any interference with the current market price. Equation (3a) shows that the demand impact of the current market price is as well totally unaffected by the knowledge of S. It is rather the same as in the absence of any private information. This is explained by the fact that the information revealed by the current market price to the informed results from the knowledge that the current market price is not influenced by individual forecasting errors. A fact that is, however, also well understood by investors without private information, thus explaining that their response is c. p. the same.

The second set-up [3] is based on

$$P_1 = S + \omega \quad \text{and} \quad P_0 = d\,S - e\,X + f$$

presupposing that all privately informed investors are subject to the same forecasting error thereby excluding that individual errors cancel out in the aggregate. It is obvious that this assumption renders the current market price a worthless piece of information to those who already know the forecast as the current market price cannot tell them anything about the future market price beyond what is already revealed by the forecast. Again, economic reasoning is readily confirmed by proceeding as outlined above: Regarding

$$\text{cov}(P_1, S \mid P_0) = \text{cov}(S + \omega, S \mid P_0) = \text{var}(S \mid P_0) \quad \text{and} \quad \text{cov}(P_1, P_0 \mid S) = 0$$

yields

$$\beta_S = \frac{\dfrac{\text{cov}(P_1, S \mid P_0)}{\text{var}(S \mid P_0)}}{\text{var}(P_1 \mid S, P_0)} = \frac{1}{\text{var}(P_1 \mid S, P_0)} = \frac{1}{\text{var}(P_1 \mid S)} = \frac{1}{\text{var}(\omega)} \tag{2b}$$

and

$$\beta_{P_0} = \frac{\text{cov}(P_0, P_1)}{\text{var}(P_0)} \left(\frac{1}{\text{var}(P_1 \mid S, P_0)} - \beta_S \right) = 0 \quad \text{q.e.d.} \tag{3b}$$

REFERENCES

[1] Admati, A. R. (1985), A noisy rational expectations equilibrium for multi-asset securities markets, *Econometrica*, 629 - 657
[2] Braun, T. (1990), Hedging mit fixen Termingeschäften und Optionen, Heidelberg: Physica
[3] Grossman, S., and J. E. Stiglitz (1980), On the impossibility of informationally efficient markets, *American Economic Review*, 393 - 408
[4] Hellwig, M. (1980), On the aggregation of information in competitive markets, *Journal of Economic Theory*, 477 - 498
[5] Gennotte, G., and H. Leland (1990), Market liquidity, hedging, and crashes, *American Economic Review*, 999 - 1021

Optimal Control of Investment, Level of Employment and Stockkeeping[1]

M. H. Breitner, B. Koslik, O. von Stryk and H. J. Pesch

Mathematisches Institut der Technischen Universität München,
Postfach, D-80290 München

Numerical simulations of microeconomic processes usually suffer from poor models and therefore often can not exhibit real phenomenons. We present a new, very complex model of an enterprise – deduced from the model of Lesourne at al. (1978) and Feichtinger at al. (1986), see Koslik et al. (1993) – including own capital distributed among the enterprise (part X) and alternative capital assets (part X_m), outside capital Y, level of employment L, a stock S and a submodel with production and selling. The interest rate for outside capital ρ_k and the interest rate for alternative own capital assets ρ_m are taken from the real values of the last ten years (May 1983 to May 1993)[2]. For the inflation i we take $i := \rho_m - 0.05$. For the own capital X, the management of the enterprise has to pay a risk premium $\rho_{r,1} X$ or $\rho_{r,2} X$ dependend on the risk of the business.

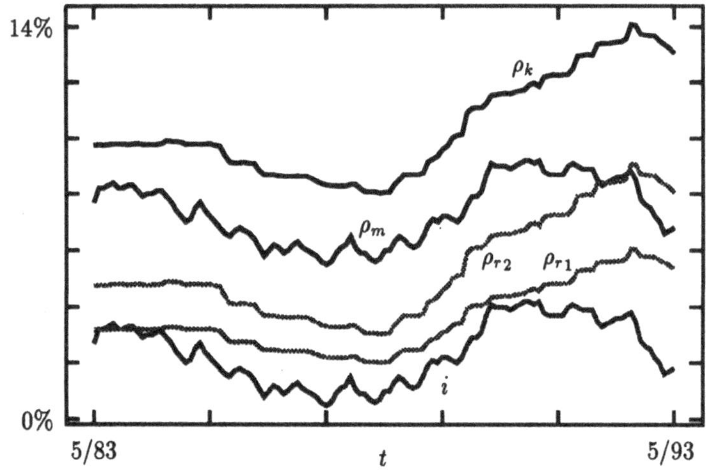

Fig. 1: Interest rate for outside capital ρ_k, interest rate for alternative own capital assets ρ_m, risk premium rates for the own capital in the enterprise X ρ_{r1} and ρ_{r2} and inflation rate i.

[1]This research has been supported by the Deutsche Forschungsgemeinschaft within the project "Anwendungsbezogene Optimierung und Steuerung" and by the Bavarian Consortium on High Performance Scientific Computing (FORTWIHR)

[2]The authors would like to thank P. Sollinger, HYPO-Bank Zentrale München, for providing us with the interest rates ρ_k and ρ_m for the last ten years.

The whole enterprise can be described by the following differential equations

$$
\begin{aligned}
\dot{S} &= S_c\,, \\
\dot{L} &= L_c\,, \\
\dot{Y} &= Y_c\,, \\
\dot{X} &= +I + (1-\tau)\cdot(P - \rho_r \cdot X)\,, \\
\dot{X}_m &= -I + (1-\tau)\cdot X_m \cdot \rho_m\,, \\
\dot{X}_r &= (1-\tau)\cdot \rho_r \cdot X\,, \\
\dot{d} &= -d \cdot \ln(1+i)\,,
\end{aligned}
$$

with

$$F = \alpha \cdot (X+Y)^{\alpha_K} \cdot L^{\alpha_L}\,,$$

and

$$P = \frac{1}{d}\cdot(p\cdot(F-S_c) - \sigma\cdot S - \omega\cdot L) - \rho_K \cdot Y - \delta\cdot(X+Y)\,.$$

Here the dot denotes the derivative w. r. t. the time $t \in [0, t_f]$. The horizon t_f is fixed at 10 years. $S_c \in [S_{c\,\min}, S_{c\,\max}]$ is the control for the stock S, $L_c \in [L_{c\,\min}, L_{c\,\max}]$ is the control for the employment level L, $Y_c \in [Y_{c\,\min}, Y_{c\,\max}]$ is the control for the outside capital Y and the investment $I \in [I_{\min}, I_{\max}]$ is the control for the own capital distribution among the enterprise X and alternative capital assets X_M. τ is the tax rate, F is the output, p the selling price, σ are the storage charges, ω are the labor costs, δ is the rate of depreciation, P is the profit and d is the reciprocal total inflation since $t = 0$. The simple bounds for the state variables must not be violated at any time $t \in [0, 10]$: $0 \le S \le 1000$, $0 \le L$, $0 \le Y$, $0 \le X$ and $0 \le X_m$. In addition the important borrowing limit $Y \le 0.8 \cdot X$ and the minimum production limit $F \ge S_c$ must be obeyed. The management of the enterprise tries to maximize the total profit at the end of the planing period (May 1993) with the help of the control functions $S_c(t)$, $L_c(t)$, $Y_c(t)$ and $I(t)$. Therefore the goal in the optimal control problem can be formulated as

$$X(t_f) + X_m(t_f) + (1-\tau)\cdot p \cdot \frac{S(t_f)}{d(t_f)} \quad \longrightarrow \quad \textbf{max !}\,.$$

The optimal control problem has been solved with the help of the new collocation method DIRCOL, see von Stryk 1992. The major advantages of this direct method are:

- Non differentiable model functions, e.g. ρ_k and ρ_m, can be handled, since no explicit numerical integration of the differential equations is done.
- The large domain of convergence enables the computation of the optimal solution even with a poor initial guess.
- Although the calculation of the adjoint differential equations is not necessary, the direct collocation method DIRCOL yields accurate estimates for the adjoint variables. These estimates facilitate the use of an highly accurate indirect optimization method, e.g. the multiple shooting method.

The optimal management of the enterprise under consideration for the last ten years can be seen in Figs. 1 – 9, where the dots are placed at the position of the collocation nodes.

Figs. 1 – 8 show the optimal solution for $\rho_r = \rho_{r,1}$ and Fig. 9 enables the comparison for $\rho_r = \rho_{r,2}$. The optimization of the enterprise requires about one and a half year in both cases. After this initial phase the influence of the economic cycles on the optimal capital partition can be obtained in Fig. 2 and Fig. 9 and the optimal controls I and Y_c for the capital flow are depicted in Fig. 3 and Fig. 4. Note that the optimal linear controls I and Y_c are controlled singular most the time.

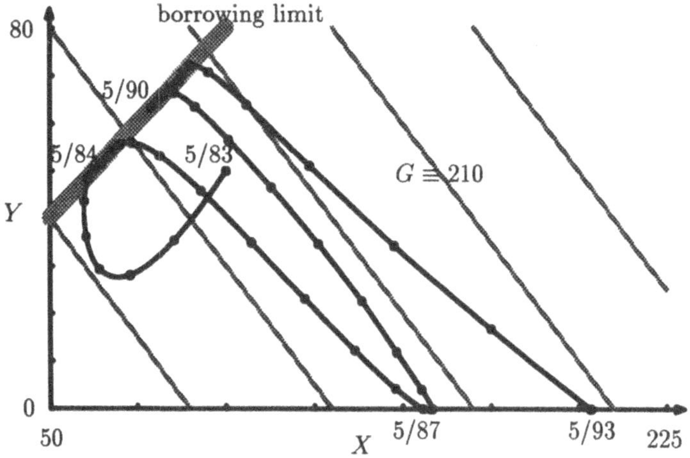

Fig. 2: Risk premium $\rho_r = \rho_{r1}$. Outside capital Y versus own capital in the enterprise X (black curve), borrowing limit (thick gray line) and lines of constant joint capital $G := X + Y$ (thin gray lines).

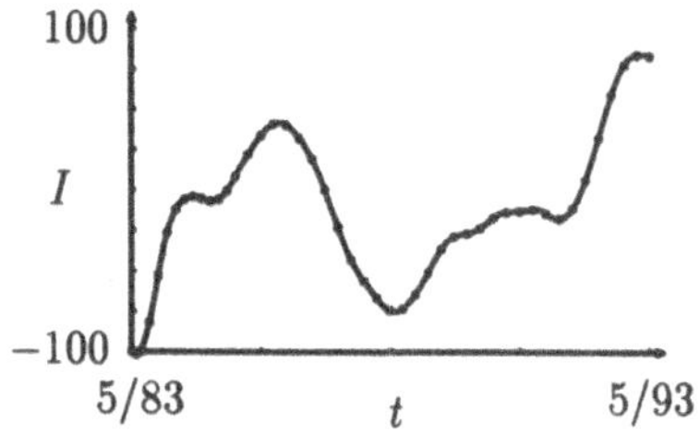

Fig. 3: Control I for the own capital partition.

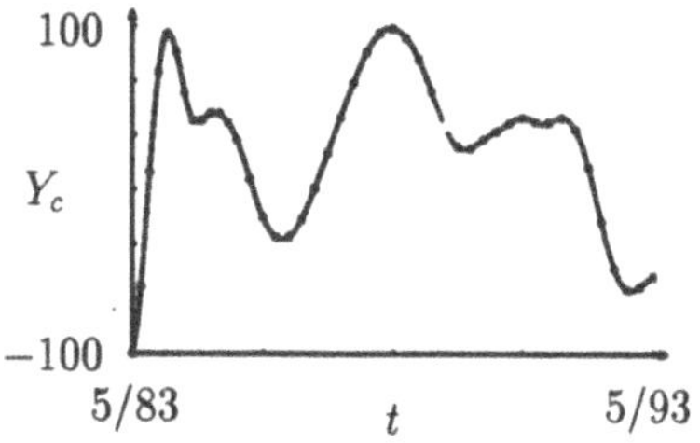

Fig. 4: Control Y_c for the outside capital.

The optimal level of employment and the optimal stock are shown in Fig. 5 and Fig. 6 .

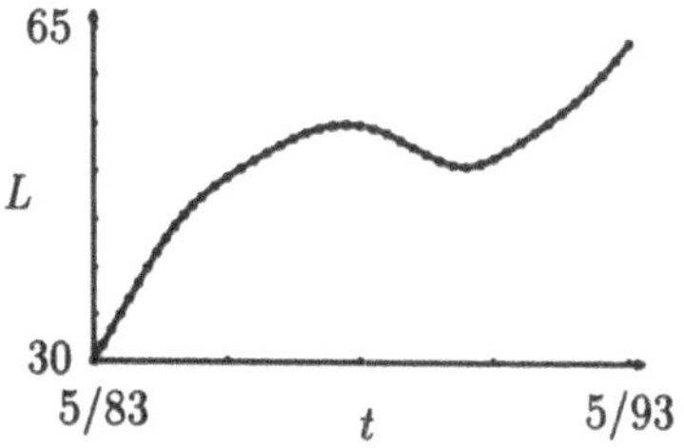

Fig. 5: Level of employment L.

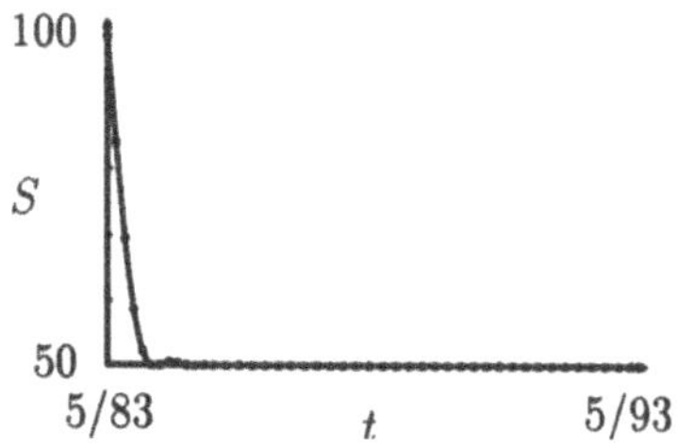

Fig. 6: Stock S.

The part of the own capital invested in alternative capital assets, e.g. fixed-interest securities, is shown in Fig. 7. The reciprocal total inflation d, see Fig. 8, enables the computation of the actual prices and costs at any time for a varying inflation.

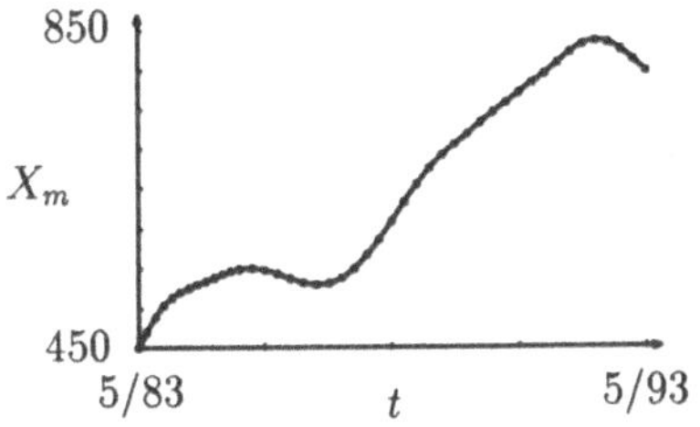

Fig. 7: Alternative own capital assets X_m.

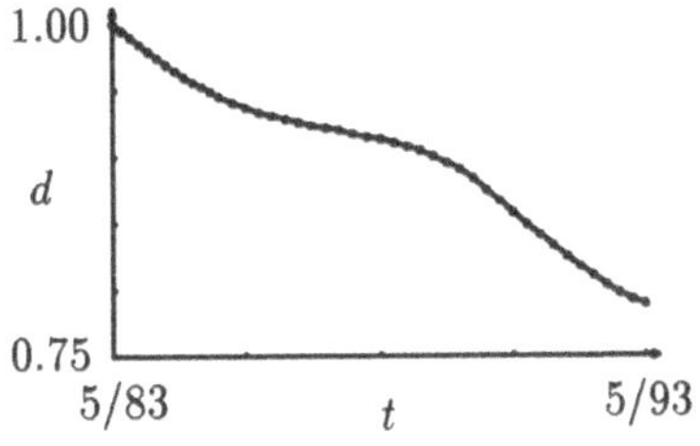

Fig. 8: Reciprocal total inflation d.

For $\rho_r = \rho_{r2}$ the borrowing limit $Y \leq 0.8 \cdot X$ once reached stays active for all t, see Fig. 9.

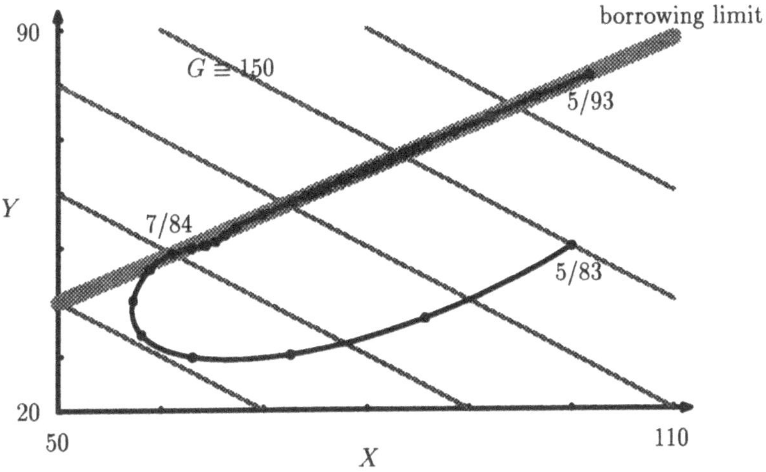

Fig. 9: Risk premium $\rho_r = \rho_{r2}$. Outside capital Y versus own capital in the enterprise X (black curve), outside capital limit (thick gray line) and lines of constant joint capital $G := X + Y$ (thin gray lines).

References

Feichtinger, G., Hartl, R.F. (1986): *Optimale Kontrolle ökonomischer Prozesse.* Walter de Gruyter, Berlin, New York.

Koslik, B., Breitner, M. H., Stryk, von, O., Pesch H. J. (1993): *Modeling, Optimization and Worst Case Analysis of a Management Problem.* Report 465, Deutsche Forschungsgemeinschaft, Schwerpunkt "Anwendungsbezogene Optimierung und Steuerung".

Lesourne, J., Leban, R. (1978): *La Substitution capital-travail au cours de la croissance de l'entreprise.* Rev. d'Economie Politique 4, pp 540 - 564.

Stryk, von, O. (1992): *Direct and Indirect Methods for Trajectory Optimization.* Annals of Operations Research 37, pp. 357 – 373.

COMPUTATIONAL COMPLEXITY IN INFINITE COMBINATORIAL STRUCTURES

Valentin E. Brimkov, Reneta P. Barneva†

Operations Research Section

Institute of Mathematics, Bulgarian Academy of Sciences,

1113 Sofia, BULGARIA

† University of Mining and Geology,

1156 Sofia, BULGARIA

The theory of computation and complexity deals with combinatorial problems set on finite combinatorial structures, and the algorithm complexity is measured with respect to an appropriate defined input length. At the same time, many problems can be defined on infinite structures (as infinite graphs, sets, etc.), presentable by infinite inputs. In such case the classical complexity theory becomes impracticable.

The paper proposes an approach to treatment of questions concerning the complexity of algorithms and corresponding problems, defined on infinite combinatorial structures. The introduced model can be also considered as natural framework for problems providing incremental search, where the information comes online, during the process of solving.

The main ideas are illustrated on some concrete examples. Algorithms for solving some of the problems are sketched, unsolvability of others is commented, and a comparison to the problems in the finite case is given.

MODEL

We will consider problems in the following general setting. The search problem $\Pi = (I_\Pi, S_\Pi)$ is supposed to be defined on a combinatorial structure $\mathcal{S}$ of arbitrary nature, presented by an input I_Π and having a set of solutions S_Π. $\mathcal{S}$ could be a graph, a family of subsets of some ground set, etc. We assume that the problem has to be solved by some Solver $\mathcal{M}$, that is in a position to perform various types of operations $t_1, \ldots, t_k$, depending on the problem nature.

$\mathcal{M}$ must realize some aim a priori defined (to find some special subgraph of a graph, or a special subset in a given family of sets). In addition we suppose that $\mathcal{M}$ disposes of incomplete, local information about the ground structure, i.e. in general $\mathcal{M}$ does not know $\mathcal{S}$ a priori, but completes the knowlege about it dynamically, during solving the problem, following some local-search-type algorithm.

This model generalizes the traditional one, where we could think that at the initial moment the known data (neighbourhood of $\mathcal{S}$) includes all the structure. Such approach also allows to consider problems where $\mathcal{S}$ is given by infinite input.

We presented the model on informal level because of its generality, but it could be precised in any concrete case, as it will be done in the next section. In some cases it would be convinient to think that the input data is received from some oracle, which has to be asked for additional information.

Supposing $\mathcal{M}$ can perform different operations, different types of complexity (eventually uncomparable each to other) correspond to them. In the classical complexity theory the most important type of complexity - the computational one, is measured with respect to the input size of the problem, but for problems with infinite inputs this is impossible. Our approach to the complexity in infinite structures is the following.

First, let us note that in the finite case, in generally, the algorithms use all the input in order to produce a solution, so that it could be said that the algorithm complexity (and correspondingly the problems' ones) is measured with respect to the volume of the data used. At the same time, it is possible for many individual problems to find the solution applying some local-search-type algorithm that manipulates only a part of the input (it is typical in cases when superfluous information is given). About the infinite case, it is clear that the problem has to be solved by algorithm using only a finite part of the infinite input. So, there are reasons to consider some data subset as an adequate characteristic of the input, if the knowlege of this subset allows to solve the problem in finite time.

Let A_Π be an algorithm such that if $\mathcal{M}$ follows it, a search problem Π will be solved in finite number of steps, and let for every individual input $i_\Pi \in I_\Pi$, $i_\Pi^{A_\Pi}$ denotes the data really used by A_Π to solve the problem (again the notion "really used" is to be precised in dependance on the concrete problem). According to our assumption about the different abilities of the Solver $\mathcal{M}$, A_Π can be considered as a multyalgorithm, consisting of k different algoritms $A_\Pi^1, \ldots, A_\Pi^k$ corresponding to the various types of operations, and different types of complexity – one per each of the algorithms – can be examined. All these complexities will be measured with respect to a basic one – *data complexity* $\mu(i_\Pi^{A_\Pi})$, that reflects in some appropriate way the volume of the used data $i_\Pi^{A_\Pi}$ defined above (in many cases it is most naturally function μ to give the number of elementary data units as numbers, graph vertices, elements of sets, etc., which are manipulated by the algorithm during its work). The complexity c_i of A_Π^i reflects the loss of operations during the work of A_Π^i. It is a function that to every (natural) number n juxtaposes the maximal (over all individual problems Π_n for which A_Π^i needs data complexity $n = \mu(i_\Pi^{A_\Pi})$) number of operations of type t_i, spent for solving the individual problems of Π_n.

We say that the (sub)algorithm $A_\Pi^i (1 \leq i \leq k)$ is a polynomial one if for every individual problem i_Π the number of steps performed till obtaining the solution is bounded by a polynomial of the corresponding data complexity $\mu(i_\Pi^{A_\Pi})$. The algorithm A_Π is polynomial if every A_Π^i is polynomial for $i = 1, \ldots, k$, and A_Π is exponential if some of its complexities are exponential functions of the data complexity. The problem Π is called polynomially solvable if there exists a polynomial algorithm A_Π such that the Solver $\mathcal{M}$, performing A_Π, will realize the aim a priori set.

Such approach allows to evaluate the algorithms and problems complexity in infinite structures. Let us, however, note that if it is necessary to compare the complexities of two algorithms for one problem, it would be needed first to receive a relation for their data complexities, after to compare the corresponding complexity functions, and finally to obtain the relation between the algorithm complexities as a superposition of the above two relations.

EXAMPLES

We consider graph problems, supposing for simplicity that graphs are displaced on the plane, that the Solver $\mathcal{M}$ is able to move along the edges of the graph which are streight line segments, and that it possesses a "vision" in radius r, can make computations, can store some data, as well as to measure passed distances. So we can talk about computational complexity, moving complexity (passed distance or number of passed edges), measuring complexity (number of performed measurings), memory complexity (the necessary memory volume). In the case of infinite graphs, we will suppose that V (being an infinite set) does not contain cluster points, and that for every fixed node $v \in V$ its degree is finite. First we will consider the well known

Path Problem (PP). Given a graph G with positive weights of its edges and two fixed vertices s and t (with known coordinates with respect to some fixed coordinate system), find a (Shortest, Longest) simple path (SPP, LPP) from s to t.

It is well known that on finite graphs the PP and SPP are polynomially solvable, for example by the Dijkstra's algorithm (DA) [3]; even if G is a disjoint graph and s and t belong to different connective components and there is no path between them, this can be checked in polynomial time [5]. It is known also that the LPP is NP-hard [4].

On connected infinite graphs, the PP and SPP are polynomially solvable, too. Really, DA could be applied, and in finite number of steps the target vertex will be reached. It is easy to see that the number of calculations, movings from one vertex to another, measurings (of angles or passed distances), and used memory are restricted by a polynomial of the data complexity, measured, for example, in number of visited edges.

At the same time, the LPP is unsolvable, as it easily follows from the infinity of the graph.

The SPP and LPP are both unsolvable if the weights can be positive and negative numbers, as well as if G is disjoint and s and t belong to different connective components.

Spanning Tree Problem (STP). Given a graph G with positive weights of its edges and a set $W \subseteq V$ of k fixed vertices of G (with known coordinates), find a (Shortest, Longest) Spanning Tree (SSTP, LSTP) for these vertices.

It is well known that if G is a finite graph and $W = V$ then the SSTP and LSTP are polynomially solvable, for example by the Prim's algorithm (PA) [6], and if $|W| \leq |V|$ (Steiner Minimal Tree (SMT)) the SSTP is NP-hard [4].

What about infinite graphs? First, let us mention that it is possible to construct in polynomial time a spanning tree (but not at all costs a shortest one) performing the following simple heuristic algorithm.

Spanning Tree Algorithm (STA). 1° Starting from some vertex $v_i \in W (1 \leq i \leq k)$ and applying consequently some polynomial algorithm for SPP (e.g. DA), construct shortest paths p_j from v_i to v_j for all $1 \leq j \leq k, j \neq i$; 2° Applying the PA on the graph obtained as an union of p_j, construct a spanning tree for W.

A shortest spanning tree can be found in exponential time. It is enough to show how to reduce the SSTP on an infinite graph G to a SSTP (SMT) with the same W on a finite graph.

Shortest Spanning Tree Algorithm (SSTA). 1° Performing STA, find a spanning tree T_W for W; 2° Calculate the sum Σ of all the weights of edges in T_W; 3° For every $v_i \in W$ construct a graph $G_i^\Sigma = (V_i^\Sigma, E_i^\Sigma)$ with vertices and edges belonging to simple paths from v_i with length not greater than Σ (it can be done, for example, by performing a variant of the Bredth-First-Search Algorithm) [5]; 4° Construct a graph $\bar{G}^\Sigma = (\bar{V}^\Sigma, \bar{E}^\Sigma) = \bigcup_{i=1}^k G_i^\Sigma$ with $\bar{V}^\Sigma := \bigcup_{i=1}^k V_i^\Sigma, \bar{E}^\Sigma := \bigcup_{i=1}^k E_i^\Sigma$; 5° Generate the set $\tau = \{\ h : h$ is a spanning tree of $\bar{G}^\Sigma\ \}$; 6° For every h generate the set $\tau_W(h) = \{\ h_W : h_W$ is a subtree of h which is a spanning tree of $W\ \}$; 7° Chose a shortest tree h_W^* in the set $\bigcup_{h \in \tau} \tau_W(h)$.

Because of the positiveness of the weights, the procedure of constructing G_i^Σ is finite for every i. It is clear also that the shortest spanning tree of W belongs to $\bar{G}^\Sigma$, because Σ is an upper bound for its general weight, and that the tree h_W^* is a shortest spanning tree of W.

It is easy to realize that the LSTP is unsolvable, as well as both the SSTP and LSTP if positive and non-positive weights are allowed. It is the case also for disjoint graphs, if there are at least two elements of W belonging to different connective components.

In fact, the connectivity question can be answered for some infinite graphs with special geometric structure. For example, it is the case for the so called convex graphs, introduced in [1], [2] and possessing some good algorithmic properties. In [2] n-dimensional convex graphs were considered and two algorithms for the PP were presented, as one of them (called Snake-Algorithm (SA)) uses constant memory only. Here we will recall the definition of convex graphs in the plane.

The plane graph $G = (V, E)$ (where V is a countable subset of R^2 without cluster points and E is a set of segments with end-points - elements of V) is called *convex graph* if

(1) all the internal faces of G are bounded convex polygons, and

(2) the union of the points of all faces and edges of G is a convex 2-dimensional polyhedron.

Now, let G be an infinite disjoint graph - union of convex graphs G_i (finite or infinite), so that each of them satisfies the additional condition

(3) if G does not cover all the plane, then the boundary of the union of all faces of G does not contain a ray.

It can be shown that the connectivity of such graphs can be verified by an algorithm (based on the SA), which is polinomial with respect to the number of calculations, measurings, passed edges or distance, and uses constant volume of memory.

REFERENCES

[1] Brimkov V E (1992) Graph problems under incomplete information. Proc. of the Internat. Simposium on Methodology of Mathematical Modelling. Varna 1992. 253-257

[2] Brimkov V (1992) A class of Graphs with good communicativeness, Proc. 17th Symposium uber OR, Hamburg, August 1992, 112-113

[3] Dijkstra E W (1959) A Note on two problems in connection with graphs, Numerische Mathematik, 1, 269-271

[4] Garey M R, Johnson D S (1979) Computers and intractability: a guide to the theory of NP-completeness, San Francisco: W.H.Freeman & Co

[5] Mehlhorn K (1984) Data structures and algorithms 2: Graph algorithms and NP-completeness, Springer Verlag (Chapter 4)

[6] Prim R (1957) Shortest connection network and some generalizations, BSTJ, 36, 1389-1401

On the 2D Knapsack Problem with Real Coefficients under the Blum-Shub-Smale Computational Model *

Valentin E. Brimkov, Stefan S. Danchev
Operations Research Section
Institute of Mathematics, Bulgarian Academy of Sciences,
1113 Sofia, BULGARIA

1 Introduction

Many problems arising in various branches of computational mathematics (in particular numerical analysis and scientific computations) have as natural domains real or complex numbers. This has motivated research derected to developing of extention of the classical theory of computation and complexity, dealing with combinatorial problems presentable over integers. The basic new conceptions, definitions and results can be found, for example, in [1]. We will mention here only that, according the new computational model, every arithmetic operation $(+, -, *, /)$ is assumed to be underlying one, performable in unique time.

A main theme in the initial research is the comparison of the results over the integers with ones over the reals, that gives deeper understanding to the basic concepts of decidability, computability, complexity, etc.

The present paper is an additional step in this direction.We consider the well known Knapsack Problem (KP) with two variables
(1) $\max\{\ c_1x + c_2y\ :\ a_1x + a_2y \leq b,\ x, y \in Z_+\ \}$,
where $c_1, c_2, a_1, a_2, b \in R_+$. It is well known that if the coefficients are rational, the problem can be solved in polynomial time in the sense of the complexity theory over the integers [3]. The same is the case if at least one of x and y is not required to be non-negative. In contrast, we have obtained that in the real data case there is no algorithm solving (1) if x and/or y may be negative (section 2). It is true also that, in terms of the new computational model, the problem (1) is intractable. In the basic section 3 a new algorithm is proposed that solves (1), and bounds for the algorithm's complexity are given.

*This work has been partially supported by the Ministry of Science and Higher Education - National Found Science Researches under contract No MM-13/91

Finally, we sketch a modification of the algorithm for solving in integers of 2-dimensional linear optimization problem with many linear constraints.

2 Some Preleminary Results

First, let us mention that if at least one component of the solution is not required to be non-negative, the problem (1) turns out algorithmically unsolvable (in contrast to the corresponding integer knapsack problem). More precisely, it is true

Theorem 2.1. There not exists any algorithm (machine) over R which determines whether (1) has a solution or not. $\bigtriangledown$

The theorem follows from the fact that the problem for determining if the equation $ax + by = c$, where $a, b, c \in R_+$ has an integer solution, is algorithmically unsolvable (see [2], theorem 2.2).

For arbitrary $a_1, a_2, b \in R_+$ the set $\{ (x, y) \;:\; a_1x + a_2y \leq b,\ x \text{ and } y \in Z_+ \}$ is finite and there is a trivial algorithm solving the problem. Having in mind the notion of complexity and polynomiality of algorithms given in [1], we see that a polynomial algorithm for (1) has to solve the problem in constant time. The following theorem shows that in this sense, the considered problem is intractable.

Theorem 2.2. There is no constant time algorithm solving (1). $\bigtriangledown$

It is proven in [1] that the operation $[x]$ (the greatest integer in x) needs $\Omega(\log_2 x)$ basic arithmetic operations. Sometimes, it is naturally to consider this operation as basic one, performable in unique time. We have proven that the theorem 2.2 remains true in this case, either. The proof is based on the following well known results.

Lemma 2.3. [5] There is no constant time algorithm over R that finds the Greatest Common Divisor (GCD) of two integers. $\bigtriangledown$

Lemma 2.4. [6] If $a, b, c \in Z_+$, $GCD(a, b) = 1$ and $c \geq ab - a - b + 1$, then the equation $ax + by = c$ has non-negative integer solution. $\bigtriangledown$

3 Algorithm

The algorithm uses as subroutine the Generalized Eucledean Algorithm (GEA), executed for a and b, $a \geq b > 0$. We set $q_{-2} = 1, p_{-2} = 0, \varepsilon_{-2} = a, q_{-1} = 0, p_{-1} = 1, \varepsilon_{-1} = b$ and for $n \geq 0$ $\varepsilon_n = \varepsilon_{n-2} - r_n\varepsilon_{n-1}$, $q_n = q_{n-2} - r_nq_{n-1}$, $p_n = p_{n-2} - r_np_{n-1}$, where $r_n = [\frac{\varepsilon_{n-2}}{\varepsilon_{n-1}}]$. It is the case

Lemma 3.1. For $n \geq 0$ and for every integer pair $(p, q) \neq (0, 0)$ with $|p| < |p_{n+1}|$ or $|q| < |q_{n+1}|$, is fulfilled $|qa + pb| \geq \varepsilon_n$. $\bigtriangledown$

Lemma 3.2. Let $S \subset Z_+^2$, $p, q \in Z_+$ and $a_1, b_1, a_2, b_2 \in R_+$ be such that every (x_1, y_1), (x_2, y_2) from S satisfy $|x_2 - x_1| \leq q$, $|y_2 - y_1| \leq p$, and there is no rational fraction with denominator not greater than q or numenator not greater than p. Then there exists a point $(x^*, y^*) \in S$ maximazing bilaterally over S the functions $a_1x + b_1y$ and $a_2x + b_2y$. $\bigtriangledown$

Further an informal description of the algorithm follows.

First, we execute n times GEA on a_1 and a_2, where n is the minimal index for which $\varepsilon_n = 0$ (in the case $\frac{a_1}{a_2} \in Q$), or $|q_n| \leq \frac{b}{a_1}, |q_{n+1}| > \frac{b}{a_1}$, or $|p_n| \leq \frac{b}{a_2}, |p_{n+1}| > \frac{b}{a_2}$. If $\varepsilon_n = 0$, we consider the line $|p_n|x + |q_n|y = [\frac{|p_n|}{a_1}b]$, otherwise - the line $\frac{x}{a'} + \frac{y}{a''} = 1$ where $a' \in Q \cap (\frac{b}{a_1}, \frac{b+\varepsilon_n}{a_1})$, $a'' \in Q \cap (\frac{b}{a_2}, \frac{b+\varepsilon_n}{a_2})$. In the both cases we have lines with integer coefficients, which will be denoted further by $A_1x + A_2y = B$. From lemma 3.1 it follows that there is at most one point $(x_0, y_0) \in Z^2_+$ between this line and the line $a_1x + a_2y = b$.

On the second stage, we execute m times the GEA on c_1 and c_2, where m is the minimal index for which $\varepsilon_m = 0$ (in the case $\frac{c_1}{c_2} \in Q$), or $|q_m| \leq \frac{b}{a_1}, |q_{m+1}| > \frac{b}{a_1}$, or $|p_m| \leq \frac{b}{a_2}, |p_{m+1}| > \frac{b}{a_2}$. From the Theory of the Diophantine Approximations it follows that there is no rational fraction with denominator not greater than $|q_{m+1}|$ and numenator not greater than $|p_{m+1}|$ in the open interval with end-points $\frac{|p_{m+1}|}{|q_{m+1}|}$ and $\frac{c_1}{c_2}$. From lemma 3.2 we obtain that there exists a point $(x^*, y^*) \in Z^2_+$, $a_1x^* + a_2y^* \leq b$ maximazing $c_1x + c_2y$ and $|p_m|x + |q_m|y$ on the set $\{ (x, y) : a_1x + a_2y \leq b,\ x, y \in Z_+ \}$. Let $C_1 := |p_m|$, $C_2 := |q_m|$.

As a third stage, we solve the integer knapsack problem $\max\{ C_1x + C_2y : A_1x + A_2y \leq B,\ x, y \in Z \}$, and let $\{ (x_i, y_i) : x_i = x_1 + (i-1)C_2, y_i = y_1 - (i-1)C_1,\ 1 \leq i \leq k \}$ be the set of the solutions. We set $(x^*, y^*) := (x_1, y_1)$ if $\frac{C_1}{C_2} > \frac{c_1}{c_2}$, and $(x^*, y^*) := (x_k, y_k)$ if $\frac{C_1}{C_2} < \frac{c_1}{c_2}$. If $a_1x^* + a_2y^* \leq b$, then (x^*, y^*) is a solution of (1). Otherwise, $(x^*, y^*) \equiv (x_0, y_0)$ (the unique non-negative integer point between $a_1x + a_2y = b$ and $A_1x + A_2y = B$). Then we set $b := a_1x^* + a_2y^*$, find $a' \in Q \cap (\frac{b-\varepsilon_n}{a_1}, \frac{b}{a_1})$, $a'' \in Q \cap (\frac{b-\varepsilon_n}{a_2}, \frac{b}{a_2})$, and as before, solve the corresponding integer knapsack problem, which solution will be a solution of (1). The case $\frac{C_1}{C_2} = \frac{c_1}{c_2}$ (i.e. $\frac{c_1}{c_2} \in Q$) can be considered in analogical manner.

It is easy to verify that the algorithm's complexity is $P(\log \frac{c}{\varepsilon})$, where P is a polynomial and $\varepsilon = \min \{ |qa - pb| : q \leq \frac{c}{a}, p \leq \frac{c}{b},\ (p, q) \in Z^2_+ \setminus (0, 0) \}$.

Further, we will sketch an anlogical method for solving more general 2-dimwnsional linear optimization problem

(2) $\max \{ c_1x + c_2y : a_{i1}x + a_{i2}y \leq b_i,\ i = 1, \ldots, k;\ x, y \in Z_+ \}$

where c_j,a_{ij},b_i are reals.

First, let us mention that the case of non-negative c_j,a_{ij},b_i, known as Multiple Knapsack Problem, can be directly reduced to at most k KPs.

In the general case, let us denote $S_A = \{ (x, y) : a_{i1}x + a_{i2}y \leq b_i,\ i = 1, \ldots, k;\ x, y \in A \}$, and mention that the extremal points and directions of S_R can be found trivially in $O(k \log_2 k)$ operations. Two cases are possible.

(A) S_R is bounded, i.e. it is a convex polygone (the case $S_R = 0$ is trivial). Then we determine p and q such that $p \geq \max_S |y_2 - y_1|$, $q \geq \max_S |x_2 - x_1|$, and define S as follows: For every constraint $a_{i1}x + a_{i2}y \leq b_i$ apply the GEA on $|a_{i1}|$ and $|a_{i2}|$ until $\varepsilon_n = 0$ or $|q_n| \leq q, |q_{n+1}| > q$ or $|p_n| \leq p, |p_{n+1}| > p$. Determine a corresponding constraint $A_{i1}x + A_{i2}y = B_i$ with integer coefficients in analogical manner as in the algorithm for (1). Then for $S = \{ (x, y) : A_{i1}x + A_{i2}y \leq B_i,\ i = 1, \ldots, k;\ x, y \in Z \}$ we have

(3) $S_Z \subseteq S$ and $|S \setminus S_Z| \leq k$.

For the objective function $c_1x + c_2y$ apply the GEA on $|c_1|$ and $|c_2|$ until $\varepsilon_m = 0$ or $|q_m| \leq q, |q_{m+1}| > q$ or $|p_m| \leq p, |p_{m+1}| > p$, and set $C_1 := sgn(c_1)|p_m|$, $C_2 := sgn(c_2)|q_m|$. After solve the optimization problem $\max_S C_1x + C_2y$ by some polynomial algorithm over integers (say, the Lenstra's one [4]). If the solution $(x^*, y^*) \in S_Z$, it is a solution of (2); else we "cut" the point (x^*, y^*) as in the algorithm for (1) and continue the same procedure. From (3) we obtain that after not more than k itterations we will find a solution of (2).

(B) S_R is unbounded (excluding the case $S_R = R^2$). It can be described a procedure (denoted further by ε-Algorithm) based on the GEA, which for every input a,b and $c \in R$ and some fixed point $(x_0, y_0) \in Z^2$, constructs monotone sequences $\{x_i\}$ and $\{y_i\}$ (finite or infinite), such that $c - \varepsilon_i < ax_i + by_i \leq c$ for $i = 0, 1, \ldots$. We will use the ε-Algorithm for solving the case (B). Two subcases are possible.

(B1) S_R is a strip between two parallel straight lines, i.e. $S_R = \{(x,y) : b_1 \leq a_1x + a_2y \leq b_2;\ x, y \in R\}$. Apply the ε-Algorithm on a_1,a_2 and b_2 finding an integer point in S_R, or until establisting that there not exists one. In the first case S_Z is infinite, and if $(c_1, c_2) \neq const(a_1, a_2)$, the objective function is unbounded; otherwise, $\sup_{S_Z} c_1x + c_2y$ is known, it cannot be found algorithmically (see the theorem 2.1), but using the ε-Algorithm the problem can be solved with arbitrary preciseness. In the second case $S_Z = 0$.

(B2) The boundary of S_R consists of not more than $k-2$ segments and two rays. Then a point $(\bar{x}, \bar{y}) \in Z^2 \cap S_R$ is searched, by applyng the ε-Algorithm for one of the rays. If there is no such point (it is possible only if the rays are parallel) then $S_Z = 0$; otherwise $(\bar{x}, \bar{y}) \in S_Z$. Now, if the function $c_1x + c_2y$ is unbounded over S_R, it is unbounded over S_Z also; if $\max_{S_R} c_1x + c_2y$ is attainable over the points of some of the rays, then $\sup_{S_Z} c_1x + c_2y$ is known, it cannot be found algorithmically (see the theorem 2.1), but using the ε-Algorithm the problem can be solved with arbitrary preciseness; otherwise $\max_{S_Z} c_1x + c_2y = \max\{c_1x + c_2y : (x,y) \in S_Z, c_1x + c_2y \geq c_1\bar{x} + c_2\bar{y}\}$, which is an optimization problem over bounded domain, i.e. we reduced (B) to (A).

References

[1] Blum L, Shub M, Smale S (1989) *On a theory of computation and complexity over the real numbers: NP-completenes, recursive functions and universal machines*, Bull. Amer. Math. Soc. (N.S.), Vol. 21, 1, 1-46

[2] Brimkov V E, Danchev S S (1993) *An example of exact computation over the reals*, Proc. of the Internat. Conf. on Mathematical Modelling and Scientific Computation, September 1993, Sozopol (to appear).

[3] Hirschberg D S, Wong C K (1976) *A polynomial-time algorithm for the knapsack problem with two variables*, J. Assoc. Comput. Mach. 23, 147-154

[4] Lenstra H V Jr (1983) *Integer programming with a fixed number of variables*, Mathematics of Operations Research, Vol. 8, No 4, November 1983

[5] Mansour Y, Schieber B, Tiwari P (1988) *Lower bounds for integer greatest common divisor computations*, Proc. 29th Ann. Symp. on Found. of CS, Oct 24-26, 54-63

[6] Sylvester J (1884) *Mathematical question*, Educational Times, Vol. 41, p. 21

The Job-Shop Problem and Immediate Selection

Peter Brucker, Bernd Jurisch, Andreas Krämer
Universität Osnabrück
Fachbereich Mathematik/Informatik
Postfach 44 69
D-49069 Osnabrück
Germany

In a job-shop scheduling problem we have n jobs $J_1, \ldots, J_n$ to be processed on m different machines $M_1, \ldots, M_m$. Each job J_i consists of a number n_i of operations $O_{i1}, \ldots, O_{in_i}$ which have to be processed in this order. Operations O_{ij} can be processed only by one machine $\mu_{ij} (i = 1, \ldots, n; j = 1, \ldots, n_i)$. Denote by p_{ij} the corresponding processing time. We assume that all processing times are integer numbers. There is only one machine of each type which can only process one operation at a time. Operations must be processed without preemption. Moreover, a job cannot be processed by two machines at the same time. For each machine M_k we have to find an ordering of all operations to be processed on M_k such that the maximal completion time $C_{\max}$ of all jobs is minimal.

This problem is one of the most difficult NP-hard scheduling problems. A 10-job, 10 machine problem formulated in 1963 (Muth & Thompson[1963]) has been solved only recently (Carlier & Pinson [1989]). The algorithm developed by Carlier and Pinson is a branch and bound method which is based on the disjunctive graph formulation of the job-shop problem. Other branch and bound algorithms have been developed recently (Applegate & Cook [1990], Brucker et al. [1991]).

The efficiency of all these branch and bound methods relies on the concept of immediate selection introduced by Carlier and Pinson. By immediate selection disjunctions, i.e. order relations between operations which have to be processed on the same machine, are fixed before branching. An order relation can be fixed if the reverse order relation yields a solution which does not improve the best solution found so far.

In Carlier & Pinson [1990] presented an $O(n^2)$-algorithm which usually fixes a large number of disjunctions. Recently they proposed an $O(\max\{n \log n, d\})$-version of their algorithm

(Carlier & Pinson [1993]). Here n is the number of operations to be scheduled on the same machine and d denotes the number of disjunctions to be fixed. The algorithm considers all pairs (O_i, O_j) of operations to be processed on this machine and decides whether a disjunction between O_i and O_j can be fixed. Besides these conditions for pairs of operations Deweß [1991] derived conditions for triples of operations which allow to fix additional disjunctions. We will generalize both concepts by

- deriving conditions for fixing disjunctions which are based on r-sets of operations to be processed on the same machine where $r \geq 2$ is an arbitrary integer
- simplifying the conditions given by Deweß
- describing algorithms for checking these conditions.

We will present an $O(\max\{n \log n, d\})$-algorithm which fixes all disjunctions derived by so called cliques as the algorithm of Carlier and Pinson does. Our algorithm is based on alternative concepts. Due to these concepts the correctness proof is much simpler than the correctness proof in Carlier & Pinson [1990].

For checking 3-set conditions we present an $O(n^2)$-algorithm improving the approach of Deweß for checking 3-sets considerably. Finally we will report on the computational results we got by replacing the algorithm of Carlier and Pinson by these new algorithms in a branch and bound method presented in Brucker et al. [1991].

In our paper we will first introduce the job-shop problem. Then the typical situation in a node of the search tree of a branch and bound method is described. The method is based on the disjunctive graph formulation of this problem. There we have a set of already fixed order relations between operations to be scheduled on the same machine. Using these relations a head r_i and a tail q_i may be calculated for each operation i. Furthermore let UB be an integer upper bound for the optimal solution value of the problem. Usually UB is the value of the best solution found so far. If we want to improve this best solution each operation i must be finished not later than the due date $d_i := UB - q_i - 1$. Thus, operation i must be processed within the time window specified by the interval $[r_i, d_i]$.

Then we will present two concepts for immediate selection. They use the time windows of the operations. The first concept based on so called cliques was introduced by Carlier and Pinson

[1989]. Roughly speaking a clique (J, c) consists of a set of operations J (to be processed on the same machine) which must be scheduled within a certain time interval because of the operations' heads and due dates. Hence the capacity of the machine to process other operations during this interval is bounded. Thus, if the processing time of an operation c exceeds this bound, it must be scheduled either before or after all operations of J.

The second concept was introduced by Deweß [1991]. It uses so called r-set conditions. This means that an operation i must be scheduled before an operation j if there exists a set J of operations with r elements $(i, j \in J)$ such that every sequence of operations of J in which j is scheduled before i does not respect the time windows given by the heads and due dates.

Next we will describe algorithms to check the conditions induced by the two concepts. The first algorithm fixes disjunctions which may be derived from cliques. It has complexity $O(\max\{n \log n, d\})$ where d is the number of disjunctions which will be fixed. This algorithm consists of two steps:

First heads and due dates of all operations to be scheduled on the same machine are improved. Therefore we calculate the earliest possible completion time s_c of operation c under the assumption that all operations respect their time windows and preemption is allowed. Then we can improve the head of operation c to $s_c - p_c$ for the schedules without preemption. This needs $O(n^2)$ (respectively $O(n \log n)$) time for all operations to be scheduled on the same machine. The $O(n \log n)$-version is based on a sophisticated datastructure which enables to decrease n different values by a constant amount in $O(\log n)$ steps.

Then using the improved heads and tails we may fix all disjunctions induced by cliques in $O(\max\{n \log n, d\})$ time.

The second algorithm checks the conditions induced by triples, i.e. 3-sets. The idea is to calculate a lower bound for the total length of all parts of operations which must be scheduled between the head of operation j and the due date of operation i if we assume that j is scheduled before i. Hence i must be scheduled before j if this lower bound exceeds the length of the interval. E.g. a very simple lower bound is $p_i + p_j$. We will give an $O(n^2)$-algorithm for calculating such a bound for all pairs of operations (O_i, O_j) to be processed on the same machine.

Finally we will report on the computational results. We implemented the different algorithms for immediate selection in a branch and bound algorithm (Brucker et al. [1991]) for solving the job-shop problem.

Of course, the number of search tree nodes did not change when we used our clique algorithm instead of Carlier and Pinson's one. But the running time was always improved by approx. 3-4% using our $O(n^2)$-algorithm.

We also implemented the $O(\max\{n \log n, d\})$-version to check clique conditions. We got an increase in the running time of approx. 35-40% for problems with 10 jobs, approx. 20-25% with 15 jobs, approx. 15-20% with 20 jobs and approx. 15% with 30 jobs. Hence we may expect a better running time performance for problems with more jobs. The triple algorithm provided quite surprising results. In general it needed approx. 10-15% search tree node less than the clique algorithm. The running time varied in a range of $\pm 10\%$ of the amount given by the clique algorithm. We also found out that the triple algorithm fixes considerably more arcs than only the arcs induced by triples.

References

D. Applegate, W. Cook [1990] A Computational Study of Job Shop Scheduling, CMU-CS-90-145, to appear in ORSA Journal of Computing.

P. Brucker, B. Jurisch, B. Sievers [1991] A Branch & Bound Algorithm for the Job-Shop Scheduling Problem, to appear in Discrete Applied Mathematics.

J. Carlier, E. Pinson [1989] An algorithm for solving the job-shop problem. Management Science 35, pp. 164-176.

J. Carlier, E. Pinson [1990] A Practical Use of Jackson's Preemptive Schedule for Solving the Job Shop Problem, Annals of Operations Research 26, pp. 269-287.

J. Carlier, E. Pinson [1993] Adjustment of Heads and Tails for the Job-Shop Problem, Preprint.

G. Deweß [1991] Ein Existenzsatz für Packungsprobleme mit Konsequenzen für die Berechnung optimaler Maschinenbelegungspläne, Working paper, Universität Leipzig.

J.F. Muth, G.L. Thompson [1963] Industrial Scheduling, Englewood Cliffs, N.J., Prentice Hall.

The Advantage of and System Support for Combined Bankassurance Products

Hans Ulrich Buhl, Klaus Sandbiller, Andreas Will
Fachbereich Wirtschaftswissenschaften, Universität Gießen
Licher Straße 70, D-35394 Gießen, Germany

1 Introduction

Banking and insurance companies are both facing the problem of losing market shares with their core products sold via traditional marketing channels. In Germany the share of banking products sold in branches dropped from 98% in 1970 to 85% in 1987; the share of insurance products sold by the traditional exclusive agents dropped from roughly 90% to 70% in the same period and is expected to fall far below 50% at the end of the century (Krupp (1993); Schweickert (1993)). The bankassurance strategies in the financial services markets combine efforts to *integrate* insurance and banking *products* as well as the corresponding *marketing channels*. Suitable *combined bankassurance products* with provable customer advantages are one key for the success of these strategies; this is the topic of Chapter 2. The second key for success is to provide customer benefits by enabling the stationary and mobile marketing channels with the knowledge and capacity to offer and contract bankassurance products in an efficient way. Chapter 3 deals with the *system support* necessary for spreading knowledge and capacity in these channels; furtheron, first experiences from a prototype developed within the ALLFIWIB-project funded by the Deutsche Forschungsgemeinschaft are sketched.

2 The Advantage of Combined Bankassurance Products

For customer decision support in the financial services field comparisons of e.g. loan interest rates offered by different banks or premiums for life policies offered from insurance companies are usual and widespread. The success of independent agents working together with a variety of financial services companies is largely based on such, often "computer-supported", comparisons of *given*, standardized offerings. Optimization of such offerings resulting in individual, tailored solutions for the special customer problem, however, is - due to complexity - hardly observable. In contrast to that, it turns out that such "local" optimization of single bankassurance products already may prove very profitable for both the customer and supplier when compared to usual standardized products. For instance, when working on the ALLFIWIB-project the following results could be derived:

- Under german tax conditions leasing one-time-payments at one of three distinct points of time are optimal whenever the lessor and the lessee calculate with different tax or interest rates.

Compared to usual contracts with constant leasing rates such optimized payment streams are always - and often considerably - better. In extreme cases the net present value of a leasing rate paid may be smaller than the tax benefit resulting from it; thus the net present value after taxes of both the lessor and the lessee may be positive and can be increased arbitrarily while the corresponding disadvantage of the fisc also increases unbounded (Buhl, Erhard (1991); Buhl (1994a)).

- If the lessor has a larger tax rate than the lessee, then for both of them the advantage of a real estate lease increases with the share of the building costs. Conversely, if the lessor's tax rate is smaller than the one of the lessee, then the advantage of the lease increases with the share of the ground (Will et al. (1993)).

- Also, due to the german corporate taxes, commercial loans without any interest and discharge payments up to contract end prove optimal compared to all other loan types (Buhl (1994b)).

- For both the investor and the issuing bank or firm zerobonds are better than all straight bonds, whenever bonds are profitable for them in the after tax world at all. A life policy is better than all bonds, whenever the german tax subsidy requirements are met (Buhl et al. (1993b)).

Integrating the results of such local optimizations into a *combined bankassurance solution* may prove very profitable for both an investor and his financial services provider, as the following example from Buhl et al. (1993b) illustrates:

Example: If an investor calculates the net present value after tax for a 1 Mio DM office building financed with funds from his private domain, he obtains a negative value of 555 KDM as a reference solution.

Neglecting transaction costs, standard leasing and loan offers for the 1 Mio DM investment as well as a straight bond for the private funds may improve the reference solution for the investor only by less than 1% while the financial services firm may calculate a net present value advantage of not more than roughly 16,000 DM. Including transaction costs the business is likely to be unprofitable for both the investor and the financial services firm.

The combined bankassurance solution consists of the following locally optimized single bankassurance products: a lease with upfront-one-time-payment, a loan without any interest and discharge payments up to contract end and a zerobond for the private funds. The net present value advantage of this solution is roughly 280,000 DM for the investor and 66,000 DM for the financial services provider. It may be further improved by replacing the zerobond by a suitable life policy with tax subsidy requirements met yielding a net present value advantage *larger* than the one of the reference solution. Thus, it is even possible, that the investor can finance the building with a *positive* total net present value over a 22-year-period, as considered in the example.

Such examples show the competitive and business potential for combined bankassurance solutions compared to the traditional core products of the financial services providers. As one main reason for the profitability of these combined solutions the lacking neutrality and the inefficiency of the german tax system is identified, particularly the following fact is key: Interest rates contained in leases, loans, straight bonds, zerobonds and insurance products are all taxed differently at either the supplier or the customer or both. This opens up a considerable optimization potential for the "coalition" of the financial services provider and its customer in nearly all practically relevant cases. The next chapter deals with the question, how such solutions may be generated by combining knowledge based techniques with methods from distributed artificial intelligence.

3 System Support for Combined Bankassurance Products

The discussion of combined bankassurance products highlighted the complexity of obtaining solutions to financial problems that are advantageous for both, the customer and the supplier. Obviously, system support is necessary to cope with this complexity (Buhl et al. (1993a)). As described in more detail in Buhl, Will (1993), König (1993), and Mack et al. (1993) the following system support is applicable, at least in principle, for both the branches and the mobile marketing channel, if access from the customer's site - e.g. via ISDN - to the data and solution agents in the network of the financial services provider is possible.

To cope with the complexity problem first, we propose a concept of *cooperating knowledge based systems* as an adequate support to elaborate and offer combined bankassurance products (see e.g. Buhl, Will (1993); König (1993); König et al. (1993)). For each financial domain, e.g. bonds or loans, a knowledge based system works as an expert (a so called "domain-agent") selecting and/or configuring solutions to a given problem. While working on problem solving a domain-agent applies rules like those presented in Chapter 2 for leasing and loans in order to obtain an advantageous or even optimal solution. Implementing each domain-agent as a separately running software process (e.g. on a local area network of workstations) the performance of the problem solving process can be improved by concurrently elaborating competing solutions to the same problem (e.g. leasing vs. loan for a financing problem). Moreover, the realization of this concept simplifies maintaining and extending the knowledge bases by the experts of the respective supplying firm. Embedding the domain-agents in a decentral Multi-Database-Server-Architecture provides the necessary remote access to all required customer and product data (König (1993)).

For implementing the idea of offering combined solutions of several locally optimized products *cooperation* of the domain-agents is necessary. This cooperation can be adequately supported by a *blackboard* as a common accessible database to store customer problems and residual problems as well as the corresponding solutions (Mack et al. (1993)). A homogeneous, payment-stream-based representation-form of both problems and solutions on the blackboard allows the agents to "understand" each problem. For example, the leasing-agent offers an optimized contract with an upfront-one-time-payment although the customer wishes to pay constant rates. The residual problem of financing the one-time-payment will then be written on the blackboard to be solved by other domain-agents, e.g. the loan-agent. In addition to this implicit way of cooperation of the domain-agents we provide a "combination-agent" with explicit knowledge overlapping several domains. If in a specific situation like the one from the example above such knowledge a priori suggests a good combination of different products the combination-agent is able to decompose the complex problem into partial problems to be solved by the single domain-agents. In this sense the combination-agent initiates explicitly combined solutions and thus helps to reduce search-time. Also, this explicit knowledge may lead to a better solution than the search process.

Based on the concept presented, a first prototype was developed within the project ALLFIWIB. Four domain-agents for loans, leasing, bonds, and life insurance as well as a combination-agent and communication and control modules were implemented. Testing activities proved the general practicablity of the ideas sketched. In the simple model framework of the prototype with deterministic payments and with only a few rules even "mixed" problems starting with periods of saving, a following real estate investment and subsequent periods of financing could be solved by the system of cooperating agents. Currently we work on improving the prototype and extending the knowledge bases with e.g. the economic knowledge from the references cited below.

4 References

Buhl H U (1994a) Leasing bei einheitlichem Kalkulationszins vor Steuern. Zeitschrift für Betriebswirtschaft 64, 1

Buhl H U (1994b) Optimale Kreditfinanzierung. Zeitschrift für Betriebswirtschaft 64, 4

Buhl H U, Erhard N (1991) Steuerlich linearisiertes Leasing - Kalkulation und Steuerparadoxon. Zeitschrift für Betriebswirtschaft 61, 12: 1355-1375

Buhl H U, Hasenkamp U, Müller-Wünsch M, Roßbach P, Sandbiller K (1993b) WI-State of the Art: Wettbewerbsorientierte IT-Unterstützung in der Finanzberatung. Wirtschaftsinformatik 35, 3: 262-279

Buhl H U, Sandbiller K, Will A (1993b) Vorteilhaftigkeit und Systemunterstützung kombinierter Allfinanzangebote. Disc.-paper No. 48, Lehrstuhl für BWL-Wirtschaftsinformatik, Universität Gießen

Buhl H U, Will A (1993) Unterstützung von Allfinanz-Angebotsprozessen mit verteilten wissensbasierten Systemen (ALLFIWIB). Information Management 2: 42-50

König H-J (1993) Dezentrale Datenhaltung in der Allfinanzkundenberatung. Informationstechnik it-ti 1: 45-54

König H-J, Roemer M, Sandbiller K, Weinhardt C, Will A (1993) Ein verteiltes Problemlösungssystem für die Allfinanz-Kundenberatung. Tagungsband des Gründungsworkshops der Fachgruppe 'Verteilte Künstliche Intelligenz' der Gesellschaft für Informatik

Krupp G (1993) Bankstrategien im Versicherungsgeschäft. Die Bank 6: 332-337

Mack B, Roemer M, Sandbiller K, Will A (1993) Problemlösungsmodelle der verteilten künstlichen Intelligenz für die Allfinanz-Kundenberatung. Disc.-paper No. 43, Lehrstuhl für BWL-Wirtschaftsinformatik, Universität Gießen

Schweickert K D (1993) Hat Ausschließlichkeitsvermittlung Zukunft? bank und markt 5: 21-22

Will A, Buhl H U, Weinhardt C (1993) Immobilienleasing und Steuern im Allfinanz-Kontext. Zeitschrift für Betriebswirtschaft 63, 9

UTILIZATION OF INTEGER PROGRAMMING FOR THE OPTIMIZATION OF CLASS TIMETABLES

José Vicente Caixeta Filho
João Carlos Vianna de Oliveira
Campus "Luiz de Queiroz"
Universidade de São Paulo
Av. Pádua Dias, 11 - 13.418-900 Piracicaba, SP - BRAZIL

1. Aim

The high schools usually have, at the beginning of each academic year, problems to define the timetables for their classes, mainly due to the restrictions in the time availability of the teachers. In view of that, it is proposed a modeling structure to help in this kind of time tabling, based on mathematical programming algorithms.

2. Modeling structure

The proposed model is basically founded upon a 0-1 integer programming structure, which means that the decision variables for the problem will represent, under optimal conditions, the subjects that should occur for each class, along the week, by each different teacher. Since this type of structure could imply in a high number of variables, resulting in a combinatorial explosion, it was decided to interpret the decision variable as representative of the teacher-subject status, i.e., because not necessarily all the teachers are able to be responsible for all subjects, this status would consider only the possible combinations. Therefore, for this study, when referring to a *subject*, this considers implicitly the combination *teacher-subject*. In view of that, the proposed modeling structure considers the following definitions:

n = number of subjects, m = number of classes, o = number of periods during the day in which subjects are taken, p = number of weekdays in which subjects are taken;

X_{ijkl} = 0-1 decision variable, representing the possible occurrence of a subject i, for the class j, in the period k, in the weekday l;

c_{ijkl} = pseudo-cost associated to the decision variable X_{ijkl}, and inicially set equal to 1.0;

A_{ijkl} = parameter type 0-1, indicating the availability of a subject for a class in a determined period of a weekday;
TOT_{ij} = total number of periods during the week in which the subject i should be offered to the class j;
R_{ikl} = parameter representing the number of classes having the same subject i, in a determined period k of a weekday l.

It is also assumed that the schools have as their main objective to achieve the maximum possible number of subjects, that is:

$$\text{Max} \sum_{i=1}^{n}\sum_{j=1}^{m}\sum_{k=1}^{o}\sum_{l=1}^{p} c_{ijkl}X_{ijkl} \tag{2.1}$$

and the following constraints taken into consideration:

$$X_{ijkl} \leq A_{ijkl} \tag{2.2}$$

that is, a subject will be offered or not in a determined period of some weekday, respecting the availability of that subject;

$$\sum_{i=1}^{n} X_{ijkl} \leq 1.0 \tag{2.3}$$

that is, in each class, it could happen a maximum of one subject in a determined period of each weekday;

$$\sum_{j=1}^{m} X_{ijkl} \leq R_{ikl} \tag{2.4}$$

that is, each subject can be offered in a determined period of a weekday to one or more classes;

$$\sum_{k=1}^{o}\sum_{l=1}^{p} X_{ijkl} \leq TOT_{ij} \tag{2.5}$$

that is, each subject can be offered according to the weekly frequency expected for each class;

$$\sum_{i=a}^{a} \sum_{j=1}^{m} X_{ijkl} + \sum_{i=b}^{b} \sum_{j=1}^{m} X_{ijkl} \leq 1.0, \text{ for } 1 \leq a,b \leq n \quad (2.6)$$

that is, for the cases in which a teacher is responsible for more than one subject, these correspondent times must not be coincident.

3. Discussion of the results

Once it was assumed that the use of this modeling structure would be responsibility of the high schools themselves, the compatible mathematical programming software tested for that should be available for microcomputers, the most common computational platform obtainable in that category of schools.

To select the software, it was used a survey conducted by Sharda (1992), taking into account the potential power of this type of tool with respect to manipulation of large and dense matrices, which certainly demand great amount of RAM memory as well long processing times. In view of that, it was utilized the OSL (IBM, 1991) code, incorporated to the optimization language GAMS (Brooke et al., 1992), under various microcomputer configurations.

Specifically for the most representative model processed for this study, built for a representative high school at the São Paulo State, Brazil, it was generated a matrix with 7,671 rows, 34,801 columns and 93,482 non-zero elements, which required, according to the solving strategy used, an average of 20 Mb of RAM memory in a microcomputer 486 DX with a clock of 66 MHz.

The obtained results attested the efficiency of GAMS/OSL, specially regarding the linear solution. However, the search for the integer solution was not equally efficient, mainly due to the fact the algorithm used for that is based on branch-and-bound techniques.

Given the integer solution is attained from the initial linear solution (which could be got through different algorithms available in OSL, including the very convergent ones for some classes of problems, such the interior point methods), the execution time consumed was considered satisfactory.

However, to get a greater efficiency to achieve the integer solution, the following solving strategies available for OSL were tested:

a) variation in the criteria for absolute and relative optimization. When the integer solution (*I*), in terms of the value of the objective function, is not exactly equal to the linear solution (*L*), the relaxation of the tolerance for valid absolute (*I* - *L*) and relative (*I/L*) intervals may imply more reasonable solutions for the problem.
b) variation in the values of some pseudo-costs. If the obtained integer solution does not consider some key-subjects of the school, priorities can be given to force the presence of the corresponding variables into the basis. This can be done with the use of solving strategies available for GAMS/OSL (such as strategies 8, 16 or 32) or, eventually, by altering the values of the pertinent c_{ijkl} in the objective function.
c) relaxation of the constraints. Identified which constraints are the most binding ones, those ones could be merely removed or have their respective RHS relaxed. It is recommended, however, that this strategy be applied only to the inequality constraints.

It has also to be considered that the evaluation of those results can be facilitated if a friendly report generator is available, once the organization of those results with the default status of GAMS/OSL can be a very complex task. GAMS/OSL has some alternatives for that, as well permits the integration with routines developed under other languages.

4. References

Brooke A, Kendrick D, Meeraus A (1992) GAMS: a user's guide - release 2.25. Scientific Press, San Francisco.
IBM Corporation (1991) Introducing the Optimization Subroutine Library - release 2. IBM, Kingston.
Sharda R (1992) Linear programming software for personal computers: 1992 survey. OR/MS Today 19(3): 44-60.

A SEQUENTIAL GENERALIZED QUADRATIC PROGRAMMING ALGORITHM USING EXACT L_1 PENALTY FUNCTIONS

Eduardo Casas
Depto. de Matemática Aplicada y Ciencias de la Computación
E.T.S.I. de Caminos – Universidad de Cantabria
Cecilia Pola
Depto. de Matemáticas, Estadística y Computación
Facultad de Ciencias – Universidad de Cantabria
39071–Santander, Spain

INTRODUCTION

We consider a nonlinear programming problem having equality and inequality constraints:

$$\text{(NLP)}\left\{\begin{array}{ll}\text{Minimize} & f(x),\\ \text{subject to} & g_i(x)=0\ ,\quad i\in E_1,\\ & g_i(x)\le 0\ ,\quad i\in I_1,\\ & c_i^T x=b_i\ ,\quad i\in E_2,\\ & c_i^T x\le b_i\ ,\quad i\in I_2\ ;\end{array}\right.$$

$f, g_i : R^n \longrightarrow R$ being smooth functions and E_1, I_1, E_2 and I_2 being finite sets with cardinals n_e, n_i, m_e and m_i respectively.

The aim of this paper is to present some theoretical properties of a nonlinear programming algorithm that combines generalized quadratic programming with a line search rule which is based on an l_1 penalty function. The algorithm computes a sequence (x^k, λ^k) with $x^{k+1} = x^k + \rho_k d^k$, where the search direction d^k is either solution, denoted by $\hat{d}^k$ (basic step), of the following generalized quadratic programming problem

$$(GQP)_k\left\{\begin{array}{ll}\text{Minimize} & \Psi(d)=\alpha_k q_k(d)+h(g(x^k)+\nabla g(x^k)^T d),\\ \text{subject to} & c_i^T d=0\ ,\quad i\in E_2\ ;\\ & c_i^T d\le b_i-c_i^T x^k\ ,\quad i\in I_2\ ;\end{array}\right.$$

with $\alpha_k > 0$,

$$q_k(d)=\frac{1}{2}d^T B_k d+\nabla f(x^k)^T d+f(x^k),$$

B_k being an $n\times n$ symmetric positive definite matrix, and $h : R^{n_e+n_i} \longrightarrow R$ defined by

$$h(y)=\sum_{i\in E_1}|y_i|\ +\ \sum_{i\in I_1}\max\{y_i,0\};$$

or $d^k = \hat{d}^k + \rho_k \bar{d}^k$, $\bar{d}^k$ (second order correction) being solution of the problem

$$(GQP)_k'\left\{\begin{array}{ll}\text{Minimize} & \alpha_k q_k(\hat{d}^k+d)+h(g(x^k+\hat{d}^k)+d^T\nabla g(x^k)),\\ \text{subject to} & c_i^T(\hat{d}^k+d)=0\ ,\quad i\in E_2\ ;\\ & c_i^T(\hat{d}^k+d)\le b_i-c_i^T x^k\ ,\quad i\in I_2\ ;\end{array}\right.$$

and the stepsize ρ_k is computed by a line search rule to give a suitable reduction of the penalty function $\phi : R^n\times(0,+\infty)\longrightarrow R$ given by

$$\phi(x,\nu)=\nu f(x)\ +\ h(g(x)).$$

This method is related to that of Fletcher (1981, 1982, 1987) who uses a trust region method instead of a line search rule.

Our algorithm incorporates an automatic adjustment rule for the selection of the penalty parameters α and ν in every iteration and these parameters are allowed to take different values, $\alpha_k \neq \nu_k$; see Casas and Pola (1993). In this paper we report numerical evidence for the usefulness of this approach, which is the main novelty of our algorithm.

We prove global convergence of our algorithm without any assumption of linear independence of the constraint gradients. Under the usual hypotheses, a superlinear convergence rate can be obtained, provided the unit stepsize is eventually accepted. To avoid the Maratos effect (see Maratos (1978)) and to accept the steplength $\rho_k = 1$ at least for the final iterations, our algorithm uses the second order correction suggested by Fletcher (1981) and follows a search arc to determine ρ_k.

THE ALGORITHM

We will give a simplified description of our algorithm. For details see Casas and Pola (1993).

Parameters and data: $\sigma \in (0, 0.5]$, $0 < \beta_1 < \beta_2 < 1$ and $\beta_3 > 0$. x^1 satisfying the linear constraints of (NLP), $B_1 \in R^{n \times n}$ being symmetric positive definite and $\nu_1, \alpha_1 > 0$.

1. Set $k = 1$.

2. Set $\rho = 1$.

3. Compute $\hat{d}^k$ by solving the generalized quadratic problem $(GQP)_k$. If $\hat{d}^k = 0$, STOP.

4. Compute $\hat{x}^k = x^k + \hat{d}^k$.

• If

$$\phi(\hat{x}^k, \nu_k) \leq \phi(x^k, \nu_k) + \sigma\rho[W_k(\hat{d}^k) - W_k(0)], \tag{1}$$

where $W_k(d) = \nu_k q_k(d) + h(g(x^k) + \nabla g(x^k)^T d)$, then set $d^k = \hat{d}^k$, $x^{k+1} = x^k + d^k$. Go to Step **6**.

• Otherwise

- If one of the two following conditions holds

$$\begin{array}{ll} 1. & h(g(x^k) + \nabla g(x^k)^T \hat{d}^k) > 0, \\ 2. & g_i(x^k) + \nabla g_i(x^k)^T \hat{d}^k \neq 0, \ \forall i \in E_1 \cup I_1, \end{array}$$

then set $tag = 0$ and go to Step **5**.

- Otherwise compute $\bar{d}^k$ by solving the generalized quadratic problem $(GQP)'_k$.

  • If some of the following conditions is satisfied

$$\begin{array}{ll} 1. & h(g(x^k + \hat{d}^k) + \nabla g(x^k)^T \bar{d}^k) > 0, \\ 2. & \|\bar{d}^k\| \geq \beta_3 \|\hat{d}^k\|, \end{array} \tag{2}$$

  then set $tag = 0$ and go to Step **5**.

  • In the other case, take $\hat{x}^k = x^k + \hat{d}^k + \bar{d}^k$
    – If (1) holds, then take $d^k = \hat{d}^k + \bar{d}^k$ and $x^{k+1} = \hat{x}^k$. Go to Step **6**.
    – Otherwise, set $tag = 1$ and go to Step **5**.

5. Compute

$$\rho = \begin{cases} \beta_1 \rho & \text{if } \ \phi(\hat{x}^k, \nu_k) \geq \phi(x^k, \nu_k), \\ \beta_2 \rho & \text{otherwise;} \end{cases} \quad \text{and} \quad \hat{x}^k = \begin{cases} x^k + \rho \hat{d}^k & \text{if } \ tag = 0, \\ x^k + \rho(\hat{d}^k + \rho \bar{d}^k) & \text{if } \ tag = 1. \end{cases}$$

• If (1) holds, then take $\rho_k = \rho$,

$$d^k = \begin{cases} \hat{d}^k & \text{if } \ tag = 0, \\ \hat{d}^k + \rho_k \bar{d}^k & \text{if } \ tag = 1. \end{cases}$$

and $x^{k+1} = \hat{x}^k$. Go to Step **6**.

• Else repeat Step **5**.

6. Generate a symmetric positive definite matrix B_{k+1}. Set $k = k + 1$. Go to Step **2**.

Remark.

The penalty parameter ν_k of the merit function ϕ may be different to the parameter α_k of the generalized quadratic problems. A priori the values of these parameters may be changed from one iteration to another. The adaptation rules for ν_k and α_k are now briefly described.

The algorithm will get α_k constant after a finite number of iterations. At the beginning of each iteration we have an estimation from the last iteration. A priori this value can be increased or decreased. The aim of decreasing it is to try to avoid the violation of the constraints in the computation of the basic step (that is to avoid $h(g(x^k) + \nabla g(x^k)^T \hat{d}^k) > 0$) and the aim of increasing it is to obtain more accurate results by the generalized quadratic programming code, simply by minimizing the influence of rounding errors.

Moreover in each iteration we try to choose a value for ν_k according to the twofold objective of minimizing the function f and obtaining a feasible point. Since the role played by the parameters α_k and ν_k in the algorithm is different, then, *a priori*, there is no reason to take $\alpha_k = \nu_k$. In fact, in the numerical tests, we have observed that the choice of $\nu_k > \alpha_k$ is often better for a faster progress of the algorithm. We take ν_k verifying the assumption A1(iii) below and we require one condition to increase ν_k: the algorithm should have exhibited some progress. To measure this progress we introduce the sequences:

$$\gamma_k = \|\nabla f(x^k) + \sum_{i \in E_1 \cup I_1} (\hat{\lambda}_i^k/\alpha_k)\nabla g_i(x^k) + \sum_{i \in E_2 \cup I_2} (\hat{\lambda}_i^k/\alpha_k)c_i\|, \text{ for } k = 1, 2, \ldots$$

where $\hat{\lambda}^k$ is the Lagrange multiplier vector associated with the constraints of $(GQP)_k$ and we define $\gamma_{1,0} = \gamma_1$,

$$\gamma_{k,0} = \begin{cases} \gamma_k & \text{if } \gamma_k < \dfrac{\gamma_{k-1,0}}{1 + \beta_4 \gamma_{k-1,0}}, \\ \gamma_{k-1,0} & \text{otherwise ;} \end{cases} \quad \text{for } k = 2, 3, \ldots, \text{with } \beta_4 > 0 \text{ fixed.}$$

To keep ν_k invariable when the previous strategy implies a small variation in the value of this parameter, it can be advisable to introduce the following device: fixed $\epsilon > 0$,

$$\text{if } \left|\frac{\nu_{k-1}}{\nu_k} - 1\right| < \epsilon, \text{ then we set } \nu_k = \nu_{k-1}. \tag{3}$$

Unlike the algorithm of Mayne and Polak (1982), where only decrease of ν_k is allowed, our algorithm can sometimes increase this parameter.

GLOBAL AND LOCAL CONVERGENCE

In this section global convergence and local superlinear convergence results are given. Firstly let us note that if $\hat{d}^k = 0$ in the k-th iteration, then the algorithm stops in Step 3 and $(x^k, \hat{\lambda}^k)$ satisfies the first order necessary conditions for the following penalty problem

$$(NLPP) \begin{cases} \text{Minimize} & \phi(x, \nu) \\ \text{subject to} & c_i^T x = b_i \ , \quad i \in E_2 \ ; \\ & c_i^T x \le b_i \ , \quad i \in I_2 \ ; \end{cases}$$

with $\nu = \alpha_k$. If furthermore $h(g(x^k)) = 0$, then $(x^k, \hat{\lambda}^k/\nu)$ is a Kuhn–Tucker pair for problem (NLP).

In the rest of the section we will assume that $\hat{d}^k \neq 0$ for all k. Moreover we make the following hypotheses

Assumptions A1. **i.** $f, g_i : R^n \longrightarrow R$ ($i \in E_1 \cup I_1$) are continuously differentiable, $\{x^k\}$ is bounded.

ii. The matrices B_k are uniformly bounded and satisfy the condition

$$\exists\, \mu > 0, \text{ such that } (\hat{d}^k)^T B_k \hat{d}^k > \mu \|\hat{d}^k\|^2 \quad \forall\, k. \tag{4}$$

iii. $\nu_k \in [\nu_{min}, \nu_{max}]$ $(0 < \nu_{min} \le \nu_{max} < \infty)$ satisfies that

$$\nu_k = \alpha_k \qquad \text{if } h(g(x^k) + \nabla g(x^k)^T \hat{d}^k) > 0, \tag{5}$$

$$\nu_k \|\tilde{\lambda}^k\|_\infty \le \alpha_k \text{ and (3) holds} \qquad \text{otherwise.} \tag{6}$$

where $\tilde{\lambda}^k$ is the Lagrange multiplier vector associated with the constraints of $(GQP)_k$ corresponding to the index set $E_1 \cup I_1$.

We also assume that the linear constraints of (NLP) are consistent.

Theorem 1 Assumptions A1 and $\nu_k \leq \nu_{k-1}$ if $\gamma_{k-1,0} \neq \gamma_{k-1}$, imply that $\liminf_{k\to\infty} \gamma_k = 0$.

Now we assume that the sequence generated by the algorithm $\{x^k\}$ converges to a local solution $\bar{x}$ of (NLP) and we study the admissibility of unit steps when x^k is near the solution.

We make the following assumptions:

Assumptions A2. i. $f, g_i : R^n \longrightarrow R$ $(i \in E_1 \cup I_1)$ are two times continuously differentiable, $x^k \rightarrow \bar{x}$ and $(\bar{x}, \bar{\lambda})$ is a Kuhn–Tucker pair for problem (NLP).

ii Matrices B_k are uniformly bounded and satisfy the condition

$$\exists\, \mu_1 > 0, \text{ such that } (d)^T B_k d > \mu_1 \|d\|^2 \quad \forall\, d \in R^n,\ \forall\, k.$$

Assumption A3. $\{\nabla g_i(\bar{x})\}_{i \in A(\bar{x})_1}$ are linearly independent and, being $A(\bar{x})_1 = E_1 \cup (A(\bar{x}) \cap I_1)$ and $A(\bar{x})_2 = E_2 \cup (A(\bar{x}) \cap I_2)$ with $A(\bar{x})$ the index set associated with constraints that are active at $\bar{x}$,

$$< \{\nabla g_i(\bar{x})\}_{i \in A(\bar{x})_1} > \cap < \{c_i\}_{i \in A(\bar{x})_2} > = \{0\}.$$

Assumption A4. $(\bar{x}, \bar{\lambda})$ satisfies the strict complementarity condition, that is

$$\begin{aligned} \bar{\lambda}_i + |g_i(\bar{x})| > 0 \quad &, \quad \forall\, i \in I_1, \\ \bar{\lambda}_i + |b_i - c_i^T \bar{x}| > 0 \quad &, \quad \forall\, i \in I_2. \end{aligned} \tag{7}$$

Assumption A5. $\max\{|\bar{\lambda}_i| : i \in E_1 \cup I_1\}\alpha_{min} < 1$, where $\alpha_{min} > 0$ is the smallest value that the parameters α_k can take.

Assumption A6. $(\bar{x}, \bar{\lambda})$ verifies the second order sufficiency condition, that is

$$d^T(\nabla^2 f(\bar{x}) + \sum_{i \in E_1 \cup I_1} \bar{\lambda}_i \nabla^2 g_i(\bar{x}))d > 0, \quad \forall\, d \in R^n \text{ such that:}$$

$$\begin{aligned} d^T \nabla g_i(\bar{x}) = 0, \qquad & i \in E_1 \cup (A(\bar{x}) \cap I_1), \\ d^T c_i = 0, \qquad & i \in E_2 \cup (A(\bar{x}) \cap I_2). \end{aligned}$$

We have the following results

Theorem 2 Under assumptions A1(iii), A2-A6 and $P_k[\nabla^2_{xx} L(\bar{x}, \bar{\lambda}) - B_k\,]\hat{d}^k = o(\|\hat{d}^k\|)$ with $P_k = I - N(x^k)[N(x^k)^T N(x^k)]^{-1} N(x^k)^T$, then the algorithm sets $\rho_k = 1$, for all k large enough.

Theorem 3 Under assumptions A1(iii), A2-A6 the superlinear convergence holds:

$$\lim_{k \rightarrow +\infty} \frac{\|x^{k+1} - \bar{x}\|}{\|x^k - \bar{x}\|} = 0.$$

References

[Casas E. and Pola C. (1993)] A sequential generalized quadratic programming algorithm using exact l_1 penalty functions. Núm 6/1993, Depto. de Matemáticas, Estadística y Computación, Univ. de Cantabria (Spain).

[Fletcher R. (1982)] Penalty functions. In A. Bachem, M. Grötschel, and B. Korte, editors, Math. Programming. The State of The Art, pages 87–114, Bonn. Springer–Verlag.

[Fletcher R. (1981)] Second order corrections for non-differentiable optimization. In G.A. Watson, editor,Lecture Notes in Mathematics 912, pages 16–31, Berlin, 1982. Numerical Analysis Dundee 1981, Springer–Verlag.

[Fletcher R. (1987)] Practical Methods of Optimization. John Wiley & Sons, Chichester and New York, second edition.

[Maratos N. (1978)] Exact Function Penalty Algorithms for Finite Dimensional and Control Optimization Problems. PhD thesis, Imperial College, University of London.

[Mayne D.Q. and Polak E.D. (1982)] A superlinearly convergent algorithm for constrained optimization problems. Math. Programming Stud., 16:45–61.

EVENTMAN - A BUSINESS EVENT TRACKING SYSTEM

Drago Čepar, Franci Mulec
Jožef Stefan Institute, Ljubljana, Slovenia

1. Introduction

In the paper we describe a groupware computer system for supporting the debt-recovery process in the legal department at Ljubljanska banka. A similar system is described in Kiel (1993). The benefits of such systems are also described in Opper and Weiss (1992). In Section 2, we describe the present computer-supported work process and compare it with the former manual process. The computer system considerably reduces the reaction time of employees. In Section 3 we discuss the possibilities and consequences of changing the work process, which is possible with Eventman. The work process is described by a simple queuing model with serial and parallel connections of service channels. We present some simulation results obtained by GPSS.

2. The Work Process in the Department

The department recovers different overdue liabilities from the bank's customers. It has a secretary, five lawyers and a file. The file is divided among five lawyers, so that every lawyer has his own subset of cases. The secretary receives documents and telephone calls (they will be uniquely referred to as events) from other bank departments, courts and bank customers. She finds out to which case a document belongs, to which lawyer the case belongs and on the basis of this information, she passes a document or a telephone call to a lawyer. (Figure 1).

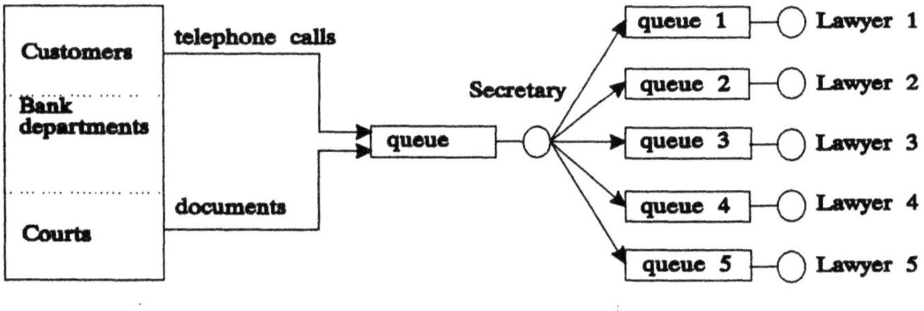

Figure 1. Model of the work process

2.1. The Manual Procedure

When the secretary received a telephone call, she examined the book of about 500 pages. She found out to which case the telephone call was related and usually also to which lawyer the case belonged. If she didn't find that information in the book, she asked the lawyers. When she found the owner of the case, she connected the phone call to him. When the secretary received a document, she registered it in the book and the same procedure followed. Processing each event took the secretary 5 minutes on average. When a lawyer received a telephone call, he had to walk from his desk to the cabinet, take the corresponding folder from the file, go back to his desk, look over the case documents, and then answer the phone call. Afterwards, he had to put the folder of the case back to the cabinet. When he received a document and surveyed it, he decided on the next action and put the document in the folder of the case. For this procedure, he spent 20 minutes for an event on average.

2.2. The Computer-Supported Procedure

Eventman is PC-DOS-based software for tracking events like phone calls and documents. It consists of a computer database of events and bank customers and user-friendly software, which enables its users to inquire about these events and customers. Among other information it contains information about the status of the case and the identity of the lawyer to whom the case belongs. The system helps the user by reminding him of possible actions he can take given the specific status of the case on the basis of the history of the case.

Now when a secretary receives a call or a document, she identifies the case and the appropriate lawyer by entering one or two keywords into the computer on her desk. Then she enters basic data about the event into the computer system and passes the call or the document to the lawyer. The time needed for this procedure is 3 minutes for an event on average.

When the lawyer receives the document, he usually doesn't have to walk away from his desk. He can find basic data about the case and its history on the computer on his desk. When he receives the document, he confirms this on a computer and chooses the next action. He puts the document in a folder of the case. The time needed for this procedure is 5 minutes for an event on average.

Year	Cases	Events	Lawyers	Cases/lawyer	Ev./lawyer
1980	200	10	3	67	3
1990	2000	60	4	500	15
1993	2800	89	5	560	18

Table 1. Number of cases and the average daily workload in the department.

The department began using Eventman at the end of 1990. It decreased the time the secretary needs for handling an event from 5 to 3 minutes and decreased the time a lawyer needs from 20 to 5 minutes on average. Therefore today, 5 lawyers and one secretary can handle about 50% more events than in 1990, and 9 times more than in 1980, when the department had 3 lawyers (see Table 1). Today a lawyer handles 6 times more events than in 1980. We accomplished this without organizational changes merely by reducing response times. We point out, that without the introduction of a computer-supported system, the greater number of cases appointed to each lawyer - 8 times more in 1993 than in 1980 - would have increased the search time and so the average time for handling an event would also have increased.

3. Changing Work Process

We will try to answer the question of whether we could further improve the present work process. With its comprehensive history, data and and process storage and description, computer support allows each lawyer to handle any event. What would happen, if every lawyer could work on all cases? We simulated two alternatives of the system from Figure 1 with VAX GPSS which is described in Martin (1985). The first alternative resumes the present work process, where every lawyer is responsible for his subset of cases. Events come into the system randomly with respect to lawyers. The result of the simulation is the same as if the secretary randomly passed the event to one of the five lawyers without considering the length of his queue. We denote this system Random. In the second alternative, the secretary passes the event to the lawyer with the shortest queue. When there are several equally short queues, the priority sequence is 1, 2, 3, 4, 5. We denote this system Minimal. We simulated 10 workdays for each alternative. We assumed an exponential distribution of interarrival times with a mean of 324 seconds (89 events per workday). The exponential distribution has higher probability for short times. This is realistic, because many events, especialy documents, come in batches, where interarrival time is 0. We assumed an exponential distribution of service times with a mean of 3 minutes for secretary and 5 minutes for lawyer. This is also a realistic assumption, because 30% of events are telephone calls, where service times are shorter than the average. From these 10 simulations, we calculated the average, minimal and maximal utilisation of lawyers for Random and Minimal models (Table 2).

		Lawyer 1	Lawyer 2	Lawyer 3	Lawyer 4	Lawyer 5
Random	MEAN	0.189	0.169	0.154	0.176	0.196
	MIN	0.128	0.086	0.109	0.087	0.092
	MAX	0.338	0.219	0.204	0.262	0.267
Minimal	MEAN	0.646	0.226	0.043	0	0
	MIN	0.575	0.168	0	0	0
	MAX	0.747	0.335	0.101	0.025	0

Table 2. Daily utilisation of lawyers for Random and Minimal model (10 simulations).

Random model. The maximal daily utilisation of a lawyer for this kind of work was 34%. However a lawyer doesn't only do the work described. We want him to do as much other work as possible. What amount of work can we assign to him? We assume that the bank takes this 34% as a real maximum, or it accepts the risk associated with its uncertainty. As it is not predictable which of the lawyers will get this maximal load, each lawyer in the department has at most 66% time available for other tasks, which must be done on the same day. For that reason, the sum of available time of lawyers is 0.661*5 = 3.31 days or 26.48 hours. It is also important that we can not miss any of the lawyers from the office.

Minimal model. We know, that the first lawyer has the most work, the second less and the last the least. If we assume the maximal utilisations from table 2, we can calculate the available time of lawyers 0.253+0.665+0.899+0.075+1 = 3.792 days or 30.34 hours, which is 3.86 hours more compared to the previous model. Lawyer 5 is now totaly available for other work, if necessary relocated (holidays, bussines trip, training).

Aditional secretary. We expect that the number of events will increase in 3 to 4 years by 100%. Calculations show that in this case we have to hire another secretary. This diminishes the secretary's mean service time to 1.5 minutes. If we retain five lawyers, the batch of 10 simulations for each alternative shows that the Minimal model gives us 8.04 hours more for other work than the Random one. With the Random model we can't miss any lawyer, whereas with the minimal model, lawyer 5 with his 0.039 maximal load is available for other work.

Aditional secretary and three lawyers. The bank plans to hire 3 more lawyers and 1 additional secretary. Our 10 simulations show that the difference in availability of lawyers for other work between the Minimal and the Random model is 14.1 hours. Under the present working practices (Random model) it will be possible to assign any of eight lawyers only for 52% of the time (4.16 hours) to other work. In the suggested work process (Minimal model) we will have 2 lawyers freely available.

4. Conclusion

The improvements reported in section 2 are the results of shorter response times which are the consequence of computer support of the office work. The work organization is not altered. But computer support can be still more valuable, because it allows for new ways of work organization. We have examined one of these possible new ways and found out its advantages. The new work organization described by the Minimal model takes advantage of computer speed and well-structured work it requires and promotes. It is typical for state of the art of computer aplications in this field that the first half is implemented almost everywere but the second part seldom.

References

Kiel D (1993) Implementing a microcomputer-based work reporting and monitoring system for Government Services, Journal of End User Computing, vol. 5, no. 1, 18-25, USA.

Martin D M (1985) General Purpose Simulation System, Simulation Software Ltd, London, UK.

Opper S, Weiss H F (1992) Technology for Teams, Van Nostrand Reinhold, New York, USA.

Demographer - a new version

Drago Čepar, Erika Uršič, Rok Založnik
Jožef Stefan Institute, Ljubljana

1. Introduction

Demographer is a software package for population projections based on mathematical model which gives the dependence among number of births, population pyramid, fertility ratios and survival ratios. The model and the program structure are briefly described in Sec. 2. In the new version some transformations and new possibilities are added. In Sec. 3 transformations of death rates to survival ratios are described. When transforming five year survival ratios to one year survival ratios, the approximation error can be diminished by including the information of some demographically similar population. This new feature is described in Sec. 4. A simple algorithm for approximating changes of one year fertility ratios on the basis of changes of total number of births has been included. It is described in Sec. 5. Some interesting results related to decay time of decreasing population are given in Sec. 6.

2. Basic features of the program

Basic algorithm of the program is described by the following equations:

$$N_{s,i+1}^{t+1} = N_{s,i}^{t} \cdot P_{s,i}, \qquad i = 0,1,2,\ldots 83, \qquad s = 1,2 \quad , \qquad N_{s,85}^{t+1} = N_{s,84}^{t} \cdot P_{s,84} + N_{s,85}^{t} \cdot P_{s,85} \quad ,$$

$$B = \tfrac{1}{2} \cdot \sum_{j=15}^{49} (N_{2,j}^{t} + N_{2,j+1}^{t+1}) \cdot R_j, \qquad N_{1,0}^{t+1} = 0.517 \cdot B \cdot P_1' \qquad , N_{2,0}^{t+1} = 0.483 \cdot B \cdot P_2' \ .$$

$N_{s,i}^{t}$ is the number of males (s=1) or females (s=2) belonging to i^{th} age group (defined as [i,i+1) for i=0,1,...,84 and [i,∞) for i=85) in year t. R_j, i=15,16,...,49 are one year specific fertility ratios; $P_{s,i}$, s=1,2, i=0,1,...,85 are one year specific survival ratios and P_s' are survival ratios for infant children. These equations are a specific case of Leslie models described in [1].

Fertility and survival ratios and sex/age population distribution are usually given for five year groups. So, we provided for the possibilities of transformations from five year to one year data. These possibilities as described in [2] are included in the program.

The program has the following structure: central procedure which controls the program flow and takes care of everything that happens in the program; transformations including approximations of one year data from five year data; output of the results in graphical or tabular form, to screen or to the printer; data base containing fertility ratios, survival ratios and population pyramids for 12 European countries. To run it we need: a PC compatible personal computer with 1 floppy disc (1.2M), hard disc recommended; 1M RAM; graphic card HERCULES, EGA, VGA or compatible; DOS 3.0 or higher. The old version of the program and its results are more fully described in [3]. In what follows we describe the features which were not included in the old version.

3. Converting death rates to survival ratios

In statistical sources five year death rates $m_{s,0}$, $m_{s,1-4}$, $m_{s,5-9}$, $m_{s,10-14}$, $\ldots, m_{s,80-84}$, m_{85+} for men(s=1) and women(s=2) are usually given. These have to be transformed to five year survival ratios ${}^5P_{s,0}$, ${}^5P_{s,1-4}$, ${}^5P_{s,5-9}, \ldots$, ${}^5P_{s,80-84}$, ${}^5P_{s,85+}$, and these according to the formulas given in [2] to one year survival ratios to feed the annual model. The transformations of five year death rates to five year survival ratios are given by :

$$ {}^5P_{s,0} = 1 - m_{s,0}, \quad {}^5P_{s,1-4} = 1 - \frac{8 \cdot m_{s,1-4}}{2 + 4 \cdot m_{s,1-4}}, \quad {}^5P_{s,i-(i+4)} = 1 - \frac{10 \cdot m_{s,i-(i+4)}}{2 + 5 \cdot m_{s,i-(i+4)}}, \quad i = 5,10,\ldots,80 \ , $$

$$ {}^5P_{s,85+} = 1 - \frac{10 \cdot m_{s,85+}}{2 + 5 \cdot m_{s,85+}}. $$

4. Approximating survival ratios for ages 74 to 85

It was observed, that the error in converting five year survival ratios to one year survival ratios is greater for ages 74 to 85. If we know annual survival ratios for some other population which we consider similar in this aspect, we can use them to get better approximations for our population. The approximation is given by

$$ k_i = \frac{\sum_{j=i-10}^{i-1} P_{s,j}}{\sum_{j=i-10}^{i-1} P^{SL}_{s,j}} \ , \quad P_{s,i} = P^{SL}_{s,i} \cdot k_i \ , \quad i = 74,\ldots,85 $$

, where $P^{SL}_{i,s}$ are one year survival ratios of the similar population. To use this feature, we have to include one year specific survival ratios $P^{SL}{}_{s,i}$ in the program data base previously.

5. Approximating fertility ratios using number of newborns

Usually we get one year specific fertility ratios $R_{i,t}$ in the statistic literature with a few years delay, whereas the annual number of births B_t is available with only a few months delay. In the first approximation we can assume that all age-specific fertility ratios are proportional to the total number of births. If we want to use the newest data in the forecast, we can use the relation $R_{i,t} = R_{i,t_0} \cdot B_t / B_{t_0}$, where t is the last year for which the number of newborns is known and t_0 is the last year for which the fertility ratios are available.

6. Decay time

The program with its computation possibilities allows us to analyze the decay time of decreasing population. We define $T_{1/2}$ as the time in which the total number of people is reduced by half. Obviously $T_{1/2}$ is defined only when survival ratios and fertility ratios are such, that in the long run the population will decrease. Let us assume that all proportions

R_i / R, i=15,..., 49 remain constant when $R=\sum_{i=15}^{49} R_i$ is changed. In this case we can get $T_{1/2}$ as a function of total fertility rate R. The results for the case of Slovenia are shown in Figure 1. We can read from the graph, that $T_{1/2}$ is defined for $0 \leq R < 2.11$. For R>2.11 population will eventually grow according to the annual model. If no children are born (R=0) population will halve in 39 years, if fertility of 1991 (1992) is sustained, it will halve in 71 (77) years.

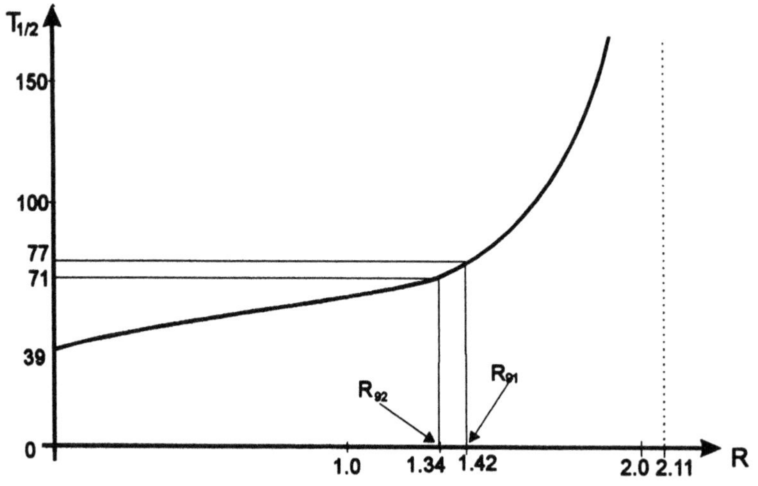

Figure 1. The decay time $T_{1/2}$ for Slovene population with fertility ratios structure 1992, population pyramid 1992 and survival ratios 1986.

Of course we could also make other assumptions on the way one year fertility ratios are changed. We could also be interested in studying $T_{1/2}$ as a function of other model parameters. It is the aim of the next version of our program to make function in Figure 1 and other ones available in tabular and graphical form with simple macros.

7. Conclusion

Demographer gives the chance to work with population projections to everybody interested in this subject. It is clear that the far future values have little or no relevance as predictions. The annual model described in Sec. 2 assumes nonexistence of migrations and long term invariability of fertility and survival ratios, which are unrealistic assumptions. Nevertheless the obtained results can be valuable as a possible way of illustrating the values of present survival and fertility ratios. The program can be used for teaching and simulation purposes. We continue to work on it and are willing to cooperate with other researchers on the subject. On request we will make population projections for any country, state or community, provided input data is supplied.

8. References

[1] Leslie P.H. The use of matrices in certain population mathematics, Biometrika 33, 183 - 212, 1945.

[2] Čepar D., Gosar L., Uršič E., Natural growth population models, Operations research "91, P Gritzmann, R.Hettich, R.Horst, E.Sachs, editions, Physica-Verlag 1992, p.p. 305 - 308.

[3] Čepar D. Habinc R. Uršič E., Založnik R., Demographer, Operations research "92, A.Karmann, K.Mosler, M.Schader, G.Uebe, editions, Physica-Verlag, Heidelberg 1993, p.p. 339 - 342

The 1-part m-machine cyclic scheduling problem in robotic cells

Yves Crama
Joris van de Klundert
Faculty of Economics
University of Limburg
P.O. Box 616, 6200 MD Maastricht
The Netherlands

We consider a flow shop consisting of m machines, an input device and an output device, in which one type of product is to be produced. There are no buffers in the flow shop and the transportation of items between machines is taken care of by a robot. The 1-part cyclic scheduling problem consists in finding the shortest cyclic schedule for the robot, i.e. a schedule that outputs one part in each cycle, can be repeated infinitely many times and has maximum throughput rate. The problem has been solved by Sethi et al. (1992) in the case where $m \leq 3$. We present an algorithm solving the 1-part cyclic scheduling problem in polynomial time for arbitrary values of m. Our approach is based on dynamic programming techniques.

A first constructive result concerning the 1-part cyclic scheduling problem is given in Sethi et al. (1992). Define activity A_i as unloading machine M_i and subsequently loading machine M_{i+1} (where the input device is M_0 and the output device is M_{m+1}). Call the sequence in which the activities are executed in a cyclic schedule a 1-part cycle. It is easy to see that every 1-part cycle corresponds exactly to a permutation of the activities. Conversely, it can be shown that every permutation of the activities defines a feasible 1-part cycle.

Theorem 1. (Sethi et al. (1992)) In a robotic cell with m machines, there are exactly $m!$ 1-part cycles.

Observe that a schedule, as opposed to a cycle, must specify loading and unloading times for each machine. Then the next question is, given a 1-part cycle, i.e. a permutation of the activities, what is the shortest schedule compatible with this cycle? We call a schedule

1-periodic if it has constant cycle time, i.e. if the time between two executions of the same activity is equal to the cycle time. Similarly, a schedule that repeats every n periods is called n-periodic. Using max-algebra (Cunninghame-Green (1979), Cohen et al. (1985)) it is possible to derive the following theorem :

Theorem 2. There is no periodic schedule with shorter mean cycle time than a shortest 1-periodic cyclic schedule.

Hence, we may restrict the analysis to 1-periodic schedules. The next step is to identify a set of 1-part cycles that necessarily contains an optimal cycle. For this purpose we introduce the concept of pyramidal permutations (analogously to pyramidal tours for the traveling salesman problem, see Gilmore et al. (1985); it is known that for the traveling salesman problem a shortest pyramidal tour can be computed by dynamic programming techniques in $O(n^2)$ time). More precisely, let $\pi = (A_0, A_{i_1}, \ldots, A_{i_k}, A_{i_{k+1}}, \ldots, A_{i_m})$ be a 1-part cycle, i.e. a permutation of the activities.

Definition 1. π is pyramidal if $1 \leq i_1 < \ldots i_k = m$ and $m > i_{k+1} > \ldots > i_{m-1} \geq 1$.

Theorem 3. The set of pyramidal 1-part cycles contains an optimal 1-part cycle.

Thus, in order to find a shortest cyclic schedule, we can restrict our attention to pyramidal permutations and to their associated shortest cyclic schedule. In general it is not trivial to find a shortest cyclic schedule associated with a given permutation. This can be done using max-algebra, but this method does not provide much insight. Since the structure of pyramidal permutations is fairly simple, one may wonder whether the shortest cycle time of a pyramidal cycle can be determined in an easier way. This is indeed the case. We have an $O(m)$ algorithm for computing a shortest schedule corresponding to a given 1-part cycle. In fact, our algorithm also enables us to solve the recognition version of the 1-part cyclic scheduling problem by dynamic programming techniques (the recognition version simply asks whether there exists a schedule with cycle time at most C, for some given C) :

Theorem 4. The recognition version of the 1-part cyclic scheduling problem can be solved in $O(m^2)$ time.

Moreover, making use of the structure of the solution given by the recognition algorithm, and applying this algorithm repeatedly, we can solve the optimization version in polynomial time.

Literature.

Cohen G., Dubois D., Quadrat J.P. & Viot M. (1985) A Linear System-Theoretic View of Discrete Event Processes and Its Use for Performance Evaluation in Manufacturing. IEEE Transactions on Automatic Control, vol AC-30 No. 3 pp 210-220.

Cunninghame-Green R. (1979) Minimax Algebra. Lecture Notes in Economics and Mathematical Systems. Springer Verlag. Berlin Heidelberg New York.

Gilmore P.C., Lawler E.L. & Shmoys D.B. (1985) Well Solved Special Cases. In Lawler E.L., Lenstra J.K., Rinnooy Kan A.H.G. & Shmoys D.B., The Traveling Salesman Problem : A Guided Tour of Combinatorial Optimization. Wiley Interscience Series in Discrete Mathematics. John Wiley & Sons. Chichester New York Brisbane Toronto Singapore.

Sethi S.P., Sriskandarajah C., Sorger G., Blażewicz J. & Kubiak W. (1992) Scheduling of Parts and Robot Moves in a Robotic Cell. International Journal of Flexible Manufacturing Systems 4 pp 331-358.

CONSISTENT RESTRICTED SHAPLEY VALUES

Jean Derks, Hans Peters
Department of Mathematics and Economics
University of Limburg
P.O. Box 616, NL-6200 MD Maastricht

1. Introduction We consider game-theoretic situations with an additional power structure on coalitions. A few examples are: The problem of distributing cost savings among the divisions of a large firm, constrained by existing contractual relations between these divisions; voting in political systems, where voters need the consent of their superiors or parties. A crucial assumption of our model is that this power structure is fixed and does not depend on the particular situation at hand. For example, the problem of distributing cost savings may occur at regular intervals, e.g. in each production planning period, but the existing power structure is fixed over several of these periods. Given this assumption, a natural further assumption is that this power structure is reflected by the game-theoretic solution concept. In this paper, we formulate axioms for such a solution concept. These axioms are inspired, on the one hand, by our assumption concerning the nature of the power structure, on the other hand by the following consideration of consistency: The solution should prescribe to a subset of players the same distribution they would receive if they would play a certain reduced game on their own. Our main result is the characterization of a class of coalition-restricted Shapley values.

For more details and proofs the reader is referred to Derks and Peters (1993b).

2. Definitions and axioms Let $Z \subseteq \mathbb{N}$ denote the set of potential *players*. ($\mathbb{N}$ is the set of natural numbers, $\subseteq$ denotes inclusion and $\subset$ denotes strict inclusion.) A *coalition* is a finite subset of Z. A *game* is a pair (N, v), where N is a coalition and $v : 2^N \to \mathbb{R}$ is a function with $v(\emptyset) = 0$. $\mathcal{G}$ denotes the set of all games. For $(N, v) \in \mathcal{G}$ and $M \subseteq N$, in $(M, v) \in \mathcal{G}$ the map v is the restriction to 2^M. A *value* is a map ψ assigning a vector in $\mathbb{R}^N$ to every game $(N, v) \in \mathcal{G}$, to be interpreted as a solution of the game. A well-known value is the *Shapley value* (Shapley, 1953).

For a given value ψ a coalition S is called *ψ-effective* if for all games $(N, v), (N, w) \in \mathcal{G}$ with $v(T) = w(T)$ for all $T \neq S$, $T \subseteq N$, and with $v(S) \neq w(S)$, we have $\psi(N, v) \neq \psi(N, w)$. A coalition S is called *ψ-ineffective* if for all games $(N, v), (N, w) \in \mathcal{G}$ with $v(T) = w(T)$ for all $T \neq S$, $T \subseteq N$, we have $\psi(N, v) = \psi(N, w)$.

Our crucial assumption concerning the power structure among coalitions is reflected by the following axiom.

Axiom 1 Every coalition S is either ψ-effective or ψ-ineffective.

Also the second axiom concerns the power structure among coalitions.

Axiom 2 For all coalitions S and T, if S and T are ψ-effective, then so is $S \cup T$.

It is assumed that in every game (N, v) some maximal ψ-effective coalition is formed and that the worth $v(S)$ of this coalition is distributed among the players of N. (A coalition $S \subseteq N$ is *maximally ψ-effective in* N if it is ψ-effective and every $S \subset T \subseteq N$ is not ψ-effective.) This is formalised by the following requirement.

Axiom 3 For all $(N, v) \in \mathcal{G}$, $\sum_{i \in N} \psi_i(N, v) = v(S)$ for some maximal ψ-effective coalition S in N.

Obviously, under Axiom 2, such a maximal ψ-effective coalition is unique.

Players i and j are *ψ-symmetric* in a coalition N if for every ψ-effective coalition $S \subseteq N$, we have $i \in S$ if and only if $j \in S$. A player is a *dummy* in a coalition N if he is not a member of any ψ-effective coalition in N.

Axiom 4 For all $(N,v) \in \mathcal{G}$ and $i,j \in N$, if i and j are ψ-symmetric in N, then $\psi_i(N,v) = \psi_j(N,v)$. If, furthermore, player i is a dummy, then $\psi_i(N,v) = 0$.

The next axiom is a consistency property closely related to that introduced by Hart and Mas-Colell (1989) for the Shapley value. Let $(N,v) \in \mathcal{G}$, and $U \subseteq N$ such that $N \backslash U$ is a ψ-effective coalition. The *reduced game* $(N\backslash U, v_{\psi,U})$ is defined as follows. For every $S \subseteq N \backslash U$,

$$v_{\psi,U}(S) = \sum_{i \in S} \psi_i(S \cup U, v).$$

Thus, in the reduced game, the worth of coalition S is equal to what the players in S receive together if they would play the (restriction of the) original game with the coalition U. The following axiom of *consistency* (or *reduced game property*) requires that in the reduced game the players do not redistribute the total of what they receive in the original game.

Axiom 5 For every $(N,v) \in \mathcal{G}$ and every $U \subseteq N$ with $N\backslash U$ ψ-effective, we have $\psi_i(N\backslash U, v_{\psi,U}) = \psi_i(N,v)$ for every $i \in N \backslash U$.

The consistency axiom will be used to relate distributions assigned by ψ across games with distinct numbers of effective coalitions. As a starting point we assume distributions for certain games with exactly two effective coalitions. This is done in our final axiom.

Axiom 6 Let S,T be ψ-effective coalitions.
(a) If $S \subset T$ and T contains no other ψ-effective proper subcoalition, then $\sum_{i \in S} \psi_i(T,v) = v(S) + |S|/|T|[v(T) - v(S)]$ for all $(T,v) \in \mathcal{G}$.
(b) If $S \cap T = \emptyset$ and both contain no ψ-effective proper subcoalitions, then $\sum_{i \in S} \psi_i(S \cup T, v) = v(S) + |S|/(|S| + |T|)[v(S \cup T) - v(S) - v(T)]$ for all $(S \cup T, v) \in \mathcal{G}$.

3. A characterization As in the preceding section, let Z be the set of potential players. Let Ω be a (finite or infinite) collection of coalitions with the property that for every pair of elements of Ω either their intersection is empty or one is contained in the other. Let $\bar{\Omega}$ be the collection of coalitions obtained by taking finite unions of elements of Ω. We call Ω an *admissible structure* (a.s.)

For $(N,v) \in \mathcal{G}$ and Ω an a.s. we define *dividends* $\Delta_v^\Omega(S)$ for coalitions $S \in \bar{\Omega}$ recursively, as follows.

$$\Delta_v^\Omega(S) = \begin{cases} v(S) & \text{if } S \text{ is a minimal element of } \Omega \\ v(S) - \sum_{T: T \subset S, T \in \bar{\Omega}} \Delta_v^\Omega(T) & \text{otherwise.} \end{cases}$$

Then a value φ^Ω on $\mathcal{G}$ is defined as follows. For every $(N,v) \in \mathcal{G}$ and every $i \in N$,

$$\varphi_i^\Omega(N,v) = \sum_{S: i \in S \subseteq N, S \in \bar{\Omega}} \Delta_v^\Omega(S)/|S|.$$

Observe that, if Ω consists of all 1-person coalitions, then φ^Ω is the Shapley value. In general, we call φ^Ω a *restricted Shapley value*. These values form a subclass of the values introduced earlier in Derks and Peters (1993a).

We can now state the main result of the paper.

THEOREM *A value ψ on $\mathcal{G}$ satisfies Axioms 1-6 if, and only if, $\psi = \varphi^\Omega$ for some admissible structure Ω.*

Remark: The a.s. Ω in this theorem consists exactly of all those ψ-effective coalitions which are not a union of smaller ψ-effective coalitions.

4. Related literature Recently, restrictions on coalitions in games have been discussed by several authors.

The restricted Shapley values introduced above are members of a larger class, introduced and characterized in Derks and Peters (1993a). Related works are Gilles and Owen (1991), Gilles *et al.* (1992), Faigle and Kern (1992), Hsiao and Raghavan (1990).

Details and proofs of the work described in this summary can be found in Derks and Peters (1993b). The main result and its proof are inspired by Hart and Mas-Colell (1989). Also the concept of a *potential* on the class of games $\mathcal{G}$, as introduced in the last mentioned paper, can be adapted to the situation where restrictions on coalitions exist.

5. References

Derks, J., and H. Peters (1993a): "A Shapley Value for Games with Restricted Coalitions", *International Journal of Game Theory*, 21, 351–360.

Derks, J., and H. Peters (1993b): "Consistent Restricted Shapley Values", Working Paper, University of Limburg, forthcoming.

Faigle, U., and W. Kern (1992): "The Shapley value for cooperative games under precedence constraints", Memorandum 1025, Faculty of Applied Mathematics, University of Twente, The Netherlands.

Gilles, R.P., and G. Owen (1991): "Games with permission structures: the disjunctive approach", Working Paper, Department of Economics, VPI & SU, Blacksburg.

Gilles, R.P., G. Owen, and R. van den Brink (1992): "Games with permission structures: the conjunctive approach", *International Journal of Game Theory*, 20, 277–293.

Hart, S., and A. Mas-Colell (1989): "Potential, Value, and Consistency", *Econometrica*, 57, 589–614.

Hsiao, C.-R., and T.E.S. Raghavan (1990): "Shapley value for multi-choice cooperative games", to appear in *Games and Economic Behavior*.

Shapley, L.S. (1953): "A value for n-person games". In: A.W. Tucker, H.W. Kuhn (eds.), *Contributions to the Theory of Games II*, 307–317, Princeton University Press, Princeton, NJ.

MODEL OF OPTIMIZATION OF WOOD WASTE PROCESSING IN SLOVENIA

Srečko Devjak, Mirko Tratnik, Franc Merzelj,

University of Ljubljana, Biotechnical Faculty, Department of Wood Science and Technology,
Rožna dolina, Cesta VIII/34, Ljubljana, Slovenia

PROBLEM

Processing of wood waste produced in sawmills and of timber which is too small for woodworking purposes is an important activity of primary timber industry in Slovenia, both from economical and ecological points of view (manufacture of particle boards and fiberboards, pulp production). The economic aspect of wood waste processing concerns the need for efficient operation of processing facilities above a profitability threshold. And the ecological aspect refers to ecological soundness of products and the environmental strain produced by processing technologies and resulting products. Closing down of non-profitable wood waste processing facilities, on the other hand, would only lead to additional problems connected with transportation and processing. The optimization model discussed in the following approaches the problems of wood waste processing from the above perspective.

MODEL

The process is divided into phases (Devjak, 1987) and includes the following conditions: the structure of available timber at its origin, the structure of wood waste resulting from mechanical processing, the conditions relating to distribution, and technological and economic considerations.

The conditions of structure and available timber volume according to woods of origin

$$\sum_h \sum_i x_{hij} - x_j = 0 \quad H=1,2,...,H \; i=1,2,...,I2 \; j=1,2,...J$$

$$x_{hij} - a_{hij} * x_j = 0 \tag{1}$$

where:

x_{hij} - quantity of i-type timber of a tree species h at a place of origin j

x_j- total available timber volume at a place of origin j

a_{hij} - portion of i-type timber in the total available timber at a place of origin j

Indexes i = 1,2,..., I1 indicate such types of timber as are suitable for mechanical processing. For the waste resulting from such processing the following applies:

$$x_{hij} - xn_{hij} - x'_{hij} = 0 \tag{2}$$

$b_{hgij} * x'_{hij} - y_{hgj} = 0$

$g = l_2 + 1, l_2 + 2, \ldots, l'$, $\quad h=1,2,\ldots,H \quad j=1,2,\ldots J$

xn_{hij} - non-processed quantity of i-type timber of a treespecies h at a place of origin j

b_{hgij} - standard for g-type mechanical processing waste of i-type timber of a tree species h at a place of origin j

y_{hgj} - quantity of g-type waste of a tree species h at a place of origin j resulting from primary timber processing

The conditions concerning the distribution of total wood waste are expressed by the following equations:

$$x_{hij} - xn_{hij} - \sum_l \sum_k z_{hijkl} = 0 \qquad i=l_1+1, l_1+2, \ldots, l2 \tag{3}$$

$$y_{hgj} - yn_{hgj} - \sum_l \sum_k z_{hijkl} = 0 \qquad g=i=l_2+1, l_2+2, \ldots, l'$$

where:

yn_{hgj} - quantity of g-type excess waste of a tree species h at a place of origin j

z_{hijkl} - quantity of i-type waste of a tree species h transported form a place of origin j to a processing location k by a means of transportation l

Distribution of wood waste from a particular place according to processing locations:

$$\sum_j \sum_l z_{hijkl} - v_{hik} = 0 \tag{4}$$

v_{hik} - input quantity of i-type ($i=l_1+1,\ldots,l_2$, $l_2+1,\ldots,l'$) waste of a tree species h for processing k

The equation for the structure of input primary material for processing k:

$$v_{hik} + vp_{hik} - \sum_m c_{hikm} * v_{km} \tag{5}$$

$$\sum_h \sum_i (v_{hik} + vp_{hik}) - \sum_m v_{km} = 0$$

$i=l_1+1,\ldots,l_2$, $l_2+1,\ldots,l'$ $\qquad m=1,2,\ldots,M$

where:

c_{hikm} -portion of i-type primary material of a tree species h in the structure of the input for processing k using technology m

v_{phik} - quantity of i-type waste of a tree species h for processing k- supplies from outside the location

v_{km} - processed timber volume at a processing facility k using technological process m

In determining c_{hikm} coefficients the use of special optimization models seems reasonable (Tratnik, 1983).

Scope of production at a final processing facility k:

$$\sum_{m} (vkm /dkm - wkm) = 0 \qquad (6)$$

d_{km} - standard of wood waste use by technology m for wood waste processing k per product unit of technology m

w_{km} - scope of production of processing k by using technology m

Economic conditions involve income and expenditure. Let us assume the following:

$$Pk = \sum_{m} w_{km} * c_{km} \qquad (7)$$

P_k - income of processing k
c_{km} - price of products of processing k using technology m

$$S'_k = \sum_{h} \sum_{i} \sum_{j} \sum_{l} z_{hijkl} * s_{hijkl} + \sum_{h} \sum_{i} vp_{hik} * c_{hik} \qquad (8)$$

S'_k - value of purchased waste for processing location k
s_{hijkl} - transportation costs and purchase price per unit of z_{hijkl},,.

c_{hik} - purchase price per unit of vphik

$$S''_k = \sum v_{km} * s_{km} \qquad (9)$$

S''_k - processing costs of processing location k
s_{km} - processing costs per unit of v_{km}

The difference between income and expenditure (R_k) of a processing location k:

$$P_k - S'_k - S'_k > R_k \qquad (10)$$

Assuming P_k as a condition required to reach a profitability threshold, we introduce u_k, so that

$$P_k - S'_k - S'_k + u_k = R_k \qquad (11)$$

thus avoiding inconsistency of the model (L. Martič, 1978).

In addition to the above mentioned conditions and any other conditions that may be considered, the following are considered as variables: x_{hij}, x_j, xn_{hij}, y_{hgj}, yn_{hgj}, z_{hijkl}, v_{hik}, vp_{hik}, v_{km}, w_{km} and u_k conditions of nonnegativity.

The form of criterial function will vary with the aim of optimization, for example:

a) Minimization of transportation of wood waste at the greatest possible quantity of processed wood waste from a particular location:

$$\text{Min.} \left(\sum_h \sum_i \sum_j \sum_k \sum_l z_{hijkl} * d_{jkl} + \sum_h \sum_i \sum_j vp_{hik} * d'\right)$$

where:

d_{jkl} - distance between a place of origin j and a processing location k when using transportation l

d' - Max. (djkl), a conditions which, for reasons of consistency of the model, allows wood waste to be purchased outside a particular location, however, at less favorable cost.

b) Economic optimization of wood waste processing:

The criterion used is the difference between income and expenditure. Income is expressed by equation (7). Expenditure includes the costs expressed in equations (8) and (9), the costs of reaching a profitability threshold uk and the costs in connection with unused wood waste:

$$\sum_h \sum_g \sum_j xn_{hij} * s'_{hij} + \sum_h \sum_i \sum_j yn_{hgj} * s'_{hgj} *S'''$$

where:

s'_{hij} - cost of unused unit of xnhij

s'_{hgj} - cost of unused unit of ynhgj

In this case, the criterion has the following form:

$$\text{Max.} \left(\sum_k (P_k - S'_k - S''_k - u_k) - S'''\right)$$

The nature of the problem is often such as to bring the model within the area of target or multicriterial programming.

REFERENCES

- Devjak, S.: Ekonomska optimizacija razporejanja in predelav lesne mase območja. Doktorska disertacija, Univerza Ljubljana, Ekonomska fakulteta v Ljubljani, 1987.
- Martič, L.: Višekriterialno programiranje, Informator, Zagreb, 1978.
- Tratnik, M.: Ekonomika optimizacije proizvodnje ivernih plošč glede na debelino ivernih plošč in vrste uporabljenega lesa. Doktorska disertacija, Univerza Ljubljana, Biotehniška fakulteta.

- Devjak, S.: Economic optimization of distribution and processing of available timber of a particular area. Doctoral thesis, University of Ljubljana, Faculty of Economics of Ljubljana, 1987.
- Martič, L.: Multicriterial programming, Informator, Zagreb, 1978.
- Tratnik, M.: Economic optimization in particle board production with respect to thickness of particle boards and types of timber used. Doctoral thesis, University of Ljubljana, Biotechnical Faculty.

ON UNIFORMIZATION FOR CONTINUOUS-TIME MARKOV CHAINS

Nico M. van Dijk *
University of Amsterdam

Abstract

The method of uniformization or randomization for continuous-time Markov chains is shown to be extendable to chains with

(i) time-inhomogeneous and
(ii) unbounded

transition rates. Some approximate computational aspects are addressed also. A special application of uniformization of actual interest is included.

1. INTRODUCTION

Continuous-time Markov chains are widely applicable for modelling practical situations that evolve continuously in time with jumps or changes at specific epochs. Particularly, applications are found in telecommunications (teletraffic analysis, broadcasting), computer performance evaluation (computer networks), manufacturing (material handling systems, assembly lines), inventory theory, maintenance analysis and reliability.

In dealing with continuous-time Markov chains the technique of uniformization, motivated by results in [4], has been shown to be a powerful tool for both computational and theoretical purposes over the last decades (cf. [2], [3], [5]). An elegant survey is given in [2].

So far, however, this technique seemed to be restricted to chains of which the transition rates are **time-homogeneous** and **uniformly bounded**. Though the first condition is reasonably justified for steady state situations it is less realistic for transient analysis. Conversely, while transition rates usually remain stochastically bounded over finite time intervals, the second condition can easily be violated in practical situations. For example, it already fails for the classical $M \mid M \mid \infty$ - infinite server queue.

This paper aims to show that the first condition is not required while the second can be circumvented in an approximative manner. Roughly speaking the presented versions are similar in spirit to the standard case in that one can sample event epochs by a **Poisson process** while at these epochs events take place according to **conditional jump** probabilities.

The results can be of practical interest for approximative procedures in combination with random sampling such as by Monte-Carlo simulation, by finite grid approximation or by iterative numerical computation. Further research in these directions is suggested.

* Correspondence address:
Professor N.M. van Dijk, Dep. of Econometrics, Roetersstraat 11,
1018 WB Amsterdam, The Netherlands

2. STANDARD UNIFORMIZATION

Consider a continuous-time Markov chain with countable state space S and transition rates

$$q(i,j)$$

for a transition from a state i into another state j, where we assume these rates to be uniformly bounded (in literature already referred to as *uniformizable.*). That is, for some finite constant $B < \infty$ and all $i \in S$.

$$q(i) = \Sigma_{j \neq i}\, q(i,j) \leq B \,. \tag{2.1}$$

Let P_t denote the corresponding transition matrix over a period of time t. The following result can then be proven (e.g. [2], [3], [4], [5]) and is generally referred to as *uniformation* or *randomization* for reasons of interpretation as given below:

$$P_t(i,j) = \sum_{k=0}^{\infty} \frac{(tB)^k}{k!}\, e^{-tB}\, P^k(i,j) \tag{2.2}$$

where P^k represents the k-th matrix power of the one-step uniformization matrix P defined by:

$$P(i,j) = \begin{cases} q(i,j)/B & (j \neq i) \\ 1-\sum_{j \neq i} q(i,j)/B & (j = i) \end{cases} \tag{2.3}$$

Uniformization interpretation

1. One way to interpret (2.2) and (2.3) is that dummy transitions i→i are introduced as possible events while the *holding times* up to a next event, which may include dummy events, have been *uniformized* to be the same for all states i to be exponential with parameter B. Given that an event occurs a transition takes place proportional to the transition rates at that instant.

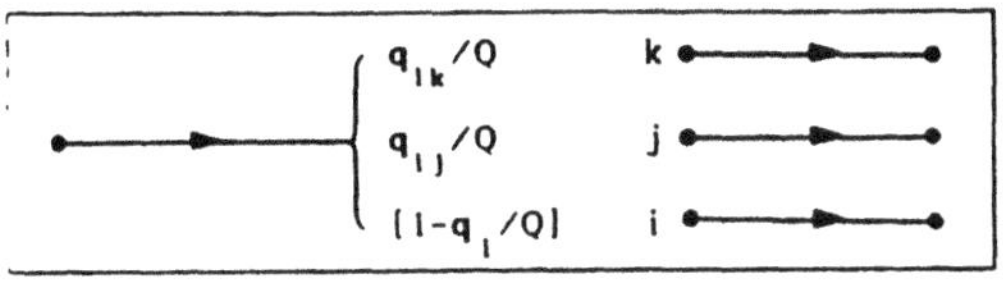

2. Another way to look at uniformization is based on the fact that events generated by a Poisson process are uniformly distributed. Hence, if k-events have taken place, the *epochs* of these events are spread according to a k-fold *uniform* distribution. Once these epochs are sampled, the conditional jump probabilities are proportional to the corresponding rates at these epochs.

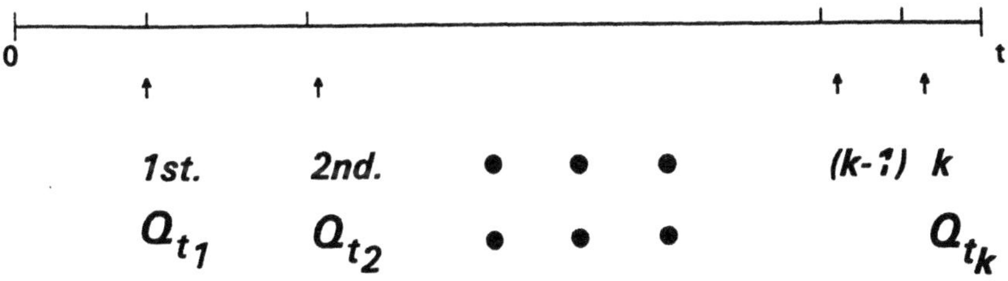

3. INHOMOGENEOUS CASE

Now consider a time-inhomogeneous in which the transition rates q(i,j) as described have become time-dependent as:

$$q_t(i,j)$$

at time t where these rates are assumed to be right-continuous in t for any fixed i,j. Furthermore, for given fixed Z assume that for some constant $B < \infty$, all $i \in S$ and $t \leq Z$:

$$q_t(i) = \sum_{j \neq i} q_t(i,j) \leq B \tag{3.1}$$

Let $P_{s,t}(i,j)$ denote the transition probability to observe the system instate j at time t given that it was in state i at time s. Furthmermore, for all $t \leq Z$ define the unformized transition matrix P_t by similar to (2.3) by:

$$P_t(i,j) = \begin{cases} q_t(i,j)/B & (j \neq i) \\ 1-\sum_{j \neq i} q_t(i,j)/B & (j=i) \end{cases}$$

The following result can then be proven in line with the second interpretation given above. The proof is based on the existence of a unique semigroup that satisfies strong regularity infinitesimal conditions in combination with a so-called minimal construction for Markov jump processes (cf. [1]).

Theorem 3.1. *For all $s \leq t \leq Z$ and any (i,j), we have:*

$$P_{s,t}(i,j) = \sum_{k=0}^{\infty} \frac{(t-s)^k B^k}{k!} e^{(t-s)B} \int_s^t \int_s^t \cdots \int_s^t \left[P_{t_1} P_{t_2} \ldots P_{t_k}(i,j) \right] d\bar{H}(t_1,t_2,\ldots,t_k) \tag{3.3}$$

$$\{t_1 \leq t_2 \leq t_k\}$$

where $d\bar{H}(t_1,t_2,\ldots,t_k)$ is the density of a k-dimensional uniform distribution at $[s,t] \times [s,t] \times \ldots \times [s,t] \subset R^k$ and where $P_{t_1} P_{t_2} \ldots P_{t_k}$ is the standard matrix product of the transition matrices at times $t_1, t_2, \ldots, t_k$ as per (2.3).

Remark 3.1. Expression (3.3) can be simplified by substituting

$$d\bar{H}(t_1,\ldots,t_k) = \frac{k!}{(t-s)^k} dt_1 \ldots dt_k. \tag{3.4}$$

The form (3.3) however directly corresponds to the second interpretation above and the form (2.3) in the homogeneous case. It reduces to (2.3) when substituting (3.4) and $\mathbf{P} = \mathbf{P}_t$ for all t .

Remark 3.2 *(Truncation)*

With $P^L_{s,t}$ the truncated version of (3.3) at level $k \leq L$ and with $||.||$ denoting the standard supremum norm, one directly derives:

(3.5) $$|| \bar{P}^L_{s,t} - P_{s,t} || \leq \sum_{k=L+1}^{\infty} \frac{(t-s)\, B^k}{k!} e^{-(t-s)B} \leq \frac{(t-s)^L B^L}{L!}$$

Remark 3.3 *(Discrete approximization)*

Expression (3.3) can still be impractical as it requires one to store a continuum, of matrices as well as to perform a continuous integration. To this end, a discrete-grid approximation can be suggested where we assume that the transition rate matrix $Q_t = (q_t(i,j))$ with diagonal elements $-q_t(i)$, satisfies a Lipschitz grid condition:

(3.6) $$||Q_{nh+\Delta t} - Q_{nh}|| \leq \Delta t\, K \qquad \text{for all } \Delta t \leq h \text{ and } nh \leq Z$$

where h is some fixed gridsize $h \leq 1/B$ and K some constant. Let $n_i = [t_i h^{-1}]$ where $[x]$ is the integer such that $[x] \leq x < [x]+1$, and denote by $\bar{H}(n_1, n_2, \ldots, n_k)$ the probability mass function of the order statistics $n_1 \leq n_2 \leq \ldots \leq n_k$ of a k-dimensional uniform distribution at $\{n, n+1, \ldots, m-1\}^k$ where $n = [sh^{-1}]$ and $m = [th^{-1}]$. Now let $P^h_{s,t}$ be the finite-grid approximation matrix defined by

(3.7) $$P^h_{s,t} = \sum_{k=0}^{\infty} \frac{(t-s)^k B^k}{k!} e^{-(t-s)B} \times \left\{ \sum_{n}^{m-1} \sum_{n}^{m-1} \ldots \sum_{n}^{m-1} \left[P_{n_1 h} P_{n_2 h} \ldots P_{n_k h} \right] \bar{H}(n_1, n_2, \ldots, n_k) \right\}_{\{n_1 \leq n_2 \leq \ldots \leq n_k\}}$$

Then

(3.8) $$\boxed{|| P^h_{s,t} - P_{s,t} || \leq h\,(t-s) K}$$

Remark 3.4 *(Computation by simulation)*

To compute (3.3) also Monte-Carlo simulation can be suggested say as follows.
First truncate as per (3.5) at level L. Next compute the Poisson probabilities for each $k \leq L$. For fixed k now do the following:

Step 1:	*Generate k random numbers $x_i \in [s,t]$.*
Step 2:	*Take their order statistics $t_i = \hat{x}_1 \leq t_2 = \hat{x}_2 \leq \ldots \leq t_k = \hat{x}_k$.*
Step 3:	*Compute (approximate or simulate) the matrix product: $P_{t_1}, P_{t_2} \ldots P_{t_k}$.*
Step 4:	*Repeat step 1-step 3 for a prescribed number of times and average out.*

4. APPROXIMATE UNIFORMIZATION

In this section we consider an approximate uniformization procedure from homogeneous Markov chains that do not necessarily satisfy the condition (2.1). Let us first present a simple example.

M | M | ∞-example. Consider an infinite server queue with Poisson arrival rate λ and exponential service rate μ per server. Hence,

$$(4.1) \qquad q(i,j) = \begin{cases} \lambda & j = i+1 \\ i\mu & j = i-1 \end{cases}$$

which violates (2.1) for any **B** so that we cannot define the uniformization matrix (2.3). Instead, consider a fixed N, typically to be thought of as large and define the matrix $\mathbf{P}^N$ as follows:

For i < N:

$$(4.2a) \qquad P^N(i,j) = \begin{cases} \lambda \,/\, [\lambda+N\mu] & (j = i+1) \\ i\mu \,/\, [\lambda+N\mu] & (j = i-1) \\ 1 - [\lambda+i\mu] \,/\, [\lambda+N\mu] & (j = i) \end{cases} \qquad \begin{matrix} \textit{(Jump with probability)}: \\ [\lambda+i\mu] \,/\, [\lambda+N\mu] \end{matrix}$$

For i > N:

$$(4.2b) \qquad P^N(i,j) = \begin{cases} \left[\dfrac{\lambda}{\lambda+i\mu}\right] & (j = i+1) \\ \left[\dfrac{i\mu}{\lambda+i\mu}\right] & (j = i-1) \end{cases} \qquad \textit{(Jump with probability 1)}$$

Then with π and π^N the steady state vectors of the original M|M|∞-queue and the Markov chain with this transition matrix one can prove that for some constant C:

$$(4.3) \qquad \boxed{\| \pi^N - \pi \| \le \frac{C}{N}}$$

By enlarging N an approximation by (4.2) thus becomes asymptotically exact.

General case

The idea from the example above can be generalized as follows:

- Take **B** arbitrary large and let $h = 1/\mathbf{B}$
- Define the jump-probability matrix $\mathbf{P}^B$ by:

$$J(i) = \min\left[1, h \sum_{j \neq i} q(i,j)\right] \tag{4.4}$$

$$P^B(i,j) = \begin{cases} 1 - J(i) & (j = i) \\ J(i)\left[\dfrac{q(i,j)}{\sum_{k \neq i} q(i,k)}\right] & (j \neq i) \end{cases} \tag{4.5}$$

In words that is, with probability J(i) a jump will take place in state i and given that a jump takes place, the actual transition will be proportional to the corresponding transition rates in that state. Then, with π and π_B the corresponding steady state vectors as determined by:

$$\pi \mathbf{Q} = 0 \qquad \text{and } \pi^B \mathbf{P}^B = \pi^B, \tag{4.6}$$

it can be proven that for some constant C:

$$\|\pi^B - \pi\| = h C = \frac{C}{B} \tag{4.7}$$

The approximate uniformization (4.5) thus becomes asymptotically exact for B tending to infinity.

5. A SPECIAL APPLICATION

As a special application of uniformization of increasing actual interest in present-day communications, consider a cellular mobile communication system with call requests arriving at cell j with Poisson arrival rate μ_j, exponential call duration or holding time with parameter μ and handover rates λ_{jk} to move from cell j to another call k during a call. (Roughly speaking that is, in a small interval of time Δt a call (driver) in cell j might move to a neighbouring cell k with probability $\lambda_{jk}\Delta t + 0(\Delta t)$).

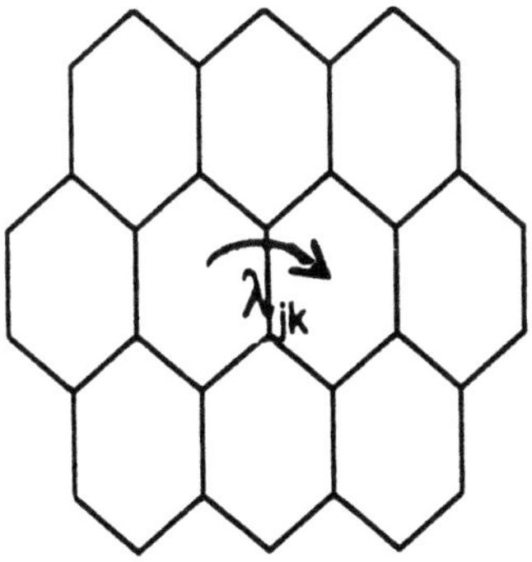

As a form of uniformization and due to the exponential underlying structure we can then also regard this system as a queueing network with a call j represented as a station j, with an exponential service parameter:

$$\mu_j = \mu + \sum_k \lambda_{ik}$$

and (conditional) routing probabilities:

$$p_{jk} = \begin{cases} \mu / \mu_j & (k=0) \quad \text{(complete)} \\ \lambda_{jk} / \mu_j & (k \neq j,0) \quad \text{(handover to k)} \end{cases}$$

to move to another station k or leave the system for k=0 upon service completion at station j. The system is hereby reformulated in the standard framework of a queueing network from which results, such as the celebrated product form expression below for the numbers n_i of ongoing calls in cell i, can be concluded directly

$$\pi(n_1,\dots,n_N) = c \prod_i \frac{1}{n_i!} \left[\frac{\lambda_i}{\mu_i}\right]^{n_i} \quad ; \lambda_j = \nu_j + \sum_i \lambda_i p_{ij} \quad (j = 1,\dots,N)$$

References

1. Gihman, I.I. and Skorohod, A.V. (1979): "Controlled Stochastic Processes". *Springer*, Berlin.

2. Grassman, W. (1990): "Finding Transient Solutions in Markovian Event Systems through Randomization". *Proceedings of "The First International Conference on the Numerical Solution of Markov Chains*. Januari 8-10, Raleigh, NC. 375-385.

3. Gross, D. and Miller, D.R. (1984): "The Randomization Technique as a Modelling Tool and Solution Procedure for Transient Markov Processes". *Oper. Res.* 32, 343-361.

4. Jensen, A. (1953): "Markovian Chains as an Aid in the Study of Markov Processes". *Skan. Aktuarietdskr.* 36, 87-91.

5. Melamed, B. and Yadin, M. (1984): "Randomization Procedures in the Computation of Cumulative-Time Distributions over Discrete State Markov Processes". *Oper. Res.* 32, 926-943.

6. Van Dijk, N.M. (1989): "Aproximation Uniformization for Continuous-Time Markov Chains with an Application ro Performability Analysis". *Stochastic Process Appl.* 40, 339-357.

Crew scheduling for an Urban transit company

K. DJELLAB, G. FLEURY, M. GOURGAND, A. QUILLIOT.
Laboratoire d'Informatique
63177 AUBIERE Cedex. FRANCE

Abstract : After a presentation of the problem : crew scheduling for drivers in an urban transit company, we exhibit the difficulties of this kind of optimization problem.

Afterward, an algorithm which is a coupling between a stochastic (annealing-like) algorithm and linear programming is proposed to solve it.

This algorithm is used to constitute the timetable for bus drivers of the T2C company (buses of the city of Clermont-Ferrand) and some of the obtained results are given.

To conclude, the efficiency of this approach is demonstrated by comparisons with various softwares proposed to the T2C by specialized companies. Moreover the structure of our algorithms allows to solve many other kinds of timetable problems. In any urban transit company, to answer the demand, and to improve the working conditions, and to maximize its profit (minimizing its manpower), appears highly combinatoric optimization problems. Many constraints need to be satisfied, a lot of them being "soft" constraints. The combinatoric of the problem is not easily reduced by these constraints. The cost function becomes usually vague and it is no more necessary to find the best solution, but only a good one.

Key words : Linear programming, Stochastic methods, Timetable.

1) Description of the problem : The crew scheduling problem is to cover the whole bus schedule the workdays remaining feasible, and the total cost becoming minimal. A task is a segment of working time on a bus, between two relief points (where a new driver can replace the previous driver of the vehicle). The moving durations (necessitated to go from a relief point to another one) are known. A workday is a feasible sequence of tasks attributed to one driver. These workdays are gathered in different grids, according to geographical or timing constraints. Each workday belongs to exactly one grid, and can be cut in two straight pieces (with a break for dinner), or not. The constraints are :

1_ the number of diary straights and their relative duration,
2_ duration and position of the break between two successive straights.
3_ duration, total spread, and position of the workday,
4_ number of workdays in each grid,
5_ moving times between two relief points (such a break is paid and must be avoided, if possible),
6_ mean duration of the workdays of each grid,
7_ compatibility between grid and vehicle blocks.

1-1) The difficulties of the problem : This problem has been shown to be NP-hard [3]. Moreover,

1) the set of all possible workdays is not partitioned by any constraint.
2) The geographically limited one straight piece workdays can be done either in the morning or in the afternoon.
3) Some of the constraints are not strict : some of them can be "desirable". One (or even more) of the workdays can slightly violate a "strict" constraint. The dates of a non commercial task can be slightly modified, if necessary. Some of the constraints cannot be known before the whole schedule is constructed.
4) Nevertheless, some (too rare) extreme tasks are devoted to precise grids.

As for most of these kinds of problems, the cost function is not exactly defined, and the quality of a schedule is not easy to be quantified. Therefore, it seems to be very hard to automatically create a exactly satisfying crew schedule.

3) Resolution algorithm : The proposed algorithm is constituted by three levels.

3-1) Description of the third level (tasks assignment) : The (linearized) problem is to devote each free task to a workday. Let S be a set of workdays, and T a set of tasks, the constraints on the (S,T) pair will be introduced as a dynamic cost function $C \ : \ S \times T \ \rightarrow \ N \cup \{+\infty\}$ calculated by :

Function Cost Input : (i :workday, j :task); Output : (cost : integer)
Begin
If at less one constraint is violated by assignment of task j to workday i
then $C_{ij} := +\infty$
Else do
$cost \leftarrow 0$;
For each soft constraint k do $cost \leftarrow cost + Coef_k \times \delta_k$
end if
End.

where $Coef_k$ points out the weight of the k constraint and δ_k measure its violation. For each couple (S,T) one construct the compatibility graph $G = (S \cup T, E)$ defined by :

$$i \in S \ j \in T \quad ij \in E \iff C_{ij} < \infty$$

Once the compatibility graph is construct with the C_{ij} cost on the edges, we solve the corresponding problem applying the transport algorithm [5] to (P) :

$$\begin{cases} Min \sum_{i=1}^{i=n} \sum_{j=1}^{j=m} C_{ij} \ x_{ij} \\ \sum_{i=1}^{i=n} x_{ij} \ = \ 1 \quad j = 1,...,m \quad (1) \quad \sum_{j=1}^{j=m} x_{ij} \ = \ 1 \quad i = 1,...,n \quad (2) \\ \sum_{i=1}^{i=n} x_{i(m+1)} \ = \ n - m \ si \ n \ > \ m \ (3) \ \sum_{j=1}^{j=m} x_{(n+1)j} \ = \ m - n \ si \ m \ > \ n \ (4) \end{cases}$$

where : $x_{ij} = \begin{cases} 1 & when \ the \ task \ \ j \ is \ assigned \ to \ workday \ \ i \\ 0 & else \end{cases}$

Assignment procedure :
I/O (S :workday set; T :tasks set)
Begin
Repeat For all i in S, j in T do $C_{ij} := Cost(i,j)$
Remove the isolated vertex
Solve the linear program $P_{(S,T)}$, *let* x^* *its optimal solution*
For all i in S, j in T do
If $x^*_{ij} = 1$ *and* $C_{ij} < \infty$ *then assign task j to workday i*
end (For)
$S \leftarrow update(S)$; $T \leftarrow update(T)$
Until $(S = \emptyset)$
End

3-2) Description of second level (Stochastic algorithm) :

descent Procedure :
I/O : two states : (S_c, T_c) *(current state) and* (S_r, T_r) *record state);*

```
        an integer : c (parking meter);
Begin
        extract (S1,T1) at random in V(Sc,Tc)
        If H(S1,T1) ≤ H(Sc,Tc) then
                If H(S1,T1) < H(Sc,Tc) then c ← 0
                        If H(S1,T1) ≤ H(Sr,Tr) then (Sr,Tr) ← (S1,T1)
                        end if
                end if
                (Sc,Tc) ← (S1,T1);
        end if
        c ← c+1
End.
Jump procedure :
        I/O : two states : (Sc,Tc) (current state) et (Sr,Tr) (record state);
        an integer : c (parking meter);
Begin
        extract at random (S1,T1) in W(Sc,Tc) (Level 3)
        If H(Sc,Tc) ≠ H(S1,T1) then
                If H(S1,T1) ≤ H(Sr,Tr) then (Sr,Tr) ← (S1,T1)
                end if
                c ← 0
        end if
        c ← c+1; (Sc,Tc) ← (S1,T1)
End.
Kangaroo program
Begin
        Fix A (the maximal number of parking before a jump)
        Choose one initial state (Sc,Tc) (Level 3)
        c ← 1; (Sr,Tr) ← (Sc,Tc)
        Repeat
                If c ≤ A then descent((Sc,Tc);(Sr,Tr);c)
                else jump((Sc,Tc);(Sr,Tr);c)
        Until : (Sr,Tr) is advisable
End.
```

The choices for $\mathcal{V}$ and $\mathcal{W}$ will be detailed hereafter.

3-3) Level one description (Improving when the residu becomes weak) : The transit company wishes a solution with weak residue. One or more workday can be eliminated as soon as a solution with a weak residue is obtained. For this, it suffices to suppress one workday from the workdays set S_k and to place their tasks in the free tasks set T_k. As soon as the new residue is weak enough, a new workday can be eliminated else the third level process go on.

The goal of two and three levels of the algorithm is to minimize the number of used workdays. To eliminated workdays one choose the grid whose number of workdays is the greater in front of that is wished, and suppress its less used workday.

We proved the convergence of the proposed algorithm.

4) Application :

4-1) Obtained results : The number of workdays is about 200, among them 65% are straight ones, the remaining are two straights ones. The total number of tasks is about 2100.

For testing, a sub-problem suffices.

Grid	Workdays nb		Mean time working		Time
nb	obtained	wish	obtained	wish	improducting/working
1	56 %	52 %	7h26	7h23	4.3 %
9	32 %	34 %	8h59	9h14	5.0 %
16	12 %	14 %	7h15	7h23	5.2 %

Fig 11. Results obtained quality.

4-2) CPU time : Solving an example of 400 tasks and 40 workdays necessitates 0.2s on a 28 Mips computer.

4-3) Choices of $\mathcal{V}$ et $\mathcal{W}$:

a) Empty k workdays becoming unactive.
b) Crew the active workdays with the remaining tasks.
c) For each unactive workday do :
let this workday be active and crew.

The number k of emptied workdays is chosen according to the size of the problem. Here it has been chosen to constitute 1.5% of the total number of workdays for $\mathcal{V}$ and 3% for $\mathcal{W}$.

5) Conclusion :

1) Our program has been compared to known specific softwares on the same samples and gives as good as, or better results. Moreover, it allows :

a) "some" unassigned tasks (a wish of the transit company).
b) the crew scheduling can be constructed from an existing one.

2) The program is very flexible and can be used with about any constraint.

3) It allows to schedule other manpower, for instance timetables, football competition... as soon as

a) one task can only be assigned to one person.
b) one person can, at any time, be assigned to only one task.
c) task duration must be known and can variate.
d) the necessary ressources must be known, and can be consumable.

BIBLIOGRAPHY

[1] E.-Molimard (1993). *Rapport de DEA.* Centre universitaire de sciences et techniques (C.U.S.T.), génie informatique. Université Blaise-Pascal, Clermont-Ferrand-II.

[2] Djellab K. (1993). *Hypergraphes et Ordonnancement.* Thèse en préparation. Université Blaise Pascal, Clermont-Ferrand-II.

[3]Fleury G. (1993). *Méthodes stochastiques et déterministes pour les problèmes N-P-Difficiles.* Thèse. Unviversité Blaise Pascal, Clermont-Ferrand-II.

[4] Garey M.R. D.S. Johnson (1983). *Computers and Intractability.* Freeman Co. New-York.

[5] Papadimitriou C.H Steiglitz K. (1982). *Combinatorial Optimization.* Prentice-Hall.

Some Remarks on Dependence Among the Consistency Tests

Czesław Domański, Dariusz Parys
Department of Statistical Methods University of Łódź
Rewolucji 1905 Nr 41, 90-214 Łódź

1. Introduction

The analysis of statistical tests properties from the point of view of their applications, besides the power, also concerns dependence among their test functions. This problem is especially important when we verify our hypothesis by several tests. Then, in many cases it is difficult to make a decision about the verified hypothesis if the tests indications are different and their powers alike. On the other hand, there is no need of using a couple of tests of a given class if their test functions are correlated.

In the paper, we consider the problem of dependence among the following consistency tests: the Kolmogorov-Smirnov, Kuiper, Cramer-von Mises, Watson, Anderson-Darling, David-Hellwig and the Shapiro-Wilk tests.

2. Dependence Measure

Let us take a random sample

$$X_1, X_2, \ldots, X_n$$

drawn from a population of distribution F(x). On the basis of this sample we are to verify the hypothesis

$$H_0: F(x) = F_N(x)$$

($F_N(x)$ denotes the distribution function of normal distribution).

Let us fix significance level α and take into account two from the above tests. Let A_1 and R_1 denote events of accepting and rejecting the normality hypothesis, respectively, using the first test. Analogously we define events A_2 and R_2 for the second test. Thus, we have defined the two-dimensional binary distribution

$$p_{00} = P(A_1,A_2), \quad p_{01} = P(A_1,R_2),$$
$$p_{10} = P(R_1,A_2), \quad p_{11} = P(R_1,R_2).$$

Obviously, it depends on the population distribution.

For the normal distribution

$$p_{1*} = p_{10} + p_{11} = \alpha, \qquad p_{*1} = p_{01} + p_{11} = \alpha,$$

while for its alternatives,

$$p_{1*} = p_{10} + p_{11} = 1 - \beta_1, \qquad p_{*1} = p_{01} + p_{11} = 1 - \beta_2,$$

express the powers of the tests.

The dependence measure between the results of the tests can be defined in many ways as a correlation coefficient in 2 x 2 distribution. We have chosen

$$\rho = \frac{p_{11} - p_{1*}p_{*1}}{\sqrt{p_{1*}(1-p_{1*})p_{*1}(1-p_{*1})}}, \qquad (3)$$

which seems to be of the most common usage.

3. Monte Carlo Experiment

In order to estimate the dependence measure ρ between all pairs created from the above seven tests, the Monte Carlo experiment was performed. For 7 sample sizes:

$$n = 6,10,15,20,30,40,50 \qquad (4)$$

7 distribution:

normal, uniform, exponential, double exponential, Pareto, lognormal, logistic (5)

the amount of $q = 10000$ n = element simple samples was drawn.

In each sample the values of test statistics Kolmogorov-Smirnov (D), Kuiper (V), Cramer-Misses (W^2), Wastson (U^2), Anderson-Darling (A^2), David_Hellwig (DH) were computed. They were compared with their critical values on the significance levels

$$\alpha = 0.05 \text{ and } \alpha = 0.10, \qquad (6)$$

and the facts of accepting or rejecting the normality hypotheses were recorded.

Thus, for every n (4), distribution (5), α (6) and a fixed pair of tests, the numbers $q_{00}, q_{01}, q_{10}, q_{11}$ of observed events (A_1,A_2), (A_1,R_2), (R_1,R_2), respectively, were available. The quotients

$$\hat{p}_{hj} = q_{hj}/q$$

can be assumed as estimates of p_{hj} $(h,j = 0,1)$,

$$\hat{p}_{1*} = \hat{p}_{10} + \hat{p}_{11} = 1 - \hat{\beta}_1, \qquad \hat{p}_{*1} = \hat{p}_{01} + \hat{p}_{11} = 1 - \hat{\beta}_2,$$

- as estimates of tests powers, and

$$\hat{\rho} = \frac{\hat{p}_{11} - \hat{p}_{1*}\hat{p}_{*1}}{\sqrt{\hat{p}_{1*}(1-\hat{p}_{1*})\hat{p}_{*1}(1-\hat{p}_{*1})}}$$

- as an estimates of dependence coefficient ρ.

4. Conclusions

Results concerning the dependence between the normality tests can be formulated as follows:

1. The examined normality tests, except for the David-Hellwig test, are strongly correlated.
2. The highest correlation has been observed between: the Anderson-Darling (A^2) test and Watson test (U^2); the Anderson-Darling (A^2) test and Cramer-von Mises test (W^2); the Watson test (U^2) and Cramer-von Mises test (W^2); the Watson test (U^2) and Kuiper test (V). The Shapiro-Wilk test also shows a relatively high dependence on the Anderson-Darling test (A^2), Watson (U^2) and Cramer-von Mises (W^2).
3. Generally, the dependence between tests functions decreases with the growth of n.
4. Dependence between normality tests is not much affected by the type of distribution.

References

Giorgi G.M., Cinci S., (1975), Sulle funzioni discriminatorie di alcuni testes univariate di normalita. Stodi di Economia 6, 100-133

Green J.R., Hegazy Y.A.S., (1976), Powerful modified - EDF goodness-of-fit tests. JASA 71, 204-209

Pearson E.S., D'Agostino R.B., Bowman K.O., (1974), Tests for departure from normality: Comparison of powers. Biometrica 64, 231-246

Shapiro S.S., Wilk R.S., Chen M.J, (1968), A comparative study of variance test for normality. JASA 63, 1343-1372

Stephens M.A. (1974), EDF statistics for goodness-of-fit and some comparisons. JASA 69, 737-739

Is there room for convergence in the E.C.?

R.C.Douven and J.C.Engwerda
Department of Econometrics, Tilburg University,
P.O. Box 90153, 5000 LE Tilburg, The Netherlands

1 Introduction

In the Maastricht Treaty (1991) the E.C. countries specified conditions for the transition to a monetary union. Two of these conditions that are necessary for admitting a country to the monetary union are represented by convergence in consumer price inflation and convergence in long term interest rates. In our paper [1] we develop a theoretical framework which makes it possible to analyze these aspects of convergence between E.C. countries. The analysis is done in a dynamic game context, where countries, apart from minimizing individual cost functions, minimize cooperatively a convergence function. This convergence function represents the above mentioned convergence conditions. The aspect of convergence is modeled as a dynamic constraint on the individual cost functions. In this way, the costs are modeled of E.C. countries which are involved in the proces of moving towards an Economic and Monetary union, which should be established (at least) in 1999. One important result of the paper is that the maximum degree of convergence is completely determined by the non-cooperative outcome of the game. In this extended abstract we illustrate this analysis in a theoretical example. The example shows that: (1) the goals with respect to convergence can seriously influence the outcome of the game. If these goals are set too ambitious the outcome can be that countries are not willing to cooperate anymore. (2) the costs involved to obtain convergence can differ substantially between countries.

2 An example

We consider a theoretic example in a (discrete time) deterministic linear quadratic difference game framework with two players (countries). The dynamic behaviours of player 1 and player 2 are described by:

$$\begin{aligned} y_1(t) &= y_1(t-1) + u_1(t) + 0.3y_2(t-1), \qquad & y_1(0) = 1, \\ y_2(t) &= y_2(t-1) + u_2(t) + 0.6y_1(t-1), \qquad & y_2(0) = 0, \end{aligned}$$

where, for $i = 1,2$, $y_i(t) \in \mathbb{R}$ is the target variable and $u_i(t) \in \mathbb{R}$ is the instrumental variable. From the interaction terms ($0.3y_2(t-1)$ for player 1 and $0.6y_1(t-1)$ for player 2) follows that each player faces a different dynamical structure. Player 2 is more influenced by player 1 than vice versa. Each player makes his plans for the future. We assume that each player has a planning period of 2 and chooses his desired paths for the future, as follows:

$$\text{desired paths} \begin{cases} \text{player 1:} & y_1^*(1) = 2, \quad y_1^*(2) = 3 \\ \text{player 2:} & y_2^*(1) = 1.5, \quad y_2^*(2) = 3. \end{cases}$$

These desired paths reflect the policymakers own wishes of the future and are obtained independently from each other. We represent the costfunctions J_1, J_2 for every individual player by:

$$J_1 = 0.5((y_1(1) - 2)^2 + (y_1(2) - 3)^2 + u_1(1)^2 + u_1(2)^2),$$
$$J_2 = 0.5((y_2(1) - 1.5)^2 + (y_2(2) - 3)^2 + u_2(1)^2 + u_2(2)^2).$$

Each player wants to play a strategy, during his planning period, which minimizes his costs. So the control problem for every individual player ($i = 1,2$) is:

$$\min_{u_i(1),u_i(2)} J_i.$$

Because the target variable (and indirectly the instrumental variable) of each player is directly related to those of the other player, the control problem of each player depends on the actions undertaken by the other player. This gives rise to various solution concepts (see e.g. [2, 3]). From the non-cooperative solutions we will just consider the open loop Nash solution, which we denote by N^c. In the sequel we will use this solution as the threat-point. The cooperative solutions are represented by the set of Pareto solutions which can be found by solving:

$$\min_u \alpha J_1 + (1 - \alpha)J_2.$$

for $\alpha \in [0,1]$, where $u := (u_1(1), u_1(2), u_2(1), u_2(2))$. However, before playing the game both players want to be sure that there will be some degree of convergence of their target variables. In this example we assume that both players want to converge to the average of their target variables. We take as a measure for the degree of convergence the following convergence function:

$$C = \sum_{i=1}^{2}(y_i(1) - \overline{y}(1))^2 + 4(y_i(2) - \overline{y}(2))^2,$$

where $\overline{y}(t) := 0.5(y_1(t) + y_2(t))$ for $t = 1,2$. So, both players agree that they want to minimize the variance of their target variables in each period. Moreover, minimizing the variance in period 2 is given more weight than minimizing the variance in period 1, which is represented by the weights of 1 in period 1 and 4 in period 2. These weights indicate that both players find it more important that there is convergence at the end of the planning period than during the planning period.

3 Analysis of the possible outcomes

Together, the players have to take a decision about what strategy to follow. Their decision will depend upon the following set:

$$\{(J_1(u), J_2(u), C(u)) \mid u \in \mathbb{R}^4\} \tag{1}$$

Because J_1, J_2, C are strictly convex functions which are twice differentiable in u, the set of optimal strategies can be found by solving the following problem: Let $\alpha, \lambda \in [0,1]$, and

$$J(u) := (1 - \lambda)(\alpha J_1 + (1 - \alpha)J_2) + \lambda C$$

Find now for every $\alpha, \lambda \in [0,1]$:

$$u^* := \arg\min_u J(u)$$

The set of optimal control strategies can be given in the following way:

$$\{u^*(\alpha, \lambda) \mid (\alpha, \lambda) \in [0,1] \times [0,1]\}$$

Substituting these control strategies in (1) gives the following set:

$$\{(J_1(\alpha,\lambda), J_2(\alpha,\lambda), C(\alpha,\lambda)) \mid (\alpha,\lambda) \in [0,1] \times [0,1]\}.$$

In the sequel we will (by varying α and λ) analyze this set of points for the given example. In

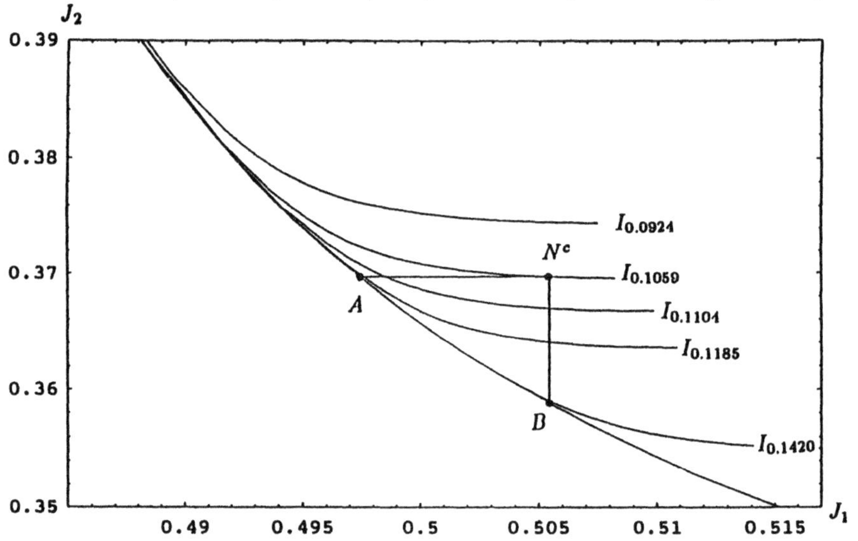

the figure above, we have projected a part of the outcomes in the J_1, J_2-plane. The interior of the triangle represents the negotiation area. An area which represents outcomes of the game for which the costs of each country seperately is lower than the costs he would have when playing the non-cooperative N^c outcome. Therefore, solutions outside the negotiation area are not likely to happen because then, at least one of the players, will play the threat point strategy. The most left (lowest) curve represents a part of the Pareto solutions. Solutions which countries would choose if they did not have to consider convergence aspects. Points above the Pareto curve correspond with outcomes where countries pay attention to the convergence criterium. In the figure we have drawn iso-convergence curves, i.e. curves with the same degree of convergence. Because countries have to stay inside the negotiation area, the degree of convergence that can be reached is limited. In the next table we show some

	J_1	J_2	C	α	λ
Cooperation					
N^c	0.505	0.370	0.1059	0.080	0.270
A	0.497	0.370	0.1258	0.625	0
B	0.505	0.359	0.1483	0.523	0
Non-Cooperation					
N^c	0.505	0.370	0.1365	-	-

characteristics of the points mentioned in the figure. In the table the cooperative outcome N^c corresponds with a strategy which yields a lower convergence value than the non-cooperative outcome N^c. The reason for this is that the non-cooperative strategy differs from the cooperative strategy. Playing the cooperative strategy gives, with the same individual costs, an increase in convergence of 0.306. Note that if the players agree on a certain degree of convergence, e.g. 0.1185, an outcome in the negotiation area on the iso-convergence line $I_{0.1185}$ will

be chosen. In this situation in almost all cases player 1 can gain more than player 2. This depends on the shape of the iso-convergence lines and ultimately can be traced back to the fact that player 1 has more influence on player 2 than vice versa.
The point with the largest degree of convergence in the negotiation area lies on the edge of the negotiation area and is exactly the N^c point which belongs to the iso-convergence line $I_{0.1059}$. We have proven in our paper [1] that if we assume strict convexity and twice differentiability of J_1, J_2, C, the outcome which corresponds with the largest degree of convergence in the negotiation area always coincides with the N^c point. To visualize this fact, we plotted in the last figure the convergence values for $0.05 \leq \alpha \leq 0.65$ and $0 \leq \lambda \leq 0.4$. The curve on the back ($\lambda = 0$) represents a subset of the Pareto solutions P. The interior of the curve drawn on the surface represents again the negotiation area. The figure suggests indeed that the N^c point corresponds with the point in the negotiation area which yields the lowest convergence value (and thus has a high degree of convergence).

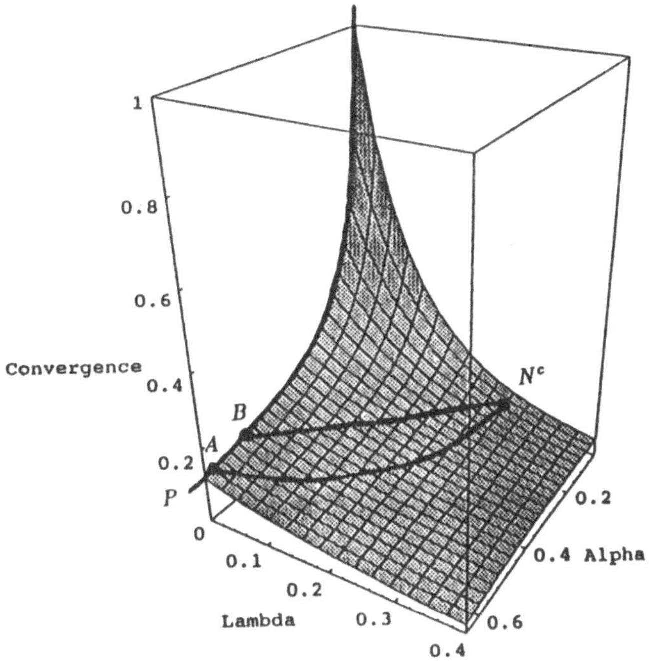

References

[1] Douven, R.C. and J.C. Engwerda, *Is there room for convergence in the E.C.?*, Discussion paper No: 9350, CentER for Economic Research, Tilburg 1993, The Netherlands.

[2] Petit, M.L., *Control theory and dynamic games in economic analysis*, Cambridge University Press, 1990.

[3] Zeeuw, A.J. de, *Difference games and linked econometric policy models*, PhD Thesis, Tilburg University, The Netherlands, 1984.

Reduced game properties of egalitarian division rules for cooperative games

Theo Driessen
Faculty of Applied Mathematics, University of Twente
Enschede, Netherlands
Yukihiko Funaki
Faculty of Economics, Toyo University, Tokyo, Japan

1. Introduction

The paper focuses on a uniform treatment of a special type of one-point solutions for cooperative games, called the egalitarian non-individual contribution (ENIC-)value. The value in question is special in the sense that it is constructed in two stages: first and foremost, each player in the game is allocated some kind of a yet unspecified individual contribution and subsequently, the surplus of the total profits is equally divided among all the players. In addition to the general setting, the unspecified notion of individual contribution will be chosen to be one of the following four particular notions:

- the individual worth of the player to participate in the game as a solitary player. The corresponding ENIC-value is known as the center of the imputation set, called CIS-value.
- the so-called separable (or marginal) contribution of the player to participate in the game as a member of the player set. The corresponding ENIC-value goes by the name of egalitarian non-separable contribution (ENSC-)value. (cf. Driessen and Funaki (1991)).
- the so-called average contribution of the player in the game which is obtainable as some average of marginal contributions of pairs of players including the player in question. The corresponding ENIC-value is called the egalitarian non-average contribution (ENAC-)value and has been studied in detail in Driessen and Funaki (1993).
- the so-called Banzhaf contribution of the player in the game which is interpretable as the average of all the player's marginal contributions to participate in the game anyhow. The corresponding ENIC-value is called the egalitarian non-Banzhaf contribution (ENBC-)value. The notion of Banzhaf contribution itself is closely related to the well-known Shapley value as well as the Banzhaf index for simple games.

The main goal of the paper is to provide an axiomatic characterization of the ENIC-value in general and the four particular ENIC-values as well. In fact, our goal is twofold because the player set may be considered as fixed or variable. Involving a fixed player set, the main Theorem 3.1 states that the ENIC-value is fully characterized by the classical axiom of relative invariance under strategic equivalence (RISE) and a modification of the classical axiom of equal treatment of substitutes in the game (ETP). Here the modified axiom requires equal value payoffs for players with identically individual contributions. Involving a variable player set, the main Theorem 4.1 states that the ENIC-value is fully characterized by RISE, ETP and a so-called consistency axiom in terms of reduced games. The notion of a reduced game has been used in axiomatizations of many other game theoretic solutions. Concerning the axiomatization of the ENIC-value in general, the reduced game is yet unspecified except for the player set, whereas the axiomatizations of the four particular ENIC-values do involve specified reduced games (cf. Corollary 4.2).

2. The class of egalitarian non-individual contribution (ENIC)-values

Let (N,v) be a *cooperative n-person game in characteristic function form* with a finite set N of n *players*, $n \geq 1$, and the *characteristic function* $v: 2^N \to \mathbf{R}$, satisfying $v(\phi)=0$, on the set 2^N of all subsets of N. A vector $x \in \mathbf{R}^N$ is said to be an *efficient payoff vector* for a game (N,v) if it meets the *efficiency* principle $\sum_{j\in N} x_j = v(N)$. The set of efficient payoff vectors for the game (N,v) is called the *pre-imputation set* for (N,v) and is denoted by $I^*(N,v)$. A *value* concept for cooperative games is a function σ such that $\sigma(N,v) \in I^*(N,v)$ for any game (N,v).

The *egalitarian non-individual contribution* (ENIC-)value allocates a yet unspecified *individual contribution* denoted by $IC_i(N,v)$ and an equal share of the *non-individual contribution* $NIC(N,v) := v(N) - \sum_{j\in N} IC_j(N,v)$ to each player i and it is formally given by $\text{ENIC}_i(N,v) := IC_i(N,v) + \frac{1}{n}NIC(N,v)$ for all $(N,v) \in G$, all $i \in N$. Firstly, if the individual contribution $IC_i(N,v)$ of any player i is chosen to be his individual worth $v(\{i\})$ in the game (N,v), then the ENIC-value becomes the *center* of gravity of the *imputation set*, called CIS-value. Secondly, if the individual contribution $IC_i(N,v)$ of any player i is chosen to be his marginal contribution from an $(n-1)$-person coalition to the grand coalition, called *separable contribution* and denoted by $SC_i(N,v) := v(N) - v(N\setminus\{i\})$, then the corresponding ENIC-value becomes the *egalitarian non-separable contribution* (ENSC-)value. Thirdly, if the individual contribution $IC_i(N,v)$ of any player i is chosen to be his *average contribution* from $(n-2)$-person coalitions to the grand coalition, defined by $AC_i(N,v) := \begin{cases} v(N) - \frac{1}{n-2}\sum_{j\in N\setminus\{i\}} v(N\setminus\{i,j\}) & \text{if } n \geq 3 \\ v(\{i\}) & \text{if } n=1 \text{ or } n=2 \end{cases}$ then the corresponding ENIC-value becomes the *egalitarian non-average contribution* (ENAC-)value. Fourthly, if the individual contribution $IC_i(N,v)$ of any player i is chosen to be the average of all his marginal contributions, called *Banzhaf contribution* and defined by $BC_i(N,v) := \frac{1}{2^{n-1}}\sum_{S\subseteq N\setminus\{i\}} [v(S\cup\{i\}) - v(S)]$ for all $n \geq 1$, then the corresponding ENIC-value becomes the *egalitarian non-Banzhaf contribution* (ENBC-)value.

AXIOM. A value σ on G is said to be *relatively invariant* under *strategic equivalence* (RISE) if $\sigma_j(N,w) = \alpha\sigma_j(N,v) + \beta_j$ for all $j \in N$, all games $(N,v) \in G$ and $(N,w) \in G$ satisfying $w(S) = \alpha v(S) + \sum_{j\in S}\beta_j$ for all $S \subseteq N$ for some $\alpha > 0$ and $\beta \in \mathbf{R}^N$.

AXIOM. A value σ on G is said to possess the *equal treatment property* (ETP) if $\sigma_i(N,v) = \sigma_j(N,v)$ for any $i,j \in N$ satisfying $v(S\cup\{i\}) = v(S\cup\{j\})$ for all $S \subseteq N\setminus\{i,j\}$.

DEFINITION. The notion IC of individual contribution is said to be *relatively invari-*

ant under *strategic equivalence* (RISE) if $IC_j(N,w) = \alpha IC_j(N,v) + \beta_j$ for all $j \in N$, all games $(N,v) \in G$ and $(N,w) \in G$ satisfying $w(S) = \alpha v(S) + \sum_{j\in S}\beta_j$ for all $S \subseteq N$ for some $\alpha > 0$ and $\beta \in \mathbf{R}^N$.

3. Axiomatizations of ENIC-values with respect to a fixed player set

Throughout this section, we fix the player set N and pay attention to an axiomatic characterization of the ENIC-value on the class G^N of games with player set N.

AXIOM. A value σ on G^N is said to possess the *equal treatment property* with respect to the notion of individual contribution (ETP_{ic}) if $\sigma_i(N,v) = \sigma_j(N,v)$ for all $i,j \in N$ in a game (N,v) satisfying $IC_i(N,v) = IC_j(N,v)$.

Theorem 3.1. *Suppose the notion IC of individual contribution satisfies RISE. Then the ENIC-value on G^N is the unique value on G^N which possesses RISE and ETP_{ic}.*

AXIOM. Let $n \geq 3$. A value σ on G^N is said to possess the *equal treatment property* with respect to the notion of individual contribution concerning 1-, $(n-1)$-, sums of $(n-2)$-person coalitions and sums of arbitrary coalitions respectively if the following condition holds for all games (N,v):

ETP^1_{ic}: $\sigma_i(N,v) = \sigma_j(N,v)$ for all $i,j \in N$ with $v(\{i\}) = v(\{j\})$

ETP^{n-1}_{ic}: $\sigma_i(N,v) = \sigma_j(N,v)$ for all $i,j \in N$ with $v(N\setminus\{i\}) = v(N\setminus\{j\})$

ETP^{n-2}_{ic}: $\sigma_i(N,v) = \sigma_j(N,v)$
for all $i,j \in N$ with $\sum_{l\in N\setminus\{i\}} v(N\setminus\{i,l\}) = \sum_{l\in N\setminus\{j\}} v(N\setminus\{j,l\})$

ETP^*_{ic}: $\sigma_i(N,v) = \sigma_j(N,v)$
for all $i,j \in N$ with $\sum_{S\subseteq N\setminus\{i\}} v(S) = \sum_{S\subseteq N\setminus\{j\}} v(S)$.

Corollary 3.2. *Let $n \geq 3$. The CIS-, ENSC-, ENAC-, ENBC-values on G^N are the unique values on G^N which possess RISE and ETP^1_{ic}, ETP^{n-1}_{ic}, ETP^{n-2}_{ic}, ETP^*_{ic}, respectively.*

4. Axiomatizations of ENIC-values with respect to a variable player set

Throughout this section, we consider the ENIC-value on the class G of all games with a variable player set. In order to axiomatize the ENIC-value on G, we make use of the notion of a reduced game. A *reduced game* is deducible from a given game $(N,v), n \geq 2$, by removing one player on the understanding that the removed player i will be paid according to a proposed payoff vector $x \in \mathbf{R}^N$. At the moment we don't specify the characteristic function $v^x : 2^{N\setminus\{i\}} \to \mathbf{R}$ except for the requirement $v^x(N\setminus\{i\}) := v(N) - x_i$ in order to meet the efficiency principle of the value.

AXIOM. A value σ on G is said to possess the *reduced game property* (RGP) with respect to a specified type of reduced games if $\sigma_j(N\setminus\{i\}, v^{\sigma(N,v)}) = \sigma_j(N,v)$ for all $(N,v) \in G$ with $n \geq 2$, all $i \in N$ and all $j \in N\setminus\{i\}$.

DEFINITION. The notion IC of individual contribution is said to be *weakly consistent* (WCONS) with respect to a specified type of reduced games if for all $(N,v) \in G$ with $n \geq 3$, all $i \in N$, there exists a constant $\alpha = \alpha(N,v,i) \in \mathbf{R}$ such that $IC_j(N\setminus\{i\}, v^x) =$

$IC_j(N,v)+\alpha$ for all $x \in \mathbf{R}^N$, all $j \in N \setminus \{i\}$.

DEFINITION. The notion IC of individual contribution is said to possess the *equal treatment property* (ETP) if $IC_i(N,v) = IC_j(N,v)$ for any $i,j \in N$ satisfying $v(S \cup \{i\}) = v(S \cup \{j\})$ for all $S \subseteq N \setminus \{i,j\}$.

Theorem 4.1. *Suppose the notion IC of individual contribution satisfies RISE, ETP and WCONS with respect to a specified type of reduced games. Then the ENIC-value on G is the unique value on G which possesses RISE, ETP and RGP with respect to that reduced game.*

In the sequel we present specified types of reduced games in order to axiomatize the four special versions of the ENIC-value mentioned in Section 2. Let (N,v) be a game with $n \geq 2, x \in \mathbf{R}^N, i \in N$ and define the corresponding reduced game $(N \setminus \{i\}, v^x)$, satisfying $v^x(N \setminus \{i\}) = v(N) - x_i$, as follows, where $\alpha = \alpha(N,v,i) \in \mathbf{R}$ is an arbitrary constant:

Type 1: $v^x(S) := v(S) + \alpha$ for all $\phi \neq S \subsetneq N \setminus \{i\}$
Type 2: $v^x(S) := v(S \cup \{i\}) - x_i + \alpha$ for all $\phi \neq S \subsetneq N \setminus \{i\}$
Type 3: $v^x(S) := \frac{|S|}{n-2}[v(S \cup \{i\}) - x_i] + \frac{n-2-|S|}{n-2}\left[\sum_{j \in N \setminus (S \cup \{i\})} v(S \cup \{j\})\right] + \alpha$ if $n \geq 4$ and, $v^x(S) := v(S) + \alpha$ if $n = 3$, for all $\phi \neq S \subsetneq N \setminus \{i\}$
Type 4: $v^x(S) := \begin{cases} \frac{1}{2}[v(S \cup \{i\}) - x_i] + \frac{1}{2}v(S) + \frac{|S| x_i}{2^{n-2}-n+1} + \alpha & \text{if } n \geq 4 \\ \frac{1}{2}[v(S \cup \{i\}) - x_i] + \frac{1}{2}v(S) + \alpha & \text{if } n = 3 \end{cases}$ for all $\phi \neq S \subsetneq N \setminus \{i\}$

The players in the reduced game of Type 1 don't cooperate with the removed player, whereas the players in the reduced game of Type 2 do cooperate with the removed player i whose reward for his cooperation within any coalition is always equal to the payoff x_i. Besides, the worth of any non-trivial coalition may be increased or decreased by some constant. In the reduced game of Type 3, the worth of a non-trivial coalition is some convex combination, depending on the coalition size, of the worth in the reduced game of Type 2 and some expression, involving the cooperation with single non-members different from the removed player i. As usual, the worth of any non-trivial coalition may be increased or decreased by some constant. In the reduced game of Type 4, the worth of a non-trivial coalition is the average of the worths in the two reduced games of Type 1 and Type 2, plus, if $n \geq 4$, some payoff depending on the coalition size.

Corollary 4.2. *The CIS-, ENSC-, ENAC-, ENBC-values on G are the unique values on G which possess RISE, ETP and RGP with respect to the reduced game of Type 1, Type 2, Type 3, Type 4, respectively.*

References

DRIESSEN, T.S.H. and Y. FUNAKI (1991): "Coincidence of and Collinearity between Game Theoretic Solutions", *OR Spektrum* 13, pp 15-30.

DRIESSEN, T.S.H. and Y. FUNAKI (1993): "The Egalitarian Non-Average Contribution Method for Cooperative Games", Memorandum No.1135, Department of Applied Mathematics, University of Twente, Enschede, The Netherlands.

DECOMPOSITION ALGORITHMS BASED ON KNOWLEDGE BASED MODELS

Ewa Dudek-Dyduch
Institute of Automatics, Staszic University
al. Mickiewicza 30, 30-059 Kraków, Poland

The paper is concern with some class of combinatorial optimization problems, namely those represented by multistage process model. A definition of multistage decision process is given as a specialized form of knowledge-based model.The different classes of decomposition algorithms based on the model are defined and analyzed in the paper. The condition for problem decomposability is given. An examples are presented.

MULTISTAGE PROCESS AS A SPECIALIZED FORM OF KNOWLEDGE BASED MODEL

The notion of a multistage decision process is widely used in optimization, but its idea has been introduced by means of examples rather than by a formal description. Let us recall the definition of multistage process given in the previous author paper.

Multistage decision (constructing) process is a process P defined as a six-touple (U,Y,y_o,f,Y_N,Y_G) where the individual elements are defined as follows: U is a decision set, Y is set of states, y_o,Y_N,Y_G are distinguished initial state and sets of not admissible and goal states, respectively, f is a partial function $f : U \times Y \to Y$ defined by means of the function $g : Y \to 2^U$ in the following way: $(u,y) \in \mathrm{Dom}\, f \Leftrightarrow u \in g(y)$.

Function f was defined as a partial function. This is so in order to deal with all the limitations concerning the control decisions in the current state in a convenient way. This is done by means of the so-called sets of possible decisions in a state y, denoted as $U_p(y)$ and defined as: $U_p(y) = \{u \in U : (u,y) \in \mathrm{Dom}\, f\}$. Thus function $g(y)$ determines the decision subset $U_p(y)$, for which function f is determined in the state y.
At the same time an individual process P is represented by a set of its trajectories. A trajectory starts from the distinguished initial state y_o and is assumed to end in the goal states set Y_G, or in the not admissible states set Y_N, or in any state for

which the set of possible decisions $U_p(y)$ is empty. It is assumed that no state of a trajectory, apart from the last one, may belong to the set Y_N or have empty set of possible decsions. A trajectory that ends in the set of the goal states Y_G is an admissible one and the decision sequence determining it is an admissible decision sequence. In other cases, a trajectory is said to be a not admissible one.
The task of optimization consists in finding such an admissible decision sequence $\tilde{u}$ which minimizes a certain criterion Q . Thus an optimization task is uniquely determined by the pair (P,Q) where process P represents all the task limitations.
A defined problem of optimization is such a set of optimization tasks which have a commonly determined set of data, common (parametric) definition of multistage process and common (parametric) definition of criterion functions.

In the most general case sets U and Y may be presented as a Cartesian product $U = U^1 \times U^2 \times \ldots U^m$, $Y = Y^1 \times Y^2 \times \ldots Y^n$. Thus a decision u as well as a state x is represented by finite sequence of values that belong to succeeding sets. There are no limitations imposed on the sets, in particular they need not be numerical ones.We will use the notions "state vector" and "control decision vector" by analogy to the classical control theory: $u = (u^1,u^2,\ldots u^m)$ $x = (x^1,x^2,\ldots x^n)$. Thus values of particular coordinates of a state as well as a control decision may be names of elements as well as some objects (e.g. finite set, sequence etc). This paper is appropriated for the processes for which at least one set is not numerical one.
Particular coordinates of the vector $u = (u^1,u^2,\ldots u^m)$ represents a separate decisions that must or may be taken at the same time. The sets Y_n, Y_F and U_p are defined by means of logical formulae. Therefore, the complete model constitutes a specialized form of a knowledge-based system.
The presented model is generalization of of the classical model of discrete dynamic systems used in control theory. The generalization lies in the fact that both the state and decision coordinates need not be numerical ones and that the definition of the sets U_p, S_N, S_F are given by means of logical formulae.

A lot of combinatorial problems can be formulated in terms of this model, e.g. optimization of discrete manufacturing processes (the symbols f,U,Y can be interpreted by means of manufacture terms), scheduling problems, traveling salesman problem, as well as classical problems considered within the frame of artificial intelligence.

PROPERTIES OF DECOMPOSITION ALGORITHMS

Decomposition method consists in dividing the problem into some partial problems to be solved separately. There are two main reason for application of the method: computational (due to large scale problems or due to possibility of parallel computing) and algorithmic one. The last reason is very vital for combinatorial problems when the partial problems are solved by means of different algorithms.

Properties of decomposition algorithms depend on:

- type of connections between the partial problems,
- properties of the partial problems algorithms.

The type of connections between the partial problems determines the order of their solving. It is defined by:

- hierarchy of independence of partial problems
- aim of solving of particular partial problems i.e. the type of information obtained as a result of solving them.

One can distinguish two types of information that are obtained: a) values of part of searched variables (e.g. sequence of the k-th coordinate of decision, denoted as $\tilde{u}^k$), b) another information (e.g. restrictions for some variables values).

Taking it into account, one can distinguished two basic types of decomposition algorithms. The first type consists in division of decision coordinates into two (or more) subsets: $u = (u^I, u^{II})$ what induces the division of control sequence $\tilde{u} = (\tilde{u}^1, \tilde{u}^2, \ldots \tilde{u}^m)$ into $(\tilde{u}^I, \tilde{u}^{II})$. Each part of the searched decision sequence is determined as a result of solving the corresponding partial problem. Concerning the second type, a role of any partial problem consists in determining values of some set of variables or only restricting this values.

EXAMPLES: algorithm for the two-machine flow shop scheduling problem with controllable job processing times Nowicki(1988) is of the first type, while algorithm for generalized Chinese postman problem presented in Dudek(1990) is of the second type.

Decomposability

Now one can formulate conditions for completely decomposability of the first type. In order to do it, the notion of so-called connection task must be defined. The task (P',Q') is said to be connected with the task (P,Q) if it satisfies the following two conditions: 1) the optimal solution of the task (P',Q') exists iff there exists the optimal solution of the task (P,Q), 2) there exists a mapping $\phi : \tilde{U}' \to \tilde{U}$ such that $\phi(\tilde{u}'^*) = \tilde{u}^*$ where $\tilde{U}',\tilde{U}$ are sets of control sequences and $\tilde{u}'^*$, $\tilde{u}^*$ are optimal control sequences of tasks P' and P respectively. Thus, when the optimal solution of the connected task has been computed then the optimal solution of the primary task can be found.

We say that problem $(\mathbb{P},\mathbb{Q})$ is first type decomposable into two independent problems iff for each task $(P,Q) \in (\mathbb{P},\mathbb{Q})$ there exists the connected task (P',Q') such that: the vectors u',y' of the connected task can be divided into two separate subsets of coordinates $u' = (u'^{I},u'^{II})$ $y' = (y'^{I},y^{II})$ such that:

- set of possible decisions $U'_p = U'^{I}_p \times U'^{II}_p$ and the logical formulae defining U'^{I}_p depends on x'^{I} and U'^{II}_p on x'^{II} only,
- function $f = (f'^{I},f'^{II})$ where $f'^{I} : U'^{I} \times Y'^{I} \to Y'^{I}$ depends on the first distinguished subset of coordinates while $f'^{II}: U'^{II} \times Y'^{II} \to Y'^{II}$ depends on the others coordinates only,
- the logical formulae defining the sets of goal states and not admissible states can be presented as conjunctions or alternatives of formulas that depend only on respective subsets of coordinates,
- performance index Q' can be presented as $Q' = Q'^{I}(\tilde{u}'^{I}) + Q'^{II}(\tilde{u}'^{II})$ or as some nondecreasing function of Q'^{I} and Q'^{II}

REFERENCES

Dudek-Dyduch E.(1990) Decomposition of optimization of discrete production processes control, Silesia Technical University Press, Automatics, vol 100, pp 13-23.

Nowicki E., Zdrzałka S. (1988) A two-machine flow shop scheduling problem with controllable job processing times. Europ.Journ.of Oper.Research, vol.34 no 2, pp.208-220.

ON SOME EXPERT CONTROL

Tadeusz Dyduch,
Sect. of Geometry and Computer Graphics,
Cracow University of Technology

EXPERT SYSTEMS

Expert Control is considered as a control performed by Expert System, i.e. a complicated computer program, composed of three parts:

- working database,
- knowledge base,
- reasoning engine.

One of the most significant feature of an expert system is ability of knowledge acquiring i.e. completing and incrementing its knowledge base. This feature, i.e. self organizing knowledge base is often utilize in support decision systems. For example, well known medical diagnosis expert systems required the rational ordering of the large amount of facts, taking into account only simple relations between parameters.

EXPERT CONTROL

Expert systems utilized in control often deal with Discrete Event Systems (DES). Expert control differs from classical control in unconventional model of control object as well as the way of choosing the decisions.

It can be applied when it is difficult to identify the physical dynamics model, or if the model is too complicated to utilize it in real time computing. A model of the controlled object is, in a matter of fact, the all knowledge base of the expert control system. Obviously, the form of the knowledge base depends on its designer. Then the form is filled up with information obtained from experts or from the other sources.

REQUIRED STATES SET AS THE MAIN PART OF KNOWLEDGE BASE

The aim of the paper is to introduce new idea of knowledge base construction, which may be used to perform expert control of some processes. This base should be create by distinguish a set of process states, which we will call Required States set (RS set). The RS set should have the following properties:
- direct aim (the objective) of the control can be expressed by means of this set i.e. should be equivalent to maintain a current state within the RS set or to bring it into the RS set,
- this set should be easy to define as well as to identify,
- for as many states as possible the following conditions should be fulfilled: a state belongs to RS set or if it does not, there exists the suitable control to lead the process state back into the RS set.

Thus, in order to acquire the knowledge from the operator of the process (the human expert of the process control) we ask him to define:
- which are the 'good enough' states (RS set),
- what are the possible controls for the process to be still in the RS set.

Therefore the description of the RS set becomes the most important part of the knowledge base. If environment influence occurs, which changes the object state, (for example disturbances, dynamic processes in controlled object, or changing demands (goals)), the expert system is searching for the control sequence, which leads the current process state back into RS set. It should result in reasonable shortening of the real time calculation, while controlling. Moreover, it should simplify the design of the control system, similarly to the programming of a robot arm movement, when it is done by leading the arm by the human operator.

EXAMPLE

Let us analyze some two-person game on the chess board, as an illustration for the former discussion.
Player A has 4 identical pieces, placed at the beginning on the

dark places a1, a3, a5, a7. Player 𝔹 has only 1 piece, placed on the chosen dark, not taken place on the board. Players move their pieces on turn. Each player moves strictly one piece to the nearest, free dark place at each turn. Player 𝔸 has to move their pieces to the nearest dark places, and move it only forward.
The game ends, when one of player has no legal move at his turn. This player lost the game.
In this game the players have not equal chances. The player 𝔸 is called a strong side, what means that for each strategy of the player 𝔹 , the player 𝔸 has a chance to win the game.
G. Owen gave the definition of such games, called them as two - person games in extensive form, on the contrary to the matrix form of the game. This games can be considered as easy to formal description examples of control of DES (Discrete Event Systems). This game has 1.006.880 different states and about 18^{24} different paths. Nevertheless, a man becomes an expert after 5 - 10 games played against experienced adversary, and can determine the RS set for effective playing this game. The RS set consists of such positions, where pieces of the player 𝔸 lie vertically, dividing the chess board into two parts with no paths between them.
Thus one can formulae the strategy for player 𝔸 to win this game (obviously this strategy exists), what seems to be hopeless before, consider the number of possibly paths. This strategy lies in bringing back the play state to the RS set.
The effective description of the RS set for this game was done along with description of the rules of control. In order to do it the symmetry in the set of states and possibility of states aggregation have been utilized. On the basis of RS set the whole game was optimized from the player 𝔸 position, by means of analyzing and optimizing the paths beginning from the RS set.
As a result system can control the game as the 𝔸 player. It contains two co - operating Mealy's automata. The first one has 4 states and describes the RS set of the game. The second automaton has 22 states, describing all the other possible paths, optimized for the side of 𝔸 player. Details about this special control can be obtained from the author or from the paper Dyduch (1981).

CONCLUSIONS

Expert control is based on the modeling of choosing the control decisions rather then on detailed, dynamic model of the controlled object, as it take place in classical control systems. The paper shows the advantages of the special formula of expert knowledge base, which can be utilize in control of some DES. Description of the special set of controlled object states is the main part of the base. This set is called RS set and serves as a basis for the control and optimization.
It is difficult to find the RS set automatically, but it can be done by human expert of control. That is thanks to human mind features such as: inclination to generalization, seeking symmetry and analogy in nature, easy ordering of fragmentary and uncompleted data.

REFERENCES

Ben-Arieh D.(1986) Knowledge Based Control System for Automated Production and Assembly. in Kusiak A. (ed.) Modelling and Design of Flexible Manufacturing Systems, Elsevier Sc.Publ., pp 347-368.

Dyduch T.(1981) Ph.D. thesis.(in polish) Academy of Mining and Metallurgy, Cracow.

Wendorff B., Warnock T., Stiller L., Mayer D., Brickner R.(1993) Bits and pieces: constructing chess endgame databases on parallel and vector architectures. Appl. Numer. Math. vol.12, pp 285-295.

Stochastic Solution of Closed Leontief Input-Output Models

Kuno Egle and Szaniszlo Fenyi
Institut für Statistik und Mathematische Wirtschaftstheorie, Universität Karlsruhe

1. The closed model

The first input-output model presented by Leontief [1936] was a closed model. A similar linear model of exchange was conceived by Gale [1960]. Their starting point is the square table of sales $x_{ij} \geq 0$ of sector i to sector j with $i, j \in N := \{1, \ldots, n\}$. Liontief assumed the proportionality $x_{ij} = a_{ij}\, x_j$ of sales with sectoral outputs $x_j \geq 0$. An input-output balance is realised if $\sum_{j \in N} a_{ij}\, x_j = x_i \ \forall\, i \in N$; in terms of the input-output matrix $A = (a_{ij})_{N \times N}$ and of the output vector $x = (x_i)_N$ this equals to

$$A\, x \;=\; x\,. \tag{1}$$

With $\mathbf{1}^T = (1, \ldots, 1)$ we also have, by Quesnay's principle,

$$\mathbf{1}^T A = \mathbf{1}^T \qquad \text{or} \qquad A^T \mathbf{1} = \mathbf{1}\,. \tag{2}$$

Contrary to (1) (2) is a formal result of price scaling.

Following Wang [1954] we could eliminate self-sales x_{ii} in (1) when using a diagonal matrix $D = \operatorname{diag}(1 - a_{ii})$, transforming (1) into $(I - A)\, D^{-1}\, D\, x = 0$ and putting $I - \tilde{A} := (I - A)\, D^{-1}$ and $\tilde{x} := D\, x$: this leads to $\tilde{A}\, \tilde{x} = \tilde{x}$ with new matrix elements $\tilde{a}_{ii} = 0$ and new outputs $\tilde{x}_i = (1 - a_{ii})\, x_i = x_i - x_{ii}$ $(i \in N)$.

In analogy to the open expenditure lag model (cf. Takayama [1974], p. 396 or Egle-Fenyi [1991]) we could give to (1) a dynamic version by

$$x_{t+1} \;=\; A\, x_t \tag{3}$$

with nonnegative starting vector x_0.

2. The associated Markov chain

From equ. (2) it is evident that A^T is a stochastic matrix. We can therefore define a Markov chain $X : \mathbf{N}_0 \times \Omega \mapsto N$ with the economic sectors as states and $P = A^T$ as matrix of transition probabilities. We assume P irreducible and primitive (cf. Cox-Miller [1965], p. 121). From an arbitrary vector $q_0 = (q_1^0, \ldots, q_n^0)^T$ of initial state probabilities $(t = 0)$ we get by recurrence

$$q_t^T \;=\; q_{t-1}^T\, P = \ldots = q_0^T\, P^t \tag{4}$$

the vector q_t of state probabilities in time $t \in \mathbf{N}$. The limit $\pi := \lim_{t \to \infty} q_t$ (to exist) is the so called vector of stationary probabilities. Trivially by the correspondence $P = A^T$ the solution of (3) behaves like $q_{t+1}^T = q_t^T P$ and that of (1) coincides with that of $\pi^T = \pi^T P$. The Markov chain defines time-varying partitions $\mathcal{P}^t = \{\Omega_i^t\}_N$ of Ω : Ω_i^t is the event to be in state i in time t; its probability is q_i^t. If $p_{ij}^{(t)}$ denotes the t-step transition probability, element of P^t, the probability of an event $\Omega_i^0 \cap \Omega_j^t$ is $q_i^0 \cdot p_{ij}^{(t)}$. The following contingency table resumes this information.

	Ω_1^t	$\cdots$	Ω_j^t	$\cdots$	Ω_n^t	
Ω_1^0	$q_1^0 p_{11}^{(t)}$	$\cdots$	$q_1^0 p_{1j}^{(t)}$	$\cdots$	$q_1^0 p_{1n}^{(t)}$	q_1^0
$\vdots$	$\vdots$		$\vdots$		$\vdots$	$\vdots$
Ω_i^0	$q_i^0 p_{i1}^{(t)}$	$\cdots$	$q_i^0 p_{ij}^{(t)}$	$\cdots$	$q_i^0 p_{in}^{(t)}$	q_i^0
$\vdots$	$\vdots$		$\vdots$		$\vdots$	$\vdots$
Ω_n^0	$q_n^0 p_{n1}^{(t)}$	$\cdots$	$q_n^0 p_{nj}^{(t)}$	$\cdots$	$q_n^0 p_{nn}^{(t)}$	q_n^0
	q_1^t	$\cdots$	q_j^t	$\cdots$	q_n^t	

Figure 1

The marginal distributions on $\mathcal{P}^0$ and $\mathcal{P}^t$ result from $P(\Omega_i^0) = \sum_j q_i^0 p_{ij}^{(t)} = q_i^0$ resp. from $P(\Omega_j^t) = \sum_i q_i^0 p_{ij}^{(t)} = q_j^t$; the components of $q_t^T = q_0^T P^t$. Under irreducibility and primitivity of P all the states are ergodic and the Markov chain is aperiodic. The elements $q_i^0 p_{ij}^{(t)}$ of the contingency table tend, with $t \to \infty$, to $q_i^0 \pi_j$, i.e. $P(\Omega_i^0 \cap \Omega_j^t) \xrightarrow{t\to\infty} P(\Omega_i^0) \cdot P(\Omega_j^\infty)$; the events Ω_i^0 and Ω_j^t are therefore asymptotically independent and the limit or stationary distribution $\pi = \lim_{t\to\infty} q_t$ has no memory w.r.t q_0. By binary coding of states, that is by assigning the i-th unit vector $e_i \in \mathbf{R}^n$ to a state i, N can be identified with $E = \{e_1, \ldots, e_n\}$, canonical basis of $\mathbf{R}^n$. A trajectory τ of length t is a sequence of states $(i_0, i_1, \ldots, i_t) \equiv (e_{i_0}, e_{i_1}, \ldots, e_{i_t})$ whose probability is $q_{i_0}^0 \, p_{i_0 i_1} \cdot \ldots \cdot p_{i_{t-1} i_t}$.

The contigency table of fig. 1 will be estimated from a sample of k trajectories of fixed length t by independent trials. With k_{ij} as number of trajectories starting in state i and ending in state j we put $k_i := \sum_j k_{ij}$ and $k^j := \sum_i k_{ij}$, where $\sum_i k_i = \sum_j k^j = k$:

	k^1	$\cdots$	k^j	$\cdots$	k^n
k_1	k_{11}	$\cdots$	k_{1j}	$\cdots$	k_{1n}
$\vdots$	$\vdots$		$\vdots$		$\vdots$
k_i	k_{i1}	$\cdots$	k_{ij}	$\cdots$	k_{in}
$\vdots$	$\vdots$		$\vdots$		$\vdots$
k_n	k_{n1}	$\cdots$	k_{nj}	$\cdots$	k_{nn}

Figure 2

In this table every row is multinomially $\mathcal{B}(k_i; p_{i1}^{(t)}, \ldots, p_{in}^{(t)})$-distributed. In general (for adjoint sampling procedures) the sizes k_i will be prescribed.

Furthermore the margin $(k^1, \ldots, k^j, \ldots, k^n)$ is multinomially $\mathcal{B}(k; q_1^t, \ldots, q_n^t)$-distributed. The parameters q_j^t are estimated by the relative frequencies $\hat{q}_j^t = k^j/k$ (cf. Johnson-Kotz [1969]). The stochastic method allows to estimate a single q_j^t. The above multinomial distribution degenerates in this case to the binomial $\mathcal{B}(k; q_j^t, 1 - q_j^t)$. The estimator $\hat{q}_t = (\hat{q}_j^t)_N$ serves to solve the dynamic model (3) via relation (4). Numerical experiments showed that this method is adapted to small t (short time dynamics). For this case of reducible A resp. P it is suffucient to study a block matrix

$$P = \begin{pmatrix} P_{11} & 0 \\ R_{21} & Q_{22} \end{pmatrix}$$

where the quadratic P_{11} and Q_{22} refer to ergodic resp. transient states. The corresponding sample contingency table allows to test on transient states. Although $\hat{q}_t$ tends to π for $t \to \infty$, an estimation of π – in view of the static model (1) via $\pi^T = \pi^T P$ – can be found directly by two methods based respectively on

Proposition 1 (cf. Kemeny-Snell [1960], p. 73, Theorem 4.2.1)
Consider a trajectory $\tau = (i_0, \ldots, i_t)$ of length t and denote by $y_i^{(t)}$ the number of occurrences of state i. Then $\lim_{t\to\infty} y_i^{(t)}/t = \pi_i$.

Proposition 2 (cf. Karlin [1966], p. 63, Theorem 1.2)
With μ_i as mean recurrence time of state i we have $\lim_{t\to\infty} p_{ii}^{(t)} = 1/\mu_i = \pi_i$.

In both cases a trajectory of big length (e.g. 10^6) has to be generated. It can be shown that the corresponding estimators are asymptotically equivalent. For illustration we use the 7×7 and 59×59 DIW input-output tables transformed to the closed 8×8 resp. 60×60 forms (see Berman-Plemmons [1979]). In the 8×8 case we generated trajectories of length 10^6 and 10^8. The following table shows an estimation of π based on the time duration method of Proposition 1 compared with exact algebraic calculations.

components of x	trajectory length 10^6	trajectory length 10^8	algebraic exact
1	.013748	.013840	.013837
2	.029377	.029142	.029121
3	.283841	.283647	.283689
4	.041835	.041874	.041887
5	.084109	.084146	.084134
6	.115008	.115117	.115097
7	.072690	.072731	.072682
8	.359392	.359501	.359552

For the estimation of a single component of π the mean recurrence time method was applied to the closed 60×60 table with encouraging results.

Literature

Berman, A., Plemmons, R. J., [1979] Nonnegative Matrices in the Mathematical Sciences. Academic Press, New York, San Francisco, London

Cox, D. R., Miller, H. D., [1965] The Theory of Stochastic Processes. Chapman and Hall, London

Egle, K., Fenyi, S., [1991] Eigenvalue estimations in input-output and growth models by Monte Carlo techniques. Discussion Paper No. 406, Institut für Wirtschaftstheorie und Operations Research, Universität Karlsruhe

Gale, D. [1960] The Theory of Linear Economic Models. McGraw-Hill, New York

Johnson, N. L., Kotz, S., [1969] Distributions in Statistics. Houghton Mifflin, Boston

Karlin, S., [1966] A First Course in Stochastic Processes. Academic Press, New York London

Kemeny, J. G., Snell, J. L., [1965] Finite Markov Chains. Reprint. D. Van Nostrand Comp., Princeton New Jersey

Leontief, W. W., [1936] Qualitative input and output relations in the economic system of the United States. Rev. Econ. Statist. 18, p. 100-125

Takayama,A., [1974] Mathematical Economics. The Dryden Press, Hinsdale, Illinois

On Connectivity of Efficient Matroid Bases

Matthias Ehrgott [1]
University of Kaiserslautern

Keywords

Matroid, basis, efficient solution, multiple objective, connectivity, algorithm.

Introduction

Let $\mathcal{M} = (N, \mathcal{I})$ be a matroid. With each element $j \in N$ we associate a weight-vector $w(j) \in I\!R_+^Q$, $Q \geq 2$. If $S \subseteq N$, the weight of S is defined as the vector with components $\sum_{j \in S} w_q(j)$. A basis B of $\mathcal{M}$ is called *efficient basis* if there is no basis B' such that $w(B') < w(B)$, i.e. if its corresponding weight-vector is vectorminimal. The multicriteria matroid optimization problem is the following:

(MCMOP) Find all efficient bases of $\mathcal{M}$.

The problem is NP-complete even for the case $Q = 2$, see [3]. Two bases are called *equivalent* if $w(B') = w(B)$. If $w(B) > w(B')$ we say that B' *dominates* B.

Despite increasing research efforts in multicriteria optimization in recent years, there are only two papers [6, 7] considering matroid optimization problems where the function to be optimized is the sum and difference of two objectives, respectively. Lexicographical and Max-Min Matroid optimization problems have been considred in [4] and [5], respectively. Several papers treat the special case of spanning tree problems with multiple objective functions [8, 9, 10, 11].

Let B, B' be two bases of the matroid $\mathcal{M}$, such that $B \backslash B' =: \{e_1, \ldots e_n\}$ and $B' \backslash B = \{f_1, \ldots f_n\}$. Then $\tau := \{f_1, \ldots f_n\} \backslash \{e_1, \ldots e_n\}$ is called $B - B'$*-exchange* or *basis-exchange w.r.t. B.* with weight $w(\tau) := \sum_{i=1}^{n} (w(e_i) - w(f_i))$. A basis-exchange τ w.r.t. B is *vectormaximal* if there is no basis-exchange τ' w.r.t. B such that $w(\tau) < w(\tau')$.

Two bases B and B' of $\mathcal{M}$ are called *neighbours* if $B' = B \backslash \{e\} \cup \{f\}$.

Definition:
The *Basisgraph* $\mathcal{B}(\mathcal{M})$ is defined by the node set

$$V(\mathcal{B}(\mathcal{M})) := \{B | B \text{ basis of } \mathcal{M}\}$$

The *Efficiencygraph* $\mathcal{EB}(\mathcal{M})$ is defined by the node set

$$V(\mathcal{EB}(\mathcal{M})) := \{B | B \text{ efficient basis of } \mathcal{M}\}$$

In both graphs edge sets are defined by all pairs of vertices that define neighboured bases.

Results and Algorithm

The first result gives a characterization of dominance and equivalence in terms of basis-exchanges.

[1] Partially supported by the Deutsche Forschungsgemeinschaft

Lemma 1:

Let B, B' be two bases and τ the $B - B'$-exchange, then:
a) $w(\tau) > 0 \Leftrightarrow B'$ dominates B.
b) $w(\tau) < 0 \Leftrightarrow B$ dominates B'.
c) $w(\tau) = 0 \Leftrightarrow B$ and B' are equivalent.

Therefore, if B is an efficient basis, B' any basis not dominated by B and B and B' are not equivalent, then neither $w(\tau) \geq 0$ nor $w(\tau) \leq 0$ for the $B - B'$-exchange τ. As such exchanges are the most important tool used in the sequel we introduce the following name: A basis exchange τ such that neither $w(\tau) \geq 0$ nor $w(\tau) \leq 0$ is called $+/-$ *exchange*.

Next we will consider basis-exchanges that are associated with two efficient bases.

Lemma 2:

If B and B' are efficient bases then either the $B-B'$-exchange τ and the $B'-B$-exchange τ' are vectormaximal $+/-$ exchanges or B and B' are equivalent.

The following result is in some sense the converse of Lemma 2.

Lemma 3:

If B is an efficient basis and τ is a vectormaximal $+/-$ exchange w.r.t to B then the basis B' defined by B and τ is efficient.

We now give two lemmas that are used to prove the main theorem of the paper.

Lemma 4:

Let B and B' be two bases of $\mathcal{M}$, such that $B \backslash B' = \{e_1, \ldots e_n\}, B' \backslash B = \{f_1, \ldots f_n\}$. Then there is a sequence of pairs $\{f_1, e_{i_1}\}, \ldots \{f_n, e_{i_n}\}$ such that if $B_0 := B$, $B_j := B_{j-1} \cup \{f_j\} \backslash \{e_{i_j}\}$, $j = 1, \ldots n$ each B_j is a basis, $B_n = B'$ and $\{e_{i_1}, \ldots e_{i_n}\} = \{e_1, \ldots e_n\}$.

Lemma 5:

Under the assumptions of Lemma 4 let C_i be the unique circuit defined by $B \cup \{f_i\}$ and $E_i := \{e_{i_1}, \ldots e_{i_{k_i}}\}$ be the elements of $B \backslash B'$ contained in C_i. Then

1. For any $j \in \{1, \ldots k_i\}$ $B \cup \{f_i\} \backslash \{e_{i_j}\}$ is a basis.
2. We can choose elements e_{i_i}, one from each E_i such that $\{e_{1_1}, \ldots e_{n_n}\} = B \backslash B'$ and $B \cup \{f_i\} \backslash \{e_{i_i}\}$ is a basis $\forall i = 1, \ldots n$.

The following theorem is the main result.

Theorem:

1. $\mathcal{B}(\mathcal{M})$ is connected.
2. $\mathcal{EB}(\mathcal{M})$ is connected.

The theorem will now be used to develop an algorithm for MCMOP. The idea is as follows: Given any efficient basis, by part 2 of the theorem we can find all efficient bases by substituting one element at a time. Let combined weights be defined as $w^*(e) = \sum_{q=1}^{Q} w_q(e)$.

STEP 1:	a) Find minimum basis w.r.t weights $w^*(e)$;
	b) Initialize: $E := \{B\}, L1 := \{B\}, L2 := \emptyset$;
STEP 2:	Choose any B from $L1$, $L1 := L1 \backslash \{B\}, L2 := L2 \cup \{B\}$;
STEP 4:	a) Find all neighbours of B;
	b) Calculate weights of the corresponding exchanges;
STEP 5:	a) Find all vectormaximal $+/-$ exchanges and all exchanges of weight 0;
	b) Let $\mathcal{B} = \{B_1, \ldots B_k\}$ be the corresponding bases. $E := E \cup \mathcal{B}, L1 := L1 \cup (\mathcal{B} \backslash L2)$;
STEP 6:	If $L1$ is empty STOP else goto STEP 2;

E is the set of efficient bases. $L1$ represents a list of candidates the neighbourhood of which has to be searched whereas $L2$ is the list of bases that have already been examined.

If $\mathcal{N}$ is the number of efficient bases the algorithm has complexity

$$O(\mathcal{N} \times (|N| \times |B|)^2 \times Q),$$

where N is the set underlying the matroid $\mathcal{M}$ and B is a basis.

References

[1] Welsh, D.J.: Matroid Theory, London, 1976

[2] Lovasz, L.; Plummer, M.D.: Matching Theory, Amsterdam, New York, Oxford, Tokio 1986

[3] Serafini, P.: Some Considerations about Computational Complexity for Multiple Objective Combinatorial Problems, Lecture Notes in Economics and Mathematical Systems 294 (1986), 222-32

[4] Zimmermann, U.: Matroid intersection problems with generalized objectives, Proc. Int. Symp. Budapest (1976), Vol. 2 383-92

[5] Granot, D.: A New Exchange Property for Matroids and Its Application to Max-Min-Problems, Zeitschrift für Operations Research 28 (1984), 41-45

[6] Minoux, M.: Solving Combinatorial Problems with Combined Min-Max Min-Sum Objectives and Applications, Mathematical Progarmming 45 (1989), 361-72

[7] Camerini, M; Mafioli, F; Martello, S; Toth, P.: Most and Least Uniform Spanning Trees, Discrete Applied Mathematics 15 (1986), 181-97

[8] Schweigert, D.: Linear Extensions and Vector Valued Spanning Trees, Methods of Operations Research 60 (1990), 219-29

[9] Schweigert, D.: Linear Extensions and Efficient Trees, Technical Report No. 172, University of Kaiserslautern, 1990

[10] Hamacher, H.W.; Ruhe, G.: On Spanning Tree Problems with Multiple Objectives, Technical Report No. 233, University of Kaiserslautern, 1993

[11] Corley, H.W.: Efficient Spanning Trees, Journal of Optimization Theory and Applications 45 (1985), 481-85

ON STOCHASTIC VECTOR OPTIMIZATION PROBLEMS WITH GENERAL STOCHASTIC PARAMETERS IN THE CONSTRAINTS USING CHANCE- CONSTRAINED APPROACH

Abou-Zaid H. El-Banna

Department of Mathematics, Faculty of Science, Tanta University, Tanta - Egypt.

In this paper, the characterizations of some basic notions of stochastic vector optimization problems with general random parameters in the constraints are presented. These notions are the set of feasible parameters, the solvability set, the stability set of the first kind and the stability set of the second kind. The chance-constrained approach is used to change the concerned problem into equivalent determinstic problem. An illustrative example is given to clarify the obtained results.

Consider the problem :

$$\text{VOP}(y) \quad \begin{cases} \min \; f_j(x), & j=1,2,\dots,L \\ \text{subject to} & \\ M(y) = \{x \in R^n \mid g_r(x,y_r) \leqq 0 \,, & r = 1,2,\dots,m\}, \end{cases}$$

where $y \in R^m$ is a random vector, $y : (\Omega,\sigma,P_w) \to (R^m,L^m,P)$ is a measurable mapping from a probability space (Ω,σ,P_w) into a Borel σ-algebra L^m, and the probability measure P inducing by y in L^m. The functions $f_j(x)$, $j=1,2,\dots,L$, $g_r(x,y_r)$, $r = 1,2,\dots,m$ are convex functions. Using chance-constrained approach VOP(y) can be written in a equivalent determinstic problem as follows [1] :

$$\text{VOP}(P) \quad \begin{cases} \min \; f_j(x), & j=1,2,\dots,L \\ \text{subject to} & \\ M(P) = \{x \in R^n \mid h_r(x) + P_r \leqq 0, & r=1,2,\dots,m, \text{ and } P_r \in (0,1)\}, \end{cases}$$

where

$$h_r(x) = - P\{y \mid g_r(x,y_r) \leqq 0\} \,, \quad r=1,2,\dots,m.$$

$x^* \in M(y)$ is an efficient solution of VOP(y), if there does not exist $x \in M(y)$ such that $f_j(x) \leqq f_j(x^*)$ for all j, $j = 1,2,\dots,L$ with strict inequality holds for at least on j with

$$P\{y \mid g_r(x^*,y_r) \leqq 0\} \geqq P_r, \quad r=1,2,\dots,m \,, \quad P_r \in (0,1).$$

The relationship between the stochastic problem VOP(y) and parametric problem VOP(P) through the basic notions of the parametric programming is given as follows :

1- <u>The set of feasible parameters</u> for problem VOP(y) is defined by :

$$U = \{y \in R^m | M(y) \neq 0 \text{ with } P\{y_r | g_r(x,y_r) \leqq 0\} \geqq P_r,\ P_r \in (0,1],\ r=1,2,\ldots,m\}$$

and the set of feasible parameters for VOP(P) is defined by :

$$U' = \{P \in R^m | P\{y_r | g_r(x,y_r) \leqq 0\} \geqq P_r\ ,\quad r = 1,2,\ldots,m\ ,\quad P_r \in (0,1)\}.$$

<u>The results</u> : i) If the st U' is closed, then U is closed.

ii) The set U' is convex.

iii) The set U is convex if $g_r(x,y_r)$ is convex in x and y_r.

2- <u>The solvability set</u> for problem VOP(y) is defined by

$$B = \{y \in R^m | \psi(y) \neq \phi \text{ with } P\{y_r | g_r(x,y_r) \leqq 0\} \geqq P_r\ ,\ P_r \in (0,1)],\quad r = 1,2,\ldots m\},$$

where $\psi(y)$ is the set of all efficient points of problem VOP(y), and the solvability set for problem VOP(P) is defined by

$$B' = \{P \in R^m | \psi(y) \neq \phi \text{ with } P\{y_r | g_r(x,y_r) \leqq 0\} \geqq P_r\ ,\quad P_r \in (0,1],\ r=1,\ldots,m\}.$$

<u>The results</u> : i) For any parameter value $y \in B$, the solvability set B is equal to the set of feasible parameters U' for the same problem.

ii) The set B' is convex.

iii) The set B is convex.

iv) If x^* is an efficient point of VOP(P) with $P_r \in (0,1]$ for all r related to VOP(y), then there is a parameter value y^* such that $x^* \in \psi(y^*)$. Moreover, one possible value y^* is given by $y_r^* = \sup\{\alpha | P\{y_r \geqq \alpha\} \geqq P_r\}$, $r = 1,\ldots,m$.

3- <u>The stability set of the first kind</u> : Suppose $y \in B$ with a corresponding efficient point x^*, then the stability set of the first kind of VOP(y) corresponding to x^* is defined by :

$S(x^*) = \{ y \in R^m | x^*$ is an efficient solution for VOP(y), with

$$P\{ y_r | g_r(x^*, y_r) \leqq 0\} \geqq P_r \ , \quad P_r \in (0,1], \quad r=1,2,\dots,m \}$$

as a similarly maner, $\grave{S}(x^*)$ can be defined.

The results : i) The set $\grave{S}(x^*)$ is starshapped with common point of visibility $P^* \leqq P(y^*)$ such that $y^* \in S(x^*)$.

ii) The set $S(x^*)$ is starshapped with common point of visibility y^* such that $P(y^*) \geqq P^*$.

iii) If $\grave{S}(x^*)$ is convex, then $S(x^*)$ is convex.

iv) If $\grave{S}(x^1) \cap \grave{S}(x^2) = \phi$, then $S(x^1) \cap S(x^2) = \phi$ where x^1, x^2 are two distinct efficient solution of VOP(y).

4- The stability set of the second kind : Let $\bar{y} \in B$ with a corresponding efficient point $\bar{x}$ in $\rho(\bar{y},J)$, where

$$\rho(\bar{y},J) = \{ x \in R^n | P\{ y_r | g_r(x,y_r) = 0\} \geqq P_r \ , \ r \in J \subset \{1,2,\dots,m\} ,$$

$$P\{ y_r | g_r(x,y_r) < 0\} \geqq P_r \ , \ r \notin J\} .$$

Then the stability set of the second kind of VOP(y) corresponding to $\rho(\bar{y},J)$ is defined by :

$$Q(\rho(\bar{y},J)) = \{ y \in B | \psi(y) \cap \rho(\bar{y},J) \neq \phi\} ,$$

where $\psi(y)$ is the set of all efficient points of VOP(y). Also, as a similarly maner, $\grave{Q}(\rho(\bar{y},J))$ can be defined.

The results : i) If the functions $f_j(x)$, $j=1,2,\dots,m$ are strictly convex and $y^1, y^2 \in B$, $y^1 \neq y^2$ with $\rho(y^1,J^1) \neq \rho(y^2,J^2)$ and $\grave{Q}(\rho(P^1,J^1)) \cap \grave{Q}(\rho(P^2,J^2)) = \phi$, then $Q(\rho(y^1,J^1)) \cap Q(\rho(y^2,J^2)) = \phi$.

ii) If the side $\rho(\bar{y},J)$ indicates a point of the feasible domain U, then the stability set of the first kind coinside with the stability set of the second kind corresponding to that point.

Remark : An illustrative example is given to clarify the obtained results.

REFERENCES

[1] Chankong, V. and Haimes, Y. " Multiobjective decision making theory and methodology ", North-Holand (1983).

[2] Guddat, J., Vasquez, F., Tammer, K., and Wendler, K. " Multiobjective and stochastic optimization based on parametric optimization " Akad. Verlag Berlin (1985).

[3] Osman, M. " Qualitative analysis of basic notions in parametric convex program I (parameters in the constraints) Appl. Math. CSSR Akad. Prague (1976).

[4] Osman, M., El-Banna, A. and Youness, E. " On a general class of parametric convex programming problems " Advances in Modelling & Simulation, AMSE press, Vol. 5, N° 1, p. 37 - 47 (1986).

[5] El-Banna, A. and Youness, E. " On some basic notions of stochastic multiobjective programming problems with random parameters in the constraints " to appear in Microelectronics and Reliability Journal (1993).

Existence of an optimal sampling frequency for LQ-controlled economic systems

Jacob Engwerda
Department of Econometrics
Tilburg University
P.O. Box 90153, 5000 LE Tilburg
The Netherlands

Abstract: In this paper we present sufficient conditions for the existence of an optimal frequency for sampling an economic system. We assume that the underlying economy is described by a linear continuous-time system containing an exogenous component, and that the policymakers want to minimize a social welfare function. This welfare function is a continuous-time quadratic tracking equation over an infinite planning horizon with positive semi-definite weighting matrices.

Introduction

It will be clear that increasing the sampling frequency of an economy brings on additional costs of data gathering, whereas the additional information that can be extracted from this data for the system will, in general, decrease on an increasing sampling frequency (since e.g. the data is corrupted by noise). Therefore, the problem arises to weigh out the advantage of an increase in the performance of the system and the additional cost of data gathering.
There is an extensive ongoing literature dealing with various problems concerning sampled data systems (see e.g. Astrom et al. (1990) and Engwerda et al. (1992) for references). Main research performed in this area has been done in the field of control engineering, in particular from a digital control point of view. However, usually, the considered systems do not contain exogenous deterministic variables, a characteristic which typically occurs in macro-economic systems. Furthermore the fact that extra sampling brings on additional costs is also a point that is rarily addressed to in this literature. Both these points motivate therefore the study of this paper: how often should a controlled economic system be sampled.
The answer to this question depends, amongst othors, on which performance criterion (c.q. goals) the policymakers are striving for. We will assume that they are looking for a policy which succeeds in tracking an a priori specified path for their target variables. Furthermore, the policy has to satisfy some additional requirements like being robust for unmodeled disturbances and staying close to some prespecified policy path (see e.g. Pitchford et al. (1977), Preston et al. (1982) and Engwerda (1990) for references). In Engwerda (1990) this economic stabilization problem is formalized as an infinite horizon quadratic tracking problem and solved in case the considered system is discrete time. We will take up this approach for sampled continuous time systems. First we formalize the continuous time control problem, and then we transform it into an equivalent discrete time problem which can be solved using the analysis of Engwerda et al. (1992). An explicit expression for the performance criterion is presented under some smooth conditions. This expression is used to draw conclusions w.r.t. the existence question of an optimal sampling frequency for the system.

II. Problem statement

Consider a system described by the following linear, finite-dimensional differential equation:

$$\dot{y}(t) = Ay(t) + Bu(t) + Cx(t), \quad t \in [t_o, t_N] \tag{1}$$

where y is an n-dimensional output vector, u is an m-dimensional control vector, and x is an p-dimensional uncontrollable deterministic vector (which is piecewise continuous in time). The social welfare function the policymakers like to minimize is given by:

$$\lim_{N\to\infty} J(u(\cdot), t_0, t_N) := (z(t_N) - z^*(t_N))^T \tilde{H}(z(t_N) - z^*(t_N)) +$$

$$\int_{t_0}^{t_N} \{(z(t) - z^*(t))^T \tilde{\tilde{Q}}(z(t) - z^*(t)) + (u(t) - u^*(t))^T \tilde{R}(u(t) - u^*(t))\}dt \tag{2}$$

Here $\tilde{\tilde{Q}}$, $\tilde{R}$ and $\tilde{H}$ are symmetric positive definite weight matrices, and $z(t) = Dy(t)$ (with D full row rank) the target variables.
Assuming, for simplicity reasons, equidistant sampling instances (i.e. $t_{k+1} - t_k = \Delta, k = 0, \ldots, N-1$), the observations we make on system (1) are then provided by the following discrete-time system

$$y_{k+1} = \phi(\Delta)y_k + \Gamma(\Delta)u_k + d_k(\Delta), \quad k = 0, 1, \ldots, N-1, \tag{3}$$

where $\phi(\Delta) := e^{A\Delta}$, $\Gamma(\Delta) := \int_{t_k}^{t_k+\Delta} e^{A(t_k+\Delta-s)}Bds$, $u_k = u(t_k)$, and $d_k(\Delta) := \int_{t_k}^{t_k+\Delta} Cx(s)ds$. Furthermore $J(u(\cdot), t_0, t_N)$ can be rewritten as

$$(y_N - y^*(t_N))^T H(y_N - y^*(t_N)) + \sum_{k=0}^{N-1} \{y_k^T Q y_k + 2y_k^T M u_k + u_k^T R u_k + 2y_k^T v_k + 2w_k^T u_k + z_k\}, \tag{4}$$

where $Q := \int_{t_k}^{t_k+\Delta} \phi^T(t, t_k)\tilde{Q}\phi(t, t_k)dt$, $M := \int_{t_k}^{t_k+\Delta} \phi^T(t, t_k)\tilde{Q}\Gamma(t, t_k)dt$, $R := \int_{t_k}^{t_k+\Delta}[\tilde{R} + \Gamma^T(t, t_k)\tilde{Q}\Gamma(t, t_k)]dt$, $v_k := \int_{t_k}^{t_k+\Delta} \tilde{Q}(d(t, t_k) - y^*(t))dt$, $w_k := \int_{t_k}^{t_k+\Delta}[\Gamma^T(t, t_k)\tilde{Q}(d(t, t_k) - y^*(t)) - Ru^*(t)]dt$, $z_k := \int_{t_k}^{t_k+\Delta}[(y^*(t) - d(t, t_k))^T \tilde{Q}(y^* - d(t, t_k)) + u^{*T}(t)Ru^*(t)]dt$ and $\phi(t, t_k) := e^{A(t-t_k)}$, $\Gamma(t, t_k) := \int_{t_k}^{t} \phi(t, s)Bds$, $d(t, t_k) := \int_{t_k}^{t} \phi(t, s)Cx(s)ds$, $y(t) := \phi(t, t_k)y(t_k) + \Gamma(t, t_k)u(t_k) + d(t, t_k)$, with $\tilde{Q} := D^T\tilde{\tilde{Q}}D$, $H := D^T\tilde{H}D$, $y^* := D^T(DD^T)^{-1}z^*$.
Note that all these matrices and variables depend on the length of the time intervals between two sampling instances. For notational simplicity this dependency is omitted.
Before we study this optimization problem, we first consider the question which target paths can be tracked by system 1. This, since it does not make any sense to study tracking problems in case the desired path can not be tracked whatever control sequence is used. As we are dealing with sampled systems, where the control is assumed to be piecewise constant, it seems reasonable to consider only desired paths which are generated by piecewise constant controls. So, the following definition makes sense.

Definition 1:
A target path $z^*(\cdot)$ is called asymptotically admissible for system (1) at time $t = 0$ for

$y(0) = \bar{y}$ if there exists a piecewise constant control sequence $u(\cdot)$ such that $z(t) - z^*(t) \to 0$ for $t \to \infty$. (Here we assume again that the target variables $z(t)$ satisfy $z(t) = Dy(t)$.) In that case $u(\cdot)$ is called a successful control. □

It it is easily shown that a target path $z^*(\cdot)$ is asymptotically admissible for $\bar{y}$ at $t = 0$ iff. there exists a piecewise constant $u^*(\cdot)$ and an $\epsilon(\cdot)$, with $\epsilon(t) \to 0$ as $t \to \infty$, such that

$$\dot{y}^*(t) = Ay^*(t) + Bu^*(t) + Cx(t), y^*(0) = \bar{y}; z^*(t) = Dy^*(t) + \epsilon(t). \tag{5}$$

In the rest of this paper we will assume that the target path mentioned in the social welfare function is asymptotically admissible and that the corresponding control sequence $u^*(.)$ is a successful one. Using these properties we have the following result

Theorem 2:
Let (ϕ, Γ) be stabilizable, (D, ϕ) detectable. Let $z^*(.)$ be an asymptotically admissible target path and $u^*(.)$ a corresponding successful control.
Then, the optimal control minimizing $\lim_{N\to\infty} J(u(\cdot), 0, N)$ w.r.t. (3) exists and, moreover, stabilizes the closed loop system. Furthermore, the welfare loss equals

$$J^*(\Delta) := \min_u \lim_{N\to\infty} J_N(u(\cdot), 0, N) = \sum_{k=0}^{\infty} r(k), \tag{6}$$

where $r(k) = -\bar{h}_{k+1}^T(R + \Gamma^T K\Gamma)^{-1}\Gamma(\Gamma^T\bar{h}_{k+1} + 2\bar{w}_k) - \bar{w}_k^T(R + \Gamma^T K\Gamma)\bar{w}_k + \bar{z}_k$. Here $\bar{v}_k^T := \int_{t_k}^{t_{k+1}} \epsilon^T(t)\tilde{\tilde{Q}}D\phi(t, t_k)dt$, $\bar{w}_k^T := \int_{t_k}^{t_{k+1}} \epsilon^T(t)\tilde{\tilde{Q}}D\Gamma(t, t_k)dt$, $\bar{z}_k^T := \int_{t_k}^{t_{k+1}} \epsilon^T(t)\tilde{\tilde{Q}}\epsilon(t)dt$, and $\bar{h}_k := \sum_{i=k}^{\infty}(\phi - \Gamma G)^{T^{i-k}}\{-G\bar{w}_i + \bar{v}_i\}$. Furthermore, K satisfies $K = Q + \phi^T K\phi - (M + \Gamma^T K\phi)^T(R + \Gamma^T K\Gamma)^{-1}(M + \Gamma^T K\phi)$ and $G = (R + \Gamma^T K\Gamma)^{-1}(\Gamma^T K\phi + M^T)$.

III. Existence of an optimal sampling frequency

We now consider the question whether there exists an optimal sampling rate for the system (1). Optimal in the sense that the sum of performance cost (6) and the cost of sampling the system, J_s, is minimized w.r.t. the sampling frequency. Obviously, the outcome of this optimization process depends on the initial state of the system (1) and on the prespecified output and control paths. So a basic problem, we will not deal with here, is to investigate how robust the optimal sampling frequency is for changes in the initial state and reference paths. Before this problem becomes actual, however, first the question arises whether always an optimal sampling frequency exists. In case the reference paths are such that for a certain sampling frequency the admissibility property is lost, our object function becomes a discontinuous function of the sampling frequency. This makes it in practice much harder to solve this optimization problem. Therefore it seems reasonable to consider only those reference paths that are asymptotically admissible for all sampling periods between zero and some a priori predetermined upperbound for the sampling period T. We have the following result.

Lemma 3:
An asymptotically admissible target path $z^*(t)$ for the continuous time system (1) satisfying (5), is asymptotically admissible for every sampling period Δ, $0 \le \Delta \le T$, if the following conditions are satisfied:

i) All (D, A)-observable eigenvalues λ, with $Re\lambda \geq 0$, are controllable.
ii) $u^*(t)$ becomes periodically constant (with period T) if $t \rightarrow \infty$. □

Another point that may cause loss of continuity of the object function is that stabilizability and detectability of the continuous time system do not imply, in general, that the sampled system has these properties too. The next lemma gives sufficient conditions under which the sampled system is both stabilizable and detectable for every choice of the sampling period $\Delta \in [0, T]$.

Lemma 4:
Let (A, B) be stabilizable.
Then $(\phi(\Delta), \Gamma(\Delta))$ is stabilizable for all $\Delta \in [0, T]$ if for all eigenvalues $\lambda, \mu \in \sigma(A) \cap \mathbf{C}_b$, $\lambda - \mu \neq \frac{2\pi i}{\theta} \forall \mid \theta \mid < T$. Here $\mathbf{C}_b := \{z \in \mathbf{C} \mid Re z \geq 0\}$. □

Using Weierstrass's theorem and relationship (6) the existence question raised at the beginning of this section can now be solved.

Theorem 5:
Assume that the cost of sampling the system, J_s, is a continuous function of the sampling rate. Furthermore, let (A, B) be stabilizable, (D, A) detectable and $\lambda - \mu \neq \frac{2\pi i}{\theta} \forall \mid \theta \mid < T$; $\lambda, \mu \in \sigma(A) \cap \mathbf{C}_b$, where T is some upperbound for the sampling period.
Then, if $z^*(\cdot)$ is an asymptotically admissible target path for the continuous time system (1) generated according to (5) where $\epsilon(t)$ converges exponentially fast to zero, there exists a sampling rate minimizing $J_s(\Delta) + J^*(\Delta)$. □

We conclude this section by noting that similar to Levis et al. (1971) one can show that, under the conditions mentioned above, $J^*(\Delta)$ is a monotonically non-decreasing function of Δ. This establishment may be helpful in actually calculating the optimal sampling frequency.

References:

Aström, K.J., Wittenmark, B., 1990, Computer Controlled Systems (Englewood Cliffs, N.J., Prentice-Hall).
Engwerda, J.C., 1990-a, The solution of the infinite horizon tracking problem for discrete-time systems possessing an exogenous component, Journal of Economic Dynamics and Control, Vol. 14, pp. 741-762.
Engwerda, J.C., Willigenburg, L.G. van, 1992, LQ-control of sampled continuous-time system in: Strejc V. (ed.), Proceedings of the 2nd IFAC workshop on system structure and control, IFAC, Prague, Czechoslovakia, pp. 128-131.
Levis, A.H., Schlueter, R.A., Athans, M., 1971, On the behavior of optimal linear sampled data regulators, Int. J. Contr., 13, pp. 343-361.
Preston, A.J., Pagan, A.R., 1982, The Theory of Economic Policy (New York, Cambridge University Press).
Pitchford, J.D.,Turnovsky, S.J., 1977, Applications of Control Theory to Economic Analysis (Amsterdam, North-Holland).

Approximating the core of euclidean TSP games

U. Faigle and W. Kern, University of Twente
S. Fekete and W. Hochstättler, Universität Köln

Traveling Salesman games are quite well-studied examples of socalled **cooperative games**. Formally, such games are defined as follows.

Definition: Let N be a finite set, the set of **players**. A **cooperative game** is defined by a function

$$c: 2^N \to \mathbb{R},$$

i.e., a function which associates a **cost** c(S) to every **coalition** $S \subseteq N$. The coalition N is also referred to as the **grand coalition**.

Example: Let $N \subseteq \mathbb{R}^2$. For each $S \subseteq N$, let

$$c(S) := \text{length of a shortest TSP tour through all points in } S \cup \{0\}.$$

The game defined this way is called a **euclidean TSP game** (cf. [Potters et al. 92]). Consider, for example, the points $i \in N$ as locations of universities and suppose that a speaker, who is located at the origin is to give a talk at each of the $n = |N|$ universities. The cost of a shortest round trip visiting all universities $i \in N$ is given by c(N). The problem is now to allocate this cost c(N) of the grand coalition in a fair way to the individual universities in the following sense:

Definition: A vector $x \in \mathbb{R}^N$ is called a **fair allocation**, if

(i) $$\sum_{i \in N} x_i = c(N)$$

(ii) $$\sum_{i \in S} x_i \le c(S) \qquad \forall\, S \subseteq N.$$

The set of all fair allocations is called the core of the game. ∎

Condition (ii) above states that, if the cost is allocated according to $x \in \mathbb{R}^N$, then no coalition S would be better off if it broke off the grand coalition and invited the speaker to visit only the universities $i \in S$.

It can be shown, however, that the core of a TSP-game may be empty. In this case, once may try instead to look for **ϵ-approximately fair allocations** (cf. [Faigle/Kern 93]), which arise from replacing condition (ii) above by

$$\text{(ii')} \qquad \sum_{i \in S} x_i \le (1+\epsilon)\ c(s) \qquad \forall S \subseteq N.$$

Of particular interest is, of course, the minimum value of $\epsilon > 0$ such that (i) and (ii') are solvable. The following example shows, that, in general, the value of ϵ has to be approximately at least equal to $\frac{1}{3}$.

Example: Consider a set of 3m points arranged in 3 columns of m points each. Each column has length 1, say, and the distance between two adjacent columns equals $d \approx \frac{1}{m}$. An optimal TSP tour through all points is indicated below:

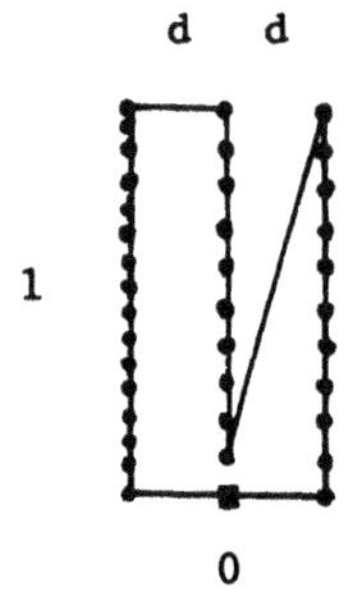

The length of this tour equals $c(N) \approx 4$. One the other hand, the coalition S_{ij} made up of columns i and j $(i,j = 1,2,3)$ has clearly cost $c(S_{ij}) \approx 2$. Hence

$$x(S_{12}) \le (1+\epsilon) \cdot c(S_{12})$$
$$x(S_{13}) \le (1+\epsilon) \cdot c(S_{13})$$

$$x(S_{23}) \le (1+\epsilon) \cdot c(S_{23})$$

implies $2 \cdot x(N) \le (1+\epsilon) \cdot 3c(S_{ij}) \approx (1+\epsilon)6$.
Hence $x(N) = c(N) \approx 4$ implies $\epsilon \approx \frac{1}{3}$.

It can be shown (cf. [Faigle et al, 93]) that $\epsilon = \frac{1}{2}$ can always be achieved. The proof is based on the well-known TSP relaxation due to Held and Karp. Consider the modified game

$$c_{HK}(S) := \min \sum d_{ij} z_{ij}$$

$$\sum_{i \in T,\, j \in S \setminus T} z_{ij} \ge 2 \qquad \forall\, \phi \ne T \subset S \cup \{0\}$$

$$z_{ij} \ge 0 \qquad \forall\, i,j \in S \cup \{0\}.$$

Here, obviously, the d_{ij} denote the euclidean distances between points $i,j \in S \cup \{0\}$.
It can be shown, using a standard argument based on the LP-dual of this optimization problem, that this modified game has nonempty core [cf. [Faigle et al. 93] for details and an intuitively appealing geometric interpretation of a corresponding fair allocation). Together with the well-known fact that $c_{HK}(N) \ge \frac{2}{3} c(N)$, this implies that ϵ-approximately fair allocations exist for $\epsilon = \frac{1}{2}$. A famous conjecture on the Held-Karp lower bound states that even $c_{HK}(N) \ge \frac{4}{3} c(N)$ holds. If this were true, then the above approach would even yield the sharp bound $\epsilon = \frac{1}{3}$.
Combining theoretical results from [Steele 90] and numerical experiments mentioned in [Goemans 90], one is led to believe that $\epsilon \approx 0.013$ suffices with high probability, if all points are independently drawn from the uniform distribution on $[0,1]^2$, (cf. [Faigle et al, 93]). A major open problem is whether with probability tending to 1 as $n = |N| \to \infty$, actually $\epsilon = 0$ suffices for random problems.

References

U. Faigle, S. Fekete, W. Hochstättler, W. Kern: "On approximately fair cost allocations in euclidean TSP-games", working paper, University of Twente, 1993

U. Faigle, W. Kern (93): "On some approximately balanced combinatorial cooperative games", ZOR (to appear)

M. Goemans, "Analysis of LP-relaxation for a class of connectivity problems" PHD thesis, MIT, Massachusetts, 1990

J. Potters, I. Curiel, S. Tijs: "Traveling Salesman games", Math. Progr. 53 (1992), 199-211.

J.M. Steele, "Probabilistic and worst case analysis of classical problems of combinatorial optimization in euclidean space", Mathematics of OR, 15 (4), 1990, 749-770.

LP–Relaxations for the Edge–Weighted Subclique Problem

U. Faigle* R. Garbe K. Heerink B. Spieker
Department of Applied Mathematics
University of Twente
P.O. Box 217
7500 AE Enschede
The Netherlands

1 Introduction

We investigate the problem of finding the best subclique of a given size in a complete edge–weighted graph. This problem was formulated by Späth [S 85], who reports numerical results indicating that simple exchange heuristics perform very well on the problem. On the other hand, our problem is closely related to the well–studied *clique partition problem* (cf. [FSS 87], [W 86], [GW 89]), for which cutting plane algorithms appear to be quite succesfuland give tight bounds on the quality of heuristic solutions. Indeed, our problem is a partition problem where exactly one non–trivial block of a given size is allowed.

Dijkhuizen and Faigle [DF 93] developed a cutting plane algorithm for the subclique problem. Although the cutting planes could be viewed as LP–relaxations for the polytope generated by feasible (0-1)–edge–incidence vectors, the algorithm gave very poor results and typically did not even approximate the true objective function value. It is therefore a challenging problem to device an algorithm for the subclique problem that allows us to evaluate the quality of a heuristic solution by giving a good bound on the true optimum.

2 LP–Relaxations

In order to improve the LP–relaxations of [DF 93], we introduced new variables for the nodes and lifted the problem into higher dimensions. This way the problem could be approached with LP–relaxations that — in spite of added variables — are very fast to solve by any LP–solver. Our LP–formulations, moreover, allowed a Lagrangean relaxation that for each choice of parameters can be solved by a direct greedy algorithm.

It was hoped that also the heuristics could be coupled with the Lagrange relaxation in order to enhance their performance. While it turned out that this approach did not noticable improve the heuristics, we could observe that lifting the problem into higher dimensions had a substantial positive effect on the quality of the LP–relaxation. Even so, the problem is very sensitive with respect to LP–relaxations that are not chosen carefully.

*e-mail: faigle@math.utwente.nl

3 Formulations

The first integer LP–formulation is only in terms of decision variables on the edges, the y–variables:

$$\max \sum_{\substack{i,j \\ i<j}} c_{ij} y_{ij}$$

s.t.

$$y_{ij} + y_{ik} - y_{jk} \leq 1 \quad \forall\, i,j,k \quad i<j<k$$

$$\sum_{\substack{j \\ j>i}} y_{ij} + \sum_{\substack{j \\ j<i}} y_{ji} \leq b-1 \quad \forall\, i$$

$$y_{ij} + y_{jl} + y_{lm} - y_{il} - y_{jm} \leq 1 \quad \forall\, i,j,l,m \quad i<j<l<m$$

$$y_{ij} \in \{0,1\}$$

It contains three types of inequalities, which are facets of the solution polytope. The first is called *triangle inequality* and it forces the third edge of a triangle to be in the solution, whenever the other two edges are. The second is called *partition inequality* and it states that no sub–clique in the graph contains more than b nodes. The third type are the *Z–inequalities*. They make sure that there is only one clique in the solution.

In total [DF 93] give eight different types of facet inducing inequalities. At every iteration of their cutting plane method the current LP is extended with some violated constraints. The method behaves very poorly in terms of time efficiency and only for small graphs the algorithm could sometimes prove optimality.

The second formulation contains also the decision variables defined on the nodes of the graph, the x–variables:

$$\max \sum_{\substack{i,j \\ i<j}} c_{ij} y_{ij}$$

s.t.

$$y_{ij} \leq x_i \qquad \forall\, i,j\,,\ i<j$$

$$y_{ij} \leq x_j \qquad \forall\, i,j\,,\ i<j$$

$$y_{ij} \geq x_i + x_j - 1 \qquad \forall\, i,j\,,\ i<j$$

$$\sum_i x_i = b$$

$$\sum_{\substack{i,j \\ i<j}} y_{ij} = \frac{b(b-1)}{2}$$

$$y_{ij} \in \{0,1\} \qquad \forall\, i,j\,,\ i<j$$

$$x_i \in \{0,1\} \qquad \forall\, i$$

The first two constraints guarantee that if a node is not in the clique also the edges incident with this node are not. The second type of constraints says that with two nodes in the clique also the edge joining them is in the clique. The remaining are the cardinality contraints on the x and y variables and the integrality constraints.

The number of constraints of this formulation is of order n^2, while the number of constraints in the first formulation is of the order n^4 (due to the Z–inequalities). However, formulation II implies the triangle inequalities while their number is of the order n^3. This shows that by lifting the size of the formulation can be decreased.

The third formulation is an extension of the second one in the sense that all solutions which are feasible for the third formulation are also feasible for the second formulation. The cardinality constraints on the sum of the y variables is replaced by

$$\sum_{\substack{j \\ j>i}} y_{ij} + \sum_{\substack{j \\ j<i}} y_{ji} = (b-1)\, x_i \quad \forall\, i,$$

i.e., cardinality constraints on the sum of the y variables per node.

4 Lagrangean Dual vs. LP–Relaxation

In the following we will show that the two methods to obtain a lower bound, namely the Lagrangean dual and the LP–relaxation, will provide the same lower bound for formulation II. In the Lagrangean dual formulation we do not dualize all but only the two first types of constraints:

$$\min_{\lambda,\mu\geq 0} \max_{x,y} \; -\sum_{i<j} \mu_{ij}$$
$$+\sum_{i<j}(c_{ij}+\lambda_{ij}+\lambda_{ji}-\mu_{ij})\,y_{ij}$$
$$+\sum_{i}\Big(-\sum_{j\neq i}\lambda_{ij}+\sum_{j>i}\mu_{ij}+\sum_{j<i}\mu_{ji}\Big)x_i$$

s.t.

$$\sum_{i} x_i = b$$
$$\sum_{i<j} y_{ij} = \frac{b(b-1)}{2}$$
$$y_{ij} \in \{0,1\} \qquad \forall\, i,j \;,\; i<j$$
$$x_i \in \{0,1\} \qquad \forall\, i$$

We see that for any fixed λ and μ, x and y can be determined by simply ordering the coefficients and setting b x-variables to 1 and $b(b-1)/2$ y-variables to 1. That means that we get integral solutions without using the integrality constraints. Thus the Lagrangean dual of the LP has the same optimal value as the Lagrangean dual of the LP-relaxation and therefore the same optimal value as the LP-relaxation itself.

5 Experiments

In order to get lower bounds we solved the Lagrangean dual and the LP-relaxation. We wrote a C program using a sort of steepest decent algorithm to compute the Lagrangean dual solution. The LP-relaxations were solved using CPLEX.

To obtain upper bounds we started with an initial clique which is improved by means of 2-exchanges between nodes. We used two different 2-exchange heuristics. The first heuristic does the first possible exchange that improves the current clique. The second, however, does the best possible exchange.

We used 3 different ways to determine the initial clique. First we took the feasible clique provided by the x-variables of the solution of the Lagrangean dual. Secondly we used a random clique. And thirdly we used a greedy heuristic that orders all nodes using the sum of the weights of all incident edges. To get a sub-clique of size b it simply takes the b nodes with greatest values.

To be able to make a better comparison we took the test-data published by Späth, which have also been used by Dijkhuizen & Faigle, together with some randomly generated graphs with cardinality up to 200. The weights on the edges were varied and we looked for sub-cliques of different sizes.

6 Numerical Results

Here we give some representative results of the many test-results we got.

The first figure shows the difference between the LP-relaxation of formulation II (dashed curve) and the LP-relaxation of formulation III (solid curve). We can not only see that the LP-relaxation of formulation III is more tight but also that for large sub-cliques the gap between the lower and upper bound tends to zero.

The second figure shows the results for a graph on 50 nodes. The x-axis shows the size of the subclique and the y-axis shows the ratio between the value of the initial clique and the value of the best found clique. The figure shows that the initial clique from the optimal Lagrangean dual solution (dashed curve) is not significantly better than a random clique (broken curve). The heuristic (solid curve) seems to come up with the best initial cliques. The figure also shows that for great subcliques the initial clique is already very close to the best found value.

7 Späth's Results

These are results of formulations II and III for the Späth test problem, which was stated as a minimization problem. The graph contained 25 nodes and the weights of the edges varies between 1 and 1.000. The third column contains the upper bounds Späth found with his heuristics. We were not able to improve any of these upper bounds. Especially for large sub-cliques we were often able to prove optimality using the lower and upper bounds.

k	Formulation II	Formulation III	Späth
3	83.65	105.55	147
4	292.80	352.94	529
5	727.50	840.80	1522
6	1412.43	1630.19	2675
7	2407.67	2777.47	4441
8	3873.82	4301.57	6975
9	5780.86	6270.68	9765
10	8102.92	8700.52	13492
11	10876.71	11595.74	17166
12	14200.44	15121.25	21680
13	19702.60	20735.00	26911
14	27312.06	28223.50	33182
15	35329.62	36237.28	39890
16	43738.00	44656.87	47008
17	52551.82	53430.73	54340
18	61753.41	62437.00	62437
19	71331.55	71733.00	71733
20	81267.00	81276.00	81276
21	92333.00	92333.00	92333
22	103648.00	103648.00	103648
23	115403.00	115403.00	115403

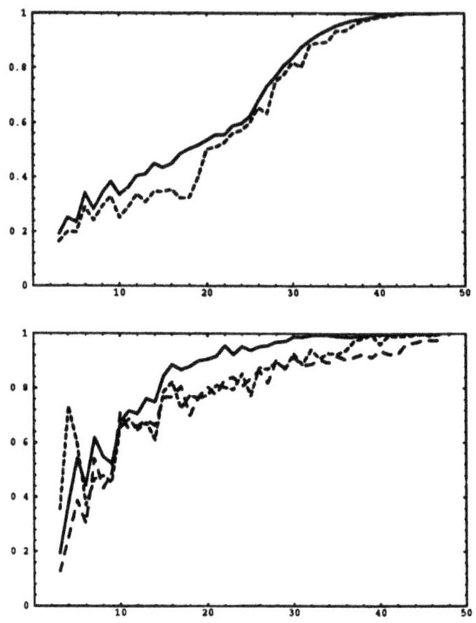

8 Conclusions & Improvements

We showed that the formulation of a combinatorial optimization problem has great influence in numerical experiments. Formulations which seem more difficult in the first place can sometimes give a better approximation of the solution polytope. Lifting a formulation can yield such an improved formulation.

In the case of the maximum sub-clique problem lifting yields better results. The larger the sub-cliques, the better the heuristics performed and for large sub-cliques we were able to prove optimality in most cases.

Some other facet inducing inequalities could be added to the LP-formulation in order to make it more tight. However, the number of the facet inducing inequalities we excluded is very large. For example, the number of Z-inequalities is of the order n^4. Adding all these inequalities would result in an intractably large LP-formulation. Therefore, a cutting plane approach using the third formulation should probably give some improvements.

References

[DF 93] G. Dijkhuizen and U. Faigle: "A cutting-plane approach to the edge-weighted maximal clique problem", *European Journal of Operational Research* 95, 1993, pp. 121–130.

[FSS 87] U. Faigle, R. Schrader, and R. Suletzki: " A cutting-plane algorithm for optimal graph partitioning", *Methods of Operations Research* 57, 1987, pp. 109–116.

[GW 89] M. Grötschel and Y. Wakabayashi: "A cutting plane algorithm for a clustering problem", *Mathematical programming B* 45, 1989, pp. 59–96.

[S 85] H. Späth: "Heuristically determining cliques of given cardinality and with minimal cost within weighted complete graphs", *Zeitschrift für Operations Research* 29, 1985, pp. 125–131.

[W 86] Y. Wakabayashi: "Aggregation of binary relations: Algorithmic and polyhedral investigations", Doctoral Dissertation, University of Augsburg, Germany.

On the Equilibrium Dynamics of a Two-Sector Overlapping-Generations Model with Heterogeneous Capital Goods

Karl Farmer

Institute of Economics, University of Graz

Schuberstraße 6A, A-8010 Graz, Austria

INTRODUCTION

In a magisterial work Galor (1992) has analysed the equilibrium dynamics of a two-sector overlapping-generations model with one homogeneous capital good. In contrast to the well-known result that the dynamics of capital accumulation is asymptotically stable if the consumption good sector is relatively more capital-intensive than the investment good sector (see Uzawa (1961) and Inada (1966) on non-overlapping-generations two-sector growth models with one homogeneous capital good), Galor (1992) detected the saddle-path property of the equilibrium dynamics which is characteristic of (also one-sector) optimal growth models and multi-sector descriptive growth models with heterogeneous capital goods.

This extented abstract reports the approach and main results of a paper (see Farmer, 1993) which analyses the equilibrium dynamics of a specific two-sector overlapping-generations economy with two heterogeneous capital goods and sectoral immobile capital services.

Because of the heterogeneity of capital the equilibrium dynamics of the capital stocks and the relative capital prices is higher dimensional than the two-dimensional equilibrium dynamics in Galor's paper.

In order to able to reduce the dimension of the equilibrium dynamics in our model and to be able to apply the fine techniques which Galor (1992) has developed Morishima's (1977) assumption of static expectations of relative capital prices is introduced. But only the additional assumption that the production elasticity of capital in the x-sector equals 0.5 makes the equilibrium dynamics two-dimensional.

Under theses assumptions the saddle-path stability properties of the capital equilibrium dynamics in the proposed model setting are precisely exhibited and the differences from Galor's results are enumerated.

THE MODEL ECONOMY: A LOG-LINEAR LEONTIEF-COBB-DOUGLAS EXAMPLE

In the following model economic activity is performed over an infinity of discrete time periods. In any period of time indexed by $t = 0,\ldots$ two goods X and Y are produced using two factors, labour services ($N^x(t)$, $N^y(t)$) and capital services ($D^x(t)$, $D^y(t)$). Both products are consumed and invested.

The labour force is exogenously fixed at $L(t) = L$ (= no growth of labour force). The capital services are immobile between the production sectors implying sector-specific prices of capital services $Q^x(t)$ and $Q^y(t)$. Labour is perfectly mobile at the competitively determined wage rate $W(t)$.

At any period of time there are two households, an old and a young one, indexed by 2 and 1, respectively. At the beginning of period t the old household holds stocks of X- and Y-commodities produced during t-1. In order to finance its X-consumption expenditures $P^X(t)\cdot C^{2,X}(t)$, the typical old household uses the rental income $Q^X(t)\cdot K^X(t-1) + Q^Y(t)\cdot K^Y(t-1)$ on the accumulated quantities of X- and Y-commodities produced during t-1.

At the beginning of any period the typical young household receives the wage income $W(t)$ which it uses to finance the "one-period forward" (Foley, 1975) purchases of the X and Y product for investment ($K^X(t)$ and $K^Y(t)$) and for Y-consumption $C^{1,Y}(t)$ at the one-period forward prices $P^X(t)$ and $P^Y(t)$.

The budget constraints in the first and second period of the planning horizon of the young household take the following form:

$$P^X(t)\cdot K^X(t) + P^Y(t)\cdot\left[C^{1,Y}(t) + K^Y(t)\right] = W(t)$$

$$P^{X,E}(t+1)\cdot C^{2,X}(t+1) = Q^{X,E}(t+1)\cdot K^X(t) + Q^{Y,E}(t+1)\cdot K^Y(t)$$

$P^{X,E}(t+1)$ denote the expected forward price and $(Q^{X,E}(t+1), Q^{Y,E}(t+1))$ the expected rental prices of commodities X and Y produced during period t.

Production occurs within each period according to constant returns to scale production functions $X(.)$ and $Y(.)$ which are invariant through time.

In order to simplify computations the following production functions $Y(.)$ and $X(.)$ are assumed:

$$Y(.) = min\left\{\frac{N^Y}{b_0}, \frac{D^Y}{b_1}\right\},\ 0 < b_0,\ 0 < b_1 < 1$$

$$X(.) = (N^X)^{1-\alpha}\cdot(D^x)^{\alpha},\ 0 < \alpha < 1.$$

Individuals are identical within as well as across generations. Individuals live two periods. Individuals born at time t are characterized by their intertemporal utility function $U(.)$:

$$U(.) = log\, C^{1,Y}(t) + \gamma\cdot log\, C^{2,X}(t+1),$$

$$0 << \gamma < 1,\ \gamma = \frac{1}{1+\theta},\ \theta > 0.$$

In accordance with Morishima's (1977) Walras' interpretation it is assumed that the young household form static expectations with respect to the market prices of the retirement period.

THE SADDLE-PATH CHARACTERISTICS OF THE EQUILIBRIUM DYNAMICS

The equilibrium dynamics of x- and y-investment quantities - given $K^X(-1), K^X(-2), K^Y(-1), K^Y(-2)$ - takes the following form:

$K^X(t) =$

$$K^X(t-1)^{\alpha} \cdot \left[1 - \left(\frac{b_0}{b_1}\right) \cdot K^Y(t-1)\right]^{1-\alpha} - \left(\frac{\gamma}{1+\gamma}\right) \cdot \alpha \cdot (1-\alpha) \cdot \left[1 - \left(\frac{b_0}{b_1}\right) \cdot \Gamma^Y(t-1)\right]^{1-2\alpha} \cdot \Gamma^X(t-1)^{2\alpha-1}$$

$$K^Y(t) = \frac{1}{b_1} \cdot K^Y(t-1) - \frac{1}{(1+\gamma)} \cdot \frac{1}{b_0} + \frac{\alpha \cdot b_1}{b_0 \cdot (1+\gamma)} \cdot (K^X(t-1))^{\alpha-1} \cdot \left[1 - \left(\frac{b_0}{b_1}\right) \cdot K^Y(t-1)\right]^{1-\alpha}$$

$$\Gamma^X(t) = K^X(t-1)$$

$$\Gamma^Y(t) = K^Y(t-1)$$

It is not difficult to see that the unique, positive fixed-point solution of this four-dimensional system of first-order difference equations reads as follows:

$$(K^X)^* = (\Gamma^X)^* = \left(\frac{\gamma}{1+\gamma}\right) \cdot \alpha^{\frac{1}{1-\alpha}} > 0$$

$$(K^Y)^* = (\Gamma^Y)^* = \left(\frac{1}{1+\gamma}\right) \cdot \left(\frac{b_1}{b_0}\right) > 0$$

The Jacobian J^* of this four-dimensional dynamical system at the fixed-point reduces to two dimensions by assuming $\alpha = 0.5$ *and* equals:

$$J^* = \begin{bmatrix} 1 & -\left(\frac{b_0}{4 \cdot b_1}\right) \\ -\left(\frac{2 \cdot b_1}{b_0 \cdot \gamma}\right) & \left[\left(\frac{1}{b_1}\right) - \left(\frac{1}{2 \cdot \gamma}\right)\right] \end{bmatrix}$$

One can show (see Farmer, 1993) that

(i) if $\theta \leq \frac{3}{5} + \left(\frac{4}{5}\right)\cdot\left(\frac{1}{b_1} - 1\right)$ *and* $b_1 \neq 0$*, the unique fixed-point is globally saddle-path stable, i. e. one eigenvalue is greater than 1, the other smaller than* $|1|$*;*

(ii) if not, the fixed-point is asymptotically unstable, i. e. both eigenvalues are greater than $|1|$.

This result shows the main difference between Galor's two-sector OLG-model with *homogeneous* capital and our two-sector OLG-model with *heterogeneous* capital: While in Galor's homogeneous-capital model there are parameter constellations which imply locally asymptotical *stable* fixed-points in our model the fixed-point is either *saddle-point stable* or *asymptotically unstable* but *never asymptotically stable..*

REFERENCES:

K. FARMER (1993), On the equilibrium dynamics of a two-sector overlapping-generations model with heterogeneous capital goods, unpubl. manuscript, Graz.

O. GALOR (1992), A two-sector overlapping-generations model: a global characterization of the dynamical system, in: *Econometrica* 60 (6), 1351-1386.

K-I. INADA (1966), Investment in fixed capital and the stability of growth equilibrium, in: *Review of Economic Studies* 33, 19-29.

M. MORISHIMA (1977), *Walras'Economics*, Cambridge, C.U.P.

H. UZAWA (1961), On a two-sector model of economic growth, in: *Review of Economic Studies* 29, 40-47.

NEW RESULTS ON A NEWTON-TYPE METHOD FOR LCP

Andreas Fischer
Department of Mathematics
Dresden University of Technology
Mommsenstr. 13, D-01062 Dresden

For treating monotone linear complementarity problems (LCP) a damped Newton-type method has been suggested recently, see Fischer(1992). It is based on an transformation of the LCP

$$Mx + q - y = 0, \quad x^T y = 0, \quad x \geq 0, \quad y \geq 0,$$

where the positive semidefinite matrix M and the vector $q \in R^n$ are given, into the equivalent nonlinear system of equations

$$T(x,y) := \begin{bmatrix} Mx + q - y \\ \phi(x^1, y^1) \\ \vdots \\ \phi(x^n, y^n) \end{bmatrix} = 0$$

with the mapping $\phi : R^2 \to R$ defined by $\phi(a,b) := \sqrt{a^2 + b^2} - a - b$.

Beside some global convergence results (obtained by a step length procedure and a suitable perturbation of the iterates) it could be shown that the method converges locally Q-quadratically to a solution, if the LCP is uniquely solvable and the solution (x^*, y^*) satisfies a strong second order condition

$$x^T M x > 0 \text{ for all } x \neq 0 \text{ with } x^i = 0 \text{ if } y^{*i} > 0. \tag{1}$$

However, no strict complementarity condition $(x^* + y^* > 0)$ is required. Moreover, practical experience shows that the method frequently converges superlinearly also if this second order condition is violated. The paper summarizes results which give a theoretical background for this observation. Some relations to interior-point methods are discussed.

THE ALGORITHM

Compared with the cited paper the algorithm given below uses a different perturbation rule, cf. Fischer(1993). The merit function $\tau : R^n \times R^n \to R$ is defined by $\tau(x,y) := \|T(x,y)\|$, where $\|.\|$ denotes the maximum-norm for vectors or a compatible matrix norm.

S0: Choose $(x_0, y_0) \in R^n \times R^n$ and $\mu \in (0, \frac{1}{2}]$. Set $k := 0$.

S1: If $\tau(x_k, y_k) = 0$, then stop.

S2: Determine $(\Delta x_k, \Delta y_k) \in R^n \times R^n$ such that

$$G(x_k, y_k)\begin{pmatrix}\Delta x_k\\ \Delta y_k\end{pmatrix} + T(x_k, y_k) = 0$$

S3: Find the largest number $t_k \in \{ (\frac{1}{2})^j \mid j \in N\}$ such that

$$\tau(x_k + t_k\Delta x_k\, ,\, y_k + t_k\Delta y_k) \le (1 - \mu\, t_k)\tau(x_k, y_k).$$

Set $x_{k+1} := x_k + t_k\Delta x_k$, $y_{k+1} := y_k + t_k\Delta y_k$ and $k := k + 1$.

Go to S1.

In view of the subsequent definition the matrix $G(x, y)$ can be regarded as a perturbation of the Jacobian $\nabla T(x, y)$ if it exists. Let

$$G(x,y) := \begin{bmatrix} M & -\mathrm{diag}(-1) \\ \mathrm{diag}(\gamma^i(x,y)) & \mathrm{diag}(\nu^i(x,y)) \end{bmatrix},$$

where for $i \in I := \{1, \ldots, n\}$ with $(x^i, y^i) \neq (0, 0)$ the entries of the diagonal matrices are given by

$$\gamma^i(x,y) := \begin{cases} \partial_1\phi(x^i, y^i) & \text{if } |\partial_1\phi(x^i, y^i)| > \sigma(x^i) \\ -\sigma(x^i) & \text{otherwise} \end{cases}$$

$$\nu^i(x,y) := \begin{cases} \partial_2\phi(x^i, y^i) & \text{if } |\partial_2\phi(x^i, y^i)| > \sigma(y^i) \\ -\sigma(y^i) & \text{otherwise} \end{cases}$$

with $\sigma(a) := 0.01(1 + a^2)^{-1} \min\{\tau^2(x, y), 1\}$ for $a \in R$.
Also for nondifferentiable points of T the matrix $G(x, y)$ is well defined by setting $\gamma^i(x, y) := -1$ and $\nu^i(x, y) := -\sigma(0)$ for the case that $(x^i, y^i) = (0, 0)$.

RESULTS

Let us denote the solution set of the LCP by $S(M, q)$. Moreover, the distance of a point $z \in R^n \times R^n$ from a nonempty set $W \subset R^n \times R^n$ is given by $\mathrm{dist}[z, W] := \inf_{w \in W} \|z - w\|$

Theorem 1:
For all starting vectors (x_0, y_0) the algorithm is well defined. Each accumulation point of the sequence $\{(x_k, y_k)\}$ solves the LCP.

For $\alpha \in [0, \frac{1}{2})$ let ϵ_α be defined by $\epsilon_\alpha := \min\{\epsilon, \epsilon^{1/(2\alpha - 1)}\}$.

Theorem 2:
Let the solution set $S(M,q)$ of the LCP be nonempty and bounded. Then, there exists $\epsilon > 0$ such that the following holds:
If there is $\alpha \in [0, \frac{1}{2})$ and $k_0 \in N$ with

$$\text{dist}[(x_{k_0}, y_{k_0}), S(M,q)] \leq \epsilon_\alpha, \tag{2}$$

$$\max\{x^i_{k_0}, y^i_{k_0}\} \geq 2\tau(x_{k_0}, y_{k_0})^\alpha \quad (i \in I) \tag{3}$$

then

$$t_k = 1 \quad \text{and} \quad \tau(x_{k+1}, y_{k+1}) \leq C\tau(x_k, y_k)^{2-\alpha}$$

is valid for all $k \geq k_0$ with some constant $C \geq 1$.

Theorem 3:
In addition to the assertion of Theorem 2 (and under the assumptions used there) there exists a constant $\bar{C} \geq 1$ such that

$$\text{dist}[(x_{k+1}, y_{k+1}), S(M,q)] \leq \bar{C}\text{dist}[(x_k, y_k), S(M,q)]^{2-\alpha}$$

for all $k \geq k_0$.

REMARKS

Remark 1:
In contrast to interior-point methods no polynomial complexity is known for the method described above. However, the iterates (x_k, y_k) are not restricted to the positive orthant R^n_{++}. Moreover, in case that the LCP has an unique solution (x^*, y^*), which satisfies the strong second order condition (1) but violates the strict complementarity condition, then whereas the described algorithm converges Q-quadratically a number of interior-point methods cannot converge locally superlinearly, see Ye/Anstreicher(1991).

Remark 2:
For proving the above results on superlinear convergence in particular some ideas developed for interior point methods (see e.g. Kojima/Mizuno/Yoshise(1991), Wright(1992)) were suitably modified, for details see Fischer(1993). By the definition of $G(x,y)$, (in general) as a special perturbation of $\nabla T(x,y)$, the local convergence behaviour of the present algorithm becomes similar to such interior-point methods.

Remark 3:
The assumptions of Theorem 2 imply the existence of a strict copmlementary solution $(\hat{x}, \hat{y}) \in S(M,q)$. Whereas for the special case of an arbitrary solvable linear program written as LCP such a solution exists, this need not hold for general solvable monotone LCP. Although (in contrast to some interior-point methods) there is no guarantee, that in

the sense of conditions (2) and (3) a certain iterate (x_{k_0}, y_{k_0}) is sufficiently close to such a strict complementary solution, almost all tests showed a superlinear convercence behaviour. The closer is α to $\frac{1}{2}$ the weaker is condition (3) but the smaller is ϵ_α. It is not clear what happens if $\alpha \in (\frac{1}{2}, 1]$.

Remark 4:
Note, that without additional assumtions or modifications the existence of an accumulation point of the iterates (cf. Theorem 1) is not ensured.

REFERENCES

Fischer, A.: A globally and locally quadratically convergent Newton-type method for positive semidefinite linear complementarity problems. Preprint MATH-NM-04-1992, Department of Mathematics, University of Technology Dresden, submitted for publication.

Fischer, A.: On the local superlinear convergence of a Newton-type method for LCP under weak conditions. Preprint MATH-NM-07-1993, Department of Mathematics, University of Technology Dresden

Kojima, M.; Mizuno, S.: Yoshise, A.: An $O(\sqrt{n}L)$ iteration potential reduction method for linear complementarity problems. Mathematical Programming 50(1991), 331-342

Wright, S. J.: An infeasible interior point algorithm for linear complementarity problems. Preprint MCS-P331-0991, Mathematics and Computer Science Division, Argonne National Laboratory, Argonne, IL 1992

Ye, Y.; Anstreicher, K.: On quadratic and $O(\sqrt{n}L)$ convergence of a predictor-corrector algorithm for the linear complementarity problem. Working Paper 91-20, Department of Management Sciences, University of Iowa City, Iowa City, IA, 1991 to appear

ROUTING IN MESHES USING LINEAR ASSIGNMENT PROBLEM

D. Fortin A. Tusera
INRIA
Domaine de Voluceau
Rocquencourt B.P. 105
78153 Le Chesnay Cedex
FRANCE

Introduction

Given a 2D array of nodes (either switches at a circuit level or PEs at an interconnection network level), and given a related set of statically known nets, we aim at routing each net such that the final routes use only lowest level of edges in the array and no short-circuit occurs. From practice, we learnt that simulated annealing may fail to route some very regular problem although we was able to route it by hand; so, we try to pose this problem in a different framework to take into account the deficiencies of simulated annealing. Finally, we conjecture that an algorithm which respects the topology of the given network (here a grid) will be able to make a global decision early in the process, avoiding *desperate* local decision late in the process. This leads to a divide-and-conquer scheme on a quad-tree basis in our case: for each net crossing the subdivision, we (partially) route it using only free edges at the corresponding level (from coarsest to finest) and we prevent infeasibility of further subproblems by checking that the number of crossing in every row and column of finer levels is less than the number of nodes in it. Writing down all of these conditions amounts to the three-dimensional linear assignment problem with side constraints (3D-LAP):

$$\max_x z = \sum_{i=1}^{n} \sum_{j=1}^{m} \sum_{k=1}^{p} c_{ijk} x_{ijk} \tag{1}$$

$$\sum_{j=1}^{m} \sum_{k=1}^{p} x_{ijk} \leq 1 \ , \ \forall i \tag{2}$$

$$\sum_{i=1}^{n} \sum_{k=1}^{p} x_{ijk} \leq 1 \ , \ \forall j \tag{3}$$

$$\sum_{i=1}^{n} \sum_{j=1}^{m} x_{ijk} \leq 1 \ , \ \forall k \tag{4}$$

$$\sum_{i=1}^{n} \sum_{j=1}^{m} \sum_{k=1}^{p} a_{ijkl} x_{ijk} \leq b_l \ , \ \forall l \qquad , \text{ where } b_l \leq \max(m,p) \tag{5}$$

$$x_{ijk} \in \{0,1\} \tag{6}$$

1 Removing constraints

The very particular structure of the right handside of the constraints (it remains less than the number of nodes in the checked edge) affords to remove every constraint by introducing 2 new dimensions; it yields to a *standard* sparse 5D-LAP. The only trick relies on the magnitude of the introduced costs to guarantee that the optimum do not lay in the empty part. Following Frieze and Yadegar (1981), we state a decomposition theorem: any nD-LAP is decomposable in a direct product of 2D-LAP ⊗ (n-1)D-LAP by relaxing n-2 dimensions; in above case, it means to solve 5D-LAP as a 2D-LAP ⊗ (2D-LAP ⊗ 3D-LAP). The 3D-LAP involved in this sequence happens to be crucial since 2D-LAP is known to have a polynomial time solution.

2 Solving 3D-LAP

Balas and Saltzman (1991) reported that subgradient method with Lagrangean multipliers associated to trivial facets has a tendency to zig-zag among a set of lower and upper bounds and consequently, to fail in difficult problems. So, they introduced class 2 cliques of the intersection graph (defined in Balas and Saltzman (1989)) as a Lagrangean relaxation technique : they reported an improved behavior of subgradient method but some shadow remains about the different parameters used.

3 An improved heuristic for 3D-LAP

Let us assume a cube problem of size n, Balas and Saltzman's improvement requires $o(n^3)$ Lagrangean multipliers; this strongly limits the use of added facets ($o(n^6)$ class 3 cliques, $o(n^5)$ facets associated to shortest odd-holes (length 5) and an exponential growth of facets associated to longer odd holes). We propose to adopt the following heuristic about introducing facets relaxation :

1. look for facets in a neigborhood of the current lower and upper bound ; we only introduce facets violated by upper bound and satisfied with equality by lower bound. This drastically cuts the number of corresponding facets ($o(n)$ class 2 cliques, $o(n^2)$ class 3 cliques and $o(n^3)$ facets associated to length 5 odd-holes. In a first attempt, we tried a less strict neighborhood of the lower bound (a ball around the lower bound at increasing distance from it) without improved results ($o(n^2)$ class 2 such cliques). Of course, we substitute a new set of facets whenever the current one is fully satisfied,

2. separate step lengths ; in standard method, a trust region is defined to estimate parameter applied to multiplier computation, yielding a half credit to unique step length ; we successfully split the trust region according to the different facets used (half credit for trivial facets then half credit of remaining part for class 2 cliques etc...)

3. weighted importance of step lengths ; the more we get closer to the optimum (given by the gap between upper and lower bound objective function), the less we give credit to trivial facets since they are a local approximation of the polytope worse than non trivial facets.

All our tests confirm that neighborhood and separate step lengths on class 2 cliques compare favorably to Balas and Saltzman's improvement (the same number of iteration upto 2 or 3) with the reported saving in the number of multipliers. We are currently under incorporating class 3 cliques.

We are aware of *standard* Camerini, Fratta and Maffioli (1975) improvement related to a trust region in computed direction of subgradient ; a second order correction of direction is brought to the new direction with keeping track of the former one ; here too, a half credit in the new direction is adopted. While we have checked that this technique prevents zig-zaging as well, we do not still introduce it in our experimentations, leaving a gap for improvements.

4 Conclusion

We proposed to deal with static routing in a 2D array in a more parallel framework than simulated annealing. In the course of comparing this approach with the latter one, we faced a nD-LAP problem which has been studied to our knowledge, upto $n = 3$; we proposed an improved heuristic to solve difficult problems. This technique does not depends on the n-dimensional figure, so we will try it in future work to the nD-LAP Polytope whose structure is much more complex than 3D-LAP since webs and antiwebs occur in intersection graph whenever n is over 4.

References

[Bal89] M.J. Balas, E. Saltzman. Facets of the three-index assignment polytope. *Discrete Applied Mathematics*, 23:201–229, January-February 1989.

[BS91] E. Balas and M.J. Saltzman. An algorithm for the three-index assignment problem. *Operations Research*, 39(1):150–161, January-February 1991.

[CM75] L. Camerini, P.M. Fratta and F. Maffioli. On improving relaxation methods by modified gradient techniques. *Mathematical Programming Study*, 3:26–34, 1975.

[FY81] A.M. Frieze and J. Yadegar. An algorithm for solving 3-dimensional assignment problem with application to scheduling a teaching practice. *J.Oper.Res.Soc*, 32:989–995, 1981.

On Stochastic Dynamic Optimization in Discrete Time

Karl Frauendorfer

Institute for Operations Research
University of St. Gallen
Bodanstr. 6, CH-9000 St. Gallen

We consider the following stochastic control problem of discrete finite time with full state information

$$\phi(x_0) := \min\ E_\pi\ [\sum_{t=0}^{T-1} \rho_t(\eta_t, x_t, \pi_t(x_t)) + b(x_T)]$$
$$s.t.\ x_{t+1} = f_t(x_t, \pi_t(x_t), \xi_t) \quad t = 0, 1, \cdots, T-1 \tag{1}$$

X_t and U_t denote the state space and the control space both equipped with the Borel field. The objective is to minimize the total expected cost over all admissible *control policies* $\pi = \{\pi_t; t = 0, \cdots, T-1\}$ where $\pi_t : X_t \to U_t$. The dynamical system is characterized through the state equations in (1). Let $(\eta_t, \xi_t) \in \mathbb{R}^{K_t} \times \mathbb{R}^{L_t}$ $(t = 0, \cdots, T-1)$ denote the random disturbances of the dynamical system, which may depend on current state x_t. The corresponding probability measure is therefore a *transition probability* denoted $P(\eta_t, \xi_t | x_t)$. The control action $u_t = \pi_t(x_t)$ has to be chosen prior to the outcome (η_t, ξ_t). State x_t is random as it depends on the uncertain outcome ξ_t; additionally, x_t depends on the control policy π_{t-1} so that the expectational operator E in (1) is taken with respect to the underlying policy π. (Measurability and integrability of the involved functions are assumed.)

The dynamic version of control problem (1) is given through backwards recursion for $t = T-1, \cdots, 0$

$$\phi_T(x_T) = b(x_T) \tag{2.1}$$

$$\phi_t(x_t) := \min_{u_t \in U_t} \int \rho_t(x_t, u_t, \eta_t) + \phi_{t+1}(f_t(x_t, u_t, \xi_t))\ dP_t(\eta_t, \xi_t | x_t) \tag{2.2}$$

yielding the optimal value $\phi_0(x_0)$ of problem (1).

Many practical problems (e.g. in finance, economics) require that decisions be made periodically over time with respect to uncertain (random) data. Thinking of problems in the field of asset and liability management (e.g.), one may model the stochastic interest rates as η_t and the stochastic volumes of assets or liabilities as ξ_t.)
If the probability measure of the random data (η_t, ξ_t) depends on the state or decision we are in the *control* case (see e.g. [1],[2], [4],[10],[13],[14]). To the contrary, if (η_t, ξ_t) depends on the history $(\eta_1, \xi_1), \cdots, (\eta_{t-1}, \xi_{t-1})$ then we are in the *multistage*

case (see e.g. [3],[5],[7],[11],[12]). The difference is seen mainly in the methodologies, which can be usefully applied: discretizing the probability measure in the multistage setting, yields multistage programs, for which structural properties (like convexity of the involved functions in the state and decision variables) may be exploited through well-established methods within mathematical programming. In control problems convexity is unlikely preserved after integration and minimization in (2), if the probability measure depends on current state, as in the above. This requires the application of the dynamic programming technique, which on the one hand requires the Markovian property of the state equation. On the other hand, dynamic programming leads to a globally optimal solution (as opposed to various mathematical programmaing methods) and has a wider scope of applicability, since it can handle difficult constraints sets such as discrete sets.

From a computational view point the curse of dimensionality amounts to computational complexities (inherent in both cases), which are in many cases insurmountable. Apart from special cases this requires to discretize the spaces so that the minimization and integration is carried out for an affordable number of discretization points. Here, we shall focus on discretizing the probability space.

For any state x_t at time t we denote with $\Theta_t(x_t)$, $\Xi_t(x_t)$ regular simplices in $\mathbb{R}^{K_t}, \mathbb{R}^{L_t}$, where $\Theta_t(x_t) \times \Xi_t(x_t)$ is supposed to cover the support of (η_t, ξ_t). Let $Q_t^l(\eta_t, \xi_t|x_t)$ and $Q_t^u(\eta_t, \xi_t|x_t)$ be the associated barycentric approximations (see [6],[8]) on $(\Theta_t(x_t) \times \Xi_t(x_t), \mathcal{B}^{K_t+L_t})$ with $\mathcal{B}^{K_t+L_t}$ being the Borel field. Then, in case that the integrands $(\eta_t, \xi_t) \to \rho_t(x_t, u_t, \eta_t) + \phi_{t+1}(f_t(x_t, u_t, \xi_t))$ are continuous saddle functions on $\mathbb{R}^{K_t} \times \mathbb{R}^{L_t}$ for any feasible (x_t, u_t), we obtain due to [8] :

$$\begin{aligned} &\int [\rho_t(x_t, u_t, \eta_t) + \phi_{t+1}(f_t(x_t, u_t, \xi_t))] dQ_t^l(\eta_t, \xi_t|x_t) \leq \\ \leq &\int [\rho_t(x_t, u_t, \eta_t) + \phi_{t+1}(f_t(x_t, u_t, \xi_t))] dP_t(\eta_t, \xi_t|x_t) \leq \\ \leq &\int [\rho_t(x_t, u_t, \eta_t) + \phi_{t+1}(f_t(x_t, u_t, \xi_t))] dQ_t^u(\eta_t, \xi_t|x_t). \end{aligned} \tag{3}$$

According to [8], we define auxiliary functions $\psi_{t-1}(x_{t-1})$, $\Psi_{t-1}(x_{t-1})$ backwards for $t = T-1, \cdots, 0$:

$$\psi_T(x_T) = b(x_T) = \Psi_T(x_T) \tag{4.1}$$

$$\psi_t(x_t) := \min_{u_t \in U_t} \int [\rho_t(x_t, u_t, \eta_t) + \psi_{t+1}(f_t(x_t, u_t, \xi_t))] dQ_t^l(\eta_t, \xi_t|x_t) \tag{4.2}$$

$$\Psi_t(x_t) := \min_{u_t \in U_t} \int [\rho_t(x_t, u_t, \eta_t) + \Psi_{t+1}(f_t(x_t, u_t, \xi_t))] dQ_t^u(\eta_t, \xi_t|x_t) \tag{4.3}$$

and get minorants and majorants for the value functions of the given problem; i.e.

$$\psi_t(x_t) \leq \phi_t(x_t) \leq \Psi_t(x_t) \; . \tag{5}$$

At each time we obtain lower and upper values for the given state, anticipating optimal policies in the future, which provide information on the goodness of the current approximation.

If the distribution functions of the transition probabilities $P_t(\eta_t, \xi_t | x_t)$ can be modelled as $R_t((\eta_t + H_t^\Theta(x_t), \xi_t + H_t^\Xi(x_t)$ - where R_t denotes a regular distribution function and $H_t^\Theta(x_t), H_t^\Xi(x_t)$ are mappings with proper dimensions - then the integral becomes

$$\int [\rho_t(x_t, u_t, \eta_t - H_t^\Theta(x_t)) \ + \phi_{t+1}(f_t(x_t, u_t, \xi_t - H_t^\Xi(x_t))] dR_t(\eta_t, \xi_t). \qquad (6)$$

We note that the saddle property of the integrand in (6) is preserved for any x_t. This allows to determine the barycentric approximations - denoted $R_t^l(\eta_t, \xi_t)$, $R_t^u(\eta_t, \xi_t)$ - of the probability measure given by $R_t(\eta_t, \xi_t)$. The associated corresponding auxiliary functions read as

$$\psi_t(x_t) := \min_{u_t \in U_t} \int \rho_t(x_t, u_t, \eta_t - H_t^\Theta(x_t)) + \phi_{t+1}(f_t(x_t, u_t, \xi_t - H_t^\Xi(x_t)) \ dR_t^l(\eta_t, \xi_t)$$

$$(7)$$

$$\Psi_t(x_t) := \min_{u_t \in U_t} \int \rho_t(x_t, u_t, \eta_t - H_t^\Theta(x_t)) + \phi_{t+1}(f_t(x_t, u_t, \xi_t - H_t^\Xi(x_t)) \ dR_t^u(\eta_t, \xi_t).$$

The advantageous feature of the above transformation is that we may now apply the barycentric approximations (as outlined in [6], [8]) *independent* of the current state. This certainly reduces the complexity with respet to the probability space. The goodness of the approximate problems induced by (7) can be improved through simplicial partitions of the underlying probability spaces (in a similar way as in [6]). If the sequences of partitions represent refinements then monotonicity of the auxiliary functions follows immediately from Theorem 16.2 in [6], implying that the corresponding approximate values behave monotonously. If, additionally, the cells become arbitrarily small (w.r.t. the diameter) and the integrands, value functions respeectively, are lower-semicontinuous in (x_t, u_t), in x_t respectively, pointwise- and epi-convergence of the auxiliary functions can be shown.
The price we have to pay for the transformation in (6) is that cost function and state equation loose linear or quadratic terms with respect to state x_t and decision u_t in case of control problem (1) being linear-quadratic.

References

1. M. AOKI: *Optimization of Stochastic Systems - Topics in Discrete-Time Dynamics*; Academic Press 1989

2. D. P. BERTSEKAS: *Dynamic Proramming - Deterministic and Stochastic Models*; Prentice-Hall 1987

3. J. BIRGE and R. J.-B. WETS: *Stochastic Programming, Part I, II*; Proceedings of the 5th International Conference on Stochastic Programming, Ann Arbor, Michigan, August 13-18, 1989; Annals of Operations Research 30-31 (1991)

4. M.A.H. DEMPSTER: On Stochastic Programming II: Dynamic Problems Under Risk; Research Report DAL TR 86-5, Dalhousie University (1986)

5. Y. ERMOLIEV and R. J.-B. WETS: *Numerical Techniques for Stochastic Optimization*; Springer-Verlag (1988)

6. K. FRAUENDORFER: *Stochastic Two-Stage Programming*; Lecture Notes in Economics and Mathematical Systems 392, Springer-Verlag (1992)

7. K. FRAUENDORFER: Multistage Stochastic Programming: Error Analysis for the Convex Case; (to appear in *Zeitschrift for Operations Research* 39/1 1994)

8. K. FRAUENDORFER: Stochastic Dynamic Optimization: Modelling and Methodological Aspects; Working Paper, Institute for Operations Research, University of St. Gallen 1994

9. K. FRAUENDORFER: Barycentric Scenario Trees in Convex Multistage Stochastic Programming; Working Paper, Institute for Operations Research, University of St. Gallen 1994

10. O. HERNANDEZ-LERMA and W. J. RUNGGALDIER : Monotone Approximations for Convex Stochastic Control Problems; (to appear in *Journal of Estimation, Control and Systems* 1993)

11. R.T. ROCKAFELLAR and R. J.-B. WETS: Nonanticipativity and L^1-Martingales in Stochastic Optimization Problems; *Math. Prog. Study* 6 (1976) 170-187

12. R.T. ROCKAFELLAR and R. J.-B. WETS: The Optimal Recourse Problem in Discrete Time: L^1-Multipliers for Inequality Constraints; *SIAM J. Control and Optimization* 16/1 (1978) 16-36

13. R.T. ROCKAFELLAR and R. J.-B.- WETS: Generalized Linear-Quadratic Problems of Deterministic and Stochastic Optimal Control in Discrete Time; *SIAM J. Control and Optimization* 28/4 (1990) 810-822

14. P. VARAIYA and R. J.-B. WETS: Stochastic Dynamic Optimization: Approaches and Computation; in. M. Iri, K. Tanabe (eds.), Mathematical Programming (KTKSci Publ.) Tokyo (1990) 309-332

A Reexamination of Utility Functions Derived from Demand Functions

Susanne Fuchs-Seliger
Institut für Wirtschaftstheorie und OR
Universität (TH) Karlsruhe

1. Introduction

In this paper the existence of a continuous utility function generating a given demand function will be reconsidered. We shall see that Hurwicz' and Uzawa's hypotheses [5], together wih certain additional conditions, imply the existence of a continuous utility function on the range of the demand function. Specifically, taking results of A. Mas-Codell [7] and M. Jackson [6] further, it will be shown that non-inferior demand functions can also be generated by continuous utility functions when, more generally, the range S of these demand functions is a convex subset of $\mathbb{R}^n_+$. Therefore, the range of the demand functions may also be a ray from the origin. In the theory of revealed preference A. Mas-Colell has been concerned with the continuity of a generating utility function in the case when the demand function is non-inferior and has the range $\mathbb{R}^n_{++}$. In integrability theory, M.Jackson [6] assumed strong non-inferiority instead of non-inferiority in order to show the existence of a continuous utility function generating the given demand function when the demand function has the range $\mathbb{R}^n_+$ (Theorem 2 in [6]). However, as we will see, our weaker condition is sufficient. In contrast to Jackson and Mas-Colell in this paper another method of proof, which is by supporting hyperplanes, is applied in order to show the existence of a continuous utility function generating a given demand function. This method of proof will be applied not only in integrability theory but also in the theory of revealed preference. Finally, we will establish two further conditions under which continuity of the generating utility function can be shown.

2. Non-Inferior Demand Functions and Continuous Utility Functions

We start our investigation of continuous utility functions in integrability theory recalling the conditions of Hurwicz and Uzawa [5].

(A) The mapping h: $\mathbb{R}^n_{++} \times \mathbb{R}_+ \to \mathbb{R}^n_+$, $x = h(p,M)$, is supposed to be the individual's demand function. We denote a price vector by p, the individual's income by M and a commodity bundle by x;

(B) h satisfies the budget equality $p \cdot h(p,M)=M$, $\forall\, p \in \mathbb{R}^n_{++}$, $M \in \mathbb{R}_+$;

(C) for every $i \leq n$ the demand for the ith commodity $x_i = h_i(p,M)$ possesses a differential,

(D) for any real numbers a', a" with $0 < a' < a''$ there exists a positive real number $K_{a'a''}$ such that for each i=1,2,3,...,n the inequality

$$\left|\frac{\partial h_i(p,M)}{\partial M}\right| \leq K_{a'a''},$$

for all $(p,M) \in \mathbb{R}^n_{++} \times \mathbb{R}_+$, and $a' \leq p_j \leq a''$, j=1,2,...,n holds;

(E) the corresponding Slutzky-Hicks matrix is symmetric and negative semidefinite.

Under these conditions for some fixed $p^* \in \mathbb{R}^n_{++}$ there exists an upper semicontinuous utility function $U_{p^*}(x)$ generating[1] h, such that

$$U_{p^*}(x) = \mu(p^*;p,M),$$

and (p,M) is any pair with $(p,M) \in \mathbb{R}^n_{++} \times \mathbb{R}_+$ for which $x = h(p,M)$, (see [5], p.125).

The function $\mu(p;p°,M°)$ is the solution of the system of partial differential equations

$$\frac{\partial \mu(p;p^0,M^0)}{\partial p_i} = h_i(p,\mu(p;p^0,M^0)),$$

together with $\mu(p°;p°,M°)=M°$, given the initial value $(p°,M°) \in \mathbb{R}^n_{++} \times \mathbb{R}_+$ (see[5],p.124).

Throughout this paper the range of h will be denoted by S. We will consider another condition, which together with the hypotheses (A)-(E) yields continuity of $U_{p^*}(x)$ on S, where S is a convex subset of $\mathbb{R}^n_+$. This condition is:

(γ) $M > M' \Rightarrow h(p,M) \geqq h(p,M'),\ \forall p \in IR^n_{++}$ and $M, M' \in IR_+$.

Demand functions satisfying condition (γ) are called "non-inferior". Since the budget equality is assumed, condition (γ) is equivalent to:

(γ') $M > M' \Rightarrow h(p,M) \geqq h(p,M') \wedge h(p,M) \neq h(p,M'),\ \forall p \in IR^n_{++}$ and $M, M' \in IR_+$.

---

[1] $U_{p^*}(x)$ generates the given demand function means, for all x in the range of h such that $px \leq M$, $x \neq h(p,M) \Rightarrow U_{p^*}(h(p,M)) > U_{p^*}(x)$ (Hurwicz and Uzawa [5], Lemma 8)

Before we present the main result of this paper we shall establish an auxiliary lemma.

__Lemma 1__

Assume that h satisfies the conditions (A)-(E) and let S be a convex subset of the $\mathbb{R}^n_+$. Then for all $x \in S$: $R(x)=\{z \in S \mid U_{p^*}(z) \geq U_{p^*}(x)\}$ is a convex set.

The main result of our paper is the following:

__Theorem 1__

If a demand function $h : \mathbb{R}^n_{++} \times \mathbb{R}_+ \rightarrow \mathbb{R}^n_+$ satisfies the conditions (A)-(E) and (γ)

and has the range $S \subseteq \mathbb{R}^n_+$, where S is a convex set, then U_{p^*} is continuous on S.

The proof uses the notion of lower boundary points[2] and a theorem on supporting hyperplanes of convex sets.

In the theory of revealed preference it can also be shown that non-inferiority implies the existence of a continuous utility function generating the given demand function. We assume the following hypotheses (see [10] and [3]):

(AI) The demand function h: $\mathbb{R}^n_{++} \times \mathbb{R}_+ \rightarrow \mathbb{R}^n_+$, $x=h(p,M)$, is supposed to be continuous;

(AII) the range of h, denoted by S, is a convex subset of $\mathbb{R}^n_+$;

(AIII) $\forall\ (p,M) \in \mathbb{R}^n_{++} \times \mathbb{R}_+,\ p \cdot h(p,M) = M$;

(AIV) for any $p^\circ, p^1 \in \mathbb{R}^n_{++}$, and $p(t)=tp^\circ+(1-t)p^1$ for $t \in\ ]0,1[$, there exists $K \in \mathbb{R}_{++}$, such that $\forall\ t \in\ ]0,1[\ , \forall\ M',M'' > 0,\ \| h(p(t),M')-h(p(t),M'') \| \leq K | M'-M'' |$.

In order to establish the next hypothesis we must preliminarily recall the definition of the relation "revealed preferred" which is

$xRy :\Leftrightarrow \exists (p,M): x=h(p,M) \wedge py \leq M \wedge x \neq y.$

The next hypothesis requires R^* to be asymmetric:

(AV) $\quad xR^*y \Rightarrow \neg(yR^*x),\ \forall x,y \in S.$

(AV) is known as the Strong Axiom of Revealed Preference.

---

[2] Suppose X is a convex set. Then x° is called a "lower boundary point" of X, if x° is a boundary point of X and for all $x \in \overline{X}$ we have, $x \leq x^\circ \Rightarrow x=x^\circ$, where $\overline{X}$ denotes the closure of X.

Theorem 2

If we assume conditions (AI)-(AV) and (γ), then the existence of a continuous utility function generating the given demand function follows.

In the theory of revealed preference as well as in integrability theory the same method of proof leads to a continuous utility function generating a non inferior demand function.

The last theorem uses the conditions:

(α) For every sequence $<(p^k,M^k)>$ we have,

$$\left[\lim_{k\to\infty} h(p^k,M^k)=\bar{x}>0 \;\wedge\; \lim_{k\to\infty} p^k=\bar{p}\geq 0 \wedge \bar{p}\neq 0\right] \;\Rightarrow\; \bar{p}>0$$

and

(β) Consider $x^1=h(p^1,M^1)$ and $x^2=h(p^2,M^2)$. If $\neg(x^1>0)$ and $p^1x^1>p^1x^2$, then there exists $x^3=h(p^3,M^3)$ such that $x^3\leq x^1$, $x^1\neq x^3$, and $p^3x^2<p^3x^3$.

Then we can demonstrate

Theorem 3

Assume (α) and (β) and conditions (A)-(E) with the additional requirement that the range of h be the $\mathbb{R}^n_+$. Then the utility function U_{p^*} is continuous on $\mathbb{R}^n_+$.

References

[1] Debreu, G.: Theory of Value, New York 1959

[2] Fuchs-Seliger, S.: On the Continuity of Utility Function in the Theory of Revealed Preference. International Economic Review 41, 1988, pp. 69-78.

[3] Fuchs-Seliger, S.: On Continuous Utility Functions Derived from Demand Functions. Journal of Mathematical Economics, 12, 1983, pp. 19-32.

[4] Hurwicz, L. and Richter, M.: Revealed Preference without Demand Continuity Assumptions. In J.S. Chipman, et al., eds.: Preferences, Utility, and Demand, New York 1971, pp. 59-76.

[5] Hurwicz, L. and Uzawa, H.: On the Integrability of Demand Functions. In J.S. Chipman, et al., eds.: Preferences, Utility, and Demand, New York 1971, pp. 114-148.

[6] Jackson, M.O.: Integration of Demand and Continuous Utility Functions. Journal of Economic Theory, 38, 1986, pp. 298-312.

[7] Mas-Colell, A.: On Revealed Preference Analysis. Review of Economic Studies, 45, 1978, pp. 121-131.

[8] Nicaido, H.: Introduction on Sets and Mappings in Modern Economics, Amsterdam, London, 1970

[9] Stigum, B.P.: Revealed Preference - A Proof of Houthakker's Theorem. Econometrica, 41, 1973, pp. 411-423.

[10] Uzawa, H.: Preferences and Rational Choice in the Theory of Consumption. In J.S. Chipman, et al., eds.: Preferences, Utility, and Demand, New York 1971, pp. 7-28.

EXACT MATROID PARITY AND POLYNOMIAL IDENTITIES [1]

G. Galbiati, Università di Pavia, Pavia, Italy
F. Maffioli, Politecnico di Milano, Milano, Italy

1 Exact matroid parity

The main problem we consider looks for a base of exact value in an integrally weighted represented matroid subject to parity conditions: we call this problem Exact Parity Base (XPB). The problem is NP-complete since it generalizes Subset Sum [Garey & Johnson (1978)]. It is however solvable in random pseudo-polynomial (r.p.p.) time and algorithms for doing this are reviewed in this work. Challenging open problems are solving the corresponding optimization problem by a (random) polynomial algorithm and solving XPB in pseudo-polynomial time: this is sofar possible only for some special cases [Barahona & Pulleyblank (1987)].

We are given a matroid $(S, \mathcal{F})$, where S is the ground set and $\mathcal{F}$ is the family of the independent sets. We assume that the matroid has even rank $2n$ and is represented over the rationals by a matrix M. This means that: 1) there is a one-to-one correspondence between elements of S and columns of M; 2) independent sets in $\mathcal{F}$ correspond to sets of linearly independent columns of M; 3) a base of the matroid correspond to a full-rank square submatrix of M.

We further assume that the elements of the ground set are an even number $2m$ and are partitioned into m pairs. Hence $M = (\boldsymbol{a}_1 \mid \boldsymbol{b}_1 \mid \ \ldots \ \mid \boldsymbol{a}_m \mid \boldsymbol{b}_m)$, where for $j = 1, \ldots, m$, the symbol $\boldsymbol{a}_j$ (or $\boldsymbol{b}_j$) not only denotes a column of M, but also the corresponding element of S, and $\{\boldsymbol{a}_j, \boldsymbol{b}_j\}$ indicates the j-th pair of elements. A base of the form $\{\boldsymbol{a}_{j_1}, \boldsymbol{b}_{j_1}, \ldots, \boldsymbol{a}_{j_n}, \boldsymbol{b}_{j_n}\}$ is called a *parity base* of M, and is identified by the set $X = \{j_1, \ldots, j_n\} \subseteq \{1, \ldots, m\}$.

Should some elements of M be noninteger it would be immediate to obtain another $2n \times 2m$ matrix, having integer elements, and still representing $(S, \mathcal{F})$. Therefore, in the sequel we shall assume without loss of generality that the matroid will be represented by (and identified with) an integer matrix M. The XPB problem can be stated as follows.

Exact Parity Base (XPB)

Input - A represented matroid $M = (\boldsymbol{a}_1|\boldsymbol{b}_1| \ldots |\boldsymbol{a}_m|\boldsymbol{b}_m)$, of rank $2n$, whose columns are partitioned into m pairs $\{\boldsymbol{a}_j, \boldsymbol{b}_j\}$, $j \in E = \{1, \ldots, m\}$.

[1] Partially supported by a Research Project "Algoritmi, modelli di calcolo e strutture informative" of the Italian Ministry of University and Scientific and Technological Research.

- A nonnegative integer weight w_j, for each $j \in E$.

- A nonnegative integer W.

Output - YES, if there exists a parity base of M whose weight is exactly W, i.e. a set $X = \{j_1, \dots, j_n\} \subseteq E$ such that $(\boldsymbol{a}_{j_1}|\boldsymbol{b}_{j_1}|\dots|\boldsymbol{a}_{j_n}|\boldsymbol{b}_{j_n})$ has rank $2n$ and $\sum_{j \in X} w_j = W$.

- NO, otherwise.

Important special cases of XPB are the following

Exact Intersection Base (XIB)

Input - Two represented matroids of rank n, $M_1 = (\boldsymbol{a}_1 \mid \dots \mid \boldsymbol{a}_m)$ and $M_2 = (\boldsymbol{b}_1 \mid \dots \mid \boldsymbol{b}_m)$, with ground set $E = \{1, \dots, m\}$.

- A nonnegative integer weight w_j assigned to each $j \in E$.

- A nonnegative integer W.

Output - YES, if there exists an *intersection base* of M_1 and M_2 whose weight is exactly W, i.e. a set $X = \{j_1, \dots, j_n\} \subseteq E$ such that both $(\boldsymbol{a}_{j_1} \mid \dots \mid \boldsymbol{a}_{j_n})$ and $(\boldsymbol{b}_{j_1} \mid \dots \mid \boldsymbol{b}_{j_n})$ have rank n, and $\sum_{j \in X} w_j = W$.

- NO, otherwise.

Exact Perfect Matching (XPM)

Input - A graph $G = \{(1, \dots, 2n), E\}$ with $2n$ vertices and $m = \mid E \mid$ edges.

- A nonnegative integer weight w_e assigned to each edge $e \in E$.

- A nonnegative integer W.

Output - YES, if G contains a perfect matching X of weight exactly W, i.e. such that $\sum_{e \in X} w_e = W$.

- NO, otherwise.

2 Some algebraic results

In the following, matrices are on the integers and are written either in standard or in column notation. Let $\Gamma = (\gamma_{ij})$ be a $2n \times 2n$ skew-symmetric matrix and let P be the set of partitions into pairs of the set $(1, 2, \dots, 2n)$. If $\pi = \{\{i_1, j_1\}, \dots, \{i_n, j_n)\}\}$ is one of these partitions, let $\sigma(\pi)$ be the sign of the permutation

$$\begin{pmatrix} 1 & 2 & \dots & 2n-1 & 2n \\ i_1 & j_1 & \dots & i_n & j_n \end{pmatrix}$$

and let $\alpha(\pi) = \sigma(\pi) \prod_{h=1}^{n} \gamma_{i_h j_h}$. Then the *Pfaffian* of Γ is defined as [Lang (1965), Lovász & Plummer (1986)] $\text{pf}(\Gamma) = \sum_{\pi \in P} \alpha(\pi)$.

In [Galbiati & Maffioli (to appear)] an algorithm for exactly computing the Pfaffian of a $2n \times 2n$ integer matrix is described. This algorithm is inspired by the algorithm in [Edmonds (1967)] for computing determinants and requires $O(n^3)$ arithmetic operations in the ring of integers.

The first result we state in this section is contained in Theorem 1 which uses the notion of *wedge product* $\boldsymbol{u} \wedge \boldsymbol{v}$ of two (column) vectors $\boldsymbol{u} = (u_1, \dots, u_r)^T$, $\boldsymbol{v} = (v_1, \dots, v_t)^T$, defined as the $r \times r$ skew-symmetric matrix $W = (w_{ij})$, with $w_{ij} = u_i v_j - u_j v_i$, i.e. $\boldsymbol{u} \wedge \boldsymbol{v} = \boldsymbol{u}\boldsymbol{v}^T - \boldsymbol{v}\boldsymbol{u}^T$. The proof of Theorem 1 uses ideas contained in the proof of Theorem 3 of [Lovász (1979)], and is based on the two following lemmas.

Lemma 1. *For any pair of column vectors $\boldsymbol{u}$, $\boldsymbol{v}$ of dimension r, and any square matrix Γ of order r, $\Gamma\boldsymbol{u} \wedge \Gamma\boldsymbol{v} = \Gamma(\boldsymbol{u} \wedge \boldsymbol{v})\Gamma^T$.*

Lemma 2. *If $\Gamma = (\boldsymbol{u}_1 \mid \boldsymbol{v}_1 \dots \boldsymbol{u}_n \mid \boldsymbol{v}_n)$ is a $2n \times 2n$ matrix with n paired columns $\{\boldsymbol{u}_i, \boldsymbol{v}_i\}$, $i = 1, \dots, n$, and matrix Δ is defined as*

$$\Delta = \sum_{j=1}^{n} z_j(\boldsymbol{u}_j \wedge \boldsymbol{v}_j),$$

z_j being a variable associated with the pair of columns $\boldsymbol{u}_j$ and $\boldsymbol{v}_j$, then

$$\text{pf}\,(\Delta) = z_1, \dots, z_n \det\,(\Gamma).$$

Theorem 1. *Let M be a $2n \times 2m$ matrix with paired columns $(\boldsymbol{a}_1 \mid \boldsymbol{b}_1 \mid \dots \mid \boldsymbol{a}_m \mid \boldsymbol{b}_m)$, $m \geq n$. Consider the $2n \times 2n$ skew-symmetric matrix*

$$C = \sum_{j=1}^{m} z_j(\boldsymbol{a}_j \wedge \boldsymbol{b}_j),$$

z_j being a variable associated with the pair of columns $\boldsymbol{a}_j$ and $\boldsymbol{b}_j$. Then

$$\text{pf}\,(C) = \sum_{1 \leq j_1 < \dots\, j_n \leq m} z_j \,\dots\, z_{j_n} \delta(j_1, \dots, j_n)$$

where $\delta(j_1, \dots, j_n) = \det\,(\boldsymbol{a}_{j_1} \mid \boldsymbol{b}_{j_1} \mid \dots \mid \boldsymbol{a}_{j_n} \mid \boldsymbol{b}_{j_n})$.

For the proofs of all results reported above and in the following the reader is referred to [Camerini, Galbiati, Maffioli (1992)]. The second result of this section is Theorem 2, which can be seen as a consequence of Theorem 1.

Theorem 2. *Let M' be a $n \times 2m$ matrix with paired columns $(a'_1 \mid b'_1 \mid \ldots \mid a'_m \mid b'_m)$, $m \geq n$. Consider the square matrix of order n*

$$D = \sum_{j=1}^{m} z_j (a'_j b'^T_j),$$

z_j being a variable associated with the pair a'_j, b'_j. Then

$$\det(D) = \sum_{1 \leq j_1 < \ldots j_n \leq m} z_{j_1} \ldots z_{j_n} \delta'(j_1, \ldots, j_n)$$

where $\delta'(j_1, \ldots, j_n) = \det(a'_{j_1} \mid \ldots \mid a'_{j_n}) \det(b'_{j_1} \mid \ldots \mid b'_{j_n})$.

Finally, the last result we need is proved in [Schwartz (1980)] and is used in probabilistic methods for testing whether a polynomial is identically zero:

Theorem 3. *Let $Q(x)$, $x = (x_1, \ldots, x_m)$, be a polynonial of degree n in m variables. Let $\bar{x}$ be chosen randomly in $\{1, \ldots, J\}^m$, $J \in N$. If $Q(x) \not\equiv 0$, then $\Pr\{Q(\bar{x}) = 0\} \leq n/J$.*

3 Random pseudo-polynomial algorithms

To each instance of problem XPB we associate a $2n \times 2n$ skew-symmetric matrix C, defined as follows:

$$C = \sum_{j=1}^{m} x_j y^{w_j} (a_j \wedge b_j).$$

Notice that the j-th pair, $j \in E$, is tagged with a variable x_j and the variable y raised to a power corresponding to the weight of the pair, so that C depends on y and a vector $x = (x_1, \ldots, x_m)^T$. Therefore C can be denoted as $C(x, y)$.

Theorem 1 with $z_j = x_j y^{w_j}$, $j = 1, \ldots, m$, tells us that:

1. pf(C) is a polynomial in the variables $x_1, \ldots, x_m, y$ which can be written as

$$\sum_{1 \leq j_1 < \ldots < j_n \leq m} x_{j_1} \ldots x_{j_n} \, y^{\omega(j_1, \ldots, j_n)} \delta(j_1, \ldots, j_n)$$

   with $\omega(j_1, \ldots, j_n) = \sum_{1 \leq h \leq n} w_{j_h}$ and $\delta(j_1, \ldots, j_n) = \det(a_{j_1} \mid b_{j_1} \mid \ldots \mid a_{j_n} \mid b_{j_n})$;
2. each monomial of pf(C) corresponds to a parity base of M;
3. the degree of y in each monomial is the weight of the corresponding parity base.

It would however be a task of exponential complexity to obtain explicitly the monomials of pf(C), since this would amount to enumerate all parity bases of M. Instead, we may express the pfaffian of C as the following polynomial in y:

$$P(x,y) = \text{pf}\ (C(x,y)) = \sum_{t=0}^{p-1} Q_t(x)\ y^t,$$

where $p-1$ is any upper bound to the maximum weight of a parity base, and each coefficient $Q_t(x)$ is a polynomial in x sum of all terms

$$x_{j_1}\ \dots\ x_{j_n}\ \delta(j_1, \dots, j_n),$$

with $1 \leq j_1 < \dots < j_n \leq m$ corresponding to parity bases of weight t. It follows that there exists a parity base of weight W if and only if $Q_W(x) \not\equiv 0$.

Theorem 2 of Section 2 suggests therefore to test whether $Q_W(\bar{x}) \neq 0$, where $\bar{x}$ is a vector chosen randomly in $\{1, \dots, J\}^m$. Since $Q_W(\bar{x})$ is a specific coefficient of the polynomial $P(\bar{x}, y)$, its computation can be done for instance through polynomial interpolation, by evaluating $P(\bar{x}, y)$ for p different values of y.

The following procedure (where w is the vector with components w_j, $j \in E$) can thus be seen to be an r.p.p. algorithm for the XPB problem, with probability of a wrong answer bounded above by the rational $\varepsilon = 1/\rho$, ρ being a preassigned positive integer.

Procedure XPB (n, m, M, w, W, ρ):
1. find an integer p larger than the maximum weight of a parity base of M;
2. **if** $W \geq p$ **then return** 'NO';
3. $J := n\rho$;
4. choose randomly $\bar{x}$ in $\{1, \dots, J\}^m$;
5. compute the $2n \times 2n$ skew-symmetric matrix $C(\bar{x}, y) = \sum_{j=1}^m \bar{x}(a_j \wedge b_j) y^{w_j}$;
6. compute the coefficient $Q_W(\bar{x})$ of the term y^W of $P(\bar{x}, y) = \text{pf}(C(x, y))$;
   comment this computation can be done, for instance, by evaluating $P(x, y)$ for $y = 0, \dots, p-1$ and interpolating;
7. **return if** $Q_W(\bar{x}) = 0$ **then** 'NO' **else** 'YES'.

The previous discussion implies that if the matroid has no parity base of weight W, then procedure XPB always answers correctly, whereas the answer may be wrong when such a parity base exists. The probability of a wrong answer in the latter case is that of the event $Q_W(\bar{x}) = 0$, given $Q_W(x) \not\equiv 0$. By Theorem 3, this probability is not greater than $n/J = 1/\rho = \varepsilon$.

A careful analysis of the complexity of procedure XPB shows that it depends heavily on the way chosen to implement line 6. If the simple Newton's interpolation is utilized the algorithm requires $O(pn^2 m \log U + p^2)$ arithmetic operations (in the ring of integers), with $p = nU$, $U = \max\{w_j : j \in E\}$. Better complexity results can be obtained using more sophisticated interpolation techniques, more extensive randomization and faster arithmetics working over finite fields [Camerini, Galbiati, Maffioli (1990)].

Note that procedure XPB does not construct a parity base of weight W when the answer is 'YES'. If this is required, line 7 of XPB can be substituted by:

7. **return if** $Q_W(\bar{x}) = 0$ **then** 'NO' **else** XPBC ($\bar{x}$)

where XPBC(x) is the following deterministic procedure:

Procedure XPBC (x):
1. $X := \{i \in E : x_i \neq 0\}$;
2. **if** $|X| = n$ **then return** X **else**
    begin
3.   **comment** since $Q_W(x) \neq 0$, **then** $|X| > n$;
            repeat
4.   choose any $j \in X$;
5.   **for each** $i \in E - \{j\}$ **do** $x'_i := x_i$;
6. $x'_j := 0$;
7.   compute the coefficient $Q_W(x')$ of the term y^W of $P(x', y)$;
8. $X := X - \{j\}$
            until $Q_W(x') \neq 0$;
9.   XPBC(x')
    end

The correctness of procedure XPBC follows easily from ideas in the proof of Theorem 3 of [Lovász (1979)]. Specifically, for the set X computed in line 1, the following equality holds

$$\sum_{j \in X} Q_W(x^j) = (|X| - n) Q_W(x)$$

where x^j is the vector whose components are

$$x_i^j = \begin{cases} x_i & \text{if } i \in E - \{j\}, \\ 0 & \text{if } i = j. \end{cases}$$

As a consequence, at line 3 we do not only know that $|X| > n$ and $Q_W(x) \neq 0$, but also that $Q_W(x^j) \neq 0$ for at least one $j \in X$. Thus the loop beginning with line 4 must terminate for some vector x' satisfying the condition $Q_W(x') \neq 0$.

It is easy to see that the time complexity of XPBC is at most m times that of XPB.

For problems XIB and XPM special versions of the above procedures yield better worst-case complexities. In particular for XPM we have $O(pn^2 \log U + pn^3 + p^2)$ arithmetic operations.

The parallel complexity of XPB has been addressed in [Galbiati & Maffioli (1992)] where it is shown to be in the class arithmetic RNC^2 (under the similarity assumption).

4 Image problems

Weighted combinatorial problems (WCP) are in general defined on the basis of the following *input* data.

- *A ground set* $E = \{e_1, e_2, \dots, e_m\}$ of m elements;
- a nonempty family $\mathcal{F} \subseteq 2^E$ of *feasible sets*, defined concisely through an ad-hoc property π as

$$\mathcal{F} = \{I \subseteq E : \pi(I) \text{ is true}\};$$

- *a weighting function* $w : E \to Z$ of the elements of E into the integers;
- an *objective function* $f : 2^E \to Z$, extending w to the subsets of E.

The availability of two procedures which, using time polynomial in m, test membership in $\mathcal{F}$ and compute $f(I)$, respectively, for any given $I \subseteq E$, is assumed.

Given (the input of) a WCP, let

$$\begin{aligned}
\psi_1 &:= \min\{f(I) : I \in \mathcal{F}\}, \\
\psi_2 &:= \min\{f(I) : I \in \mathcal{F} \text{ and } f(I) > \psi_1\}, \\
&\vdots \\
\psi_k &:= \min\{f(I) : I \in \mathcal{F} \text{ and } f(I) > \psi_{k-1}\}, \\
&\vdots
\end{aligned}$$

and let K be the smallest integer s.t.

$$\{I : I \in \mathcal{F} \text{ and } f(I) > \psi_K\} = \phi.$$

We call the vector $\psi = (\psi_1, \psi_2, \dots, \psi_K)$ the *image* of the given WCP.

Let ξ be the event that *any one* among the values $Q_t(\bar{x})$, $t = 0, 1, \dots, p-1$ comes out to be zero, when the polynomial $Q_t(x)$ is not identically zero. Then from Theorem 3 it follows that the probability $\Pr(\xi)$ is not greater than pn/J.

Given n, p and a prescribed upper bound ε to $\Pr(\xi)$, i.e. to the probability of error, the required value of J is thus

$$J = \lceil \frac{pn}{\varepsilon} \rceil. \quad (1)$$

A random pseudo-polynomial procedure for computing the image of an instance of XPB is then the following:

Procedure PARIMAGE (n, m, M, w, J, p):
1. choose randomly $\bar{x} = (\bar{x}_1, \ldots, \bar{x}_m)$ in $\{1, \ldots, J\}^m$;
2. $C := (0)$;
3. **for** $i = 1$ to m **do** $C := C + \bar{x}_i y^{w_i}(a_i \wedge b_i)$;
4. compute the coefficients of the polynomial in y, $\mathrm{pf}(C) = \sum_{j=0}^{p-1} q_j y^j$;
5. $K := 0$;
6. **for** $j := 0$ to $p-1$ **do if** $q_j \neq 0$ **then**
   begin
7. $\quad \psi_k := j$;
8. $\quad K := K + 1$;
   end

It can be proved that the complexity of procedure PARIMAGE, in terms of arithmetic operations, is $O(n^2 m + pn^3 \log p)$, while it reduces to $O(pn^3 \log p)$ in the case of perfect matchings of a graph. These complexity results derive straightforwardly from those concerning algorithm 3 in [Camerini, Galbiati, Maffioli (1990)].

5 Extensions, open problems and final remarks

Let us first remark that multi-weighted versions of the exact problems reviewed in this work can also be addressed and solved with r.p.p. algorithms. The substantial difference in such solution algorithms consists in tagging each element of a k-weighted problem with the help of a vector $y = (y_1, \ldots, y_k)$ instead of a single variable y. This implies that in the algorithms the polynomials utilized in line 5 are multi-variable polynomials, requiring multi-variate interpolating techniques, as proposed for instance in [Camerini et alii (1992)].

Another remark is that some exact versions of min-cost (integral) flow problems are solvable by r.p.p. algorithms because of the close relationship between flow networks and matching optimization theory. In fact, it is well-known [Papadimitriou & Steiglitz (1982)] that the Minimum Cost Flow problem (minimizing the cost of a flow of prescribed value between a source and a sink, in a capacitated network) can be polynomially reduced to the Uncapacitated Transportation problem (minimizing the cost of a flow between sources and sinks, in an uncapacitated, bipartite network), which in turn can be transformed (via a pseudo-polynomial reduction [Lawler (1976)]) into the Minimum Cost Perfect Matching problem (minimizing the cost of a perfect matching in a bipartite graph). These two reductions are easily seen to preserve the costs of the corresponding integral solutions, and therefore they also apply to the exact versions of the same problems provided the underlying graph is acyclic.

From a practical point of view it is very important to explore if algebraic methods of the kind surveyed here could help solving optimization problems more efficiently: an important step in this direction would be to find a r.p. algorithm for finding a parity base of maximum weight in a given represented matroid.

For further applications in the realm of strongly NP-hard problems the reader is addressed to [Barvinok (1992)], whereas a recent contribution in the field of parallel algorithms and complexity taking advantage of similar techniques is [Narayanan, Saran, Vazirani (1992)].

References

Barahona F, Pulleyblank W R (1987) Exact arborescence, matching and cycles. Discrete Applied Mathematics 16: 91-100

Barvinok A I (1991) Optimization problems on matroids and exponential sums. Proc. 2nd IPCO Conference. Pittsburgh. 316-333

Camerini P M, Galbiati G, Maffioli F (1992) Random pseudo-polynomial algorithms for exact matroid problems. Journal of Algorithms 13: 258-273

Camerini P M, Galbiati G, Maffioli F (1991) The image of weighted combinatorial problems. Annals of Operations Research 33: 181-197

Camerini P M, Galbiati G, Maffioli F (1990) Modular arithmetic and randomization for exact matroid problems. Proc. of the 1st IPCO Conference. Waterloo. 101-114

Edmonds J (1967) System of distinct representatives and linear algebra. Journal of Research of the National Bureau of Standards B. 71; 241-245

Galbiati G, Maffioli F (to appear) On computation of Pfaffians

Galbiati G, Maffioli F (1992) Constructing an exact base is in RNC^2. Parallel Processing Letters 2: 301-309

Garey M, Johnson D (1978) Computers and Intractability. Freeman. San Francisco, CA

Lang S (1965) Algebra. Addison-Wesley. Reading, MA

Lawler E L (1976) Combinatorial Optimization: Networks and Matroids. Holt, Rinehart & Winston. New York

Lovász L (1979) On determinants, matchings and random algorithms. Fundamentals of Computation Theory 79: 565-574

Lovász L, Plummer D (1986) Matching Theory. North-Holland. Amsterdam

Narayanan H, Saran H, Vazirani V V (1992) Randomized parallel algorithms for matroid union and intersection, with application to arborescences, and edge-disjoint spanning trees. Proc. 3rd SODA. 357-366

Papadimitriou C H, Steiglitz K (1982) Combinatorial Optimization: Algorithms and Complexity. Prentice-Hall. Englewood Cliffs, WJ

Schwartz J T (1980) Fast probabilistic algorithms for verification of polynomial identities. Journal of the ACM 27: 701-717

Structural Exchange Rate Relationships in the Foreign Exchange Markets

Tilmann Gerhards
University of Karlsruhe
and
SGZ-Bank AG
P.O. Box 6960
D-76049 Karlsruhe
Germany

Introduction

Existing exchange rate theory concentrates on the two-country framework. But there is little empirical support for the validity of theoretical models such as monetary or asset market approaches to exchange rate determination. Moreover, only few papers discuss exchange rate behaviour within a multi-country framework. Therefore this paper instead focuses on the joint behaviour of five major bilateral U.S. dollar exchange rates since the breakdown of the Bretton-Woods system.

Considering the most important industrial countries the question arises, whether there exist valid long-run and/or short-run relationships among their exchange rates and, if being the case, whether plausible interpretations can be offered. Within this context it is also of an interest to evaluate aspects and influences of the Exchange Rate Mechanism of the European Monetary System (EMS).

Among others, multivariate cointegration methods are applied in this study. If a set of exchange rates is cointegrated then, although each series may be individually non-stationary (e.g. integrated of order one, I(1)), there must exist at least one linear combination which is stationary (I(0)). And this linear combination can be thought of as a long-run relationship where the exchange rate series tend to move together over time (see Engle and Granger [1987] for further details).

Econometric Methods

To evaluate the ideas from above the vector autoregression (VAR) framework is used. Consider a VAR of the following form

$$x_t = \Pi_1 x_{t-1} + \ldots + \Pi_k x_{t-k} + \epsilon_t, \ t=1,2, \ldots T, \qquad (1)$$

where x_t is a $(p \times 1)$ vector of I(1) variables, Π_i are $(p \times p)$ matrices of coefficients and ϵ_t is a vector of Gaussian errors. A maximum likelihood method to test for cointegration within a multivariate framework is provided by Johansen [1988] and Johansen and Juselius [1990], therefore we only give a brief description here.

Consider equation (1) in an error-correction-form:

$$\Delta x_t = \Gamma_1 \Delta x_{t-1} + \ldots + \Gamma_{k-1} \Delta x_{t-k+1} + \Pi x_{t-k} + \epsilon_t, \tag{2}$$

where $\Gamma_i = -I + \Pi_1 + \ldots + \Pi_i$, $i = 1, \ldots, k-1$ and $\Pi = -(I - \Pi_1 - \ldots - \Pi_k)$. It is obvious from (2) that all terms except Πx_{t-k} are stationary by definition. Therefore the equation system (2) is consistent only if $\Pi = 0$, or if the coefficients of Π are such that Πx_t is a stationary process. The latter case implies that $\text{rank}(\Pi) = r < p$. The cointegration hypothesis is formulated as:

$$\Pi = \alpha \beta', \tag{3}$$

where α and β are $(p \times r)$ matrices of rank r. The rows of β' form the r distinct cointegration vectors such that, for x_t as a non-stationary process, $\beta' x_t$ is stationary.

Johansen demonstrates that a likelihood ratio test statistic, so called trace statistic, for the null hypothesis of, at most, r cointegration vectors is

$$Q(\text{Trace}) = T \sum_{i=r+1}^{p} \ln (1 - \hat{\lambda}_i), \tag{4}$$

where $\hat{\lambda}_i$ denote the squared canonical correlations between the x_{t-k} and Δx_t series. A second likelihood ratio statistic for testing that there are at most r cointegration vectors against the alternative of $r+1$ is given by

$$Q(\lambda_{max}) = T \ln (1 - \hat{\lambda}_{r+1}). \tag{5}$$

Both tests have nonstandard distributions under the null hypothesis, but critical values have been generated by Monte Carlo methods. Direct hypotheses on the cointegration vectors such as tests for weak exogeniety, long-run exclusion of variables from β and structural tests on the form of β can be formulated as well and are described in Johansen and Juselius [1990].

Empirical results and discussion

In this study we used bilateral quarterly nominal exchange rates between the United States and Germany, the United Kingdom, Japan, Switzerland and France. The empirical analysis was performed for the five-variable vector x'=(DEM/USD, GBP/USD, JPY/USD, CHF/USD, FRF/USD) and all series were put in logarithmic form. We conducted two cointegration exercises, one for the time before the inception of the exchange rate mechanism of the EMS (1973 - 1979) and one for the period from 1979 till the end of 1991.

The empirical results, reported in table 1, indicate that there exist stationary long-run relationships between the levels of these exchange rates. For the EMS period both tests, the λ_{max} as well as the trace statistics, suggest one significant cointegration vector on the 5% level, whereas for the pre-EMS period this evidence is only supported by the trace test.

Table 1
Cointegration Results.

H_0	Eigen-value	λ_{max} Test	Critical Value 5%	Trace Test	Critical Value 5%
		VAR Model 1979:2 - 1991:4			
$r \leq 4$	0.046	02.355	08.083	02.355	08.083
$r \leq 3$	0.154	08.350	14.595	10.705	17.844
$r \leq 2$	0.179	09.864	21.279	20.569	31.256
$r \leq 1$	0.313	18.798	27.341	39.367	48.419
$r=0$	0.533	38.116**	33.262	77.484**	69.977
		VAR Model 1973:1 - 1979:1			
$r \leq 4$	0.089	02.232	08.083	02.232	08.083
$r \leq 3$	0.318	09.184	14.595	11.416	17.844
$r \leq 2$	0.441	13.959	21.279	25.375	31.256
$r \leq 1$	0.593	21.562	27.341	46.937	48.419
$r=0$	0.682	27.466	33.262	74.403**	69.977

** indicate significance on the 5% level. Critical values for the λ_{max} and trace statistics are taken from Johansen and Juselius [1990].

Imposing several likelihood ratio tests on the form of the cointegration vectors (table 2) for the different periods leads to further results: Since the inception of the EMS the German mark-U.S. dollar rate together with the British pound and Swiss franc rate are cointegrated and form a stationary linear combination. The exchange rate between the U.S. dollar and the EMS currency French franc adjusts to this long-run relationship but has no influence upon the form of the cointegration vector. Including Italian lira in the vector leads to the same conclusions as for the French franc, these EMS currencies adjust to the cointegration vector but have no influence on the form of β. On the contrary the Japanese Yen-U.S. dollar rate is relatively independent from the other exchange rates. Concerning the pre-EMS period the DEM/USD-rate is the only series were both hypotheses, for weak exogeniety as well as for long-run exclusion from β, are rejected, but further tests are inconclusive.

Dynamic simulations using forecast error variance decompositions and impulse responses (see Sims [1980]) were also applied. The results indicate that impulses in the DEM/USD-rate are followed by similar reactions of the other series whereas this is not observed vice versa. This evidence is stronger within the EMS period than in the pre-EMS period. Since the start of the EMS a major part of the variability of forecast errors of all exchange rates except the JPY/USD-rate are explained by innovations in the DEM/USD-rate (more than 40% over all forecast horizons of up to 24 steps). In the pre-EMS period own innovations in the exchange rate series account for a larger part of the variance of forecast errors.

It can be summarized that our results support the evidence of an increasing importance of the German mark-U.S. dollar rate for the other European exchange rates on the one hand and a relatively independent role of the Japanese Yen-U.S. dollar rate on the other hand.

Table 2
Likelihood Ratio Tests

Variable	Weak Exogeniety ($\chi^2(1)$)	Long-Run Exclusion from β ($\chi^2(1)$)
	VAR Model 1979:2 - 1991:4	
DEM/USD	07.17***	5.14**
GBP/USD	11.00***	7.27***
JPY/USD	02.25	0.21
CHF/USD	09.34***	7.96***
FRF/USD	12.93***	1.31
Hypothesis on vector β and α $(\beta_1, \beta_2, 0, \beta_4, 0)$ $(\alpha_1, \alpha_2, 0, \alpha_4, \alpha_5)$	3.68 ($\chi^2(3)$) 0.30	
	VAR Model 1973:1 - 1979:1	
DEM/USD	04.15**	4.25**
GBP/USD	04.41**	0.61
JPY/USD	00.95	5.00**
CHF/USD	03.37*	0.00
FRF/USD	01.00	0.06
Hypothesis on vector β and α $(\beta_1, 0, \beta_3, 0, 0)$ $(\alpha_1, \alpha_2, 0, \alpha_4, 0)$	10.12 ($\chi^2(5)$) 0.07*	

*, **, *** indicate significance on the 10%,5% and 1% level. The applied likelihood ratio tests are described in Johansen und Juselius [1990].

References

Engle, R. F., Granger, C. W. J. 1987. Co-integration and Error Correction: Representation, Estimation, and Testing. Econometrica, 55, 2, 251-276.

Johansen, S. 1988. Statistical Analysis of Cointegration Vectors. Journal of Economic Dynamics and Control, 12, 231-254.

Johansen, S., Juselius, K. 1990. Maximum Likelihood Estimation and Inference on Cointegration - With Application to the Demand for Money. Oxford Bulletin of Economics and Statistics, 52, 2, 169-210.

Sims, C. A. 1980. Macroeconomics and Reality. Econometrica, 48, 1-48.

SPECTRAL MOMENTS OF GRAPHS AND SOME APPLICATIONS

Dieter Gernert
Technische Universität München (Fak. WS)
Arcisstr. 21, D-80290 München

1. Introduction and notation

The spectral moments S_k (k = 1,2,...) of a graph G, which are defined as the sum over the kth powers of all eigenvalues of the adjacency matrix A(G), have a lot of interesting properties. Here a geometrical interpretation, their connection with the coefficients of the characteristic polynomial of G, several inequalities, relations with other graph invariants, and some number-theoretical properties are presented. Possible applications are related to proofs in graph theory, the evaluation of certain graph-theoretical properties, and the counting of special subgraphs.

Only finite undirected graphs (without loops or multiple edges) are considered. As usual, G is a graph with p vertices and q edges, and $\bar{G}$ is its complementary graph; c_k is the number of cycles with k vertices in G, d_i the degree of the vertex v_i, s_{d2} the sum over all d_i^2, ω the cardinality of the greatest clique, and g denotes the girth (length of the shortest cycle in G). K_i denotes a complete graph with i vertices, and N(H) the number of subgraphs isomorphic to H in G.

2. Geometrical interpretation and elementary properties

Since the adjacency matrix A(G) is real and symmetric, all its eigenvalues λ_i are real. Each spectral moment S_k (defined as above) is equal to the number of all closed walks of length k in G; in a "walk" edges may be passed more than once (see e.g. Cvetković 1980). It follows easily that

$$S_1 = 0$$

$S_2 = 2q$

$S_3 = 3c_3.$

By counting the walks of length 4 and 5 we get

$$S_4 = 8c_4 + 2s_{d2} - 2q \qquad (1)$$

$$S_5 = 10c_5 + 10N(K_3+e) + 30c_3. \qquad (2)$$

3. Connections with the characteristic polynomial

The characteristic polynomial of a graph G, which is defined as the characteristic polynomial of its adjacency matrix A(G), can be written as

$$X(G,x) = x^p + r_1x^{p-1} + r_2x^{p-2} + \dots + r_{p-1}x + r_p.$$

For the first coefficients we find (Biggs 1974):

$r_1 = 0$

$r_2 = -q$

$r_3 = -2c_3.$

Formulas for r_4 and the following coefficients require a theorem which expresses r_k by the numbers of specific subgraphs of G (Biggs 1974). In the case of r_4 this leads to

$$r_4 = N(2K_2) - 2c_4. \qquad (3)$$

Some applications will be discussed in Sect. 6. Since the spectral moments S_k are elementary symmetric functions of the roots of $X(G,x)$, they are connected with the coefficients r_k by Newton's equations (see e.g. Bôcher 1925). With $S_1 = r_1 = 0$ and $S_2 = 2q$ we arrive at

$$S_4 = 2q^2 - 4r_4. \qquad (4)$$

Next, (3) allows to derive bounds for r_4:

Lemma 1: If G is a connected graph with p vertices then

$$-3N(K_4) \leqslant r_4 \qquad (5)$$

$$-3\binom{p}{4} \leqslant r_4 \leqslant (p-2)(p-3)/2. \qquad (6)$$

Proof: If $p \leqslant 3$ then $r_4 = 0$, and for the rest we assume $p \geqslant 4$. Each induced subgraph of G with 4 vertices (named H) is considered separately. If H is isomorphic to K_4 then by virtue of (3) H contributes three copies of $2K_2$ and three 4-cycles. From (3) it follows that $r_4(H) = -3$. If H is of any other type we have $r_4(H) \geqslant 0$. Summation over all induced subgraphs with

4 vertices leads to (5). The minimum stated in (6) is assumed if and only if G is the K_p. The upper bound in (6) is reached if and only if G is the path P_p, where $c_4(P_p) = 0$ and $N(2K_2)$ can be computed easily. (QED)

From (5) and (6) upper and lower bounds for S_4 can be derived by substituting in (4).

4. Inequalities related to spectral moments

An upper bound for the greatest eigenvalue λ_1 follows from (1) and the definition of S_4 (Roth 1993):

$$\lambda_1{}^4 \leq 8c_4 + 2s_d{}^2 - \omega + 1 - 2q.$$

Here it is used that at least $\omega - 1$ eigenvalues are less than or equal to -1. A counting of all closed walks of length 6 yields a complicated expression, which can be simplified for graphs with girth g 7:

$$\lambda_1{}^6 \leq 9s_{d2} - \omega + 1 - 16q.$$

5. Congruences and similar properties

To any walk there exists another walk with opposite orientation, and hence all S_k are even. For prime k a theorem by Schönemann (1839) states that $S_k \equiv S_1$ (mod k), which finally supplies

$$S_k \equiv 0 \pmod{2k} \qquad \text{(if k is an odd prime)}$$

For k = 5 this is illustrated by (2).

For odd g we have $S_i = 0$ for all i with i odd, $i < g$, and $S_g = 2gc_g$ (see (2) again). For even subscripts we find

$$S_2 \equiv S_4 \equiv S_6 \equiv 2q \pmod 4 \qquad (7)$$

$$S_6 \equiv 2q + 2c_4 \pmod 6.$$

A study of possible walks shows that (7) cannot be extended to greater subscripts (Roth 1993).

6. Some applications

Newton's inequality for polynomials all of whose roots are real can be applied to X(G,x):

$$r_3^2 > 4r_2r_4/3.$$

Substitutions for the r_k together with (4) lead to

$$12c_3^2 > q(S_4 - 2q^2).$$

Evidently, this new lower bound for c_3 is relevant only if $S_4 - 2q^2 > 0$. As a consequence of $S_4 - 2q^2 = -4r_4$ (from (4)) it makes sense to distinguish between "r_4-negative graphs", "r_4-balanced graphs", and "r_4-positive graphs" according to $r_4 < 0$, $= 0$, > 0. The proofs of the following lemmas are easy.

Lemma 2: If G includes no subgraph K_4 then $r_4(G) \geq 0$.

Lemma 3: If G is completely bipartite then $r_4(G) = 0$.

Lemma 4: If G is a graph such to each subgraph H isomorphic to K_4 (if any) there exists an unconnected edge then $r_4 \geq 0$.

It follows from Lemma 4 that r_4-negative graphs have a diameter $d \leq 3$ and a dominating cycle.

Spectral moments of G and its complement $\overline{G}$ are interrelated:

$$S_2 + \overline{S}_2 = p(p - 1)$$

$$S_3 + \overline{S}_3 = 6(c_3 + \overline{c}_3) = 3s_{d2} + (p - 1)(p^2 - 2p - 6q).$$

In the latest step a theorem by Lovász (1979) was used.

Relations like those presented above become useful also within knowledge-based systems (Gernert 1989, with further references) which include a multitude of relations between graph invariants and permit to support graph-theoretical proofs and the design of algorithms.

References

Biggs N (1974) Algebraic graph theory. Cambridge University Press, London

Cvetković D M, Doob M, Sachs H (1980) Spectra of graphs. Academic Press, New York

Gernert D (1989) A knowledge-based system for graph theory. Methods of Operations Research 63: 457-464

Lovász L (1979) Combinatorial problems and exercises. North-Holland, Amsterdam

Roth I (1993) Das Spektrum der Adjazenzmatrix und der Laplace-Matrix von Graphen. Unpublished diploma thesis, TU München

Schönemann T (1839) Theorie der symmetrischen Funktionen der Wurzeln einer Gleichung. J.r.a.Math. 19: 231-243, 289-308

Polymatroids, Bipartite Graphs And The Cone Of Boolean Submodular Functions

Eberhard Girlich, Michael Höding
Fakultät für Mathematik, Technische Universität
PSF 4120, 39016 Magdeburg, Germany

1 Introduction

Polymatroids ([2, 5]), a special class of polytopes, can be used for the description of feasible solution sets of discrete optimization problems. For any *polymatroid* holds

$$P(r) = \{x \in \mathbb{R}_n^+ : \sum_{i \in S} x_i \leq r(S), S \subseteq N = \{1, 2, \ldots, n\}\},$$

where $r(S)$ is a submodular, isotone and normalized *rank function* ($r : 2^N \to \mathbb{R}$).

A set S is *r-closed*, if for all S', $S \subset S' \subseteq N$ the function $r(S)$ is strictly isotone. A set S is *r-inseparable*, if for all two disjoint subsets S_1 and S_2 of S with $S_1 \cup S_2 = S$ holds $r(S_1) + r(S_2) > r(S)$. We denote by $R(r)$ the set of all non-empty r-closed and r-inseparable sets. $R(r)$ is called *facet-poset*.

Two polytopes P_1, P_2 are *combinatorial equivalent* ([3]), if there exists an isomorphism ϕ from P_1 to P_2 such that for all $F_1 \subset F_2 \subset P_1$ the relation $\phi(F_1) \subset \phi(F_2) \subset \phi(P_1) = P_2$ is satisfied.

By $f(P)$ we denote the *structural vector* of the polytope P such that the component $f_i(P)$ $(i = 0, 1, \ldots, n-1)$ of $f(P)$ is the number of i-dimensional faces of the polytope P.

Theorem 1 *If P_1 is combinatorial equivalent to P_2, then the structural vectors $f(P_1)$ and $f(P_2)$ are equal.*

For an n-dimensional polymatroid $P(r)$ we conclude, that $f_{n-1}(P(r)) = |R(r)| + n$. By a *polymatroid type* $P(r)$ we denote the representative of a class of combinatorial equivalent polymatroids.

We can classify the polymatroid types by the number of elements of $R(r)$. Let us remark that the type of polymatroids does not only depend from $R(r)$ but from the relations between the values of the function $r(S)$, $S \in R(r)$, too.

2 The cone of the Boolean submodular functions and bipartite graphs

The *Boolean submodular, isotone and normalized function* $r_J(S)$ is defined by $r_J(S) = 1$, if $S \cap J \neq \emptyset$ and $r_J(S) = 0$ otherwise. We can describe special rank functions $r(S) \in H(n)$ by a positive linear combination of the Boolean submodular functions

$r_J(S)$ in the following way:

$$r(S) = \sum_{j=1}^{2^n-1} b_j r_{J_j}(S) = \sum_{j\in I_S} b_j r_{J_j}(S) = \sum_{j\in I_S} b_j, \quad b_j \geq 0,$$

where $I_S = \{j : S \cap J_j \neq \emptyset, b_j > 0\}, \quad S, J_j \subseteq N.$

The set of these rank functions $r(S)$ is a simplicial cone denoted by $H(n)$. For $n = 2$ the cone $H(n)$ is equal to the cone $A(n)$ of all submodular, isotone and normalized rank functions. In the case of $n \geq 3$ the cone $H(n)$ is a proper subset of the cone $A(n)$.

Theorem 2 *Let $r(S)$ and $r^*(S)$ be elements of $H(n)$, differing only by the values of the positiv b_j. Then the facet-posets $R(r)$ and $R(r^*)$ of the polymatroids $P(r)$ and $P(r^*)$ are equal.*

Theorem 3 *For each face F of the cone $H(n)$ holds, that every function $r(S)$ of the interior of F generates the same polymatroid type $P(r)$.*

We can assign the sets J_j, where j is an element of the set of the indices of the positive b_j, to (0,1)-columns in a matrix $Q = \|q_{ij}\|_{n\times t}$ with $q_{ij} = 1$ if $i \in J_j$ and $q_{ij} = 0$ otherwise. The matrix Q can be identified as a qualification matrix of a problem of optimal unification (POU) ([5]). Obviously we can interprete the matrix $Q = (q_{ij})$ as a corresponding adjacency matrix of a bipartite graph $G = (V_1, V_2; E)$, with t different columns $(1 \leq t \leq 2^n - 1)$ and n rows, such that $\sum_{j=1}^{n} q_{ij} \neq 0$ for all $i \in \{1, 2, \ldots, n\}$.

The number of matrices Q (bipartite graphs) is an upper bound for the number of polymatroid types of $H(n)$. A trivial upper bound for the number of different bipartite graphs is $2^{2^n-1} - 1$. By an algorithm for enumeration of matrices Q we obtain 51845646 matrices for $n = 5$.

References

[1] Bixby R E, Cunningham W H, Topkis D M (1985) The partial order of a polymatroid extreme point. Mathematics of Operations research 10: 367-378

[2] Edmonds J (1970) Submodular functions, matroids and certain polyhedra. Proceeding of the Calgary International Conference on Combinatorial Structures and Their Applications. Gordon and Breach, New York: 69-87

[3] Emelicev V A, Kovalev M M, Kravzov M K (1984) Polytopes, Graphs and Optimization. Cambridge University Press

[4] Fujishige S (1991) Submodular functions and optimization. Annals of discrete mathematics 47, North-Holland

[5] Girlich E, Kowaljow M M (1981) Nichtlineare diskrete Optimierung. Akademie Verlag Berlin

EXPECTED WASTE FOR A BIN-PACKING ALGORITHM USING ITEMS THAT ARE EXPONENTIALLY DISTRIBUTED

Walter Goessens
UFSIA, Universiteit Antwerpen
Prinsstraat 13
B-2000 Antwerpen

INTRODUCTION

With some probability-calculations, we will describe and evaluate an algorithm for the famous bin-packing problem. Given lengths $(l_i)_{i \geq 1}$ of items, we want to find a way of packing these in bins of given size c. A rather simple algorithm consists in packing these items into such bins, as long as they can be packed with a rest length that is less than a given length R_{max}. So, no rest length of at least R_{max} can be considered as being 'garbage' and is therefore saved for later use. When the lengths of the items are known to follow a certain probabilistic distribution, a problem consists in finding the expected waste of a bin. We will calculate this expected waste when the lengths are exponentially distributed.

DEFINITIONS

$X_i =$ the length of item number i, independently and exponential(α)

$n =$ the number of items

$c =$ the (unique) size of the bins

$N = max\{k : \sum_{i=1}^{k} X_i \leq c\} =$ the number of items fitting into one bin

$U = \sum_{i=1}^{N} X_i =$ the occupied space in a bin

$W = c - U =$ the waste in a bin

$R_{max} =$ the maximum length that can be considered as 'garbage'

$\alpha =$ the parameter of the exponential distribution of the lengths of the items

$\nu = E[N] = \alpha c =$ the average number of items in a bin

$\nu_p = \alpha(c - R_{max}) =$ the average number of items fitting into $c - R_{max}$

$\varepsilon = \frac{R_{max}}{c} =$ the maximal waste fraction in a bin

$I_l(z) =$ the modified Bessel-function of order l (see Abramovitch 1970)

RELATED DISTRIBUTIONS

Theorem 1:

N is Poisson-distributed with mean ν.

Theorem 2:

$\forall w \in]0, c[: f_W(w) = \sum_{n=1}^{\infty} \alpha.\frac{\nu^n e^{-\nu}}{n!(n-1)!}.[\alpha(c-w)]^{n-1}.e^{-\alpha(c-w)}$

$Pr[W = c] = Pr[N = 0] = e^{-\nu}$

$Pr[W = 0] = Pr[W \geq 0] - \lim_{x \to 0^+} Pr[W \geq x] = 1 - \sum_{n=1}^{\infty} e^{-2\nu} \frac{\nu^n}{n!} \sum_{i=0}^{n-1} \frac{\nu^i}{i!}$

EXPECTED WASTE

Expected waste for this algorithm $= E[W|0 \le W \le R_{max}] = \frac{\int_0^{R_{max}} w f_W(w) dw}{Pr[0 \le W \le R_{max}]}$

$$\int_0^{R_{max}} w f_W(w) dw = ce^{-2\nu}\left[I_0(2\nu) + I_1(2\nu)\right]$$
$$-ce^{-\nu(2-\epsilon)}\left[I_0(2\nu\sqrt{1-\epsilon}) + \sqrt{1-\epsilon} I_1(2\nu\sqrt{1-\epsilon})\right]$$

$$Pr[0 \le W \le R_{max}] = (1 - e^{-\nu(1-\epsilon)} I_0(2\nu\sqrt{1-\epsilon}))$$

Theorem 3: Expected waste for this algorithm =

$$\frac{ce^{-\nu}\left[I_0(2\nu) + I_1(2\nu)\right] - ce^{-\nu(1-\epsilon)}\left[I_0(2\nu\sqrt{1-\epsilon}) + \sqrt{1-\epsilon} I_1(2\nu\sqrt{1-\epsilon})\right] + c}{(1 - e^{-\nu(1-\epsilon)} I_0(2\nu\sqrt{1-\epsilon}))}$$

BIBLIOGRAPHY

M. Abramovitch and I.A. Stegun (1970) Handbook of Mathematical Functions, Dover Publications, Inc., New York.

ALGORITHMS FOR THE CAPACITATED-CHINESE-POSTMAN-PROBLEM IN MIXED GRAPHS

Peter O. K. Greistorfer
Department of Industrial Management
Karl-Franzens-Universität Graz
Hans-Sachs-Gasse 3, A-8010 Graz

1. INTRODUCTION

This paper is concerned with a routing-problem that arises in a variety of practical situations, e.g. in the case of household refuse collection and winter gritting or during the work of postmen and electricity- or gas-meter readers. This type of Vehicle-Routing-Problem (VRP) is called the Capacitated-Chinese-Postman-Problem (CCPP), a special instance of the general class of Capacitated-Arc-Routing-Problems (Bodin et. al. (1983), Golden et. al. (1983)). The *model* of the CCPP can be described as an arc-routing version of the well-known node-oriented ***standard*** VRP. Let $H=(V,E,c,q)$ be a given graph with set of nodes V and set of edges E and let $c: E \to \mathbb{R}^+$ ($d: E \to \mathbb{Z}^+$) be a cost (demand) function assigning a positive real (integer) to each edge in H. The fleet of vehicles is homogenous, i.e. each vehicle has a capacity W and there is no restriction on the number of vehicles. Each edge demand must be satisfied by one vehicle i, which drives on route R_i. The cost of R_i, which starts and ends at the depot node, is $c(R_i)$. Minimizing the total cost, the sum over all $c(R_i)$, one has to determine a set of routes, called touring schedule T.

2. BASIC APPROACH

If in a solution of the CCPP all edges are traversed exactly *once*, the underlying graph is *Eulerian* and T consists of exactly one route R_1. Such a route is called an *Euler tour*. In this uncapacitated case $c(R_1)$ equals the total length of the graph H, which is the sum of all edge costs called $c(H)$. This result *cannot* be achieved in two cases: firstly, if W is big enough to satisfy the total demand, but H is non-Eulerian (a feasible route is called *postman tour*) and secondly, if W is not big enough (a non-Eulerian graph might be another reason too). In the latter case T consists of more than one route and in both cases there is at least one edge which has to be traversed a second time. Out of these considerations the lower bound for $c(T)$, the cost of any schedule T, equals $c(H^\varepsilon)$. Therefore the overall algorithm which has been designed is a two-step approach: In the *first step* a graph H is made Eulerian by duplicating certain edges and in the *second step*, the true routing step, T is constructed for the Eulerian graph H^ε obtained from the first step. For non-Eulerian directed and undirected graphs the first step can be solved optimally in polynomial time. In doing so the directed duplication problem is reduced to a ***transportation problem*** and the undirected one to a *matching-problem*. In both cases the optimality conditions for a graph to be Eulerian are comparatively simple: The in-degree at every node must equal the out-degree in the directed case and there must not be an odd-degree node in an undirected graph. For more information see e.g. Domschke (1985) and Lawler (1976). The main task of this paper is to study the mixed duplication case for which no polynomial algorithm is known. Here a new heuristic branch-and-bound algorithm is introduced. This will be done in the section 3. For the *second step*, the routing step, two procedures have been designed: a *sequential* and a *parallel* approach, which are outlined in section 4. The paper finishes with a brief analysis of computational results in section 5.

3. CYCLE DECOMPOSITION ALGORITHM FOR MIXED NON-EULERIAN GRAPHS

The node conditions for the directed and undirected graphs cannot be transformed to the mixed case in a proper way. There is "only" a so-called *cut-condition*, an extension of the node conditions mentioned, which has to be met for *every* subset of the node set of a graph. Ford and Fulkerson (1974) prove that the cut condition is necessary and sufficient. They propose a flow method which detects subsets violating the cut condition. The duplication procedure for non-Eulerian mixed graphs is based on *another* alternative Eulerian graph property. This procedure consists of two subroutines. The first of them generates a feasible solution (FS subroutine) and the second one, a greedy-improvement algorithm (GI subroutine), tries to improve the result obtained . Both combined constitute the cycle decomposition branch-and-bound algorithm (CDBA). Let $H=(V,E,c)$ be an arbitrary (directed, undirected or mixed) graph. Then we denote a set of not necessarily distinct cycles, $S=\{\zeta_1,..., \zeta_m\}$, with $m\geq 1$, as a *cycle cover* if E(S), the edge set of S, which is defined by the union of all cycle edges $E(\zeta_i)$, equals the edge set E(H) of the graph:

$$E(S) \; := \bigcup_{i=1}^{m} E(\zeta_i) = E(H) \; .$$

S is called a *cycle decomposition* S^* if, for $0\leq i<j\leq m$, $E(\zeta_i) \cap E(\zeta_j)=\emptyset$. If $m=1$, then S (S^*) contains only ζ_1, a postman tour (Eulerian tour). For the mixed duplication case we now use the fact that *every* Eulerian graph has at least one cycle decomposition (Fleischner 1990) and that for any (weakly) connected graph a cycle cover can be built. Each cycle cover S containing only oriented cycles induces an Eulerian orientation D^ε. Therefore the objective of finding a cost-benefical duplication for the non-Eulerian graph can be transformed to the objective of finding a cost-benefical cycle cover S, which itself is a cycle decomposition S^* for the induced graph D^ε. The basic idea of CDBA is the construction of various cycle covers and the selection of the best one from which D^ε can easily be derived. The search for S is organized within a heuristic branch-and-bound technique and this is what the FS subroutine does: Let $H=(V,E,c)$ be a mixed graph and S_P an incomplete cycle cover, where *incomplete* means that there is at least one edge of E that is not contained in some cycle of S_P. If all the edges of S_P

$$E(S_P) \; := \bigcup_{\zeta_i \in S_P} E(\zeta_i)$$

are removed from H, the subgraph $T_P := (V(T_P) \subseteq V(H), E(T_P) = E(H) \setminus E(S_P), c)$ remains. Depending on the next edge from $E(T_P)$, e.g. e_1 or e_2, for which a cycle ζ_1 or ζ_2 is to be built, two (cost-) alternative cycle covers $S_P \cup \zeta_1$ and $S_P \cup \zeta_2$ can be formed. On the other hand this also means that after removing edges $E(\zeta_1)$ and $E(\zeta_2)$ from T_P, two new smaller subgraphs remain. For a more formal explanation we assume that a branch-and-bound tree has already been built during the procedure. Every node of the tree corresponds to a certain problem, solved or not. Unsolved problems have no successor in the tree and are terminal nodes. Now we examine a certain terminal problem P_ν. P_ν is the partial problem number ν, which is generated from (the solved) predecessor problem P. At every node of the tree a new cycle for the given incomplete cycle cover is constructed. P_ν has been created by a branching operation at P, the nomination of an edge $e_\nu \in E(T_P)$ not contained in S_P. Now problem P_ν may be stated as follows: "Find a cycle ζ_ν in such a way that the resulting subgraph $T_\nu := (V(T_\nu) \subseteq V(H), E(T_\nu) = E(H) \setminus E(S_\nu), c)$, where $S_\nu := S_P \cup \zeta_\nu$, can be made Eulerian at minimal cost". The cycle is found - and this is part of the heuristic idea - by determining a shortest path joining the head and the tail of e_ν. The way we do this depends on e_ν, directed or not, and on the graph T_P. First we search for ζ_ν in T_P. If there is no path, ζ_ν is found in H. If e_ν is undirected, a concept of productivity-surplus is used to select from alternative possibilities (Greistorfer (1993)). - The second subroutine of CDBA, the GI subroutine, tries to improve the constructed directed Eulerian graph D^ε. During the FS subroutine it is possible that two or more different cycles together form an unproductive new one. The GI subroutine has the task of removing these multi-cycles: In successive iterations and beginning with the graph D^ε, the biggest unproductive cycle is deleted from the current graph until no additional cost reductions are possible.

4. ROUTING STEP

There are two alternative procedures: The *sequential* route-first-cluster-second procedure follows an idea well-known from literature (Domschke 1985): One big Eulerian tour, the solution of the uncapacitated problem, is split into parts according to vehicle capacity. Subsequently, the resulting schedule may be improved by a heuristic packing algorithm. In the *parallel* procedure both steps, routing and clustering, are combined. The parallel approach is an adaption of the savings idea for node-oriented VRPs, proposed by Clarke and Wright (1964).

5. COMPUTATIONAL RESULTS

All the methods have been implemented by means of a PASCAL program running on PCs. To comment the results of step 1 for mixed graphs the following two strategies are compared: the Eulerian graph obtained by CDBA (FS and GI subroutine) and the Eulerian graph obtained by a so-called greedy-duplication (GD algorithm). In the GD algorithm first a directed Eulerian graph is built, without branching and bounding, by determining shortest cycles only in H, in the same way as CDBA does at every node of the decision tree when there is no cycle in T_P. After that this graph is improved by the GI subroutine. The test sample of 32 graphs consists of 19 planar graphs constructed by hand, of 12 simulated non-planar graphs and 1 real world example, the centre of Graz, a mixed graph with 344 nodes, 274 undirected and 217 directed edges. In 5 cases CDBA could not generate a better result than the GD algorithm. The remaining 27 CDBA-results were better up to 18.8% with an average of 8.3%, 6.0% and 11.0% for constructed, simulated and real world example(s) respectively. The quality of the two routing procedures is also measured with percentage numbers (similar to Eglese and Li 1992): the *schedule efficiency* $SE_i\%:=c(H^{\varepsilon})\cdot 100/c(T)$ and the *routing efficiency* $RE_i\%:=c(H)\cdot 100/c(T)$. Index $i=1,2,3$ denotes the kind of schedule, which is computed for different capacities: a small (2 routes), medium (about 5 routes) and big schedule (up to 16 routes). The average results $øSE_i$ and $øRE_i\%$ are shown in the following table. They have been calculated by taking the better schedule in each case: the sequential or the parallel one. The parallel approach performs better with 65% of all data samples. The entry in the last column, $RE\%^{max}:=c(H)\cdot 100/c(H^{\varepsilon})$, is the upper bound of routing efficiency:

graphs	$øSE_1\%$	$øSE_2\%$	$øSE_3\%$	$øRE_1\%$	$øRE_2\%$	$øRE_3\%$	$øRE\%^{max}$
directed	98. 1	90. 0	80. 0	71. 2	66. 8	62. 1	72. 2
undirected	97. 9	89. 0	75. 3	87. 8	81. 1	68. 2	89. 6
mixed	95. 3	86. 0	71. 6	71. 6	68. 8	54. 7	78. 4

Quality of results: Schedule efficiency and routing efficiency

REFERENCES

Bodin L. D., B. L. Golden, A. A. Assad and M. O. Ball (1983) Routing and scheduling of vehicles and crews: The state of the art. *Comput. & Ops. Res* 10: 63-211.

Clarke G. and J. Wright (1964) Scheduling of vehicles from a central depot to a number of delivery points. *Ops Res.* 12: 568-581.

Domschke W. (1985) *Logistik: Rundreisen und Touren.* 2nd Ed. R. Oldenbourg-Verlag. München - Wien.

Eglese R. W. and L. Y. O. Li (1992) Efficient routeing for winter gritting. *J. Opl Res. Soc.* 43: 1031-1034.

Fleischner H. (1990) *Eulerian graphs and related topics.* Part 1 Vol. 1. North-Holland. Amsterdam - New York - Oxford - Tokyo.

Ford, Jr. L. R. and D. R. Fulkerson (1974) *Flows in networks.* 6th Ed. Princeton University Press. Princeton/New Jersey.

Golden B. L., J. S. Armon and E. K. Baker (1983) Computational experiments with algorithms for a class of routing problems. *Comput. & Ops. Res.* 10: 47-59.

Greistorfer P. O. K. (1993) *Lösungsverfahren für kantenorientierte Tourenplanungsprobleme in gemischten Graphen.* Ph.D., Dept. of Industrial Management, Karl-Franzens-Universität Graz.

Lawler E. L. (1976) *Combinatorial optimization: Networks and matroids.* Holt, Rinehart & Winston. New York - Chicago - San Francisco.

HUMAN CAPITAL AND INTERNATIONAL CAPITAL FLOWS

Thomas Gries,
University of Göttingen, Germany

In the traditional Heckscher-Ohlin type of trade and growth theory, capital mobility is not integrated. Embodied in products, factor mobility takes place by the way of commodity trade. As a consequence, H.-O. theory implies factor price equalization. Therefore, there are only few proposition to combine Heckscher-Ohlin trade theory and international factor mobility. The first approach is proposed in a model, which is frequently called the Kemp-Jones model [Ruffin (1984)]. The reason for capital mobility in this kind of model is a deviation in productivity. This recardian type of argument can not only imply trade, but also international mobility of capital. A second incentive for capital mobility was brought up by Fischer/Frenkel (1972). In the Fischer/Frenkel approach installation costs of capital induce capital mobility. Generally, capital mobility was discussed more as a problem of monetary macroeconomics than as component of pure trade theory. In the subsequent paragraphs a different view of integrating capital mobility into H.-O. trade theory is suggested [see also Gries (1993)]. Four characteristics modifying standard neoclassical open economy growth theory are important:

- The small open economy produces with three factors of production (labor, real capital and human capital). The production process described by the foreign exchange production function [see Findlay (1973,1984)]. Real capital and human capital are accumulated over time and labor is exogenously growing.
- A country's economic fundamentals are characterized by the local immobile factor endowment [*characteristic endowment*], namely labor and human capital. Human capital is identified as the 'peoples skills'. Human capital is 'embodied' in the population, and therefore is an immobile factor.
- Making use of results well known in labor economics, human capital and real capital are poor substitutes in the production process. In a survey on human capital Hamermesh (1986) finds: "Perhapss the most consistent finding is that non production workers (presumable skilled labor) are less easily substitutable for physical capital than are production workers (unskilled labor). Indeed, a number of the studies find that nonproduction workers and physical capital are *p*- complements. This supports Rosens' (1968) and Griliches (1969) results on capital- skill complementary hypothesis"(Hamermesh 1986, p. 461).

- The accumulation of human capital is determined by portfolio decisions and an intertemporal optimal program. Accumulated local human capital determines the local requirements of real capital. Real capital is supplied totally elastic on world markets and employed on a 'normal' level of utilization. Real capital will never be the limiting factor for a potential momentary rise in production.

These general characterizations lead to a standard intertemporal optimization problem. From the first order conditions we obtain an extended Ramsey Rule and a steady state solution for the economy's optimal per capita wealth and human capital intensity. From these variables all major variables can be derived (e.g. income per capita, the position of specialization and comparative advantages, international capital flows and international factor price deviations).

The most interesting results are summarized as follows: A country originally can be defined by the '*characteristic parameters*'. The country's 'characteristic parameters' (namely the rate of time preference, the elasticity of intertemporal substitution in consumption and the vector of portfolio parameters) determine intertemporal accumulation, portfolio decision, and eventually the country's '*characteristic endowment*'. The 'characteristic endowment' determines the international position of comparative advantage, guides the direction of flows of mobile real capital and determines the incentives for a potential mobility of normally immobile factors.

a. Since we used the foreign exchange production function, every human capital intensity represents a certain sector. Therefore a country's optimal relative factor abundance defines the pattern of specialization and trade. In this respect the model is a dynamic generalized version of H.-O. theory. Trade is induced through factor endowments, which are determined by optimal accumulation and portfolio decisions.

b. The portfolio decision determines the local endowment of human capital and the potential supply of mobile real capital. If the stock of accumulated human capital is small, little real capital is needed in domestic production. For a given world interest rate the required real capital is absorbed from internal and external sources. The domestic excess supply (demand) is provided to (taken from) the world markets of real capital. As a result of optimal intertemporal and portfolio decisions a country may accumulate little human capital, and therefore will attract little real capital. The lack of domestic opportunities to invest will channel wealth accumulation to world markets. A capital outflow can be observed even for a poor country with little capital endowment.

c. As a property of a homogeneous production function, every human capital intensity implies a different marginal productivity. Different countries with different 'characteristic endowments' and different optimal human capital abundance realize different marginal rates of substitution. Therefore, the factor price equalization theorem does not hold. Steady state specialization patterns imply factor prices differentials and generate permanent incentives for the mobility of normally immobile factors like labor and human capital.

Several fields of policy implications can be suggested: ***Human capital accumulation:*** Human capital is the central element of this approach. The portfolio decision on human capital accumulation is a key component in determining a country's 'characteristic endowment', and -as a result- the country's general economic performance. Therefore, political implications are plain. All policies rising human capital accumulation will attract additional real capital for domestic production and improve the general economic situation. Among many other factors determining the portfolio decisions, the distribution of wealth and income may be an important parameter.

Capital flight: The expression *capital flight* is usually associated with capital moving in a direction not expected from looking at the real economic fundamentals. The outflow of capital from poor countries with poor capital endowments and expected high returns is often regarded as capital flight. In this approach the mechanism is different: If the stock of accumulated human capital is small, little real capital is needed in domestic production. Little human capital attracts only a small amount of real capital. Capital outflow can be observed even for a poor country with little capital endowment. The *flight* of capital indicates a lack of opportunities to invest due to missing human capital.

With respect to international transfer payments a second implication seems important: Internal or external development policies that simply increase the availability of capital without strong implication for human capital accumulation, will have little success. Simple transfers of money will not be effective as developing strategy.

Direct investments Permanent factor price differentials due to different pattern of specialization induce incentives for the mobility of normally immobile factors. The larger the difference in human capital intensity between two countries, the larger the factor price differential and the stronger the incentives for factor mobility. When investors from industrialized countries notice large returns on human capital, bundles of the general immobile human capital and complementary real capital will move via direct investment to developing countries. Human capital may become partly mobile by direct investments. An increasing international migration of labor is a signal for a partly moving labor force.

References:

Findlay, R. (1973), International trade and Development Theory, Columbia University Press, New York.

Findlay, R. (1984), Growth and Development in Trade Models, in: Jones, R.W. / Kenen, P.B. (eds.), Handbook of International Economics, 1, 185-236.

Fischer, S. / Frenkel, J. (1972), Investment, the Two-Sector Model and Trade in Debt and Capital Goods, Journal of International Economics, 2, 211-233.

Gries, T., (1993), Human Capital, Comparative Advantages and International Factor Mobility, Discussion Paper, Department of Economics University of Goettingen, No. 63.

Ruffin, R.J. (1984), International Factor Movements, in: Jones, R.W. / Kenen, P.B. (eds.), Handbook of International Economics, 1, 185-236.

COMPUTER SIMULATION FOR IMAGE RECONSTRUCTION FROM A VERY LIMITED NUMBER OF PROJECTIONS

Nadezhda Gubareny
Institute of Simulation Problems in
Power Engineering
15 General Naumov St.
USS 252680 Kiev-164
Ukraine

Our work is devoted to the elaboration of methods, algorithms and application package for reconstruction from a very limited number of projections with a strong noisy. Such problems exist, for example, in geophysics, by exploitation of oil and gas deposits, in optic, in reseach of plasma and of combustion processes in the internal-combustion engine. One of our problems is to restore tomogramms obtained by means of optical measurements. In this case the input data are the interferogramms which are representated by summary image of refrective index distribution in cross section of phase object. An essentional difference between this problem and the problems of traditional image reconstruction lies in the fact that initial data are not given by a set of projections which each taken separately but by means of summary image. We suggest new iterative algebraic algorithm SUM for solving this problem. In the bases of it there put the relaxation algorithm ART-3 obtained by Herman (1975) for solving the system of linear double-sided inequalities. The algorithm SUM was realised in the form of application programms for IBM PC/AT. It were conducted the computer simulations on a number of model 2-dimentional and 3-dimentional objects and was treated the interferogrammes obtained by research of concrete physical procedures. It was shown that this algorithm gives better results as compared with another wellknown algorithms, removes artifacts and permits a strong noisy of input data.

Herman G.T. (1975) A relaxation method for reconstructing objects from noisy x-rays. Math. Programming 8: 1-19.

CAPACITATED LOT-SIZING WITH LINKED PRODUCTION QUANTITIES OF ADJACENT PERIODS

Knut Haase, Andreas Drexl
Institut für Betriebswirtschaftslehre
Christian-Albrechts-Universität zu Kiel
Olshausenstr. 40, FRG-24118 Kiel

1. Introduction

The well-known Capacitated Lot-Sizing Problem (CLSP) is based on the assumption that for each lot in a period setup costs are incurred. The setup costs of a CLSP solution can be reduced by linking the production quantities of an item which is scheduled in two adjacent periods. Therefore we propose the CLSP with linked lot-sizes, denoted by CLSPL.

The CLSPL is formulated as a mixed-integer programming model. For the heuristic solution of the CLSPL we introduce a sampling method which is backward oriented and relies on so-called randomized regrets.

The algorithm for the Discrete Lot-Sizing and Scheduling Problem (DLSP), introduced in [4], can be used for solving the CLSPL. In addition, a solution of the Dixon-Silver heuristic [cf. 3] can be transformed into a CLSPL solution, too. Computational results show, that the sampling method is more efficient.

2. The CLSP with Linked Lot-Sizes (CLSPL)

A single-stage system is considered, where a number of different items $j=1,\dots,J$ have to be manufactured on one machine. The time horizon T is segmented into a finite number of time periods $t=1,\dots,T$ with equal length. The machine is available with C_t capacity units in period t. To setup the machine for item j causes s_j setup costs. Inventory costs of h_j are incurred to hold one unit of item j one period in inventory. The demand for item j in period t, d_{jt}, has to be satisfied without delay (shortages are disallowed). Producing one unit of item j absorbs p_j capacity units (finite production speed). *We assume that the setup state can be preserved between two adjacent periods.* The objective is to minimize the sum of setup and holding costs. We propose to consider the following capacitated lot-sizing problem with linked lot-sizes, denoted by CLSPL:

$$\min \sum_{j=1}^{J}\sum_{t=1}^{T}\left[s_j(x_{jt}-z_{jt})+h_j I_{jt}\right]$$

subject to

$$I_{j,t-1} + q_{jt} - I_{jt} = d_{jt} \qquad (\forall j,t)$$

$$\sum_{j=1}^{J} p_j q_{jt} \le C_t \qquad (\forall t)$$

$$B \cdot x_{jt} - q_{jt} \ge 0 \qquad (\forall j,t)$$

$$\sum_{j=1}^{J} z_{jt} \le 1 \qquad (\forall t)$$

$$z_{jt} - x_{j,t-1} \le 0 \qquad (\forall j,t)$$

$$z_{jt} - x_{jt} \le 0 \qquad (\forall j,t)$$

$$1 - \sum_{j=1}^{J} x_{jt} + J \cdot v_t \ge 0 \qquad (\forall t)$$

$$z_{jt} + z_{j,t-1} + v_{t-1} \le 2 \qquad (\forall j,t)$$

$v_t \ge 0$ $(\forall t)$, $I_{jt}, q_{jt} \ge 0$ $(\forall j,t)$, $x_{jt}, z_{jt} \in \{0,1\}$ $(\forall j,t)$ where

v_t = a variable indicating whether more than one item is produced in period t $(v_t > 0)$ or not $(v_t = 0)$,

x_{jt} = a binary variable indicating whether a quantity is produced for item j in period t (x_{jt}=1) or not (x_{jt}=0),

z_{jt} = a binary variable indicating whether the quantities of item j in period t-1 and period t are linked (z_{jt}=1) or not (z_{jt}=0),

and $I_{j0}=0$, $v_0=0$, $x_{j0}=0$, $z_{j0}=z_{j1}=0$ (j=1,...,J).

A similar model for the multi-machine case with setup times has been presented in [2].

3. A Sampling Method for the CLSPL

Let $D_{jt} := \max\left\{0, \sum_{\tau=t}^{T}(d_{j\tau} - q_{j\tau})\right\}$ $(\forall j,t)$,

$$TRC := \sum_{j=1}^{J} p_j D_{j1},$$

$$nd_{jt} := \begin{cases} 0 & \text{if } t = 0 \\ t & \text{if } d_{jt} > 0 \\ nd_{j,t-1} & \text{otherwise} \end{cases} \qquad (\forall j,t),$$

$$CC_t := \sum_{\tau=1}^{t} C_\tau \qquad (\forall t),$$

$$r_{jt}(i) := \begin{cases} (1-\gamma)h_j D_{jt} - \gamma \cdot s_j & \text{if } (j \neq i) \wedge (D_{jt} > 0) \\ (1-\gamma)h_j D_{j,nd_{j,t-1}} & \text{if } (j = i) \wedge (TRC \leq CC_{nd_{j,t-1}}) \\ -\infty & \text{otherwise} \end{cases} \quad (\forall j; \gamma \in [0,1]), \text{ and}$$

$$\rho_{jt}(i) := \begin{cases} 0 & \text{if } r_{jt}(i) = -\infty \\ \left(r_{jt}(i) - \min\{r_{kt}(i) \mid \forall k \wedge r_{kt}(i) > -\infty\} + \varepsilon\right)^{\delta} & \text{otherwise} \end{cases} \quad (\delta \geq 0, \varepsilon > 0).$$

BACLSPL, the method for solving the CLSPL incorporates the following two main ideas:

(i) Lot-sizing and scheduling is done backward oriented starting in period T.

(ii) The regrets $\rho_{jt}(i)$ are used in a randomized way to decide which item(s) should be produced in a specific period.

4. Computational Results

The solution quality of BACLSPL is compared with the solution quality of the DLSP-algorithm in [4]:

	TV11 1)	TV12	TV13	TV14
reduced costs 2) of DLSP	8080	7090	6840	6840
BACLSPL 3)	7470	6980	6800	6660

1) published in [5] 2) defined and determined in [4]

3) $\varepsilon=1$, $\delta\in[0,9]$, 1000 executions of BACLSPL

In [1] 120 instances are reported. The instances are solved with the Dixon-Silver (DS) heuristic. A DS-schedule can be improved by linking of production quantities and producing the lots as late as possible. We use BACLSPL in a *deterministic version*, i.e. the item with maximal $r_{jt}(i)$ is scheduled. The average procentage deviations between the upper bounds of DS and BACLSPL, i.e. $\Delta Z=100\cdot(\overline{Z}_{DS} - \overline{Z}_{BACLSPL})/\overline{Z}_{BACLSPL}$) and the average computation times of BACLSPL (in brackets) are as follows:

	(J,T)=(50,8)	(J,T)=(20,20)	(J,T)=(8,50)
average 1) ΔZ [CPU-time] 2)	0.45 [10,5 sec.]	7.19 [3 sec.]	11.05 [1,7 sec.]

1) 40 instances per entry 2) 80486-CPU with 50 MHz

4. Summary

The CLSP with linked lot-sizes (CLSPL) provides a better solution quality than the DLSP and the CLSP. For the heuristic solution of the CLSPL an efficient backward oriented method is introduced which relies on randomized regrets.

References

[1] **Cattrysse, D., Maes, J., Van Wassenhove, L.N.**, "Set Partitioning and column generation heuristics for capacitated lotsizing", European J. of Operational Research, Vol. 46 (1990), pp. 38-47.

[2] **Dillenberger, C., Escudero, L.F., Wollensak, A., Zhang, W.**, "On solving a large-scale resource allocation problem in production planning", in: Operation research in production planning and control, Fandel, G. et al. (eds.), Springer Verlag Berlin 1992, pp. 105-119.

[3] **Dixon, P.S., Silver, E.A.**, "A heuristic solution procedure for multi-item single-level, limited capacity, lot-sizing problem", Journal of Operations Management 2/1, (1981), pp. 23-29.

[4] **Fleischmann, B.**, "The discrete lot-sizing and scheduling problem", European J. of Operational Research, Vol. 44 (1990), pp. 337-348.

[5] **Thizy, J.-M., Van Wassenhove, L.N.**, "Lagrangean relaxation for the multi-item capacitated lot-sizing problem: A heuristic implementation", IIE Transaction, Vol. 17 (1985), pp. 308-313.

The equal gain splitting rule for sequencing situations and the general nucleolus

Herbert Hamers, Imma Curiel, Jos Potters, Stef Tijs

Tilburg University, P.O. Box 90153, 5000 LE Tilburg, The Netherlands

In a one machine sequencing situation there is a queue of agents, each with one job, before a machine. Each agent (player) has to process his job on the machine. The finite set of agents is denoted by $N = \{1, ..., n\}$.

By a bijection $\sigma : N \to \{1, ..., n\}$ we can describe the position of the agents in the queue. Specifically, $\sigma(i) = j$ means that player i is in position j. We assume that there is an initial order $\sigma_0 : N \to \{1, ..., n\}$ on the jobs of the players before the processing of the machine starts. W.l.o.g. we assume that σ_0 is defined by $\sigma_0(i) = i$ for all $i \in N$. The processing time p_i of the job of player i is the time the machine takes to handle this job. Further, it is assumed that every agent has an affine cost function $c_i : [0, \infty) \to \mathbf{R}$ defined by $c_i(t) = \alpha_i t + \beta_i$ with $\alpha_i > 0, \beta_i \in \mathbf{R}$.

A sequencing situation as described above is denoted by (N, p, α), where $N = \{1, ..., n\}, r = (r_i)_{i\in N}$ and $\alpha = (\alpha_i)_{i\in N}$. The vector $\beta = (\beta_i)_{i\in N}$ is omitted in the description of the sequencing situation since for each order σ the fixed costs of β are constant.

For player $i \in N$ we define the following sets with respect to the initial order σ_0. The head of player i is the set $\{1, 2, ..., i\}$ and the tail of player i is the set $\{i, i + 1, ..., n\}$. The family set of coalitions consisting of all heads and all tails is denoted by $\mathcal{H}$.

The completion time of a player i if processed according to a bijection $\sigma : N \to \{1, ..., n\}$ is equal to $C(\sigma, i) := \sum_{j:\sigma(j)\leq\sigma(i)} p_j$. The total costs of $c_\sigma(S)$ of a coalition $S \subset N$, is given by

$$c_\sigma(S) := \sum_{i\in S} \alpha_i(C(\sigma, i)) + \beta_i.$$

The (maximal) cost savings of a coalitions S depend on the set of admissable rearrangements of this coalition. A bijection $\sigma : N \to \{1, ..., n\}$ is called admissable for S if it satisfies the following two conditions:

(i) The completion time of each agent outside the coalition S is equal to his completion time in the initial order: $C(\sigma_0, i) = C(\sigma, i)$ for all $i \in N \backslash S$.

(ii) the players of S are not allowed to jump over players outside S:

$$\{1, ..., i\} \cap N \backslash S = \{j \mid \sigma(j) < \sigma(i)\} \cap N \backslash S \quad \text{for all } i \in S.$$

The set of admissable rearrangements for a coalition S is denoted by Σ_S.

Given a sequencing situation (N, p, α) the corresponding sequencing game is defined in such a way that the the worth of a coalition S is equal to the maximal cost savings the coalition can achieve by means of an admissable rearrangement. Formally we have,

$$v(S) = \max_{\sigma \in \Sigma_S} \{\sum_{i \in S} (\alpha_i C(\sigma_0, i) + \beta_i) - \sum_{i \in S} (\alpha_i C(\sigma, i) + \beta_i)\}.$$

The Equal Gain Splitting (EGS) rule, introduced by *Curiel, Pederzoli* and *Tijs (1989)*, in a sequencing situation (N, p, α) is defined for all $i \in N$ by

$$EGS_i(N, p, \alpha) := \frac{1}{2} \sum_{j<i} g_{ji} + \frac{1}{2} \sum_{j>i} g_{ij}$$

Here $g_{ij} := \max\{\alpha_j p_i - \alpha_i p_j, 0\}$ represents the gain attainable for player i and j in case player i is directly in front of player j. Note that the optimal order of a queue can be obtained from the initial order by switching neighbours only. Hence, in the EGS rule a player is assigned half of the gains of all neighbour switches he is actually involved in to obtain the optimal order. This paper characterizes in terms of efficiency and the fair head-tail split property the EGS rule.

Definition 1 *Let (N, v) be a sequencing game. Then a vector $x \in R^n$ sastisfies the fair head-tail split property if*

$$v(S) - \sum_{j \in S} x_j + \frac{1}{2} \Delta_S = v(S^c) - \sum_{j \in S^c} x_j + \frac{1}{2} \Delta_S \text{ for all } S \in \mathcal{H}$$

where $\Delta_S = v(N) - v(S) - v(S^c)$.

Hence, the fair head-tail split property tells that there is an equal share of the marginal benefit of the union of a head and its complement.

Theorem 1 *Let (N, v) be the sequencing game corresponding to the sequencing situation (N, p, α). Then $EGS(N, p, \alpha)$ is the unique rule that satisfies efficiency and the fair head-tail split property.*

The head tail core $C^{\mathcal{H}}(v)$ of a sequencing game (N, v) is defined by

$$C^{\mathcal{H}}(v) = \{x \in \mathbf{R^n} \mid x(N) = v(N), \sum_{j \in S} x_j \geq v(S) \text{ for all } S \in \mathcal{H}\}.$$

Theorem 2 $\qquad C^{\mathcal{H}}(v) = conv\{h^J \mid h^J \in E\}.$

where h^J corresponds to the solutions of the set of equations

$$\begin{array}{ll} \sum_{k=1}^{k=i} x_k = v(N) - v(\{i+1, ..., n\}) & i \in J \\ \sum_{k=1}^{k=i} x_k = v(\{1, ..., i\}) & i \in N \backslash J \end{array}$$

Theorem 3 *Let (N, p, α) be a sequencing situation and (N, v) the corresponding sequencing game. Then $EGS(N, p, \alpha) = \frac{1}{2^{n-1}} \sum_{J \subset N} h^J$.*

In *Maschler, Potters* and *Tijs(1993)* a general nucleolus is introduced on the class of truncated games, an extension of the class of cooperative games. The general nucleolus of the truncated game $(N, \mathcal{H}, v, \Pi)$ is defined by

$$\mathcal{N}(N, \mathcal{H}, v, \Pi) = \{x \in \Pi \mid \Theta \circ F(x) \preceq_L \Theta \circ F(y) \text{ for all } y \in \Pi\}.$$

where $\Pi := \{x \in \mathbf{R^n} \mid \sum_{j \in N} x_j = v(N)\}$.

Theorem 4 *Let $(N, \mathcal{H}, v, \Pi)$ be a truncated game of the sequencing game (N, v) corresponding to (N, p, α). Then $EGS(N, p, \alpha)$ coincides with $\mathcal{N}(N, \mathcal{H}, v, \Pi)$.*

References:

CURIEL I., PEDERZOLI G., TIJS S. (1989), Sequencing games, *European Journal of Operational Research*, **40**, 344-351.

MASCHLER M., POTTERS J. , TIJS S. (1992), The general nucleolus and the reduced game property, *International Journal of Game Theory*, 85-106.

POTTERS J., CURIEL I., RAJENDRA PRASAD V., TIJS S., VELTMAN B. (1993), Sequencing and Cooperation, *To appear in: Operations Research.*

POTTERS J., CURIEL I., RAJENDRA PRASAD V., TIJS S., VELTMAN B.(1993), Cooperation in one machine scheduling, *To appear in: Zeitschrift für Operations Research.*

POTTERS J., REIJNIERSE H. (1992), Γ component additive games, *Research Memo Nijmegen University.*

Consequentialism, Non-Archimedean Probabilities, and Lexicographic Expected Utility

PETER J. HAMMOND

Department of Economics, Stanford University, CA 94305-6072, U.S.A.

Latest version: August 1992. An incomplete earlier version, last revised in August 1988, was entitled "Consequentialism, Extended Probabilities, and Lexicographic Expected Utility." In June 1992 an extensive revision was incorporated in a presentation to the Second Workshop on "Knowledge, Belief and Strategic Interaction: The Problem of Learning" at Castiglioncello (Livorno), Italy.

Abstract

Earlier work (Hammond, 1988a, b) on dynamically consistent "consequentialist" behaviour in decision trees was unable to treat zero probability events satisfactorily. Here the rational probability functions considered in Hammond (1992), as well as other non-Archimedean probabilities, are incorporated into decision trees. As before, the consequentialist axioms imply the existence of a preference ordering satisfying independence. In the case of rational probability functions, those axioms, together with continuity and a new refinement assumption, imply the maximization of a somewhat novel lexicographic expected utility preference relation. This is equivalent to maximization of expected utility in the ordering of the relevant non-Archimedean field.

Non-Archimedean Expected Utility

ma la natura la dà sempre scema
similemente operando all'artista
c'ha l'abito dell'arte e man che trema

Dante, *La Divina Commedia, Vol. III: Paradiso* (Canto XIII, 76–78)†

1. Introduction and Outline

1.1. Consequentialism in Single Person Decision Theory

The consequentialist approach to single-person decision theory, with uncertainty described by specified objective probabilities, was expounded in Hammond (1988a, b). In fact the latter paper also deals with states of nature and subjective probabilities. Here non-Archimedean subjective probabilities will not be considered at all, but left for later work.

This consequentialist approach is based on three axioms. Of these, the first requires behaviour to be well defined for an (almost) unrestricted domain of finite decision trees with: (i) decision nodes where the agent makes a move; (ii) chance nodes at which random moves occur with specified positive probabilities; (iii) and terminal nodes which result in a single consequence within a specified domain of relevant consequences. It follows that behaviour in any such tree results in a set of probability distributions over consequences. The second axiom requires behaviour to be dynamically consistent in continuation subtrees, in the sense that behaviour at any decision node is the same in a subtree as in a full tree. And the third is the "consequentialist choice" axiom, requiring that the set of possible random consequences of behaviour in any decision tree of the domain be explicable as the choice of desirable random consequences from the set of random consequences that the tree makes feasible.

† "But Nature fumbles, with no sure command
Over her tools, like an artificer
Who know his trade but has a trembling hand."

Dante Alighieri the Florentine, *The Divine Comedy, Cantica III: Paradise*; translated (rather freely) by D.L. Sayers and B. Reynolds (Penguin: Harmondsworth, 1962).

The earlier work then showed how these three consequentialist axioms imply the existence of a preference ordering (i.e., a complete and transitive weak preference relation) defined on the space of random consequences. Moreover, this ordering must satisfy Samuelson's (1952) independence axiom. In this way, two of the most important and even controversial axioms of standard decision theory become implications of apparently weaker and possibly more appealing axioms of the consequentialist reformulation. Thereafter, an extra condition of continuity of behaviour with respect to changing probabilities leads to the preference ordering having an expected utility representation.

1.2. Consequentialism in Game Theory

This paper is the second in a series whose purpose is to extend the scope of this consequentialist approach from single-person decision trees to multi-person extensive games. In fact, a decision tree is nothing more than a one person "consequentialist extensive game" of perfect and complete information. The difference from the usual notion of a game in extensive form comes about because no payoffs are specified. Instead, terminal nodes are assumed to result in pure consequences within the specified domain of consequences. Then the existence of a payoff function defined on this domain of consequences is not assumed, but becomes an important implication of consequentialism.

The main obstacle to this extension of consequentialism comes about because the earlier single person theory excludes zero probability chance moves — it is in this sense that the domain of allowable decision trees is *almost* rather than fully unrestricted. Such a restriction is excusable in single person decision theory where there are no good reasons for retaining zero probability events. In multi-person game theory, however, testing to see whether a particular profile of strategies for each player constitutes an equilibrium involves seeing what happens when any player deviates and then all the other players react according to their presumed equilibrium strategies. Yet these reactions are behaviour in the face of events which are supposed to have probability zero, since that is supposed to be the probability of any player deviating from equilibrium. So one is faced with the need to update probabilities in a Bayesian manner even though a zero probability event has occurred. For this reason, the zero probability restriction makes it difficult to apply consequentialist decision theory to multi-person games in a way that yields subgame perfect or other kinds of refined equilibria. The task of this work is to remove this burdensome restriction.

Not surprisingly, the zero probability problem has already led several game theorists to extend the space of ordinary probabilities in various ways. In particular, Selten (1975) and Myerson (1978) considered "trembles." Kreps and Wilson (1982), and then Blume, Brandenburger and Dekel (1991a, b) considered lexicographic hierarchies of probabilities. Myerson (1986) considered complete conditional probability systems. Finally, McLennan (1989a, b) considered logarithmic likelihood ratio functions whose values can be infinite. Hammond (1992) shows that all of these different extensions, when suitably formulated, are in fact equivalent to each other, and also to a particular space of "conditional rational probability functions."

In decision trees, it is usual to specify independent probabilities at each separate chance node. After all, in principle any causes of dependence can and should be modelled within the structure of the tree itself. Then, however, it is particularly important to be sure that the entire joint distribution of all chance moves is determined uniquely from the marginal probability distributions over the chance moves at each separate chance node of the decision tree. In the case of ordinary probabilities, this is trivial because joint probabilities are found by simply multiplying appropriate marginal probabilities. Yet Hammond (1992) also shows how the equivalent sets of extended probabilities mentioned in the previous paragraph all fail this crucial test. That is, many different joint extended probability distributions over nature's possible strategies in the decision tree can arise from the same collection of independent marginal probability distributions over nature's moves at different chance nodes. This is because such extended probabilities lack the structure of an algebraic field in which the operation of multiplication is well defined.

1.3. Consequentialism with Non-Archimedean Probabilities

So it seems necessary to work with a richer space of extended probabilities, for which multiplication and other algebraic field operations are well defined. There should also be an ordering relation rich enough to give meaning to the statements that probabilities are non-negative or positive and that they are larger or smaller. Now, within an ordered field such as the real line $\Re$, the *Archimedean axiom* states that, for any positive number r, there is an integer n for which $n\,r > 1$. Overcoming the zero probability problem seems to require some kind of *non-Archimedean* ordered field in which this axiom is violated. Obviously, any such field must have at least one positive "infinitesimal" element ϵ with the property that $n\epsilon < 1$ for every positive integer n, even though ϵ is positive. It follows that any such positive infinitesimal must be smaller than any positive real number; in particular, it cannot be a real number itself.

Section 2 below therefore begins by briefly reviewing the definition and key properties of non-Archimedean ordered fields. Particular attention is paid to the elementary field $\Re(\epsilon)$ whose use was recommended in Hammond (1992). Its members are rational functions in a single infinitesimal variable denoted by ϵ. For any finite support in an appropriate sample space, Section 2 proceeds to consider a corresponding set of elementary non-Archimedean probabilities. In the case when the field is $\Re(\epsilon)$, such probabilities are called "rational probability functions" (or RPF's).

It then becomes natural to consider in Section 3 decision trees having RPF's or other non-Archimedean instead of ordinary positive probabilities attached to each chance move in the tree. Behaviour in such trees gives rise to *non-Archimedean consequences* — i.e., RPF's or more general non-Archimedean conditional probability distributions over the domain of relevant consequences. Within the corresponding domain of finite *non-Archimedean consequentialist decision trees* the previous consequentialist axioms can be applied almost without change. Most implications are also the same as in Hammond (1988a, b), since virtually all the arguments in those two papers apply to probabilities taking values in a general ordered field, and not just to those taking values in the Archimedean ordered field $\Re$. In particular, the three "consequentialist" assumptions mentioned in Section 1.1 imply the existence of a revealed preference ordering. And this ordering must satisfy Samuelson's (1952) independence axiom.

The set of preference orderings that satisfy the independence axiom on the space of relevant non-Archimedean random consequences is actually very large. Many such orderings, however, pay no attention to the interpretation of ϵ as an infinitesimal. In addition, recall that the only motivation which has been offered for non-Archimedean probabilities is to resolve the zero probability problem mentioned in Section 1.2. Now, were zero probabilities to be allowed, the problem they create is that the usual decision criteria generate behaviour sets that are too large. Accordingly, Section 4 proposes an additional and rather natural refinement axiom. This requires that in any decision tree whose chance moves have non-Archimedean probabilities differing only infinitesimally from those in an ordinary decision tree with real probabilities, behaviour with non-Archimedean probabilities should refine that with ordinary probabilities. It is then shown how this refinement axiom implies that the strict preference relation over non-Archimedean random consequences must be refine the corresponding relation over ordinary random consequences. And, in the special case of RPF's, there must be a unique extension which can be regarded as a lexicographic hierarchy of preference orderings over ordinary random consequences.

Another part of the theory where the non-Archimedean field structure makes some difference is in the continuity condition set out in Section 5 as a necessary and sufficient condition for expected utility maximization. Within a general non-Archimedean field the construction used by Herstein and Milnor (1953) and others to determine the real values of a von Neumann-Morgenstern utility function is invalid, since it relies upon a continuity or "Archimedean" axiom. Nevertheless, the theory presented here is meant to extend the earlier standard theory of expected utility and subjective probability, so it seems reasonable to retain this Archimedean axiom for the subspace of decision trees with real valued positive probabilities. In combination with the earlier axioms concerning behaviour in decision trees, this *restricted continuity* axiom implies that, when probabilities are described by RPF's, all the preference orderings making up the lexicographic hierarchy described in Section 4 can be represented by the expected value of the same von Neumann-Morgenstern utility function. A particular feature of the new lexicographic expected utility criterion is that it generalizes the standard criterion presented by Blume, Brandenburger and Dekel (1991a, b). For example, it allows and even requires expected utility hierarchies of differing lengths to be compared.

Now, the expectation of any real valued utility function with respect to some non-Archimedean probability distribution is itself a member of the non-Archimedean ordered field introduced in Section 2. As Section 6 shows, the new lexicographic expected utility criterion is equivalent to maximizing non-Archimedean expected utility with respect to the ordering of the field $\Re(\epsilon)$ in which RPF's take their values.

Finally, Section 7 gathers together all the consequentialist axioms and their implications that have been set out in previous sections. They imply the existence of a unique class of cardinally equivalent von Neumann-Morgenstern utility functions such that consequentialist behaviour must be "non-Archimedean" Bayesian rational in the sense that it maximizes the lexicographic expected utility preference criterion set out in Section 4. Moreover, any behaviour which is non-Archimedean Bayesian rational in this sense will satisfy the consequentialist axioms. This is the main theorem of the paper.

2. Non-Archimedean Probabilities

2.1. General Non-Archimedean Ordered Fields

An *ordered field* $\langle \mathbb{F}, +, \cdot, 0, 1, > \rangle$ is a set $\mathbb{F}$ together with: (i) the two algebraic operations $+$ (addition) and $\cdot$ (multiplication); (ii) the two corresponding identity elements 0 and 1; (iii) the binary relation $>$ which is a total order of $\mathbb{F}$ satisfying $1 > 0$. The set $\mathbb{F}$ must be closed under its two algebraic operations. The usual properties of real number arithmetic also have to be satisfied — i.e., addition and multiplication both have to be commutative and associative, the distributive law must be satisfied, and every element of $x \in G$ must have both an additive inverse $-x$ and a multiplicative inverse $1/x$, except that $1/0$ is undefined. The order must be such that $y > z \iff y - z > 0$, while the set of positive elements in $\mathbf{F}$ must be closed under both addition and multiplication. Both the real line and the rationals are important and obvious examples of ordered fields. The set $Q(\sqrt{2})$ of real numbers expressible in the form $a + b\sqrt{2}$ for some pair of rationals $a, b \in Q$ is a somewhat less familiar example.

Any ordered field $\mathbf{F}$ has positive integer elements $n = 1, 2, \ldots$ which can be found by forming the sums $n = 1 + 1 + \ldots + 1$ of n copies of the element $1 \in \mathbf{F}$. Then $\mathbb{F}$ is said to be "Archimedean" if, given any $x > 0$ in $\mathbf{F}$, there exists such a positive integer n for which $n\,x > 1$. So any non-Archimedean ordered field must have at least one *positive infinitesimal* ϵ with the property that $n\,\epsilon \leq 1$ for all positive integers n.

The introduction claimed that the set of real valued probabilities needs extending for a fully satisfactory decision theory. In future, therefore, $\mathbf{F}$ will always be a non-Archimedean ordered field that extends the real line $\Re$. Now, for any positive $r \in \Re$, there exists an ordinary positive integer n satisfying $1/n < r \in \mathbf{F}$. Any positive infinitesimal $\epsilon \in \mathbf{F}$ must therefore satisfy $\epsilon \leq 1/n < r$, and so must be smaller than any positive real number.

For any $x \in \mathbf{F}$, let $|x|$ denote x if $x \geq 0$ and $-x$ if $x < 0$. Say that any $x \in \mathbf{F}$ is *infinitesimal* if $|x| < r$ for all (small) real $r > 0$, and that x is *finite* if $|x| < r$ for some (large enough) real r. Any $x \in \mathbf{F}$ is said to be *infinite* if and only if it is not finite. Any non-zero $x \in \mathbf{F}$ is therefore infinitesimal if and only $1/x$ is infinite.

Next, given any finite $x \in \mathbf{F}$, the two sets $\{r \in \Re \mid r > x\}$ and $\{r \in \Re \mid r \leq x\}$ partition the real line $\Re$, and so form a Dedekind cut. The usual properties of the real line then ensure that there is a unique ${}^0x \in \Re$, called the *real part* of x, defined by

$$^0x := \inf\{r \in \Re \mid r > x\} = \sup\{r \in \Re \mid r \leq x\}.$$

For any real $r > 0$, note that $x - r < {}^0x < x + r$. Define ${}^\epsilon x := x - {}^0x$. Then $|{}^\epsilon x| < r$ for all real $r > 0$, so ${}^\epsilon x$ is infinitesimal. Since $x = {}^0x + {}^\epsilon x$, it is natural to call ${}^\epsilon x$ the *infinitesimal part* of x.

2.2. An Elementary Non-Archimedean Ordered Field

Since decision and game theory would seem to require some non-Archimedean ordered field $\mathbf{F}$ containing $\Re$ as a subfield, it is natural to explore the simplest such field. This must contain at least one positive infinitesimal ϵ. So no candidate for the field $\mathbf{F}$ can possibly be simpler than the one that results from appending ϵ to $\Re$, and then closing the resulting set $\Re \cup \{\epsilon\}$ under the operations of addition, subtraction, multiplication, and division except by zero. The result of this closure is a field denoted by $\Re(\epsilon)$ that has been discussed by Robinson (1973, p. 88–9) in particular. Its members are all the "rational" functions which can be expressed as ratios

$$f(\epsilon) = \frac{A(\epsilon)}{B(\epsilon)} = \frac{a_0 + a_1\epsilon + a_2\epsilon^2 + \cdots + a_n\epsilon^n}{b_0 + b_1\epsilon + b_2\epsilon^2 + \cdots + b_m\epsilon^m} = \frac{\sum_{i=0}^n a_i\epsilon^i}{\sum_{i=0}^m b_i\epsilon^i} \tag{1}$$

of two polynomial functions $A(\epsilon), B(\epsilon)$ of the indeterminate ϵ with real coefficients; moreover not all the coefficients of the denominator $B(\epsilon)$ can be zero.

Now, one can simplify (1) by successively: (i) eliminating any leading zeros $a_0 = a_1 = \ldots = a_{k-1} = b_0 = b_1 = \ldots = b_{j-1} = 0$; (ii) dividing both numerator and denominator by the leading non-zero coefficient b_j of the denominator; (iii) cancelling any positive powers of ϵ that are common to all terms of both numerator and denominator and relabelling the coefficients a_i, b_i accordingly. The result is that any $f(\epsilon) \in \Re(\epsilon)$ given by (1) gets put into its *normalized form*

$$f(\epsilon) = \frac{\sum_{i=k}^n a_i\epsilon^i}{\epsilon^j + \sum_{i=j+1}^m b_i\epsilon^i} \tag{2}$$

for some integers $j, k, m, n \geq 0$ such that $j = 0$ or $k = 0$ (or both). Moreover $a_k \neq 0$ unless $f(\epsilon) = 0$. Note too that each real number $r \in \Re$ can be simply expressed in the form (2) by writing $r = r/1 \in \Re(\epsilon)$, with $j, k, m, n = 0$ and $a_0 = r$.

It remains to be shown that $\Re(\epsilon)$ really is a non-Archimedean ordered field. The binary relation $>$ will be defined so that $y > z \iff y - z > 0$ where, for any $x = f(\epsilon) \in \Re(\epsilon)$ in its normalized form (2), one has $f(\epsilon) > 0$ if and only if $a_k > 0$. Recalling that ϵ is intended to be an infinitesimal, this condition is entirely natural because it is equivalent to having $f(r)$, the corresponding real valued rational function of the real variable r, be positive for all small positive r. For later reference, note that $>$ is effectively a lexicographic relation. For if $f(\epsilon)$ is given by (1), then $f(\epsilon) > 0$ if and only if $a_k/b_j > 0$, where a_k and b_j are the first non-zero coefficients of the numerator and denominator respectively.

From the above definition, it is easy to check that $>$ is asymmetric and transitive, while either $f(\epsilon) > 0$ or $f(\epsilon) < 0$ unless $f(\epsilon) = 0$. So $>$ is indeed a total order. And it is easy and routine to check that the corresponding set of positive elements is closed under addition and multiplication. Finally, $\Re(\epsilon)$ is non-Archimedean because $1 > 0$ and so the order $>$ defined above satisfies $1 - n\epsilon > 0$ for every positive integer n.

Let $f(0) \in \Re$ denote the value at $r = 0$ of the corresponding polynomial function $f(r)$ of the real variable r. Then it is easy to see that any $f(\epsilon) \in \Re(\epsilon)$ given by (2) is infinitesimal if and only if $k > j = 0$, so that $f(0) = 0$. And any such $f(\epsilon)$ is infinite if and only if $j > k = 0$, so that $f(0)$ is undefined. Finally, whenever $f(\epsilon) \in \Re(\epsilon)$ is finite, $f(0)$ is equal to its real part ${}^0 f(\epsilon)$.

Choosing a more appropriate algebraic field in which probabilities can be defined is an important first step. And for the purposes of this paper and some later work in decision and game theory, the field $\Re(\epsilon)$ appears to be rich enough. However, some further extensions of $\Re(\epsilon)$ are eventually going to be necessary so as to accommodate countably additive non-Archimedean probability measures, continuous strategy spaces, etc. — for example, the set $\Re^*(\epsilon)$ mentioned in Hammond (1992), whose members are power series $\sum_{k=0}^{\infty} a_k \epsilon^k$ with real coefficients $a_0, a_1, a_2, \ldots$. Accordingly, much of the paper actually works with a general non-Archimedean ordered field $\mathbf{F}$ that extends $\Re(\epsilon)$. This field could be as rich as the whole non-standard real line ${}^*\Re$ of "hyperreals," or it could be one of many possible sub-fields of ${}^*\Re$, including $\Re^*(\epsilon)$.

2.3. A Positive Cone

Probabilities are always non-negative. Avoiding the zero probability problem requires them all to be positive. In fact, when requiring a probability to have some positive non-Archimedean value $p \in \mathbf{F}$, a more restrictive condition than $p > 0$ will be used. Probabilities will actually be given values in some convex *non-Archimedean positive cone* $\mathbf{P}$ — that is, in a set $\mathbf{P} \subset \mathbf{F}_+ := \{x \in \mathbf{F} \mid x > 0\}$ containing all the positive reals and at least one infinitesimal, such that $\mathbf{P}$ is closed under addition, multiplication and division. Of course, such a cone cannot be closed under subtraction. So it is natural to have $\mathbf{P}$ as a minimal set in $\mathbf{F}$ with these properties. The members of such a $\mathbf{P}$ will be described as *strongly positive.*

When $\mathbf{F} = \Re(\epsilon)$, let $\mathcal{P}(\epsilon)$ denote the set of all $f(\epsilon) \in \Re(\epsilon)$ given by (1) whose real coefficients a_i ($i = 0$ to I) and b_j ($j = 0$ to J) are all non-negative, while $f(\epsilon) \neq 0$. Equivalently, the numerator and denominator of $f(\epsilon)$ must each contain at least one positive real coefficient, and no negative coefficient. Obviously $\mathcal{P}(\epsilon)$ is the smallest set containing both the positive part of the real line and ϵ which is also closed under addition, multiplication and division. The set $\mathcal{P}(\epsilon)$ is therefore a convex non-Archimedean positive cone, implying that one can take $\mathbf{P} = \mathcal{P}(\epsilon)$.

2.4. Non-Archimedean Probabilities

Let Ω be a non-empty sample space. Note carefully that Ω is not required to be finite. Let F any non-empty finite subset of Ω. A $\mathbf{P}$*-probability on* (or *with support*) F is a mapping $p(\cdot) : 2^\Omega \to \mathbf{P} \cup \{0\}$ which is defined on the domain 2^Ω of all subsets of Ω, and satisfies the three axioms:

(i) $p(E) \in \mathbf{P}$ whenever $E \cap F \neq \emptyset$;

(ii) $p(E) = 1$ whenever $F \subset E \subset \Omega$;

(iii) $p(E \cup E') = p(E) + p(E')$ whenever $E, E' \subset \Omega$ are such that $E \cap E' = \emptyset$.

From axioms (ii) and (iii) it follows that, whenever $E \cap F = \emptyset$, then

$$1 = p(E \cup F) = p(E) + p(F) = p(E) + 1$$

and so $p(E) = 0$. Actually, apart from (i), these are the usual axioms of probability theory, but with $p(E)$ taking values in $\mathbf{P} \cup \{0\}$ instead of $\Re_+$. However, axiom (i) strengthens the usual condition that $p(E) \geq 0$ for all $E \subset F$. To justify this strengthening, recall that the only reason for introducing extended and non-Archimedean probabilities has been the need to overcome the zero probability problem in decision and game theory. Note too that $p(E)$ is allowed to be an arbitrarily small strongly positive infinitesimal in $\mathbf{P}$.

Let $\Delta^0(F;\mathbf{P})$ denote the set of all such $\mathbf{P}$-probabilities with support F. This set is obviously an extension of the set $\Delta^0(F)$ of ordinary probability distributions with support F. Let $\Delta(\Omega;\mathbf{P})$ denote the set of all $\mathbf{P}$-probabilities that belong to $\Delta^0(F;\mathbf{P})$, for some finite $F \subset \Omega$. Thus all the members of $\Delta^0(F;\mathbf{P})$ definitely have F as their support, whereas members of $\Delta(\Omega;\mathbf{P})$ have supports which can be any finite subset of Ω.

As usual with finitely supported probability distributions, any $p(\cdot) \in \Delta^0(F;\mathbf{P})$ is completely determined by its values $p(\{\omega\})$ on the singleton subsets $\{\omega\}$ $(\omega \in F)$. With the customary slight abuse of notation, write these values as $p(\omega)$ $(\omega \in F)$, all of which must be strongly positive. Moreover, it must be true that $p(\omega) = {}^0p(\omega) + \eta(\omega)$, where the real part ${}^0p(\cdot)$ is an ordinary probability distribution in $\Delta(F)$, while each $\eta(\omega)$ is infinitesimal in $\mathbb{F}$, and also $\sum_{\omega \in F} \eta(\omega) = 0$. For any $\omega \in F$ it is necessary to have ${}^0p(\omega) > 0$ or $\eta(\omega) \in \mathbf{P}$ (or both).

In the special case when $\mathbf{P} = \mathcal{P}(\epsilon)$, such non-Archimedean probabilities will be called *rational probability functions* (or RPF's). Let $\Delta^0(F;\epsilon)$ denote the set of all such RPF's with support F. And let $\Delta(\Omega;\epsilon)$ denote the set of all RPF's that belong to $\Delta^0(F;\epsilon)$, for some finite $F \subset \Omega$.

Members of $\Delta^0(F;\epsilon)$ have probabilities given, for all $\omega \in F$, by rational functions

$$p(\omega;\epsilon) = \frac{A(\omega;\epsilon)}{B(\omega;\epsilon)} = \frac{a_0(\omega) + a_1(\omega)\,\epsilon + a_2(\omega)\,\epsilon^2 + \cdots + a_{I(\omega)}(\omega)\epsilon^{I(\omega)}}{b_0(\omega) + b_1(\omega)\,\epsilon + b_2(\omega)\,\epsilon^2 + \cdots + b_{J(\omega)}(\omega)\epsilon^{J(\omega)}} = \frac{\sum_{i=0}^{I(\omega)} a_i(\omega)\,\epsilon^i}{\sum_{j=0}^{J(\omega)} b_j(\omega)\,\epsilon^j}$$

of the form (1). Here the coefficients $a_i(\omega)$ $(i = 0$ to $I(\omega))$ and $b_j(\omega)$ $(j = 0$ to $J(\omega))$ are all non-negative real numbers and, for any $\omega \in F$, neither all the $a_i(\omega)$ nor all the $b_j(\omega)$ are zero. Now, the finite collection $B(\omega;\epsilon)$ $(\omega \in F)$ of polynomials has a positive lowest common denominator which will be written as $L(\epsilon) := \sum_{h=0}^{H} \ell_h\,\epsilon^h$. For all $\omega \in F$ one has

$$p(\omega;\epsilon) = \frac{L(\omega;\epsilon)}{L(\epsilon)} = \frac{\sum_{h=0}^{H} \ell_h(\omega)\,\epsilon^h}{\sum_{h=0}^{H} \ell_h\,\epsilon^h}, \text{ where } L(\omega;\epsilon) := \frac{A(\omega;\epsilon)\,L(\epsilon)}{B(\omega;\epsilon)}. \tag{3}$$

After repeating the operations used to obtain the normalized form (2) of a general rational function (1) — i.e., eliminating any leading zeros, cancelling redundant powers of ϵ, and dividing by the leading coefficient of the denominator — one obtains the *normalized form*

$$p(\omega;\epsilon) = \frac{p_0(\omega) + \sum_{h=1}^{H} \ell_h(\omega)\,\epsilon^h}{1 + \sum_{h=1}^{H} \ell_h\,\epsilon^h}. \tag{4}$$

Here $\sum_{\omega\in F} p_0(\omega) = 1$ and $\sum_{\omega\in F} \ell_h(\omega) = \ell_h$ for $h = 1$ to H. Moreover $p_0(\omega)$ must be equal to the real part ${}^0p(\omega;\epsilon)$ of $p(\omega;\epsilon)$, for all $\omega \in F$. In particular $p_0(\cdot) \in \Delta(F)$ is an ordinary probability distribution.

An alternative form of (4) will be used in Section 4 below. This comes from dropping any terms for which $\ell_h = 0$, letting H denote the remaining set of those integers h with $\ell_h > 0$. Then (4) becomes

$$p(\omega;\epsilon) = \frac{\sum_{k\in K} \ell_k\, p_k(\omega)\,\epsilon^k}{\sum_{k\in K} \ell_k\,\epsilon^k} \tag{5}$$

where $p_k(\omega) := \ell_k(\omega)/\ell_k$ for $k \in K$ and all $\omega \in F$. Then $0 \in K$, $\ell_0 = 1$, and $p_k(\cdot) \in \Delta(F)$ for all $k \in K$.

Finally, note that (5) can be regarded as specifying probabilities

$$p^*(k,\omega;\epsilon) := \frac{\ell_k\, p_k(\omega)\,\epsilon^k}{\sum_{j\in K} \ell_j\,\epsilon^j}$$

as functions of ϵ on the extended sample space $\mathcal{N} \times \Omega$, where $\mathcal{N}$ denotes the set of non-negative integers, to be interpreted as various orders in a lexicographic hierarchy (cf. Blume *et al.*, 1991a, b). This is equivalent to compounding the ordinary conditional distributions $p^*(\omega|k) := p_k(\omega)$ (all $\omega \in F$ and $k \in K$) with the particular RPF $\ell(\cdot;\epsilon) \in \Delta(\mathcal{N};\epsilon)$ given by

$$\ell(k;\epsilon) := p^*(\{k\} \times \Omega;\epsilon) = \frac{\ell_k\,\epsilon^k}{\sum_{j\in K} \ell_j\,\epsilon^j} \quad \text{(all } k \in K\text{)}.$$

2.5. Independence

Suppose that the finite non-empty sample space Ω is the n-fold Cartesian product $\prod_{s=1}^{n} \Omega^s$. Suppose that, for $s = 1$ to n, there are $\mathbf{P}$-probability distributions $p^s(\cdot) \in \Delta^0(F^s; \mathbf{P})$ with respective finite supports $F^s \subset \Omega^s$. Then these n distributions are said to be *independent* if their joint distribution has support $F = \prod_{s=1}^{n} F^s$ and is described by the unique $\mathbf{P}$-probability distribution $p(\cdot) \in \Delta(F; \mathbf{P})$ that satisfies

$$p(\prod_{s=1}^{n} E^s) = \prod_{s=1}^{n} p^s(E^s) \quad \text{whenever } E^s \subset F^s \ (s = 1, 2, \ldots, n).$$

This corresponds to the strongest of the three definitions of independence in Blume *et al.* (1991a) and in Hammond (1992). And it is the only one of the three allowing the joint distribution to be inferred uniquely from the independent marginal distributions.

2.6. Non-Archimedean Conditional Probabilities

Suppose that $p(\cdot) \in \Delta^0(F; \mathbf{P})$ is any $\mathbf{P}$-probability distribution on the finite subset $F \subset \Omega$. Then the non-Archimedean conditional probability

$$P(E|E') := p(E)/p(E') \in \mathbf{P} \tag{6}$$

is certainly well defined whenever $\emptyset \neq E \subset E' \subset F$. The zero probability problem has therefore been resolved.

Consider the case when $\mathbf{P} = \mathcal{P}(\epsilon)$ and $p(\cdot; \epsilon) \in \Delta^0(F; \epsilon)$ is any RPF on the finite subset $F \subset \Omega$. Then the non-Archimedean conditional probability (6) takes the form

$$P(E|E'; \epsilon) := p(E; \epsilon)/p(E'; \epsilon) \in \mathcal{P}(\epsilon) \tag{7}$$

where $p(E; \epsilon)$ and $p(E'; \epsilon)$ are rational functions in $\mathcal{P}(\epsilon)$, and so therefore is $P(E|E'; \epsilon)$. Since ϵ is an infinitesimal, it is tempting in this case to consider the ordinary conditional probabilities that are defined by the limit

$$P(E|E') := \lim_{r \to 0+} P(E|E'; r), \tag{8}$$

of the positive real valued rational function $P(E|E'; r)$ as r tends to zero through ordinary positive real values. The conditional probabilities $P(E|E')$ $(\emptyset \neq E \subset E' \subset F)$ then form a *complete conditional probability system* (or CCPS) on F, of the kind studied by Rényi (1955, 1970), Lindley (1965), and Myerson (1986), amongst others. Each such CCPS is obviously represented by an equivalence class of RPF's, where any two RPF's $p(\cdot;\epsilon), q(\cdot;\epsilon) \in \Delta^0(F;\epsilon)$ are to be regarded as equivalent if and only if

$$\lim_{r\to 0+} p(E;r)/p(E';r) = \lim_{r\to 0+} q(E;r)/q(E';r) \text{ whenever } \emptyset \neq E \subset E' \subset F. \tag{9}$$

Moreover, as pointed out in Hammond (1992), each such equivalence class of RPF's can be represented by a single *conditional rational probability function* satisfying the property that

$$p(\omega;\epsilon) = \frac{p_{k(\omega)}(\omega)\, \epsilon^{k(\omega)}}{\sum_{k=0}^{K} \epsilon^k} \tag{10}$$

for all $\omega \in F$, where $p_k \in \Delta^0(F_k)$ are ordinary probability distributions whose supports

$$F_k = \{\, \omega \in F \mid p_k(\omega) > 0 \,\} = \{\, \omega \in F \mid k(\omega) = k \,\} \quad (k = 0 \text{ to } K) \; .$$

form a partition of F. However, considering only such CCPS's loses a lot of valuable relevant information. For, as discussed in Section 1.2, the joint distribution of several independent random variables is only uniquely determined from the marginal distributions when non-Archimedean probabilities are represented by RPF's in general form, with values in an algebraic field.

3. Non-Archimedean Consequentialist Behaviour

3.1. Non-Archimedean Consequentialist Decision Trees

Let Y be a given domain of consequences which could conceivably occur. As remarked in Section 1.1, consequentialism in single-person decision theory considers dynamically consistent behaviour β in an almost unrestricted domain $\mathcal{T}(Y)$ of consequentialist finite decision trees. These are decision trees in the sense of Raiffa (1968), except that payoffs are not specified. Instead, any terminal node x in any tree $T \in \mathcal{T}(Y)$ has an associated consequence $y = \gamma(x)$ within the consequence domain Y.

This paper will consider instead the set $\mathcal{T}(Y;\mathbb{P})$ of $\mathbb{P}$-*consequentialist* finite decision trees. Each member of $\mathcal{T}(Y;\mathbb{P})$ is a collection

$$T = \langle N, N^*, N^0, X, N_{+1}(\cdot), n_0, \pi(\cdot|\cdot), \gamma(\cdot)\rangle \tag{11}$$

whose eight component parts are described and interpreted as follows:

(i) N is a non-empty finite set of *nodes* of the tree T, which is partitioned into the four disjoint sets N^*, N^0, N^1, and X having properties (ii)–(vii) below;

(ii) N^* is the (possibly empty) set of *decision nodes*;

(iii) N^0 is the (possibly empty) set of *chance nodes*;

(iv) X is the non-empty set of *terminal nodes*;

(v) $N_{+1} : N \twoheadrightarrow N$ is the *immediate successor* correspondence which, so that T really is indeed a tree, must satisfy:

(a) $\forall n \in N : \; n \notin N_{+1}(n)$;

(b) $\forall n \in N : \; N_{+1}(n) = \emptyset \iff n \in X$;

(c) $\forall n, n' \in N : \; N_{+1}(n) \cap N_{+1}(n') \neq \emptyset \iff n = n'$;

and must also generate an acyclic binary *successor* relation $\succ$ on N, defined by the property that $n' \succ n$ if and only if there exists a chain $n_1, n_2, \ldots, n_k$ in N such that $n_1 = n$, $n_k = n'$ and $n_{j+1} \in N_{+1}(n_j)$ for $j = 1$ to $k - 1$;

(vi) n_0 is the unique *initial node* in N satisfying $\forall n \in N : \; n_0 \notin N_{+1}(n)$;

(vii) at each chance node $n \in N^0$, there is a non-Archimedean conditional probability distribution $\pi(\cdot|n) \in \Delta(N_{+1}(n); \mathbb{P})$ over the set $N_{+1}(n)$ (whose members are to be interpreted as the possible chance moves from n to each succeeding node $n' \in N_{+1}(n)$);

(viii) $\gamma : X \to Y$ is the *consequence mapping*, indicating the consequence $\gamma(x)$ of reaching each terminal node x.

Most of this definition is identical to that in Hammond (1988a, b, Section 2). Natural nodes and sets of possible states of the world are not considered, since consideration of subjective probabilities has been left for a later paper. Otherwise, only the concept of $\mathbb{P}$-probability in part (vii) and the consequence mapping in part (viii) are different. The latter has been changed so that each terminal node x gives rise to just one sure consequence $\gamma(x) \in Y$, rather than to a probability distribution over Y. The change is just to make clear how all uncertainty is eventually resolved within a decision tree. The proof of the Refinement Lemma in Section 4.1 below contains an example illustrating this definition.

Where it is desirable to emphasize dependence on T, I shall write $N(T)$, $N^*(T)$, etc.

3.2. Dynamically Consistent Behaviour

As in the earlier work described in Section 1.1, it will now be assumed that *behaviour* is formally described by a correspondence β with a domain consisting of all pairs (T, n) satisfying $T \in \mathcal{T}(Y; \mathbf{P})$ and $n \in N^*(T)$. Its value is a *behaviour set* $\beta(T, n)$, which is a non-empty subset of the appropriate set $N_{+1}(T, n)$ of all decisions that are feasible at the decision node n of the tree T in the domain $\mathcal{T}(Y; \mathbf{P})$ of non-Archimedean consequentialist decision trees.

Now, given any decision tree $T \in \mathcal{T}(Y; \mathbf{P})$ and any fixed node $\bar{n}$ of T, there is a "subtree" of T or a *continuation from* $\bar{n}$ with

$$T(\bar{n}) := \bar{T} = \langle \bar{N}, \bar{N}^*, \bar{N}^0, \bar{X}, \bar{N}_{+1}(\cdot), \bar{n}_0, \bar{\pi}(\cdot|\cdot), \bar{\gamma}(\cdot) \rangle. \tag{12}$$

To define $T(\bar{n})$ explicitly, first let $N(n) := \{ n' \in N \mid n' \succ n \text{ or } n' = n \}$ denote the set of nodes in N which either succeed or coincide with n. Then $T(\bar{n})$ is the decision tree with the initial node $\bar{n}_0 := \bar{n}$, the set of nodes $\bar{N} := N(\bar{n})$ and with all of the other sets, correspondences, and functions $\bar{N}^*, \bar{N}^0, \bar{X}, \bar{N}_{+1}(\cdot), \bar{\pi}(\cdot|\cdot), \bar{\gamma}(\cdot)$ of (12) given by appropriate restrictions of $N^*, N^0, X, N_{+1}(\cdot), \pi(\cdot|\cdot), \gamma(\cdot)$ to the smaller set of nodes $\bar{N}$. From this definition it is obvious that $T(\bar{n})$ meets all the criteria set out in Section 3.1 above, and so is itself an non-Archimedean consequentialist decision tree in $\mathcal{T}(Y; \mathbf{P})$.

Suppose that n is any decision node of a tree $T \in \mathcal{T}(Y; \mathbf{P})$ with the set of nodes N. When the agent comes to make a decision at node n, the remaining decision problem is really sufficiently described by the tree $T(n)$. Behaviour at node n must therefore be described by $\beta(T(n), n)$ as well as by $\beta(T, n)$. Thus it will also be assumed that behaviour is *dynamically consistent* in the sense that $\beta(T, n) = \beta(T(n), n)$ at all decision nodes n of every tree $T \in \mathcal{T}(Y; \mathbf{P})$. This consistency condition is entirely natural since, as discussed in Hammond (1988a, b), it is satisfied even by a naïve agent who neglects changing tastes altogether. Of course, a naïve agent's actual behaviour usually departs from planned behaviour. Also, except in very special cases, naïve behaviour violates consequentialism, as defined below (cf. Hammond, 1976).

From now on only consistent behaviour will be considered, and will be called simply *behaviour*.

3.3. Non-Archimedean Consequences of Behaviour

Finally, it will be presumed that the domain of consequences has been specified broadly enough to capture everything that is relevant for the agent's behaviour. Then "consequentialism" means that in all decision trees in the domain, including the "continuation subtrees" of any tree, the agent's behaviour gives rise to a non-empty set of possible "chosen" random consequences which depends only upon the feasible set of random consequences. Before this can be formalized it is obviously necessary to see first what the feasible set and choice set are in any tree $T \in \mathcal{T}(Y; \mathbb{P})$.

Let $\Delta(Y; \mathbb{P})$ denote the set of all $\mathbb{P}$-probabilities when the sample space is taken to be the consequence domain Y. It turns out that, in any tree $T \in \mathcal{T}(Y; \mathbb{P})$, any kind of feasible behaviour must yield a random consequence belonging to some non-empty *feasible set* $F(T) \subset \Delta(Y; \mathbb{P})$. Moreover, behaviour β must yield a random consequence belonging to some non-empty *(revealed) choice set* $\Phi_\beta(T) \subset F(T)$. This is best demonstrated by using backward recursion to construct, in successively larger and larger subtrees $T(n)$ with earlier and earlier initial nodes n in $N(T)$, the corresponding pairs of subsets $F(T, n)$ and $\Phi_\beta(T, n)$ of $\Delta(Y; \mathbb{P})$. Moreover, backward induction can be used to show that

$$\emptyset \neq \Phi_\beta(T, n) \subset F(T, n) \subset \Delta(Y; \mathbb{P})$$

at every node $n \in N(T)$. Finally, of course, one works back to the initial node n_0 at which $F(T) = F(T, n_0)$ and $\Phi_\beta(T) = \Phi_\beta(T, n_0)$, so that

$$\emptyset \neq \Phi_\beta(T) \subset F(T) \subset \Delta(Y; \mathbb{P}).$$

The backward recursion and backward induction start at the terminal nodes $x \in X$ where only a single consequence $\gamma(x)$ is possible. Then

$$\emptyset \neq F(T, x) = \Phi_\beta(T, x) = \{\delta_{\gamma(x)}(\cdot)\} \subset \Delta(Y; \mathbb{P}) \tag{13}$$

where $\delta_{\gamma(x)}(\cdot)$ denotes the unique degenerate $\mathbb{P}$-probability distribution in $\Delta^0(\{\gamma(x)\}; \mathbb{P})$ with $\delta_{\gamma(x)}(\{\gamma(x)\}) = 1$. At previous nodes $n \in N \setminus X$, both $F(T, n)$ and $\Phi_\beta(T, n)$ are calculated from the values of $F(T, n')$ and $\Phi_\beta(T, n')$ at all nodes $n' \in N_{+1}(n)$ which immediately succeed n. There are two different cases — cf. Hammond (1988b, Section 4).

Case 1. At any decision node $n \in N^*$ one has

$$\emptyset \neq \Phi_\beta(T,n) := \bigcup_{n' \in \beta(T,n)} \Phi_\beta(T,n') \subset F(T,n) := \bigcup_{n' \in N_{+1}(n)} F(T,n') \subset \Delta(Y;\mathbf{P}). \tag{14}$$

Case 2. At any chance node $n \in N^0$ one has

$$\begin{aligned} \emptyset \neq \Phi_\beta(T,n) &:= \sum\nolimits_{n' \in N_{+1}(n)} \pi(n'|n)\, \Phi_\beta(T,n') \\ \subset F(T,n) &:= \sum\nolimits_{n' \in N_{+1}(n)} \pi(n'|n)\, F(T,n') \subset \Delta(Y;\mathbf{P}). \end{aligned} \tag{15}$$

These constructions (14) and (15) evidently work just as well in the set $\Delta(Y;\mathbf{P})$ as they did before in $\Delta(Y)$. The proof of the Refinement Lemma in Section 4.1 provides a simple example of how they work in practice.

3.4. Non-Archimedean Consequentialist Behaviour

The *non-Archimedean consequentialist choice axiom* requires behaviour β to reveal a unique *non-Archimedean consequence choice function* C_β with the property that

$$\Phi_\beta(T) = C_\beta(F(T)) \tag{16}$$

in all the trees $T \in \mathcal{T}(Y;\mathbf{P})$. In particular, the structure of the decision tree must be irrelevant to consequentialist behaviour.

3.5. Ordinality and Independence

So the three consequentialist axioms require that the behaviour sets $\beta(T,n)$: (i) are non-empty subsets of $N_{+1}(n)$ defined at every decision node n of every tree $T \in \mathcal{T}(Y;\mathbf{P})$; (ii) satisfy the consistency condition $\beta(T(n),n') = \beta(T,n')$ at all decision nodes n' of any subtree $T(n)$ of a tree $T \in \mathcal{T}(Y;\mathbf{P})$; (iii) satisfy the consequentialist choice axiom (16).

The arguments of Hammond (1988b, Sections 5 and 6) can now be applied virtually without change, and so will not be repeated here. They show first that consequentialist behaviour β reveals, not only a consequence choice function C_β, but also a corresponding *consequence preference ordering* R — i.e., a complete transitive binary relation — on the set $\Delta(Y;\mathbf{P})$ of $\mathbf{P}$-probabilities. Thus, for every $T \in \mathcal{T}(Y;\mathbf{P})$, one has

$$\Phi_\beta(T) = \{\, \lambda \in F(T) \mid \mu \in F(T) \Longrightarrow \lambda \; R \; \mu \,\}.$$

Second, on the space $\Delta(Y)$ of ordinary probability distributions, which is of course a subset of $\Delta(Y;\mathbb{P})$, it was shown that the *independence condition* due to Samuelson (1952) is another implication of consequentialism. For all ordinary probability distributions $\lambda, \mu, \nu \in \Delta(Y;\mathbb{P})$ and all real numbers α with $0 < \alpha < 1$, independence requires that

$$\lambda \; R \; \mu \iff [\alpha \lambda + (1-\alpha)\nu] \; R \; [\alpha \mu + (1-\alpha)\nu]. \tag{17}$$

Exactly the same arguments now imply the *non-Archimedean independence condition* on $\Delta(Y;\mathbb{P})$. For all $\lambda, \mu, \nu \in \Delta(Y;\mathbb{P})$ this requires that

$$\lambda \; R \; \mu \iff \frac{\alpha \lambda + \theta \nu}{\alpha + \theta} \; R \; \frac{\alpha \mu + \theta \nu}{\alpha + \theta} \tag{18}$$

whenever $\alpha, \theta \in \mathbb{P}$, so that $\alpha\,(\alpha+\theta)^{-1}$ and $\theta\,(\alpha+\theta)^{-1}$ can be regarded as $\mathbb{P}$-probabilities over a pair of disjoint states.

In Hammond (1988b, Section 8) it is also shown that any preference ordering R over the set $\Delta(Y)$ satisfying the independence condition (17) generates a consequentialist and dynamically consistent behaviour norm on the "almost unrestricted domain" of all finite consequentialist decision trees having strictly positive ordinary probabilities at all chance nodes. It is important to consider only trees in this almost unrestricted domain because, if a completely unrestricted domain of finite consequentialist decision trees were allowed instead, then the implication would be that all random consequences in each space $\Delta(Y)$ must be indifferent, and so the behaviour norm must satisfy $\beta(T,n) = N_{+1}(T,n)$ at every decision node n of every tree in the unrestricted domain. Here, a corresponding result is true, but on the less restricted domain $\mathcal{T}(Y;\mathbb{P})$ of finite consequentialist decision trees having strongly positive non-Archimedean probabilities at all chance nodes. For any preference ordering R over the set $\Delta(Y;\mathbb{P})$ satisfying the new independence condition (18) will generate a consequentialist and dynamically consistent behaviour on this domain. Once again, the proof is exactly the same as before.

4. Lexicographic Refinements

4.1. A Refinement Axiom

There are many different preference orderings R on $\Delta(Y;\mathbf{P})$ satisfying independence (18). Some of these are implausible, however. For consider the case when $\mathbf{P} = \mathcal{P}(\epsilon)$. Let $v : Y \to \Re$ be any von Neumann-Morgenstern utility function defined on the set Y of all possible sure consequences. Then, for each positive real number r, there is a corresponding ordering R_r with the property that

$$p\ R\ q \iff \sum_{y \in Y} [p(y;r) - q(y;r)]\, v(y) \geq 0 \tag{19}$$

whenever $p, q \in \Delta(Y;\epsilon)$, where $p(y;r)$ and $q(y;r)$ denote the real numbers obtained by regarding p and q as functions of the real variable r instead of the infinitesimal ϵ. The preferences defined by (19) obviously satisfy independence (18), as well as the restricted continuity condition to be considered later. Yet such orderings pay no attention to the intended interpretation of ϵ as an infinitesimal. A further assumption is needed.

As explained in Hammond (1992), the reason for introducing probabilities with values in a general non-Archimedean cone $\mathbf{P}$ is to refine consequentialist behaviour in trees having zero probabilities at some chance nodes, while leaving unaffected such behaviour in trees having positive probabilities at all chance nodes. Now, given any non-Archimedean tree $T \in \mathcal{T}(Y;\mathbf{P})$ as in Section 3.1, let ${}^0T \in \mathcal{T}(Y)$ be the corresponding ordinary tree obtained when every non-Archimedean probability $\pi(n'|n) \in \mathbf{P}$ ($n \in N^0$, $n' \in N_{+1}(n)$) in T is replaced by its corresponding real part ${}^0\pi(n'|n) \in \Re$. Also, to ensure that ${}^0\pi(n'|n) > 0$ throughout ${}^0T$, remove the entire subtree ${}^0T(n')$ from ${}^0T$ whenever ${}^0\pi(n'|n) = 0$ for some node $n' \in N_{+1}(n)$ immediately succeeding the chance node $n \in N^0$.

The *refinement axiom* then requires that at any decision node $n \in N^*({}^0T) \subset N^*(T)$, one must have $\beta(T,n) \subset \beta({}^0T,n)$. In particular, if $n \in N^*({}^0T)$ is such that $\beta({}^0T,n) = \{n'\}$ for some unique $n' \in N_{+1}(n)$, then it must be true that $\beta(T,n) = \{n'\}$ as well. Actually, it will be enough to assume this weaker condition in what follows. The main implication of this refinement axiom is the following Lemma, whose conclusion could almost have been stated as an alternative to the axiom.

REFINEMENT LEMMA. *In combination with the consequentialist axioms of Section 3.5, the refinement axiom implies that, whenever $p, q \in \Delta(Y;\mathbf{P})$ and ${}^0p\ P\ {}^0q$, then $p\ P\ q$.*

PROOF: First, let

$$Y_p := \{\, y \in Y \mid p(y) > 0 \,\} \quad \text{and} \quad Y_q := \{\, y \in Y \mid q(y) > 0 \,\}$$

denote the finite supports of the two distributions $p, q \in \Delta(Y; \mathbf{P})$. Then consider the particular finite decision tree $T \in \mathcal{T}(Y; \mathbf{P})$ with initial node n_0, which is the only decision node, while the other nodes satisfy:

$$N_{+1}(n_0) = N^0 = \{\, n_p, n_q \,\} \quad \text{and} \quad X = X_p \cup X_q$$

where $X_p := N_{+1}(n_p) = \{\, x_p(y) \mid y \in Y_p \,\}$ and $X_q := N_{+1}(n_q) = \{\, x_q(y) \mid y \in Y_q \,\}$.
Suppose too that the probabilities and consequences in T are given by

$$\pi(x_p(y)|n_p) = p(y) \quad \text{and} \quad \gamma(x_p(y)) = y \ (\text{all } y \in Y_p);$$

$$\pi(x_q(y)|n_q) = q(y) \quad \text{and} \quad \gamma(x_q(y)) = y \ (\text{all } y \in Y_q).$$

Then the backward recursion construction of Section 3.3 shows that

$$\Phi_\beta(T, x_p(y)) = F(T, x_p(y)) = \{\delta_y\} \ (\text{all } y \in Y_p);$$

$$\text{and} \quad \Phi_\beta(T, x_q(y)) = F(T, x_q(y)) = \{\delta_y\} \ (\text{all } y \in Y_q)$$

at the terminal nodes, while

$$\Phi_\beta(T, n_p) = F(T, n_p) = \sum\nolimits_{x \in X_p} \pi(x|n_p)\, F(T, x) = \sum\nolimits_{y \in Y_p} p(y)\, \{\delta_y\} = \{p\};$$

$$\Phi_\beta(T, n_q) = F(T, n_q) = \sum\nolimits_{x \in X_q} \pi(x|n_q)\, F(T, x) = \sum\nolimits_{y \in Y_q} q(y)\, \{\delta_y\} = \{q\}.$$

at the chance nodes. So finally the feasible set is

$$F(T) = F(T, n_0) = F(T, n_p) \cup F(T, n_q) = \{p\} \cup \{q\} = \{\, p, q \,\} \subset \Delta(Y; \mathbf{P}).$$

Also the set of revealed consequences is $\Phi_\beta(T) = \Phi_\beta(T, n_0)$, where

$$p \in \Phi_\beta(T, n_0) \iff n_p \in \beta(T, n_0) \quad \text{and} \quad q \in \Phi_\beta(T, n_0) \iff n_q \in \beta(T, n_0).$$

Now ${}^0T$ differs from T only in replacing the probabilities $p(y)$ and $q(y)$ by their respective real parts ${}^0p(y)$, ${}^0q(y)$, while also excluding altogether any terminal nodes $x_p(y)$ or $x_q(y)$ for which ${}^0p(y) = 0$ or ${}^0q(y) = 0$, as appropriate. So a similar construction in ${}^0T$ shows that $F({}^0T) = \{\, {}^0p, {}^0q \,\} \subset \Delta(Y)$. Then the hypothesis ${}^0p \; P \; {}^0q$ implies $\Phi_\beta({}^0T) = \{{}^0p\}$. This obviously requires $\beta({}^0T, n_0) = \{n_p\}$. But then the refinement axiom, even in its weak form, implies $\beta(T, n_0) = \{n_p\}$. Therefore $\Phi_\beta(T) = \{p\}$, implying that $p \; P \; q$. ∎

This lemma already gives the beginnings of a lexicographic preference criterion. It is incomplete, however, because in the case when ${}^0p \; I \; {}^0q$ nothing yet has been said about what higher criterion determines whether or not $p \; P \; q$.

4.2. Lexicographic Preferences

This section will consider RPF's with values in $\mathcal{P}(\epsilon)$ and show that there must be a complete lexicographic preference criterion in this special case. To this end, let

$$p(y;\epsilon) = \frac{\sum_{i\in I} P_i\, p_i(y)\, \epsilon^i}{\sum_{i\in I} P_i\, \epsilon^i} \quad \text{and} \quad q(y;\epsilon) = \frac{\sum_{j\in J} Q_j\, q_j(y)\, \epsilon^j}{\sum_{j\in J} Q_j\, \epsilon^j} \tag{20}$$

be any two RPF's $p, q \in \Delta(Y;\epsilon)$ that have been expressed in the form (5). In particular, it must be true that $0 \in I \cap J$, $P_0 = Q_0 = 1$, while $P_i > 0$, $p_i(\cdot) \in \Delta(Y)$ (all $i \in I$) and $Q_j > 0$, $q_j(\cdot) \in \Delta(Y)$ (all $j \in J$). Now these two RPF's can be given the common denominator

$$\sum_{k\in K} R_k\, \epsilon^k := \sum_{i\in I} P_i\, \epsilon^i \times \sum_{j\in J} Q_j\, \epsilon^j$$

where $K := I + J$ (as the sum of the two sets of integers) and $R_k := \sum_{(i,j)\in H_k} P_i\, Q_j$ with $H_k := \{\, (i,j) \in I \times J \mid i + j = k \,\}$ (all $k \in K$). These definitions, together with the previously specified properties of I, J, P_i ($i \in I$), Q_j ($j \in J$), also imply that $0 \in K$, while $R_0 = 1$ and $R_k > 0$ ($k \in K$). Then one has

$$p(y;\epsilon) = \frac{\sum_{i\in I} P_i\, p_i(y)\, \epsilon^i \times \sum_{j\in J} Q_j\, \epsilon^j}{\sum_{k\in K} R_k\, \epsilon^k} = \frac{\sum_{k\in K} \sum_{(i,j)\in H_k} P_i\, p_i(y)\, Q_j\, \epsilon^k}{\sum_{k\in K} R_k\, \epsilon^k}. \tag{21}$$

Now define $p_k^*(\cdot), q_k^*(\cdot) \in \Delta(Y)$ (all $k \in K$) so that

$$p_k^*(y) := \sum_{(i,j)\in H_k} \frac{P_i\, Q_j}{R_k}\, p_i(y) \quad \text{and} \quad q_k^*(y) := \sum_{(i,j)\in H_k} \frac{P_i\, Q_j}{R_k}\, q_j(y). \tag{22}$$

With this definition, (21) implies that

$$p(y;\epsilon) = \frac{\sum_{k\in K} R_k\, p_k^*(y)\, \epsilon^k}{\sum_{k\in K} R_k\, \epsilon^k} \quad \text{and similarly} \quad q(y;\epsilon) = \frac{\sum_{k\in K} R_k\, q_k^*(y)\, \epsilon^k}{\sum_{k\in K} R_k\, \epsilon^k}.$$

So, after dropping the function arguments from the notation, one has

$$p = \frac{\sum_{k\in K} R_k\, p_k^*\, \epsilon^k}{\sum_{k\in K} R_k\, \epsilon^k} \quad \text{and} \quad q = \frac{\sum_{k\in K} R_k\, q_k^*\, \epsilon^k}{\sum_{k\in K} R_k\, \epsilon^k}. \tag{23}$$

Next, for any integer $m \in K$, define the following three subsets of K:

$$K_{<m} := \{\, k \in K \mid k < m \,\}; \quad K_{>m} := \{\, k \in K \mid k > m \,\}; \quad K_{\geq m} := \{\, k \in K \mid k \geq m \,\}.$$

Furthermore, define

$$R^m(\epsilon) := \sum\nolimits_{k\in K_{\geq m}} R_k\,\epsilon^k, \quad p^m := \frac{\sum_{k\in K_{\geq m}} R_k\, p_k^*\, \epsilon^k}{R^m(\epsilon)}, \quad q^m := \frac{\sum_{k\in K_{\geq m}} R_k\, q_k^*\, \epsilon^k}{R^m(\epsilon)}. \tag{24}$$

Then one can rewrite (23) as

$$p = \frac{\sum_{k\in K_{<m}} R_k\, p_k^*\, \epsilon^k + R^m(\epsilon)\, p^m}{\sum_{k\in K_{<m}} R_k\, \epsilon^k + R^m(\epsilon)}; \quad q = \frac{\sum_{k\in K_{<m}} R_k\, q_k^*\, \epsilon^k + R^m(\epsilon)\, q^m}{\sum_{k\in K_{<m}} R_k\, \epsilon^k + R^m(\epsilon)}.$$

In case $p_k^* \; I \; q_k^*$ for $k \in K_{<m}$, it follows from repeated application of the independence condition (18) that $p \; R \; q \iff p^m \; P \; q^m$.

Now, dividing by $R^m\, \epsilon^m$ all the terms of both numerator and denominator in the definitions of p^m, q^m in (24) gives

$$p^m = \frac{p_m^* + \sum_{k\in K_{>m}} R_k\, p_k^*\, \epsilon^{k-m}/R^m}{1 + \sum_{k\in K_{>m}} R_k\, \epsilon^{k-m}/R^m} \quad \text{and} \quad q^m = \frac{q_m^* + \sum_{k\in K_{>m}} R_k\, q_k^*\, \epsilon^{k-m}/R^m}{1 + \sum_{k\in K_{>m}} R_k\, \epsilon^{k-m}/R^m}.$$

The real parts of these probability distributions are therefore ${}^0p^m = p_m^*$ and ${}^0q^m = q_m^*$. Combining the above results with the refinement lemma then shows that, in case $p_k^* \; I \; q_k^*$ for all $k \in K_{<m}$, one has

$$p_m^* \; P \; q_m^* \iff {}^0p^m \; P \; {}^0q^m \Longrightarrow p^m \; P \; q^m \iff p \; P \; q$$

and so $p_m^* \; P \; q_m^* \Longrightarrow p \; P \; q$. Finally, in case $p_k^* \; I \; q_k^*$ for all $k \in K$, repeated application of the independence condition (18) shows that $p \; I \; q$. So it has been proved that

THEOREM. *For all pairs of RPF's $p, q \in \Delta(Y;\epsilon)$ given by (20), one has*

$$p \; P \; q \iff \langle p_k^* \rangle_{k\in K} \; P_L \; \langle q_k^* \rangle_{k\in K}$$

where $\langle p_k^* \rangle_{k\in K}, \langle q_k^* \rangle_{k\in K} \in \Delta^K(Y)$ are the lexicographic hierarchies of probability distributions whose members are given by (22), and where P_L is the lexicographic preference criterion defined by

$$\langle p_k^* \rangle_{k\in K} \; P_L \; \langle q_k^* \rangle_{k\in K} \iff \exists m \in K : p_k^* \; I \; q_k^* \; (\text{all } k \in K_{<m}) \; \& \; p_m^* \; P \; q_m^*.$$

5. Continuity and von Neumann-Morgenstern Utility

5.1. Continuous Preferences

In Section 3.5 it was claimed that consequentialist behaviour in trees $T \in \mathcal{T}(Y; \mathbf{P})$ must maximize a preference ordering R on $\Delta(Y; \mathbf{P})$ satisfying the independence axiom (18). So two of Herstein and Milnor's (1953) three axioms which imply expected utility maximization are satisfied. But discontinuous lexicographic preferences are still possible, even in trees with strictly positive ordinary probabilities at chance nodes. In single person decision theory, the motivation for avoiding such discontinuities is not entirely clear, beyond analytical convenience and a feeling that continuity is anyway rather natural. In the case of n-person game theory, however, continuity of behaviour as common expectations vary is crucial for the existence of equilibrium in general games.

Thus, in order to derive expected utility maximization, an axiom of continuity as probabilities vary — or what some have called an "Archimedean" axiom — will be added. The following was included as the third and last axiom in Herstein and Milnor's (1953) simplification of the original von Neumann and Morgenstern (1943) formulation:

Restricted Continuity Axiom. *If $\lambda, \mu, \nu \in \Delta(Y)$ with $\lambda \; P \; \mu$ and $\mu \; P \; \nu$, then there exist α and θ with $0 < \alpha < \theta < 1$ such that:*

$$[(1-\alpha)\,\lambda + \alpha\,\nu] \; P \; \mu \quad \text{and} \quad \mu \; P \; [(1-\theta)\,\lambda + \theta\,\nu].$$

As Herstein and Milnor show, this assumption, together with the fact that R is a preference ordering on $\Delta(Y)$ satisfying the independence axiom (17), implies the existence of a real-valued von Neumann-Morgenstern utility function (NMUF) v on Y such that

$$\lambda \; R \; \mu \iff \mathbf{E}_\lambda \, v \geq \mathbf{E}_\mu \, v \tag{25}$$

for all $\lambda, \mu \in \Delta(Y)$, where

$$\mathbf{E}_\lambda \, v := \sum\nolimits_{y \in Y} \lambda(y)\, v(y) \tag{26}$$

denotes the expected value of v with respect to λ, and $\mathbf{E}_\mu \, v$ is defined similarly.

The two NMUF's v, $\tilde{v}$ on Y are said to be *cardinally equivalent* if there exist real numbers $\rho > 0$ and α such that $\tilde{v}(y) \equiv \alpha + \rho v(y)$ on Y. Then, as is well known, there is a unique cardinal equivalence class of NMUF's whose expected values all represent the ordering R on $\Delta(Y)$.

5.2. Continuous Behaviour

Rather than assume directly continuity of preferences on the domain of ordinary probabilities $\Delta(Y)$, however, it is in the spirit of consequentialist decision theory to postulate continuity of behaviour instead, whether or not that behaviour is in fact consequentialist. Accordingly, let T be any ordinary decision tree in $\mathcal{T}(Y)$, with strictly positive real probabilities at all its chance nodes. Let n^* be any decision node of T, and n^0 any chance node of the subtree $T(n^*) \in \mathcal{T}(Y)$ whose initial node is n^*. Consider now a family of ordinary decision trees $T^\pi \in \mathcal{T}(Y)$ in which only the probability distribution $\pi = \pi(\cdot|n^0) \in \Delta(N_{+1}(n^0))$ at the chance node n^0 varies. To ensure that $\pi(n) > 0$ for all $n \in N_{+1}(n^0)$ and so that $T^\pi \in \mathcal{T}(Y)$, remove from T the entire subtree $T(n)$ following any node $n \in N_{+1}(n^0)$ with $\pi(n) = 0$. All the other features of the decision trees T^π should be entirely independent of the probabilities π.

Now, the behaviour set $\beta(T^\pi, n^*)$ at the fixed decision node $n^* \in N^*$ is well defined and varies with π. Accordingly, one obtains a correspondence $\pi \mapsto\!\!\!\!\to \beta(T^\pi, n^*)$ whose graph is

$$G_\beta(T, n^*, n^0) := \{\, (\pi, n) \in \Delta(N_{+1}(n^0)) \times N_{+1}(n^*) \mid n \in \beta(T^\pi, n^*) \,\}.$$

Since $\Delta(N_{+1}(n^0))$ is compact while $N_{+1}(n^*)$ is a finite set, this correspondence will have a compact graph, and so be upper hemi-continuous, provided that its graph is a closed set. So behaviour β is said to be *continuous* provided that $G_\beta(T, n^*, n^0)$ is indeed closed, for every decision tree $T \in \mathcal{T}(Y)$, decision node $n \in N^*(T)$, and chance node $n^0 \in N^0(T(n^*))$. Formally, this is weaker than the stronger condition which requires β to be jointly continuous as *all* probabilities vary in each decision tree. In combination with the other axioms, however, the weaker continuity condtion used here is actually equivalent to joint continuity.

The proof given in Hammond (1988b, Section 9) shows how such continuous behaviour implies the Herstein-Milnor (Restricted) Continuity Axiom stated in Section 5.1. Then there must indeed exist a unique cardinal equivalence class of von Neumann-Morgenstern utility functions whose expected values are maximized by the random consequences of behaviour in the restricted trees of $\mathcal{T}(Y)$.

6. Non-Archimedean Expected Utility

6.1. Representing Lexicographic Preferences

Suppose that non-Archimedean probabilities are RPF's taking values in the positive cone $\mathcal{P}(\epsilon)$. Suppose that the restricted continuity axiom of Section 5.1 is satisfied by consequentialist behaviour in the domain $\mathcal{T}(Y;\epsilon) := \mathcal{T}(Y;\mathcal{P}(\epsilon))$ of all finite decision trees with such RPF's attached to their chance nodes. Then the restriction of the ordering R to $\Delta(Y)$ is represented by the expected value of an NMUF $v : Y \to \Re$, as in (25).

Define the ordinary real valued expected utility function $U : \Delta(Y) \to \Re$ so that

$$U(\lambda) := \mathbf{E}_\lambda v = \sum\nolimits_{y \in Y} \lambda(y)\, v(y) \tag{27}$$

for all $\lambda \in \Delta(Y)$. This definition can now be extended from ordinary probability distributions to RPF's in an obvious way. The result will be the *non-Archimedean expected utility function* $U(\cdot;\epsilon) : \Delta(Y;\epsilon) \to \Re(\epsilon)$ which is defined so that, given any

$$p = p(y;\epsilon) = \frac{\sum_{i \in I} P_i\, p_i(y)\, \epsilon^i}{\sum_{i \in I} P_i\, \epsilon^i} \in \Delta(Y;\epsilon),$$

one has

$$U(p;\epsilon) := \mathbf{E}_p v = \sum\nolimits_{y \in Y} p(y;\epsilon)\, v(y) = \frac{\sum_{i \in I} P_i \sum_{y \in Y} p_i(y)\, v(y)\, \epsilon^i}{\sum_{i \in I} P_i\, \epsilon^i} = \frac{\sum_{i \in I} P_i\, U(p_i)\, \epsilon^i}{\sum_{i \in I} P_i\, \epsilon^i}. \tag{28}$$

Suppose that the refinement axiom of Section 4.1 is imposed in addition. Section 4.2 characterized the resulting lexicographic preferences. Now these preferences can be interpreted as maximizing expected utility with respect to the total ordering on the space $\Re(\epsilon)$. To see this, let $p, q \in \Delta(Y;\epsilon)$ be any pair of rational functions of ϵ taking the form (20). They can be given a common denominator and put in the form

$$p = \frac{\sum_{k \in K} R_k\, p_k^*\, \epsilon^k}{\sum_{k \in K} R_k\, \epsilon^k} \quad \text{and} \quad q = \frac{\sum_{k \in K} R_k\, q_k^*\, \epsilon^k}{\sum_{k \in K} R_k\, \epsilon^k}$$

as in (23) of Section 4.2, with the ordinary probability distributions $p_k^*(\cdot), q_k^*(\cdot) \in \Delta(Y)$ given by (22), and with $R_k > 0$ (all $k \in K$). So $U(p;\epsilon) > U(q;\epsilon)$ in $\Re(\epsilon)$ if and only if

$$\frac{\sum_{k \in K} R_k\, U(p_k^*)\, \epsilon^k}{\sum_{k \in K} R_k\, \epsilon^k} - \frac{\sum_{k \in K} R_k\, U(q_k^*)\, \epsilon^k}{\sum_{k \in K} R_k\, \epsilon^k} = \frac{\sum_{k \in K} R_k\, [U(p_k^*) - U(q_k^*)]\, \epsilon^k}{\sum_{k \in K} R_k\, \epsilon^k} > 0 \text{ in } \Re(\epsilon),$$

or if and only if

$$\sum\nolimits_{k\in K} R_k\,[U(p_k^*) - U(q_k^*)]\,\epsilon^k > 0 \text{ in } \Re(\epsilon). \tag{29}$$

But (29) is true if and only if the following lexicographic criterion is satisfied: there must exist an integer $m \in K$ for which $U(p_k^*) = U(q_k^*)$ whenever $k \in K$ with $k < m$, while $U(p_m^*) > U(q_m^*)$. However, for all $k \in K$ one has $U(p_k^*) > U(q_k^*) \iff p_k^*\ P\ q_k^*$. Also, the theorem stated at the end of Section 4.2 shows that

$$p\ P\ q \iff \exists m \in K : p_k^*\ I\ q_k^*\ (\text{all } k < m)\ \&\ p_m^*\ P\ q_m^*.$$

Finally, therefore, this chain of equivalences shows that $U(p;\epsilon) > U(q;\epsilon)$ in $\Re(\epsilon)$ if and only if $p\ P\ q$. This is true for all pairs $p, q \in \Delta(Y;\epsilon)$. So the preference ordering R is perfectly represented by the non-Archimedean expected utility function $U(\cdot;\epsilon)$, provided that the (lexicographic) total ordering in $\Re(\epsilon)$ is applied to each pair of non-Archimedean expected utilities.

6.2. Why Refinement is Needed

LEMMA. *Suppose that $f(\epsilon), g(\epsilon) \in \mathcal{P}(\epsilon)$ with $f(\epsilon) > g(\epsilon)$. Suppose too that $p, q \in \Delta(Y;\epsilon)$ with $p\ P\ q$. Then, given any other $h(\epsilon) \in \mathcal{P}(\epsilon)$ and the two members $p_f, p_g \in \Delta(Y;\epsilon)$ defined by*

$$p_f := \frac{f(\epsilon)\,p + h(\epsilon)\,q}{f(\epsilon) + h(\epsilon)} \quad \text{and} \quad p_g := \frac{g(\epsilon)\,p + h(\epsilon)\,q}{g(\epsilon) + h(\epsilon)},$$

it must be true that $p_f\ P\ p_g$.

PROOF: For the non-Archimedean expected utility function $U(\cdot;\epsilon)$ which represents R on $\Delta(Y;\epsilon)$, one has

$$\begin{aligned} U(p_f) - U(p_g) &= \frac{f(\epsilon)\,U(p;\epsilon) + h(\epsilon)\,U(q;\epsilon)}{f(\epsilon) + h(\epsilon)} - \frac{g(\epsilon)\,U(p;\epsilon) + h(\epsilon)\,U(q;\epsilon)}{g(\epsilon) + h(\epsilon)} \\ &= \frac{[f(\epsilon) - g(\epsilon)]\,h(\epsilon)}{[f(\epsilon) + h(\epsilon)]\,[g(\epsilon) + h(\epsilon)]}\,[U(p;\epsilon) - U(q;\epsilon)] > 0 \end{aligned}$$

when $f(\epsilon) > g(\epsilon)$ and $p\ P\ q$, because then $f(\epsilon) - g(\epsilon)$, $f(\epsilon)$, $g(\epsilon)$, $h(\epsilon)$, and $U(p;\epsilon) - U(q;\epsilon)$ are all positive elements of $\Re(\epsilon)$. ∎

This lemma is important because it shows the need to distinguish the two members $f(\epsilon), g(\epsilon) \in \mathcal{P}(\epsilon)$ whenever $f(\epsilon) \neq g(\epsilon)$. For if these two were not distinguished, the corresponding two members $p_f, p_g \in \Delta(Y;\epsilon)$ would have to be regarded as identical, and so indifferent according to the conditional relation I. But then, since the order $\geq$ on $\Re(\epsilon)$ is total, one of the pair $f(\epsilon)$, $g(\epsilon)$ is greater than the other — say, $f(\epsilon) > g(\epsilon)$. Finally, the Lemma would imply that $p\ I\ q$ for all $p, q \in \Delta(Y; \epsilon)$, so that all random consequences would have to be indifferent. For this reason, non-trivial consequentialist decision theory requires all the different members of $\mathcal{P}(\epsilon)$ to be distinguished.

7. Main Theorem

For the case when probabilities take strongly positive values in the particular non-Archimedean field $\Re(\epsilon)$, the five assumptions introduced in previous Sections are:

A1) **Unrestricted Domain:** There is a non-empty behaviour set $\beta(T, n) \subset N_{+1}(n)$ at every decision node n of every tree T in the domain $\mathcal{T}(Y; \epsilon)$ of finite decision trees having (strongly positive) $\mathcal{P}(\epsilon)$-valued probabilities at all chance nodes and consequences in Y at all terminal nodes.

A2) **Dynamic Consistency:** Whenever $T \in \mathcal{T}(Y; \epsilon)$ and n' is a decision node of the subtree $T(n)$, then $\beta(T(n), n') = \beta(T, n')$.

A3) **Consequentialist Choice:** There is a revealed consequence choice function C_β such that the set $\Phi_\beta(T)$ of possible random consequences of behaviour β in any tree $T \in \mathcal{T}(Y; \epsilon)$ satisfies $\Phi_\beta(T) = C_\beta(F(T))$, where $F(T)$ is the set of random consequences which are feasible in T.

A4) **Refinement:** Given any tree $T \in \mathcal{T}(Y; \epsilon)$, let ${}^0T \in \mathcal{T}(Y)$ be the tree which is derived from T by replacing the $\mathcal{P}(\epsilon)$-valued probabilities $\pi(n'|n; \epsilon)$ $(n' \in N_{+1}(n))$ at each chance node n of T by their corresponding real parts ${}^0\pi(n'|n)$, followed by omitting any nodes which can only be reached with probability zero according to the probabilities ${}^0\pi$. Then one should have $\beta(T, n) \subset \beta({}^0T, n)$ at every decision node n of ${}^0T$.

A5) **Restricted Continuity:** For every ordinary decision tree $T \in \mathcal{T}(Y)$, decision node n^* in T, and chance node n^0 in the subtree $T(n^*)$ with initial node n^*, the correspondence $\pi \mapsto\!\!\!\rightarrow \beta(T^\pi, n^*)$ from real valued probabilities $\pi \in \Delta(N_{+1}(n^0))$ to behaviour at n^* in the tree $T^\pi \in \mathcal{T}(Y)$ with probabilities π at n^0 has a closed graph.

Now:

MAIN THEOREM.

(1a) Any behaviour satisfying the first four axioms A1)–A4) above reveals a (complete and transitive) preference ordering R defined on $\Delta(Y;\epsilon)$ with the properties that:

(i) There is a restricted preference ordering ${}^0R$ on the space $\Delta(Y)$ which, whenever $\lambda, \mu, \nu \in \Delta(Y)$ and $0 < \alpha < 1$, satisfies the independence condition

$$[\alpha\,\lambda + (1-\alpha)\,\nu]\;{}^0R\;[\alpha\,\mu + (1-\alpha)\,\nu] \iff \lambda\;{}^0R\;\mu.$$

(ii) Suppose that

$$p = \frac{\sum_{k\in K} R_k\, p_k^*\, \epsilon^k}{\sum_{k\in K} R_k\, \epsilon^k} \quad \text{and} \quad q = \frac{\sum_{k\in K} R_k\, q_k^*\, \epsilon^k}{\sum_{k\in K} R_k\, \epsilon^k}$$

are any two RPF's in $\Delta(Y;\epsilon)$ that have been given a common denominator, while $R_k > 0$ and $p_k^*, q_k^* \in \Delta(Y)$ for all $k \in K$, where K is a non-empty set of non-negative integers. Then one has $p\;P\;q$ if and only if the lexicographic criterion

$$\exists m \in K : p_k^*\;{}^0I\;q_k^*\;(k < m\;\&\;k \in K) \quad \text{and} \quad p_m^*\;{}^0P\;q_m^*$$

is satisfied.

(1b) Conversely, if R is any ordering defined on $\Delta(Y;\epsilon)$ that is derived by applying the lexicographic criterion in part (ii) of (1a) to an ordering ${}^0R$ on $\Delta(Y)$ satisfying the independence condition in part (i) of (1a), then behaviour that maximizes R in each decision tree of $\mathcal{T}(Y;\epsilon)$ will satisfy A1)–A4).

(2a) Behaviour will satisfy all five axioms A1)–A5) above only if, in addition, there is a unique cardinal equivalent class of NMUF's $v : Y \to \Re$ for which

$$\lambda\;{}^0R\;\mu \iff \sum_{y\in Y} [\lambda(y) - \mu(y)]\, v(y) \geq 0 \text{ whenever } \lambda, \mu \in \Delta(Y),$$

in which case the ordering R on $\Delta(Y;\epsilon)$ is the unique ordering induced by applying the (lexicographic) total order $\geq$ in $\Re(\epsilon)$ to values $U(p;\epsilon)$ of the non-Archimedean expected utility function that is defined for all $p \in \Delta(Y;\epsilon)$ by

$$U(p;\epsilon) := \sum_{y\in Y} p(y;\epsilon)\, v(y).$$

(2b) Conversely, maximizing the non-Archimedean expected value of any such NMUF in the (lexicographic) order of $\Re(\epsilon)$ will generate behaviour satisfying A1)–A5).

PROOF: First, (1a) is proved by combining the arguments of Hammond (1988a and b, Sections 5 and 6) — see also Section 3.5 above — with the Theorem of Section 4.2. Conversely, (1b) is proved by a dynamic programming argument like that in Hammond (1988b, Section 8); the refinement axiom A4) is then obviously satisfied because of the lexicographic criterion in part (ii) of (1a).

For (2a), Section 5 explained why A5) would imply the existence of a unique cardinal equivalent class of NMUF's, and then Section 6.1 showed that behaviour would maximize non-Archimedean expected utility in the (lexicographic) total order $\geq$ of $\Re(\epsilon)$. Conversely, the single hypothesis of (2b) obviously implies all the hypotheses of (1b), so A1)–A4) will be satisfied. Furthermore, behaviour in ordinary decision trees with random consequences in $\Delta(Y)$ will maximize ordinary expected utility and so satisfy the restricted continuity axiom A5). ∎

An important corollary of this Main Theorem is that all attempts to treat as equivalent any pair of non-Archimedean probability distributions having different values in $\mathcal{P}(\epsilon)$ are doomed to fail. For, when combined with the five axioms set out above, any such attempt leads to the unacceptable conclusion that all non-Archimedean random consequences are indifferent — see Section 6.2.

ACKNOWLEDGEMENTS

During the academic year 1986–7, some initial work for this and related papers was generously supported by the Guggenheim Foundation and by C.O.R.E. at the Université Catholique de Louvain. Much of a preliminary draft was written during a fruitful visit to the Department of Economics at Princeton University in the Spring of 1987. Later, in Spring 1988 I received support from the Deutsche Forschungsgemeinschaft through Sonderforschungsbereich 303 while visiting the University of Bonn.

The work reported here and in related papers owes its origins to particularly useful interaction with Adam Brandenburger and Eddie Dekel. C.O.R.E. also provided the opportunity for many helpful discussions with Jean-François Mertens. Earlier versions were incorporated in presentations to the conference on "Sequential Equilibria and Structural Stability" at Luminy, January 1987, to the workshop on "Game Theory in the Behavioral Sciences" at the Zentrum für Interdisziplinäre Forschung at the University of Bielefeld in April 1988, and to the mathematical economics seminars at Princeton, Stanford, Harvard, and Bonn Universities. Other improvements and encouragement have resulted from helpful comments by several seminar participants, Bill Zame, Reinhard Selten, Barry Nalebuff, Avinash Dixit, and Andrew Caplin in particular. My thanks to all the above individuals and institutions.

REFERENCES

L. BLUME, A. BRANDENBURGER AND E. DEKEL (1991a), "Lexicographic Probabilities and Choice Under Uncertainty," *Econometrica*, **59**: 61–79.

L. BLUME, A. BRANDENBURGER AND E. DEKEL (1991b), "Lexicographic Probabilities and Equilibrium Refinements," *Econometrica*, **59**: 81–98.

P.J. HAMMOND (1976), "Changing Tastes and Coherent Dynamic Choice," *Review of Economic Studies*, **43**: 159–173.

P.J. HAMMOND (1988a), "Consequentialism and the Independence Axiom," in *Risk, Decision, and Rationality: Proceedings of the 3rd International Conference on the Foundations and Applications of Utility, Risk, and Decision Theories* edited by B. Munier (Dordrecht: D. Reidel), pp. 503–516.

P.J. HAMMOND (1988b), "Consequentialist Foundations for Expected Utility," *Theory and Decision*, **25**: 25–78.

P.J. HAMMOND (1992), "Elementary Non-Archimedean Representations of Probability for Decision Theory and Games," preprint, Department of Economics, Stanford University.

I.N. HERSTEIN AND J. MILNOR (1953), "An Axiomatic Approach to Measurable Utility," *Econometrica*, **21**: 291–297.

D. KREPS AND R. WILSON (1982), "Sequential Equilibrium," *Econometrica*, **50**: 863–894.

D.V. LINDLEY (1965), *Introduction to Probability and Statistics from a Bayesian Viewpoint, Part 1: Probability*. Cambridge: Cambridge University Press.

A. MCLENNAN (1989a), "The Space of Conditional Systems is a Ball," *International Journal of Game Theory*, **18**: 125–139.

A. MCLENNAN (1989b), "Consistent Conditional Systems in Noncooperative Game Theory," *International Journal of Game Theory*, **18**: 141–174.

R. MYERSON (1978), "Refinements of the Nash Equilibrium Concept," *International Journal of Game Theory*, **7**: 73–80.

R. MYERSON (1986), "Multistage Games with Communication," *Econometrica*, **54**: 323–358.

H. RAIFFA (1968), *Decision Analysis: Introductory Lectures on Choices under Uncertainty*. Reading, Mass.: Addison-Wesley.

A. RÉNYI (1955), "On a New Axiomatic Theory of Probability," *Acta Mathematicà Academiae Scientiarum Hungaricae*, **6**: 285–335.

A. RÉNYI (1970), *Probability Theory*. New York: Elsevier.

A. ROBINSON (1973), "Function Theory on Some Nonarchimedean Fields," *American Mathematical Monthly: Papers in the Foundations of Mathematics*, **80**: S87–S109.

P.A. SAMUELSON (1952), "Probability, Utility, and the Independence Axiom," *Econometrica*, **20**: 670–678.

R. SELTEN (1975), "Re-examination of the Perfectness Concept for Equilibrium Points of Extensive Games," *International Journal of Game Theory*, **4**: 25–55.

J. VON NEUMANN AND O. MORGENSTERN (1943, 1953), *Theory of Games and Economic Behavior (3rd. edn.)*. Princeton: Princeton University Press.

BOLTZMANN-LIKE AND FORCE MODELS FOR BEHAVIORAL CHANGES

Dirk Helbing
II. Institute for Theoretical Physics
University of Stuttgart
Pfaffenwaldring 57/III, 70550 Stuttgart, Germany

Abstract

It is shown, that BOLTZMANN-like equations allow the formulation of a very general model for behavioral changes. This model takes into account spontaneous (or externally induced) behavioral changes and behavioral changes by pair interactions. As most important social pair interactions imitative and avoidance processes are distinguished. The resulting model turns out to include as special cases many theoretical concepts of the social sciences, e.g. the multinomial logit model, the logistic equation, the gravity model and the game dynamical equations.

A KRAMERS-MOYAL expansion of the BOLTZMANN-like equations leads to BOLTZMANN-FOKKER-PLANCK equations, which allow the introduction of "social forces" related to an idea of LEWIN. Social forces reflect the social influences of, for example, norms, the public opinion and trends on behaviorial changes. They are not only given by external factors (the environment) but also by the interactions of the individuals. Variations of the individual behavior are taken into account by diffusion coefficients. The force model can e.g. be applied to group dynamics, opinion formation, and the behavior of pedestrians.

The Boltzmann-like behavioral model

Let us consider a population consisting of a great number $N \gg 1$ of individuals. Concerning a special topic of interest, these individuals show at each time t one behavior $\boldsymbol{x}(t)$ of several possible behaviors $\boldsymbol{x}_i$ combined in the set Ω.

Due to the "freedom of will" one cannot expect a deterministic theory for the temporal change $d\boldsymbol{x}/dt$ of the individual behavior $\boldsymbol{x}(t)$ to be realistic. However, one can construct a model for the change of the *probability distribution* $P(\boldsymbol{x},t)$ of behaviors $\boldsymbol{x}(t)$ within the given population ($P(\boldsymbol{x},t) \geq 0$, $\sum\limits_{\boldsymbol{x}\in\Omega} P(\boldsymbol{x},t) = 1$). A theory of this kind is, of course, stochastic. In order to take into account several ***types** a* of behavior, we may distinguish *A **subpopulations** a* consisting of $N_a \gg 1$ individuals ($\sum\limits_{a=1}^{A} N_a = N$). Then, the following relation holds:

$$P(\boldsymbol{x},t) = \sum_{a=1}^{A} \frac{N_a}{N} P_a(\boldsymbol{x},t) . \qquad (1)$$

Our goal is now to find a suitable equation for the probability distribution $P_a(\boldsymbol{x},t)$ of behaviors within subpopulation a ($P_a(\boldsymbol{x},t) \geq 0$, $\sum\limits_{\boldsymbol{x}\in\Omega} P_a(\boldsymbol{x},t) = 1$). If we neglect memory effects, the desired equation has the form of a *master equation* (HELBING 1992a, 1992b, 1993b):

$$\frac{d}{dt}P_a(\boldsymbol{x},t) = \sum_{\substack{\boldsymbol{x}'\in\Omega \\ (\boldsymbol{x}'\neq\boldsymbol{x})}} \Big[w^a(\boldsymbol{x}|\boldsymbol{x}';t)P_a(\boldsymbol{x}',t) - w^a(\boldsymbol{x}'|\boldsymbol{x};t)P_a(\boldsymbol{x},t)\Big]. \tag{2}$$

$w^a(\boldsymbol{x}'|\boldsymbol{x};t)$ is the ***effective transition rate*** (i.e., transition probability per time unit) from behavior $\boldsymbol{x}$ to behavior $\boldsymbol{x}'$ and takes into account the behavioral variations between the individuals (occuring even within the same type a of behavior!). For models of behavioral changes the following special form of $w^a(\boldsymbol{x}'|\boldsymbol{x};t)$ has found to be suitable (HELBING, 1992b, 1993b):

$$w^a(\boldsymbol{x}'|\boldsymbol{x};t) := \nu_a(t)R_a(\boldsymbol{x}'|\boldsymbol{x};t) + \sum_{b=1}^{A}\nu_{ab}(t)\Big[f^1_{ab}(t)P_b(\boldsymbol{x}',t) + f^2_{ab}(t)P_b(\boldsymbol{x},t)\Big]R^a(\boldsymbol{x}'|\boldsymbol{x};t). \tag{3}$$

Inserting (3) into (2), we obtain the BOLTZMANN-like behavioral model. Obviously, it depends quadratically on the probability distributions $P_b(\boldsymbol{y},t)$, which is due to pair interactions between individuals. In (3),

- $\nu_a(t)$ is a measure for the rate of spontaneous (or externally induced) behavioral changes within subpopulation a.
- $R_a(\boldsymbol{x}'|\boldsymbol{x};t)$ [resp. $R^a(\boldsymbol{x}'|\boldsymbol{x};t)$] is the *readiness* for an individual of subpopulation a to change the behavior from $\boldsymbol{x}$ to $\boldsymbol{x}'$ spontaneously [resp. in pair interactions].
- $\nu_{ab}(t) \equiv N_b\,\widetilde{\nu}_{ab}(t)$ is the *interaction rate* of an individual of subpopulation a with individuals of subpopulation b.
- $f^1_{ab}(t)$ is a measure for the frequency of *imitative processes*

  $$\boldsymbol{x}',\boldsymbol{x}' \longleftarrow \boldsymbol{x},\boldsymbol{x}' \qquad (\boldsymbol{x}\neq\boldsymbol{x}'), \tag{4}$$

  where an individual of subpopulation a takes over the behavior $\boldsymbol{x}'$ of an individual of subpopulation b. The total frequency of imitative processes is proportional to the probablility $P_b(\boldsymbol{x}',t)$ of behavior $\boldsymbol{x}'$ within subpopulation b.
- $f^2_{ab}(t)$ is a measure for the frequency of *avoidance processes*

  $$\boldsymbol{x}',\boldsymbol{x} \longleftarrow \boldsymbol{x},\boldsymbol{x} \qquad (\boldsymbol{x}\neq\boldsymbol{x}'), \tag{5}$$

  where an individual of subpopulation a changes the behavior $\boldsymbol{x}$ to another behavior $\boldsymbol{x}'$ if meeting an individual of subpopulation b with the same behavior (defiant behavior, snob effect). The total frequency of avoidance processes is proportional to the probablility $P_b(\boldsymbol{x},t)$ of behavior $\boldsymbol{x}$ within subpopulation b.

For $R^a(\boldsymbol{x}'|\boldsymbol{x};t)$ we take the quite general form

$$R^a(\boldsymbol{x}'|\boldsymbol{x};t) = \frac{e^{U^a(\boldsymbol{x}',t)-U^a(\boldsymbol{x},t)}}{D_a(\boldsymbol{x}',\boldsymbol{x};t)} \tag{6}$$

with $D_a(\boldsymbol{x}',\boldsymbol{x};t) = D_a(\boldsymbol{x},\boldsymbol{x}';t) > 0$ (cf. HELBING, 1992b, 1993b). Then, the readiness $R^a(\boldsymbol{x}'|\boldsymbol{x};t)$ for an individual of subpopulation a to change the behavior from $\boldsymbol{x}$ to $\boldsymbol{x}'$ will be the greater,

- the greater the *difference* of the *utilities* $U^a(.,t)$ of behaviors $\boldsymbol{x}'$ and $\boldsymbol{x}$ is,
- the smaller the *incompatibility ("distance")* $D_a(\boldsymbol{x}',\boldsymbol{x};t)$ between the behaviors $\boldsymbol{x}$ and $\boldsymbol{x}'$ is.

Ansatz (6) is related to the *multinomial logit model.* It assumes *utility maximization* with incomplete information about the exact utility of a behavioral change from $\boldsymbol{x}$ to $\boldsymbol{x}'$ (cf. HELBING, 1992b).

The resulting behavioral model turns out to include as special cases many theoretical concepts of the social sciences, e.g. the logistic equation, the gravity model and the game dynamical equations (i.e., the evolutionary game theory) (cf. HELBING 1992b, 1993a, 1993b). Computer simulations of the BOLTZMANN-like equations (2), (3), (6) are discussed and illustrated in HELBING (1992b, 1993b). Two examples are given below. The above figures depict imitative behavior of subpopulation $a = 1$, whereas the figures below illustrate avoidance behavior of subpopulation $a = 2$.

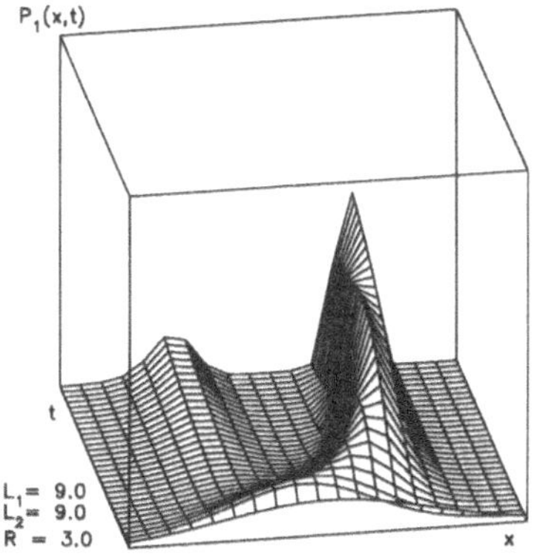

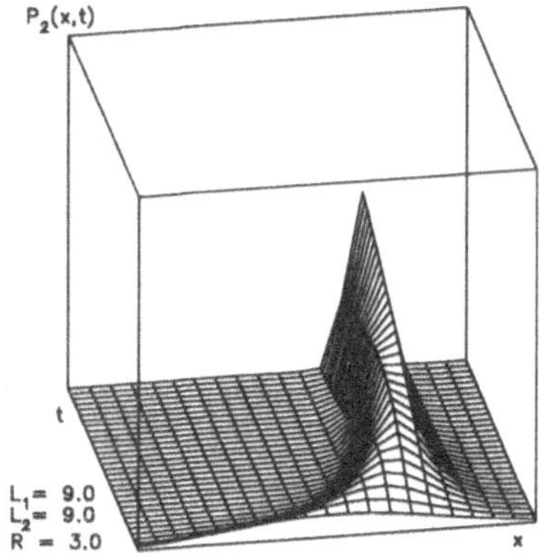

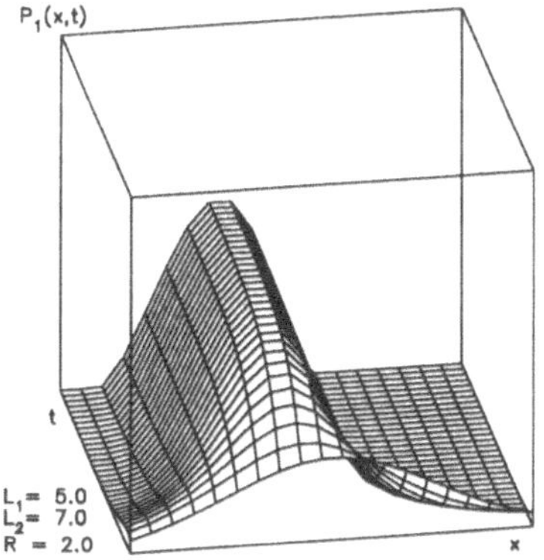

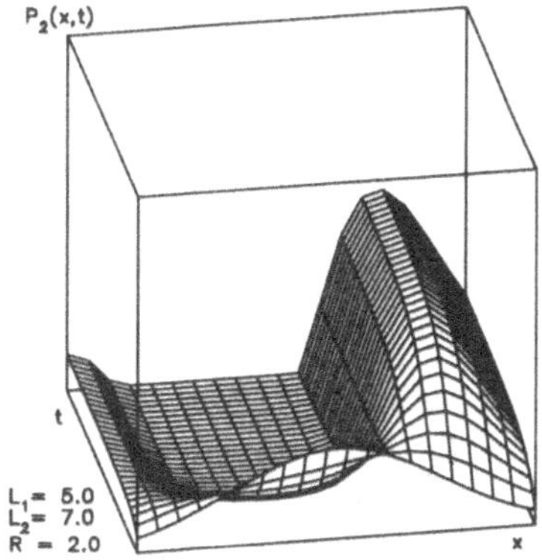

Reformulation in terms of a force model

We shall now assume the set Ω of possible behaviors to build a *continuous* space. The n dimensions of this space correspond to different characteristic *aspects* of the considered behaviors. In the continuous formulation, the sum in (2) has to be replaced by an integral:

$$\frac{d}{dt} P_a(\boldsymbol{x}, t) = \int\limits_{\Omega} d^n x' \left[w^a(\boldsymbol{x}|\boldsymbol{x}'; t) P_a(\boldsymbol{x}', t) - w^a(\boldsymbol{x}'|\boldsymbol{x}; t) P_a(\boldsymbol{x}, t) \right] . \tag{7}$$

A reformulation of the BOLTZMANN-like equations (7), (3) via a second order TAYLOR approximation (KRAMERS-MOYAL expansion) leads to a kind of *diffusion equations*: the socalled BOLTZMANN-FOKKER-PLANCK *equations* (HELBING, 1992a, 1992b, 1993b)

$$\frac{\partial}{\partial t} P_a(\boldsymbol{x}, t) = -\sum_{i=1}^{n} \frac{\partial}{\partial x_i} \left[K_{ai}(\boldsymbol{x}, t) P_a(\boldsymbol{x}, t) \right] + \frac{1}{2} \sum_{i,j=1}^{n} \frac{\partial}{\partial x_i} \frac{\partial}{\partial x_j} \left[Q_{aij}(\boldsymbol{x}, t) P_a(\boldsymbol{x}, t) \right] \tag{8a}$$

with the effective *drift coefficients*

$$K_{ai}(\boldsymbol{x}, t) := \int\limits_{\Omega} d^n x' \, (x'_i - x_i) w^a(\boldsymbol{x}'|\boldsymbol{x}; t) \tag{8b}$$

and the effective *diffusion coefficients*

$$Q_{aij}(\boldsymbol{x},t) := \int\limits_{\Omega} d^n x' \, (x'_i - x_i)(x'_j - x_j) w^a(\boldsymbol{x}'|\boldsymbol{x};t) \,. \tag{8c}$$

Whereas the drift coefficients $K_{ai}(\boldsymbol{x},t)$ govern the systematic change ("drift", motion) of the distribution $P_a(\boldsymbol{x},t)$, the diffusion coefficients $Q_{aij}(\boldsymbol{x},t)$ describe the spread of the distribution $P_a(\boldsymbol{x},t)$ due to fluctuations resulting from the individual variation of behavioral changes.

The BOLTZMANN-FOKKER-PLANCK equations (8a) are equivalent to the stochastic equations (LANGEVIN equations)

$$\frac{dx_i}{dt} = F_{ai}(\boldsymbol{x},t) + \sum_{j=1}^{n} G_{aij}(\boldsymbol{x},t)\xi_j(t) \tag{9a}$$

with

$$K_{ai}(\boldsymbol{x},t) = F_{ai}(\boldsymbol{x},t) + \frac{1}{2} \sum_{j,k=1}^{n} \left[\frac{\partial}{\partial x_k} G_{aij}(\boldsymbol{x},t) \right] G_{ajk}(\boldsymbol{x},t) \tag{9b}$$

and

$$Q_{aij}(\boldsymbol{x},t) = \sum_{k=1}^{n} G_{aik}(\boldsymbol{x},t) G_{akj}(\boldsymbol{x},t) \tag{9c}$$

(cf. HELBING, 1992b). For an individual of subpopulation a the last term of (9a) describes the contribution to the change of behavior $\boldsymbol{x}$ that is caused by behavioral fluctuations $\boldsymbol{\xi}(t)$. Since the diffusion coefficients $Q_{aij}(\boldsymbol{x},t)$ and the coefficients $G_{aij}(\boldsymbol{x},t)$ are usually small quantities, we have $F_{ai}(\boldsymbol{x},t) \approx K_{ai}(\boldsymbol{x},t)$ (cf. (9b)), and (9a) can be put into the form

$$\frac{d\boldsymbol{x}}{dt} \approx \boldsymbol{K}_a(\boldsymbol{x},t) + \textit{fluctuations}. \tag{10}$$

Whereas the fluctuation term describes individual behavioral variations, the vectorial quantity $\boldsymbol{K}_a(\boldsymbol{x},t)$ drives the systematic change of the behavior $\boldsymbol{x}(t)$ of individuals of subpopulation a. Therefore, it is justified to denote $\boldsymbol{K}_a(\boldsymbol{x},t)$ as *social force* acting on individuals of subpopulation a.

Social forces reflect the social influences of, for example, norms, the public opinion and trends on behavioral changes. They are not only given by external factors (the environment), but also by the interaction of the individuals, since they depend on the behavioral distributions $P_b(\boldsymbol{y},t)$ (cf. (3), (8b)).

The social force model is related with LEWIN's (1951) social field theory. It is very useful for the description of opinion formation, the behavior of pedestrians, or group dynamics (HELBING 1991, 1992b, 1993b).

Literature

D. Helbing (1991) A mathematical model for the behavior of pedestrians. *Behavioral Science* **36**, 298–310.

D. Helbing (1992a) Interrelations between stochastic equations for systems with pair interactions. *Physica A* **181**, 29–52.

D. Helbing (1992b) *Stochastische Methoden, nichtlineare Dynamik und quantitative Modelle sozialer Prozesse.* Doctoral dissertation, University of Stuttgart; published by Shaker Verlag, Aachen, 1993.

D. Helbing (1993a) Stochastic and Boltzmann-like models for behavioral changes, and their relation to game theory. *Physica A* **193**, 241–258.

D. Helbing (1993b) Boltzmann-like and Boltzmann-Fokker-Planck equations as a foundation of behavioral models. *Physica A*, in print.

K. Lewin (1951) *Field Theory in Social Science.* Harper & Brothers, New York, 1951.

Value Preserving Intertemporal Portfolio Selection

Klaus Hellwig and Thomas Wiesemann
Abteilung Betriebswirtschaft
Universität Ulm
Helmholtzstr.18, D-89069 Ulm, Germany

1 Motivation

The traditional approach to the intertemporal portfolio and consumption problem is to determine a portfolio that maximizes the expected value of consumption for a given utility function. However, this approach has been criticized in several ways. Empirical results revealed severe and persistent violations of the underlying von Neumann-Morgenstern-axioms of rational choice (see for example Allais and Hagen (1979)). The diversity of objectives pursued by an investor when making his portfolio decision may not be adequately capturable in single utility numbers (see for example Sen (1990)). If more than one decision maker is involved the utility function of a 'representative investor' has to be found. This leads to the problem of aggregating different utilities and it is far from obvious how that should be done.

An alternative way to solve the portfolio problem is as follows. In a first step principles are formulated reflecting the objectives pursued by investors and acceptable to the majority of decision makers involved. A second step is to prove the existence of portfolio stategies satisfying these principles. In accordance with this approach we present a portfolio decision based on two principles: absence of arbitrage and value preservation. Absence of arbitrage assures that the portfolio stategies employed are dynamically efficient. Value preservation means that the present value of consumption has to be sustained over all time periods planned. While the no-arbitrage-profit principle is self-evident, the value preservation principle seems to be appropriate especially for institutional investors, like investment companies.

2 The Model

An investor with initial endowment $K > 0$ faces the problem of choosing among a certain number of securities at trading dates $t = 0, \dots, T-1$, where T is a fixed planning horizon. The investor is able to describe the uncertain future by an event tree. The nodes of the tree are termed states. The set of all states is denoted by $S = \{0, 1, \dots, n\}$, where $n+1$ is the total number of states. The set of states at time t is denoted by S_t. The conditional probability for occurence of state s ($s = 1, \dots, n$), provided that the preceeding state has been realized, shall be denoted by $0 < \pi_s \leq 1$. Associated with the given securities is a payoff matrix $A \in \mathbf{R}^{(n+1)\times m}$, where m is the total number of distinct investment opportunities. We assume $m \leq n$ and hence allow for dynamically incomplete markets. The components of a column of A are the unit cashflows of a specific security. If, for example, a security i can be chosen in state s', then $a_{s'i} = -1$, $0 \leq a_{si} < \infty$ for all states following s' and $a_{si} = 0$ otherwise. The amount invested in security i shall be denoted by x_i. Thus a portfolio strategy is given by a vector $x = (x_1, \ldots, x_m)^T \in X$, where $X \subset \mathbf{R}^m$ is the set of feasible trading strategies. Associated with each portfolio strategy is a vector of consumption $c = (c_0, \ldots, c_n)^T \in \mathbf{R}^{n+1}$. Let $b = (K, 0, \ldots, 0)^T \in \mathbf{R}^{n+1}$, then c is related to x by $c = Ax + b$. We call a pair (x, c) a feasible portfolio and consumption strategy if $x \in X$ and $c = Ax + b$. It will be assumed, that the investor wants to invest K at $t = 0$. Therefore $c_0 = 0$.

In order to operationalize the two principles a set

$$P = \{p = (p_0, \ldots, p_n)^T \in \mathbf{R}^{n+1} : p > 0, \sum_{s=0}^{n} p_s = 1\}$$

of state prices is introduced. Let $(\bar{x}, \bar{c})$ be feasible. Then $(\bar{x}, \bar{c})$ is said to permit arbitrage if and only if a feasible pair $(\hat{x}, \hat{c})$ exists such that $\hat{c} \geq \bar{c}$, $\hat{c} \neq \bar{c}$. Hence, it is easy to verify that $(\bar{x}, \bar{c})$ does not permit arbitrage if and only if a price vector $\bar{p} \in P$ exists such that $\bar{x}$ is an optimal solution of

$$\max_{x \in X} \{\bar{p}^T A x\}. \tag{1}$$

This assures that $(\bar{x}, \bar{c})$ is a dynamically efficient portfolio and consumption strategy. As a second principle, the present value of consumption is required to be preserved throughout the planning period. To determine the present value at $t = 0$ for a given vector of state prices $\bar{p} \in P$, let $(\bar{x}, \bar{c})$ be a feasible arbitrage-free portfolio and consumption strategy associated with $\bar{p}$. Then the present value at time $t = 0$ is given by

$$V(\bar{p}) = \bar{q}^T \bar{c},$$

where $\bar{q} = \frac{1}{\bar{p}_0} \bar{p}$ is a normalization of $\bar{p}$ necessary to relate state prices to the beginning of the plannig period. Let $s \in \{1, \ldots, n\}$ and s' be the state preceeding s. Then

$$1 + \bar{r}_s(\bar{p}) = \pi_s \frac{\bar{q}_{s'}}{\bar{q}_s}$$

is one plus the portfolio return between states s' and s. Now it can be shown that $V(\bar{p})$ is preserved over time if and only if

$$\bar{c}_s = \begin{cases} \bar{r}_s(\bar{p}) V(\bar{p}) & \text{if } s \in S_t,\ t = 1, \ldots, T-1 \\ \bar{r}_s(\bar{p}) V(\bar{p}) + V(\bar{p}) & \text{if } s \in S_T. \end{cases} \tag{2}$$

Definition 1 *A feasible pair $(\bar{x}, \bar{c})$ satisfying (1) and (2) for some $\bar{p} \in P$ is called a value preserving portfolio and consumption strategy.*

Let $(\bar{x}, \bar{c})$ be value preserving with price vector $\bar{p}$. Then it can be shown that

$$V(\bar{p}) = K + \max_{x \in X} \{\bar{q}^T A x\}.$$

Since $\max_{x \in X} \{\bar{q}^T A x\} \geq 0$, K is a lower bound for V. As a result, for a value preserving solution at least the initial capital is preserved.

3 Existence

We prove the existence of value preserving portfolio and consumption strategies by proving the existence of economic equilibria using a fixed-point argument. Let P^* be an (arbitrary) convex and compact subset of P. For any $\bar{p} \in P^*$ let $x(\bar{p})$ be the set of optimal solutions of (1) and $c(\bar{p})$ be a consumption plan according to (2). The set of excess demand vectors corresponding to $\bar{p}$ is then given by

$$D(\bar{p}) = c(\bar{p}) - Ax(\bar{p}).$$

Define

$$\phi(\bar{p}) = \left\{\hat{p} \in P^* : \hat{p}^T y = \max_{p \in P^*}\{p^T y\} \text{ for some } y \in D(\bar{p})\right\}.$$

Then ϕ is a correspondence mapping P^* into the set of all subsets of P^*. We show that ϕ is an upper semi-continuous and convex-valued correspondence and then by Kakutani's (1941) theorem conclude that a fixed-point $\bar{p} \in P^*$ of ϕ exists. We make the following assumption.

(A) The amount x_i invested in the ith investment opportunity has upper and lower bounds k_i^u, k_i^l such that $-\infty < k_i^l \le 0 \le k_i^u < \infty$ for all $i = 1, \dots, m$. This includes the possibility to invest sufficiently high amounts in a riskless security at single period risk-free interest rates $r_t \ge 0$, $t = 0, \dots, T-1$.

Thus portfolio strategies are restricted by

$$x \in X = \{x \in \mathbf{R}^m : k_i^l \le x_i \le k_i^u \text{ for all } i = 1, \dots, m\}.$$

This includes possible short-sale constraints. Using a proof given by Hellwig (1992) it is now easy to show that there is a $P^* \subset P$ such that $0 \in D(\bar{p})$ for any fixed-point $\bar{p}$ of ϕ. This proves the following theorem.

Theorem 1 *Given (A), there exists a value preserving portfolio and consumption strategy for the intertemporal portfolio and consumption problem.*

4 Applications and extensions

We reduce the multi-period model to a single-period portfolio selection model, which was discussed in detail by Hellwig (1993). We show applications to the pricing of options and other derivative securities. Thus option prices are determined without knowing an investor-specific utility function even in the case of incomplete markets when the Cox-Ross-Rubinstein (1979) option pricing formula fails to hold. So-called value preserving option trading strategies are developed. Furthermore, extensions of the model are discussed including arbitrary concave cashflow functions, indivisibility constraints of the investment opportunities, fixed state-contingent wage-income streams and the introduction of state-dependent ex ante growth rates.

5 References

ALLAIS, M. and HAGEN, O. (1979): *Expected utility hypothesis and the Allais paradox.* D. Reidel Publishing Company, Dordrecht.

COX, J., ROSS, S.A. and RUBINSTEIN, M. (1979): Option pricing: A simplified approach. *Journal of Financial Economics*, 7, 229-263.

HELLWIG, K. (1992): Ertragswerterhaltung und ökonomisches Gleichgewicht. *Discussion Papers in Economics, Abteilung Betriebswirtschaft, Universität Ulm.*

HELLWIG, K. (1993): A present value approach to the portfolio selection problem. In FLAVELL, R. (ed.) *Modelling Reality and Personal Modelling. Contributions to Management Science.* Physica-Verlag, Heidelberg.

KAKUTANI, S. (1941): A generalization of Brouwer's fixed-point theorem. *Duke Mathematical Journal*, 8, 451-459.

SEN, A. (1990): Rational Behaviour. In EATWELL, J., MILGATE, M. and NEWMAN, P. (eds.) *Utility and Probability.* Macmillan Press, London and Basingstoke.

GENERATING CONVEX POLYOMINOES AT RANDOM

W. Hochstättler, C. Moll, University of Cologne
Martin Loebl, Praha

1 Introduction

Unit squares having their vertices at integer points in the Cartesian plane are called **cells**. A **polyomino** is a connected finite subset of cells in the grid. The number of cells is the **area** of the polyomino. The length of the boundary is called its **perimeter**.
Polyominoes have been studied – essentially – from two points of view. The question how to tile the plane with polyominoes is adressed (among others) in [Ber81], [Con90], [Mar91]. On the other hand several authors treat enumerative questions concerning polyominoes (cf. [Ben74], [Pol69]). The asymptotic behaviour of certain types of polyominoes has several applications to problems arising in percolation theory in statistical physic (cf. [Gutt88], [Lin88]). For a survey on recent results concerning the enumeration of polyominoes see [Del91].
A polyomino is called **convex**, if the intersection with any horizontal or vertical line is connected. A few years ago M.-P. Delest and G. Viennot ([Del84]) found that the number of convex polyominoes of perimeter $2n+8$ is given by $P_{2n+8} = (2n+11)4^n - 4(2n+1)\binom{2n}{n}$. The proof of this formula is not bijective and thus does not provide a possibility to generate them at random.
In this talk we present a new recursion formula for the number P_n of convex polyominoes of given perimeter n. We will construct a bijection from $\{1,\dots,P_n\}$ into the set of polyominoes with perimeter n. This bijection leads to a polynomial time algorithm that generates polyominoes with fixed perimeter with uniform probability. Furthermore, we suggest a simple probabilistic algorithm with linear running time for this task.

2 A Bijection

A polyomino P of perimeter n determines a smallest rectangle $r(P)$ of perimeter n which circumscribes it. A rectangle s of height 1 is called a **strip**. We consider each polyomino as a sequence of strips $(s_1,\dots,s_k)$, where s_1 is the topmost strip and s_k is the downmost strip of the polyomino. Fixing an embedding of a strip s we denote by $L(s), R(s)$ the horizontal coordinates of the leftmost, resp. rightmost point of s.
Let $P = (s_1,\dots,s_k)$ be a polyomino, s_l the downmost strip with $L(s_l)$ minimal and s_r the downmost strip with $R(s_r)$ maximal. We partition the set $(s_1,..,s_k)$ as follows:

i. the **top** $s_1,\dots,s_{min(l,r)}$,

ii. the **interior** $s_{min(l,r)+1},\dots,s_{max(l,r)}$,

iii. the **bottom** $s_{max(l,r)+1},\dots,s_k$.

Given a polyomino it is an easy task to construct its partition into top, interior and bottom.
We consider three different types of polyominoes, polyominoes with empty interior and empty bottom, polyominoes with empty bottom and non-empty interior and polyominoes with non-empty bottom.
In our bijection we construct a convex polyomino P strip by strip starting from the top. Given a partially constructed polyomino $\tilde{P}$, determined by a sequence of strips $s_1, .., s_j$, we consider the set of all possible extensions of $\tilde{P}$ to a convex polyomino P.

Lemma 1 *Let $\tilde{P} = (s_1, \ldots, s_j)$ be a convex polyomino of perimeter $\tilde{n}$.*

- *Then the set of all extensions $(s_{j+1}, \ldots, s_k)$ of $\tilde{P}$ to a convex polyomino $P = (s_1, \ldots, s_k)$ is determined by the type of $\tilde{P}$ and the last strip s_j.*

- *The number of possible extensions of $\tilde{P}$ to a convex polyomino P of perimeter n only depends on $\tilde{m}$, the length of the bottom line of $\tilde{P}$, and $\tilde{l} = n - \tilde{n} + \tilde{m}$, the remaining length, that is the length of the path replacing the bottom line in P and the type of $\tilde{P}$.*

Lemma 1 leeds to a recursion formula for the following numbers: $N_b(\tilde{m}, \tilde{l})$, $N_i(\tilde{m}, \tilde{l})$ and $N_t(\tilde{m}, \tilde{l})$ - the number of possible extensions in the three cases - and for P_n - the total number of polyominoes. The recursion formula induce a tree, where the leaves are the polyominoes of a given perimeter, interior nodes are partially constructed polyominoes and the root is the empty polyomino. The numbers N_b, N_i, N_t and P_n associated with the interior nodes, resp. the root, give the number of leaves of the corresponding subtrees.
Every embedding of such a tree in the euclidian plane rises to a linear order on the leaves and hence a numbering of the polyominoes of perimeter n. The set of numbers of the leaves in its subtree is an intervall.
We use this fact to compute the bijection between the polyominoes of perimeter n and the intervall $[1, P_n]$ which proceeds as follows:
Given a polyomino $p = (s_1, \ldots, s_k)$ we build the partition of the polyominoes of perimeter n induced by their first strip. The ordering of the terms in the recursion formula yields a partition of the interval $[1, P_n]$. Thus s_1 determines an interval I_1. Applying this procedure recursively – always taking into account the type of the already touched part of p – we end up in a leaf of the tree with interval $[j, j]$.
On the other hand, given a number j in $[1, P_n]$ we compute the partition of the interval $[1, P_n]$, fix the corresponding strip s_1 and proceed recursively.
The depth of the tree and its maximum degree is bounded by $\frac{n-2}{2}$. Hence the above computations can be performed in $O(n^3)$, ($O(n^2)$ using uniform measure) after a preprocessing time of $O(n^5)$ ($O(n^3)$ memory) for the computation of the numbers N_b, N_i, N_t and P_n.

3 A probabilistic algorithm

The algorithm described in the last chapter has a huge memory requirement. Furthermore, an exact long integer arithmetic is necessary to compute random polyominoes of large perimeter with this approach. Thus this method is hardly applicable for practical use. We will discribe a very simple probabilistic algorithm with linear time and space requirement. Using the formula for the total number of convex polyominoes with fixed perimeter, we prove that this algorithm succeeds with asymptotic probability 0.5.

A well known approach to count polyominoes is to study the language, which is defined by the boundaries of convex polyominoes encoded as sequences of 'L'eft, 'R'ight, 'U'p and 'D'own moves. To develop a probabilistic algorithm we first collect some obvious properties of these cyclic 'LURD'-sequences.

Let P be a convex polyomino of perimeter n, T the cyclic 'LURD'-sequence encoding the boundary of P, $l(r,u,d)$ the number of 'L's ('R's, 'U's, 'D's resp.) in T. Furthermore, let $T_{UD}(T_{LR})$ denote the cyclic 'UD' ('LR') subsequences of T, then the following holds:

i. $l = r > 0$, $u = d > 0$

ii. There is a unique $L =: L_0$ $(R =: R_0)$ with successor R (L) in T_{RL} and its successor in T is a U (D).

iii. There is a unique $U =: U_0$ $(D =: D_0)$ with successor D (U) in T_{UD} and its successor in T is an R (L).

iv. The smallest rectangle Q circumscribing P is of height u and width l.

Every LURD-sequence with these properties represents a closed walk in the rectangle Q, that touches every side only once in the correct order and has no reverse step. A LURD-sequence with these properties encodes a convex polyomino if and only if the induced path is simple. Checking simplicity of a LURD-sequence can be done in linear time. In most cases LURD-sequences with (i)-(iii) encode simple paths.

In order to build such LURD-sequences, we consider words on the alphabet $\{V, H\}$ and map the LURD-sequences to vertical-horizontal-sequences writing an 'V' for every 'U' and 'D' and an 'H' for every 'L' and 'R'. In addition we store the number of 'L's before the first 'R' (the distance of the starting point U_0 to the left side of the rectangle). This enables us to reconstruct the LURD-sequence from the corresponding VH-sequence. We can encode LURD-sequences as a pair of a binary string of length n and a number k in $0, \ldots, \frac{n}{2} - 1$. The properties of LURD-sequences corresponding to polyominoes can be transformed to properties of $VH-k$-encodings. This allows us to eliminate some more redundancy of the VH-k-encoding - to reduce our encoding to a binary string of length $n - 6$ and a k in $0, \ldots, \frac{n}{2}$ - and leeds to sufficiant conditions to classify all VH-k-encodings corresponding to LURD-sequences with (i)-(iii).

In order to generate a random polyomino of perimeter n we repeat the following algorithm:

(1) Choose a number k in $0, \ldots, \frac{n}{2}$ and a binary string of length $n - 6$.

(2) Generate a VH-k encoding of length n.

(3) If the VH-k encoding doesn not correspond to an $LURD$-encoding with (i)-(iii), then return $fail$.

(4) Construct the corresponding LURD-sequence.

(5) If the path induced by this sequence is not simple then return *fail* else return the LURD-sequence.

In fact this algorithm has the following properties:

- If this function returns an LURD-sequence, then this sequence encodes the boundary of a convex polyomino.
- Every convex polyomino is generated with uniform probability.
- The function returns a polyomino with asymptotic probability 0.5.
- The function has linear running time.

The convergence of the probability towards 0.5 is very fast. It is thus possible to generate large random polyominoes effectively with our algorithm.

References

[Ben74] E. Bender: Convex n-ominoes *Discr. Math. 8 (1974) 219 - 226*

[Ber81] C. Berge, C. C. Chen, V. Chvatal and C. S. Seow: Combinatorial properties of polyominoes *Combinatorica 1 (1981) 217 - 224*

[Con90] J. H. Conway and J. C. Lagrias: Tiling with polyominoes and combinatorial group theory *J. Comb. Th. A53 (1990) 183 - 208*

[Del84] M. P. Delest and G. Viennot: Algebraic languages and polyominoes enumeration *Theor. Comp. Sci. 34 (1984) 169 - 206*

[Del91] M. Delest: Polyominoes and animals: Some recent results *J. Math. Chem. 8 (1991) 3 - 18*

[Gol89] S. Golomb: Polyominoes while tile rectangles *J. Comb. Th. A51 (1989) 117 - 124*

[Gutt88] A. J. Guttmann: The number of convex polygons on the square and honeycomb lattices *J. Phys. A21 (1988) 467 - 474*

[Lin88] K. Y. Lin and S. J. Chang: Rigorous results for the number of convex polygons on the square and honeycomb lattices *J. Phys. A21 (1988) 2635 - 2642*

[Mar91] G. E. Martin: Polyominoes: A Guide to Puzzles and Problems in Tiling *Mathematical Association of America Spectrum Series 1991*

[Pol69] G. Pólya: On the number of certain lattice polygons *J. Comb. Th. 6 (1969) 102 - 105*

A NEW LINEAR TIME ALGORITHM FOR COMPUTING THE CONVEX HULL OF A SIMPLE POLYGON

W. Hochstättler, S. Kromberg, C. Moll
Mathematisches Institut
Universität zu Köln
Weyertal 86-90, D-50931 Köln, Germany

1. INTRODUCTION

The problem of determining the convex hull of a simple polygon has received a lot of attention in the early eighties. The first linear time algorithm for this task was proposed by Sklansky (1972). Sklansky's Algorithm can be described as follows:
Start at an extreme point of the polygon. Delete all left turns while moving around the polygon in clockwise direction. After each step backtrack until the path from the starting point to the point currently considered given by the not (yet) deleted points has right turns only.
The problem with this algorithm is that the lastmentioned path may become self-intersecting and that the algorithm therefore fails in some cases. Its asset is the simplicity of its idea and that it requires only very little global information about the given simple polygon in advance – its orientation and an extreme point.
The algorithm presented in this note supplements Sklansky's algorithm in a simple way assuring that the current path from the starting point to the currently considered point is always simple and consists of right turns only.
Like Sklansky's and different from other (correct) $O(n)$-algorithms for computing the convex hull of a simple polygon our algorithm only requires that the simple polygon be given in clockwise orientation and that the starting point is known to be an extreme point of the convex hull. From then on the decision whether or not to delete a point is based solely on local information. Our algorithm thus can not only be regarded as being simpler than the algorithms in McCallum, Avis (1979), Ghosh, Shyamasundar (1983), Bhattacharya, Elgindy (1984), it also provides new insight into the structure of the problem.

2. DEFINITIONS AND NOTATION

In this note the term *point* refers to a point in the Euclidean plane represented by its coordinates. For two points $p = (x, y)$ and $q = (x', y')$ in the plane $\det(p, q)$ denotes $xy' - x'y$ and $[p, q]$ denotes the line segment $\{\lambda p + (1 - \lambda)q \mid \lambda \in [0, 1]\}$. If p and q are different, $L(p, q)$ denotes the directed line through p and q directed from p to q. We say a point r is to the *right* of (respectively *on*, *left* of) $L(p, q)$ if $\det(p - q, r - q)$ is positive (respectively zero, negative) and denote by $H(p, q)$ the halfspace of points on or to the right of $L(p, q)$.
The term *polygon* refers to a piecewise linear closed curve in the plane. A polygon is represented by a sequence $P = p_1 \dots p_n$ of points in the order they are encountered as the curve is traversed.

The points p_i $(1 \leq i \leq n)$ are referred to as the *turn points* of the polygon, p_i is a *right turn* (respectively *left turn*) or a *convex turn point* (respectively *reflex turn point*) of P if p_{i+1} is to the right (respectively left) of $L(p_{i-1}, p_i)$ (indices read modulo n). A polygon is *convex* if all its turn points are convex.

Given a polygon $P = p_1 \dots p_n$ and $i, j \in \{1, \dots, n\}$, we let $Path_P(p_i, p_j)$ denote the path in P from p_i to p_j which follows the orientation of P. $Path_P(p_i, p_j)$ is *convex* if all turn points different from p_i and p_j that are visited by the path are convex turn points of P. If $Path_P(p_i, p_j)$ is simple and all turn points visited by the path are contained in $H(p_i, p_j)$, we let $K_P(p_i, p_j)$ denote the union of the bounded regions enclosed by the polygon $p_i p_{i+1} \dots p_j$ and its boundary.

The convex hull of a set S of points is denoted $conv(S)$. It is wellknown that $conv(S)$ is a (convex) polyhedron, if S is finite. Its vertices are also called *extreme points* of $conv(P)$.

A simple polygon is *clockwise oriented* if its interior lies to the right as the polygon is traversed. It follows from the Jordan Curve theorem that for a simple clockwise oriented polygon $P = p_1 \dots p_n$ and the extreme points $p_{i_1}, \dots, p_{i_k}$ of $conv(P)$ where $1 \leq i_1 < i_2 < \dots < i_k \leq n$ one has that $p_{i_1} \dots p_{i_k}$ represents the simple convex polygon that is the boundary of $conv(P)$.

3. THE ALGORITHM

Before formally stating our algorithm we give an informal description of its operation pointing out where it supplements Sklansky's algorithm.

The algorithm requires that the input polygon be given in clockwise orientation and that the starting point is an extreme point of the convex hull. As, however, it is easy to find such a point and determine the orientation of a simple polygon in linear time, this assumption does not restrict its generality. The input polygon is stored in a doubly linked list S.

Like Sklanskys', the algorithm leaves S unchanged and moves to the next point, if the currently stored polygon has a right turn at the currently considered point, named p_{run}. If not, we initialize p_{head} to the successor of the currently considered point and p_{tail} to its predecessor. Now we alternate the following two steps:

If the path given by the (current) predecessors of p_{tail} followed by p_{head} has a left turn at p_{tail}, we backtrack p_{tail} until the resulting path has right turns only.

If the successor of p_{head} lies inside the polygon formed by the original path from p_{head} to p_{tail} and $[p_{tail}, p_{head}]$, we advance p_{head} to the first point outside of this polygon.

If none of the two conditions holds, we remove the points between p_{tail} and p_{head}.

The algorithm stops once it reaches the starting point.

input: A sequence of points $p_1 \dots p_n$ stored in a doubly linked list representing a clockwise oriented simple polygon with the property that p_1 is an extreme point of $conv(P)$

output: A subsequence $p_{i_1} (= p_1) \dots p_{i_k}$ representing the simple convex polygon that is the boundary of $conv(P)$

(1) $p_{run} :=$ succ(p_1)

(2) **if** $p_{run} = p_1$ **stop**

(3) **if** succ(p_{run}) is to the right of $L($pred$(p_{run}), p_{run})$ **then**

```
(4)         p_run := succ(p_run) and go to (2)
(5)  else
(6)         p_head := succ(p_run)   p_tail := pred(p_run)
(7)         decrease p_tail until p_head is to the right of L(pred(p_tail), p_tail)
(8)         L := L(p_tail, p_head)
(9)         if succ(p_head) is on or right of L and to the left of L(pred(p_head), p_head) then
(10)              increase p_head until p_head is to the left of L and go to (7)
(11)        succ(p_tail) := p_head   pred(p_head) := p_tail
(12)        p_run := p_head   and go to (2)
```

4. CORRECTNESS OF THE ALGORITHM

Crucial observations for proving the correctness of our algorithm are stated in the following Lemma. We abbreviate $K_P(p_i, p_j)$ by $K(p_i, p_j)$.

Lemma 1 *Let $P = p_1 \dots p_n$ be the input polygon of the algorithm. If $P' = p_{i_1} \dots p_{i_k}$ $(1 \leq i_1 < i_2 < \dots < i_k \leq n)$ denotes the subsequence of P consisting of either*

the currently stored predecessors of p_{run} $(= p_{i_k})$ in line **(2)**

or the currently stored predecessors of p_{tail} $(= p_{i_{k-1}})$ followed by p_{head} $(= p_{i_k})$ in line **(7)**,

then the following holds:

(i) $i_1 = 1$ *and* $k \geq 2$,

(ii) $Path_{P'}(p_{i_1}, p_{i_k})$ *is simple and convex,*

(iii) $\forall\, 1 \leq \lambda \leq k-1 :\ Path_P(p_{i_\lambda}, p_{i_{\lambda+1}}) \subseteq \bigcap_{\mu=1}^{\lambda} H(p_{i_\mu}, p_{i_{\mu+1}})$

(iv) $\forall\, 1 \leq \lambda \leq k\ \forall\, 1 \leq \mu \leq \lambda - 2 : p_{i_\lambda} \notin K(p_{i_\mu}, p_{i_{\mu+1}})$,

(v) all points p_j that were discarded (i.e. $1 \leq j \leq i_k$, $p_j \notin P'$) are not extreme points of $conv(P)$.

The proof of the Lemma is by induction. It follows from the Lemma that when the algorithm reaches p_1 the currently stored polygon is simple and convex, and all points that were discarded are not extreme points of $conv(P)$. As the algorithm obviously runs in linear time we thus have:

Theorem 1 *The algorithm presented in 3. finds the convex hull of a simple polygon in linear time.*

REFERENCES

Bhattacharya B, Elgindy H (1984) A New Linear Convex Hull Algorithm for Simple Polygons. IEEE Trans. Inform. Theory, vol. IT-30, no. 1: 85-88

Ghosh S, Shyamasundar R (1983) A Linear Time Algorithm for Obtaining the Convex Hull of a Simple Polygon. Patt. Recogn., vol. 16, no. 6: 587-591

McCallum D, Avis D (1979) A Linear Algorithm for Finding the Convex Hull of a Simple Polygon. Inform. Proc. Lett., vol. 9, no. 5: 201-206

Sklansky J (1972) Measuring concavity on a rectangular mosaic. IEEE Trans. Comput. 21: 1355-1364

A PRODUCTION-TRANSPORTATION PROBLEM WITH STOCHASTIC DEMAND AND CONCAVE PRODUCTION COSTS

Kaj Holmberg
Department of Math., Linköping Institute of Technology, S-581 83 Linköping, Sweden
Hoang Tuy
Institute of Mathematics, P.O. Box 631, Bo Ho, Hanoi, Vietnam.

The problem of transporting goods from a set of supply points (factories) to a set of demand points (customers) so as to minimize linear transportation costs is well known and very efficient solution methods exist. In the well-known facility location problem one also includes fixed charges for the supply points. On the other hand, in ordinary transportation problems, stochastic demand has been introduced and modelled by convex costs, yielding the Stochastic Transportation Problem, [STP], solved by for example the methods in Cooper and LeBlanc (1977) and Holmberg and Jörnsten (1984). However, the simultaneous use of these generalizations has recieved little attention until now. Only a few suggestions for solution methods can be found, LeBlanc (1977), Franca and Luna (1982). In this paper we consider generalizing this problem even further, by introducing general concave costs at the supply points, as well as convex costs at the demand points. Fixed charges are not the only cost structures that occur when producing goods at a factory. Economies of scale very often yield other concave cost functions.

We consider a transportation problem with m supply points and n demand points. Let z_i be the amount that is shipped out of supply point i, y_j the amount that is shipped into demand point j and x_{ij} the amount that is shipped from supply point i to demand point j. $g_i(z_i)$ (assumed to be concave) is the cost of producing z_i units at supply point i. The maximal capacity is denoted by S_i. The demand, d_j, at demand point j is assumed to be stochastic. If y_j units are actually received then a penalty cost $q_j(y_j, d_j)$ is incurred. In most cases of interest, each expected penalty $f_j(y_j) = E[q_j(y_j, d_j)]$ is a convex function, see Cooper and LeBlanc (1977). The linear transportation costs have unit costs c_{ij}.

$$
\begin{aligned}
v^* = \quad \min \quad & \sum_{i=1}^{m}\sum_{j=1}^{n} c_{ij}x_{ij} + \sum_{i=1}^{m} g_i(z_i) + \sum_{j=1}^{n} f_j(y_j) \\
\text{s.t.} \quad & \sum_{i=1}^{m} x_{ij} = y_j \quad j = 1,\dots,n \qquad (1) \\
& \sum_{j=1}^{n} x_{ij} = z_i \quad i = 1,\dots,m \qquad (2) \\
& 0 \le z_i \le S_i \quad i = 1,\dots,m \qquad (3) \\
& x_{ij} \ge 0 \quad \forall\, i,j \qquad (4)
\end{aligned}
\qquad [P]
$$

Certainly the introduction of concave costs makes the problem difficult. The objective function is a sum of three terms: a linear transportation cost, a convex shortage penalty and a concave production cost. It is neither convex nor concave, but a *d.c. function*, i.e. a function that can be represented as a difference of two convex functions, Horst and Tuy (1993). The problem of minimizing a d.c. function under linear constraints is a nonconvex global optimization problem, which may have multiple local minima with substantially different values, Tuy (1987), Horst and Tuy (1993). Such multiextremal problems cannot be solved by standard methods of nonlinear programming which can at best locate a local minimum.

The constraints of [P] are of transportation type and the objective function is separable. Furthermore, if the concave term in the objective function is linearized, then the problem becomes a [STP]. It turns out that by exploiting all these additional structures it is possible to devise a solution method capable of solving fairly large problems. Specifically, using the fact that the nonconvex component of the objective function involves only a part of the variables, we can reduce the problem to a d.c. optimization problem of much smaller dimension than the original one, Tuy (1992). Next, this reduced problem can be solved by a branch and bound procedure in which branching is performed by partitioning the space into rectangles (to take account of the separability of the variables) while bounding is based on solving subproblems of the form [STP] (to take advantage of the availability of efficient algorithms for [STP]). Computational experiments indicate that the algorithm obtained that way can solve problems with up to 100 supply points and 500 demand points in reasonable time. It should be noted that at present, for most global optimization algorithms, problems of this size are considered difficult.

Let us mention two special cases of [P]. The first one is obtained by letting g_i consist of a fixed charge, and called the Stochastic Transportation-Location Problem, [STLP], treated in LeBlanc (1977) and Franca and Luna (1982). The other special case is the [STP], which has been treated in many papers and can be solved quite efficiently, for example with the Frank-Wolfe method in Cooper and LeBlanc (1977) and LeBlanc, Helgason, and Boyce (1985), and by combinations of separable programming, Lagrangean relaxation with subgradient optimization and mean value cross decomposition (Holmberg (1992)) in Holmberg (1993).

Problem [P] has $mn + m + n$ variables, while only m are nonconvex: $z_1, \ldots, z_m$ and very often $m \ll n$, though n may be fairly large. We propose a solution method which reduces [P] to a d.c. optimization problem in R^m, then solves the latter by a branch and bound procedure in which bounding is based on solving subproblems of the form of [STP].

Specifically, for a given z in the rectangle $\Omega = \{z : 0 \le z \le S := (S_1, ..., S_m)\}$, consider the problem [Q(z)], which is [P] with z fixed, with objective function value $\varphi(z)$.

Proposition 1 *$\varphi(z)$ is a convex function and [P] is equivalent to*

$$\min\{\varphi(z) + g(z) : z \in \Omega\} \qquad [P^*]$$

in the sense that the two problems have equal optimal values and if (x^*, y^*, z^*) solves [P] then z^* solves $[P^*]$ and conversely if z^* solves $[P^*]$ then (x^*, y^*, z^*) solves [P], where (x^*, y^*) is an optimal solution of $[Q(z^*)]$.

At each iteration, a rectangular partition of the feasible domain is available as a result of previous subdivisions. This partition is then refined by choosing a "promising" rectangle in the partition and subdividing it via some (w, i). Both the choices of the candidate M for further subdivision and the parameters (w, i) of subdision are guided by the lower bounds assigned to every member of the partition.

For any rectangle $M = [p, q]$ contained in the feasible domain Ω, let $L_{M,i}(.)$ be the affine function which agrees with $g_i(.)$ at the endpoints of the segment $[p_i, q_i]$ and $L_M(x) = \sum_{i=1}^{m} L_{M,i}(z_i)$. Furthermore, let $\beta(M)$ be the objective function value of the convex program, [CP(M)], obtained by replacing $g(z)$ in [P] by $L_M(x)$ and adding the constraint $z \in M$.

Proposition 2 $\beta(M) \leq \min\{\varphi(z) + g(z) : z \in M\}$

Clearly each [CP(M)] is a convex problem which differs from the [STP] only by the additional constraint $p \leq z$. Therefore, the lower bounding subproblem for each partition rectangle can be solved by adapted versions of the algorithms in Holmberg (1993). We now state Algorithm 1.

Initialization
Take a subrectangle M_1 of Ω which is known to contain a global optimal solution of [P*]. Let z^1 be the best feasible point available, INV (incumbent value) $= \varphi(z^1) + g(z^1)$. Set $\mathcal{M}_1 = \mathcal{P}_1 = \{M_1\}, k = 1$.

Iteration $k = 1, 2, \ldots$

(i) For each $M \in \mathcal{P}_k$ solve the convex program [CP(M)] obtaining its optimal value $\beta(M)$ and optimal solution $(\bar{x}(M); \bar{y}(M), \bar{z}(M))$. Update INV and z^k.

(ii) Delete all $M \in \mathcal{M}_k$ such that $\beta(M) \geq$ INV$-\varepsilon$. Let $\mathcal{M}'_k$ be the collection of remaining members of $\mathcal{M}_k$. If $\mathcal{M}'_k = \emptyset$ then terminate: z^k is a global ε-optimal solution of [P*]. Otherwise choose $M_k \in \operatorname{argmin}\{\beta(M) : M \in \mathcal{M}'_k\}$.

(iii) Let $w^k = \bar{z}(M_k)$. Select $i_k \in \operatorname{argmax}\{g_i(w_i^k) - L_{k,i}(w^k)\}$, where $L_{k,i}(z)$ stands for $L_{M_k,i}(z)$, and divide M_k via (w^k, i_k). Let $\mathcal{P}_{k+1}$ be the partition of M_k and $\mathcal{M}_{k+1} = (\mathcal{M}'_k \setminus \{M_k\}) \cup \mathcal{P}_{k+1}$. Update INV by setting z^{k+1} equal to the best among z^k and all $w(M), M \in \mathcal{M}_k$. Set $k \to k+1$ and go back to (i).

Theorem 1 *For $\varepsilon > 0$ Algorithm 1 is always finite. For $\varepsilon = 0$, either Algorithm 1 is finite or it generates an infinite sequence $\{z^k\}$ every cluster point of which is a global optimal solution of [P*] .*

We have tested two branch-and-bound methods, one where the subproblem is solved by separable programming combined with mean value cross decomposition, Holmberg (1993), and one where the subproblem is solved with the Frank-Wolfe method used in Cooper and LeBlanc (1977), with modifications similar to those suggested in LeBlanc et al. (1985). The last one is found to be rather stable, while the first one often outperforms the other and sometimes is much worse. We believe that these difficulties are due to the practical difficulties when solving the linear minimal cost network flow problems arising in the primal subproblem in mean value cross decomposition. Both the costs and the capacities have to be integers in such a code, so we have to deal with both non-integral costs and non-integral capacities by scaling them. In order to keep the method as stable as possible, we decided to sacrifice a little of the speed, and use the modified Frank-Wolfe method.

The concave cost functions are chosen to be of the form $g_i(z_i) = \begin{cases} d_i z_i^{a_i} & \text{if } z_i > 0 \\ 0 & \text{if } z_i = 0 \end{cases}$ where d_i is obtained by multiplying a random nuber with a chosen weight, c_g. The exponents a_i are randomly generated in an interval $[\underline{a}, \bar{a}]$, where $\underline{a} \geq 0$ and $\bar{a} < 1$. The parameters c_g, $\underline{a}$ and $\bar{a}$ have proved to affect the difficulty of the problem very much, so different values have been tested. For applications in chemical industry, the exponents a_i mostly lie in the interval [0.6, 0.7]. We can note that $g_i(z_i)$ is continuous if $a_i > 0$, while if $a_i = 0$, it is a step function, i.e. a fixed charge, so if $a_i = 0 \; \forall i$, the special case STLP is obtained.

We have solved a total of 74 randomly generated problems in various sizes, from 10 origins and 50 destinations to 100 origins and 500 destinations. The largest problem has 50.000 x-variables, 500 y-variables and 100 z-variables. Among these problems we have some instances of STLP of the same size as in LeBlanc (1977) and some of the same size as in Franca and Luna (1982). The main test problems are 13 problems of the size $m = 50$ and $n = 300$ with $a_i \in [0.1, 0.6]$, 5 problems of the same size with $a_i \in [0.6, 0.7]$ and 5 problems of the largest size, $m = 100$ and $n = 500$ with $a_i \in [0.6, 0.7]$. Finally, we have solved 20 instances of STLP, 10 of the size $m = 20$ and $n = 100$ and 10 with $m = 25$ and $n = 200$. The value of c_g has a strong effect on the difficulty of solving the problems. For small values and large values of c_g the problems are easy and solved in a couple of seconds or at most a minute. However, somewhere between these extremes, we find a sharp increase in difficulty, where the solution times increase to up to 10 minutes for the 50×300-problems and to more than an hour for the hardest of the 100×500-problems.

References

Cooper, L., and LeBlanc, L. J. (1977), "Stochastic transportation problems and other network related convex problems", *Naval Research Logistics Quarterly* 24, 327–336.

Franca, P. M., and Luna, H. P. (1982), "Solving stochastic transportation-location problems by generalized Benders decomposition", *Transportation Science* 16, 113–126.

Holmberg, K. (1992), "Linear mean value cross decomposition: A generalization of the Kornai-Liptak method", *European Journal of Operational Research* 62, 55–73.

Holmberg, K. (1993), "Efficient decomposition and linearization methods for the stochastic transportation problem", Research report LiTH-MAT-R-1993-10, Department of Mathematics, Linköping Institute of Technology, Sweden.

Holmberg, K., and Jörnsten, K. (1984), "Cross decomposition applied to the stochastic transportation problem", *European Journal of Operational Research* 17, 361–368.

Horst, R., and Tuy, H. (1993), *Global Optimization* (Second edition), Springer-Verlag, Berlin.

LeBlanc, L. J., Helgason, R. V., and Boyce, D. E. (1985), "Improved efficiency of the Frank-Wolfe algorithm for convex network programs", *Transportation Science* 19, 445–462.

LeBlanc, L. J. (1977), "A heuristic approach for large scale discrete stochastic transportation-location problems", *Computers & Mathematics with Applications* 3, 87–94.

Tuy, H. (1987), "Global optimization of a difference of two convex functions", *Mathematical Programming Study* 30, 150–182.

Tuy, H. (1992), "The complementary convex structure in global optimization", *Journal of Global Optimization* 2, 21–40.

BICONVEX QUADRATIC MAXIMIZATION SUBJECT TO LINEAR CONSTRAINTS

Stane Indihar
Faculty of Business Economics
SLO-62000 Maribor, Razlagova 14, Slovenia

We shall be concerned with the following special nonlinear programming problem

$$\max\left\{f(x,y)\,|\,x\in X, y\in Y\right\} \tag{1}$$

where

$$f(x,y) = a^Tx+b^Ty+x^TCy+x^TEx+y^TFy$$

$$X = \left\{x\in\mathbf{R}^m\,|\,Ax\le p, x\ge 0\right\} \qquad Y = \left\{y\in\mathbf{R}^n\,|\,By\le q, y\ge 0\right\}$$

$$A \in \mathbf{R}^{s\times m},\quad B\in\mathbf{R}^{t\times n},\quad C\in\mathbf{R}^{m\times n},\quad p\in\mathbf{R}^s,\quad q\in\mathbf{R}^t$$

$$E \in \mathbf{R}^{m\times m},\quad F\in\mathbf{R}^{n\times n}$$

We assume that E,F are positive semi-definite matrices and X,Y are nonempty (bounded or unbounded) polyhedral convex sets.

If E = 0, F = 0, then problem (1) is well-known bilinear programming (BLP) problem which has been studied by several authors (for references see for instance [1], [3]) who have developed different approaches for solving it.

Since the functions $f(x,y^0)$, $f(x^0,y)$ ($x^0\in X$, $y^0\in Y$ are fixed vectors) are convex quadratic functions we could say, analogously to BLP, that problem (1) is a convex biquadratic maximization problem.

Problem (1) belongs to the class of multiextremal global optimization problems. It is a generalization of the problem studied in [2]. Namely, the assumption about the boundedness of X and Y, which has been included in [2] in this work is omited.

Let us define the function

$$g(x) = \max_{y\in Y} f(x,y) = a^Tx+x^TEx+x^TEx+\max_{y\in Y}((b+C^Tx)^T+y^TFy)$$

It can be shown that it is convex.

Introducing the function $g(x)$ problem (1) can be transformed into a convex maximization problem

$$\max\left\{g(x)\,|\,x\in X\right\} \tag{2}$$

The connection between problems (1) and (2) gives the following theorem.

Theorem 1 If $(\tilde{x},\tilde{y})\in X\times Y$ is an optimal solution of (1) then $\tilde{x}$ is an optimal solution of (2) and $f(\tilde{x},\tilde{y})=g(\tilde{x})$. Conversely, if $\tilde{x}$ solves (2) and $g(\tilde{x})=f(\tilde{x},\tilde{y})$, where $\tilde{y}$ is an optimal solution of the problem

$$\max\left\{f(\tilde{x},y)\,|\,y\in Y\right\}$$

then $(\tilde{x},\tilde{y})$ solves (1).

On the basis of this theorem we can apply for solving problem (1) a method for convex maximization over a polyhedral convex set. Since problem (1) has similar properties as BLP-problem, we will propose for solving problem (1) Thieu's [3] outer-approximation algorithm. This finite algorithm has the following features:

1. it does not assume that X, Y are bounded sets,
2. it constructs a finite sequence of polyhedral convex sets containing X
   $S_0\supset S_1\supset S_2\supset\ldots\supset X$,
3. for an obtained S_k it examines if $g(x)$ is bounded on extreme halflines of S_k or if there exists a vertex of S_k, which is also a vertex of X, for which the function $g(x)$ reaches the maximum value on S_k.

References

Horst, R. and Tuy, H., Global Optimization, Springer-Verlag, Berlin Heidelberg 1990.

Indihar, S., A generalization of bilinear programming, First Balkan Conference on Operational Research Proceedings, Thessaloniki 17-20 October 1988, 326-335.

Thieu, T.V., A note on the solution of bilinear programming problems byreduction to concave minimization, Mathematical Programming 41 (1988) 49-53.

K-FOLD COMPLEMENTARITY PROBLEM AND THE ORDER COMPLEMENTARITY PROBLEM

G. ISAC
Department of Mathematics
Collège militaire royal de
St-Jean, St-Jean, Québec,
Canada, J0J 1R0

1. Introduction

We consider in this paper the k-Fold Complementarity Problem. This problem is the mathematical model used in Economics in the study of distributive problems [11]. We show that the k-Fold Complementarity Problem is equivalent to an Order Complementarity Problem, and by this way, we have that this problem is naturally prepared to apply a topological index defined using the homotopy. We give some existence theorems and some comments about the computation of solutions.

2. The k-Fold Complementarity Problem

Consider a distributive problem involving n agents and k goods. $\mathbf{R}^k_+$ stands for the consumption set of jth consumer, (j=1,2,3....,n) and a point $x \in \mathbf{R}^{nk}_+$ denotes an *allocation,* that can be written as: $x = (x_1, \ldots, x_n)$, where $x_j = (x_{j1}, x_{j2}, \ldots, x_{jk})$, for all j=1,2,..,n. We consider the following problem. Given a vector of utility values $v = (v_1, \ldots, v_n) \in \mathbf{R}^n$, find the amount of goods and their corresponding distribution so that, these utility levels are actually reached, and if some agent ends up with utility grater than his component v_j, than he must receive no goods. If $u_j : \mathbf{R}^{nk}_+ \to \mathbf{R}$ denotes the jth agent's payoff function, we have the n-vector function of agent's payoffs $u(x) = [u_1(x), \ldots, u_n(x)]$, for all $x \in \mathbf{R}^{nk}_+$. Now, our problem becomes

$$\begin{cases} \text{find } x \in \mathbf{R}^{nk}_+ \text{ such that } u(x) \geq v \\ \text{and } u_j(x) > v_j \Rightarrow x_j = 0, \; (j = 1, \ldots, n) \end{cases} \tag{1}$$

If 0_n (resp. 0_k) denotes the origin of $\mathbf{R}^n$ (resp $\mathbf{R}^k$). and F(x):=u(x)-v, for all $x \in \mathbf{R}_+^{nk}$, then problem (1) has the following form named "the k-Fold Complementarity Problem"

$$(k-F,CP):\begin{cases}\text{find } x \in \mathbf{R}_+^{nk} \text{ such that } F(x) \geq 0_n \\ \text{and } F_j(x) > 0 \Rightarrow x_j = 0_k, \ (j=1,\ldots,n)\end{cases}$$

3. The Order Complementarity Problem

We consider on $\mathbf{R}^{nk}$ the ordering "$\leq$" defined by the cone $\mathbf{R}_+^{nk}$. With respect to this ordering $\mathbf{R}^{nk}$ is a vector lattice and we denote: $x \wedge y = \inf(x,y)$, $x \vee y = \sup(x,y)$.
Given n operators $T_1, T_2, \ldots, T_r : \mathbf{R}_+^{nk} \to \mathbf{R}_+^{nk}$ the General Order Complementarity Problem associated to $\{T_i\}_1^n$ and $\mathbf{R}_+^{nk}$ is ,

$$GOCP(\{T_i\}_1^r, \mathbf{R}_+^{nk}):\begin{cases}\text{find } x_0 \in \mathbf{R}_+^{nk} \text{ such that} \\ \wedge(T_1(x_0), T_2(x_0), \ldots, T_r(x_0)) = 0\end{cases}$$

This important problem was studied in [2], [4-9]. Consider now the problem (k-F,C). If $k \geq 2$ we define $\psi : \mathbf{R}_+^n \to \mathbf{R}^{nk}$ by $\psi(x_1,\ldots,x_n) = (\underbrace{x_1,\ldots,x_1}_{\text{k-times}},\ldots,\underbrace{x_n,\ldots,x_n}_{\text{k-times}})$. We put $T_1(x) = I(x)$ (the identity mapping) and $T_2(x) = \psi(F(x))$, for all $x \in \mathbf{R}_+^{nk}$.

Proposition. *The problem (k-F,CP) is equivalent to the problem* $GOCP(\{T_i\}_{i=1}^2, \mathbf{R}_+^{nk})$.

4. A topological index with respect to a cone

The problem $GOCP(\{T_i\}_{i=1}^n, \mathbf{R}_+^n)$ was studied by the classical topological degree in [1], [2], [3]. Our principal instrument in this paper, to study the problem $GOCP(\{T_i\}_{i=1}^2, \mathbf{R}_+^n)$, defined before, is the topological index introduced by Opoitsev in [10]. We say that a continuous mapping $f : \mathbf{R}_+^{nk} \to \mathbf{R}^{nk}$ is $\mathbf{R}_+^{nk}$-*admissible* mapping , if it does not carry the boundary points of $\mathbf{R}_+^{nk}$ into $\mathrm{int}\mathbf{R}_+^{nk}$. Using a special homotopy for $\mathbf{R}_+^{nk}$-admissible mappings we define the expressions: ind(f,0)=1; ind(f,0)=0; ind(f,∞)=1 and ind(f,∞)=0. It is important to remark that to define this index we use only the homotopy.

5. Existence results

We present several existence results for the problem (k-F,CP). Let $\mathcal{T}:\mathbf{R}_+^{nk} \to \mathbf{R}^{nk}$ be the mapping $\mathcal{T}(x) = T_1(x) \wedge T_2(x)$, for all $x \in \mathbf{R}_+^{nk}$. The results presented in this paper are based on the following theorems.

Theorem 1.

The function $\mathcal{T}(x)$ *is* R_+^{nk}*-admissible and if* $ind(\mathcal{T}, \infty) = 1$ *then the problem (k-F,CP.) has at least one solution* $x_* \in \mathrm{R}_+^{nk}$.

Theorem 2. *Let the* R_+^{nk}*-indices at the origin and at infinity of* $\mathcal{T}$ *be defined and let* $ind(\mathcal{T}, 0) \neq ind(\mathcal{T}, \infty)$. *Then the problem (k-F,CP) has at least one nonzero solution* $x_* \in R_+^{nk}$

6. Approximation methods

In this section we comments several numerical methods for the problem (k-F, CP*)* based on its equivalence with an Order Complementarity Problem.

7. Comments

The problem (k-F,CP*)*, with F à Z-function, was studied in [11] as an optimization problem. In this paper we use the nonlinear analysis.

References

[1]. GARCIOA C. B., GOULD F. J. and TURNBULL T R. (1983) Complementary cones and degree in linear complementarity problems. In: Homotopy Methods and Global Convergence (Eds.:B.C.Eaves, F.J.Gould, H.O.Peitgen and M.J. Todd) Plenum Press: 91-144

[2]. GOWDA M.S. and SZNAJDER R. (1992) The generalized order linear complementarity problem. Preprint, University of Maryland, Baltimore, County.

[3]. HOW R. (1983) On a class of linear complementarity problems of variable degree In: Homotopy Methods and Global Convergence (Eds.:B.C.Eaves, F.J.Gould, H.O Peitgen and M.J. Todd) Plenum Press: 155-178

[4]. ISAC G. (1992) Complementarity problems. Lecture Notes in Math. Nr.1528, Springer-Verlag

[5]. ISAC G. (1992) Iterative methods for the general order complementarity problem. In: Approximation Theory, Spline Functions and Applications (Ed. S.P. Singh), Kluwer Academic Publishers: 365-380

[6]. ISAC G. and KOSTREVA M. (1991) The generalized order complementarity problem. J. Opt. Theory Appl. 71 Nr.3: 517-534

[7]. ISAC G. and KOSTREVA M. (1991) Kneser's theorem and the multivalued general order complementarity problem. Appl. Math. Lett. 4 Nr.6: 81-85

[8]. ISAC G. and KOSTREVA M. (1992) The implicit general order complementarity problem and Leontief's input-output model. Preprint, Royal Military College of St-Jean

[9]. ISAC G. and Goeleven D. (1993) The general order complementarity problem: models and iterative methods. Annal Oper. Res. (Forthcoming)

[10]. OPOITSEV V. I. (1979) Existence theorems in problems of system statics. Transl. Avtomatika i Telemekhanika Nr.3: 85-95

[11]. VILLAR A. (1992) Operator theorems with applications to distributive problems and equilibrium models. Lecture Notes in Economics and Mathematical Systems Nr.377, Springer-Verlag .

A Fault Diagnosis Information System Using Temporary Relations between Symptoms

Stephan Jacobs
Lehrstuhl für Informatik V, RWTH Aachen
Ahornstr. 55, 52056 Aachen, Germany

Introduction

Finding faults in a technical or medical system is a well known problem where much experience was gained from several applications within the last decade (Horn, 1990). Most of them are interactively used, rulebased systems. Frequently appearing symptoms are related to hypothized faults. On the other hand there are monitoring systems which observe e.g. technical processes or human patients. Monitoring systems generate messages periodically (e.g. oil-temperature and oil-pressure in a car) or in special predefined situations (e.g door is open while driving). The increasing use of monitoring systems which leads to a large number of to be diagnosed messages demands the use of a combination of fault diagnosis and monitoring systems. However the combination of the different approaches leads to several problems. Temporary relations between symptoms have to be considered in an appropriate representation of faults.

- The temporal order of symptoms is not observed in traditional "snapshot diagnosis". But ordering of symptoms can be used to differ between faults. Because of causal relations the situations Symptom "S1 before S2" can be interpreted differently from the situation "S2 before S1".
- Because of the spatial range of the machine and because of the delay of some reactions faults and their related symptoms does not appear at the same moment but within an interval. The question now is to choose the range of the interval in which all symptoms have to appear.

Additional problems arise concerning the operating of the system. The symptoms of different monitors arrive like a stream of signals. They have to be interpreted continuously. Questions apply to the synchronization of the incoming signals and the diagnosis system.

- When does the diagnosis has to be started ?
- How are symptoms treated, which appear during a diagnosis ?

Finally monitoring is not only made to enter into a log, but to recognize critical situations and react to it immediately. So there are requirements that systems should react in real-time, i.e. within a predefined interval.

Concept

The relationship between faults F_i and Symptoms S_j is often described with rules similar to the following: $F_1 \Leftarrow$. The fault is defined by a set of symptoms. However there is no ordering of symptoms, nor a statement of an interval in which the symptoms have to arrive. Taking a formal-language-perspective (Hopcroft et al., 1988) the set of symptoms can be interpreted as several words. Each symptom is interpreted as a letter, and each combination of all symptoms S_1, ... S_j is an accepted word of the language F_1. Changing from sets to languages an ordering is introduced. As formal languages have there equivalents within finite state machine (FSM), these machines can be used to analyze the incoming symptoms. E.g. the rule $F_1 \Leftarrow S_1, S_2, S_3$, the language $F_1 = \{S_1S_2S_3, S_1S_3S_2, ..., S_3S_2S_1\}$ and the FSM in figure 1 all represent the same relationship between faults and symptoms (Hopcroft et al., 1988, Dorn, 1992). The FSM has to be interpreted in the following way. The circle represent states and the arrow possible transitions between the states. The empty state is the starting state and the bold state is the finite state. If a symptom S_j arrives and an transition labeled with this symptom leads from the actual to another state, one can move to this new state. If a symptom leads to the finite state the fault is detected. The FSM in figure 1 represents all combination of sequences of three symptoms.

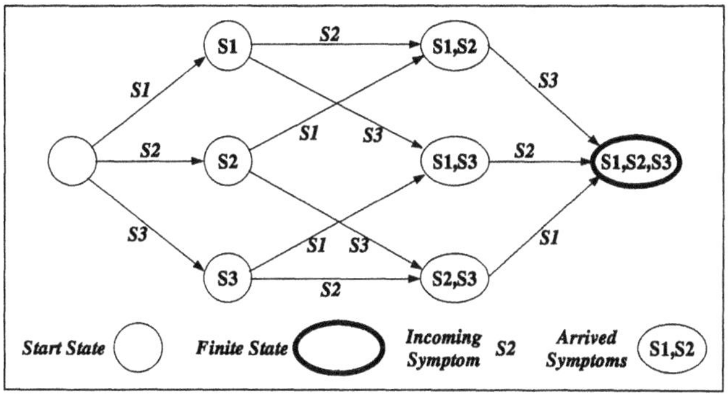

Figure 1 Finite state machine representing all orders of symptoms S_1, S_2, S_3

Introducing partial ordering by explicit declaration of sequences. the FSM will be reduced. If e.g. it is required that S_2 arrives before S_3, that means $F_1 \Leftarrow S_1, S_2, S_3; S_2 < S_3$, the FSM is reduced as some states and transitions are illegal now. In fact the FSM in figure 2 will accept only the sequences of S_1, S_2 and S_3, where S_2 arrives before S_3.

Combining diagnosis and monitoring systems it has to be possible to declare a time window (Krebs et al., 1991), (Nejdl et al., 1992), a pre-defined interval in which all symptoms indicating a fault have to arrive. The range of the window has to be set to the maximum expected time period where symptoms relevant to the fault will receive. The time window is started with the

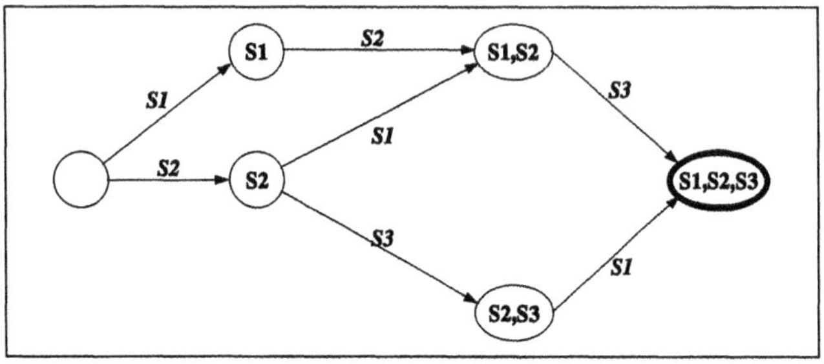

Figure 2 Finite Automaton with partial ordering of symptoms

first incoming symptom, and is closed either by arriving a finite state within the finite automaton or if the time of the window is expired. It is no problem to put a whole FSM into one time window. Additionally time windows can be used to describe temporal constraints to parts of the FSM. If e.g. S_1, S_2 have to arrive within 10 seconds and S_3 has to arrive within 6 seconds after the FSM is started, that means $F_1 \Leftarrow S_1, S_2, S_3; S_2 < S_3; S_1, S_2 \epsilon [0s : 10s], S_3 \epsilon [0s : 6s]$ this can be described within the FSM by labeling the transitions (cf. fig. 3). The time window is started

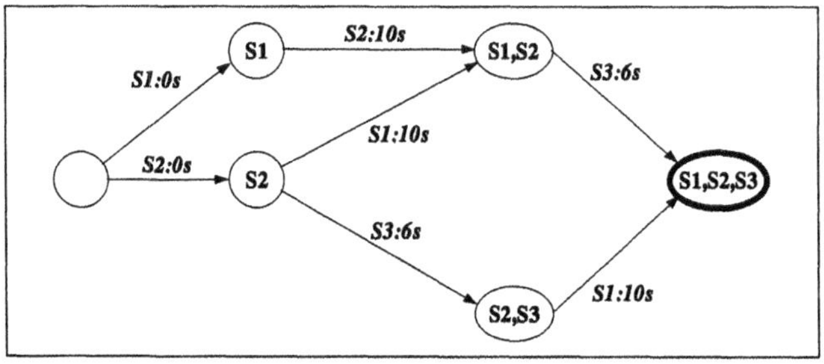

Figure 3 Introducing time windows to the FSM by labeling transitions

with the first incoming symptom. As the window is started by this symptom the transition is labeled with a *0* (e.g. S_1*:0s*). When the next symptom arrives the time is compared relative to the time window. If the symptom arrives in time, one changes the state as before. If the symptom arrives out of time, the window is closed. It's important to notice that the time has to be labeled not to the state but to the transition. If a state can be reached by two ways, sometimes the transitions have different time-labels, i.e. a possible label for the state would be ambiguous (in fact in some complicate cases even the labels for the transitions are ambiguous and must be declared and corrected at run-time). E.g. in figure 3 the last symptom can either be S_1 or S_3. If S_3 is the last symptom, the time interval has to be set to 6 seconds. If S_1 is the last symptom, S_3 is already received in time and so the weaker interval is relevant.

Using labeled FSMs the representation of faults and their related symptoms in consideration of temporal ordering and intervals is possible. Moreover the FSMs lead to a simple implementation.

Implementation

For each fault a FSM is implemented (Hüsgens, 1993). Each FSM is represented as a graph. A diagnosis now is the attempt to find a fault (in the language perspective this is a word) in the incoming stream of symptoms (in the language perspective these are the letters). A diagnosis is successful, if the word (fault) is found, i.e. if the FSM got into the finite state. Each incoming symptom is used as a trigger. It can start a new diagnosis, i.e. it starts a new process as an instance of the FSM, or it can lead to a state transition of waiting FSMs, if it is the appropriate symptom. For that at each time several processes run in parallel each waiting for a symptom. A copy of the incoming symptom is sent as a message to every process.

In contrast to usual diagnosis systems, which open a backward window as a snapshot, our approach "looks" forward, each symptom can start a new diagnosis. Usual systems work on global knowledge (the whole window), whereas our diagnosis processes only have to work on the actual symptom. Hence they consume only a minimum of computing power. Usual systems have to work up past symptoms when starting a diagnosis, whereas our diagnosis-processes are always up to date. On the other hand the number of processes increases with the number of possible faults and with the number of incoming symptoms. Moreover faults, which are described by several unordered symptoms, lead to huge FSMs. So if faults are described by a set of symptoms, the representation by FSM seems to be inappropriate. However the concept of parallel processes can be used anyway using another data-structure (e.g. sets).

A first version of the system is implemented on a 386 PC under OS/2. It is used to control a furnace within the metal industry.

References

Dorn, J., 1992, "Temporal Reasoning in Sequence Graphs", Proceedings of the 10th International Conference on Artificial Intelligence (AAAI'92), 1992

Hopcroft, J., Ullman, J., 1988, "Einführung in die Automatentheorie, formale Sprachen und Komplexitätstheorie", Addsion-Wesley

Horn, W., 1990, "Anwendungen von Expertensystemen" in Gottlob, G., Frühwirth T., Horn, W., (eds.), "Expertensysteme" (in German), Springer, pp. 61-72

Hüsgens, J., 1993, "Zeitabhänigige Regeln in einem Diagnosesystem zur Fehlererkennung in Produktionsprozessen", (in German), Working Paper, RWTH Aachen,

Krebs, V., Respondek, T., 1991, "Automatisierung komplexer chemicher Prozesse durch Echtzeit Expertensysteme", (in German) atp-Softwareexpress, 33(2), 1991

Nejdl, W., Pfau-Wagenbauer, M. 1992, "Integrating Model-Based and Heuristic Features in a Real-Time Expert System for Power Distribution Networks", IEEE Expert, Feb. 1992

On the Solution of Linear Vector Optimization Problems in the Image Space

Johannes Jahn
Institut für Angewandte Mathematik
Universität Erlangen-Nürnberg
Martensstr. 3, D-91058 Erlangen

1 Introduction

The considered linear vector optimization problem reads as follows

$$\left.\begin{array}{c} \min Cx \\ \text{subject to the constraints} \\ Ax \leq b \\ x \in \mathbb{R}^n \end{array}\right\} \quad (1)$$

where C is a real (m,n) matrix, A is a real (p,n) matrix, b is an element of $\mathbb{R}^p$ and $\leq$ has to be understood in a componentwise sense. Throughout we assume that the constraint set $S := \{x \in \mathbb{R}^n \mid Ax \leq b\}$ is nonempty. The set S is a convex polytope in $\mathbb{R}^n$ and the image set $P := \{Cx \mid x \in S\}$ of the objective mapping is also a convex polytope ([5, p. 307]).

Definition 1 An element $\bar{y} \in P$ is called *minimal* (or *efficient*) if there is no $y \in P$ with $y \leq \bar{y}$ and $y \neq \bar{y}$. An element $\bar{x} \in S$ is called a *minimal solution* (or an *Edgeworth-Pareto optimal point* or a *functional efficient point*) of the vector optimization problem (1), if $C\bar{x}$ is a minimal element of P.

Every minimal vertex of P is the image of a vertex of S which is a minimal solution of the problem (1). Simple examples show that in general the number of minimal vertices of P is much smaller than the number of vertices of S which are minimal solutions. Dauer and Liu [3] discuss this fact with a linear vector optimization problem with $n = 52$ variables, $p = 20$ constraints and $m = 3$ objectives. It turned out that the set P has 21 minimal vertices and the set S has 60 vertices which are minimal solutions. This is based on the different dimensions of the spaces: S is a subset of $\mathbb{R}^{52}$ and P is contained in $\mathbb{R}^3$. In general, for a linear vector optimization problem the dimension of the image space is small whereas the dimension of the preimage space of the objective mapping may be very large, and therefore investigations of the vertices of P instead of S are important.

2 Main Results

Since P s a convex polytope, it can be written in the form

$$P = \{y \in I\!R^m \mid Dy \leq e\} \tag{2}$$

where D is a real (k, m) matrix and $e \in I\!R^k$ is a given vector. In special cases the set P can be formulated more explicit ([1, Thm. 2.1], [2, Thm. 2.6] and [4]). It is often difficult to give a formula for the unknown terms D and e. The following proposition gives a very special and simple result.

Proposition 1 If the matrix C is regular, then $P = \{y \in I\!R^m \mid AC^{-1}y \leq b\}$.

So, under the assumption of Proposition 1 we obtain $D = AC^{-1}$ and $e = b$. In order to get a characterization of certain minimal elements of P we introduce the notion of a proper facet.

Definition 2 Let the set P be given by (2). If for an arbitrary $i \in \{1, \ldots, k\}$ the set

$$P_i := \{x \in P \mid d_i^\top y = e_i\}$$

(where $d_i^\top$ denotes the i-th row of the matrix D and e_i denotes the i-th component of the vector e) is nonempty, then P_i is called a *facet* of P. The set P_i is called a *proper facet*, if there exists some $\bar{y} \in P_i$ such that

$$d_j^\top \bar{y} < e_j \text{ for all } j \in \{1, \ldots, k\}, j \neq i.$$

With the following theorem we present a characterization of a proper facet of P which consists only of minimal elements.

Theorem 1 Let the set P be given by (2). Then every proper facet $P_i := \{y \in P \mid d_i^\top y = e_i\}$ consists only of minimal elements of the set P if and only if $d_i \in I\!R^m$ has only negative components.

In the case of a convex polyhedron P (i.e. $m = 3$) the notion of proper facets can be extended to the notion of proper edges.

Definition 3 Let the set P be given by (2) with $m = 3$. If for arbitrary $i, j \in \{1, \ldots, k\}$, $i \neq j$, the set

$$E_{i,j} := \{y \in P \mid d_i^\top y = e_i \text{ and } d_j^\top y = e_j\}$$

is nonempty (where $d_i^\top$ denotes the i-th row of the matrix D and e_i denotes the i-th component of the vector e), then $E_{i,j}$ is called an *edge* of P. An edge $E_{i,j}$ is called a *proper edge* of P, if there exists some $\bar{y} \in E_{i,j}$ such that

$$d_s^\top y < e_s \text{ for all } s \in \{1, \ldots, k\}, s \neq i, s \neq j.$$

The following algorithm can be used for the determination of all minimal elements of proper facets and proper edges of the convex polyhedron P.

Algorithm 1

Step 1: Determine the index set
$I_1 := \{i \in \{1, \ldots, k\} \mid d_i \text{ has only negative components}\}$.

Step 2: Determine the set I_2 of pairs
$(i, j) \in (\{1, \ldots, k\} \setminus I_1) \times (\{1, \ldots, k\} \setminus I_1)$ of indices $i \neq j$ with the following properties:

(a) The system
$$Dy \leq e, d_i^\top y = e_i, d_j^\top y = e_j$$
has at least one solution $y \in \mathbb{R}^3$.

(b) The linear optimization problem
$$\min \alpha$$
subject to the constraints
$$\lambda d_{i_l} + \mu d_{j_l} \leq \alpha \text{ for } l = 1, 2, 3$$
$$0 \leq \lambda \leq 1,\ 0 \leq \mu \leq 1,\ \alpha \leq 0$$
has a negative minimal value.

Step 3: Determine a subset M of minimal elements of P as union of minimal proper facets and minimal proper edges in the form
$$M = \bigcup_{i \in I_1} \{y \in P \mid d_i^\top y = e_i\}$$
$$\cup \bigcup_{(i,j) \in I_2} \{y \in P \mid d_i^\top y = e_i \text{ and } d_j^\top y = e_j\}.$$

Theorem 2 Let the set P be given by (2) with $m = 3$. Then Algorithm 1 determines minimal facets and minimal edges of P where at least all minimal proper facets and minimal proper edges of P are determined.

For the missing proofs and further details we refer to [6].

References

[1] J.P. Dauer, "Analysis of the Objective Space in Multiple Objective Linear Programming", *J. Math. Anal. Appl.* 126 (1987) 579–593.

[2] J.P. Dauer, "Numerically Analyzing Linear Multicriteria Optimization Problems", in: W. Stadler (ed.), *Multicriteria Optimization in Engineering and in the Sciences* (Plenum Press, New York, 1988), p. 27–47.

[3] J.P. Dauer and Y.-H. Liu, "Solving Multiple Objective Linear Programs in Objective Space", *European J. Oper. Res.* 46 (1990) 350–357.

[4] J.P. Dauer and O.A. Saleh, "A Representation of the Set of Feasible Objectives in Multiple Objective Linear Programs", *Linear Algebra Appl.* 166 (1992) 261–275.

[5] D. Gale, *The Theory of Linear Economic Models* (McGraw-Hill, New York, 1960).

[6] J. Jahn, "On the Determination of Minimal Facets and Edges of a Convex Polytope" (manuscript, University of Erlangen-Nürnberg, 1993).

BIFURCATED ROUTING WITH TRANSITION COSTS

Anne De Jongh
Service Mathématique de la Gestion
Université Libre de Bruxelles
Boulevard du Triomphe, CP 210/01, B-1050 Brussels

A transmission network can be viewed as a graph where the nodes are the cities and the arcs are the communication means between these cities. We consider here two common problems that often arise when we want to route a communication demand on the network:
The first one is that node and arc failures can happen. To avoid it, the operators often route the communication demand on two paths between the source and the sink. The second one is that new arcs may have been added to the network, with a different technology in comparison with the original arcs. The routing of a flow from one technology to another requires the working of a special appliance and causes a cost called "transition cost", which has to be added to the traditional routing cost. We will deal here with networks on which two different technologies are installed.

There exist four different bifurcated routing problems for transmissions. All of them can be transformed into a problem of flow of value two and minimum cost on an adequate network with unit capacities on all arcs.
(P1) **Finding two different arc disjoint paths between the source (s) and the sink (t) without transition costs.** This problem has been studied by Suurballe and Tarjan (1984) who have developed an augmenting path algorithm to solve it.
(P2) **Finding two different arc disjoint paths with transition costs.** This problem can be solved by applying the augmenting path algorithm to a network where all the nodes, except s and t have been splitted into two nodes, one for the entering and leaving arcs of technology 1 and the other for the arcs of technology 2. These two nodes are linked together by two arcs whose cost is equal to the transition cost.
(P3) **Finding two node disjoint paths without transition costs.** We can solve this problem by applying the same algorithm to a network where each node is also splitted into two nodes, but this time, one node is for the arcs entering the original node and the other one for the arcs leaving it. The first node is linked to the second by an arc of cost zero.

(P4) **Finding two node disjoint paths with transition costs.** This problem is not so easy to solve and merits a special study.

First of all, it can be shown by a reduction of 3-SAT that this problem is strongly NP-hard.

On the hand, we consider the two following heuristics:
H1 : This heuristic is the same as in (P3), except that once we have the two paths, we compute the transition costs and add them to the routing costs. It is clear that this heuristic often fails to provide a good solution.
H2 : We transform the network such as mentioned in (P2), then compute a first min-cost path with Dijkstra's algorithm, forbid the intermediate nodes of the obtained solution and finally compute a second min-cost path, again with Dijkstra's algorithm. This second heuristics seems to provide quite better results than H1 but can sometimes give bad results. We provide a worst-case bound for H2 and show that it is the best possible.

On the other hand, after giving a good formulation of the problem, we consider a Lagrangean relaxation of this formulation. Specifically, we relax the constraint that force the two paths to be node disjoint. H1 and H2 are used to give an upper bound to the Lagrangean solution, and the method used to solve the relaxation is an interesting adaptation of the augmenting path algorithm.

Finally, the Lagrangean relaxation is embedded into a branch and bound procedure.
We tested the whole procedure on a lot of problems created by the network generator NETGEN, and on the Belgian telephone network.

Reference :

Suurballe J.W., Tarjan R.E. (1984) A quick method for finding shortest pairs of disjoint paths. Networks, vol 14, 325-336.

Batch Sequencing with Sequence Dependent Setup-Times and -Costs: A Comparison of Logic and Mixed Integer Programming Approaches

Carsten Jordan, Andreas Drexl, Institut für Betriebswirtschaftslehre, Christian-Albrechts Universität zu Kiel, Olshausenstr. 40, D-24118 Kiel

We consider a batch sequencing model were a number of jobs has to be processed on a single machine. The set of job is partitioned into classes, and a sequence-dependent setup-time is needed when switching from jobs in one class to another. For each jobclass holding costs are given, for each job its deadline, its processing time and an earliness weight proportional to the processing time and holding costs of the class are given. All jobs must be sequenced on a single machine so that each job is processed between time zero and its deadline. Four different objectives are considered: first to minimize the sum of sequence-dependent setup-costs (between classes) and weighted earliness for each job completed before its deadline (Case I). Second, only the sequence-dependent setup costs (Case II), third only the sum of earliness costs has to be minimized (Case III). Fourth, the problem may be viewed as a Constraint Satisfaction Problem (Case IV).

The aim is to compare modelling and solution performance of two different general solvers for this example problem (cf. [3]).

A very concise conceptual model formulation of the above problems can be obtained taking decision variables as *indexes* (cf. [4]). This formulation is implemented in the constraint propagation/logic programming language CHARME.

For the different objectives (Cases) two different mixed integer programming (MIP) formulations are used: With sequence-dependent setup-costs in the objective (Cases I and II) in formulation MIP A decision variables state, that two jobs are sequenced *directly* after each other (cf. [1]). For Cases III and IV another formulation MIP B can be used to reduce the number of binary variables (cf. [2]). The mixed-integer programming formulations are solved by OSL, a state-of-the-art MIP solver.

For instances with tighter constraints in Cases I and II the logic programming solver outperforms the MIP solver. In the other cases performance of the logic programming solver is worse.

Comparing modelling with the two different solvers we observe that the number of constraints is linear in the number of jobs for the conceptual formulation versus its square for the MIP formulations. Moreover, to achieve comparable performance two different MIP formulations had to be used versus only one for the logic programming solver.

References

[1] Blazewicz, J., M. Dror and J. Weglarz, 1991. Mathematical programming formulations for machine scheduling: a survey, *European Journal of Operations Research,* Vol. 51, pp. 283-300.

[2] Coleman, B.J., 1993. A simple model for optimizing the single machine early/tardy problem with sequence dependent setups, *Production and Operations Management*, Vol.1, pp. 225-228.

[3] Jordan, C. and A. Drexl, 1993. A Comparison of Logic and Mixed-Integer Programming Solvers for Batch Sequencing with Sequence-Dependent Setups, Working paper, Universität Kiel.

[4] Woodruff, D.L. and M.L.Spearman, 1992. Sequencing and batching for two classes of jobs with deadlines and setup times, *Production and Operations Management*, Vol.1, pp. 87-102.

COLLECTIVE SELFORGANIZED COMPUTER PROCESSES IN DIGITAL NETWORK STRUCTURES

Alexandr Katkov
Institute of Simulation Problems in
Power Engineering
15 General Naumov St.
USS 252680 Kiev-164
Ukraine

Collective selforganized computer processes arise in digital network structures under following necessary conditions: in the first the system must be globally parallel, in the second its behaviour must be nonprogrammed and defined only by physical properties of components. Last condition fulfils when there are not any systems of synchronization which does computer processes invarianting to individual physical properties of system components. On the one side it doesn't permit to use potentially more high speed of operation components, and on other side it blocks arising of selforganized computer processes which distinguish in some cases by high efficiency. Under fulfilment of necessary conditions as pointed out above in digital network structures orienting for solving equations of Laplace, Puasson, it researched two tipes of selforganized computer processes. First of them observed in digital network structure in elements of which there was not fixed the end moment of transitional process and new operands entered to logging in before end of operation fulfilment over preceding ones. For finding of stable state that is solving of equation system it used stochastic generation process of initial system state from which its path to stable state is defined only by physical properties of components. The second process is researched in network structure which elements had simple construction of end moment locking in of transitional process that was the signal for taking to logging in of new operand element to computer. In such case there were arised computer processes in the form of chaotic relaxation (Chasan D.,Miranker W., 1969).

Chasan D.,Miranker W. (1969) Chaotic relaxation. Linear Algebra and its Appl. 2: 199-222.

LINEAR DEPENDENCES OF RANDOM VARIABLES AND SIMULATION

Ivan Kavkler, Lilijana Arih
School of Business and Economics, University of Maribor
Razlagova 14, 62000 Maribor, Slovenia

In the optimization model SLOM - Stochastic Linear Optimization Model (see Kavkler et al. (1991)) n interdependent normally distributed random variables appear, for which a suitable random sample exists. The set of all variables has to be split into the subset of exogenous and the subset of endogenous variables. Because the exogenous variables are correlated in practical cases, it was necessary to find new linear expressions of endogenous variables with exogenous variables. These expressions, generalized linear multiple regressions, were found by using factor analysis (see Kim, Mueller (1988)). According to our expectations, the obtained results are quite good for poor correlated exogenous variables.

A generalized linear multiple regression

Let

$$y_j, \qquad j = 1, 2, \ldots , n \tag{1}$$

be the normally distributed random variables, by which the considered process is representatively described, and let

$$Y_{(N,n)} = \left[y_{ij} \right]_{(N,n)} \tag{2}$$

be the random sample associated to the variables (1). Let

$$x_j, \qquad j = 1, 2, \ldots, n \tag{3}$$

be the standardized random variables of (1).

By using the correlation matrix

$$R = \left[r_{ij} \right]_{(n,n)} \tag{4}$$

and the factor analysis, the variables (3) can be expressed by the equation

$$x = Qf + e, \tag{5}$$

where

$x \in \mathbb{R}^n$ is the vector of the variables (3),

$f \in \mathbb{R}^m$, $m < n$, is the vector of common factors,

$e \in \mathbb{R}^n$ is the vector of residuals, and

$Q \in \mathbb{R}^n \times \mathbb{R}^m$ is the matrix of factor loadings.

If m uncorrelated random variables from (3) exist ($x_1, x_2, \ldots, x_m$), it is possible to express the other variables by linear multiple regression

$$x_{en} = R_3 x_{ex} + e_{en}$$

where

$x_{ex} \in \mathbb{R}^m$ is the vector of exogenous variables from (3),

$x_{en} \in \mathbb{R}^{n-m}$ is the vector of endogenous variables from (3),

$e_{en} \in \mathbb{R}^{n-m}$ is the vector of residuals of endogenous variables.

The matrix R_3 is defined by the equation

$$R = \begin{bmatrix} I_m & R_{2(m,n-m)} \\ R_{3(n-m,m)} & R_{4(n-m,n-m)} \end{bmatrix}. \tag{6}$$

In this case the vector $x_{ex} = f$ is a solution of the equation (5). Following this fact a generalized linear multiple regression for poor correlated exogenous variables was developed by using factor analysis.Let the rows of the matrix Q in (5) be permutated so that for the rows 1, 2, ..., m holds

$$\sum_{i=1}^{m-1} \sum_{j=i+1}^{m} | r_{ij} | \text{ --> min} \tag{7}$$

and let the new matrix Q' be partitioned as

$$Q' = \begin{bmatrix} Q_{1(m,m)} \\ Q_{2(n-m,m)} \end{bmatrix}. \tag{8}$$

Without loosing on generality we can assume

$$x_{ex} = \left[x_1, x_2, \dots, x_m\right] \quad \text{and}$$

$$x_{en} = \left[x_{m+1}, x_{m+2}, \dots, x_n\right] .$$

The equation (5) can be transformed to

$$x_{ex} = Q_1 f + e_{ex}, \qquad (9)$$

$$x_{en} = Q_2 f + e_{en}. \qquad (10)$$

By the fact that Q_1^{-1} in practical cases, because of (7), exists and that the usual conditions for uncorrelated f, e_{ex}, e_{en} are fulfilled, from the equation (9) it follows on average

$$\tilde{x}_{en} = Q_2 Q_1^{-1} \tilde{x}_{ex}, \qquad (11)$$

where $\tilde{x}_{ex}$, $\tilde{x}_{en}$ are vectors of deterministic continous variables which mean the changeable means of variables (3).

The elements of the matrix

$$B = Q_2 Q_1^{-1} \qquad (12)$$

represent the generalized regression coefficients in the case of normally distributed, standardized and poor correlated exogenous random variables.

Validation of the obtained generalized regression coefficients

The quality of the obtained equation (11) was verified by simulation experiments. The random sample for the variables (3) was obtained from a random sample for m uncorrelated, normally distributed, standardized random variables z_j according to the equation

$$x = Az + e,$$

where $z^T = [z_1, z_2, \dots, z_m]$. The matrix A enables to create the expected interdependences of variables (3). These dependences are given by the matrix

$$C = A_2 A_1^{-1} ,$$

where the matrices A_2 and A_1 were obtained from the matrix A in the same way as the matrices Q_2 and Q_1 from the matrix Q. The distance

$$d(C,B) = \sum_{j=1}^{n-m} \sum_{i=1}^{m} |c_{ji} - b_{ji}|$$

was taken as the criterion for the quality of the obtained generalized linear multiple regression.

In the case m = 3, n = 5 with the correlation matrix

$$R = \begin{bmatrix} 1.000 & .457 & .768 & -.164 & -.047 \\ .457 & 1.000 & .248 & -.046 & -.674 \\ .768 & .248 & 1.000 & -.037 & .230 \\ -.164 & -.046 & -.037 & 1.000 & .272 \\ -.047 & -.674 & .230 & .272 & 1.000 \end{bmatrix}$$

as exogenous variables x_2, x_3, x_4 were chosen according to (7). The matrices B, C, R' and the distances d(C,B) and d(C,R') were calculated. The elements of the matrix R' are the regression coefficients for the case of uncorrelated exogenous variables.

$$C = \begin{bmatrix} .256 & .828 & -.154 \\ -1.010 & .636 & .285 \end{bmatrix} \qquad B = \begin{bmatrix} .297 & .848 & -.147 \\ -.945 & .563 & .294 \end{bmatrix}$$

$$R' = \begin{bmatrix} .457 & .768 & -.164 \\ -.674 & .230 & .272 \end{bmatrix} \qquad \begin{aligned} d(C,B) &= 0.215 \\ d(C,R') &= 1.026 \end{aligned}$$

References:

Kavkler I., L.Arih, Š.Zorko : A Stochastic Linear Optimization Model. Economic Analysis 25 (1991), 176-186.

Kim J.-O., C.W.Mueller : Factor Analysis - Statistical Methods and Practical Issues. Sage Public., Beverly Hills, London, 1988.

HETEROGENEITY AND MULTIVARIATE LOGISTIC DISTRIBUTIONS

Lothar Knüppel
Universität Osnabrück
Rolandstraße 8, D-49069 Osnabrück

1 Introduction

Heterogeneity of populations, sets of objects, supply, or demand in statistical models often is ignored or described outside and prior to statistical model analysis such that this analysis runs for fictitious independent and mean objects or on an aggregate level. The reasons are lack or complexity of appropriate models incorporating heterogeneity and comfortable results for i.i.d. variables from sampling theory. Complete heterogeneity has to include and describe two essential aspects (1) different individual behavior and (2) dependence of this behavior. For aspect (1) convolution and compounding of sufficiently flexible distributions are well-established techniques. With respect to univariate logistic distributions these techniques were used since Dubey (1969) to produce many satisfying results (Knüppel 1986). For aspect (2) multivariate extensions are self-suggesting.
But multivariate logistic distributions, derived as compounds, copulas, conditionals, extensions, or else, since Gumbel's bivariate logistic distributions (1961) are known to be rather rigid in their description of dependence structures. An exception seems to be the multivariate form of Satterthwaite/Hutchinson's bivariate logistic distribution (1978). The richness of this multivariate distribution here is analyzed with respect to its individual models and their dependencies; comparisons to contingency-type logistic distributions are given, demonstrating its appropriateness in describing heterogeneity aspect (1) and its superiority in (2).

2 Derivation and properties of a p−variate logistic distribution

Let $X_1, \dots, X_p$, given θ, be independent random variables (rvs), each having a type-one Extreme-value distribution with distribution function (df) F_i and individual parameters a_i' and $b_i > 0$, where the location parameters a_i' depend on the common parameter θ such that

$$a_i'(\theta) = a_i + b_i \cdot \ln(b_i\theta) \qquad \theta > 0 \qquad i = 1, \dots, p \tag{1}$$

Parameter θ describes the "similarity" because of dependence. The joint distribution of $X_1, \dots, X_p$, given θ, is the product $\prod_{i=1}^p F_i(x_i|\theta)$. Now, applying Dubey's idea (Dubey 1969) to this multivariate case, let θ be rv with $\theta \sim$Gamma(t, λ) across the population. Then the joint marginal distribution of $X_1, \dots, X_p$, describing dependent individual behavior, is

$$F(x_1, \dots, x_p) = \int_0^\infty \prod_{i=1}^p F_i(x_i|\theta) g(\theta) d(\theta) = (\lambda^t/\Gamma(t)) \int_0^\infty \theta^{t-1} \exp(-\theta \cdot \lambda c_p) d\theta \tag{2}$$

where C_r is the rv $C_r := [1 + \sum_{i=1}^r (b_i/\lambda) \cdot \exp(-(x_i - a_i)/b_i)]$ with here $r = p$ and value c_p.

By transformation to the Gamma-integral we obtain a logistic df defined by Johnson (1987)

$$F(x_1,\dots,x_p) = [1+\textstyle\sum_{i=1}^{p}(b_i/\lambda)\exp(-(x_i-a_i)/b_i)]^{-t} \tag{3}$$

$$-\infty < x_i < +\infty; a_i \in \mathbb{R}; b_i, t, \lambda > 0; i = 1,\dots,p.$$

F is called p-variate generalized logistic distribution. It includes (1) Malik-Abraham's multivariate logistic, if $t = 1$ and $p = 1, 2, \dots$, (2) Gumbel's bivariate logistic, if $t = 1$ and $p = 2$, and Satterthwaite-Hutchinson's bivariate logistic, if $t = 2$ and $p = 2$.

$F(x_1,\dots,x_p)$ is the "rich" alternative to "poor" models, where $a_1 = \dots = a_p = \bar{a}$, $b_1 = \dots = b_p = \bar{b}$, and θ constant or θ ~Exponential are assumed, i.e. where neither heterogeneity aspect (1) nor (2) or only a simple form of (1) are present.
As F is a location-scale distribution, we set $a_i = 0, b_i = 1; i = 1,\dots,p$ for further analysis.

Theorem 1: Let the p-dimensional rv $(X_1,\dots,X_p)$ have the p-variate logistic (3). Then
(P1) each X_i has a univariate logistic marginal $F(x_1,\dots,x_p) = [1+(1/\lambda)\exp(-x_i)]^{-t}$
(P2) the joint marginal distribution of $(X_1,\dots,X_n)$ with $n < p$ is an n-variate logistic (3)
(P3) the rvs $X_{n+1},\dots,X_p$ are dependent by the common mixing distribution of the independent rvs $X_1,\dots,X_n$, given θ, with conditional probability density functions (pdfs) which are not $(p-n)$-variate logistic
(P4) multivariate Exponential and Extreme-Value distributions result, if $t \to 0$ or $t \to \infty$.

Properties (P1) and (P2) are obvious by inserting $p = 1$ and $p = n$ into equation (3). Property (P3) is obtained e.g. by applying the simplifying transformation $Y_i = X_i + \ln(\lambda \cdot c_n); i = 1,\dots,p$. Then the rvs $Y_{n+1},\dots,Y_p$ have the joint conditional df

$$F(y_{n+1},\dots,y_p|y_1,\dots,y_n) = \left[1+\textstyle\sum_{n+1}^{p}\exp(-y_i)\right]^{-(t+n)} \tag{4}$$

where the power demonstrates that the conditional distributions are not $(p-n)$-variate logistic. Johnson gave (P1) and relations to the multivariate Burr and Pareto-distributions (Johnson 1987). Individual behavior may be generalized to X_i ~generalized Extreme-value (a_i, b_i, s) with shape parameter s distributed across the population. Then pdfs and extended results to (P4) are available, but no closed forms of dfs, e.g. of (3) or (4), exist.

3 Bivariate analysis, correlation and regression

According to (3) and (P1)-(P3), two rvs X and Y have the standard form df and properties

$$F(x,y;t) = [1+e^{-x}+e^{-y}]^{-t} \qquad t > 0 \tag{5}$$

(P4) both marginals $F_X(x;t)$ and $F_Y(y;t)$ of (5) are univariate logistic
(P5) $F(x,y;t) = F(y,x;t)$, i.e. symmetry to $x = y$
(P6) X and Y are not independent, as $F(x,y)$ cannot be factorized to logistic marginals
(P7) $F(0,0) = 1/3^t \neq P(X \geq 0, Y \geq 0)$ for any $t > 0$.

The distribution of the probability mass on the x/y-quadrants and the dependence between the individual rvs X and Y are determined by t (cf. figure 1).

Fig. 1: Probability mass distribution

	$x<0$	$x>0$
$y>0$	$1/2^t - 1/3^t$	$1 - 2(1/2^t) + 1/3^t$
$y<0$	$1/3^t$	$1/2^t - 1/3^t$

In comparison with Gumbel's bivariate distribution, properties (P5) and (P6) hold for both the Gumbel and the logistic distribution, properties (P4), (P5), (P7) are not restricted to $t = 1$. The probability mass and its mode can be shifted from the third to the first quadrant along the line $x = y$ by increasing parameter t. And we have no longer $f(-x, -x) > f(x, x)$ as given by Gumbel. There is a growing "concentration" of probability mass to $x = y \to \infty$ as t is increased.

The bivariate logistic pdf has its mode at $x_{mod} = y_{mod} = \ln t$ with

$$f(x_{mod}, y_{mod}) = (1 + 1/t)(1 + 2/t)^{-(t+2)} \tag{6}$$

and $f(x_{mod} = 0, y_{mod} = 0) = 2/27$, if $t = 1$. Its df contour lines meet a hyperbolic equation

$$e^{-x} + e^{-y} = 1/c^{1/t} - 1 \qquad 0 \leq c = F(x, y; t) \leq 1 \tag{7}$$

By conditional and bivariate generating functions the conditional expectation, conditional variance and Bravais-Pearson-coefficient of correlation are obtained:

$$E(X|y; t) = \ln F_Y(y; t = 1) + \Psi(t + 1) - \Psi(1) = E(X; t) + 1/t - \ln(1 + e^{-y}) \tag{9}$$

$$Var(X|y; t) = \Psi'(t + 1) + \Psi'(1) \tag{10}$$

$$r(t) = \Psi'(t)/(\Psi'(t) + \Psi'(1)) = 1/(1 + \Psi'(1)/\Psi'(t)) \qquad t > 0 \tag{11}$$

where Ψ is the digamma function. $E(X|y; t)$ is a nonlinear increasing function of y, called regression curve. Its increase is determined by y, its asymptotic level $x = \Psi(t + 1) - \Psi(1)$ is determined by t. The intersection point of the regression curves $E(X|y, t)$ and $E(Y|x, t)$ is at $(\ln i, \ln i)$ where $i = \exp[\Psi(t+1) - \Psi(1)] - 1$. The conditional variance is constant and smaller than the unconditional variance by t^{-2} at any y, but $E(X|y; t) > E(X; t)$, if $y > \ln(e^{1/t} - 1)$. Given y, the conditional variance decreases as t is increased. If $t = 1$, equations (7) and (8) together with recursion properties of the digamma function and $\Psi'(1) = \pi^2/6$ reproduce the simple results of Gumbel's bivariate logistic distribution. Instead of Gumbel's restriction to $r = 0.5$ here we have correlations with $0 < r(t) < 1$ and $r(t) \to 0$, if $t \to \infty$, i.e. if there is an increasing variation between individual behaviors. But negative coefficients $r(t)$ are not possible. Satterthwaithe/Hutchinson (1978) gave similar forms of (9)-(11) and found that other measures like grade correlation and Kendall's τ give no explicit results.

4 Bivariate $C-$type logistic distributions

Bivariate distributions with explicit parameter ρ of association, contingency, or correlation are called C-type distributions. Parameter ρ may be introduced to (5) by adding a mixed term into the squared bracket. Thus a $C-$type bivariate logistic distribution is defined by

$$F(x,y;\rho,t) = [1 + e^{-x} + e^{-y} + \rho e^{-x-y}]^{-t} \qquad (-1 < \rho < +1) \qquad (12)$$

Equation (12) has a simple form, but its pdf, and particularly its conditional pdfs, generating functions, and moments are complicated and uncomfortable, even if $t = 1$. They depend on x and ρ by a function $d(x;\rho) = (1-\rho)/(1+\rho e^{-x})$, e.g.

$$E(Y|x;\rho,t=1) = d(x;\rho) - \ln(1 - d(x;\rho)/\rho)$$
$$Var(Y|x;\rho,t=1) = \pi^2/3 - (d(x;\rho))^2 \qquad \text{if } t = 1.$$

Another way to find a logistic $C-$type is its definition as a member of a $C-$type system. The Farlie-Gumbel-Morgenstern (FMG) system by means of two univariate logistic dfs F_X, F_Y with parameters t_X and t_Y may be specified such that a bivariate FGM logistic df results:

$$F(x,y;\rho,\theta) = F_X \cdot F_Y \cdot [1 + \rho(1-F_X)(1-F_Y)] \qquad \theta = (t_X, t_Y) \qquad (15)$$

with symmetry $F(x,y;\rho,\theta) = F(y,x;\rho,\theta)$, if $t_x = t_Y$. As it is defined by its univariate marginals only, its joint pdf f, product moments, and regression curves depend on marginal dfs F_X, F_Y and pdfs f_X, f_Y. E.g. the conditional expectation is

$$E(X|y;\rho,\theta) = E(X;\rho,\theta) + [\textstyle\int x(1-2F_X)dF_X] \cdot \rho(1-2F_Y) \qquad (16)$$

which is linear in F_Y. The Bravais-Pearson coefficient reflects two ways of dependence (ρ, t)

$$r(\rho,\theta) = \rho[Var(X;\rho,t_x)Var(Y;\rho,t_y)]^{-1/2} \cdot \textstyle\int(1-F_X)\mathrm{dx} \cdot \int(1-F_Y)\mathrm{dy} \qquad (17)$$

Some simplifications are obtained, if $t_x = t_y$. If moreover $t_x = t_y = 1$, then

$$r(\rho) = 3\rho/\pi^2 \qquad \text{with } |r(\rho)| < 0.304 \qquad (18)$$

as $-1 \leq \rho \leq +1$. If $t_x \neq 1$ and $t_y \neq 1$, coefficient r remains small. For, continuous bivariate FGM distributions always have $|r| \leq 1/3$ (Schucany/Parr/Boyer 1978) and thus, in spite of two dependence parameters, are restricted to the description of weak linear dependence.

Similar results hold for the Plackett system of bivariate logistic $C-$type distributions.

References:

Gumbel, E.J. (1961): Bivariate logistic distributions. JlAmStatAss, 56, 335-349.

Johnson, M.E. (1987): Multivariate Statistical Simulation. New York: Wiley.

Knüppel, L. (1986): Some properties of a generalized logistic distribution for reliability nad life-time applications. Methods of Operation Research, 57, 199-210.

Satterthwaite, S.P.; Hutchinson, T.P. (1978): A generalisation of Gumbel's bivariate logistic distribution. Metrika, 25, 163-170.

Competitive Advantages through Flexible Design of Decentralized Information Systems

Hans-Jürgen König
Fachbereich Wirtschaftswissenschaften, Universität Gießen
Licher Str. 60, 6300 Gießen, Germany

In contrast to widespread mainframe-based architectures, decentralized corporate information systems offer adaptability in a world of changing business-constraints to support corporate goals in a flexible way. Beyond this, a goal-oriented decentralized corporate-wide system and application architecture provides competitive advantages by differentiation from architectures of competitors in the market. This paper presents an economic decision model to support information managers in selecting and designing goal-oriented system and application architectures in a changing economic world.

1 Introduction

Information technology (IT) should be applied to support a company's *competitive goals* [3]. The information system (IS) of a company has to be designed goal-oriented with respect to a lot of technical and business constraints. *Technical constraints* e.g. in the area of compatibility, heterogenity, interoperability, integrity, security or performance are understood in depth [4]. The primary challenge is to deal with *business constraints*. A *competitive* IS has to support *customer needs* to strengthen a company's competitive position in the market to increase a company's profitability in the short run as well as in the long run. This requires an *integrated design* of a company's IS and a company's *organizational structures* and *business processes*. A lot of constraints result from present and future customer needs, from competitive structures in the market and generally from the state and development of the national economy and international markets. An IS is composed of its *system architecture* and its *application architecture*. The system architecture includes hardware, system software like operating systems and communication software, and the system topology. The application architecture on the other hand includes data, knowledge and functions relevant for a company's business activities. Conventional centralized system architectures of competing companies are very similar. They hardly provide design-alternatives for a company to differentiate from competitors. Especially an integrated design of system architecture and naturally distributed organizational structures is nearly impossible. In conventional IS-environments only the application architecture allows for differentiation between competitors to gain competitive advantages. *Present* available IT allows for a design of *decentralized* corporate IS based on computer-networks and on heterogeneous interoperable platforms with distributed applications based on the peer-to-peer-paradigm or the client-server-paradigm [1],[4]. A "good" IS allows for *economical* adaptations to support changing requirements in a changing world. Unfortunately, literature in areas of management science and computer science *hardly provides a well-founded theoretical basis* to design such good IS, that is to exploit the gained *degrees of freedom* modern IT provides.

2 The Model

$x_t \in X$ ($y_t \in Y$), $t = 0,...,T$, denotes an instance of a company's system (application) architecture at a period of time t. A changing economic world implies changes in the requirements of a company's IS. $u_t(x_t,y_t)$ is the expected (opportunistic) *cash-inflow* provided by use of a company's IS in t. Due to changing requirements, which are modeled in the time-dependent function u_t, the same IS can cause different cash-inflows in different periods. $u_t(x_t^*,y_t^*) = \max\{u_t(x_t,y_t) | x_t \in X, y_t \in Y\}$ denotes the maximum cash-inflow that can be achieved in t by selecting and implementing the most adequate IS. An *inadequate* or technical *incompatible* IS can cause a negative cash-inflow ($u_t(x_t,y_t) < 0$). In order to adapt the IS to the requirements, a company may decide to change its system and/or application architecture. $v_t(x_{t-1},x_t)$ ($w_t(y_{t-1},y_t)$) denotes the singular non-negative *cash-outflow* caused by a change from x_{t-1} to x_t (y_{t-1} to y_t)) in the beginning of period t. v_t and w_t are time-dependend in a changing world. In case of $x_{t-1} = x_t$ ($y_{t-1} = y_t$), it is $v_t(x_{t-1},x_t) = 0$ ($w_t(y_{t-1},y_t) = 0$).

A *rational* company will *not* try to implement (x_t^*,y_t^*) in $t = 1,...,T$, because this strategy may cause significant cash-outflows by adapting the IS to new requirements in an optimal way. A rational company will try to fit the requirements with respect to the inevitable cash-outflows by starting in (x_0,y_0):

$$\min_{x_t,y_t}\left\{\sum_{t=1}^{T}\left(u_t(x_t^*,y_t^*)-u_t(x_t,y_t)+v_t(x_{t-1},x_t)+w_t(y_{t-1},y_t)\right)q^{-t}\right\} \tag{1}$$

The resulting *IS-migration-path* (x_t^0,y_t^0), $t = 1,...,T$, is *optimal* with respect to the *net present value criterion* [5]. q denotes the time-invariant discounting rate. (1) describes the decision problem of a company's information management with respect to a *dynamic* and *uncertain* future. In practice, a company has to restrict the consideration to *some relevant* system and application architectures to reduce complexity. It is also difficult to estimate the future shape of the functions **u**, **v** and **w**. *Well-founded subjective estimations* may all the same be achievable by consulting experts in the areas of management science and computer science. Decision criterion (1) *smoothes* the IS-migration-path over time: If a dynamic world causes 'chaotic jumps' in the requirements definitions, an optimal IS may be far from (x^*,y^*) in some periods. (1) also helps to explain the *time lag* between availability of new information technologies and use of these technologies. A new technology may cause future cash-inflows by satisfying future requirements, which are discounted in the model. The implementation of new technologies yet causes cash-outflows at present.

3 Centralized vs. Decentralized Corporate Information Systems

At present, most companies use centralized mainframe-based system-architectures to satisfy the demand for relevant information of their organizational units. A centralized IS hardly allows for changes in its system architecture. The ability to quickly service customer needs is widely accepted as an important *competitive factor* e.g. in financial services companies. This requires the availability of local processing power at all company's customer interfaces. This also requires a flexible remote access to corporate or public data- and knowledge bases and application servers. If strategies and organizational stuctures change, if business activities are expanded or if customer's preferences change, new or restructured organizational units may ask for local processing power and for access to (additional) remote informational resources. A classical centralized mainframe-based system-architecture *cannot* satisfy this demands. In a centralized system architecture, $\mathbf{x}$ is therefore assumed to be *fix* over time $\left(\mathbf{x}=\bar{\mathbf{x}}\right)$.

A centralized IS only allows for changes in the application architecture due to changing requirements. The range of those changes ist thereby more *limited* as it is in decentralized system architectures, because powerful kinds of modern applications like *cooperating* and *competing* software *agents* in intelligent distributed problem solving systems [2] based on peer-to-peer or client-server software technology hardly kann be supported in a centralized mainframe-based system-architecture. In a centralized system architecture, the decision problem is reduced as follows:

$$\min_{y_t}\left\{\sum_{t=1}^{T}\left(\mathbf{u}_t\left(\bar{\mathbf{x}},\mathbf{y}_t^*\right)-\mathbf{u}_t\left(\bar{\mathbf{x}},\mathbf{y}_t\right)+\mathbf{w}_t(\mathbf{y}_{t-1},\mathbf{y}_t)\right)\mathbf{q}^{-t}\right\} \tag{2}$$

The resulting *IS-migration-path* for a *centralized* IS $\mathbf{y}_t^{o'}$, t = 1,...,T, is *optimal* with respect to the *net present value criterion.* Many companies think about *downsizing* or *rightsizing* their centralized IS. They face the problem of uncertainty, if such a step was *economically advantageous.* Pros and cons are discussed a lot in practice, but *well-founded decision models are hardly to find.* (1) and (2) may be useful to face this problem by *comparing* the optimal IS-migration-path in the centralized case and in the decentralized case, both initialized with the *present* centralized IS $\left(\bar{\mathbf{x}},\mathbf{y}_0\right)$. *Downsizing* is economically *advantageous* if

$$\sum_{t=1}^{T}\left(\mathbf{u}_t\left(\mathbf{x}_t^{o},\mathbf{y}_t^{o}\right)-\mathbf{u}_t\left(\bar{\mathbf{x}},\mathbf{y}_t^{o'}\right)-\mathbf{v}_t\left(\mathbf{x}_{t-1}^{o},\mathbf{x}_t^{o}\right)-\mathbf{w}_t\left(\mathbf{y}_{t-1}^{o},\mathbf{y}_t^{o}\right)+\mathbf{w}_t\left(\mathbf{y}_{t-1}^{o'},\mathbf{y}_t^{o'}\right)\right)\mathbf{q}^{-t}>0 \tag{3}$$

The optimal IS-migration-paths are results of *dynamic optimization.* Therefore *no* alternative can be identified as *general advantagous.* An exact result has to be calculated for a concrete scanario. The following *informal interpretation* of (3) yet gives some *hints,* that in many cases downsizing or rightsizing may be the *better* choice: To make the interpretation more easy, it is assumed, that changes of the application architecture cause in both alternatives by and large the same cash-outflow. It results:

$$\sum_{t=1}^{T}\left(\mathbf{u}_t\left(\mathbf{x}_t^{o},\mathbf{y}_t^{o}\right)-\mathbf{u}_t\left(\bar{\mathbf{x}},\mathbf{y}_t^{o'}\right)-\mathbf{v}_t\left(\mathbf{x}_{t-1}^{o},\mathbf{x}_t^{o}\right)\right)\mathbf{q}^{-t}>0 \tag{4}$$

Because of the additional degrees of freedom, it can be assumed, that $\mathbf{u}_t\left(\mathbf{x}_t^*,\mathbf{y}_t^*\right)>\mathbf{u}_t\left(\bar{\mathbf{x}},\mathbf{y}_t^*\right)$, t = 1,...,T, holds. In many cases, the difference may be significant. The first change of the system architecture in the decentralized case $\mathbf{v}_1\left(\bar{\mathbf{x}},\mathbf{x}_1^{o}\right)$ leaving the present centralized world can be assumed as *most significant* and costly. Changes in system architecture in following periods can be assumed as *incremental* and less costly. In following periods, $u_t(x_t^*, y_t^*) - u_t(x_t^o, y_t^o) > 0$ can thus be assumed as small. The same holds for $u_t\left(\bar{x}, y_t^*\right) - u_t\left(\bar{x}, y_t^{o'}\right) > 0$, because changes in system architecture can not apply and changes in application architecture are considered as less significant. From a very *heuristic* viewpoint follows the economical dominance of downsizing if the discounted sum of differences of the cash-inflow maximizing ISs dominates the first period cash-outflow of moving the centralized system architecture to a decentralized system architecture. Because of v_1, u_1 is assumed to be the same in both alternatives.

$$\sum_{t=2}^{T}\left(u_t(x_t^*, y_t^*) - u_t\left(\bar{x}, y_t^*\right)\right)q^{-t} > v_1\left(\bar{x}, x_0^o\right) \qquad (5)$$

The right-hand side of (5) kann be estimated by experts. The left-hand side does not require dynamic optimization. In many long term considerations, downsizing may thus be advantageous.

4 Conclusion

Present available IT allows for a *flexible goal-oriented* design of a company's IS. Through orientation towards present and future needs of a company's *information logistics*, IS becomes a powerful tool to defend and increase a company's *competitive* position in the market. Flexibility of an IS-architecture is the link between goal-orientation and *strategic fit* on the one hand and economical operations and change management on the other hand. This paper presented an *economic model* to provide optimal decisions on the design of a company's system and application architecture in a *changing world.* It considers the need for a flexible IS-design to satisfy the *changing requirements* and proposes *migration paths* to IS-architectures, which allow for low-cost adaptations to changing requirements. It is also shown, that the model can be *applied* to support *downsizing* and *rightsizing* decisions. In this context, the model was informally reduced to an *easy-to-use-heuristic.*

References:

[1] König, H.-J.: Dezentrale Datenhaltung in der Allfinanzkundenberatung, in: Informationstechnik und technische Informatik it+ti, 1/1993, S. 45-55

[2] König, H.-J., Roemer, M., Sandbiller, K., Weinhardt, Ch., Will, A.: *Ein verteiltes Problemlösungssystem für die Allfinanzkundenberatung*, in: Müller, J. (Hrsg.): Gründungsworkshop der GI-Fachgruppe Verteilte Künstliche Intelligenz, DFKI, Document D-93-06, Saarbrücken, 1993

[3] McNurlin, B.C., Sprague, R.H.: Information Systems Management in Practice, Prentice-Hall, London, 1989

[4] Mullender, S.: Distributed Systems, Addison Wesley, Reading, 1989

[5] Weston, J.F., Copeland, T.E.: Managerial Finance, 9. Ed., The Dryden Press, Fort Worth, 1992

Long run simulation of the German social security system

Günter Köpp and Götz Uebe
Institut für Statistik und quantitative Ökonomik
Universität der Bundeswehr Hamburg
22039 Hamburg, Germany

1. Introduction

As is well known by most recent public discussion social security systems of all industrial societies pass through a most dramatic change: an ever smaller working population has to support a continuously growing older population, placing an enormous financial stress on a system which was designed at a completely different demographic and economic environment. The abstract is to sketch a numerical simulation model, by which a long run projection of the German social security system can be analyzed. In modeling social security four central properties must be taken care of: (i) social security is a subsystem of economics and demography, (ii) the system is of great inertia, slowly moving, yet with strong effects, (iii) a formally simple setup, yet with confusing detail, and (iv) a system of extreme dominance of legal constructions, enforceable in court.

2. Abstract of simulation model

The central accounting identity is the equality of total revenue and total expenditures: the current maintenance of the equilibrium of a system "pay as you go"

$$E_t \equiv A_t \text{ (E_t total revenue; A_t total expenditure).}$$

This is an "ideal", yet not attainable relation, hence

$$\Delta_t \equiv E_t - A_t \Leftrightarrow E_t = A_t + \Delta_t, \qquad (1)$$

(Δ_t definition of excess of total revenue, respectively of expenditures).
Current reserve (a first legal restriction of social security) (S_t)

$$S_t = S_{t-1} + \Delta_t, \; S_t \geq A_t / 12. \qquad (2)$$

This legal restriction is the natural policy point for the change of the rate of contribution. If the restriction is violated (i.e. S too low) the rate must go up (based on the philosophy of (1)), and if S is too high, the rate should go down. In addition, changes should not occur, unless a specific threshold is exceeded, in order to exclude continuous and erratic changes. This is modeled by a reaction function.

Revenues consist of five main components: compulsory contributions of members (B_t), federal subsidy (BZ_t), other government contributions (SEr_t), capital returns (VE_t) and other revenues (SE_t).

$$E_t \equiv B_t + BZ_t + SEr_t + VE_t + SE_t. \tag{3}$$

Compulsory contributions of members (B_t) are linked to the demographic pyramid

$$B_t = b_t \left(\sum_{j=1}^{2} \sum_{i=1}^{100} a_{i,t}^j P_{i,t}^j øve_{i,t}^j \right), \tag{4}$$

(j=1,2 male resp. female population; b_t global rate of contribution; $a_{i,t}$ percentage share of members of age i; $P_{i,t}$ number of persons of age i; $øve_{i,t}$ mean income subject to social security taxation).

Social security membership is a complicate legal construct, depending on whether a person contributes to, resp. receives from social security, depending on size of income and age, and depending on subsidiary legal entitlements (e.g. maternity, draft).

Federal subsidy (BZ_t) a second legal reaction function, is essentially an adaptive, legally required mechanism, e.g. after the reform act of 1992 by the new scheme)

$$BZ_t = BZ_{t-1} \frac{E_{t-2}}{E_{t-3}} \frac{b_t}{b_{t-1}} \text{ or } BZ_t = BZ_{t-1} \frac{NE_{t-2}}{NE_{t-3}} \frac{b_t}{b_{t-1}} \tag{5}$$

(b_t rate of contribution, E_t wage income per capita; NE_t net wage income per capita).

The generation of net, resp. gross wage income per capita is either modeled by

$$E_t = \alpha_{6,1} E_{t-1} + \alpha_{6,2}, \text{ or } NE_t = \left(\alpha'_{6,1} NE_{t-1} + \alpha'_{6,2}\right)\left(1 + \frac{b_t - b_{t-1}}{2}\right) \tag{6}$$

Other government contributions (SEr_t) are modeled by a simple linear relation

$$SEr_t = \alpha_{7,1} SEr_{t-1} + \alpha_{7,2} + \alpha_{7,3} d_7 + KLG_t \text{ (}d_7\text{ a dummy variable)} \tag{7}$$

Capital returns (VE_t) in distinction to the above the system of "pay as you go" depend on stock of assets and the term structure

$$VE_t \equiv rl_t RV_{t-1} + rk_t S_{t-1} \tag{8}$$

(RV_t other assets; S_t current reserve; rl_t rate of return, long term; rk_t rate of return, short term). The stock of assets, and the rates of interest, after some experimentation were found to be best modeled by an autoregressive, resp. linear relations:

$$RV_t = \alpha_{9,1} RV_{t-1} + \alpha_{9,2} + \alpha_{9,3} d_9, rk_t = \alpha_{9,4} rk_{t-1} + \alpha_{9,5}, rl_t = \alpha_{9,6} rl_{t-1} + \alpha_{9,7} \tag{9}$$

(d_9 dummy-variable). Other revenues (SE_t) are small "almost" negligible, and they are fixed to be a constant:

$$SE_t = \alpha_{10,1}. \tag{10}$$

Similarly to the revenues for the expenditure account only a few main items have to be considered, i.e. the expenditure account is given by

$$A_t \equiv R_t + RH_t + KV_t + KLG_t + BEr_t + VV_t + SA_t, \tag{11}$$

(social security payments (R_t), costs of rehabilitations (RH_t), health insurance contributions (KV_t), compensation of children education (KLG_t), refunds (BEr_t), administrative expenditures (VV_t), other expenditures (SA_t)). Basically they are selfexplanatory.

Social security payments (R_t) are a function of demography and legal entitlements:

$$R_t = \sum_{j=1}^{2} \sum_{k=1}^{12} \sum_{i=1}^{100} RB^j_{i,k,t}\, a^j_{i,k,t}\, P^j_{i,t} \tag{12}$$

(j=1,2 male resp. female population; k denotıng the main types of social security entitlement (k=1,...,12); $RB_{i,k,t}$ average monthly payment of type k and age i; $a_{i,k,t}$ percentage share of recipients of age i; $P_{i,t}$ number of persons of age i.).

Most of these items flow from the demography model, which is part ot the simulation model [see Köpp - Uebe].

The percentage share of recipients ($a_{i,k,t}$) is a plain reformulation of the total numbers:

$$a_{i,k,t} = \frac{A_{i,k,prog\text{-}1}}{P_{i,prog\text{-}1}} \tag{13}$$

($A_{i,k,prog-1}$ number of persons of age i and type k; $P_{i,prog-1}$ projected number of persons of age i).

Average monthly payment of type k and age i in year t ($RB_{i,k,t}$) is the third set of important legal reaction rules, the new adaption rule (of 1992) for the monthly pension, which essentially is of the structure:

$$\text{monthly pension}_t = \text{individual pension credits} \times \text{pension type factor} \times \text{actual pension value}_t. \tag{14}$$

The actual pension value (aRw_t) is given by

$$aRw_t = aRw_{t-1} \frac{E_{t-1}}{E_{t-2}} \frac{NQ_{t-1}}{NQ_{t-2}} \frac{RQ_{t-2}}{RQ_{t-1}}, \tag{15}$$

(E_t gross wage income per capita; NQ_t net wage ratio = the ratio of net to gross wage income; RQ_t net pension ratio = the ratio of net to gross pension, see equ. 6).

The net pension ratio (RQ_t) results by deduction of the health insurance:

$$RQ_t = 1 - kvb_t / 2 \quad (kvb_t \text{ health insurance rate}). \tag{16}$$

The average monthly amount paid out of pension k is a complicate average of two semi-annual rates: From January to June, resp. from July to December

$$\text{ø}mr_{i,k,t} = \text{ø}mr_{i,k,t-1} \qquad \text{ø}mr_{i,k,t} = (aRw_t / aRw_{t-1})\, \text{ø}mr_{i,k,t-1} \tag{17}$$

($\text{ø}mr_{i,k,t}$ average monthly amount paid out of pension k to age i), hence the average annual amount paid out of pension k to age i is given by

$$RB_{i,k,t} \equiv 6 \times \text{ø}mr_{i,k,t-1} + 6 \times \text{ø}mr_{i,k,t} \tag{18}$$

Costs of rehabilitations (RH_t)

$$RH_t = \alpha_{19,1} RH_{t-1} + \alpha_{19,2} \tag{19}$$

Health insurance contributions (KV_t)

$$KV_t = \frac{kvb_t}{2} R_t \tag{20}$$

Compensation of children education (KLG_t), a new type of rent and a very complicate legal construction, is based on the number of children, the legal time of introduction, the female cohort, and a specific entitlement rate:

$$KLG_t = \frac{1}{3} \sum_{i=T_0}^{T_1-1} P_{i,t}^{w} \, AnzK \; 0.0115 \; abg_t + \sum_{i=T_1}^{100} P_{i,t}^{w} \, AnzK \; 0.0115 \; abg_t \qquad (21)$$

($P_{i,t}^{w}$ number of privileged females (from the demography model); AnzK number of children per female; abg_t basis of entitlement; T_0, T_1 years of legal introduction).

$$abg_t = \alpha_{22,1} \, abg_{t-1} + \alpha_{22,2} \qquad (22)$$

Refunds of contributions (BEr_t) are essentially constant, even though bussiness cycle may play a role.

$$BEr_t = \alpha_{23,1} + \alpha_{23,2} \, d_{23} \; (d_{23} \text{ dummy-variable}) \qquad (23)$$

Administrative costs (VV_t) again (see e.g. (22)) are modeled autoregressively:

$$VV_t = \alpha_{24,1} \, VV_{t-1} + \alpha_{24,2} \qquad (24)$$

Other expenditures (SA_t), similarly to the approach taken for the other items in revenues (see above (10)), are designated to be negligible, resp. a constant item:

$$SA_t = \alpha_{25,1}. \qquad (25)$$

3. Outline of simulation and summary

The model of section 2 can be varied interactively according to various scenarios of economic growth, demographic developments, change of parameters and structure of submodel. The results correspond to the complexity of the social security model:
(i) Due to the immense detail, scenario changes are presented by tabular surveys.
(ii) As a general conclusion one must emphasize the usual policy motivation of economic analyis: Long run position of German social security due to the messy detail is difficult to evaluate. However, if the past is any guide, the funds and arrangements of the present social security system will have little bearing on its long run future. Any analysis is of limited use [see Smith]. The ongoing discussion will reshape and "improve" the system.

4. References

Smith, D. P.: Formal demography, Plenum Press, New York, 1992.

Köpp G., Uebe G.: Eine Langzeitprognose für die deutsche Bevölkerung, Discussion Papers in Statistics and Quantitative Economics, No. 52, Hamburg, 1992.

Modelling Simulated Annealing with History Dependent Cooling Schedules

Michael Kolonko,
Institut für Mathematik
Universität Hildesheim,
Marienburger Platz 22, D-31141 Hildesheim

1. Standard simulated annealing

Simulated annealing (SA) is a stochastic iterative method for finding the minimum of a cost function $c : S \to \mathbb{R}_+$. In its standard setup it uses a Markov matrix $(G(x,y))_{x,y\in S}$ to produce a new candidate y at random from the neighbourhood of the present solution $x \in S$. The candidate y becomes the new solution with probability $\alpha_n(x,y)$ and is rejected with probability $1 - \alpha_n(x,y)$. Most applications use

$$\alpha_n(x,y) := \min\left\{1, \exp\left(-\frac{c(y)-c(x)}{t_n}\right)\right\}$$

where $(t_n)_{n\geq 0}$ is a sequence of positive constants ('temperatures') converging to zero.

The standard mathematical model (see e.g. Anily/Federgruen (1987)) uses an inhomogeneous Markov chain $(X_n)_{n\geq 0}$ with transition matrices $P_n(x,y) := G(x,y)\alpha_n(x,y)$ for $x \neq y$. Then conditions on the prespecified sequence $(t_n)_{n\geq 0}$ are given such that $(X_n)_{n\geq 0}$ is strongly ergodic with limiting distribution $\pi_\infty :=$ uniform distribution on optimal states. The resulting optimal temperature schedule requires $(t_n)_{n\geq 0}$ to decrease logarithmically with n.

2. A semi-inhomogeneous Markov chain

We present a model which allows more general ways of changing the temperature: we call a process $(X_n, T_m)_{n\geq 0, m\geq 1}$ a **semi-inhomogeneous Markov chain** if (with $S_m = \sum_{i=1}^m T_m$, $S_0 = 0$)

$$P(X_{n+1} = j \mid X_0, \ldots, X_n, S_0, \ldots, S_m, S_m \leq n < S_{m+1}) = P_{m+1}(X_n, j)$$
$$P(T_{m+1} = k \mid X_0, \ldots, X_{S_m}, \ldots, X_{S_m+k}, \ldots, X_n, S_0, \ldots, S_m, T_{m+1} \geq k)$$
$$= g_k^{(m+1)}(X_{S_m}, \ldots, X_{S_m+k})$$

for suitable $P_{m+1}, g_k^{(m+1)}$. This means that $(X_n)_{n\geq 0}$ has a constant transition matrix P_{m+1} during the random time intervals $[S_m, S_{m+1})$ whose duration does not depend on the state history outside of that interval. Note that

$$P(X_{n+1} = j \mid X_0, \ldots, X_{S_m}, \ldots, X_n, S_0, \ldots, S_m) = P(X_{n+1} = j \mid X_{S_m}, \ldots, X_n),$$

i.e. $(X_n)_{n\geq 0}$ is not a Markov chain.

We have two applications in mind.

3. Simulated annealing without rejections

Greene/Supowit (1986) introduced a variant of SA in which the 'temperature' is changed only after a new state has been accepted. This fits into our model with

$$T_{m+1} = \min\{k \geq 1 \mid X_{S_{m+k}} \neq X_{S_m}\},\ m \geq 1.$$

One can show that then $X_{S_{m+1}}$ and T_{m+1} are even conditional independent given X_{S_m}. Greene/Supowit suggest to skip all 'rejections' and to generate the next solution directly according to $P_{X_{S_{m+1}}|X_{S_m}}$. They show that this is advantageous for particular graph partition problems. In general however we can show that if $P_{X_{S_{m+1}}|X_{S_m}}$ is simulated using the classical acceptance/rejection scheme then we are back at the standard simulated annealing with temperatures kept fixed during rejections.

4. Stepwise Cooling

The analysis mentioned in 1. leads to logarithmically decreasing t_m, involving large estimated constants. As this is too slow in practical problems, one often proceeds heuristically: the temperature t_m is kept fixed for a 'long' time N, then it is assumed that the stationary distribution π_m belonging to P_m has been reached and t_m is lowered (steeper than logarithmically). Then, if $\pi_m \to \pi_\infty$, we shall asymptotically simulate the distribution π_∞ which is concentrated on the optimal states. In our framework we can show that there is a semi-inhomogeneous Markov chain $(X_n, T_m^*)_{n\geq 0, m\geq 1}$ such that

$$P(X_S = i) = \pi_m(i) \quad \text{and} \quad \lim_{m\to\infty} P(T_m^* \leq k) = 1\ ,\ k \geq 0$$

for any convex $m \to t_m$, i. e. there is a sequence of randomized stopping times T_m^* converging in probability to 0 such that the distribution of the embedded process converges to π_∞. The proof uses ideas of Aldous/Diaconis (1987) on strong stationary times in homogeneous Markov chains. To transfer this concept to the non-Markovian $(X_n)_{n\geq 0}$ we used a second semi-inhomogeneous Markov chain which behaves like $(X_n, T_m)_{n\geq 0, m\geq 1}$ up to the M-th breakpoint S_M and then becomes homogeneous (a 'decoupling' argument).
Though not constructive this result shows that the heuristics used in practice have an optimal theoretical counterpart.

5. References

1. Aldous D, Diaconis P (1987) Strong uniform Times and finite random walks. Adv. Appl. Prob. 8 : 69–97
2. Anily S, Federgruen A (1987) Simulated Annealing Methods with General Acceptance Probabilities. J. Appl. Prob. 24 : 657–667
3. Greene J. W., Supowit K. J. (1986) Simulated Annealing without Rejecting Moves . IEEE Trans. on CAD CAD-5, No.1 : 221–228

Intelligent Multiple Criteria Decision Support

Ewa Konarzewska Gubała
Department of Operations Research
Oskar Lange Academy of Economics in Wrocław
53-345 Wrocław, ul. Komandorska 118\120, Poland

Abstract: The idea of the intelligent multiple criteria decision support system is presented. The system architecture contains an intelligent module to selection of the appropriate problem structure and multiple criteria decision making method. This architecture is implemented by a prototype system COMPROMISE.

Introduction

The managerial applications of *Operations Research* show two main tendencies recently:
(1) in the theoretical domain - the searching for and developing "soft" approaches and methods for modelling and solving semistructured decision problems,
(2) in the application area - the intensive using of information technology, mainly in Decision Support System (DSS) and Expert System (ES) framework to implement *OR* "soft" approaches.

Multiple Criteria Decision Support Systems

Multiple Criteria Decision Support Systems (MCDSS) are considered as specific class of DSSs employing various Multiple Criteria Decision Making (MCDM) methods. These systems interactively assist the decision maker in evaluating and comparing decision alternatives by making use of objective and subjective data, models and knowledge. MCDSSs cover a wide range of semistructured decision problems characterised by the multiplicity of the conflicting objectives and by the need of an active presence of decision maker during the decision process.

The typical architecture of DSS is composed of a Data Base, a Model Base, a Dialogue Base and the software managing the above bases. According to *Jelassi (1987)* MCDSSs typology the most popular are systems of first generation, i.e. stand-alone systems including only one MCDM method and a more or less rudimentary user interface. To this kind of systems belong, e.g.: ADBASE *(Steuer 1983-89)*, ELECTRE III, IV *(Skalka et al. 1984-86)*, ELECTRE I, IS *(Roy, Skalka, 1985--87)*, VIMDA *(Korhonen, Laakso 1987)*, BIPOLAR *(Konarzewska 1988-89)*, ARIADNE *(Goicoechea, Fu Li, 1989)*, ELECCALC *(Kiss et al., 1991)* etc....

The next step towards the idea of the integrated DSS components has been made by the including a Model Base with a variety of models to the system architecture and full integration with the Data Management System. There are some good examples of these systems: MIRACLE *(Bernabeu, Winkels 1981)*, DIDAS *(Lewandowski et al., 1985)*, PREFCALC *(Jacquet-Lagreze, Jelassi, 1983-87)*, BARG *(Bronisz et al., 1989)*.

The use of Expert Systems technology

Recently, there has been increasing interest in integrating the decision analysis and ES technology. An excellent survey on this subject is provided by *White (1990)*. *Ozernoy and Bordetski (1992)* review several recent applications of ES for MCDM sorting them into three groups:
- Rule-based MCDM Expert Systems, e.g. EXTRA *(Pasche, 1991)*
- Systems for MCDM methods' selection, e.g. ADVISOR *(Ozernoy, 1991)*
- Negotiation and Group Decision Support Systems, e.g. NEGOPLAN *(Matwin et al., 1989)*.

The DSS using an ES technology referred as the Knowledge-based DSS or Intelligent Decision Support System (IDSS) introduces a new aspect of decision support - an ability of "problem recognition". This is an important modelling feature at least for two reasons:

(1) It makes possible the mixing of algorithmic and heuristic methods in solving the ill structured problems:

(2) It makes possible support the user in the choice phase as well as in the problem formulation or intelligence phase (according to Simon paradigm).

The last one is exceptionally important in our opinion. In presence of variety MCDM models and methods, the conceiving problem structure and its solution concept are the crucial aspects of MCDM modelling. Usually, one assumes that this stage is done out of DSS. The intelligent support based on the MCDM expert knowledge and on the rich model base seems to be prospective mission for ES technology in MCDSSs.

COMPROMISE: Intelligent Multiple Criteria Decision Support System

General description. COMPROMISE is an integrated, interactive and intelligent MCDSS that works in IBM PC environment. It has been designed and developed in 1990 (version 1.0) and 1991 (version 2.0) by E. Konarzewska-Gubała, J. Majchrzak, M. Nowiński, M. Rymarczyk and L. Warężak from OR Department of Wrocław Academy of Economics. (The project was supported by Polish Scientific Committee-KBN in framework of Program 10.VI.6: *Computer optimisation and its managerial applications*, co-ordinated by Prof. W. Bukietyński.)

The support provided by the system concerns three major phases of decision making process:

(1) Problem identification (intelligence). This step involves the intelligent user interface in order to identify user problem and to suggest him/her the relevant model of quantitative analysis.

(2) Problem analysis (design). At this step the pre-determinate model of user problem is constructed and the analysis is called for.

(3) Decision searching (choice). In this phase the final decision is developed interactively using the possible results of the analysis.

DSS architecture. COMPROMISE is composed of seven subsystems. Phase (1) is performed by knowledge based subsystem EXPERT. Steps (2) and (3) are supported by the specific COMPROMISE subsystems: ND-MOLP, F-MOLP, BIPOLAR, ELECTRE, PROMET and FILTR They contain ***the Model Base*** of system COMPROMIS (MOLP and BIPOLAR can be used as independent stand-alone systems). The following models and methods have been included:
- **ND-MOLP** (Non Dominated solutions of MultiObjective Linear Programming) contains ADBASE method (quotation of original, licensed software *"ADBASE: MOLP-Computer Package" by Steuer, 1989)*

• **F-MOLP** (Final solutions of MOLP) contains MOLP models with different scalarisation functions: weighted, fractional, lexicographic and distance (*Konarzewska, 1980)*

• **FILTER** contains the "filtering" procedures of non dominated solution sets in singling decision problems; procedures are developed by Steuer as an integrated part of *"ADBASE..."* package.

• **BIPOLAR** contains the model BIPOLAR developed and implemented (*Konarzewska,1989)* as a stand-alone MCDSS for discrete alternatives evaluations using the bipolar reference system

• **ELEKTRA** contains the modified ELECTRE IV method based on preference credibility structure in discrete decision problems *(version presented in Skalka et al., 1986)*

• **PROMET** contains the PROMETHEE I and II methods of discrete decision analysis using the generalised criterion concept *(version presented in Brans et al., 1986)*

The Knowledge Base (in subsystem **EXPERT**) is oriented to the selection of MCDM model and method from the library of ***Model Base*** (if it is possible). Its construction is founded on the binary tree. The inference engine uses the forward chaining algorithm. Several attributes are selected that may uniquely characterise the models in the knowledge base. The selection of the appropriate method depends on the users responses which indicate whether a particular attribute is essential in the method selection

The Dialogue Base is designed on two levels:
(a) The system level gives the user possibility of the using of Model Base and Knowledge Base: it guides him/her to the choice of appropriate problem formulation (model) and
(b) The subsystems level enables problem modelling:(according to the model chosen in (a)) and interactive analysis of decision alternatives.

The Data Base is created on subsystem's level in form of files for analysed application.

Range of decision problems In the MCDM methodology the problem structure and solution concept (e.g. a form of scalarization function) closely depend on the information elicited from decision maker about his/her objectives and preferences *(Konarzewska-Gubala, 1980).*

The implemented model base and knowledge base, completed by information provided by users allow to analyse the relatively large range of MCDM problems using the COMPROMISE:system. These problems may be characterised by:

- selection, sorting and decisions ordering,
- discrete and continuous alternatives sets,
- quantitative and qualitative criteria,
- preference description and preference construction,
- dominance and outranking preference relational systems.

Technical characteristics. COMPROMISE can be installed on any PC AT/386/486 with at least 640 KB RAM. It was developed in C (BIPOLAR, ELECTRA, PROMET, F-MOLP), Fortran (ND-MOLP) and Prolog (EXPERT).

Conclusions

(1) The integration of MCDM methodology with DSS and ES technology is recognised as a prospective field of research and application

(2) The knowledge based technology can play useful role in assisting all phases of decision process, not only the choice phase.
(3) The COMPROMISE system has been presented. It belongs to the MCDSS generation that intensively uses the model base and knowledge base as the elements of its architecture.
(4) The most important features of COMPROMISE are: the model selection capability and the covering by system the relatively wide range of model situations.
(5) The improving of COMPROMISE is designed by application of professional ES shell and using its explanation capabilities.

References

Bernabeu YA, Winkels HN (1981) MIRACLE: Une méthode interactive de réduction, d'amélioration et de classification evolutiv. *Document du LAMSADE*:16, .Paris
Brans JP, Vincke Ph, Mareschal B (1986) How to select and how to rank projects: The PROMETHEE method *European Journal of Operational Research* 24:228-238
Bronisz P, Kruś L, Kręglewski T (1989) BARG: A DSS for multicriteria bargaining problem. Systems Research Istitute Warsaw
Goicoechea A, Fu Li (1989) On the use of multiple attributes and imperfect information with ARIADNE to rank alternative systems. *Report S-7, STATCOM INC.*, Virginia
Jacquet-Lagreze E (1983) PREFCALC-Evaluation et décision multicritére. *Euro-Decision,* Paris
Jelassi MT (1987) From stand-alone methods to integrated and intelligent DSS. In: Sawaragi et al. (eds) Toward Interactive and Intelligent Decision Support Systems . *Lecture Notes in Economics and Mathematical Systems* vol.285. Springer Verlag. Berlin Heidelberg New York
Kiss L, Martel JM, Nadeau R (1991) ELECCALC: A DSS for modeling the decision maker's preferences. Faculté des Sciences de l'Administration, Université Laval, Québec
Konarzewska-Gubała E (1980) Multiobjective Programming . Polish Scientific Publishers. Warszawa *(in Polish)*
Konarzewska-Gubała E (1989) BIPOLAR: Multiple Criteria Decision Aid using Bipolar Reference System. *Documents du LAMSADE:* 56. LAMSADE .Paris
Korchonen P, Laakso J (1986) A visual interactive method for solving multiple criteria problem. *European Journal of Operational Research:*24:277-287
Matwin S, Szpakowicz S, Koperczak Z, Kersten GE, Michałowski W (1989) NEGOPLAN: An expert system shell for negotiation support. *IIII Expert, vol. 4, 4: 50-62*
Pasche C (1991) EXTRA: An expert system for multicriteria decision making. *European Journal of Operational Research* 52: 224-234
Roy B, Hugonnard JG (1982) Ranking of suburban line extension projects on the Paris metro system by a multicriteria method. *Transportation Research*: 164 4: 153-171
Skalka JM, Bouyssou D, Bernabeu YA (1986) ELECTRE III et IV. Aspects methodologiques et guide d'utilisation. *Documents du LAMSADE:* 25. LAMSADE .Paris
Steuer R (1989) ADBASE Transmittal Package (Version 9/89). Department of Management Science and Information Technology University of Georgia, Georgia USA.
Ozernoy VM, Bordetski AB (1992) Using Expert System Technology for Multiple Criteria Decision Making: a survay. *Proceedings of X Int. Conference on MCDM Taipei, July 1992* vol. II: 271-280.
Ozernoy VM (1991) Developing an Interactive DSS for discrete alternative MCDM method selection. In: Korhonen P et al. (eds) MultipleCriteria Decision Support. Springer Verlag: 242-257
White CC (1990) A survey on the integration of decision anallysis and expert systems for decision support. *IEEE Transactions on Systems, Man and Cybernetics, vol. SMC 20, 2: 158-164*

PROGRAM ALLOCATION PREDICTION BY NEURAL NETWORKS

A. Krysiak, F Seredynski
Institute of Computer Science of
Polish Academy of Sciences
Ordona 21, 01-237 Warszawa, POLAND

Abstract:

The paper presents the problem of program graph allocation on parallel computer and proposes the solution based on the model of multilayer neural network with backpropagation learning schedule.

Keywords: parallel computers, program allocation, neural networks

The execution of programs on parallel multiprocessor systems requires the optimal allocation of program graph into the graph of the system. The program graph allocation can be defined as an optimization problem and solved in several ways. The most common solution is based on boolean matrix algebra and 0-1 programming.
Each allocation (mapping) of program graph into the processors array is defined as a boolean matrix with rows corresponding to the program graph nodes: $p_1,\ldots,p_k$ and columns corresponding to the processing nodes: $n_1,\ldots.,n_q$. There is also a cost function assigned to each allocation and defined as a sum of the local costs of processing and communication over all the program nodes and system nodes. The optimization process is a process of finding the allocation which minimize the cost function (see Berman [1987]).
Another approach is based on dynamic allocation of nodes according to the principles of the Boltzmann Machine, where the program graph is migrating within the graph of the system until the optimal allocation is found (see Aarts [1989]).
This paper suggests different approach to solving the aforementioned problem, which is based on the model of the multilayer Neural Network (see also Dodd [1989]).

The network taken under consideration consists of three layers of processing elements (neurons):

- input layer: $X=(x_1,\ldots,x_n)$,
- "hidden" layer: $H=(h_1,\ldots,h_l)$,
- output layer: $Y=(y_1,\ldots,y_m)$

where elements of each layer are connected to all elements of the previous layer. In our model each input and output neuron corresponds to one of the system nodes (processing units) from the set: $N=(n_1,\ldots,n_q)$. On the other hand the numerical value of each input and output of the network represents the number (index) of program node from the set: $P=(p_1\ldots,p_k)$ allocated in the corresponding node of the system. Hence we can write that: IF x_i=j THEN (j-th program node is allocated in i-th system node) where: i=1..q and j=1..k.

The aforementioned neural network was "trained" with the use of standard error backpropagation algorithm (see Hinton [1989]). During the training process certain allocation is coded onto the inputs of the network, which produces another allocation on its outputs. Both allocations are compared in terms of the cost function and better one is chosen as a training set. If network actually produced better allocation the learning step is skipped (the connection weights are not changed) and another allocation is presented. The process is repeated until no better allocation can be found in a given number of steps.

During the operation phase the previously trained network is automatically generating consecutive allocations, starting from a given state (e.g. all program nodes in one system node). Each allocation produced by the network during operation is fed back to the inputs of the network only if it is better (i.e. has the lower cost function) than the previous allocation presented to the network (if it is not then the previous allocation is modified and the process is continued).

The network has been tested on the problem of allocating the program graph with 8 nodes (modules) on the graph of 16 processors (matrix of 4x4). The neural network had 16 input nodes, 16 output nodes (one for each system node) and 10 nodes in the hidden layer. The cost function (calculated for each allocation) was defined as: (see Seredynski [1991]).

$$C_{ij} = C'_{ij} + C''_{ij} = \frac{1}{2}\sum_{g=1}^{q} [t_{ig} d(i,g)] + \sum_{g=1}^{k} (b_{ig})$$

where:

C'_{ij} -communication time of i-th program node allocated in j-th system node,

C''_{ij} -processing time of i-th program node in j-th system node,

t_{ig} -data transfer time between i-th program module and its g-th neighbor (allocated in g-th system node),

d(i,g)-distance between i-th and g-th nodes of the system,

b_{ig} -processing time of i-th and g-th program modules (if both are allocated in the same system node).

The system shows a tendency to decrease the cost of consecutive allocations and finally settled in the state representing the optimal allocation (minimizing the cost function).

REFERENCES:

Aarts H.L., Korst J.H. (1989) - Computation in Massively Parallel Networks Based on the Boltzmann Machine. Parallel Computing, No.9(1989), pp.129-145.

Berman F. (1987) - On Mapping Parallel Algorithms into Parallel Architectures. Journal of Parallel and Distibuted Computing, No.4(1987), pp.439-458.

Dodd N. (1989) - Graph Matching by Stochastic Optimization Applied to the implementation of Multi-layer Perceptrons on Transputer Networks. Parallel Computing, 10(1989),pp.135-142.

Hinton G.E. (1989) - Connectionist Learning Procedures. Artificial Intelligence No.40(1989).

Seredynski F. (1991) - Task Allocation by a Team of Learning Automata. ISMIS'91, Charlotte N.C. USA, Oct 16-19 1991.

AN ASSESSMENT OF FLEXIBILITY CONCEPTS AND THEIR PRACTICAL USEFULNESS TO DECISION MODELLING

Anne Ku
London Business School
Sussex Place, Regent's Park
London NW1 4SA
United Kingdom

The idea of flexibility appears in many disciplines. It refers to having or offering many different choices or functions. Flexibility is a way of dealing with uncertainty. In spite of its popularity, flexibility has not received the formal recognition worthy of mature and well-defined concepts like optimality or profitability. Its usefulness may have been overlooked, particularly its potential contribution to aspects of modelling that are not well served by existing ideas. For example, many types of uncertainties in large-scale and long term investment planning are inadequately treated by standard optimisation techniques. This paper invites a fresh approach to uncertainty modelling by use of flexibility concepts from a decision analysis perspective.

FLEXIBILITY

The word "flexibility" or "flexible" is used much more often today than it was a decade ago. In banking and finance, investors' preference for flexibility translates into the notion of liquidity, or the ease in which assets can be transformed. In operations management, flexible manufacturing systems replace the function and product-specific machines of the past. In the labour markets, employers are giving flexi-time and flexible hours to attract better skilled workers. In turn, a multi-skilled worker can have more job opportunities. Flexible information systems offer users more functionality. The so-called "dash for gas" in the present UK Electricity Industry refers to the rapid build-up of a flexible technology called combined cycle gas turbine which can be quickly built off-site in small but modular unit sizes. In all of these areas, flexibility represents a desirable property or goal.

However, the meaning of flexibility is not easy to grasp. In many situations the word is used haphazardly, often in the absence of a better one. Over-use has led to confusion and poor understanding. In spite of its wide application, flexibility is neither necessary nor sufficient. As a result, it has not been successfully unified or classified. Instead of attempting to develop yet another formal definition, this paper distills common characteristics from the ways in which it is used in different disciplines. Several recurrent themes are also identified from the applications and interpretations of flexibility. This analysis unifies different uses of flexibility in a conceptual framework.

CONCEPTUAL FRAMEWORK

There are many well-defined concepts closely associated with flexibility. The relationships between them, as shown by triangles in the following figure, help to clarify our understanding of flexibility.

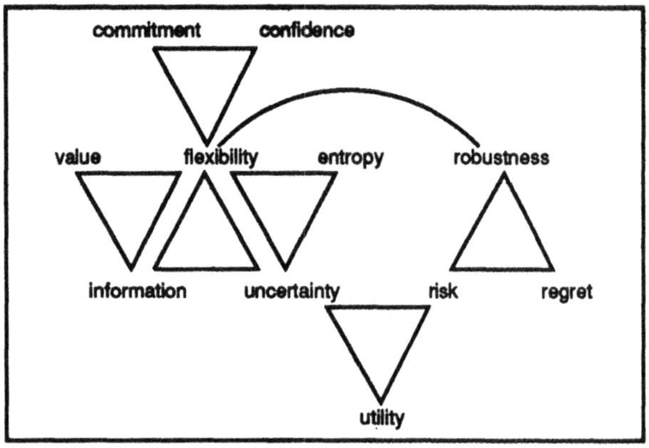

Conceptual Framework

In this framework, the arc between "flexibility" and "robustness" represents the two types of flexibility observed by Gupta and Buzacott (1988), Mandelbaum (1978), Eppink (1978), and Ansoff (1968). They see two fundamental ways of responding to change. Active or action flexibility is the ability to respond by changing or reacting. Passive or state flexibility, on the other hand, exists when there is no need to react because of immunity, insensitivity, or tolerance. This second type of flexibility is better known as robustness.

Flexibility, whether active or passive, is closely associated with uncertainty. Merkhofer (1975) states that the value of flexibility is related to the the value of information in decision analysis. Flexibility is needed when you have less than perfect information. The more flexibility you have, the greater is the value of your information gathering. Similarly, the more information you expect to obtain, the more valuable flexibility is to you. Flexibility is desirable when you are uncertain about what actions to take. Flexibility provides a way of coping with uncertainty though not necessarily reducing it. For example, before making the first of a series of decisions, you may possess the greatest flexibility. Yet you also face the greatest uncertainty. Once you make a decision, you reduce the uncertainty (by forgoing other options) as well as the flexibility you once had. This close relationship between flexibility and uncertainty suggests the possibility of using uncertainty measures to value flexibility. The second law of thermodynamics states that a system left on its own will tend towards maximum disorder. Entropy is a measure of this disorder in physics, randomness in nature, and uncertainty in information theory. Maximum uncertainty occurs in a system when the probability of changing into any other state is equal. [Given n possible states, entropy is highest when the probability of state transition is 1/n.] Likewise, maximum flexibility occurs when each alternative has an equal chance of being selected. Pye (1978) and Kumar (1987) are among the chief supporters of entropy as a measure of flexibility. Finally, by applying utility theory to the individual's preference for flexibility, Montenegro (1978) introduces flexibility profiles as a useful tool in modelling.

Risk is a negative consequence of uncertainty. Robustness allows one to avoid risk by means of immunity, insensitivity, or tolerance. Like flexibility, robustness does not remove or necessarily reduce uncertainty, but it does provide a kind of coping mechanism. One way to reduce risk is to select the course of action that minimises your future regret. Turning this around, we can use the expected regret decision criterion as a way to increase robustness.

Commitment, confidence, and flexibility are also related in a similar fashion. If you are unsure about your preferences and also not confident of your model, then you will be reluctant to commit yourself to a course of action. In this case, you would seek flexibility, for instance, by delaying the decision until you have more information.

MEASURES AND DECISION CRITERIA

The above framework provides a basis for the development of operational measures and decision criteria. Several measures have already been proposed in the literature, most notably in doctoral theses on this subject. The most common ones are introduced here.

The most popular by far is the size of choice set or the number of choices. This can be directly deduced from the inherent meaning of flexibility. It is countable, simple, and feasible. However, it gives no indication of the degree of differentiation among the choices or their attractiveness. Furthermore, the number of choices depends on the partitioning of the choice set as well as the stage in the decision process.

Some commentators see flexibility as the ease of transition from one state to another. Ease is a function of cost and time, reflecting the freedom of choice. Unfortunately, it is not self-evident or sufficient to explain the amount of flexibility.

The logarithmic measure of entropy has long been established and accepted in the natural sciences and more recently in information theory. Though neat and self-contained, it fails to link information with decisions. Furthermore, since entropy does not discriminate between states, it can lead to bad decisions.

Along with the above, Mandelbaum (1978) suggests ways of increasing flexibility, such as decomposing a decision into sequential stages, postponing actions, and partitioning the choice set. A decision criterion that allows this should differentiate between decision paths. "Satisficing" rather than optimising has been observed by Simon (1961) as a more practicable decision strategy. By the same reasoning, Mandelbaum and Buzacott (1990) and Heimann and Lusk (1976) point out that a satisficing decision criterion gives more flexibility.

CONCLUSIONS

Flexibility is widely believed to be desirable and useful. Nonetheless without a clear definition, it remains elusive. The conceptual framework presented here organises concepts of flexibility into related themes and thereby provides a basis for the development of operational measures and decision criteria. The next step is to test them in decision modelling.

REFERENCES

Ansoff, H.I. (1968) *Corporate Strategy,* Penguin Books

Eppink, Derk Jan (1978) *Managing the Unforeseen: a study of flexibility,* PhD Thesis, Free University of Amsterdam

Gupta, D. and Buzacott, J.A. (1988) A framework for understanding flexibility of manufacturing systems, *Technical Report,* University of Waterloo

Heimann, Stephen R.and Edward J. Lusk (1976) Decision Flexibility: An Alternative Evaluation Criterion, *Accounting Review,* Vol. 51, pp 51 - 64

Kumar, V. (1987) Entropic measures of manufacturing flexibility, *International Journal of Production Research,* Vol. 25 No. 7, pp 957 - 966

Mandelbaum, Marvin (1978) *Flexibility and Decision Making - An Exploration and Unification,* PhD Thesis, University of Toronto

Mandelbaum, Marvin and John Buzacott (1990) Flexibility and decision making, *European Journal of Operational Research,* Vol. 44, pp. 17 - 27

Merkhofer, M.W. (1975) *Flexibility and Decision Analysis,* PhD Thesis, Stanford University

Montenegro, J.L.A. (1978) *Planning Telecommunication Systems: A Normative Approach,* PhD Thesis, University of Pennsylvania

Pye, Roger (1978) A Formal, Decision-Theoretic Approach to Flexibility and Robustness, *Journal of Operational Research Society,* Vol. 29 No. 3, pp. 215 - 227, Pergamon Press plc

Simon, Herbert (1961) *Administrative Behaviour,* Macmillan, New York

Some results concerning the complexity of interval edge-colorings of graphs

Marek Kubale
Dept. of Foundations of Informatics
Technical University of Gdańsk
PL-80952 Gdańsk

The interval coloring of a weighted graph so that each edge receives a number of consecutive colors and no two colors of the edges at any vertex are the same is a generalization of the classical edge-coloring problem to graphs with integer weights on the edges. In this contribution we consider the complexity of this problem in some of its more interesting special cases. Obviously, finding of an optimal solution to interval edge-coloring problem is NP-hard, as it is already NP-complete to determine the chromatic index of a simple graph. Therefore, we assume some strong restrictions on the length of coloring intervals and the structure of a graph. In this way we obtain a number of result about special cases that are either positive (i.e. polynomially solvable subproblems) or negative (i.e. NP-completeness proofs).

1. Introduction

As mentioned above, the general problem of interval coloring of edges is NP-hard. However, unlike the usual problem, the interval edge-coloring remains NP-hard for some highly structured families of graphs for which polynomial time algorithms for the classical problem are known (e.g. complete graphs, bipartite graphs [1], trees [5]). Nevertheless, in view of potential applications in scheduling and timetabling it would be desirable to have efficient algorithms for polynomially solvable subproblems. This note focuses on such special cases involving sparse graphs. In this way we determine to some extent a line of demarcation between P and NP-complete problems of interval coloring the edges of sparse graphs.

We consider graphs $G = (V,E)$ with $n = |V|$ vertices and $m = |E|$ edges. To make the inclusion relation between families of graphs clearer, we allow singular loops at vertices although multiple edges between vertices are not permitted. In addition, we consider two kinds of edge weighting functions: arbitrary and binomial. A weighting function $F: E \to N$ is said to be *arbitrary* if N is the set of all positive integers. A weighting function is called *binomial* if its range is restricted to 2 element set $\{1,l\} \subset N$, i.e. $F: E \to \{1,l\}$.

In the sequel we consider the complexity of interval coloring for the following types of graphs: complete, bipartite, trees, caterpillars, stars, paths. In Figure 1 we give containment relations for these classes of graphs.

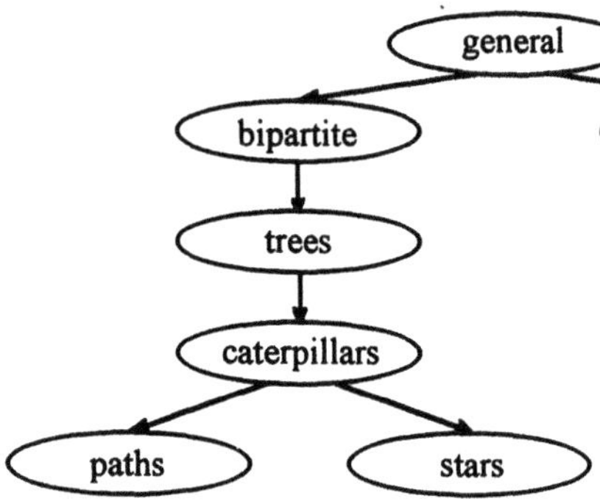

Fig.1. Containment relations.

2. Arbitrary edge weights

In the case of arbitrary edge weights the problem is NP-complete for all graphs of Fig. 1 except paths. The strongest result of this kind is as follows.

Theorem 2.1. INTERVAL EDGE-COLORING *is* NP-*complete even if G is a star with a loop at each noncentral vertex.*

The proof is by transformation from PARTITION problem. Given a set A of positive integers $\{a_1,a_2,\ldots,a_m\}$ with half of its sum equal to b, we construct a star with edge weights a_i $(i = 1,\ldots,m)$ and m loops of weight b. It is easy to see that there exists a PARTITION of A if and only if G can be colored within $2b$ colors.

On the other hand, every path P can be optimally colored with Δ colors, where Δ is the maximum weighted degree of P. The algorithm runs in two passes through P. Firstly, we find the value of Δ, secondly, we assign alternately two extremal intervals in range $[1,\ldots,\Delta]$ to consecutive edges. In this way we obtain

Theorem 2.2. *If G is a path then a chromatic interval coloring can be found in linear time.*

3. Binomial edge weights

We begin with

Theorem 3.1. INTERVAL EDGE-COLORING *is* NP-*complete if G is a binomial complete graph.*

The proof of this theorem by reduction from CHROMATIC INDEX is given in [4].

The broadest class of graphs that we are able to color in polynomial time are trees. An algorithm for optimal coloring of a binomial tree T with maximum degree d in $O(dn)$ time was presented in [6]. This algorithm runs in $O(n^2)$ worst-case time and $O(n^{3/2})$ on average. The algorithm takes advantage of intricate labelling of the edges of T. Summing up we have

Theorem 3.2. *If G is a binomial tree than a chromatic interval coloring can be found in* $O(n^2)$ *time.*

Applying a different approach the author was able to give a linear time algorithm for caterpillars with hairs of arbitrary length [3]. However, the problem of interval edge-coloring of binomial bipartite graphs seems to be open. It would be good to know the complexity of this problem because of potential applications in the open-shop scheduling problem.

In the table below we give a complexity classification for the INTERVAL EDGE-COLORING problem.

Graphs	Edge weights			References
	uninomial	binomial	arbitrary	
general	NPC !	NPC !	NPC !	[2]
complete	$O(n^2)$	NPC !	NPC !	Thm.3.1
bipartite	$O(n^2 \log n)$	?	NPC !	[1]
trees	$O(n)$	$O(n^2)$	NPC !	[5],[6]
caterpillars	$O(n)$	$O(n)$	NPC	[3]
stars	$O(n)$	$O(n)$	NPC	Thm.2.1
paths	$O(n)$	$O(n)$	$O(n)$	Thm.2.1

NPC - NP-complete

NPC ! - NP-complete in the strong sense

$O(\cdot)$ - Complexity of an optimization algorithm

? - Open

References

[1] Cole R., Hopcroft J.E., On edge coloring bipartite graphs, *SIAM J. Computing* 11 (1982) 540-546.

[2] Holyer I., The NP-completeness of the edge coloring, *SIAM J. Computing* 10 (1981) 718-720.

[3] Kubale M., Interval edge-coloring of caterpillars with hairs of arbitrary length, *Zastos. Mat.* 19 (1987) 505-517.

[4] Kubale M., Complexity classification for interval edge-coloring of some graphs, *Proc. 33th Int. Wiss. Koll.*, Ilmenau (1988) vol. 4, 217-220.

[5] Mitchel S., Hedetniemi S., Linear algorithms for edge-coloring trees and unicyclic graphs, *Inf. Process. Lett.* 9 (1979) 110-112.

[6] Piwakowski K., Kubale M., A polynomial algorithm for edge-coloring of binomial trees, presented at *Int. Conf on Combinatorics*, Keszthely(1993).

On the Variance of the Number of Pivot Steps Required by the Simplex Algorithm

Karl-Heinz Küfer
Department of Mathematics
University of Kaiserslautern
P.O. Box 3049, D-67663 Kaiserslautern

Introduction: Excellent practical perfomance, which led to Dantzig and Hirsch's linearity conjectures on the one hand, and exponential worst-case behaviour on the other hand are the main benchmarks in complexity analysis of most variants of the simplex algorithm. Borgwardt (1982a,b) was the first to explain this embarrasing gap by means of probabilistic analysis. Using a stochastic problem simulation he proved that the number of pivot steps required by a variant of Gass and Saaty's parametric objective function algorithm —the "Schatteneckenalgorithmus (shadow vertex algorithm)"—is expected to be polynomial. But knowledge about the average complexity alone does not reveal the algorithm's properties completely. Important questions remain open. What is the probability of exponential examples? What is the probability of deviations from the mean? So, many researchers, e.g. Shamir (1987) in his survey paper, asked for higher moments or even for the distribution of the random variable "number of pivots". We are going to derive some information on the variance in this paper.
Corresponding to Borgwardt we look at linear programming problems of type

$$\max_{x \in X} v^T x\,;\; X := \{x \in \mathbb{R}^n \,|\, a_i^T x \leq 1;\; i = 1, \ldots, m\}, \tag{1}$$

where a_i, v, $x \in \mathbb{R}^n$, $m \geq n \geq 2$. The vectors a_i are supposed to be identically, independently distributed random vectors in $\mathbb{R}^n \setminus \{0\}$, whose polar representations consist of independent radial and directional parts, the first being arbitrarily distributed on $\mathbb{R}^+$ the latter being uniformly distributed on the unit sphere (rotation-invariance-property). The set X can be considered a random nonempty polyhedron in $\mathbb{R}^n$. In order to transform the problem into a geometrical setting we profit from a representation of the functional "number of pivots" on the polar polyhedron of X. Let

$$Y := \{y \in \mathbb{R}^n \,|\, x^T y \leq 1;\; x \in X\} = \mathrm{convhull}(0, a_1, \ldots, a_m) \tag{2}$$

be the polar polyhedron Y of X. Furthermore for all linear independent vectors u and v of unit length let $s_{u,v}(X)$ be defined by

$$s_{u,v}(X) := \begin{cases} \text{number of boundary simplices of } Y \text{ intersected by } cone(u,v) \text{ -1} \\ \quad \text{if } \mathbb{R}^+ u \text{ intersects a boundary simplex of } Y \\ \text{number of boundary simplices of } Y \text{ intersected by } cone(u,v) \\ \quad \text{if } \mathbb{R}^+ u \text{ doesn't intersect a boundary simplex of } Y \end{cases} \tag{3}$$

$s_{u,v}(X)$ equals the number of pivot steps, which phase II of the shadow vertex algorithm requires for maximizing the functional $v^T x$ over X, when the iteration is started with a vertex of X, whose polar vertex cone intersects $\mathbb{R}^+ u$.

Prior results: As the main step in his polynomiality proof Borgwardt estimated the expected number of pivots required by phase II from above independent from the underlying rotationally invariant distribution:

$$\mathrm{E}(s_{u,v}) \leq \frac{e\pi}{4}\left(\frac{\pi}{2} + \frac{1}{e}\right) n^3 m^{1/(n-1)}. \tag{4}$$

The average in (4) is taken on the choice of X and on u and v, where u, v are considered identically, independently distributed uniformly on the unit sphere in $\mathbb{R}^n$.
An important trick within the proof of this result is to average on the vectors u and v first, that means we look at the functional $s := \mathrm{E}(s_{u,v})$, where we average on the choice of u and v. Moments of s are much easier to analyze than those of $s_{u,v}$ because of obvious symmetry reasons. Based on these ideas Küfer (1992a,b) investigated the quotient $\frac{\mathrm{Var}(s)}{\mathrm{E}^2(s)}$ asymptotically for a subclass of the rotationally symmetric distributions—the distributions with compact support. The main result of this research is:

$$\frac{\mathrm{Var}(s)}{\mathrm{E}^2(s)} = o(1),\ m \to \infty \tag{5}$$

For more special distributions with bounded domain the rate of growth of this quotient can be given exactly. Without any condition on the underlying rotationally invariant distribution the quotient in (5) remains at least bounded in m. Unfortunately, we have $\mathrm{Var}(s) \leq \mathrm{Var}(s_{u,v})$. Thus, asymptotic equivalents of $\mathrm{Var}(s)$ can only serve as lower asymptotic bounds for $\mathrm{Var}(s_{u,v})$. So far open is the question for meaningful upper bounds.

Main result: In the present paper we can state as a first asymptotic upper bound for the variance of $s_{u,v}$:

Theorem:

For $n \geq 2$ and any rotationally invariant distribution:

$$\frac{\mathrm{Var}(s_{u,v})}{\mathrm{E}^2(s_{u,v})} = \mathcal{O}(m^{(n-2)/(n-1)}),\ m \to \infty, \tag{6}$$

The bound on the right hand side in (6) can be improved for classes of distributions.

In general we conjecture that the order of growth in m is too big. We believe that one can prove qualitatively the same results as has been cited for Var(s) but we have not succeeded in doing so up to now.

References:

[1] Borgwardt, K. H. (1977) *Untersuchungen zur Asymptotik der mittleren Schrittzahl von Simplexverfahren in der linearen Optimierung.* Dissertation, Universität Kaiserslautern.

[2] Borgwardt, K. H. (1982a) *Some Distribution-Independent Results About the Asymptotic Order of the Average Number of Pivot Steps of the Simplex Method.* Math. of O. R. 7: 441-462.

[3] Borgwardt, K. H. (1982b) *The Average Number of Pivot Steps Required by The Simplex Method is Polynomial.* ZOR 26: 157-177.

[4] Küfer, K. H. (1992a) *Asymptotische Varianzanalysen in der stochastischen Polyedertheorie.* Dissertation, Universität Kaiserslautern.

[5] Küfer, K. H. (1992b) *On the Variance of the Number of Pivot Steps Required by the Simplex Algorithm.* To appear in ZOR, Preprint Universität Kaiserslautern.

[6] Shamir, R. (1987) *The Efficiency of the Simplex Method: A Survey* Management Science 33: 241-262.

Inversion Problems In Pyramidal Classification

Rainer Lasch
Institut für Statistik und Mathematische Wirtschaftstheorie, Universität Augsburg
Memminger Str. 14, 86159 Augsburg, Germany

1 Introduction

Pyramidal classification of multidimensional data allows the construction of overlapping clusters. The pyramidal representation is a natural extension of the hierarchical classification. The graphical representaion of indexed hierarchies by dendrograms is well-known. For the graphical representation of indexed pyramids a similar procedure can be used. Milligan (1979) has shown that the most used agglomerative hierarchical techniques single and complete linkage generate hierarchical structures with monotonically increasing distance values so the resulting dendrogram is free of inversions. Transferring this agglomerative techniques to the pyramidal classification it can be shown that only the complete linkage technique generates pyramidal structures with monotonically increasing distance values. Using the single linkage technique inversions are possible in the graphical representation. For the existence of an inversion a necessary and sufficient condition is formulated.

2 Definitions and Notations

To allow an uniform formal presentation of the hierarchical and pyramidal classification the following notation is used. Subsequently let $N = \{1, ..., n\}$ be a finite set of objects.

Definition 2.1

a) *Given a set $A \subset N$ let i_{min}, $i_{max} \in A$ be the minimal and maximal elements of A according to an order Θ. The set A is* **connex** *according to Θ if*

$$(i \in N \text{ is according to } \Theta \text{ between } i_{min} \text{ and } i_{max}) \Longleftrightarrow (i \in A)$$

b) *Let $\mathcal{S}$ be a set of non-empty parts of N. An order Θ is* **compatible** *with $\mathcal{S}$ if all subsets $A \subset N$ $(A \in \mathcal{S})$ are connex according to Θ.*

Definition 2.2

Denote by $\mathcal{H}$ a set of non-empty parts of N. The set $\mathcal{H}$ will be called a **hierarchy** *if*

(1) $N \in \mathcal{H}$

(2) $\forall\, i \in N : \{i\} \in \mathcal{H}$

(3) $\forall\, A, B \in \mathcal{H}\, (A \neq B)$: $A \cap B = \emptyset$ or $A \cap B = A$ or $A \cap B = B$

Definition 2.3

Denote by $\mathcal{P}$ a set of non-empty parts of N. The set $\mathcal{P}$ will be called a **pyramid** *if*

(1) $N \in \mathcal{P}$

(2) $\forall\, i \in N : \{i\} \in \mathcal{P}$

(3) $\forall\, A, B \in \mathcal{P}\ (A \neq B):\quad A \cap B = \emptyset \quad \text{or} \quad A \cap B \in \mathcal{P}$

(4) *There exists an order Θ compatible with $\mathcal{P}$*

The sets $A, B, ...$ of $\mathcal{H}$ or $\mathcal{P}$ are called **classes** of the hierarchy or the pyramid. Comparing this two definitions, condition (3) in Definition 2.2 is on the one hand stronger than condition (3) in Definition 2.3. On the other hand for any corresponding tree representation of a hierarchy $\mathcal{H}$ there also exists an order Θ compatible with $\mathcal{H}$ if one orders for example the leaves/singletons from left to right. With this remarks it is easy to state the following proposition:

Proposition 2.4

The set of hierarchies is included in the set of pyramids.

For a useful graphical representation of hierarchies and pyramids it is necessary to introduce an index for their classes. This index indicates the heterogenity of the classes and allows a comparison of different classes by their similarity structure.

Definition 2.5

An **indexed hierarchy** *is a pair $(\mathcal{H}, f)$ where $\mathcal{H}$ is an hierarchy and f is a mapping $f : \mathcal{H} \to \mathbb{R}_+$ such that*

(1) $f(A) = 0 \iff$ *A contains only equivalent objects*

(2) $\forall\, A, B \in \mathcal{H},\ A \subsetneq B:\ f(A) < f(B)$

Definition 2.6

An **indexed pyramid** *is a pair $(\mathcal{P}, f)$ where $\mathcal{P}$ is an pyramid and f is a mapping $f : \mathcal{P} \to \mathbb{R}_+$ such that*

(1) $f(A) = 0 \iff$ *A contains only equivalent objects*

(2) $\forall\, A, B \in \mathcal{P},\ A \subset B:\ f(A) \leq f(B)$

(3) $A \subsetneq B$ and $f(A) = f(B) \Rightarrow \exists A_1, A_2 \in \mathcal{P}\ (A_1 \neq A; A_2 \neq A)$ and $A_1 \cap A_2 = A$

Example 2.7

Let $N = \{1,2,3,4\}$ be a finite set of objects. Let f be a hierarchical index given by $f(\{i\}) = 0\ \forall i \in N, f(\{1,2\}) = 1, f(\{3,4\}) = 4$ and $f(N) = 7$, then

$$\mathcal{H} = \{\{1\}, \{2\}, \{3\}, \{4\}, \{1,2\}, \{3,4\}, N\}$$

is a possible indexed hierarchy. Let f be a pyramidal index given by $f(\{i\}) = 0$

$\forall i \in N, f(\{1,2\}) = 1, f(\{2,3\}) = 2, f(\{3,4\}) = f(\{1,2,3\}) = 4, f(\{2,3,4\}) = 5$ and $f(N) = 7$, then

$$\mathcal{P} = \{\{1\},\{2\},\{3\},\{4\},\{1,2\},\{2,3\},\{3,4\},\{1,2,3\},\{2,3,4\},N\}$$

is a possible indexed pyramid which allows overlapping of clusters. For example $\Theta : 4 \prec 3 \prec 2 \prec 1$ is an order compatible with $\mathcal{P}$.

In the pyramidal and the hierarchical classification the index indicates the heterogenity of the classes that is the smaller the index of a class the more homogenious is this class. In Figure 1a the classes A and B and in Fig. 1b the class D are called **predecessors** of the class C resp. E. As can be seen each class in the pyramidal classification has at most two and in the hierarchical classification only one predecessor (Diday, E., 1987).

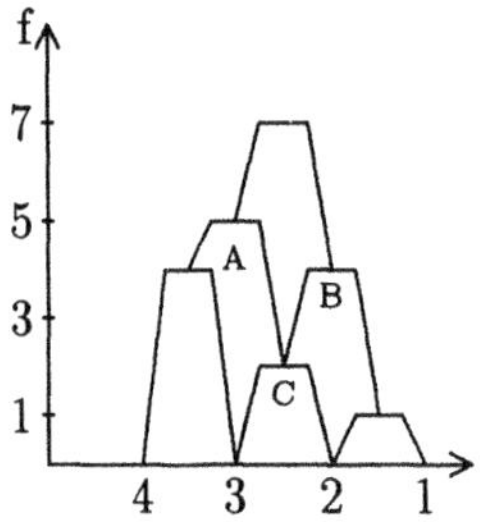

Fig. 1a : Indexed Pyramid $(\mathcal{P}, f)$

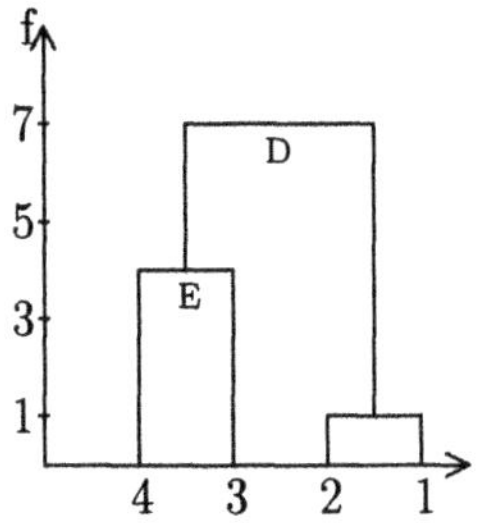

Fig. 1b : Indexed Hierarchy $(\mathcal{H}, f)$

3 Agglomerative Clustering Techniques

The agglomerative hierarchical and pyramidal techniques produce a complete sequence of non-overlapping resp. overlapping cluster solutions. They all operate in essentially the same way, proceeding sequentially from the stage in which each object is considered to be single class to the final stage in which there is a single group containing all n objects. At each stage in the procedure two groups considered to be the most similar are joined together. Once the classes are joined together they are never separated later in the process. The index of a joined class corresponds to the value of the dissimilarity index of the two classes that have formed it.

3.1 Measuring Inter-Cluster Dissimilarity

Agglomerative hierarchical or pyramidal techniques differ primarily in how they measure the distance or similarity of two clusters, where a cluster may, at times, consist of only a single object. The simplest and most frequently used inter-group measures are

$$f(K \cup L) = d(K, L) := \min\{d_{ij} | i \in K,\ j \in L\} \tag{1}$$

$$f(K \cup L) = d(K, L) := \max\{d_{ij} | i \in K,\ j \in L\} \tag{2}$$

in the hierarchical techniques and

$$f(K \cup L) = d(K,L) := \min\{d_{ij} | i \in K,\ j \in L,\ i,j \notin K \cap L\} \tag{3}$$

$$f(K \cup L) = d(K,L) := \max\{d_{ij} | i \in K,\ j \in L,\ i,j \notin K \cap L\} \tag{4}$$

in the pyramidal techniques. In the above mentioned equations $d(K,L)$ is the dissimilarity between two clusters K and L and d_{ij} is the dissimilarity between objects i and j. This, of course, could be one of a large variety of measures, including, for example, euclidean and city block distances. The dissimilarity measures in (1) or (3) are the basis of **single linkage clustering** and that in (2) or (4) are the basis of **complete linkage clustering**. These two techniques have the often desirable property that they are invariant under monotone transformations of the original inter-object dissimilarities.

The single linkage and the complete linkage clustering algorithms for the construction of a hierarchy are well-known (Opitz, O., 1980, S.96ff). Lance and Williams (1966) introduced a recurrence formula which can be used to compute the updated inter-cluster distance values resulting from the cluster fusion which occur at each level of a hierarchical clustering procedure. The recurrence formula gives the updated distance between a cluster L and a newly formed cluster $K = K_1 \cup K_2$ which was created out of the fusion of the clusters K_1 and K_2. The recurrence formula is computed as

$$\begin{aligned} d(L,K) &= \alpha_1\, d(L,K_1) + \alpha_2\, d(L,K_2) + \beta\, v(K_1,K_2) \\ &\quad + \gamma\, |d(L,K_1) - d(L,K_2)|, \end{aligned}$$

and the parameters α, β and γ define the linkage process:

- $\alpha_1 = \alpha_2 = 1/2,\ \beta = 0,\ \gamma = -1/2$ define the single linkage algorithm
- $\alpha_1 = \alpha_2 = 1/2,\ \beta = 0,\ \gamma = 1/2$ define the complete linkage algorithm

Milligan (1979) has proved that the recurrence formula generates hierarchical structures with monotonically increasing distance values if the following conditions are satisfied:

- $\gamma \geq 0:\ \alpha_1 + \alpha_2 + \beta \geq 1,\ \alpha_1, \alpha_2 \geq 0$
- $\gamma < 0:\ \alpha_1 + \alpha_2 + \beta \geq 1,\ |\gamma| \leq \alpha_1, \alpha_2$

In the hierarchical classification the single and complete linkage algorithm generates hierarchical structures with monotonic increasing distance values. If the distances are monotonically increasing, it is impossible for a cluster fused later in the hierarchy to have a distance value which is less than the distance value for a cluster fused earlier in the hierarchy. Nonmonotonic distances would imply that more objects are fused into clusters before having fused objects which are actually closer. The case of nonmonotonic distances is called **inversion**. Nonmonotonic distances should be avoided in classification algorithms because the resulting inversions are very difficult to explain.

In contrast to hierarchical classification pyramidal classification generates additionally an order Θ on the set of objects which is compatible with the proximities between this objects.

The fact that this generated order has to be compatible with the constructed set of parts is in this way difficult that only specified classes can be fused.

For the computation of the updated inter-cluster distances in the pyramidal clustering procedure it is possible to extend the recurrence formula of Lance/Williams to pyramids (Lasch, R., 1993, S. 111 ff).

Using the complete linkage algorithm one can use

$$d(L, K_1 \cup K_2) = \frac{1}{2}\, d(L, K_1) \,+\, \frac{1}{2}\, d(L, K_2) \,+\, \frac{1}{2}\, |d(L, K_1) - d(L, K_2)|.$$

The recurrence formula for the single linkage algorithm depends on the position of the classes K and L. A class K is called **left of** a class L relative to an compatible order $\prec$ if

$$(\min(K) \prec \min(L) \quad \text{and} \quad \max(K) \prec \max(L)).$$

Using the single linkage algorithm one can use

$$d(L, K_1 \cup K_2) = \min\{d(L, K_2), d(L - K_2, K_1 - K_2)\},$$

if $K_1 \cup K_2$ is left of L or

$$d(L, K_1 \cup K_2) = \min\{d(L, K_1), d(L - K_1, K_2 - K_1)\},$$

if L is left of $K_1 \cup K_2$.

Using the complete linkage algorithm the recurrence formula of the hierarchical and pyramidal classification is identical. This implies that in pyramidal classification the complete linkage algorithm generates monotonic distance values and the resulting pyramid is free of inversions.

The use of the pyramidal single linkage algorithm can generate inversions. The reason for the existence of an inversion using the single linkage algorithm is the observance of a constructed compatible order Θ. The following example illustrates this fact.

Example 3.1
Let $N = \{1, 2, 3, 4\}$ be a finite set of objects. The single linkage algorithm generate the following extended dissimilarity data. The minimal distance values in Table 1 generate

	1	2	3	4	{1,2}	{2,3}	{3,4}	{1,2,3}
1	0							
2	1	0						
3	3	1	0					
4	2	5	1	0				
{1,2}	∞	∞	∞	2	0			
{2,3}	∞	∞	∞	∞	3	0		
{3,4}	2	∞	∞	∞	∞	5	0	
{1,2,3}	∞	∞	∞	∞	∞	∞	2	0

Table 1: Extended Dissimilarity Data, Single Linkage Algorithm

the classes $\{1,2\}, \{2,3\}$ and $\{3,4\}$ on the index level $f(\{1,2\}) = f(\{2,3\}) = f(\{3,4\}) = 1$. The corresponding order $\Theta : 1 \prec 2 \prec 3 \prec 4$ is compatible with the generated set of parts. In the next step the minimal distance occurs between object 1 and class $\{3,4\}$ with $d(1,\{3,4\}) = d(1,4) = 2$. But this fusion would generate the class $\{1,3,4\}$ which is not compatible with the order Θ. Therefore the next allowable fusion is between the classes $\{1,2\}$ and $\{2,3\}$ generating the class $\{1,2,3\}$ on the level $f(\{1,2,3\}) = 3$.

Using the single linkage algorithm the dissimilarity between two classes K, L is equal to the minimal distance between pairs of objects. Considering two classes K and L with object $1 \in K$ and object $4 \in L$ one can compute $d(K,L) \leq d(1,4) < f(\{1,2,3\})$. In the course of the algorithm the classes K, L with object $1 \in K$ and object $4 \in L$ are constructed and the fusion of this classes would generate an inversion. In the next step of example 3.1 the minimal distance occurs between the classes $\{1,2,3\}$ and $\{3,4\}$ and the index of the resulting fusion generates an inversion:

$$f(\{1,2,3,4\}) = d(\{1,2,3\},\{3,4\}) = d(1,4) = 2 < f(\{1,2,3\}) = 3$$

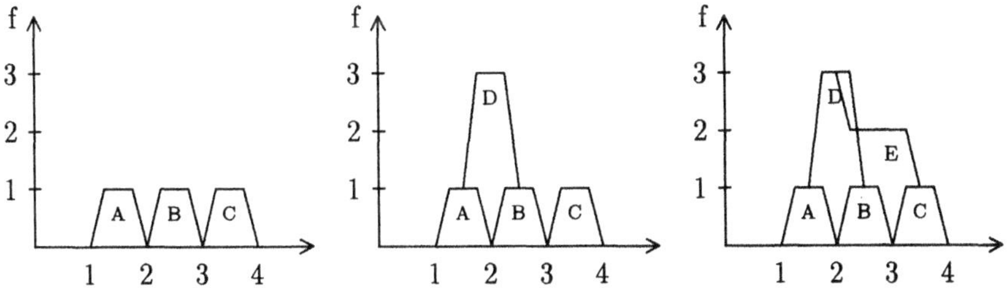

$\Theta : 1 \prec 2 \prec 3 \prec 4$
$\min\{d(K,L)\} = d(\{1\},C) = 2$
$\{1\} \cup C = \{1,3,4\}$

$d(A,B) = 3$
$A \cup B = \{1,2,3\}$

$\min\{d(K,L)\} = d(D,C)$
$d(D,C) = d(\{1\},\{4\}) = 2$

This example leads to a necessary and sufficient condition for the existence of inversions which can be used in the course of the algorithm:

Proposition 3.2

In step ν of the single linkage algorithm let J_ν be the set of classes which are not yet fused in step ν, $d_\nu^* := \min_{K,L \in J_\nu} \{d(K,L)\}$ the minimal distance between two classes and f_ν the corresponding index level:

$$\textit{Existence of an inversion} \Longleftrightarrow \exists\, \nu : \; d_\nu^* < f_\nu$$

Proof:

It is evident that $(*) \quad d_\nu^* \leq f_{\nu+1}$ and the allowable fusion of the classes K and L in step ν implies $d_\nu^* = d(K,L) = f_\nu$.

⇒: Let $d^*_\nu \geq f_\nu$ for all ν then $(*)$ implies for all ν

$$f_{\nu+1} \geq d^*_\nu \geq f_\nu,$$

that is there exists no inversion.

⇐: Consider two classes K und L with $d(K,L) = d^*_\nu$. In step $\nu + k$ $(k > 0)$ exist two classes K', L' with $K \subset K', L \subset L'$ and $d^*_{\nu+k} = d(K', L') = f_{\nu+k}$. Thus one can state:

$$\begin{aligned} f_{\nu+k} &= d(K', L') \\ &= \min\{d(i,j) \,|\, i \in K' - L',\ j \in L' - K'\} \\ &\leq d(K, L) \\ &= d^*_\nu \\ &< f_\nu. \end{aligned}$$

□

4 References

Diday, E. (1987) *Orders and overlapping clusters by pyramids,* Rapports de Recherche, I.N.R.I.A. no 730.

Diday, E., Bertrand, P. (1986) *An extension of hierarchical clustering: the pyramidal presentation,* in: Pattern Recognition in Practice II, Gelsema, E.S., Kanal, L.N. (Hrsg.), S. 411-421.

Lance, G.N., Williams, W.T. (1966) *A general theory of classificatory sorting strategies 1. Hierarchical systems,* Computer Journal, vol 9, S. 373-380.

Lasch, R. (1993) *Pyramidale Darstellung multivariater Daten,* Josef Eul, Bergisch Gladbach, Köln.

Milligan, G.W. (1979) *Ultrametric hierarchical clustering algorithms,* Psychometrika, vol 44, no 3, S. 343-346.

Opitz, O. (1980) *Numerische Taxonomie,* Fischer, Stuttgart, New York.

A Comparison of Heuristic Methods in Scheduling Flexible Assembly Systems

Georg List and Anton Nußbaumer
Extraordinariat CIM
Wirtschaftsuniversität Wien
1190 Wien
AUSTRIA

1 Introduction

For optimization problems that are NP-hard, which includes most problems arising in scheduling, there are at present no easy solutions. Classical OR-methods cannot be used, because you would need approximately 10^{36} years of time for a complete enumeration in our simplest test case, whereas an acceptable response time is about an quater of an hour. As there is currently no way to solve such problems exactly, the objective of finding the global optimum has to be changed in the target to find the best result possible over a given period.

With roots going back in the late 1960's and early 1970's heuristic methods have been object of intensive research in the last decade. The methods of tabu search, genetic algorithms and simulated annealing have been singled out by the Committee on the Next Decade of Operations Research (see [CONDOR88]) as "extremely promising" for future treatment of practical applications.

In our current research project P8199-PHY "Dynamische Ressourcenbelegungsplanung" (see [JAMMERNEGG91]) we are studying heuristic methods in process planning and control of flexible assembly systems.

2 Model

As a basic model, a FAS with four partially parallel assembly centres is examined. These four cells are supplied by AGV's. In contrast to many similar experiments in this field the system definition is made much more realistic. So the system is based on real products (toy-cars) and the influence of restrictions such as transport-times, palette-dimensions, machine-breakdowns and other stochastic events which occur in reality, are verified [GRONALT93]. SIMAN/CINEMA with Fortran subroutines is used to implement the model [SCHMID93].

Due to the existing interfaces the implementation of the tested algorithms is easily possibly by substituting the modeled system by the real system.

3 Heuristic Methods

In our current research project the following procedures are tested for efficiency in the field of flexible manufacturing:

Simulated Annealing

Simulated Annealing has become a very popular tool in combinatorical optimization since its introduction in 1982 (see [KIRKPATRICK82]). Osman and Potts [OSMAN89], as well as Ogbu und Smith [OGBU90] discussed the advantages and difficulties of this heuristic in production scheduling. On the basis of available comparisons the following can be said about this approach:

- The solutions found by the Simulated Annealing algorithm are of very good quality.
- On the other hand it requires more time than most of the other popular heuristics to evaluate these solutions.
- The following factors are important for the success of this algorithm:
  acceptance-probability, perturbance technique, kind of temperature-reduction.

Tabu-Search

Important new results in the field of Tabu-Search algorithms in application to Job Shop scheduling were found by M. Widmer [WIDMER91], whose examinations also include details such as Tooling Constraints. Of no minor interest are the examinations of Taut, who proposes Tabu Search as the most efficient heuristic in complex job-shop re-scheduling problems (see [TAUT92]). The following advantages and problems of the procedure can be found:

- The algorithm supplies good solutions without exception, which in most cases are found very quickly.
- The speed and the accuracy of the method can be varied by different parameter-settings
- The choice of the following factors is important:
  tabu-list size, solution-surroundings, number of optimization steps.

Threshold Accepting

This is one of the most recent approaches in heuristic optimization theory. Proposed in 1990 by Dueck and Scheuer [DUECK90], Threshold Accepting seems to be equivalent or even superior to the Simulated Annealing algorithm (see [ALTHOEFER91]). Until now there are no special results known about the application of Threshold Accepting in the field of production scheduling.

Genetic Algorithms

The method of Genetic Algorithms (GA) is based on the principles of Natural Selection, Inheritance and Mutation. The foundations developed by Holland et al. [HOLLAND75] have been and still are applied with success in all areas of combinatoric optimization, as, for example, Job-Shop Scheduling [DAVIS85], Travelling-Salesman problems [GREFENST85] and as *classifier-systems* [GOLDBERG89].

This technique is based on the principle, that certain structures can adjust better to the environment than others.

- The advantage of this procedure is that very less knowledge about the respective problem-structure is required. Satisfying solutions are found even for rather bad parameter settings [GOLDBERG89].
- GA's can be used not only for solving combinatoric optimization problems but also as classification tools.

For all these heuristics the following can be said: It is possible to prove that the success of the algorithms does not depend on the choice of the initial solution.

Nevertheless experiments have shown that a good starting solution contributes greatly to the efficiency of an algorithm.

4 Results and Conclusion

Partner institutions are studying other OR-Methods (Linear Programming, mixed Priority-Rules, Neural Networks) and comparisons of the different methods show that heuristic algorithms can deal with complex problems (neural network-methods can only solve simple problems, as they need a big number of training cases), and outperform mixed priority rules, that are tested on complete grids.

A combination of priority rules and heuristic methods is currently tested, and we expect further improvement from this combined algorithm.

References

[ALTHOEFER91] I. Althöfer and K.-U. Koschnick (1991). On the Convergence of "Threshold Accepting", *Applied Mathematics and Optimization* 24, pp. 183-195.

[CONDOR88] Committee on the Next Decade of Operations Research (Condor) (1988). Operations research: The next decade, *Oper. Res.* 36.

[DAVIS85] L. Davis (1985). "Job shop scheduling with Genetic Algorithms", *Proceedings of the Internat. Conference on Genetic Algorithms and their Applications.*

[DUECK90] G. Dueck, T. Scheuer (1990). Threshold accepting: A general purpose optimization algorithm appearing superior to simulated annealing, *Journal of Computational Physics* 90, pp. 161-175.

[GREFENST85] J. Grefenstette, R. Gopal, B. Rosmaita, D. Van Gucht (1985). "Genetic Algorithms for the Travelling Salesman Problem", *Proceedings of the Internat. Conference on Genetic Algorithms and their Applications.*

[GOLDBERG89] D.E. Goldberg (1989). *Genetic Algorithms in Search, Optimization and Machine Learning.* Addison-Wesley, New York.

[GRONALT93] M. Gronalt, A. Nußbaumer, M. Schmid (1993). "Beschreibung des virtuellen Unternehmens - Entwicklung der Datenstruktur", *working paper.*

[HOLLAND75] J. Holland (1975). "Adaption in Natural and Artificial Systems", *The University of Michigan Press*, Ann Arbor, Michigan.

[JAMMERNEGG91] W. Jammernegg, G. Feichtinger, H. Hruschka (1991). Projektbeschreibung: Entwicklung von Methoden zur dynamischen Ressourcenbelegungsplanung bei Flexiblen Montagesystemen.

[KIRKPATRICK82] S. Kirkpatrick, C.D. Gelatt Jr., and M.P. Vecchi (1982). Optimization by simulated annealing, *IBM Research Report RC* 9355.

[OGBU90] F.A. Ogbu, D.K. Smith (1990). "The application of the simulated annealing algorithm to the solution of the $n/m/C_{max}$ flowshop problem", *Computs. Opns. Res.* 17(3), 243-253.

[OSMAN89] I.H. Osman, C.N. Potts (1989). "Simulated annealing for permutation flowshop scheduling", *OMEGA* 17(6), pp. 551-557.

[SCHMID93] M. Schmid (1993). "Kurzbeschreibung des Simulationsmodells zur Grobsimulation", *working paper.*

[TAUT92] Th. Taut (1992). Optimization Strategies for very complex job shop re-scheduling: Tabu Search - what else?, Diplomarbeit an der Techn. Universität München.

[WIDMER91] M. Widmer (1991). "Job Shop Scheduling with Tooling Constraints: a Tabu Search Approach", *J. Opl. Res. Soc.* 42(1), 75-82.

Sequential Estimation through Estimating Equations

Ryszard Magiera
Institute of Mathematics, Technical University of Wrocław
50-370 Wrocław, Poland

Using the approach to estimation through estimating equations, the information inequalities for regular sequential estimating plans are given and an optimum property of regular maximum likelihood sequential plans is shown in a general model for stochastic processes. The optimum sequential estimating functions are obtained in the nuisance parameter case as well. Under suitable regularity conditions on stopping times and likelihood functions it is pointed out that in searching for optimum sequential estimators one can replace the maximum likelihood equation by the maximum conditional likelihood equation in order to eliminate the influence of the nuisance parameter.

Optimum Estimating Equation Plans for Stochastic Processes

Let $X(t), t \geq 0$, be a stochastic process with either discrete or continuous time and with values in $(R^k, \mathcal{B}_{R^k})$. Suppose that the distribution of $X(t)$ belongs to a family of probability measures $P_\vartheta, \vartheta \in \Theta \subset R^n$, for which the restriction to $\mathcal{F}_t = \sigma\{X(s) : s \leq t\}$, $P_{\vartheta,t}$, is dominated by the restriction μ_t of a probability measure μ to $\mathcal{F}_t$, i.e., for each $t \geq 0$ and all $\vartheta \in \Theta$, $P_{\vartheta,t} \ll \mu_t$. Moreover, assume that

$$dP_{\theta,t}/d\mu_t = L(Y(t), t, \vartheta),$$

where $Y(t), t \geq 0$, is a process with values in $(R^m, \mathcal{B}_{R^m})$ and adapted to the filtration $\mathcal{F}_t, t \geq 0$, and $L(\cdot, \cdot, \vartheta)$ is a continuous function. In the case of continuous time it is supposed that the process $Y(t), t \geq 0$, has Skorokhod paths, i.e., paths which are right-continuous and have limits from the left.

Let τ be a stopping time relative to $\mathcal{F}_t, t \geq 0$, such that $P_\vartheta(\tau < \infty) = 1$ for each $\vartheta \in \Theta$. Suppose that the process is observed during the random time interval $[0, \tau]$. Let $P_{\vartheta,\tau}$ and μ_τ denote the restrictions of P_ϑ and μ to $\mathcal{F}_\tau$. Under the conditions given above $P_{\vartheta,\tau} \ll \mu_\tau$ and

$$dP_{\vartheta,\tau}/d\mu_\tau = L(Y(\tau), \tau, \vartheta) \quad \text{(the fundamental identity of sequential analysis).}$$

Using the concept of information in estimating function theory initiated by Godambe (1960), the problem of sequential estimation in the general model for stochastic processes will be considered. Let Θ be an open interval of the real line. To estimate the parameter $\vartheta \in \Theta$, a function $D(\tau, \vartheta) = D(Y(\tau), \tau, \vartheta)$ is constructed such that for each $\vartheta \in \Theta$, $D(\tau, \vartheta)$ is $\mathcal{F}_\tau$-measurable and $E_\vartheta D(\tau, \vartheta) = 0$ (unbiasedness). For a given stopping time τ and the function D, an estimate of ϑ is determined by $\hat{\vartheta}_\tau = d(\tau) = d(Y(\tau), \tau)$ as the solution of the *estimating equation*, $D(Y(\tau), \tau, \vartheta) = 0$. The idea is to obtain an unbiased *estimating function* $D(\tau, \vartheta)$ with smaller variance $E_\vartheta D^2(\tau, \vartheta)$, such that $D(\tau, \vartheta) \cong 0$, and larger sensitivity $| E_\vartheta[\partial D(\tau, \vartheta)/\partial\vartheta] |$. By an *estimating equation plan* we shall mean any pair $\delta = (\tau, D(\tau, \vartheta))$ consisting of a finite stoping time τ and an estimating function D. If for a given stopping time τ the likelihood function $L(\tau, \vartheta)$ and the estimating function D satisfy certain regularity conditions (ensuring the interchanging of the order of differentiation and integration), then the sequential plan δ will be called a *regular estimating sequential plan*. The class of all regular estimating sequential plans will be denoted by $\mathcal{D}$.

Definition 1. *A sequential plan* $\delta^* = (\tau, D^*(\tau,\vartheta)) \in \mathcal{D}$ *is said to be optimum if*

$$E_\vartheta \left\{D^*(\tau,\vartheta)/E_\vartheta\left[\partial D^*(\tau,\vartheta)/\partial\vartheta\right]\right\}^2 \le E_\vartheta \left\{D(\tau,\vartheta)/E_\vartheta\left[\partial D(\tau,\vartheta)/\partial\vartheta\right]\right\}^2 \tag{1}$$

for all $\delta = (\tau, D(\tau,\vartheta)) \in \mathcal{D}$ *and all* $\vartheta \in \Theta$.

Theorem 1. *For all* $\delta = (\tau, D(\tau,\vartheta)) \in \mathcal{D}$,

$$E_\vartheta \left\{D(\tau,\vartheta)/E_\vartheta\left[\partial D(\tau,\vartheta)/\partial\vartheta\right]\right\}^2 \ge 1/E_\vartheta\left[\partial \log L(\tau,\vartheta)/\partial\vartheta\right]^2,$$

the equality being attained when $D(\tau,\vartheta)$ *is given by* $D^*(\tau,\vartheta) = \partial \log L(\tau,\vartheta)/\partial\vartheta$ *up to a non-zero multiplicative constant* $c(\vartheta)$ *and up to sets of* μ_τ*-measure zero.*

Theorem 1 establishes that the sequential plan $\delta_0 = (\tau, D^*(\tau,\vartheta))$ with $D^*(\tau,\vartheta) = \partial \log L(\tau,\vartheta)$ $/\partial\vartheta$ satisfies (1), and consequently that the maximum likelihood sequential estimation plan is optimum.

Optimum Estimating Equation Plans in the Nuisance Parameter Case

Assume now that $\vartheta = (\vartheta_1, \vartheta_2) \in \Theta = \Theta_1 \times \Theta_2$, Θ_1, Θ_2 being both real open intervals, where $\vartheta_1 \in \Theta_1$ is the parameter of interest, and $\vartheta_2 \in \Theta_2$ is the nuisance parameter.

The estimating equation plans, for ϑ_1, of the form $\delta = (\tau, D(\tau,\vartheta_1))$ will be considered, where τ is a stopping time relative to $\mathcal{F}_t, t \ge 0$, such that $P_\vartheta(\tau < \infty) = 1$ for each $\vartheta \in \Theta$, and $D(\tau,\vartheta_1) = D(Y(\tau),\tau,\vartheta_1)$ is the estimating function. The parameter ϑ_1 is estimated through the estimating equation $D(\tau,\vartheta_1) = 0$. It is assumed that $E_\vartheta D(\tau,\vartheta_1) = 0$ for all $\vartheta \in \Theta$ and that L and D satisfy appropriate regularity conditions. The class of all regular estimating sequential plans for ϑ_1 will be denoted by $\mathcal{D}_1$.

Definition 2. *A sequential plan* $\delta^* = (\tau, D^*(\tau,\vartheta_1)) \in \mathcal{D}_1$ *is said to be optimum if*

$$E_\vartheta \left\{D^*(\tau,\vartheta_1)/E_\vartheta\left[\partial D^*(\tau,\vartheta_1)/\partial\vartheta_1\right]\right\}^2 \le E_\vartheta \left\{D(\tau,\vartheta_1)/E_\vartheta\left[\partial D(\tau,\vartheta_1)/\partial\vartheta_1\right]\right\}^2$$

for all $\delta = (\tau, D(\tau,\vartheta_1)) \in \mathcal{D}_1$ *and all* $\vartheta \in \Theta$.

The results in what follows generalize to the sequential case and to the general model for stochastic processes the respective results of Godambe and Thompson (1974), Godambe (1976) and Ferreira (1982).

Theorem 2. *If the estimating equation plans* $\delta_1^* = (\tau, D_1^*(\tau,\vartheta_1)) \in \mathcal{D}_1$ *and* $\delta_2^* = (\tau, D_2^*(\tau,\vartheta_1))$ $\in \mathcal{D}_1$ *are both optimum, then*

$$D_1^*(\tau,\vartheta_1)/E_\vartheta\left[\partial D_1^*(\tau,\vartheta_1)/\partial\vartheta_1\right] = D_2^*(\tau,\vartheta_1)/E_\vartheta\left[\partial D_2^*(\tau,\vartheta_1)/\partial\vartheta_1\right], \ \vartheta \in \Theta, \ \mu_\tau - a.s.$$

Theorem 3. *Suppose that the sequential plan* $\delta^* = (\tau, D^*(\tau,\vartheta_1)) \in \mathcal{D}_1$ *in which* $D^*(\tau,\vartheta_1)$ *is of the form*

$$D^*(\tau,\vartheta_1) = a(\vartheta)\partial \log L(\tau,\vartheta)/\partial\vartheta_1 + r(\tau,\vartheta),$$

where $r(\tau,\vartheta) = r(Y(\tau),\tau,\vartheta)$ *is real valued and* $\mathcal{F}_\tau$*-measurable for each* $\vartheta \in \Theta$, *satisfies the condition*

$$E_\vartheta\left[r(\tau,\vartheta)D(\tau,\vartheta_1)\right] = 0 \quad \text{for all} \quad \vartheta \in \Theta \quad \text{and} \quad \delta = (\tau, D(\tau,\vartheta_1)) \in \mathcal{D}_1. \tag{2}$$

Then the sequential plan δ^* *is optimum.*

Remark. Note that the choice $r(\tau,\vartheta) = c(\vartheta)\left\{[\partial \log L(\tau,\vartheta)/\partial\vartheta_2]^2 + \partial^2 \log L(\tau,\vartheta)/\partial\vartheta_2^2\right\}$, μ_τ-a.s., ensures (2) and the unbiasedness for $D^*(\tau,\vartheta_1)$.

Theorem 3 and Remark provide a method of constructing an optimum estimating function $D^*(\tau,\vartheta_1)$ and Theorem 2 guarantees uniqueness.

Suppose now that for a given stopping time τ there exists a statistic $U(\tau) = U(Y(\tau),\tau)$ with density function $h(U(\tau),\vartheta)$ and such that the likelihood fuction $L(Y(\tau),\tau,\vartheta)$ satisfies the following assumption: a conditional density function g_U of $(Y(\tau),\tau)$ given $U(\tau)$ depends on ϑ only through ϑ_1, that is, $L(Y(\tau),\tau,\vartheta)$ takes the form

$$L(Y(\tau),\tau,\vartheta) = g_U(Y(\tau),\tau,\vartheta_1)h(U(\tau),\vartheta).$$

Next, suppose that for each fixed ϑ_1, the regular sequential plan $\delta = (\tau, D(\tau,\vartheta_1))$ is complete in the sense that for each fixed $\vartheta_1 \in \Theta_1$ the family of distributions of $U(\tau)$ is complete.

Theorem 4. *For the complete sequential plans $\delta = (\tau, D(\tau,\vartheta_1)) \in \mathcal{D}_1$, the following inequality*

$$E_\vartheta\left\{D(\tau,\vartheta_1)/E_\vartheta\left[\partial D(\tau,\vartheta_1)/\partial\vartheta_1\right]\right\}^2 \geq 1/E_\vartheta\left[\partial \log g_U(\tau,\vartheta_1)/\partial\vartheta_1\right]^2$$

is valid for all $\vartheta \in \Theta$, the equality being attained when $D(\tau,\vartheta_1)$ is given by

$$D^*(\tau,\vartheta_1) = \partial \log g_U(\tau,\vartheta_1)/\partial\vartheta_1$$

up to a non-zero multiplicative constant $c(\vartheta_1)$ and up to sets of μ_τ-measure zero.

Under the stated conditions Theorem 4 justifies replacing the maximum likelihood equation $\partial \log L(\tau,\vartheta)/\partial\vartheta_1 = 0$ by the maximum conditional likelihood equation $\partial \log g_U(\tau,\vartheta)/\partial\vartheta_1 = 0$, in order to eliminate the influence of the nuisance parameter ϑ_2.

Some Special Models

The Ornstein-Uhlenbeck process. Let $X(t), t \geq 0$, be a stochastic process satisfying the following stochastic differential equation $dX(t) = \beta[\vartheta_1 - X(t)]dt + (2\beta\vartheta_2)^{1/2}dW(t)$, where $W(t), t \geq 0$, denotes the standard Wiener process, $\vartheta = (\vartheta_1,\vartheta_2) \in \Theta = (-\infty,\infty) \times (0,\infty)$ and $\beta > 0$ is a known value.

Suppose that $X(0) = x_0$ and let τ be a stopping time determining a regular estimating plan for ϑ_1 in the case when ϑ_2 is unknown. Then Theorem 3 may be applied with $a(\vartheta) = 2\vartheta_2$ and $r(\tau,\vartheta) \equiv 0$, obtaining the optimum estimating plan $(\tau, D^*(\tau,\vartheta_1))$ with

$$D^*(\tau,\vartheta_1) = X(\tau) - x_0 + \beta\int_0^\tau X(s)ds - \beta\vartheta_1\tau$$

and $\hat{\vartheta}_{1,\tau} = \left[X(\tau) - x_0 + \beta\int_0^\tau X(s)ds\right]/\beta\tau$. For example, the estimating equation plan $(\tau_a, D^*(\tau_a,\vartheta_1))$ with

$$\tau_a = \inf\left\{t \geq 0 : X^2(t) - x_0^2 + \beta\int_0^t X^2(s)ds = a\right\}, \quad a > 0,$$

is optimum for estimating the mean value parameter ϑ_1 when the covariance parameter ϑ_2 is an unknown nuisance parameter of the process considered.

Suppose now that $X(0) \sim \mathcal{N}(\vartheta_1,\vartheta_2)$. Let τ be a stopping time determining a regular estimating plan for ϑ_1 when ϑ_2 is unknown. In this case, applying Theorem 3 with $a(\vartheta) = \vartheta_2$ and $r(\tau,\vartheta) \equiv 0$ yields the optimum estimating plan $(\tau, D^*(\tau,\vartheta_1))$ with

$$D^*(\tau,\vartheta_1) = \frac{1}{2}\left(X(\tau) + X(0) + \beta\int_0^\tau X(s)ds\right) - \vartheta_1\left(1 + \frac{\beta}{2}\tau\right)$$

and $\hat{\vartheta}_{1,\tau} = \left[X(\tau) + X(0) + \beta \int_0^\tau X(s)ds\right]/(2+\beta\tau)$.

Nonhomogeneous Poisson process. Let $N(t), t \geq 0$, be a one-dimensional, nonhomogeneous Poisson process with intensity function $\lambda(t,\vartheta)$, $\vartheta = (\vartheta_1, \vartheta_2)$. Let us consider the inverse plan defined by $\tau_0 = \inf\{t \geq 0 : N(t) = n_0\}$, where $n_0 > 1$ is a given integer. Suppose that the intensity $\lambda(t,\vartheta)$ is of the form $\lambda(t,\vartheta) = \alpha(t,\vartheta_1)\beta(\vartheta_2)$. Then the likelihood function at the stopping time τ_0 can be written in the form

$$L(\tau_0,\vartheta) = g_{\tau_0}(t_1,\ldots,t_{n_0-1},\tau_0,\vartheta_1)h(\tau_0,\vartheta_1,\vartheta_2)$$

(t_i denotes the i-th jump time of the process), where for ϑ_1 fixed the family $h(\tau_0,\vartheta_1,\vartheta_2), \vartheta_2 \in \Theta_2$, of distributions of $U(\tau_0) \equiv \tau_0$ is complete. Using Theorem 4 yields the following form of the optimum sequential estimating function for estimating ϑ_1 when ϑ_2 is the nuisance parameter:

$$D^*(\tau_0,\vartheta_1) = \sum_{i=1}^{n_0-1} \frac{\partial\alpha(t_i,\vartheta_1)/\partial\vartheta_1}{\alpha(t_i,\vartheta_1)} - (n_0-1)\frac{\int_0^{\tau_0}(\partial\alpha(s,\vartheta_1)/\partial\vartheta_1)ds}{\int_0^{\tau_0}\alpha(s,\vartheta_1)ds}. \tag{3}$$

In particular, for the Pareto process, $\alpha(t,\vartheta_1) = \vartheta_1/(1+\vartheta_1 t)$, $\beta(\vartheta_2) = \exp(\vartheta_2)$, $\vartheta_1 > 0$, $-\infty < \vartheta_2 < \infty$, equation (3) yields the optimum sequential estimating equation

$$D^*(\tau_0,\vartheta_1) = \sum_{i=1}^{n_0-1} \frac{1}{\vartheta_1(1+\vartheta_1 t_i)} - \frac{(n_0-1)\tau_0}{(1+\vartheta_1\tau_0)\log(1+\vartheta_1\tau_0)} = 0.$$

For the Weibull process, $\alpha(t,\vartheta_1) = \vartheta_1 t^{\vartheta_1 - 1}, \beta(\vartheta_2) = \exp(\vartheta_2)$, $\vartheta_1 > 0$, $-\infty < \vartheta_2 < \infty$, one obtains

$$D^*(\tau_0,\vartheta_1) = (n_0-1)\left(\frac{1}{\vartheta_1} - \log\tau_0\right) + \sum_{i=1}^{n_0-1}\log t_i,$$

$$\hat{\vartheta}_{1,\tau_0} = \frac{n_0-1}{\sum_{i=1}^{n_0-1}\log\frac{\tau_0}{t_i}}.$$

References

Ferreira PE (1982) Sequential estimation through estimating equations in the nuisance parameter case. *Ann Statist* 10: 167-173.

Godambe VP (1960) An optimum property of regular maximum likelihood estimation. *Ann Math Statist* 31: 1208-1212.

Godambe VP (1976) Conditional likelihood and unconditional optimum estimating functions. *Biometrika* 63: 277-284.

Godambe VP, Thompson ME (1974) Estimating equations in the presence of a nuisance parameter. *Ann Statist* 2: 568-574.

INFLATION AND CREDIT MARKET SHOCKS: A SIGNAL EXTRACTION PROBLEM

Kent Matthews
Liverpool Business School
98 Mount Pleasant
Liverpool, L3 5UZ, UK

Chris Ioannidis
Cardiff Business School
Colum Drive
Cardiff, CF1 3EU, UK

When credit markets are regulated by quantitative controls, shocks to this market have no implications for the rate of interest. An excess demand for credit is not reflected in the movements of the interest rate. Movements in the interest rate will solely reflect the state of liquidity preference and changes in monetary policy. When credit markets are deregulated, interest rates will respond to credit market disequilibrium. If information about the shocks are known only with a lag but interest rates are part of the current observed information set, agents face a signal extraction problem in identifying whether a movement in the rate of interest is due to a credit or monetary shock. The effect of either shock on output and the price level will depend on agents' perception of the source of the shock. This argument is demonstrated with the aid of a stylized model.

THEORETICAL MODEL

The model consists of a money market, a credit market and a surprise supply function. Expectations are rational and all variables are in logarithms except for the rate of interest which is fractional. The model is specified below with the variables taking on conventional definitions.

$M^d = P - \alpha R + Y$	demand for money
$M^s = M^* + \epsilon$	supply of money
$L^d = P + EY - \beta(R - EP_{+1} + EP) + u$	demand for credit

$D^d = P + Y + \delta R$ demand for deposits

$Y = Y^* + \mu(P-EP)$ supply of output

where u and ϵ are stochastic terms with known variances $\sigma^2(u)$ and $\sigma^2(\epsilon)$. The stochastic terms are not observed at the time expectations are formed but the rate of interest is. The demand for deposits acts as the supply of loans to the banking sector. The solution for the rate of interest is given in general terms as; $R = Au + B\epsilon$, where A and B are undetermined coefficients. For an explanation of the solution method see Minford and Peel (1983). The expected rate of interest is given by $ER = [1/\Omega]Eu + [\alpha\beta/\Omega]E\epsilon$ where $\Omega = (\alpha\beta+\delta+\beta)$ and following Graybill (1961) the expected values of u and ϵ are given by; $Eu = \phi_u(Au+B\epsilon)/A$ and $E\epsilon = \phi_\epsilon(Au+B\epsilon)/B$, where $\phi_u = A^2\sigma 2(u)/X$, $\phi_\epsilon = B^2\sigma^2(\epsilon)/X$ and $X = A^2\sigma^2(u)+B^2\sigma^2(\epsilon)$. If monetary shocks dominate, then $\phi_\epsilon \rightarrow 1$ and $\phi_u \rightarrow 0$, if credit shocks dominate, $\phi_\epsilon \rightarrow 0$ and $\phi_u \rightarrow 1$. The response of the model to shocks from either market will depend on the past history of shocks. Hence if monetary shocks dominated the past, a credit shock could be misinterpreted as a money shock and vice versa. A table of responses ares detailed below. The table of responses indicates that the effect of a credit shock on P and Y will depend on whether the recent past was dominated by one type of shock or the other.

<u>Response to shocks</u>

	u	ϵ
P	$(1/\Omega)\phi_u-\phi_\epsilon$	$\phi_\epsilon+(1-(1/\Omega)\mu)\phi_u/(1+\mu)$
Y	ϕ_ϵ	$[\mu/(1+\mu)]\phi_u$

If the history of credit and monetary shocks alter, the responses of prices and output to the shocks will also alter. The evolution of these responses are captured by Kalman filter estimation - see Athans (1974) for a discussion.

ECONOMETRIC RESULTS

The econometric results consists of two semi-reduced form models of the inflation and output growth process for the UK between 1971:1 and 1990:1. The inflation equation is a dynamic ECM specification where the error-correction term is a unique cointegrating vector consisting of inflation, the rate of growth of base money, output growth and a constant term [D_4P, D_4M, D_4Y, c] -> [1, -.998, 1.80, 0.67], see Matthews and Ioannidis (1992), where D is the difference operator ($D_4x=x_t-x_{t-4}$). Inflation is defined as the annual rate of change of the GDP deflator, money is monetary base, credit is bank and building society lending and output is GDP expenditure at factor cost in 1985 prices. In general functional form;

$$D_1D_4P = f(D_1D_4P_{-4}, D_1D4Y_{-8}, D_1D_4M_{-8}, D_4C_{-8}, D_4C_{-9}, RES_{-4})$$

$$D_1D_4Y = g(D_1D_4Y_{-4}, D_1D_4Y_{-6}, D_1D_4M_{-3}, D_1D_4M_{-4}, D_1D_4C_{-1}, D_1D_4C_{-2})$$

The evolution of the credit parameters were obtained from Kalman filter estimation. The sum of the two credit coefficients in both the inflation and growth equations are charted in charts 1 and 2 for the 1980s. The 1980s were a period of strong deregulation of financial institutions and credit markets. Quantitative controls on bank deposit creating activity was abolished in June 1980, in 1982 hire purchase controls were lifted and throughout the first half of the 80s, the banks began to compete aggressively in the mortgage market. The charts show that inflation and growth responses to credit shocks are consistent with monetary shocks dominating the first half of the 80s (Thatcher's tight monetary policy) and credit shocks dominated the second half (the Lawson boom).

CONCLUSION

Inflation and output growth have been shown to be influenced by both monetary and credit shocks. Its effects depend on agent's evaluation of the signal extraction problem. This finding has implications for the transmission mechanism and anti-inflationary central bank policy.

Chart 1

Inflation-Credit Coefficients

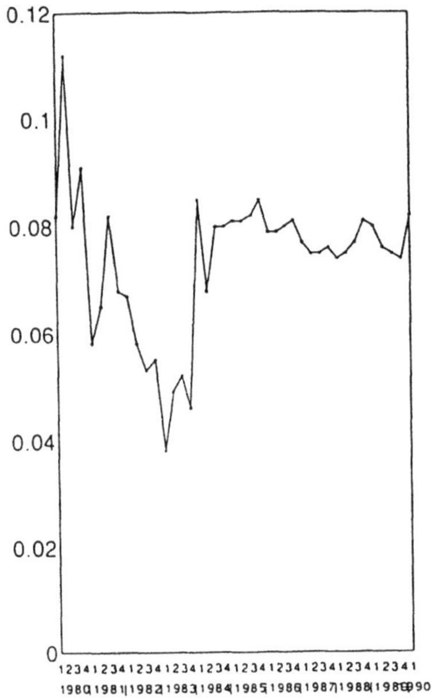

Chart 2

Output-Credit Coefficients

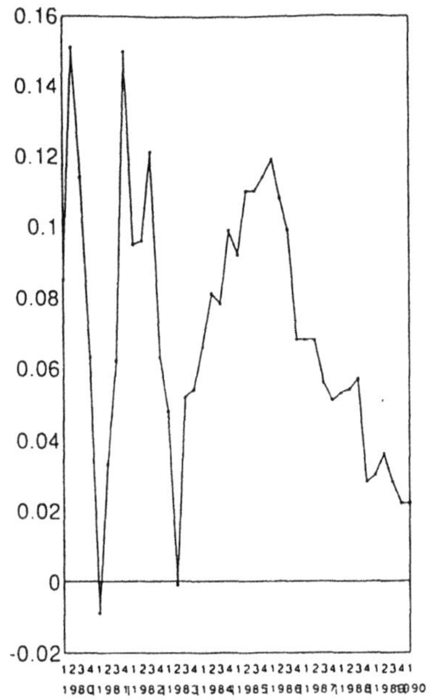

REFERENCES

Athans M (1974), "The Importance of Kalman Filtering Methods for Economic Systems", Annals of Economic and Social Measurement, 3/1

Graybill F A (1961), An Introduction to Linear Stochastic Models, Vol 1, New York: McGraw-Hill

Matthews K and Ioannidis C (1992), "Inflation: Too Much Money or Too Much Credit?", Cardiff Business School Discussion Paper series in Financial and Banking Economics, FABER/92/1/2/A.

Minford P and Peel D (1983), "Some Implications of Partial Current Information Sets in Macroeconomic Models Embodying Rational Expectations", Manchester School, Sept

THE GENERAL BUSINESS OPTIMIZATION MODEL

Ivan Meško
University of Maribor, Department of Economics
SLO-62000 Maribor, Razlagova 14, Slovenija

Tjaša Meško
University of Ljubljana, Department of Computer Science
SLO-61000 Ljubljana, Tržaška 25, Slovenija

Consider the optimization model of a business process including investment possibilities, production activities and market activities. At first we explain the decision variables and the constraints. For each activity we define a nonnegative decision variable representing the quantity of the activity. Some decision variables may be lower or upper bounded. For each investment possibility, a zero-one variable is defined. The investment should be realized if the optimal value of the zero-one variable is 1. For each element we construct a constraint to assure that the sum of the consumed and sold amount of the element is not greater than the sum of the purchased and produced amount. Here, the element is either a production element or a product.

A simple example is obtained if for each production activity the consumed quantities of the elements per unit of the production activity are known in advance. The consumed quantities can also be defined as the piecewise linear functions of decision variables [2]. If for some production activities the technological procedure must be determined by the optimization, the decision variables have to be defined in a different way. Such a phenomenon appears for example if in one phase of the production process the mixing problem arises. More decision variables are needed for a production activity if its product is a mixture. The quantity of such a production activity is defined as a sum of decision variables. The decision variable gives the quantity of the raw material consumed by the production of the mixture. We can assure the required quality of all mixtures by means of special constraints. The construction of those constraints is demonstrated on the example.

There are many possibilities for defining the objective function. If investment selection is included we can maximize the rate of return. In this case two programming problems need to be solved. The first one determines the optimal contribution without including the investment possibilities. In the second programming problem the objective function is a fraction. In the numerator we have the increase of the contribution caused by investments. Namely, from the income we subtract the variable cost, the semi fixed cost caused by investments, and the optimal objective function value of the first model. In the denominator are the invested means. If all constraints and the numerator are piecewise linear we obtain a fractional piecewise linear programming problem.

The fractional piecewise linear programming problem can be transformed into a linear mixed integer one and solved by available computer programs [4]. Using the Charnes-Cooper transformation [1], [3] we obtain a quadratic mixed integer programming problem where in addition to the linear terms, products of a zero-one variable by the new positive variable introduced by the Charnes-Cooper transformation arise. Such products can be replaced by linear terms [2], [3].

Since the general optimization model can hereby not be presented in detail, we will consider a simplified example from metallurgic industry. The market data is given in the table. For raw material B we have a supplier. The price is 6 monetary units per unit. At the most we may buy 20 units. Other market data in the table are analogous. The technological data is given by the figure. The figure is read according to the following example. One unit of ingots A is consumed while 0.8 units of sheets A and 0.2 units of cuttings A are produced per one unit of rolling A.

Table. Market activities and investments

	Element	Variable	Type	Price	Minimal	Maximal
E_1	Raw material A	y_1	Source	5		
E_2	Raw material B	y_2	Source	6		20
E_3	Foundry	y_{31}	Source			5
		y_{32}	Source			5
		u_{32}	Investment	1000		
E_6	Ingots B	z_6	Customer	7		
E_8	Sheets A	z_{81}	Customer	15	10	30
		z_{82}	Customer	15		10
		u_{82}	Investment	200		
E_9	Sheets B	z_9	Customer	12		5
		u_9	Investment	400		

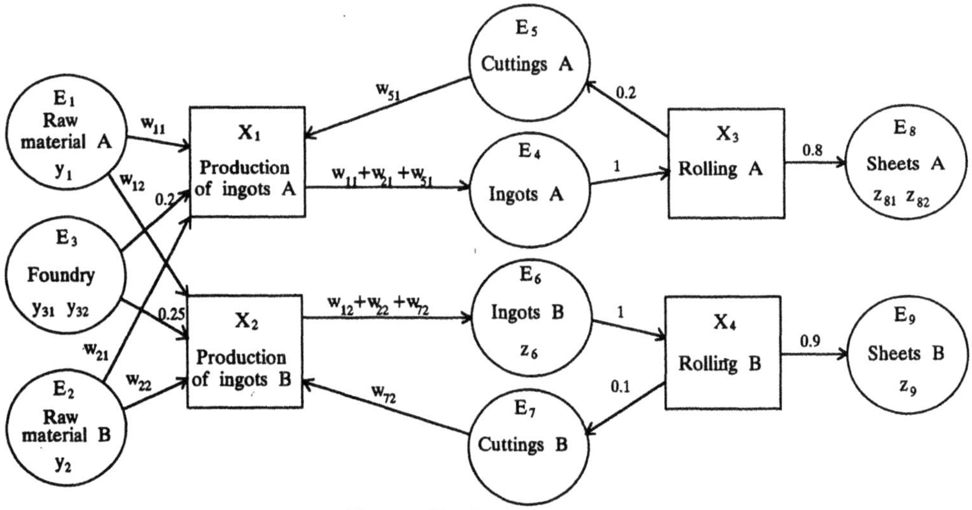

Figure. Production process

There are three investment possibilities. The semi fixed cost of each investment is 3% of the invested means. The foundry has a capacity of 5 units. By investing 1000 monetary units we obtain an additional capacity of 5 units. The upper bound of selling sheets A can be increased by 10 units if we invest 200 monetary units in the market research. In order to make the production activity rolling B operational, we have to invest 400 monetary units.

The optimal quantities of the raw materials consumed by the production of ingots have to be determined by the optimization. We have two kinds of raw materials together with cuttings at our disposal. The raw material A contains 98% of aluminium, 1% of silicium and 1% of the rest. The raw material B contains 80% of aluminium, 18.5% of silicium and 1.5% of the rest. Ingots A must contain 6.8% of silicum, no more than 1.2% of the rest, and aluminium. Ingots B must contain 3.5% of silicium, no more than 1.2% of the rest, and aluminium.

The optimization model is expressed as follows.

$$\text{maximize} \frac{7z_6 + 15z_{81} + 15z_{82} + 12z_9 - 5y_1 - 6y_2 - 30u_{32} - 6u_{82} - 12u_9 - f^*}{1000u_{32} + 200u_{82} + 400u_9}$$

subject to zero-one variables u_{32}, u_{82} and u_9, other variables are nonnegative, and

E1: $y_1 - w_{11} - w_{12} \geq 0$

E2: $y_2 - w_{21} - w_{22} \geq 0 \qquad y_2 \leq 20$

E3: $y_{31} + y_{32} - 0.2w_{11} - 0.2w_{21} - 0.2w_{51} - 0.25w_{12} - 0.25w_{22} - 0.25w_{72} \geq 0$

$y_{31} \leq 5 \qquad y_{32} \leq 5u_{32}$

E4: $w_{11} + w_{21} + w_{51} - x_3 \geq 0$

E5: $0.2x_3 - w_{51} \geq 0$

E6: $w_{12} + w_{22} + w_{72} - x_4 - z_6 \geq 0$

E7: $0.1x_4 - w_{72} \geq 0$

E8: $0.8x_3 - z_{81} - z_{82} \geq 0 \qquad 10 \leq z_{81} \leq 30 \qquad z_{82} \leq 10u_{82}$

E9: $0.9x_4 - z_9 \geq 0 \qquad z_9 \leq 5u_9$

SiA: $0.01w_{11} + 0.185w_{21} = 0.068(w_{11} + w_{21})$

SiB: $0.01w_{12} + 0.185w_{22} = 0.035(w_{12} + w_{22})$

RestA: $0.01w_{11} + 0.015w_{21} \leq 0.012(w_{11} + w_{21})$

RestB: $0.01w_{12} + 0.015w_{22} \leq 0.012(w_{12} + w_{22})$

Here, $f^* = 193.371$ is the maximal value of the function

$$f = 7z_6 + 15z_{81} - 5y_1 - 6y_2$$

subject to the same constraints and $u_{32}=u_{82}=u_9=0$.

This programming problem can be transformed into a linear mixed integer programming problem. The Charnes-Cooper transformation is used with $W_j=w_jt$, $X_j=x_jt$, $Y_j=y_jt$ and $Z_j=z_jt$, where t is the new positive variable. After the substitution of quadratic terms we obtain the following programming problem.

$$\text{maximize } 7Z_6 + 15Z_{81} + 15Z_{82} + 12Z_9 - 5Y_1 - 6Y_2 - 30r_{32} - 6r_{82} - 12r_9 - 193.371t$$

subject to the nonnegative variables, and

$u_{32} = 0 \text{ or } 1$ $\quad u_{82} = 0 \text{ or } 1$ $\quad u_9 = 0 \text{ or } 1$

$Y_1 - W_{11} - W_{12} \geq 0$ $\quad Y_2 - W_{21} - W_{22} \geq 0$ $\quad Y_2 - 20t \leq 0$

$Y_{31} + Y_{32} - 0.2W_{11} - 0.2W_{21} - 0.2W_{51} - 0.25W_{12} - 0.25W_{22} - 0.25W_{72} \geq 0$

$Y_{31} - 5t \leq 0$ $\quad Y_{32} - 5r_{32} \leq 0$

$W_{11} + W_{21} + W_{51} - X_3 \geq 0$ $\quad 0.2X_3 - W_{51} \geq 0$

$W_{12} + W_{22} + W_{72} - X_4 - Z_6 \geq 0$ $\quad 0.1X_4 - W_{72} \geq 0$ $\quad 0.8X_3 - Z_{81} - Z_{82} \geq 0$

$Z_{81} - 10t \geq 0$ $\quad Z_{81} - 30t \leq 0$ $\quad Z_{82} - 10r_{82} \leq 0$

$0.9X_4 - Z_9 \geq 0$ $\quad Z_9 - 5r_9 \leq 0$

$-0.058W_{11} + 0.117W_{21} = 0$ $\quad -0.025W_{12} + 0.15W_{22} = 0$

$-0.002W_{11} + 0.003W_{21} \leq 0$ $\quad -0.002W_{12} + 0.003W_{22} \leq 0$

$1000r_{32} + 200r_{82} + 400r_9 = 1$

$t - r_{32} - s_{32} = 0$ $\quad r_{32} - u_{32} \leq 0$ $\quad s_{32} + u_{32} \leq 1$

$t - r_{82} - s_{82} = 0$ $\quad r_{82} - u_{82} \leq 0$ $\quad s_{82} + u_{82} \leq 1$

$t - r_9 - s_9 = 0$ $\quad r_9 - u_9 \leq 0$ $\quad s_9 + u_9 \leq 1$

The optimal objective function value is 0.131. The contribution increase is 13.1% of the invested means. We should invest in the foundry and in the market research.

References

[1] Charnes, A and W. W. Cooper: Programming with Linear Fractional Functionals. Naval Research Logistic Quarterly, 6, 1962, 181-186.

[2] Meško, I.: Piecewise Linear Approximations in R^n. Operations Research Proceedings 1986, Springer-Verlag, Berlin-Heidelberg 1987, 618-625.

[3] Meško, I.: Fractional Piecewise Linear Optimization. Operations Research '91, Physica-Verlag, Heidelberg 1992, 611-612.

[4] Schrage, L.: LINDO, An Optimization Modeling System. The Scientific Press, Fourth edition, South San Francisco 1991.

TIME-SERIES FORECASTING BY PATTERN IMITATION - OUTLIERS

Barbara Motnikar, Tomaž Pisanski*
'Jožef Stefan' Institute, Jamova 39,
*University Ljubljana, Department of Mathematics and Mechanics, Jadranska 19
SLO–61111 Ljubljana, Slovenia

INTRODUCTION

We improve the *pattern-imitation* method for time-series forecasting presented in *Motnikar et al. (1992) and (1993)*. Given a univariate time-series $z_1, \ldots, z_n$, we defined its patterns $\vec{r}(t) \equiv (z_t, z_{t+1}, \ldots, z_{t+s-1})$ as vectors of s consecutive observations starting at time t, where $1 \leq t \leq n - s + 1$ and s is the pattern length. Using a certain similarity measure, we chose set $S = \{\vec{r}(t_1), \ldots, \vec{r}(t_k)\}$ of patterns sufficiently similar to the prototype pattern (denoted by $\vec{p}$), that is the last pattern before the forecast origin. We estimated a future value z_{n+l}, which is l time-steps ahead of the forecast origin n, by a linear combination of the observations following the k patterns from S, where weights w_j are determined according to the similarity between patterns $\vec{r}(t_j)$ and $\vec{p}$ ($\vec{p} \equiv \vec{r}(n - s + 1)$):

$$\hat{z}_n(l) \equiv z_n + \sum_{j=1}^{k} w_j(z_{t_j+s-1+l} - z_{t_j+s-1}) \,. \tag{1}$$

An observation z_t that is unusually large or small relative to the other values in a given stationary time-series is called an *outlier*. To define an outlier of a non-stationary time-series, we have to take into account non-stationary characteristics: trend, season, nonconstant variance and cycle. For more about time-series analysis, see *Box, Jenkins (1970)*. Typically, outliers are of two types:
(i) The measurement is observed, recorded, or entered into the computer incorrectly. This type of outlier does not influence any other observations. It is called a *Type I* outlier (additive outlier).
(ii) The measurement is correct, but represents a rare (chance) event. Usually, this type of outlier influences few subsequent observations. It is called a *Type II* outlier (innovational outlier); see *Sincich, 1991.*

If a time-series contains outliers, forecasts may be contaminated. In this paper, we discuss how Type I outliers influence time-series analysis by pattern-imitation depending on the outliers' positions in the data set and present an approach for their detection and handling.

ANALYSIS OF TIME-SERIES WITH OUTLIERS

The standard approach to outlier detection is based on the distribution function of time-series observations (e.g., *Schmid, 1990*). Since in the pattern-imitation method there are no statistical assumptions about the distribution function, we have to use a descriptive approach. We detect outliers (i) by eye; or (ii) by z-score (observations that do not fall within 3 standard deviations of the time-series mean); or (iii) by a leave-one-out (LOO) test in the position of an extreme one-step-ahead forecast error. Let us review how outliers may cause difficulties in the three phases of time-series analysis.

1. *Estimation of the model parameters.* Model parameters are estimated automatically using a cross-validation technique. Estimates are robust; they are not very sensitive to single observations. However, after elimination of outliers, more accurate values of the parameters may be obtained.

2. *Fit-quality test.* Some time-series observations are chosen as a *validation set* and are not used as input data. We estimate them by one-step-ahead forecasts and calculate their mean absolute error (MAE); this represents fit-quality. Outliers in the validation set yield an incorrect estimate of fit-quality.

3. *Forecasting future values* z_{n+l}. A time-series with outliers produces a different linear combination (1) than a time-series without outliers. The difference between them strongly depends on the outliers' positions in the data set.

   a) An outlier *in the prototype pattern* $\vec{p}$ prevents us from finding an appropriate set S.

   b) Outlier $z_{t_j+s-1+l}$ infects one component of (1). (It follows a pattern $\vec{r}(t_j) \in S$.)

   c) An outlier that eliminates a pattern from the set S reduces (1) by one component. (It changes a similar pattern to a dissimilar one.)

   d) (1) is not changed when the outlier is in a pattern or follows a pattern that is outside S.

   e) We cannot do anything with outliers *in the prediction set.* They may lead to large forecast errors.

HOW TO HANDLE OUTLIERS

Since not all outliers contaminate forecasts, we should decide whether to
(i) replace an outlier with a resonable value (e.g., obtained by a one-step-ahead forecast): this is necessary in phase 3.a and recommended in phase 3.c; or

(ii) consider an outlier as a missing observation: this is necessary in phase 2 and recommended in phase 1 and 3.b; or

(iii) do nothing: phases 3.d and 3.e.

We present a forecasting algorithm that considers outliers. The corresponding phases are written in parenthesis.

1: Estimate the model parameters by standard procedure ignoring outliers (1).

2: Using a LOO test, detect suspect outliers and denote them as missing observations. Ignoring these observations, re-estimate the model parameters.

3: Ignoring missing observations, evaluate the fit-quality test (2).

4: If the prototype pattern contains a missing value, replace it with a reasonable value (3.a).

5: Compare all patterns $\vec{r}(t)$ with prototype pattern $\vec{p}$. When a pattern $\vec{r}(t)$ with a missing observation seems similar, replace the outlier with a reasonable value. Find the set S of similar patterns (3.c).

6: Calculate forecasts $\hat{z}_n(l)$ of future values. If observation $z_{t_j+s-1+l}$ is missing, eliminate the pattern $\vec{r}(t_j)$ from the set S or replace the outlier with a reasonable value (3.b).

AN EXAMPLE

Let us consider the time-series 'Sunspot numbers'. Its analysis by the pattern-imitation method is described by *Motnikar et al. (1993)*. In the forecasting of further 15 observations beyond the origin 206, set S contains the following 11 patterns: $\vec{r}(44)$, $\vec{r}(178)$, $\vec{r}(13)$, $\vec{r}(55)$, $\vec{r}(1)$, $\vec{r}(124)$, $\vec{r}(32)$, $\vec{r}(123)$, $\vec{r}(54)$, $\vec{r}(98)$, $\vec{r}(112)$, which are ordered by similarity. Now, we reanalyse the time-series that contains two outliers: observations z_{55} and z_{90} are set to equal 1.0. Outlier z_{90} does not influence forecasts, while outlier z_{55} affects forecasts in two ways: (i) forecasts of all future values are little spoiled in phase 3.c (patterns $\vec{r}(55)$ and $\vec{r}(54)$ are eliminated from S), and (ii) forecast $\hat{z}_{206}(6)$ of z_{212} is greatly influenced in phase 3.b (the outlier follows the most similar pattern $\vec{r}(44)$). In Table 1, we compare $\hat{z}_{206}(6)$ and the MAE of forecasts, using four values of observation z_{55}: (1) original value 0.0638, (2) outlier value 1.0, (3) forecasted value $\hat{z}_{54}(1) = 0.0107$ and (4) missing value. The original value of forecasted observation z_{212} equals 0.0298.

In comparison with a time-series without outliers, forecasts of future values are greatly affected by one outlier and unaffected by another. When a destructive outlier is treated as a missing observation, forecasts are little affected and when it is properly replaced, forecasts are almost unaffected.

value of z_{55}:	original 0,0638	outlier 1.0000	forecasted 0.0107	missing
$\hat{z}_{206}(6)$:	0.090	0.255	0.088	0.092
MAE:	0.084	0.088	0.084	0.091

Table 1: Consideration of outlier's influence to the forecasts.

CONCLUSION

The majority of time-series methods use all observations to create a forecasting model. As a result, forecasts are contaminated unless we replace all outliers. However, in the pattern-imitation method, not all outliers influence forecasts. We presented different influences depending on the outliers' positions in the data set and suggested an algorithm that handles outliers. We estimate that in only 10% of positions outliers have significant impact on the forecasts of future values.

Acknowledgement. We thank Mr. Wolfgang Schmid, Ms. Regina Elsebach and Mr. Drago Čepar for their helpful discussion.

REFERENCES

Box G., Jenkins G. (1970), Time Series Analysis: Forecasting and Control, *Holden-Day, San Francisco.*

B. Motnikar, D. Čepar, P. Žunko, M. Ribarič, B. Vovk (1992), 'Time Series Forecasting by Imitation of Preceding Patterns', *Operations Research '91, Extended Abstracts of the 16th SOR (Trier, 1991); p. 272 - 275, Physica-Verlag, Springer-Verlag Company, Heidelberg.*

B. Motnikar, D. Čepar, P. Žunko, M. Ribarič (1993), 'Time Series Forecasting by Pattern Imitation - further development', *Operations Research '92, Extended Abstracts of the 17th SOR (Hamburg, 1992); p. 375-378, Physica-Verlag, Springer-Verlag Company, Heidelberg.*

Schmid W., (1990), 'Discussion of a LR Test for Detecting Outliers in Time Series Data', *Statistics & Decisions 8, p. 271-294, R. Oldenbourg Verlag, München.*

Sincich T., (1991), 'A Course in Modern Business Statistics', *Dellen Publ. Comp., San Francisco.*

Periodic networks and railway scheduling

Karl Nachtigall
Institut für Mathematik, Universität Hildesheim
Marienburger Platz 22, D-31141 Hildesheim

Consider a railway network where all trains arrive and depart regularly. We discuss the task to find a timetable which minimizes network caused waiting times for passengers changing lines. A usual approach in the railway literature is to minimize a weighted sum of waiting times arising at a selected class of change opportunities.

For the case that we only view to one station this problem is an application of the following periodic scheduling model investigated by *P. Brucker; R.E. Burkhard* and *J. Hurnik* (see [1, 2, 3]) : "How should a finite number of polygons with vertices on some circle be arranged such that some criterion function depending on the distances between adjacent vertices is minimized ?"

In order to find optimal timetables for a network with a lot of different stations we combine ideas with the concept of periodic networks. The basic ideas of this model are due to *P. Serafini* and *W. Ukovich* [7], who present a framework to find feasible schedules with respect to given time constraints.

The waiting time optimization task is formulated as a "periodic program". The decomposition of such a problem into a finite number of ordinary linear programming problems allows to develop a branch and bound method.

1 Minimizing waiting times in railway networks

Consider a periodic served railway network given by a system $\mathcal{L} := \{L_1, ..., L_n\}$ of n lines. By a line we will understand a transportation service where all trains of this line passes a certain sequence of stations with fixed interval timetable. For simplicity we assume that all lines are served with one common interval time or period τ and that the running- and stopping times of all trains addressed to L_i are fixed. Thus, scheduling line L_i is completely done by fixing one departure at the initial station to a point of time π_i. If we assume a periodic behavior with infinite horizon, then at all times $\pi_i + z\tau$ ($z \in \mathbb{Z}$) one train of line L_i will start its journey. z is said to be the number of this train.

If trains associated with different lines (say L_1 and L_2) serve the same station S, then passengers can change. By d_i (i=1,2) we denote the fixed amount of time which all trains of line L_i take to reach station S from its initial stations. s_2 indicates the duration of the stop in S of all trains addressed to L_2 and δ is the least amount of time a passenger needs to change platforms. Now, a passenger arriving with a train of line L_1 numbered by p can get the next train of L_2 leaving after $t_p := \pi_1 + d_1 + \delta + p\tau$. Hence, the waiting time is given by

$$w_{12}^S := \min_z \{\pi_2 + d_2 + s_2 + z\tau - t_p \mid \pi_2 + d_2 + s_2 + z\tau \geq t_p\}$$

In order to have more short expression we use the real function $[\,\cdot\,]_\tau : \mathbb{R} \to [0, \tau[$; $t \mapsto \min_{z \in \mathbb{Z}} \{t + z\tau \mid t + z\tau \geq 0\}$. The abbreviation $a_{12} := d_2 + s_2 - d_1 - \delta$ yields $w_{12}^S = [\pi_2 - \pi_1 - a_{12}]_\tau$. With corresponding notations, the waiting time of an arbitrary transfer possibility $(S, L_i \to L_j)$ (= changing from L_i to L_j in station S) can be calculated as

$$w_{ij}^S = [\pi_j - \pi_i - a_{ij}^S]_\tau \tag{1}$$

where a_{ij}^S is a fixed given time difference depending on the running- and stopping-times of L_i and L_j.

Now, assume that the timetable designer has selected a class $\mathcal{C}$ of transfer possibilities $c_{ij}^S := (S, L_i \rightarrow L_j)$, which are weighted with a measure ω_{ij}^S for the number of passengers who change in S from L_i to L_j. This leads to the optimization task $\sum_{c_{ij}^S \in \mathcal{C}} \omega_{ij}^S [\pi_j - \pi_i - a_{ij}^S]_\tau \rightarrow min.$

This periodic program becomes more transparent by the following graph theoretical interpretation: With every line L_i we associate a vertex i representing the event *"depart at the initial station"*, and any transfer opportunity c_{ij}^S is described by a directed edge $e = (i,j)$ linking i and j. Furthermore this edge is associated with the weight $\omega_e := \omega_{ij}^S$ and the running time difference $a_e := a_{ij}^S$. The resulting graph with vertex set V and edge set E is denoted by $\mathcal{N} = (V, E, (a_e, \omega_e)_{e \in E})$ and is said to be the change network.

If we have fixed a directed spanning tree T of $\mathcal{N}$, then every non-tree arc $a = (u,v)$ generates a unique determined directed path p_a from node u to node v in T. The network matrix with respect to this tree is defined by $\Gamma = [E, N]$, where E denotes the $k \times k$ unit matrix and the $k \times (m-k)$ matrix $N = (\gamma_{ab})$ is given by $\gamma_{ab} = \pm 1$, if p_a contains arc b in positive, negative orientation, respectively. $\gamma_{ab} = 0$, if b is not contained in p_a. k is said the cyclomatic number of $\mathcal{N}$.

Instead of the potential $\vec{\pi}$ we may use the resulting tension $\vec{x} := (\pi_j - \pi_i)_{e=(i,j)} \in \mathbf{R}^m$. Every tension is characterized by $\Gamma \vec{x} = \vec{0}$. This leads to the problem $\sum_{e \in E} \omega_e [x_e - a_e]_\tau \rightarrow min$ subject to $\Gamma \vec{x} = \vec{0}$. Substituting $x_e \rightarrow x_e - a_e$ yields with $\vec{b} := -\Gamma \vec{a}$ the problem $\sum_{e \in E} \omega_e [x_e]_\tau \rightarrow min$ subject to $\Gamma \vec{x} = \vec{b}$. As turned out in [5], we will get a similar, more general optimization model, if the periods of the lines are different. In that case for every transfer possibility c_{ij}^S the common period τ has to be replaced by the greatest common divisor $\tau_e := \gcd(\tau_i, \tau_j)$ of the periods τ_i, τ_j addressed to the lines L_i and L_j. This yields the "periodic program"

$$\sum_{e \in E} \omega_e [x_e]_{\tau_e} \rightarrow min \quad s.t. \quad \Gamma \vec{x} = \vec{b} \tag{2}$$

2 Local regions of a periodic program

The structure of periodic programming problem is illustrated by the following figure

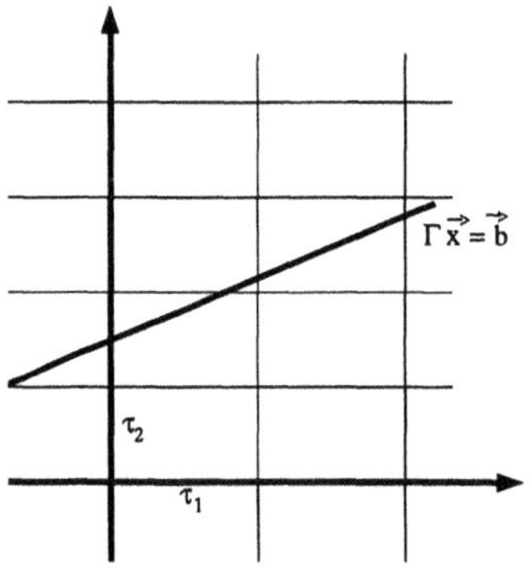

The objective f is a noncontinuous function which is periodic with respect to $\vec{\tau} = (\tau_e)$, i.e. $f(\vec{x} + \vec{\tau}) = f(\vec{x})$. For every box generated by

$$z_e \tau_e \leq x_e < (z_e + 1)\tau_e \ (e = 1, .., m)$$

the objective f is a linear mapping. Thus, periodic programming is a nonconvex optimization problem which splits into an infinite number of local regions each representing a usual linear program.

For an integral matrix Γ we denote by $[\mathrm{H}, \mathbf{0}]$ the Hermite normal form of $\Gamma \begin{pmatrix} \tau_1 & & 0 \\ & \ddots & \\ 0 & & \tau_m \end{pmatrix}$.
H is a nonsingular, lower triangular matrix, in which each row has unique maximum entry, which is located on the main diagonal of B (see [6]). By $\Gamma^+, \Gamma^- \geq \mathbf{0}$ we denote the positive and negative part of Γ, respectively. Then the set $\mathcal{Z} := \left\{\vec{z} \mid -\Gamma^-\vec{\tau} - \vec{b} \leq \mathrm{H}\vec{z} \leq \Gamma^+\vec{\tau} - \vec{b}\right\}$ is finite.

Note, that the Hermite normal form as well as the set $\mathcal{Z}$ are depending on the initial spanning tree which gives the network matrix Γ.

2.1 Theorem Every linear periodic program $\sum_{i=1}^{n} \omega_i [x_i]_{\tau_i} \to min \quad s.t. \;\; \Gamma\vec{x} = \vec{b}$ with integral data $\Gamma, \vec{b}$ and nonnegative weights $\omega_i \geq 0$ is solvable, iff $\Gamma\vec{x} = \vec{b}$ at least has one solution. In that case the solution can be solved by

$$\min_{\vec{z} \in \mathcal{Z}} \left\{\vec{\omega}\vec{x} \mid \Gamma\vec{x} = \vec{b} + \mathrm{H}\vec{z};\; \vec{0} \leq \vec{x} \leq \vec{\tau}\right\} \tag{3}$$

3 A branch and bound approach

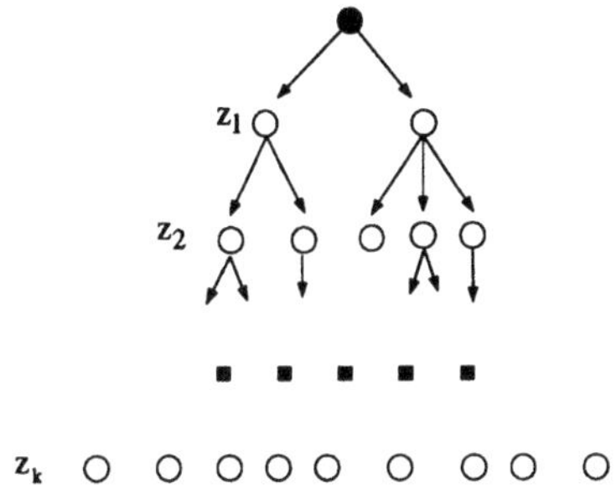

The set $\mathcal{Z}$ can be described by an arborescence of depth k (= cyclomatic number of the change network). Every path from the root to a final vertex on level k represents a feasible vector $\vec{z} \in \mathcal{Z}$. This representation indicates the use of a branch and bound (b&b) procedure. For every vertex v of this arborescence at level j we associate that problem of (3), where the first j components of $\vec{z}$ are fixed to the values of the path leading to v.

Real relaxation of the remaining components yields the lower bound :

$$S^{lower}(v) := \min \left\{\vec{\omega}\vec{x} \mid \Gamma_j\vec{x} = \vec{b}_j + \mathrm{H}_j\vec{z}_j;\; \vec{0} \leq \vec{x} \leq \vec{\tau}\right\} \tag{4}$$

where Γ_j, H_j and $\vec{z}_j$ arise by cancelling the last $k - j$ rows. For the network matrix Γ this is a problem of tension with minimum cost, which can be derived as the dual of a minimum cost flow problem (see e.g. [4]). For practical implementation of the b&b method we seperate always the vertex v with smallest evaluation $S^{lower}(v)$ which means a breadth first search.

4 Computational results

In order to test this b&b method, we used randomly generated networks. A connected network with n nodes and cyclomatic number $k \geq 1$ represents the situation to have n different railway lines and take $m := n + k - 1$ different changing possibilities into consideration for optimization. The computational experiments have indicated that instances with $k \leq 15$ can be solved with acceptable time complexity. The following graphic reports averages CPU-times depending on the cyclomatic number ranged from 5 to 15 for instances with $n = 20, 40$ and $n = 80$ nodes

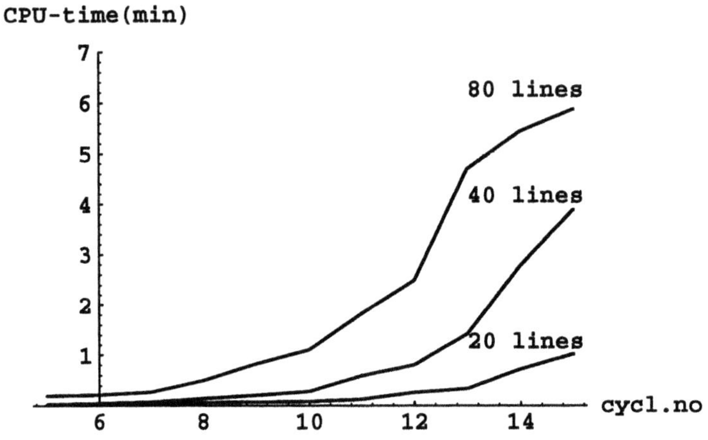

References

[1] P. Brucker, R. Burkard, and J. Hurink, *Cyclic schedules for r irregularly occuring events*, Journal of Computational and Applied Mathematics, 30 (1990), pp. 173–189.

[2] P. Brucker and J. Hurink, *A railway scheduling problem*, Zeitschrift für Operations Research, (1986), pp. A 223–A 227.

[3] R. E. Burkard, *Optimal schedules for periodically recurring events*, Discrete Applied Mathematics, (1986), pp. 167–180.

[4] M. Gondran and M. Minoux, *Graphs and algorithms.*, J. Wiley & sons, 1984.

[5] K. Nachtigall, *Time periodic network optimization*, Hildesheimer Informatik-Berichte, 8/93 (1993).

[6] A. Schrijver, *Theory of linear and integer programming.*, J. Wiley&sons, Chichester New York Brisbane Toronto Singapore, 1986.

[7] P. Serafini and W. Ukovich, *A mathematical model for periodic scheduling problems*, SIAM J. Discrete Math., 2 (1989), pp. 550–581.

A note on two person full-information best choice problems with imperfect observation

P. Neumann Z. Porosiński† K. Szajowski†*

The paper deals with the following zero-sum game version of the full-information best choice problem. Two person observe sequentially a known number of *iid* random variables from a known continuous distribution with the object of choosing the largest. The random variables cannot be perfectly observed. Each time a random variable is sampled the sampler is informed only whether it is greater than or less than some level specified by him. Players can choose at most one observation. After each sampling players take a decision for acceptance or rejection of the observation. If both want to accept the same observation the priority is given to the specified player, say Player 1. The class of adequate strategies and the suitable gain function for the problem is constructed. It is shown that the game has solution in *pure strategies*. The numerical examples are given. The random number of observations is also investigated.

The priority game with imperfect observation

Let $X_1, X_2, \ldots, X_N$, $N \in \mathbb{N}$, $N \in \mathbb{N}$, be a sequence of *iid* random variables with common and known distribution defined on a probability space $(\Omega, \mathcal{F}, \mathbf{P})$. The sequence of random variables is sequentially sampled one by one by two decision makers (players). However the observations are imperfect and the exact realized values are not known. Players specify only their level of sensitivity (impressionability) and they are able to know whether the observed random variable is greater than or less than prescribed, chosen by himself, level. After X_n is observed Player 1 has to accept or reject the observation. If he rejects it then Player 2 has to decide if he rejects the observed realization. When some player accepts the observation at a moment n, then the another one will investigate the sequence of future realizations having opportunity to accept one of them. Neither recall nor uncertainty of selection is allowed. One can say that Player 1 has priority to accept the realization. The aim of the players is to choose *the best observation* (the maximal one). The problem is the generalization of the one player full-information best choice problem with imperfect observation. The review of the related problem and results one can find the papers by Sakaguchi (1984) and Porosiński (1991).

In this paper we admit that the problem is modelled by two person zero-sum game. The similar models for the no-information case have been considered e.g. by Szajowski (1993) and Enns &

* Inst. für Mathematische Stochastik, Tech. Univ. Dresden, Mommsenstrasse 13, D-O-8027 Dresden, Germany

† Institute of Mathematics, Technical Univ. of Wrocław, Wybrzeże Wyspiańskiego 27, PL-50-370 Wrocław, Poland

Ferenstein (1987). The structure of strategy sets and the form of the gain functions are different in these problems. Let $\mathcal{F}_n = \sigma\{X_1, X_2, \ldots, X_n\}$, $n = 1, 2, \ldots, N$ and $\mathcal{S}$ is the set of stopping times with respect to $\{\mathcal{F}_n\}_{n=1}^N$. Since the observations are imperfect we admit $\mathcal{S}_0 = \{\tau \in \mathcal{S} : \tau = \inf\{1 \leq n \leq N : X_n \geq x\}, x \in \Re\}$ as the class of adequate strategies for one person decision problem. We assume that the player have $\mathcal{S}_0$ as the sets of strategies and the above described priority of Player 1 will be involved in the gain function.

Let Player 1 and Player 2 choose $x \in \Re$ and $y \in \Re$, respectively. If $x < y$ and Player 1 accepts X_s then he gets $+1$ when $\{X_1 < x, \ldots, X_{s-1} < x, X_s \geq x, X_{s+1} < X_s, \ldots, X_N < X_s\}$, -1 when there is $t > s$ such that $\{X_1 < x, \ldots, X_{s-1} < x, X_s \geq x, X_{s+1} < y, \ldots, X_{t-1} < y, X_t > \max(X_s, y), X_{t+1} < X_t, \ldots, X_N < X_t\}$ and 0 otherwise. Let $x \geq y$. In this case if Player 1 accepts X_s then he gets $+1$ when $\{X_1 < y, \ldots, X_{s-1} < y, X_s \geq x, X_{s+1} < X_s, \ldots, X_N < X_s\}$ or there is $t > s$ such that $\{X_1 < y, \ldots, X_{s-1} < y, y \leq X_s < x, X_{s+1} < x, \ldots, X_{t-1} < x, X_t \geq x, X_{t+1} < X_t, \ldots, X_N < X_t\}$, -1 when there is $t > s$ such that $\{X_1 < y, \ldots, X_{s-1} < y, X_s \geq x, X_{s+1} < y, \ldots, X_{t-1} < y, X_t > X_s, X_{t+1} < X_t, \ldots, X_N < X_t\}$ or $\{X_1 < y, \ldots, X_{s-1} < y, y \leq X_s < x, X_{s+1} < X_s, \ldots, X_N < X_s\}$ and 0 otherwise. Taking into account the above consideration we can assume that the observed random variables have the uniform distribution and the set of strategies $\mathcal{S}_0$ is equivalent to the interval $[0, 1]$. It reduces the problem to the zero-sum game on the unit square. The payoff function is the expected value of the described gain of Player 1.

The finite horizon case

Let the horizon of observation be fixed. The payoff of Player 1 for $x < y$ has the form

$$\begin{aligned}
\text{(1a)} \qquad f_N(x,y) &= \sum_{s=1}^{N} x^{s-1} \int_x^1 x_s^{N-s}\,dx_s - \sum_{t=2}^{N}\sum_{s=1}^{t-1} x^{s-1} \left(\int_x^y y^{t-s-1}\,dx_s \int_y^1 x_t^{N-t}\,dx_t \right. \\
&\quad \left. + \int_y^1 y^{t-s-1}\,dx_s \int_{x_s}^1 x_t^{N-t}\,dx_t \right) = \sum_{i=1}^{N} \frac{x^{N-i} - x^N}{i} \\
&\quad - \sum_{j=1}^{N-1} \sum_{i=j+1}^{N} \frac{x^{N-i} y^{i-j-1}}{j} \left(1 - x - (y-x)y^j - \frac{1-y^{j+1}}{1+j} \right)
\end{aligned}$$

and for $x \geq y$

$$\begin{aligned}
\text{(1b)} \quad f_N(x,y) &= \sum_{s=1}^{N} y^{s-1} \int_x^1 x_s^{N-s}\,dx_s + \sum_{s=1}^{N-1} \sum_{t=s+1}^{N} y^{s-1} \int_y^x x^{t-s-1}\,dx_s \int_x^1 x_t^{N-t}\,dx_t \\
&\quad - \sum_{s=1}^{N} y^{s-1} \int_y^x x_s^{N-s}\,dx_s - \sum_{s=1}^{N-1} \sum_{t=s+1}^{N} y^{s-1} \int_x^1 y^{t-s-1}\,dx_s \int_{x_s}^1 x_t^{N-t}\,dx_t \\
&= \sum_{i=1}^{N} \frac{y^{N-i}}{i} (1 - 2x^i + y^i) \\
&\quad + \sum_{j=1}^{N-1} \sum_{i=j+1}^{N} \left(y^{N-i} x^{i-j-1} (x-y) \frac{1-x^j}{j} - \frac{y^{N-j-1}}{j} (1 - x - \frac{1-x^{j+1}}{j+1}) \right)
\end{aligned}$$

TABLE 1

The solution of the game with fixed horizon N and the priority for Player 1

N	x^*	y^*	Value
3	0.546	0.372	0.351
4	0.647	0.510	0.338
5	0.712	0.600	0.330
6	0.758	0.662	0.326
7	0.790	0.705	0.323
10	0.852	0.792	0.317

Proposition 1. *The payoff function of Player 1 in the full-information best choice problem two person zero-sum game with imperfect information, fixed horizon N and the priority for Player 1 is given by (1). The game has a solution (x^*, y^*) in the pure strategies.*

FIG. 1. *The payoff function for $N = 5$*

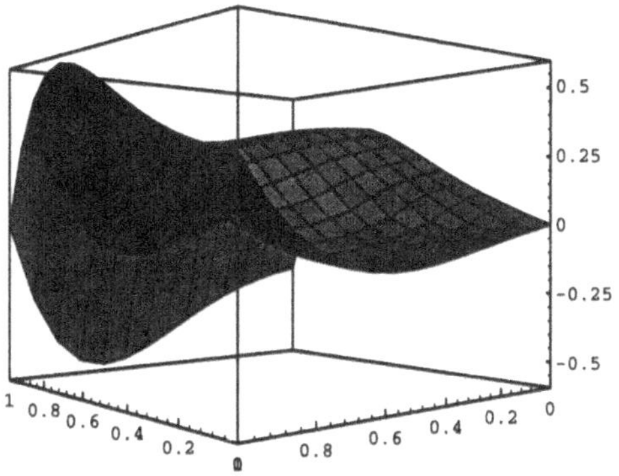

The examples of the equilibria for same horizon N are given in Table 1. The graph of the payoff function for $N = 5$ is shown on Figure 1.

Geometric N

Let N be geometric with the parameter $p \in [0,1]$, i.e. $p_k = P(N = k) = p\,q^k, p > 0, q = 1-p, k \geq 0$. The payoff function in this case is $f(x,y) = \sum_{N=0}^{\infty} p_N f_N(x,y)$, where $f_N(x,y)$ stands for the gain function for N fixed given by (1). $f(x,y)$ can be written, after simplifications, as a function $g(s,t)$ (see Figure 2) of new coordinate variables $s = p/(1-qx)$, $t = p/(1-qy)$ on $[p,1] \times [p,1]$ (this transformation keeps monotonicity)

$$(2) \qquad g(s,t) = \begin{cases} t\ln t - s\ln s - t\ln s + \frac{t^2}{s} + \frac{t^2}{s}\ln s - t^2 & \text{if } p \leq t \leq s \leq 1, \\ t\ln t - s\ln s + s - st & \text{if } p \leq s < t \leq 1. \end{cases}$$

It is very interesting and important that the gain function $g(s,t)$ depends on p only by its domain. The function $g(s,t)$ considered on unit square has a unique saddle point $(s^*, t^*) \approx (0.3196, 0.2246)$

FIG. 2. *The contour plot of the payoff function when the number of the observation has the geometric distribution*

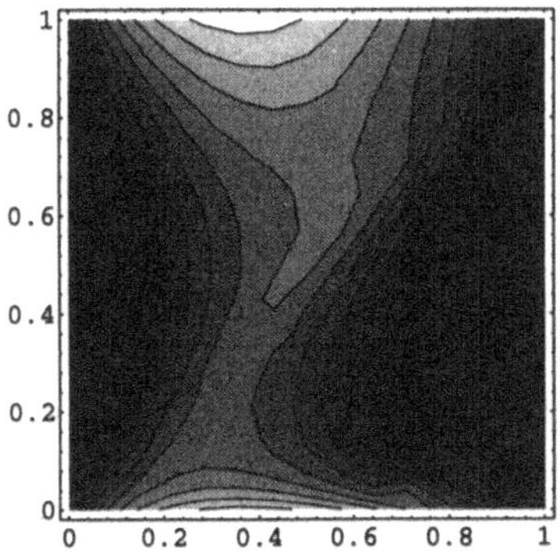

being a solution of equations

$$\begin{aligned} s(s+t)+(s^2+t^2)\ln s &= 0, \\ s+2t(1-s)+(2t-s)\ln s + s\ln t &= 0 \end{aligned}$$

in a triangle $0 \leq t \leq s \leq 1$.

Proposition 2. *For geometric N there exists a solution of the game and is of the following form depending on p:*

1. *If $p \leq t^*$ then optimal levels are $x^* = (s^* - p)/qs^*$, $y^* = (t^* - p)/qt^*$ for Player 1 and Player 2, respectively, and the value of the game $g(s^*, t^*) \approx 0.2127$ is independent of p;*
2. *If $t^* < p \leq s^*$ then optimal levels are $x^* = (s^* - p)/qs^*$, $y^* = 0$ for Player 1 and Player 2, respectively, and the value of the game is equal to $g(s^*, p)$;*
3. *If $p > s^*$ then optimal levels x^*, y^* are equal to 0 both players and the value of the game is equal to $g(p,p) = p(1-p)$.*

Remark 1. *It is interesting and quite unexpected that in all* natural *situations (i.e. when p is small, $p \leq t^* \approx 0.2246$) the value of the game is constant.*

References

E. ENNS AND E. FERENSTEIN (1987) *On a multi-person time-sequential game with priorities*, Sequential Analysis, 6, pp. 239–256.

Z. POROSIŃSKI (1991) *Full-information best choice problems with imperfect observation and a random number of observations*, Zastos. Matem., 21, pp. 179–192.

M. SAKAGUCHI (1984) *Best choice problems with full information and imperfect observation*, Math. Japonica, 29, pp. 241–250.

K. SZAJOWSKI (1993) *Double stop by two decision makers*, Adv. Appl. Probab., pp. 438 – 452.

Complexity of Optimization on Vectorweighted Bipartite Graphs

Peter NEUMAYER, Universität Kaiserslautern

Abstract: It is known that we can find a maximum matching in a weighted bipartite graph G in polynomial time, especially within $O(n^3)$ steps, with 2n is the number of vertices. In such a problem each edge of G is weighted with a real, positive number or an integer. More generally, I consider now a weighted bipartite graph with vectorweighted edges. It is shown that the decision problem for a maximum matching in a vectorweighted graph G is NP-complete. Furthermore I apply a definition of complexity concerning counting problems in order to get a more detailed insight of the problem. I use the counting-complexity according to L.G. Valiant and show that the vectorweighted bipartite matching problem is #P-complete.

Keywords: complexity, vectoroptimization

I. Introduction

I suppose that the classical concept of nondeterministic Turing machines (TM) and polynomial transformations is known to the reader, otherwise it can be found for example in [1]. Kuhn [2] has shown that the weighted matching problem is in the class $\mathcal{P}$ of problems that can be solved in polynomial time. But according to L.E. Valiant the problem of counting the number of perfect matchings (which is equivalent to the problem of calculating the permanent of a matrix) is #P-complete. This is interesting since #P is the class of difficult counting problems which contains all counting problems that are related to decision problems in $\mathcal{NP}$, for example counting the number of trees in a directed graph or maximum cliques is in #P.

Since the scalar weighted matching problem is in $\mathcal{P}$, I consider now the vector weighted matching problem and it will be shown that using vectorvalued weights for the edges the matching problem becomes $\mathcal{NP}$-complete and counting the number of efficient solutions becomes #P-complete.

II. Definitions

DEFINITION 1: A counting Turing machine is a standard nondeterministic TM with an auxiliary output device that prints in binary notation on a special tape the number of accepting computations induced by the input. It has worst-case time complexity $f(n)$ if the longest accepting computation induced by the set of all inputs of size n takes $f(n)$ steps (when the TM is regarded as a standard nondeterministic machine with no auxiliary device).

DEFINITION 2: #P is the class of functions that can be computed by counting TMs of polynomial time complexity. A function $g \in \#P$ is said to be #P-complete if all other functions in #P polynomially transform to g.

DEFINITION 3: Let $x, y \in \mathbb{R}^n$. x dominates y, that is $x > y$, if $x \neq y$ and $x_i \geq y_i$ for every component i. Let $x, y \in X \subset \mathbb{R}^n$. We say y is efficient, if there is no $x \in X$ with $x > y$.

Let M denote a matching. The weight of this matching is the sum of the weights of the edges which are contained in the matching. A matching M dominates a matching M' if the weight of M dominates the weight of M'.

III. Two Theorems

We consider now the following decision problem $\mathcal{D}$: is there a matching M' which dominates the given matching M.

THEOREM 1: Let G denote a complete vectorweighted bipartite graph with 2n vertices and let M denote a perfect matching. Then the decision problem $\mathcal{D}$ is $\mathcal{NP}$-complete.

PROOF: In order to verify a yes-instance of the algorithm we have to compare the weight of M and M'. This can be done in polynomial time and therefore the decision problem $\mathcal{D}$ is in $\mathcal{NP}$. I have to prove now the completeness of $\mathcal{D}$ in the class $\mathcal{NP}$.
I just prove the case of two components, because all cases with more than two components can be reduced to the case of two components by just choosing two components and neglecting all the others. Doing this we get the completeness of all higher dimensional cases if the two dinensional case is $\mathcal{NP}$-complete.

Let (a_i,b_i) with $i=1,\ldots,n^2$ be the weights of the edges e_i and (A,B) the sum of the weights of a given matching M. We can now reformulate our problem: is there a matching M' such that $A' = \sum_{i \in m} a_i \geq A$ and $B' = \sum_{i \in m} b_i \geq B$ and $(A',B') \neq (A,B)$. In order to prove the $\mathcal{NP}$-completeness of this problem I use the Interval-Subset-Sum problem (ISS-problem) which is known to be $\mathcal{NP}$-complete [1] and transform it to the decision problem $\mathcal{D}$. The ISS-problem consists of n numbers $c_1,\ldots,c_n$ and two bounds v,d with $v < d$ and the problem is to determine a subset k of the c_i's with $\sum_{i \in k} c_i \in [v,d]$. Let n denote the number of c_i's, then I define a complete, bipartite graph G with 2n vertices and the c_i's are the weights of a perfect matching in G and all the other edges have weights equal to zero. Thus we can assigne each subset k of the c_i's a matching in G which can be extended to a perfect matching with the same weight. On the other hand we can assigne each matching in G exactly one subset of the c_i's.

The objective $\sum_{i \in k} c_i \in [v,d]$ of the ISS-problem can be divided into two objectives for the matching problem. Let $a_i = c_i$, $b_i = d - c_i$, $A = v$ and $B = (n-1)d$, then we have

$$A' = \sum_{i \in m} a_i = \sum_{i \in m} c_i = \sum_{i \in k} c_i \geq v \text{ and } B' = \sum_{i \in m} b_i = \sum_{i \in m} d - c_i = nd - \sum_{i \in k} c_i \geq (n-1)d$$

Thus, we have a bipartite matching problem with two-dimensional vectorweighted edges and each (v,d) dominating solution of this matching problem corresponds to a solution of the ISS-problem. Vice versa each solution of the ISS-problem corresponds to a (v,d) dominating matching. ■

Let $\mathcal{E}$ denote the problem of determining the number of all nondominated matchings of a vectorweighted bipartite and complete graph G.

THEOREM 2: The counting problem $\mathcal{E}$ is #P-complete.

PROOF: According to Valiant the following statement is true. There is a function g∈ $\mathcal{FP}$ (class of functions that can be calculated in polynomial time on a deterministic Turing machine) that maps an arbitrary nondeterministic Turing machine and an input x for it to a propositional formula in 3-conjunctive normal form such that the number of satisfying assignments of g(M,x) is equal to the number of accepting computations of M on x. Because of this, for every decision problem in $\mathcal{NP}$ the corresponding counting problem is in #P. Thus our counting problem $\mathcal{E}$ is in #P, too.

Now I have to prove that any #P-complete problem transforms polynomially to $\mathcal{E}$. I choose the perfect matching problem, which is #P-complete, and transform it polynomially to $\mathcal{E}$. Let G denote a bipartite graph and m the number of edges. Then I have to choose the weights for G such that every perfect matching is efficient. Therefore I choose a m-dimensional vector for every edge, m−1 components equal to 1 and one component equal to 2, such that all weights are not comparable. Thus a matching is perfect if and only if it is nondominated in the corresponding vectorweighted graph and the number of perfect matchings is equal to the number of nondominated matchings. ■

References:

[1] Garey,M.;Johnson,D.; Computers and Intractability: A Guide to the Theory of NP-Completeness, Freeman, San Francisco 1979

[3] Kuhn, H.W.; The Hungrian Method for the Assignment Problem, Naval Research Logistics Quarterly, 2 (1955), 83-97

[5] Valiant,L.G.; The Complexity of Computing the Permanent, Theoretical Computer Sciences 8, 189-201 (1979), 189-201

[6] Valiant,L.G.; The Complexity of Enumeration and Reliability Problems, SIAM J. Comput. 8, 410-421 (1979), 410-421

SHORTEST PATH PROBLEM ON PARALLEL PROCESSORS

Vasile NICA*), Csaba FABIAN**), Zoltan KORMOS**)
*) Dept. of Ec. Cybernetics, **) Dept. of Informatics,
Academy of Economic Studies
Calea Dorobanţilor, 15-17
71131, Bucharest, ROMANIA

INTRODUCTION

Finding shortest path is a fundamental problem in the study of transportation and communication networks. Besides its own importance it appears as a subroutine in many other combinatorial optimization problems such as vehicle routing, network design or flows.

Classical methods (like Ford, Dijkstra) progressively construct paths from the initial node to all the other nodes of the network. These paths are permanently corrected in the sense of diminishing their lengths. At the end, not only shortest path to final node is obtained but all shortest paths from the initial node to the other ones.

In this paper the problem is reconsidered from the point of view of the existence of two parallel processors. Each of them applies Dijkstra's algorithm: the first starts from the initial node to the final one while the second "goes back" from the final node to the initial one. The processors work independently until they meet in some nodes; so, in a progressive manner, various paths between initial and final nodes are obtained by concatenation. From these paths, always the shortest is retained.

A lot of numerical experiments were made on a number of randomly generated networks. All of these have shown that the above search procedure needs much less time than Dijkstra's algorithm on a single processor.

DIJKSTRA'S ALGORITHM

Let $G=(N,A)$ be a directed network and let $c(i,j)$ represent the length of the arc $(i,j)\in A$. We suppose all $c(i,j)$ to be nonnegative integers. We are looking for the shortest path between two distinguished nodes s and t.

Among several method: which solve this problem, Dijkstra's algorithm seems to be the most popular. The basic idea of the algorithm is to fan out from node s and label nodes in order of their distance from s. Each node i has a label $d(i)$: the label is permanent once we know that it represents the shortest distance from s to i; otherwise it is temporary. Initially we give node s a permanent label

$d(s)=0$, and each other node j a temporary label $d(j)=c(s,j)$ if $(s,j) \varepsilon A$ or $d(j) = \infty$ otherwise. At each iteration the label of a node j is the shortest distance from the source s along paths whose internal nodes are all permanently labeled. The algorithm selects a node i^* with the minimum temporary label, makes it permanent and scans all arcs emerging from i^* to update the distance labels of adjacent nodes. When all nodes have been designated as permanently labeled, the algorithm terminates. Its correctness is based on the fact that it is always possible to designate the node with minimum temporary label as permanent.

With minor modifications, the above procedure can be applied to find shortest paths from all nodes to the final node t.

DIJKSTRA'S PARALLEL ALGORITHM

Now, imagine two persons, named RED and BLUE moving simultaneously along the edges of the network. RED starts from the initial node s and applies Dijkstra's algorithm in order to find shortest paths from s to all other nodes. To achieve his mission RED successively updates the red labels dr(i), $i \varepsilon G$ and, at every iteration, makes permanent that temporary red label with minimum value. On the other side, BLUE applies the "reverse" Dijkstra's algorithm starting from the final node t. His objective is to find shortest paths from all nodes in G to the node t. In order to do this, he iteratively updates the blue labels db(j), $j \varepsilon G$, making permanent, at every iteration, that temporary blue label with minimum value. Clearly, RED and BLUE will meet in at least one node. Such nodes will be called joint nodes. If j is a joint node the sum dr(j) + db(j) represents the length of a path from s to t. Many such paths can be obtained, but only the shortest among them is retained together with its defining joint node.

The termination of this parallel procedure is based on the following:

Theorem. When a joint node j is obtained with both red and blue labels declared permanent then dr(j) + db(j) represents the length of the shortest path from s to t.

For the algorithmic representation of the above procedure we will use the following notations:

. PR (resp. PB) set of those nodes with permanent red (resp.blue) label

. SCR (resp. SCB) set of those nodes attained by RED (resp. BLUE) along paths effectively generated by the algorithm.

. JN: current joint node

.dJN: length of the shortest path from s to t obtained by concatenation.

```
Algorithm RED
begin
      PR = {s}, SCR = {i| there exists (s,i) ε A}
      set dr(s) = 0
      if (s,i) ε A  set dr(i) = c(s,i) and pred(i) = s; otherwise dr(i) = + ∞
      set dJN = + ∞
      while SCR ≠ φ do.
      begin
            select i* ε SCR such that dr(i*) = min {dr(i), i ε SCR}
            PR = PR ∪ {i*}, SCR = SCR - {i*}
            if i* = t then STOP
            if i* ε PB and i* = JN then STOP
            for any arc (i*,j) with j ∉ PR do
                  begin
                        dr(j) = min {dr(j),dr(i*)+c(i*,j)}
                        if dr(j) was + ∞, then SCR = SCR ∪ {j}
                        if dr(j) diminished, then update pred(j) = i*
                        if db(j)<+∞ and dr(j)+db(j)<dJN then update
                        JN = j and dJN - dr(j) + db(j)
                  end
      end
end
Algorithm BLUE
begin
      PB = {t}, SCB = {j | (j,t) ε A}
      set db(t) = 0
      if(j,t) ε A set db(j) = c(j,t) and succ(j) = t; otherwise db(j) = + ∞
      set dJN = + ∞
      while SCB ≠ φ do
      begin
            select j* ε SCB such that db(j*) = min {db(j), j ε SCB}
            PB = PB ∪ {j*}, SCB = SCB - {j*}
            if j* = s then STOP
            if j* ε PR and j* = JN then STOP
            for any arc (i,j*) with i ∉ PB do
                  begin
                        db(i) = min {db(i), c(i,j*) + db(j*)}
                        if db(i) was + ∞, then SCB = SCB ∪ {i}
```

```
                if db(i) diminished then update succ(i) = j.
                if dr(i) < + ∞ and dr(i) + db(i) < dJN then
                        update JN = {i} and dJN = dr(i) + db(i)
          end
    end
end
```

NUMERICAL EXPERIMENTS

Numerical experiments have been made on a Novell network. The two parallel processors were simulated with two work stations. The geometric 50 x 50 lattice of nonnegative integers has been used to construct concrete test problems. From this lattice p% arcs were deleted in a randomly manner. Lengths of the arcs were also randomly generated in the interval [0,100]. The numerical results are given in the following table, where t_P (resp.t_D) means time needed by the parallel algorithm (resp. Dijkstra's algorithm) to solve a problem :

Initial node	Final node	$(t_P/t_D)\cdot 100$ when p=30%	$(t_P/t_D)\cdot 100$ when p=20%
1	2499	57,7	56,2
212	2042	61,5	55,4
410	1290	67,0	57
625	1825	44,9	44,8
1030	1325	54,2	55
425	1225	43,5	40,3
333	1412	68,4	67,1
1250	1290	45,3	66
Average		53,3	53,5

REFERENCES

Ahuja K., Magnanti T., Orlin J. (1988). Nework Flows. Sloan W.P. no. 2059-88. MIT. Cambridge, U.S.A.

Dijkstra E. (1959) A Note in Two Problems in Conexion with Graphs. Num. Math. 1., 269-271

Gibbons A., Rytter W. (1988). Efficient parallel algorithms. Cambridge Univ.Press, U.S.A.

Nickolson T. (1966). Finding the shortest route between two points in a network. The Comp. J. vol.9, no.3, 275-280

Bicriterial and Restrictive Planar 2-Median Problems

S. Nickel*
University of Kaiserslautern

1 Introduction

Much work has been done to extend 1-Median problems with respect to forbidden regions and barriers (see for example [Larson and Sadiq, 1983], [Hamacher and Nickel, 1991] and [Hamacher and Nickel, 1992]). But very few has been done for the multifacility case, where the new facilities also have some interaction.

The same is true for multicriterial location problems. A more general definition of multicriterial location problems in [Hamacher and Nickel, 1993] allows to state multifacility problems, but they haven't been discussed yet.

In this paper we will develop efficient algorithms which fill these two gaps a little bit.

We will present algorithms to solve the 2-Median problem for the l_1-norm with respect to a forbidden rectangle. Also an algorithm for solving bicriterial 2-Median problems (with l_1-norm) is developed.

It should be noted that the results also hold for the l_∞-case, because of the norm-converting mapping $T(X)$, which transforms a l_1-environment into a l_∞-environment and vice versa (see [Francis et al., 1992]).

We are given a set $Ex = \{Ex_1, \dots, Ex_M\}$ ($Ex_i = (a_i, b_i)$) of existing facilities and we are looking for a set $New = \{X_1, X_2\}$ ($X_i = (x_i, y_i)$) of new facilities to be located. The interaction between the new and the existing facilities is expressed by non-negative weights w_{mn} and the interaction between the two new facilities by the non-negative weight v.

The restrictive 2-Median problem (R2M) can then be written as

$$\min_{New \subseteq F} \left(f(New) := \sum_{n=1}^{2} \sum_{m=1}^{M} w_{nm} l_1(Ex_m, X_n) + v l_1(X_1, X_2) \right) ,$$

where the feasible region $F := \mathbb{R}^2 \setminus int(R)$, with $R \subseteq \mathbb{R}^2$ a connected set. The set of optimal locations for the restricted problem is called $\mathcal{X}_R^*(f)$ and the set of optimal locations for the unrestricted problem is called $\mathcal{X}^*(f)$.

*Partially supported by a grant of the Deutsche Forschungsgemeinschaft

The bicriterial 2-Median problem (B2M) is written as

$$\min_{New \subseteq F} F(New) := \begin{pmatrix} f^1(New) := \sum_{n=1}^{2}\sum_{m=1}^{M} w^1_{nm} l_1(Ex_m, X_n) + v^1 l_1(X_1, X_2) \\ f^2(New) := \sum_{n=1}^{2}\sum_{m=1}^{M} w^2_{nm} l_1(Ex_m, X_n) + v^2 l_1(X_1, X_2) \end{pmatrix},$$

where we mean minimize in the sense of finding pareto-optimal solutions. The set of pareto locations (i.e. $X \in \mathbb{R}^2$ with the property that there is no $Y \in R^2$, $X \neq Y$ with $f_1(Y) \leq f_1(X)$ and $f_2(Y) \leq f_2(X)$) is denoted $\mathcal{X}_{par}(f_1, f_2)$.

2 Basic Concepts

First we want to reformulate the objective function.

$$\begin{aligned} f(New) &= \sum_{m\in\mathcal{M}} w_{m1} l_1(Ex_m, X_1) + \sum_{m\in\mathcal{M}} w_{m2} l_1(Ex_m, X_2) + v l_1(X_1, X_2) \\ &= \underbrace{\sum_{m\in\mathcal{M}} w_{m1}|a_m - x_1| + \sum_{m\in\mathcal{M}} w_{m2}|a_m - x_2| + v|x_1 - x_2|}_{:=f_1(New)=f_1(x_1,x_2)=:f_a(X)} + \\ &\quad \underbrace{\sum_{m\in\mathcal{M}} w_{m1}|b_m - y_1| + \sum_{m\in\mathcal{M}} w_{m2}|b_m - y_2| + v|y_1 - y_2|}_{:=f_2(New)=f_2(y_1,y_2)=:f_b(Y)} \end{aligned}$$

Now we do a little further work to get rid of the absolut values in f_a and f_b. To do so we sort the a_i and b_i in ascending order, delete duplicates and get:

$$a'_1 < a'_2 < \ldots < a'_{P_a}\ , b'_1 < b'_2 < \ldots < b'_{P_b}\ .$$

Additionally we define $\mathcal{P}_a := \{1, \ldots, P_a\}$, $\mathcal{P}_b := \{1, \ldots, P_b\}$, $a'_0 := b'_0 := -\infty$ and $a'_{P_a+1} := b'_{P_b+1} := \infty$.

So we get two different subdvisions of the $\mathbb{R}^2$, namely

$$\begin{aligned} <t,s>_a &:= \left\{(x,y) : \ a'_t \leq x \leq a'_{t+1}\ ,\ a'_s \leq y \leq a'_{s+1}\right\} \text{ for } t,s \in \mathcal{P}_{a_0} := \mathcal{P}_a \cup \{0\} \\ <t,s>_b &:= \left\{(x,y) : \ b'_t \leq x \leq b'_{t+1}\ ,\ b'_s \leq y \leq b'_{s+1}\right\} \text{ for } t,s \in \mathcal{P}_{b_0} := \mathcal{P}_b \cup \{0\} \end{aligned}$$

Now we define regions

$$\begin{aligned} <t,s>^+_a &:= \{(x,y) \in <t,s>_a : \ x \geq y\} \\ <t,s>^-_a &:= \{(x,y) \in <t,s>_a : \ x < y\} \end{aligned}$$

and analogously $<t,s>^+_b$, $<t,s>^-_b$.

For a function g from $\mathbb{R}^2$ to $\mathbb{R}$ we call

$$L_=(z) := \{(x,y) : g(x,y) = z\}$$

level curve and

$$L_\leq(z) := \{(x,y) : g(x,y) \leq z\}$$

level set of g with level z.

Now we can state the main result of this section.

Theorem 2.1. *For $X = (x,y) \in <t,s>^r_\nu$, with $r \in \{+,-\}$ and $\nu \in \{a,b\}$ the set $L_=(f_\nu(X))$ is the graph of a linear function.*

3 Solving (R2M)

For $\nu \in \{a, b\}$ let

$$\begin{aligned}\mathcal{H}_\nu &:= \{(x,y) : \exists p \in \mathcal{P}_\nu \text{ s.t. } x = \nu'_p\} \\ &\cup \{(x,y) : \exists p \in \mathcal{P}_\nu \text{ s.t. } y = \nu'_p\} \\ &\cup \{(x,y) : x = y\} .\end{aligned}$$

The following result shows the combinatorial nature of our problem.

Theorem 3.1. *Let $R \subseteq \mathbb{R}^2$ be a convex set and $\mathcal{X}^*(f_\nu) \subseteq int(R)$. Then there is an optimal solution $X^*_R \in \mathcal{X}^*_R(f_\nu)$ satisfying*

1. $X^*_R \in \partial R$
2. $X^*_R \in \mathcal{H}_\nu$

Also $\mathcal{X}^*_R(f_\nu) \subseteq \partial R$.

Since we can decompose a forbidden rectangle $R = [a, b] \times [c, d]$ in forbidden regions for the first and for the second coordinate, an efficient algorithm can be stated for solving (R2M) with a forbidden rectangle. Note that Theorem 3.1 still is true for degenerate rectangles, where the coordinates of two corners are infinity.

4 Solving (B2M)

First we characterize the set of optimal locations for f^i_ν, $\nu \in \{a, b\}$ and $i = 1, 2$.

Theorem 4.1. *$\mathcal{X}^*(f^i_\nu)$ is either:*

a) *A corner point of $< s, t >^{+,-}_{f^i_\nu}$.*

b) *A line segment joining two adjacent corners of $< s, t >^{+,-}_{f^i_\nu}$.*

c) *The whole cell $< s, t >^{+,-}_{f^i_\nu}$.*

Define

$$\begin{aligned}\mathcal{X}_{1,2}(f^1_\nu, f^2_\nu) &:= \underset{X \in \mathcal{X}^*(f^1_\nu)}{\operatorname{argmin}} f^2_\nu(X) \\ \mathcal{X}_{2,1}(f^1_\nu, f^2_\nu) &:= \underset{X \in \mathcal{X}^*(f^2_\nu)}{\operatorname{argmin}} f^1_\nu(X)\end{aligned}$$

as the two lexicographic optimal location sets.

The next theorem characterizes $\mathcal{X}_{par}(f^1_\nu, f^2_\nu)$.

Theorem 4.2. *$\mathcal{X}_{par}(f^1_\nu, f^2_\nu)$ is a chain consisting of corner points, line segements and cells described in Theorem 4.1 connecting $\mathcal{X}_{1,2}(f^1_\nu, f^2_\nu)$ and $\mathcal{X}_{2,1}(f^1_\nu, f^2_\nu)$.*

Note that

Lemma 4.3. $\mathcal{X}_{par}(f^1_a, f^2_b) \times \mathcal{X}_{par}(f^1_a, f^2_b) \supseteq \mathcal{X}_{par}(f^1, f^2)$.

So our next task is to combine the elements of $\mathcal{X}_{par}(f_a^1, f_b^2)$ and $\mathcal{X}_{par}(f_a^1, f_b^2)$ in such a way that we get $\mathcal{X}_{par}(f^1, f^2)$.

For this we use a scalarization of our problem (see [Geoffrion, 1967]):

$$X_{par} \in \mathcal{X}_{par}(f^1, f^2)$$

$$\Longleftrightarrow$$

$$X_{par} \text{ solves } \min_{X \in \mathbb{R}^4} (\lambda f^1(X) + (1-\lambda) f^2(X)) \text{ for a } \lambda \text{ with } 0 < \lambda < 1$$

This equivalence holds since the minimization of f^1 and f^2 can be formulated as linear programming problems (see [Isermann, 1974]).

Theorem 4.4. *The correct pairing of the elements of $\mathcal{X}_{par}(f_a^1, f_b^2)$ and $\mathcal{X}_{par}(f_a^1, f_b^2)$ to elements of $\mathcal{X}_{par}(f^1, f^2)$ can be done effienctly using the scalarization and the fact that*

$$\min_{X \in \mathbb{R}^4} (\lambda f^1(X) + (1-\lambda) f^2(X)) =$$

$$\min_{X,Y \in \mathbb{R}^2} ((\lambda f_a^1(X) + (1-\lambda) f_a^2(X)) + (\lambda f b^1(Y) + (1-\lambda) f_b^2(Y)))$$

References

[Francis et al., 1992] Francis, R. L., Leon F. McGinnis, J., and White, J. A. (1992). *Facility layout and location: An analytical approach, 2nd Edition.* Prentice-Hall, New York.

[Geoffrion, 1967] Geoffrion, A. M. (1967). Solving bicriterion mathematical programs. *Operations Research*, 15:38–54.

[Hamacher and Nickel, 1991] Hamacher, H. W. and Nickel, S. (1991). Combinatorial algorithms for some 1-facility median problems in the plane. Technical Report 191, University of Kaiserslautern. EJOR, to appear.

[Hamacher and Nickel, 1992] Hamacher, H. W. and Nickel, S. (1992). Restricted planar location problems and applications. Technical Report 227, University of Kaiserslautern.

[Hamacher and Nickel, 1993] Hamacher, H. W. and Nickel, S. (1993). Multicriterial planar location problems. Technical report, University of Kaiserslautern.

[Isermann, 1974] Isermann, H. (1974). Proper efficiency and the linear vector maximization problem. *Operations Research*, 22:189–191.

[Larson and Sadiq, 1983] Larson, R. C. and Sadiq, G. (1983). Facility locations with the manhattan metric in the presence of barriers to travel. *Operations Research*, 31:652–669.

Optimal Solutions to Approximate Integer Programming Problems

Osman Oğuz
Department of Industrial Engineering
Bilkent University
Ankara, Turkey.

Extended Abstract The dictum "the input data is not precise anyway" is often stated in defence of the many heuristic or approximate methods developed to solve difficult problems in mathematical programming. Difficult meaning not yielding a solution in a "reasonable" amount of time. A brief survey of the literature shows that a considerable amount of effort has been spent to investigate and devise this kind of methods in the area of integer and combinatorial programming, e.g., Garey & Johnson (1979), Cornuejols et al. (1977), Balas & Martin (1980),Ibarra & Kim (1975), Sahni (1975), Lawler (1979), Magazine & Oguz (1984).

Also, data imprecision or variation is a source of great concern in linear and nonlinear programming. It has led to many forms of sophisticated mathematical analysis especially in the case of linear programming. The most prominent among these is sensitivity analysis. Strictly speaking, it is the analysis of the effect of input data changes on an optimal solution of a linear program. All well known books on the subject have chapters on sensitivity and/or post optimality analysis, e.g., Dantzig (1963), Bazaraa & Jarvis (1977), Chavatal (1983).

In the case of nonlinear programming, similar topics are discussed under names like perturbation analysis, stability analysis, or parametric analysis. A collection of articles in a special issue of Journal of Optimization Theory and Applications (JOTA) edited by A. V. Fiacco (1986) may be seen to get an idea about these. Interval analysis may also be considered in this realm. Ratschéck & Voller (1991) provide a recent review of this subject.

More recent extensions of sensitivity analysis are multiparametric analysis, linear programming with interval objective function coefficients, and tolerance analysis as reflected in the works of Zeleny (1974), Yu & Zeleny (1976), Steuer (1981), and Wendell (1985). The basic premise in sensitivity analysis and these more recent works is that the preservation of the optimality of a solution has paramount importance and no effort should be spared to make a new one available when the existing solution loses this quality due to changes in data.

When this approach is contrasted with that of the dictum mentioned above for approximate (heuristic) solutions, the inherent paradoxicality can not be missed. Data imprecision is almost a welcome relief in cases where optimal solutions are hard to find and convenient substitutes (approximate solutions) are recomended instead. When it is relatively easier to find optimal solutions, on the other hand, a myriad of ways and means of restoring optimality against the slightest variations in the input data are suggested.

This study is an attempt at reconciling these two approaches. We consider the following problem:

Max $\{z = C^T X | C| \in \Phi, X \in S\}$

where $\Phi = \{C \in Z^n | c_i \in [\alpha_i, \omega_i] \; for \; 1 \leq i \leq n\}$

$S = \{X \in Z_+^n | AX = b, b \in \Psi\}$

$\Psi = \{b \in Z^n | b_i \in [\mu_i, v_i] \; for \; 1 \leq i \leq m\}$

Z is the set of integers.

Methods of finding optimal solutions for some (but not all) instances of C and b in the given intervals will be discussed. The starting point of the discussions is a proposition based on the following two problems:

Max $\{z^1 = C^1 X | AX = b, X \in R^n\}$

and

$Max\{C^2 X | AX = b, X \in R^n\}$

Letting X^1 and X^2 be the optimal solutions of these two problems, we show that $(z^1 - z^3)/z^3 \leq 2\beta/(1-\beta)$ where $z^1 = C^1 X^1$, $z^3 = C^1 X^2$ and $\beta = Max_i |c_i^1 - c_i^2|/|c_i^2|$ for $c_i^2 \neq 0$. Then we go on to use this result in combination with the tolerance limits due to Wendell (1985) in partial coverage of the hperrectangles Φ and Ψ. The proposed techniques are demonstrated through some numerical examples.

References

Bazaraa, M.S.,and J.J.Jarvis (1977) *Linear Programming and Network Flows* , John Wiley & Sons, New York.

Balas, E.,and R. Martin (1980), "Pivot and Complement: A Heuristic for 0-1 Programming", Management Science, 26, pp.86-96.

Chvatal, V. (1983),*Linear Programming* .

Cornuejols, G., M.L. Fisher and G.L. Nemhauser (1977), "Location of Bank Accounts to Maximize Float: An Analytical Study of Exact and Approximate Algorithms", Management Science, 23, pp.789-810.

Dantzig, G.B. (1963), *Linear Programming and Extensions* , Princeton University Press.

Fiacco, A.V. (1986, editor), Special Issue on Mathematical Programming with Data Perturbations, Journal of Optimization Theory and Applications.

Garey, M.R., and D.S. Johnson (1979), *Computers and Intractibility: A Guide to the Theory of NP-Completeness* .

Ibarra, O., and C. Kim (1975),"Fast Approximation Algorithms for the Sum of Subsets Problems", J. of ACM, 22, pp.463-468.

Lawler, E.L. (1979),"Fast Approximation Algorithms for Knapsack Problems" , Mathematics of Operations Research, 14, pp.339-356.

Magazine, M.J., and O. Oguz (1984),"A Heuristic Algorithm for the Multidimensional 0-1 Knapsack Problem", European Journal of Operational Research, 16, pp.319-326.

Ratschek, H., and R.L. Voller (1991),"What Can Interval Analysis Do for Global Optimization?", Journal of Global Optimization, 1, pp.111-130.

Sahni, S. (1975), "Approximate Algorithms for the 0-1 Knapsack Problem", J. of ACM, 22, pp.115-124.

Steuer, R.E. (1981),"Algorithms for Linear Programming with Interval Objective Function Coefficients", Mathematics of Operations Research, 6, pp.333-348.

Wendell, R.E. (1985),"tolerance Approach to Sensitivity Analysis in Linear Programming", Management Science, 31, pp.564-578.

Yu, P.L., and M. Zeleny (1976),"Linear Multiparametric Programming by Multicriteria Simplex Method", Management Science, 23, pp.159-170.

Zeleny, M. (1974), *Linear Multiobjective Programming,* Spriger-Verlag, New York.

ANALYSIS OF PANEL DATA BY MEANS OF THE GAMBLER-MOVER-STAYER MODEL

Maria Overbeck-Larisch
Fachbereich MN, Fachhochschule Darmstadt
Schöfferstraße 3, 64295 Darmstadt, Deutschland

The Gambler-Mover-Stayer Model (GMS) was developed as an instrument for judging the efficiency of psychotherapeutical training projects [4]. The model requires tests at the beginning and at the end of the training and one or more additional tests when training is in progress. The test results are assumed to be of ordinal level. The times of the tests are $t=0$ (the beginning of the training), $t=1$, $t=2$, ... , $t=T$ (the end of the training). The sequence of test results of a person is denoted by x_0, x_1, ... x_T. The test results are evaluated by categorical values 1, 2, ... , C , where "1" is the best test result.

The central idea of the GMS is the differentiation of three types of pupils or patients: gamblers, (true) movers and stayers. The (true) movers form the real training group. At the beginning of the course they do not have the ability which is to be imparted, at least not in the highest degree. During the course they can improve their abilities with a certain probability, but they cannot fall off. They continually move toward the goal of the training project. Therefore they are called Movers.
In every training group we also have persons whose abilities fluctuate from time to time. At certain times they seem to have aquired a remarkable skill, but later on they seem to have lost it. For these persons a good test result at time T does not indicate the successful completion of the course. These persons do not move continually to the goal of the training program, they rather seem to gamble. Therefore they are called Gamblers. When judging the efficiency of a group training project it is of great importance, to separate the (true) movers from the gamblers.
Apart of these two groups there exists the group of Stayers, consisting of those persons, whose abilities must be constant during the complete training for two possible reasons: either a pupil or patient already has the ability which is to be imparted in the highest degree or else the person is not at all influenced by the training program.
The GMS is a Mixed Markov Model with three independent Markov chains describing the three mentioned groups of persons. It is related to the Mover-

Stayer Model well known in literature (see for instance [2]), from which however it differs by the differentiation between true movers and gamblers. Moreover the GMS generalizes the Black & White Model of Converse [1], which yields a Gambler-Stayer Model.

The mathematical formulation of the GMS is working on the following assumptions. During the training process a mover can improve his abilities with a certain probability but he cannot change for the worse. Therefore for a (true) mover the sequence $x_0, x_1, \dots, x_T$ of test results at times $t=0, \dots, t=T$ is monotone. The transition probabilities of the Markov chain describing the group of the movers satisfy the following condition with $\mathscr{C} := \{1, 2, \dots, C\}$:

$$pm_{ij} = pm_{ij}(t) = P(X_t = j \mid X_{t-1} = i) \begin{cases} = 1 & \text{for } i=j=1 \quad \text{and all } t=1,\dots,T \\ = 0 & \text{for } i<j \ (i,j \in \mathscr{C}) \text{ and all } t=1,\dots,T \\ \geq 0 & \text{for all } 2 \leq i \text{ and } j \leq i \ (i,j \in \mathscr{C}) \end{cases}$$

The test results of the gamblers look like the results of a random experiment independent of the training. Each of the categories $1, 2, \dots, C$ is assumed to occur with the same probability. Under these assumptions all transition probabilities of the corresponding Markov chain have the same value $1/C$.

So for the path probabilities $p_{i_0 i_1 \dots i_T} = P(X_0 = i_0, X_1 = i_1, \dots, X_T = i_T)$ of the complete stochastic process we have:

$$p_{i_0 i_1 \dots i_T} = \begin{cases} \eta_{i_0} * g_{i_0} * (1/C)^T + \eta_{i_0} * m_{i_0} * p^T_{m_{i_0 i_0}} + \eta_{i_0} * s_{i_0} & \text{if } i_0 = i_1 = \dots = i_T \\ \eta_{i_0} * g_{i_0} * (1/C)^T + \eta_{i_0} * m_{i_0} * \prod_{t=1}^{T} p_{m_{i_{t-1} i_t}} & \text{otherwise} \end{cases}$$

This is the equation of the Gambler-Mover-Stayer Model. Besides the transition probabilities the model contains the following parameters:

$\eta_i = P(X_0 = i)$ $(1 \leq i \leq C)$

$g_i = P(\text{a person is a gambler} \mid X_0 = i) = P(G \mid X_0 = i)$ $(1 \leq i \leq C)$

$m_i = P(\text{a person is a mover} \mid X_0 = i) = P(M \mid X_0 = i)$ $(1 \leq i \leq C)$

$s_i = P(\text{a person is a stayer} \mid X_0 = i) = P(S \mid X_0 = i)$ $(1 \leq i \leq C)$

The numbers η_i form the initial distribution of the test results. η_1 for example is the probability for a person to achieve the best possible test result at the beginning of the training. The numbers g_i or m_i or s_i are the conditional probabilities for a person to be a gambler or a mover or a stayer respectively under the condition, that at the beginning of the training this person achieves the test result i.

The parameters of the GMS are subject to the starting condition $m_1=0$ and the following restrictions:

$$\sum_{i=1}^{C} \eta_i = 1 \qquad g_i+m_i+s_i = 1 \text{ for all } 1\le i\le C \qquad \sum_{j=1}^{i} p_{m_{ij}} = 1 \text{ for all } 1\le i\le C$$

The GMS was applied to data sets coming from different psychotherapeutical research projects well known in literature [3, 5, 6] and it turned out to be an appropriate instrument for measuring the change in categorical data whenever they were the result of a kind of training.
But the scope of the GMS is not limited to psychotherapeutical training projects. It can also be a method for studying the change in public opinion during a special campaign. Let us for example assume that n persons are asked at times $t=0$, ..., $t=T$ to comment on a political statement. The answer could be agreement (level code=1), rejection (level code=3) or indifference (level code=2). If between times $t=0$ and $t=T$ the persons are influenced by a kind of campaign we exactly have the situation the GMS was developed for. If we denote by $n_{i_0 i_1 i_2 \ldots i_T}$ the number of persons, who at the time $t=\nu$ give the answer i_ν, we get as a total 3^{T+1} frequencies which enable us to estimate the parameters of the GMS. Moreover, if the goodness of fit is acceptable, it is possible within the frame of the model to judge the success of the campaign.

The GMS can also be a method for studying the consumers' behaviour under the influence of advertising. The following table contains the data of a (real) study concerning the decisions of n=452 persons when buying a special article of consumption. The data demonstrate the advertising success of several producers of this article in contest against the leading producer who controls 50% of the market. The table contains the decisions of these 452 persons at three points of time within a period of 7 months.

times	t=0	1	1	1	1	2	2	2	2
	t=1	1	1	2	2	1	1	2	2
	t=2	1	2	1	2	1	2	1	2
		134	41	37	30	43	24	33	110

It means 1: decision to buy one of the competitive products
2: decision to buy the product of the market leader

When fitting the data to a GMS with C=2 and T=2, we can restrict the parameter estimation to the parameters η_1, g_1, g_2, m_2 und $p_{m_{21}}$, which completely determine this model. (The following results were computed by the software PANMARK [7]):
The value of the Likelihood ratio statistic is $L^2=1.75$ (DF=2, Prob=0.42). So there is nothing to object to the GMS. The Maximum likelihood estimates are :

$$\hat{\eta}_1=0.5354 \qquad \hat{g}_1=0.5950 \qquad \hat{g}_2=0.4571 \qquad \hat{m}_2=0.1720 \qquad \hat{p}_{m_{21}} = 0.5261$$

About 17 percent of the persons who at time t=0 decided to buy the product of the market leader are Movers. At times t=1 or t=2 they change with a probability of about 53% to one of the competitive products. Corresponding to the assumptions of the GMS they do not change back to the product of the market leader.
The other parameters of the model can be computed from the restrictions:

$$\hat{\eta}_2=0.4646 \qquad \hat{s}_1=0.4050 \qquad \hat{s}_2=0.3709$$

By the formula of Bayes we get some further characteristic values of the model:
53.10% of the persons turn out to be Gamblers, 38.91% are Stayers.
44.28% of the Stayers continue to buy the product of the market leader.
55.72% of the Stayers are Stayers of the competitive products.

Literatur

[1] Philip E. Converse - 1964
The nature of belief systems in mass publics
In: D.E. Apter (ED.), Ideology and discontent (pp. 206-261)
New York: The Free Press

[2] Halina Frydman - 1984
Maximum Likelihood Estimation in the Mover Stayer Model
Journal of the American Statistical Association, Vol.79, (pp. 632-638)

[3] Rolf Langeheine und Frank Van De Pol - 1990
Veränderungsmessung bei kategorialen Daten
Zeitschrift für Sozialpsychologie, Bd.21, (pp. 88-100)

[4] Maria Overbeck-Larisch, Oliver Jabs - 1992
Beurteilung von Gruppentrainingsprogrammen im Rahmen eines Gambler-Mover-Stayer Modells
Zeitschrift für Sozialpsychologie (submitted)

[5] Timothy M. Morgan, Carol S. Aneshensel, Virginia A. Clark - 1983
Parameter Estimation for Mover-Stayer Models
Analyzing Depression Over Time
Sociological Methods & Research, Vol.11 No.3, (pp. 345-366)

[6] Lee M. Wiggins - 1973
Panel Analysis Latent Probability Models for Attitude and Behaviour Processes
Elsevier Scientific Publishing Company

[7] PANMARK
TURBO-PASCAL-Programm zur Analyse von Paneldaten mit Markovketten
von R.Langeheine und F.Van De Pol, 1990

AGGREGATION & CLUSTERING OF PREFERENCES: OPINION vs. ACTION

Jan W. Owsiński

Systems Research Institute
Polish Academy of Sciences
Newelska 6; 01-447 Warszawa
Poland

The paper presents and analyses a simple general model allowing valued ("fuzzy") preference coefficient expressions from a set of judges over a set of options. The main question addressed by the paper is the nature of information that can be obtained from such a construct. This information ranges from a very loose "opinion" to very strict "action definition". It is proposed that while in case of determination of opinion solutions are simple if not trivial, it is in the case of action definition that real obstacles arise. It becomes namely necessary to take into account the narrowed down tolerance of the judges as to possible divergence of the outgoing information from own preferences. This leads to the problem of simultaneous clustering - and - aggregation of preferences. This problem has not as yet found a satisfactory theoretical and algorithmic solution. The paper presents the objective function which avoids triviality of results (e.g. monotonicity with respect to cluster number), an outline of a relatively simple and quick suboptimization algorithm, and a new and natural definition of consensus for the clustering-and-aggregation problem, this definition being based upon the precepts of the algorithm used.

1. THE DECISION MAKING MODEL

We are considering the application of certain **data analysis methods** in the case of the model of **group decision making** in which n judges express their opinions as to m options in the form of pairwise preference coefficients $d^i_{kl} \in [0,1]$, where i, $i \in I=\{1,...,n\}$, denotes a judge and k,l, $k,l \in L=\{1,...,m\}$, denote options considered. Hence, the coefficients must not necessarily belong to {0,1}, but may also correspond to less definite preferences.

It is obvious that the need for allowing such "fuzzy" (or "valued") preference coefficients to be elicitated arises when the options are perceived through a number of criteria on which they may score in a very different manner, and the elicitation of these scores by every judge for every criterion would be much too cumbersome, if at all possible (considering e.g. the problem of identification of all the - independent - criteria), let alone an aggregation of these multicriteria scores into pairwise preference coefficients.

Within this framework the methods of data analysis are used to resolve, at least partially, the dilemma between **agreement** and **information**, or between opinion and **action**.

2. THE TWO EXTREMES

Thus, it is easy to see that in the space of fuzzy relations E_D, these relations being denoted $D^i = \{d^i_{kl}\}_{kl}$, $D^i \in E_D$, we can, in the extreme case, obtain in a straightforward manner the **"aggregate opinion"** of the judges that is the closest to all of the preference relations of the judges. Such an "aggregate opinion" might namely be given simply by an **average of the preference coefficient values**. Note that we do not impose here any formal restrictions on the properties of D^i (e.g. transitivity) nor on the space of these relations E_D, (e.g. metricity), since we are concerned with a practical approach, in which one can hardly encounter the cases where any of the really important constraints on relations are violated, or which can be devised in such a way as to ensure a natural fulfilment of some basic assumptions (e.g. by taking from the judges the triangular matrices of d^i_{kl}, under $d^i_{kl}=1-d^i_{lk}$). In case of need, though, we can resort to fuzzy-preference-oriented definitions, like the one of transitivity:

$$d_{kl} + d_{lh} - d_{hk} \le 2 - \varepsilon, \ \varepsilon \in [0,1],$$

where ε is the degree of fuzzy transitivity ranging from $\varepsilon=1$ (complete or "crisp" transitivity) to $\varepsilon=0$ (maximum relaxation possible), and d_{kl} are the coefficients defining the resulting "opinion", say, averages of d_{kl}^i over i.

While obtaining of the outcome in the form of such a fuzzy average may be sometimes satisfactory from the point of view of expression of the "opinion" of the judges, it may by no means be so from the point of view of "**information**" we may want from the judges, namely, in the extreme case - ordering of the options (this kind of aggregate being referred to here as "**decision**").

The response of the latter kind - i.e. the **aggregate ordering**, even for the fuzzy input case - may be obtained by the reference to the philosophy of Regnier's barycenters (Regnier, 1965), to the mathematical programming of Marcotorchino and Michaud (1979), or to the suboptimization algorithms of the present author (Owsiński and Zadrożny, 1986).

Thus, according to the latter technique, the second extreme - the ordering that is the closest to the opinion, that is: **the decision that is the closest to the opinion** - would be found with a simple exchange algorithm suboptimizing the objective function

$$Q_O(\bar{D},D,r) = \sum_{k,l}(r\bar{d}_{kl}d_{kl} + (1-r)\bar{d}_{lk}d_{lk}) \rightarrow \max_{D\in E_O} \qquad (1)$$

under usual constraints securing, this time, that d_{kl} form an ordering, where $\{\bar{d}_{kl}\}_{kl}=\bar{D}$ is the average relation from all the judges (e.g. the relation obtained in the first extreme case), $\{d_{kl}\}_{kl}=D$ is the relation we are looking for, E_O is the space of orderings, and $r\in[0,1]$ is the algorithmic coefficient. The algorithm starts functioning at $r=1$, implying the initial solution, namely $D(r=1)\equiv\{1,2,...,n\}$, i.e. the chosen lexicographical order, and then progressing through decreasing values of r and changing orderings $D(r)$ down to $D(r=0.5)$, which is the suboptimal one. At each step of a change, occurring for some r^t, a narrow class of operations is performed on the previously obtained ordering $D(r^t)$ among which the one is selected such that maximizes the resulting increment of the objective function (1). Thereby we have a simple and flexible preference aggregation algorithm, which allows, simultaneously, making of comparisons of all the feasible solutions that can be.

In addition, we obtain the sequence of values of r, $\{r^t\}_t$, $t=1,\ldots$, at which the suboptimal orderings change, and therefore also the intervals $[r^t, r^{t-1}]$ for which these consecutive suboptimal orderings (for given values of r) are valid, the length of intervals being the measure of stability of these results. In case of more than one globally suboptimal orderings $D(0.5)$ we would have a subsequence of $\{r^t\}$ in which all the values $r^{t'}$, $r^{t''}$,... are equal 0.5.

3. WHY CLUSTER?

Thus, we have an easy way to obtain an opinion, and a slightly more complicated way of obtaining the decision. The dilemma, however, would persist. Having just one ordering may be sufficient - if judges so agree - even to specify a "decision", but it still carries very little information on the **actual stances of these judges**. This is a question of no secondary importance for group decision making.

Thus, there are are at least two other problems with the analysis of the data provided by the judges, in any of the two extreme cases cited above. The aggregates for all the judges, namely, provide very little data on the **agreement measures** as to any of the aggregates (we can only assert that in the second case this agreement will in general not be higher than in the first one). We can devise variance-like indicators in order to assess the general divergence of opinions (i.e. the fuzzy preference relations), but this will be of little practical help if we do not know what is the actual structure of the set of preference relations.

Then, there is yet the question of clarity, not only for the outsiders, but for the participants of the exercise as well. The insufficiency of information can be namely seen easily if we want to interprete either of the results previously obtained in the commonly understood and accepted language of "elections" or "votings": it is only in the case of orderings that we can relatively easily reconstruct a voting situation. The fundamental question asked in the language mentioned is: what is the support for a given outcome? One could of course assume that this support is given implicitly through values of d^i_{kl}. A simple expression of such a support given implicitly by the judge i the outcome D would be

$$S(D^i,D) = 1 - \frac{2}{m(m-1)} \sum_{k,l} |d^i_{kl} - d_{kl}|$$

reaching 1 for the identical opinion (preference relation) and 0 for the "exactly opposite" one, which exists, however, only if $d^i_{kl}\in\{0,1\}$. One might suspect, though, that support, in fact, decreases much more quickly away from own D^i, perhaps even in a significantly nonlinear manner. The only way, it seems, of knowing this support would be to ask the judges directly. It is, of course, not possible to do that at the time of specification of preference relations, for technical reasons (how to express the support? with respect to what?).

Expression of support would certainly be easier a posteriori, when some reference points are already available, especially when these reference points are given as orderings.

In case of the fuzzy extreme (e.g. a simple average) there is yet, within the problem of clarity, the question of possibility of obtaining averages that are close to indifference ($\bar{d}_{kl}\approx 0.5$), thereby providing neither opinion nor information, in fact.

In such a situation a (partial) way out consists in **clustering of preference relations** with simultaneous finding of aggregate relations for clusters. In this manner we will discover the "parties" within the set of judges - if they exist - and their "core" opinions as well as decisions. It is with respect to these "cores" that we may look for support and agreement.

There are, however, no effective methods of **simultaneous finding of clusters of such relations and of the aggregates of the two types** mentioned (see Gaul and Schader, 1988, and Owsiński and Zadrożny, 1986, 1990). Thus, the present author proposes a suboptimization algorithm, based upon the cluster analysis precepts elaborated in earlier works (Owsiński, 1990). It refers to the objective function having the general form

$$Q_C(P,\{D_q\}_q,r) = rQ_D(P,\{D_q\}_q) + (1-r)Q_S(P,\{D_q\}_q) \rightarrow \max_{P\in E_P, D_q\in E_O} \qquad (2)$$

where P is the partition of the set of judges, Q_D is the function of distance of clusters of judges within the whole partition, and Q_S is the function of similarity within the clusters of judges, again over the whole partition. The algorithm starts with r=1, implying the partition $P(r=1)$ for which (2) attains maximum such that all the judges - or their preference relations - constitute separate clusters. Then, similarly as in the case of finding of the orderings so as to maximize (1), the algorithm proceeds through mergers of preference relations corresponding to judges, these mergers being the best ones from the point of view of the objective function (2). The mergers correspond to monotonically decreasing values of r. The suboptimal partition is found, again, for r=0.5. It can be shown that for quite mild conditions the cluster-wise aggregates D_q are similarly suboptimal as the clusters are. Furthermore, this way of proceeding enables formulation of a new and intuitive definition of **consensus** among judges.

If namely, the judges are asked to repeat the specification of their preference coefficients during a session, so as to obtain a better agreement among them, then the clustering-and-aggregation procedure is also repeated. If however, we retain for the consecutive rounds the same framework (scale) for the definitions of Q_D and Q_S then - provided the judges get closer to each other in terms of preference relations specified by them - it may turn out that in some of the consecutive rounds, at the level of r=0.5 we obtain **just one cluster of judges**, encompassing all of them. It would seem appropriate to refer to such a situation as to a **consensus**.

If we want to have the clusterwise aggregates to have the form of orderings, then, similarly as before, the situation gets much more complicated. The explicit form of the objective function (2) will have Q_D and Q_S defined in the following manner:

$$Q_D(P,\{D_q\}_q)=\frac{2}{p(p-1)}\sum_{q=1}^{p-1}\sum_{q'=q+1}^{p}\sum_{i\in A_q}\sum_{k=1}^{n-1}\sum_{l=k+1}^{n}(d_{lk}^{q'}d_{kl}^{i}+d_{kl}^{q'}d_{lk}^{i}) \quad (3)$$

$$Q_S(P,\{D_q\}_q)=\frac{1}{p}\sum_{q=1}^{p}\sum_{i\in A_q}\sum_{k=1}^{n-1}\sum_{l=k+1}^{n}(d_{kl}^{q}d_{kl}^{i} + d_{lk}^{q}d_{lk}^{i}) \quad (4)$$

where p is the number of clusters of judges (sought as well, of course, and not predefined), A_q is the q-th cluster composing the partition of judges denoted previously by P, and d_{kl}^q are the clusterwise preference relations aggregates ($\{d_{kl}^q\}_{kl} = D_q$) we are looking for together with A_q. The task of maximizing (2) with (3) and (4) seems to be indeed formidable.

Still, in spite of such a complicated form the problem may be approached in quite a simple manner, by first defining the orderings that are the closest to each of the initial preference relations of the judges in terms of (1), and then grouping these preference relations which have the same closest orderings. Thereby we obtain the first maximum of the function (2) with (3) and (4), correspoding to maximum value of r. Further operations, which may, as before, be limited to mergers, are already being performed in the space of orderings.

4. FINAL REMARKS

The methodology outlined aims at obtaining possibly much from a session in which judges are asked to give their opinions in the form of pairwise preference coefficients, and it provides all the information that may be wished by a session manager, falling short only in terms of strict optimisation of the objective functions formulated. It offers, of course, possibility of comparison with any other approach through the use of globally rational objective functions, and what it loses out on optimality, it compensates with its simplicity and speed.

REFERENCES

Gaul W. and Schader M., 1988: *Clusterwise evaluation of paired comparisons*. Paper for Fourth International Symposium on Applied Stochastic Models and Data Analysis: "The Ins and Outs of Solving real Problems". Nancy, December 1988, INRIA, Le Chesnay.

Marcotorchino J.-F. and Michaud P., 1979: Optimisation en Analyse Ordinale des Donnees. Masson, Paris.

Owsiński J.W. and Zadrożny S., 1986: *Structuring a regional problem: aggregation and clustering in orderings*. Applied Stochastic Models and Data Analysis, 2, 1 & 2, pp.83-95.

Owsiński J.W., 1990: *On a new quick clustering method with a global objective function*. Applied Stochastic Models and Data Analysis, 6, pp.157-171.

Owsiński J.W. and Zadrożny S., 1990: *The problem of clusterwise aggregation of preferences*. In: Decision Making Models for Management and Manufacturing, R.Kulikowski and J.Stefański, eds. Omnitech Press, Warszawa, pp.91-101.

Regnier S., 1965: *Sur quelques aspects mathematiques des problemes de classification automatique*. ICC Bulletin, 4, 1965.

Inverse Function Theorems for Nonsmooth Mappings in Banach Spaces

Zsolt Páles[1]
Fachbereich Mathematik
Universität des Saarlandes
D-66123 Saarbrücken, Deutschland

The aim of this note is to present the extension of some classical inverse and implicit function theorems to the nonsmooth situation.

The central regularity notion of the paper is the concept of strict prederivative invented by Ioffe(1981) in the theory of fans.

The central result of the paper is Theorem 1, which asserts the local surjection property for Banach space valued functions assuming the existence of a compact convex family of surjective linear operators which form a strict predrivative of the function at the given point. The proof of this result requires four corner stones of the mathematical analysis: Banach's open mapping theorem, Michael's selection theorem, Ekeland's variational principle and Kakutani's fixed point theorem. As an immediate consequence of this result, we get Grave's and Lyusternik's theorem, a generalization of Clarke's inverse function theorem and some classical inverse and implicit function theorems.

Locally Lipschitz Mappings and Strict Prederivatives

In overcoming the difficulties that are caused by the nonsmoothness of mappings, there are several efforts made by many authors. We only mention Clarke(1983), who invented the generalized gradient and generalized Jacobian and Ioffe(1981) who initiated the use of strict prederivatives of functions. We recall them now.

Let X and Y be normed spaces, $D \subset X$ be an open set and $f : D \to Y$ be an arbitrary function. A family of bounded linear operators $\mathcal{T} \subset \mathbf{B}(X,Y)$ is called a ***strict prederivative*** of f at the point $\hat{x} \in D$ if for all $\varepsilon > 0$ there

[1]The support of the Humboldt Foundation is gratefully acknowledged.

exists $\delta > 0$ such that

$$f(x') - f(x'') \in \mathcal{T}(x' - x'') + \varepsilon\|x' - x''\|B_X \qquad \text{for all} \quad x', x'' \in \hat{x} + \delta B_X$$

(here and in the sequel, B_X and B_Y denote the closed unit ball of X and Y, respectively).
Obviously, a function f admits a one element prederivative at $\hat{x}$ if and only if it is strictly Fréchet differentiable.
If X and Y are finite dimensional spaces, then the generalized Jacobian of a locally Lipschitz function f at $\hat{x}$ is defined by

$$\partial f(\hat{x}) := \overline{\text{co}}\{T \in \mathbf{B}(X,Y) \mid \exists x_n \to \hat{x} : \ \forall n \, \exists f'(x_n) \ \text{and} \ \lim_{n\to\infty} f'(x_n) = T\}.$$

This definition makes sense since f is almost everywhere differentiable by Rademacher's theorem.
The following result of Ioffe(1981) describes the connection between these two notions.

Lemma. *Let X and Y be finite dimensional normed spaces $D \subset X$ be open and $f : D \to Y$ be a locally Lipschitz function at $\hat{x} \in D$. Then $\partial f(\hat{x})$ is a compact convex strict prederivative of f at $\hat{x}$.*

Surjectivity of Nonsmooth Mappings

The main result of this paper is stated in the following surjection theorem.

Theorem 1. *Let X and Y be Banach spaces, $D \subset X$ be an open set, $f : D \to Y$, and $\hat{x} \in D$. Assume that f has a compact convex prederivative $\mathcal{T} \subset \mathbf{B}(X,Y)$ at $\hat{x}$ such that all $T \in \mathcal{T}$ are surjective. Then there exists neighborhoods $U \subset D$ of $\hat{x}$ and V of $f(\hat{x})$, a positive constant L and a function $\varphi : U \times V \to D$ such that*

$$f(\varphi(x,y)) = y \qquad \text{and} \qquad \|x - \varphi(x,y)\| \le L\|f(x) - y\|$$

hold true for all $x \in U$ and $y \in V$.

The proof of this theorem makes use of Banach's open mapping theorem, Michael's selection theorem, Ekeland's variational principle and Kakutani's fixed point theorem.
The statement of Theorem 1 can be extended to the investigation of the solvability of equations $f(p, \varphi) = y$, where the first variable of f is taken

from a topological space. Such extensions of Lyusternik's theorem can be found in Ioffe—Tihomirov(1979) in the smooth case.

As a consequence, in the smooth situation we obtain at once

Corollary 1. (The inverse function theorems of Lyusternik(1934) and Graves(1935).) *Assume that f in Theorem 2 is strictly Fréchet differentiable at $\hat{x}$ and $f'(\hat{x})$ maps X onto Y. Then the conclusion of Theorem 1 holds.*

The application of the Lemma yields

Corollary 2. (Extension of Clarke's inverse function theorem, cf. Clarke (1983).) *Let X and Y be finite dimensional normed spaces and assume that $f : D \to Y$ is a locally Lipschitz function at $\hat{x}$. Assume that the elements of $\partial f(\hat{x})$ are matrices of full rank. Then the conclusion of Theorem 1 holds.*

Inverse and implicit function theorems

When the prederivative of f consists of bijective operators, then the following more stronger statement can be verified.

Theorem 2. *Let X and Y be Banach spaces, $D \subset X$ be an open set, $f : D \to Y$, and $\hat{x} \in D$. Assume that f has a compact convex prederivative $\mathcal{T} \subset \mathrm{B}(X,Y)$ at $\hat{x}$ such that all $T \in \mathcal{T}$ are bijective. Then there exists neighborhoods $V \subset Y$ of $f(\hat{x})$ and a function $\psi : V \to D$ such that*

$$f(\psi(y)) = y \qquad \text{for} \quad y \in V$$

and $\mathcal{T}^{-1}$ is a compact prederivative of ψ at $f(\hat{x})$.

Two immediate corollaries of Theorem 2:

Corollary 3. (The classical inverse function theorem.) *Assume that f in Theorem 2 is strictly Fréchet differentiable at $\hat{x}$ and $f'(\hat{x})$ is a bijective operator. Then there exist a neighborhood V of $f(\hat{x})$ and $\psi : V \to D$ such that the conclusion of Theorem 2 holds true and ψ is strictly Frechet differentiable at $f(\hat{x})$ with $\psi'(f(\hat{x})) := (f'(\hat{x}))^{-1}$.*

Corollary 4. (The inverse function of Clarke(1976).) *Let X and Y be finite dimensional normed spaces and assume that $f : D \to Y$ is a locally Lipschitz function at $\hat{x}$. Assume that the elements of $\partial f(\hat{x})$ are invertible matrices. Then the conclusion of Theorem 2 holds with $\mathcal{T} = \partial f(\hat{x})$.*

A Lagrange Multiplier Rule

The most important application of Theorem 1 is contained in the following result which is a multiplier rule for optimum problems with nonsmooth equality constraints.

Theorem 3. *Let X and Y be Banach spaces, $D \subset X$ be an open set, $f : D \to Y$, $F : D \to \mathbf{R}$. Let $\hat{x} \in D$ be a solution of the following problem*

$$(\mathcal{P}): \qquad \text{Minimize} \quad F(x) \qquad \text{subject to} \quad f(x) = 0.$$

Assume that f and F have compact convex prederivatives $\mathcal{T} \subset \mathcal{B}(X,Y)$ and $\mathcal{S} \subset X^*$ at $\hat{x}$, respectively, such that the range of all $T \in \mathcal{T}$ is closed. Then there exist Lagrange multipliers $\lambda \in \mathbf{R}$ and $y^* \in Y^*$ satisfying

$$0 \in \lambda\mathcal{S} + y^* \circ \mathcal{T} \qquad \textit{and} \qquad |\lambda| + \|y^*\| \neq 0.$$

This result reduces to the usual Lagrange multiplier rule known for problems with equality constraints (see e.g. Ioffe—Tihomirov(1979)) if the functions f and F are smooth at $\hat{x}$.

When X and Y are finite dimensional spaces, then the statement reduces to a special case of a result due to Clarke(1983), since inequality-type constraints are not handled here.

References

Clarke, F. H. (1976) *On the inverse function theorem*, Pacific J. Math. 62: 97-102.

Clarke, F. H. (1983) *Optimization and Nonsmooth Analysis*, Canadian Math. Soc. Series of Monographs and Advanced Texts, Wiley-Interscience, New York–Chichester–Brisbane– Toronto–Singapore.

Graves, L. M. (1935) *Topics in functional calculus*, Bull. Amer. Math. Soc. 41: 641-662.

Ioffe, A. D. (1981) *Nonsmooth analysis: differential calculus of nondifferentiable mappings*, Trans. Amer. Math. Soc. 266: 1-56.

Ioffe, A. D. and Tihomirov, V. M. (1979) *Theory of extremal problems*, North-Holland, Amsterdam.

Lyusternik, L. A. (1934) *On extremum conditions for functionals*, Math. Sbornik, 41: 390-401.

KNOWLEDGE ACQUISITION THROUGH SCHEDULE DECOMPOSITION

Erwin Pesch
Faculty of Economics and Business Administration, KE, University of Limburg
P.O. Box 616, NL–6200 MD Maastricht

Introduction

A **job shop** consists of a set of different machines that perform operations on jobs. Each job has a specified processing order through the machines; that is a job is an ordered list of operations, each of which is determined by the machine it requires and by its processing time. Operations cannot be interrupted (non–preemption), each machine can handle only one job at a time, and each job can be performed on only one machine at a time. The operation sequences on the machines are unknown and have to be determined so as to minimize the makespan, i.e. the time required to complete all jobs, see the different problem formulations by Blazewicz et al. (1991) and Adams et al. (1988).

As the name suggests, **genetic algorithms** are motivated by the theory of evolution, see Goldberg (1989) and Michalewicz (1992). They have been designed as general search strategies and optimization methods.
Roughly speaking, a genetic algorithm aims at producing near–optimal solutions by letting a set of random solutions undergo a sequence of unary and binary transformations (reproduction, crossover, mutation) governed by a selection scheme biased towards high–quality solutions.

The job shop scheduling problem is a typical representative of a binary **constraint satisfaction problem (CSP)**, i.e., generally speaking, there is a set of variables each of which has its own domain of values. Find an assignment of values to variables such that a set of constraints on variable pairs is satisfied (see Dechter / Pearl (1988) and Meseguer (1989)). Assume that there is an upper bound on the makespan of an optimal schedule of the underlying job shop scheduling problem. Then computing heads and tails assigns to each operation an interval of possible start times. Considering variable domains as possible operation start times where the variables define the operations in a schedule then the disjunctive graph illustrates the job shop scheduling constraint satisfaction problem, hence it corresponds to the constraint graph (Montanari (1974)).

Consistency checks, or roughly speaking propagation of constraints will make implicitly defined constraints more visible and will prune the search tree in a branch and bound algorithm (cf. Pesch et al. (1993), Mackworth (1977)). The better the bounds the more arc directions in the disjunctive graph can be fixed during the propagation process.

Genetic Based Learning

Genetic algorithms do not fit best for scheduling problems in order to get near-optimal solutions if no improvement heuristic, such as local search, is incorporated (cf. Davis (1985), Ulder et al. (1991)) and only little work is done on genetic algorithms with respect to (job shop) scheduling, see Dorndorf / Pesch (1993), Husbands et al. (1991), and Starkweather et al. (1992). Some type of an improvement heuristic may be incorporated into the crossover operator (see Kolen / Pesch (1991), Yamada / Nakano (1992)). The strategy of Dorndorf and Pesch (1992) controls a sequence of priority rules or the machine inclusion sequence for the shifting bottleneck heuristic of Adams et al. (1988) or Balas et al. (1992) and learns to find best combinations in both cases. A different approach was followed by Storer et al. (1992). They map the original data of the underlying problem instance to slightly disturbed and genetically controlled data representing new problem instances. The latter are solved heuristically and the solution, i.e. the operations' processing orders, are considered to be solutions of the original problem.
One can use other kinds of rules which fix the order of operations on the same machine. For instance, any permutation of unscheduled operations might represent a rule (Davis (1985) and Hilliard / Liepins (1988)). The approach to search a best sequence of decision rules for selecting operations is just in line with the ideas of Fisher and Thompson (1963) on probabilistic learning of sequences consisting of two priority rules, and Crowston et al (1963) on learning how to find promising linear combinations of basic priorities.
Constraint propagation in the sense of arc- or path-consistency (Van Hentenryck et al. (1992)) generally fixes only a few most often trivial arc directions even if tight upper bounds of the makespan in an optimal schedule are applied. Remedy yields to consider subproblems (e.g. one-machine or multiple-job problems). Hence, new genetic based approaches were applied, the **one machine constraint propagation based genetic algorithm** and a **multiple job constraint propagation based genetic algorithm**. Whenever a new population is generated a local decision rule in the sense of constraint propagation in order to achieve arc- and path-consistency is applied simultaneously to each subproblem with respect to some upper bound. Feasible solutions are obtained as in Yamada / Nakano (1992). For details see Pesch (1993).

Computational Results

The probably 2 best known test problems for job shop scheduling (Fisher / Thompson (1963)): the 5 × 20, and the 10 × 10 problem the optima of which are 1165 and 930, respectively (cf. Carlier / Pinson (1990), Brucker et al. (1991), Applegate / Cook (1991)) can optimally be solved by the one machine constraint propagation based genetic algorithm. Detailed computational results compared to other local search approaches (Aarts et al. (1991), Nakano and Yamada (1991, 1992), Dell'Amico / Trubian (1993), Van Laarhoven et al. (1992)) are provided in Pesch (1993).
The constraint propagation based approaches even try to avoid the use of problem specific knowledge that is not relevant for the complete problem. Introducing problem specific knowledge makes a genetic strategy a promising alternative. This knowledge might be incorporated by the application of a heuristic performing well on the particular problem, such as the shifting bottleneck procedure for the job shop problem.

References

E.H.L. Aarts, P.J.M. van Laarhoven, and N.L.J. Ulder (1991): Local–search–based algorithms for job shop scheduling. Working paper, University of Eindhoven.

J. Adams, E. Balas, and D. Zawack (1988): The shifting bottleneck procedure for job shop scheduling. Management Science 34, 391–401.

D. Applegate and W. Cook (1991): A computational study of the job–shop scheduling problem. ORSA Journal on Computing 3, 149–156.

E. Balas, J.K. Lenstra, and A. Vazacopoulos (1992): One machine scheduling with delayed precedence constraints. Management Science Research Report MSRR–589, Carnegie Mellon University, Pittsburgh.

J. Blazewicz, M, Dror, and J. Weglarz (1991): Mathematical programming formulations for machine scheduling: a survey. European Journal of Operational Research 51, 283–300.

P. Brucker, B. Jurisch, and B. Sievers (1991): A fast branch & bound algorithm for the job–shop scheduling problem. Discrete Applied Mathematics (to appear).

J. Carlier and E. Pinson (1990): A practical use of Jackson's preemtive schedule for solving the job shop problem. Annals of Operations Research 26, 269–287.

W.B. Crowston, F. Glover, G.L. Thompson, and J.D. Trawick (1963): Probabilistic and parametric learning combinations of local job shop scheduling rules. ONR Research Memorandum No. 117, GSIA, Carnegie–Mellon University, Pittsburg, PA.

L. Davis (1985): Job shop scheduling with genetic algorithms. Proc. an Int. Conf. Genetic Algorithms and Their Applications (J.J. Grefenstette, ed.). Lawrence Erlbaum Ass., 136–140.

R. Dechter and J. Pearl (1988): Network–based heuristics for constraint satisfaction problems. Artificial Intelligence 34, 1–38.

M. Dell'Amico and M. Trubian (1993): Applying tabu–search to the job shop scheduling problem. Annals of Operations Research 41 (to appear).

U. Dorndorf and E. Pesch (1992): Evolution based learning in a job shop scheduling environment. Computers & Operations Research (to appear).

U. Dorndorf and E. Pesch (1993): Genetic algorithms for job shop scheduling. Operations Research Proc. 1992 (K.-W. Hansmann et al. eds.), Springer, Berlin, 243–250.

H. Fisher and G.L. Thompson (1963): Probabilistic learning combinations of local job-shop scheduling rules. Industrial Scheduling (J.F. Muth and G.L. Thompson, eds.). Prentice Hall, Englewood Cliffs.

D.E. Goldberg (1989): Genetic Algorithms in Search, Optimization and Machine Learning. Addison-Wesley, Reading.

P. van Hentenryck, Y. Deville, and C.-M. Teng (1992): A generic arc-consistency algorithm and its specializations. Artificial Intelligence 57, 291–321.

M.R. Hilliard and G.E. Liepins (1988): Machine learning applications to job shop scheduling. Proc. Workshop on Production Planning and Scheduling. AAAI-SIGMAN, St. Paul, MN.

P. Husbands, F. Mill, and S. Warrington (1991): Genetic algorithms, production plan optimisation and scheduling. Lecture Notes in Computer Science 496, 80–84.

A. Kolen and E. Pesch (1991): Genetic local search in combinatorial optimization. Discrete Applied Mathematics (to appear in 1994).

P.J.M. van Laarhoven, E.H.L. Aarts, and J.K. Lenstra (1992): Job shop scheduling by simulated annealing. Operations Research 40, 113–125.

A.K. Mackworth (1977): Consistency in networks of relations. Artificial Intelligence 8, 99–118.

P. Meseguer (1989): Constraint satisfaction problems: an overview. AICOM 2, 3–17.

Z. Michalewicz (1992): Genetic Algorithms + Data Structures = Evolution Programs. Springer, Berlin.

U. Montanari (1974): Networks of constraints: fundamental properties and applications to picture processing. Informations Sciences 7, 95–132.

R. Nakano and T. Yamada (1991): Conventional genetic algorithm for job shop problems. Proc. 4th Int. Conference on Genetic Algorithms and their Applications, San Diego, CA, 474–479.

E. Pesch (1993): Machine learning by schedule decomposition. Working paper, University of Limburg, Maastricht.

E. Pesch, A. Drexl, and A. Kolen (1993): Automatische Wissensakquisition mittels modellbasierter Inferenz in CHARME. Working paper, University of Limburg, Maastricht.

T. Starkweather, D. Whitley, K. Mathias, and S. McDaniel (1992): Sequence scheduling with genetic algorithms. New Directions for Operations Research in Manufacturing (G. Fandel, T. Gulledge, and J. Jones, eds.), Springer, Berlin, 129–148.

R.H. Storer, S.D. Wu, and R. Vaccari (1992): New search spaces for sequencing problems with application to job shop scheduling. Management Science 38, 1495–1509.

N.L.J. Ulder, E.H.L. Aarts, H.-J. Bandelt, P.J.M. van Laarhoven, and E. Pesch (1991): Genetic local search algorithms for the traveling salesman problem. Lecture Notes in Computer Science 496, 109–116.

T. Yamada and R. Nakano (1992): A genetic algorithm applicable to large-scale job-shop problems. Proc. 2nd. Int. Workshop on Parallel Problem Solving from Nature (R. Männer and B. Manderick, eds.), 281–290.

MULTILEVEL CONTROL OF AQUATIC ECOSYSTEMS IN LAKE

Grażyna Petriczek, Zygmunt Uhrynowski
Systems Research Institute
Polish Akademy of Sciences
01-447 Warsaw,Newelska 6,

The ecological models of lake consist of two parts. One of them describes biochemical processes, the other describes the transportation of water polluted by different substances. The biochemical part of the model concerns variations in phyto and zooplankton populations and in the concentration of such substances as phosphorus,nitrogen etc. The biochemical processes are related to the growth and mortality of organisms, nonorganic nutrients assimilation and sedimentation. The transportation part of the model reflects the structure of the spatial partition of lake. This structure has the form of the sequence of layers (segments), homogeneous from the point of view of pollutant concentration.

In ecological model under consideration we assume that the body of water is ideally mixed, i.e. the concentration of a substance in the body can be considered to be completely homogeneous - diffusion can be neglected.

These assumptions can concern either one of the layer of a lake or lakes in which the extent of turbulence due to wind, tides or other forces is so gread that for practical purposes the concentration is homogenous.

In considered model we assume that a lake is a nonstratified, well mixed reservoir, in which concentration changes of constituents depend only on time. It is assumed that the growth of plants and organisms in lake depends on the pollutant quality coefficients such as phosphorus and nitrogen. In the model the following processes are considered: zooplankton grazing, respiration, nutrients sedimentation and biodegradation.

Under above assumptions the model describing variations of nitrogen and phosphorus concentation as well as variations in phyto and zooplankton populations has the form of following differential equations :

$$\frac{dA}{dt} = (\mu_a - r_a - s_a - m_a)A - \frac{\mu_z Z}{d} - \frac{Q\,A}{V} \qquad [1]$$

$$\frac{dZ}{dt} = (\mu_z - r_z - m_z)Z - \frac{\mu_f F}{d} - \frac{Q.Z}{V} \qquad [2]$$

$$\frac{dP}{dt} = \frac{Q_d P_d}{V} + Z_p + \alpha_s P - \frac{(\mu_a - r_a)A}{\alpha_p} + \frac{r_z Z}{\alpha_p} - \frac{Q\,P}{V} +$$

$$+ k_4\, dp\, k_6 \qquad [3]$$

$$\frac{dN}{dt} = \frac{Q_d N_d}{V} + Z_n + \beta_s N - \frac{k_d N}{V} - \frac{(\mu_a - r_a)A}{\beta_p} + \frac{r_z Z}{\beta_p} +$$

$$+ k_4\, dn\, k_6 - \frac{Q\,N}{V} \qquad [4]$$

where : A , Z - are respectively phyto and zooplankton concentrations,

P , N - are respectively phosphorus and nitrogen dissolved in lake water,

Z_n , Z_p - waste loads (phosphorus and nitrogen) discharged to the lake,

Q , (Q_d) - rate of total outflow from (inflow to) the lake,

F - fish concentration.

In the above equations, the growth coefficients μ_a , μ_z , μ_f play a essential part. They are of the following nonlinear form

$$\mu_a = \mu_{amax}(T,L)\,\frac{N}{k_n + N}\;\frac{P}{k_p + P} \qquad [5]$$

$$\mu_z = \mu_{zmax}(T,L)\,\frac{A}{k_a + A} \qquad [6]$$

$$\mu_f = \mu_{fmax}(T)\frac{Z}{k_z + Z} \qquad [7]$$

As results from the equations [1] - [4] and from the relationships describing the coefficients μ_a, μ_z, μ_f, the considered aquatic ecosystem model is of nonlinear form and canbe decomposed into three interconnected submodels :

a) a submodel describing variations in phytoplankton population,
b) a submodel describing variations in zooplankton population,
c) a submodel describing variations of nitrogen and phosphorus concentrations.

The global model composed of these submodels is given by the system of ordinary nonlinear differential equations [1] - [4]. The interconnection between submodels is realized, among others, by the growth coefficients μ_a, μ_z, where μ_a is a function of nitrogen and phosphorus concentrations and μ_z is a function of the phytoplankton population.

The control objective is to determine such a strategy for waste loads discharges, which quaranteesecological equilibrium in the lake. The problem of waste load discharge optimal control we formulate as the following optimization problem :

Minimize the following performace functional :

$$J(x,u,m) = \int_{t_0}^{t_1} \left(\|(u_d - u_2)_+\|^2 + \|(x_3 - x_{3d})_+\|^2 + \|(x_1 - x_{1d})_+\|^2 \right) dt \qquad [8]$$

subject to the equations [1] - [4]

where :

$x = [x_1, x_2, x_3] = [A, Z, (P, N)]$ - is the vector of the state variables,

$u = [u_2, u_3] = [F, (Z_n, Z_p)]$ - is the vector of the control variables,

$m = [m_1, m_2, m_3]$ - is the interconnection variables given by :

$$m_1 = g_1(x_2,x_3) \quad ; \quad m_2 = g_2(x_1) \quad ; \quad m_3 = g_3(x_1,x_2) ,$$

$g_i(\ )$, i= 1,.,3 are nonlinear functions of phyto and zooplankton populations and of phosphorus and nitrogen concentrations. They are connected with the form of coefficients μ_a, μ_z .

u_d - is a desirable fish concentration,

x_{3d} - is a desirable quality level,

x_{1d} - corresponds to drinking-water quality requirements

To solve this problem we apply the two-level coordination method based on the augmented Lagrange functional associated with interaction equations : $m_i = g_i(x)$, i= 1,2,3 .

This leads to a two-level problem structure :

The first-level problem consists in independent minimization of the local functional with respect to state and control variables (for given multipliers π and interaction variables m).The first-level optimization gives optimal values of state variables x_i and control variables u_i (the fish concentration F and waste loads Z_n, Z_p) for each subsystem (submodel).

The task of the second level consists in determining such values of multipliers π and interaction variables m , which guarantee global optimum for the whole system. The Lagrange multipliers are associated with the interconnection equations.

References :

Beck M.B, G. van Straten (ed.) (1983) Uncertainty and Forecasting of Water Quality. Springer-Verlag. Berlin Heidelberg New York

Biskwas A,K (1981) Models for Water Quality Management. (Series in: Water Resources and Environmental Engineering). McGraw-Hill. New York

Somlyody L, Herodek S, Fischer J(ed.) (1983) Eutrophication of Shallow Lakes: Modelling and Management. IIASA. Laxenburg

Sonzogni W, Uttormark P, Lee G (1978) A phosphorus residence time model: Theory and Application. Water Research. vol.10 Pergamon Press

Systems Analysis for Water Quality Management. (1975) Proceedings of a Seminar Sponsored by the Regional Office for Europe of the World Health Organization. Budapest

SHORT PROOFS OF SOME THEOREMS IN PROBABILITY AND STATISTICS BASED ON A WEAK COMPACTNESS ARGUMENT FOR TESTS

D. Plachky
Institute for Mathematical Statistics
Einsteinstr. 62, D-48149 Münster

Abstract

Short proofs based on the weak compactness of tests are given for the following results:

(i) continuous dependence of the envelope power function on the level,

(ii) closedness of the range of probability measures,

(iii) characterization of weak compactness of non-randomized tests,

(iv) characterization of the equality of strong and weak convergence of tests,

(v) existence of densities according to the Radon-Nikodym theorem,

(vi) topological characterization of absolute continuity of finite measures.

The following weak compactness theorem is mainly used in statistics as a tool for the proof of the existence of optimal tests (cf. Lehmann (1986), p. 576): For some probability space $(\Omega, \mathcal{A}, P)$ and any sequence φ_n of test there exists some subsequence φ_{n_k} and some test φ satisfying $\lim_{k\to\infty} \int \varphi_{n_k} f\,dP = \int \varphi f\,dP$ for all $f \in L_1(\Omega, \mathcal{A}, P)$. Here the notion "test" stands for any $\mathcal{A}$-measurable function $\varphi : \Omega \to [0,1]$, whereas the special case $\varphi = I_A$ (indicator function for $A \in \mathcal{A}$) is called non-randomized test. The aim of this note is to show that this result admits many other applications in probability and statistics.

Example 1 Continuous Dependence of the Envelope Power Function on the Level *Let $(\Omega, \mathcal{A}, \mathcal{P})$ denote a statistical experiment, i.e. $\mathcal{P}$ is a family of probability measures on $\mathcal{A}$ and Q some fixed probbility measure on $\mathcal{A}$. Then it will be shown that the envelope power function $\beta(\alpha)$ defined by $\beta(\alpha) = \sup\{\int \varphi\,dQ : \varphi \in \Phi_\alpha\}$, depends continuously on $\alpha \in [0,1]$ for decreasing sequences, where Φ_α is the set of all level α tests with respect to $\mathcal{P}$, i.e. $\Phi_\alpha = \{\varphi$ test: $\int \varphi\,dP \leq \alpha,\ P \in \mathcal{P}\}$. Now the weak compactness theorem together with V.3.14 of*

Dunford/Schwartz (1964), p. 422, implies (without any additional assumption on $\mathcal{P}$) the existence of some $\varphi_\alpha^* \in \Phi_\alpha$ satisfying $\int \varphi_\alpha^* \, dQ = \beta(\alpha)$. In particular, for any decreasing sequence $\alpha_n \in [0,1]$ satisfying $\lim_{n\to\infty} \alpha_n = \alpha$, there exists some subsequence $\varphi\alpha_{n_k}$ and some test φ_α satisfying $\lim_{k\to\infty} \int \varphi\alpha_{n_k} dP = \int \varphi_\alpha \, dP$, $P \in \mathcal{P} \cup \{Q\}$, from which $\varphi_\alpha \in \Phi_\alpha$ follows. Furthermore, $\int \varphi_\alpha \, dQ = \beta(\alpha)$ and, therefore, $\lim_{n\to\infty} \beta(\alpha_n) = \beta(\alpha)$, is valid in the case $\alpha_n \downarrow \alpha$, since $\alpha \to \beta(\alpha)$ is monotone increasing, i.e. the left-continuity of $\alpha \to \beta(\alpha)$ on the closed unit interval has been proved. The continuity of $\alpha \to \beta(\alpha)$ on the open unit interval follows from the concavity of the envelope power function $\alpha \to \beta(\alpha)$. The concavity of the envelope power function might be derived from the existence of tests $\varphi_{\alpha_j}^* \in \Phi_{\alpha_j}$, $j = 1,2$, satisfying $\beta(\alpha_j) = \int \varphi_{\alpha_j}^* \, dQ$, $j = 1,2$, since $\beta(\lambda\alpha_1 + (1-\lambda)\alpha_2) \geq \lambda \int \varphi_{\alpha_1}^* dQ + (1-\lambda) \int \varphi_{\alpha_2}^* dQ$ is valid for any $\lambda \in [0,1]$.

In the following three examples the uniquely determined decomposition of any probability measure P according to $P = \mu_1 + \mu_2$, where μ_1 is a finite atomless measure and μ_2 is a finite atomic measure will be applied in addition to a weak compactness argument for tests. The existence of μ_j, $j = 1,2$, follows from the simple fact that μ_2 is the concentration of P on the union of a maximal set of pairwise disjoint P-atoms and μ_1 the concentration of P on the corresponding complement.

Example 2 Closedness of the Range of a Probability Measure
Taking into consideration that the range of a finite atomless measure is convex it remains to show that the range of an atomic probability measure on a σ-algebra $\mathcal{A}$ of subsets of a set Ω is closed, which follows from a weak compactness argument. For this purpose let $\{A_1^*, A_2^*, \ldots\}$ denote a maximal set of pairwise disjoint P-atoms, which implies that Ω is equal to $\bigcup_j A_j^*$ up to a P-zero set. Therefore, $\lim_{n\to\infty} \int I_{A_n} f \, dP = \int \varphi f \, dP$, $f \in L_1(\Omega, \mathcal{A}, P)$, for a sequence $A_n \in \mathcal{A}$ and some test φ implies that φ is equal up to a P-zero set to an union of sets belonging to $\{A_1^*, A_2^*, \ldots\}$. Hence, a weak compactness argument of tests implies the closedness of the range of an atomic probability measure and, therefore, the closedness of the range for any probability measure.

Example 3 Characterization of Weak Compactness of the Set of Non-randomized Tests
It has been already proved in the preceding example that a sequence of non-randomized tests I_{A_n}, $A_n \in \mathcal{A}$, satisfying $\lim_{n\to\infty} \int I_{A_n} f \, dP = \int \varphi f \, dP$, $f \in L_1(\Omega, \mathcal{A}, P)$, for some test φ implies that φ is already non-randomized up to a P-zero set, if P is atomic. Clearly, this conclusion remains valid if the sequence I_{A_n} is replaced by a generalized sequence I_{A_α}, $A_\alpha \in \mathcal{A}$ (cf. Dunford/Schwartz (1964), I.7.1, p. 26), since φ must be equal on any A_j^* to some constant c_j up to a P-zero set, where $\{A_1^*, A_2^*, \ldots\}$ denotes a maximal set of pairwise disjoint P-atoms. For the proof of the converse direction that weak compactness of the set of non-randomized tests implies that the underlying probability measure P is atomic, one might start from the atomless part μ_1 of P consisting of the concentration of P on the complement of

$\bigcup_j A_j^*$, *which will be denoted by* Ω_o *in the sequel, where* $\{A_1^*, A_2^*, \ldots\}$ *is a maximal set of pairwise disjoint* P*-atoms. The property of* μ_1 *to be atomless yields the existence of pairwise disjoint sets* $A_{(\frac{k-1}{2^n}, \frac{k}{2^n}]}$, $k = 1, \ldots, 2^n$, *satisfying* $P_1(A_{(\frac{k-1}{2^n}, \frac{k}{2^n}]}) = 2^{-n}$, $k = 1, \ldots, 2^n$, $n \in \mathbb{N}$, *and* $A_{(\frac{k-1}{2^n}, \frac{k}{2^n}]} = \bigcup_{\nu=(k-1)2^m+1}^{k2^m} A_{(\frac{\nu-1}{2^{n+m}}, \frac{\nu}{2^{n+m}}]}$, $k = 1, \ldots, 2^n$, $n, m \in \mathbb{N}$, *where* $A_{(0,1]}$ *is equal to* Ω_o *and* P_1 *stands for* $\mu_1 / P(\Omega_o)$, *if* $P(\Omega_o) > 0$ *would hold true. Now the weak compactnes argument for tests applied to the sequence of indicator functions of the sets* B_n *defined by* $\bigcup_{k=1,\, k\text{odd}}^{2^n} A_{(\frac{k-1}{2^n}, \frac{k}{2^n}]}$, $n \in \mathbb{N}$, *yields* $\lim_{k\to\infty} \int I_{B_{n_k}} f\, dP_1 = \frac{1}{2} \int f\, dP_1$ *for all* $f \in L_1(\Omega, \mathcal{A}_o, P_1|\mathcal{A}_o)$, *where* $\mathcal{A}_o$ *denotes the* σ*-algebra generated by the sets* $A_{(\frac{k-1}{2^n}, \frac{k}{2^n}]}$, $k = 1, \ldots, 2^n$, $n \in \mathbb{N}$. *In particular,* $\frac{1}{2}$ *cannot be equal to some non-randomized test up to a* P*-zero set, which is a contradiction to the assumption that the set of non-randomized tests should be weakly compact, i.e.* $P(\Omega_o) = 0$ *must be valid, which is equivalent to the property of* P *to be atomic.*

Example 4 Characterization of the Equality of Weak and Strong Convergence of Tests

Let P *denote some atomic probability measure on a* σ*-algebra* $\mathcal{A}$ *of subsets of a set* Ω. *Then* $\lim_{n\to\infty} \int \varphi_n f\, dP = \int \varphi f\, dP$, $f \in L_1(\Omega, \mathcal{A}, P)$ *for a sequence* φ_n *of tests, which converges weakly to some test* φ *implies* $\varphi_n \to \varphi$ P*-a.e., since any real-valued, measurable function is* P*-a.e. equal to some constant on any* P*-atom. Now the theorem of dominated convergence implies the strong convergence* $\lim_{n\to\infty} \int |\varphi_n - \varphi| dP = 0$ *of the sequence* φ_n *to* φ. *This conclusion remains valid for generalized sequences of tests, if one takes into consideration the main idea for the reduction of the theorem of dominated convergence for generalized sequences (cf. Dunford/Schwartz (1964), III.3.7, p. 124) to sequences. For the proof of the converse direction that the equality of strong and weak convergence of tests implies that the underlying probability measure* P *is atomic, one might start from the observation that the strong limit of a sequence of non-randomized tests must coincide up to a* P*-zero set with some non-randomized test. According to the investigations of the preceding example 3 the underlying probability measure* P *must be atomic.*

The final application of the weak compactness of tests concerns the existence of densities according to the theorem of Radon-Nikodym. For this purpose one might start from the following version of the weak compactness argument for tests: For any generalized sequence φ_α of tests there exists some generalized subsequence (subnet) φ_β and some test φ satisfying $\lim_\beta \int \varphi_\beta f\, dP = \int \varphi f\, dP$, $f \in L_1(\Omega, \mathcal{A}, P)$. This version might be proved by means of the theorem of Alaoglu (cf. Dunford/Schwartz (1964)1, V.4.2, p. 424) applied to the Hilbert space $L_2(\Omega, \mathcal{A}, P)$ without using the Radon-Nikodym theorem. Therefore, one gets a new and short proof for the theorem of Radon-Nikodym based on a weak compactnes argument as the following example shows.

Example 5 Existence of Densities According to the Theorem of Radon-Nikodym

Let μ, ν *denote finite measures on a* σ*-algebra* $\mathcal{A}$ *of subsets of a set* Ω, *where* μ *is absolutely* *continuous with respect to* ν *(symbol:* $\mu \ll \nu$*). In the sequel one starts from the special case* $\mu \leq \nu$*, from which* $\mu(A) = \int_A \varphi_{\mathcal{F}} d\nu$ *for all* $A \in \sigma(\mathcal{F})$ *and any finite subset* $\mathcal{F}$ *of* $\mathcal{A}$ *follows, where* $\varphi_{\mathcal{F}}$ *denotes the test defined by* $\sum_{k=1}^{m(n)} \frac{\mu(A_k)}{\nu(A_k)} I_{A_k}$*,* $\sigma(\mathcal{F})$ *the* σ*-algebra generated by* $\mathcal{F}$*. Here* A_k*,* $k = 1, \ldots, m(n)$*, stands for the atoms of* $\sigma(\mathcal{F})$ *satisfying* $\nu(A_k) > 0$*. Now any generalized subsequence* $\varphi_{\mathcal{F}'}$ *of the generalized sequence* $\varphi_{\mathcal{F}}$ *with weak limit* φ *as a test yields* $\mu(A) = \int_A \varphi d\nu$*,* $A \in \sigma(\mathcal{F})$*, for any finite subset* $\mathcal{F}$ *of* $\mathcal{A}$*, since for any* $\mathcal{F}$ *there exists some* $\mathcal{F}'$ *containing* $\mathcal{F}$*. Hence,* φ *is a version of the Radon-Nikodym derivative (density of* μ *with respect to* ν*)* $\frac{d\mu}{d\nu}$*. Furthermore, the original generalized sequence* $\varphi_{\mathcal{F}}$ *satisfies* $\lim_{\mathcal{F}} \int \varphi_{\mathcal{F}} f d\nu = \int \varphi f d\nu$*,* $f \in L_1(\Omega, \mathcal{A}, P)$*, since* $\frac{d\mu}{d\nu}$ *is uniquely determined up to a* ν*-zero set. The general case* $\mu \ll \nu$ *follows from the special case, which has been just investigated, by the observation that* $\frac{\varphi}{1-\varphi} I_{\{\varphi<1\}}$ *is a version of* $\frac{d\mu}{d\nu}$*, where* φ *stands for a version of* $\frac{d\mu}{d(\mu+\nu)}$*. This might be seen from the equality* $\int_A (\sum_{k=1}^{\infty} \varphi^k) d(\mu + \nu) = \int_A (\sum_{k=1}^{\infty} \varphi^{k-1}) d\mu$ *for all* $A \in \mathcal{A}$*, which implies* $\int_A (\sum_{k=1}^{\infty} \varphi^k) d\mu + \int_A (\sum_{k=1}^{\infty} \varphi^k) d\nu = \int_A (\sum_{k=0}^{\infty} \varphi^k) d\mu$ *for all* $A \in \mathcal{A}$*, i.e.* $\int_A (\sum_{k=1}^{\infty} \varphi^k) d\nu = \mu(A)$ *holds true for any* $A \in \mathcal{A} \cap \{\varphi < 1\}$*. Finally* $\nu(\{\varphi = 1\}) = 0$ *implies* $\mu(\{\varphi = 1\}) = 0$ *because of* $\mu \ll \nu$*, i.e.* $\mu(A) = \int_A \frac{\varphi}{1-\varphi} I_{\{\varphi<1\}} d\nu$ *is valid for all* $A \in \mathcal{A}$*.*

Example 6 Topological Characterization of Absolute Continuity
Let ν, μ *denote finite measure on some* σ*-algebra* $\mathcal{A}$ *of subsets of a set* Ω*. Then absolute continuity* $\nu \ll \mu$ *is equivalent to the property of* μ *and* ν *that* $\int \varphi_n f \, d\mu \to \int \varphi f \, d\mu$*,* $f \in L_1(\Omega, \mathcal{A}, \mu)$ *implies* $\int \varphi_n g \, d\nu \to \int \varphi g \, d\nu$*,* $g \in L_1(\Omega, \mathcal{A}, \nu)$*, where* φ_n*,* $n \in \mathbb{N}$*, and* φ *denotes tests. Clearly,* $\nu \ll \mu$ *is implied by this property of* μ *and* ν*. For the converse direction one might start from a sequence* φ_n *of tests satisfying* $\lim_{n\to\infty} \int \varphi_n f \, d\mu = \int \varphi f \, d\mu$*,* $f \in L_1(\Omega, \mathcal{A}, \mu)$*, for some test* φ *and select some subsequence* φ_{n_k} *such that* $\lim_{k\to\infty} \int \varphi_{n_k} g \, d\nu = \int \psi g \, d\nu$*,* $g \in L_1(\Omega, \mathcal{A}, \nu)$*, for some test* ψ *holds true. This implies* $\int_A \psi \, d\nu = \int_A \varphi \, d\nu$*,* $A \in \mathcal{A}$*, i.e.* $\psi = \varphi$ ν*-a.e. and, therefore,* $\lim_{n\to\infty} \int \varphi_n g \, d\nu = \int \varphi g \, d\nu$*,* $g \in L_1(\Omega, \mathcal{A}, \nu)$*. This conclusion remains valid for generalized sequences instead of sequences, which shows that absolute continuity* $\nu \ll \mu$ *is equivalent to the property of* μ *and* ν *that the weak topology with respect to* ν *of the set consisting of all test is coarser than the corresponding weak topology with respect to* μ*.*

References

Dunford, N. and J. Schwartz (1964): Linear Operators. Interscience Publishers, New York

Lehmann, E. L. (1986): Testing Statistical Hypotheses. J. Wiley, New York

Approximation algorithms for multi-index transportation problems with decomposable costs

M. Queyranne
University of British Columbia
Fac. of Comm. and Bus. Adm.
Vancouver, V6T 1Z2
Canada

F.C.R. Spieksma
University of Limburg
Dept. of Math.
P.O. Box 616, 6200 MD Maastricht
the Netherlands

1 Introduction

The axial multi-index transportation problem can be formulated as follows. Given are k sets A_r with $|A_r| = n_r$, for $r = 1, \ldots, k$. The cartesian product of these sets A_r, $1 \leq r \leq k$, is denoted as A, that is $A = \{a : a \in A_1 \times A_2 \times \cdots \times A_k\}$. We will refer to an element $a \in A$ as cluster a. For each cluster $a \in A$ a certain cost $c_a \in \mathbb{R}$ is specified. Further, for $r = 1, \ldots, k$, $i = 1, \ldots, n_r$, we define the sets $A_{ri} = \{a \in A : a(r) = i\}$. To each set A_{ri}, $1 \leq r \leq k$, $1 \leq i \leq n_r$ a nonnegative demand $e_{ri} \in \mathbb{R}$ is associated. The problem is now to find nonnegative real numbers x_a, $a \in A$, such that the sum of those numbers x_a for which $a(r) = i$, is equal to e_{ri} for $r = 1, \ldots k$, $i = 1, \ldots n_r$, and such that total cost, summed over all clusters, is minimized. Mathematically, the problem can be described as follows:

$$
\begin{aligned}
(kTP) \quad & \text{minimize} \quad \sum_{a \in A} c_a x_a \\
& \text{such that} \quad \sum_{a \in A_{ri}} x_a = e_{ri} \qquad r = 1, \ldots, k, \ i = 1, \ldots, n_r \\
& \qquad\qquad\quad x_a \geq 0 \qquad a \in A.
\end{aligned}
$$

In order to ensure the existence of a feasible solution, it is assumed that $K \equiv \sum_{i=1}^{n_r} e_{ri}$ for $r = 1, \ldots, k$.

This paper deals with the special case of (kTP) where the costs c_a, $a \in A$, are not arbitrarily given numbers, but are in some sense decomposable. More precisely, we will assume that there exist nonnegative numbers $d_{ij}^{A_r \times A_s}$, representing a distance between element i of A_r, $1 \leq i \leq n_r$, and element j of A_s, $1 \leq j \leq n_s$ for $r, s = 1, \ldots, k$, $r \neq s$, which determine the cost of a cluster $a \in A$. Formally, the costs c_a, $a \in A$ are defined to be decomposable if there exists a function $f : \mathbb{R}^{\binom{k}{2}} \rightarrow \mathbb{R}$ (called the cost-function) such that

$$c_a = f\left(d^{A_1\times A_2}_{a(1),a(2)},\ d^{A_1\times A_3}_{a(1),a(3)},\ \ldots,\ d^{A_1\times A_k}_{a(1),a(k)},\ d^{A_2\times A_3}_{a(2),a(3)},\ \ldots,\ d^{A_2\times A_k}_{a(2),a(k)},\ \ldots,\ d^{A_{k-1}\times A_k}_{a(k-1),a(k)}\right)$$

for all $a \in A$.

We will further assume that the distance (or length) function d satisfies the triangle inequality, that is

$$d^{A_r\times A_s}_{ij} + d^{A_s\times A_t}_{j\ell} \geq d^{A_r\times A_t}_{i\ell} \text{ for } \quad r,s,t = 1,\ldots,k,\ i = 1,\ldots,n_r,\ j = 1,\ldots,n_s,\ \ell = 1,\ldots,n_t,$$

and that d is symmetric, that is

$$d^{A_r\times A_s}_{ij} = d^{A_s\times A_r}_{ji} \qquad r,s = 1,\ldots,k,\ i = 1,\ldots,n_r,\ j = 1,\ldots,n_s.$$

A problem very closely related to (kTP) is the axial k-index assignment problem. This problem arises when $n_r = n$ for $r = 1,\ldots,k$, $i = 1,\ldots,n$, and x_a is restricted to be either 0 or 1 for all $a \in A$. In Crama and Spieksma (1992), it is proven that for $k \geq 3$ and some very simple cost-functions with the distance function d satisfying the triangle inequality, the k-index assignment problem is $\mathcal{NP}$-hard. Bandelt, Crama and Spieksma (1991) present heuristics for the multi-index assignment problem with decomposable costs, along with worst-case analyses for different specifications of the cost-function (see also Gusfield (1991)).

The purpose of this paper is to unify and extend the analyses in Bandelt et al. (1991), and to show that their results can also be applied to the multi-index transportation problem. In the next section, the heuristics are introduced, and in Section 3 a general worst-case analysis is presented.

2 The heuristics

Consider the following heuristic, consisting of two phases. The first phase amounts to solving $k-1$ ordinary (that is 2-index) transportation problems with respect to A_h and A_r for some given h, $1 \leq h \leq k$, for $r = 1,\ldots,k$. Let us denote the optimal solution to the 2-index transportation problem defined by demands e_{ri} and e_{sj} and distances $d^{A_r\times A_s}_{ij}$ for some $1 \leq r \neq s \leq k$, for $i = 1,\ldots,n_r$, $j = 1,\ldots,n_s$, by $y^{A_r\times A_s}_{ij}$. Next, in the second phase, a solution to the k-index transportation problem is constructed based on the solutions found in the first phase. We will refer to the heuristic as the single-hub heuristic. A formal description is as follows.

Step 1 Compute for some h, $1 \leq h \leq k$, $y^{A_r\times A_h}_{ij}$, for $r = 1,\ldots,k$, $r \neq h$, $i = 1,\ldots,n_r$, $j = 1,\ldots,n_h$. Set $\tilde{y}^{A_r\times A_h}_{ij} = y^{A_r\times A_h}_{ij}$ for $r = 1,\ldots,k$, $r \neq h$, $i = 1,\ldots n_r$, $j = 1,\ldots,n_h$.

Step 2 For $j := 1$ to n_h do
begin

$$
\text{inner loop}\left\{
\begin{array}{l}
q := 0 \\
a(h) := j \\
a(i) := 1 \text{ for all } i \neq h \\
\text{while } q < e_{h,a(h)} \text{ do} \\
\text{begin} \\
\quad \text{let } \ell \text{ be such that } \tilde{y}^{A_\ell \times A_h}_{a(\ell),a(h)} = \min_{r \neq h} \tilde{y}^{A_r \times A_h}_{a(r),a(h)} \\
\quad z^h_a := \tilde{y}^{A_\ell \times A_h}_{a(\ell),a(h)} \\
\quad \tilde{y}^{A_r \times A_h}_{a(r),a(h)} := \tilde{y}^{A_r \times A_h}_{a(r),a(h)} - z^h_a \text{ for all } r \neq h \\
\quad a(\ell) := a(\ell) + 1 \\
\quad q := q + z^h_a \\
\text{end;}
\end{array}
\right.
$$

end.

Notice that a solution constructed by the single-hub heuristic only depends on the distance function d, and not on the actual costs c_a, $a \in A$. Further, the single-hub heuristic gives rise to the multiple-hub heuristic in the following straightforward way: apply the single hub heuristic for $h = 1, \ldots, k$ and pick the best solution.

3 A general worst-case analysis

Consider a specific cost-function f with respect to a certain cluster $a \in A$, and define $H_a = \sum_{r=1, r\neq h}^{r=k} d^{A_r \times A_h}_{a(r),a(h)}$, also referred to as a hub. Depending on the specification of the cost-function f, it may be possible to bound c_a from above using the triangle inequality, by $\alpha_1(k) \cdot H_a$, $\alpha_1(k) \in \mathbb{R}$ for all $k \geq 2$. More formally:

$\alpha_1(k)$ equals the smallest real number for which the following condition holds: $c_a = f(d^{A_1 \times A_2}_{a(1),a(2)}, \cdots, d^{A_{k-1} \times A_k}_{a(k-1),a(k)}) \leq \alpha_1(k) \cdot H_a$, $a \in A$, for all lengths d satisfying the triangle inequality, with respect to some cost-function f, and $k \geq 2$.
For example, let f be the sum cost-function, that is

$$c_a = \sum_{r<s} d^{A_r \times A_s}_{a(r),a(s)} \text{ for all } a \in A.$$

Since

$$d^{A_r \times A_s}_{a(r),a(s)} \leq d^{A_r \times A_h}_{a(r),a(h)} + d^{A_s \times A_h}_{a(s),a(h)} \text{ for all } a \in A,$$

it follows that one needs $k-1$ hubs H_a to bound c_a from above for all $a \in A$. Hence, in case of the sum cost- function $\alpha_1(k) \leq k-1$. Of course, $\alpha_1(k)$ need not exist. Then we set $\alpha_1(k) = \infty$.

In a similar way, one can define another parameter $\alpha_2(k)$:

$\alpha_2(k)$ equals the smallest real number for which $H_a \leq \alpha_2(k) \cdot c_a$, $a \in A$, for all lengths d satisfying the triangle inequality with respect to some cost-function f, $k \geq 2$.
It is easy to see that for the sum cost case $\alpha_2(k) \leq 1$. Again, if $\alpha_2(k)$ does not exist, we set $\alpha_2(k) = \infty$.

Now, let $c(SH_h)$ denote the cost of the solution found by the single-hub heuristic, and let OPT denote the cost of an optimal solution to the k-index transportation problem with decomposable costs. We have the following theorem.

Theorem 3.1 *$c(SH_h) \leq \alpha_1(k) \cdot \alpha_2(k) \cdot OPT$ for all h.*

Evidently, the bound $\alpha_1(k) \cdot \alpha_2(k)$, $k \geq 2$, is also a valid upper bound for the ratio between the cost of the solution found by the multiple-hub heuristic and the cost of the optimal solution. Let us, in order to be able to derive a possibly better bound for the multiple-hub heuristic, introduce $\alpha_3(k)$:

$\alpha_3(k)$ equals the smallest real number for which $\sum_{r<s} d^{A_r \times A_s}_{a(r),a(s)} \leq \alpha_3(k) \cdot c_a$, $a \in A$, for all lengths d satisfying the triangle inequality, with respect to some cost-function f, $k \geq 2$.
For example, $\alpha_3(k)$ is easily seen to equal 1 in case of the sum-cost function. Again, if $\alpha_3(k)$ does not exist, let $\alpha_3(k) = \infty$.

With $c(MH)$ denoting the cost of the solution found by the multiple-hub heuristic, we have the following theorem:

Theorem 3.2 *$c(MH) \leq \frac{2\alpha_1(k)\alpha_3(k)}{k} \cdot OPT$.*

References

Bandelt, H.-J., Y. Crama and F.C.R. Spieksma (1991), "Approximation algorithms for multidimensional assignment problems with decomposable costs", to appear in *Discrete Applied Mathematics*.

Crama, Y. and F.C.R. Spieksma (1992), "Approximation algorithms for three-dimensional assignment problems with triangle inequalities", *European Journal of Operational Research*, 60, 273–279.

Gusfield, D. (1993), "Efficient methods for multiple sequence alignment with guaranteed error bounds", *Bulletin of Mathematical Biology*, 55, 141–154.

MULTICRITERIAL OPTIMIZATION IN PRODUCTION AND MANAGEMENT

Mark Rabinovitch
Engineer-economical Institute St. Petersburg
Hardtstraße 10/I, D-69124 Heidelberg

A general form of the multicriterial optimization problem (MOP) is $\max\{F(X): F=(f_1,\dots,f_m),\ X\in Q,\ Q\subset R^n,\ f_i\in C(R^1)\}$. A definition of a "decision" MOP is determined by interrelations of criteria (unordered, partially ordered, linearly ordered). For given MOP we determine an associated approximate MOP (AMOP). If $Q^*\subset Q$ is determined as the set of optimal plans of certain MOP then the set $\overline{Q}$ ($Q^*\subset\overline{Q}\subset Q$) of ε-optimal plans of associated AMOP is defined. Main questions arising in the choice of the ε-optimal plans of AMOP are discussed. We introduce a definition of ε-ordered criteria and suggest a decision concept for AMOP with ε-ordered criteria. Definitions of ε-Pareto set and εP-optimal plan are discussed. Main approaches to the choice of the εP-optimal plans for AMOP are based on reduction of the ε-Pareto set. We consider and develope certain of these.

We ground a thesis: practically all problems of production planning and management (PPM) have to be modelled as AMOP. In connection with this main principles and particularities of the multicriterial optimization in applied models PPM are considered. We argue in favour of an examination of AMOP as problems under uncertain conditions. Their indeterminacy can be reduced or removed only in the process of the problem decision by introduction of a new information. We discusse general questions arising in practical applications of AMOP in PPM. The main of these is to research qualitative and quantitative interrelations of criteria. We discusse and examine main features of the choice of ε-optimal plans in applied AMO models: a phenomenon of competitive optimal plans, exchangeability of criteria and restrictions as well as collisions appearing in a process of the final optimal plan choice by a decision making person. A problem of a vector criterion scalarization for these models is examined and a conclusion is made, that there are a few obstacles for its correct decision. The main one: it is impossible to compare different criteria, even normalized, because of insufficient and very different trustiness of an initial information.

We describe and examine optimality criteria and decision choice for three well known problems of decision making. The first one is the problem of the optimal choice of nomenclature and volumes of production in a small serial industry for a calendar period (year, quarter). It is proposed, that a capacity of an order book for the considered enterprise exceeds its available production facilities. For certain articles minimal and maximal production volumes are given as well as extreme output moments. Funds of time for the main production subdivisions are restricted , but there are certain means to increase. Given problem was traditionally modelled with the only criterion of maximal profit (or a certain equivalent one). We argue : this problem is naturally multicriterial, though the profit is the main one. We examine other criteria: minimal expence accounts for increasing of production facility, minimal expence accounts for storage of the finished production, maximal reliability of the optimal plan fulfilment by unreliable information. We discusse a question of scalarization vector criterion in this problem and argue an incorrectness of this procedure. Given criteria may have different interrelations in concrete problems, in particular they can be ε-ordered. We propose an iterative method for ε-optimal plans search, Rabinovitch (1988).

We discusse the following version of sceduling problem. Given small serial industry enterprise has a year plan with fixed production volumes. Moments of articles output aren't fixed, but they belong to certain time intervals (for instance, to quarters). The problem consist in the search of optimal moments of production output with precision to shorter intervals (for instance, to months or ten-day periods) with keeping a certain restrictions system. We suggest and argue the following optimality criteria: (1) maximal uniform work-load of main generalized production subdivisions, (2) maximal admitable concentration of output of the same production type articles, (3) minimal value of circulating capital appearing in consequence of incomplete production, (4) maximal reliability of the optimal plan fulfilment with unreliable information elements. Analysis of given criteria leads to conclusion, that (I) is the main of these. In the neighbourhood of its optimal plans set a reduction of ε-Pareto set determined by others criteria is suggested.

A following marketing model is considered. Some firm plans to begin a new or modernized production type output in order to sale it at some new as well as traditional markets. The firm has forecasts about possible tentative prices and expectable demand volumes of its production at the each market. There are some means in order to increase production facilities. The problem consist in search for optimal prices and production volumes for the each market. The following optimality criteria can be considered: (I) maximal summary sale volume, (2) maximal summary profit, (3) minimal costs of production and marketing, (4) maximal sale volume for new markets, (5) minimal expectable summary damage caused by invasion at new markets. It can be considered several interrelations of criteria in dependence upon a strategic and tactical policy of the firm. For instance, (4) and (5) can be the most important and unordered (or equally valuable), others are secondary and ε-ordered. In a generalized marketing model we consider several production types as well as an extended restrictions and parameters collection (including variable costs for reclame, service, modernization of production and so on). In the other variant of this model we have a dynamic process for prices and production volumes optimization for several periods of time. These models are suitable for practical applications. They can be used also as a part of a business game for managers teaching and training.

Literature.

Rabinovitch M (I988) Multicriterial models and methods of optimization in production planning. Leningr. University. Leningrad (Russian).

CONVEXITY-CONCAVITY: MATRICES AND MATRIX GAMES

Tadeusz Radzik
Institute of Mathematics, Technical University of Wroclaw
Wybrzeze Wyspianskiego 27, 50-370 Wroclaw, Poland

This paper characterizes some class of matrices with rows and columns having properties closely related to the convexity-concavity of functions. The matrix games described by such payoff matrices well approximate continuous games on the unit square with payoff functions $F(x,y)$ concave in x for each y, and convex in y for each x. It is shown that the optimal strategies in such matrix games have a very simple structure and a search-procedure is given. The results have a very close relationship with the results of papers: Debreu (1952), Glicksberg (1952), Radzik (1991, 1992,1993) and Shapley (1964).

Main Results

For any zero-sum two-person game considered in the paper, Player 1 is a "maximizer" while Player 2 is a " minimizer". Further, in any matrix game, denoted by Γ or $\Gamma(W)$, $W = [w_{ij}]$, $1 \le i \le m$, $1 \le j \le n$, is a $m \times n$-payoff matrix of Player 1. This player is related to the rows while Player 2 is related to the columns of W.

Now, we give the first two very natural definitions of two classes of matrices related to the convexity (concavity) property of a function $F(x,y)$ with respect to one variable. Next, these classes are fully characterized in terms of necessary and sufficient conditions.

Definition 1: A $m \times n$-matrix $W=[w_{ij}]$, $1 \le i \le m$, $1 \le j \le n$, is said to be *row-convex* if there exist a function $F_1(x,y)$ on the unit square and two strictly increasing sequences $\{x_i\}_{i=1}^{m}$ and $\{y_j\}_{j=1}^{n}$ in [0, 1], such that for all i and j, all the functions $F_1(x_i, \cdot)$ are convex and $F_1(x_i, y_j) = w_{ij}$.

Definition 2: A $m \times n$-matrix $W=[w_{ij}]$, $1 \le i \le m$, $1 \le j \le n$, is said to be *column-concave* if there exist a function $F_2(x,y)$ on the unit square and two strictly increasing sequences $\{x_i\}_{i=1}^m$ and $\{y_j\}_{j=1}^n$ in [0, 1], such that for all i and j, all the functions $F_2(\cdot,y_j)$ are concave and $F_2(x_i,y_j) = w_{ij}$

Theorem 1: A matrix $W=[w_{ij}]$, $1\le i\le m$, $1\le j\le n$, is row-convex (column-concave) if and only if there exist a sequence, $\lambda_1,\ldots,\lambda_{n-1}$ $(\tau_1,\ldots,\tau_{m-1})$ of positive numbers, such that

$$\frac{w_{i2}-w_{i1}}{\lambda_1} \le \frac{w_{i3}-w_{i2}}{\lambda_2} \le \ldots \le \frac{w_{in}-w_{i,n-1}}{\lambda_{n-1}} \quad \text{for } i=1,2,\ldots,m.$$

$$\left[\frac{w_{2j}-w_{1j}}{\tau_1} \ge \frac{w_{3j}-w_{2j}}{\tau_2} \ge \ldots \ge \frac{w_{mj}-w_{m-1,j}}{\tau_{m-1}} \quad \text{for } j=1,2,\ldots,n.\right]$$

Theorem 2: A matrix $W=[w_{ij}]$, $1\le i\le m$, $1\le j\le n$, is row-convex and column-concave if and only if there exist a continuous function $F(x,y)$ on the unit square and two strictly increasing sequences $\{x_i\}_{i=1}^m$ and $\{y_j\}_{j=1}^n$ in [0, 1], such that

(*a*) the function $F(x,y)$ is concave in x for each y, and convex in y for each x,

(*b*) $F(x_i,y_j) = w_{ij}$ for all i and j.

Definition 3: The pair (k,l) is said to be a *saddle point* of a matrix $W = [w_{ij}]$, $1\le i\le m$, $1\le j\le n$, when w_{kl} is the minimal element in the k-th row of W and maximal in the l-th column of W.

Let us denote

$$W_{kl}^{ij} = \begin{bmatrix} w_{ij} & w_{ij+l} & \cdots & w_{il} \\ w_{i+1,j} & w_{i+1,j+l} & \cdots & w_{i+1,l} \\ \cdots & \cdots & \cdots & \cdots \\ w_{kj} & w_{k,j+1} & \cdots & w_{kl} \end{bmatrix}$$

If $1\le i\le k\le m$ and $1\le j\le l\le n$, we shall say that the matrix W_{kl}^{ij} is a *submatrix* of (or *contained in*) a matrix $W = [w_{ij}]$, $1\le i\le m$, $1\le j\le n$.

Now we are ready to express our two last results.

Theorem 3: Let $W=[w_{ij}]$, $1\leq i\leq m$, $1\leq j\leq n$, be any $m\times n$-matrix which is row-convex and column-concave. Then for matrix game $\Gamma=\Gamma(W)$ and its value $v^{*}= val(\Gamma(W))$, there must occur one of the following four cases:

Case 1: There exists a saddle point (s,r) in W.
Then the pair $(\mu^{*},\nu^{*}) = (\delta_{s}, \delta_{r})$ is a pair of optimal strategies for Player 1 and 2, respectively, in Γ. The value of the game Γ is $v^{*}= w_{sr}$.

Case 2: There exists a 2×2-submatrix in W, of the form $W^{sr}_{s+1,r+1}$, without saddle points.
Then $v^{*} = val(\Gamma(W^{sr}_{s+1,r+1}))$ and the optimal strategies for Players 1 and 2 in the matrix game $\Gamma(W^{sr}_{s+1,r+1})$ are also optimal in the game $\Gamma(W)$, and they are of the form, $\mu^{*}= \lambda\delta_{s}+ (1-\lambda)\delta_{s+1}$ and $\nu^{*}= \gamma\delta_{r}+ (1-\gamma)\delta_{r+1}$ for some $0 < \lambda,\gamma < 1$.

Case 3: Cases 1 and 2 do not hold and there is a 2×3-submatrix $W^{sr}_{s+1,r+2}$ of W without saddle points.
Then $v^{*} = val(\Gamma(W^{sr}_{s+1,r+2}))$, the matrix $W^{sr}_{s+1,r+2}$ has the form

$$W^{sr}_{s+1,r+2} = \begin{bmatrix} w_{sr} & v^{*} & w_{s,r+2} \\ w_{s+1,r} & v^{*} & w_{s+1,r+2} \end{bmatrix},$$

and the optimal strategies for Player 1 and 2 in the matrix game $\Gamma(W^{sr}_{s+1,r+2})$ are of the form $\mu^{*}=\lambda\delta_{s}+ (1-\lambda)\delta_{s+1}$ and $\nu^{*}=\delta_{r+1}$ for some $0<\lambda<1$, respectively, and they remain optimal in the game $\Gamma(W)$.

Case 4: Cases 1 and 2 do not hold and there is a 3×2-submatrix $W^{sr}_{s+2,r+1}$ of W without saddle points.
Then $v^{*}= val(\Gamma(W^{sr}_{s+2,r+1}))$, the matrix $W^{sr}_{s+2,r+1}$ has the form

$$W^{sr}_{s+2,r+1} = \begin{bmatrix} w_{sr} & w_{s,r+1} \\ v^{*} & v^{*} \\ w_{s+2,r} & w_{s+2,r+1} \end{bmatrix},$$

and the optimal strategies for Player 1 and 2 in the game $\Gamma(W^{sr}_{s+2,r+1})$ are of the form $\mu^* = \delta_{s+1}$ and $\nu^* = \gamma\delta_r + (1-\gamma)\delta_{r+1}$ for some $0<\gamma<1$, respectively, and they are also optimal in the game $\Gamma(W)$.

Theorem 4: Let $W = [w_{ij}]$, $1 \le i \le m$, $1 \le j \le n$, be a row-convex and column-concave $m \times n$-matrix, such that all its 2×2-submatrices of the form $W^{ij}_{i+1,j+1}$ have saddle points. Then one of the players has a pure optimal strategy in the matrix game $\Gamma(W)$. If additionally, there is exactly one minimal element in each row of W, and exactly one maximal element in each column of W, then both players possess pure optimal strategies in $\Gamma(W)$.

References

Debreu, G (1952) A social equilibrium existence theorem. Proceedings of the National Academy of Science, 38: 886-893.

Glicksberg, I.L (1952) A further generalization of the Kakutani's Fixed Point Theorem with application to Nash equilibrium points. Proceedings of the American Mathematical Society,38: 170-174.

Radzik T (1991) Saddle point theorems. International Journal of Game Theory 20: 23-32.

Radzik T (1992) Matrix games with matrices convex in rows and concave in columns. The Indian Journal of Statistics, Series A 54: 115-122.

Radzik T (1993) Nash equilibria of discontinuous non-zero-sum two-person games. International Journal of Game Theory, 21: 429-437.

Shapley LS (1964) Some topics in two-person game. Advances in Game Theory, Ann. of Math. Studies 52:1-28

GENERALIZATIONS OF ERLANG FORMULAE AND SOME OF THEIR 2ND ORDER PROPERTIES

M.F. Ramalhoto
Instituto Superior Técnico / Universidade Aberta
Lisbon, Portugal

A. Pacheco
Instituto Superior Técnico
Lisbon, Portugal

A formula of Erlang type, denoted by $C_d(r, r\rho)$ and called 3rd (non-immediate-service) Erlang formula, is defined for the M|M|r|r+d system. This formula represents the equilibrium probability of non-immediate-service and is a function of three parameters: intensity of traffic "ρ", number of servers "r", and number of waiting positions "d". When $d = 0$, $C_0(r, r\rho)$ is the classical 1st Erlang formula and the limit of $C_d(r, r\rho)$ as d goes to $+\infty$ is the classical 2nd Erlang formula. The extra parameter d allows a unified study of the three most important Markovian queueing system - M|M|r|r, M|M|r|r+d and M|M|r - and introduces a greater flexibility in its design. It is shown that, when in equilibrium, the number of customers waiting, the number of busy servers, the waiting time in the queue and the total sojourn time in the system are distributed as a sum of two well-known random variables, weighted by the 3rd Erlang formula. Some of these results also show the influence on one hand of the 1-server-system and on the other of the infinite-server-system in the study of the r-server-system, where the 3rd Erlang formula, can indicate a "heavy" / "low" traffic situation. The equilibrium loss probability, denoted by $B_d(r, r\rho)$, and the equilibrium delay probability, denoted by $D_d(r, r\rho)$, are also rewritten in terms of $C_d(r, r\rho)$. It is shown that $B_d(r, r\rho)$ is convex in d. It is reported that, $B_d(r, r\rho)$ is convex in ρ if ρ is less than some ρ^* and concave if ρ is greater than ρ^*, for a broad range of integer values of r and d, and that the M|M|1|1 system is the only M|M|r|r+d system for which the loss probability is concave in ρ in all its range.

1. THE THIRD ERLANG FORMULA

In the M|M|r|r+d system the equilibrium probability of non-immediate-service (customer waits or is rejected), for $r \in N$, $d \in N_0$, $\rho \in R^+$ is given by,

$$C_d(r, r\rho) = \sum_{i=r}^{r+d} p_i = ((r\rho)^r/r!) \sum_{i=r}^{d} \rho^i/(\sum_{i=0}^{r-1} \rho^i/i! + ((r\rho)^r/r!) \sum_{i=0}^{d} \rho^i) \tag{1}$$

where p_i represents the equilibrium probability of i customers in the system (waiting or being served). From (1), $C_0(r, r\rho)$ is the usual 1st (loss or B) Erlang formula, denoted by B (r, rρ), and the limit of C_d (r, rρ) as d goes to infinity is the usual 2nd (delay or C) Erlang formula, denoted by C (r, rρ), which is defined just for $0 < \rho < 1$. The C_d (r, rρ) can be rewritten in terms of the inverse of B (r, rρ) as follows:

$$C_d(r, r\rho) = \left(B^{-1}(r, r\rho)\left(\sum_{i=0}^{d} \rho^i\right)^{-1} + 1 - \left(\sum_{i=0}^{d} \rho^i\right)^{-1}\right)^{-1}. \tag{2}$$

Let $N'_{r,d}$ denote the number of customers waiting in the queue; $NS_{r,d}$ denote the number of occupied servers; $N_{r,d}$ denote the number of customers in the system (waiting or being served); $T'_{r,d}$ denote the waiting time in the queue, $T_{r,d}$ denote the total sojourn time in the system. The symbol d is dropped in the case of the M|M|r system, and the symbol $\sim$ means "distributed as".

Proposition 1. For the ergodic M|M|r|r+d system, and $r \in N$, $d \in N_0$, $\rho \in R^+$

$$N'_{r,d} \sim (1-C_d(r, r\rho))\, 0 + C_d(r, r\rho)\, N_{1,d-1}$$

where P(0=o)=1 and $N_{1,d-1}$ is the random variable, number of customers in a M|M|1|1+(d-1) system with the same intensity of traffic ρ.

Proof: By (1) and after some straightforward calculations, the equilibrium probability function of $N'_{r,d}$ can be rewritten in terms of the 3rd Erlang formula as follows:

$$P(N'_{r,d} = i) = \begin{cases} 1-C_d(r, r\rho)\left(\sum_{n=1}^{d} \rho^n \Big/ \sum_{j=0}^{d} \rho^j\right), & i = 0 \\ C_d(r, r\rho)\left(\rho^i \Big/ \sum_{j=0}^{d} \rho^j\right), & i = 1, 2, \ldots, d \end{cases} \tag{3}$$

From (3),

$$(N'_{r,d} = i \mid N'_{r,d} > 0) = \rho^i \Big/ \sum_{j=0}^{d} \rho^i, \quad i = 0, \ldots, d \tag{4}$$

i.e. $(N'_{r,d} \mid N'_{r,d} > 0) \sim G(d, 1-\rho)$, where $G(d, 1-\rho)$ means the truncated geometric distribution of parameters d and (1-ρ); which is also the probability distribution of the number of customers (waiting or being served) in a M|M|1|1+(d-1) system with the same intensity of traffic ρ. The proposition follows from (3) and (4). o

As a direct consequence of proposition 1, for the ergodic M|M|r system (by taken the limits as d goes to $+\infty$, and with $0 < \rho < 1$) and $r \in N$

$$N'_r \sim (1-C(r, r\rho))\, 0 + C(r, r\rho)\, N_1 \tag{5}$$

where N_1 is the geometric random variable of parameter (1-ρ), which also represents the number of customers in a M|M|1 system.

Proposition 2: For the ergodic M|M|r|r+d system and $r \in N$, $d \in N_0$, $\rho \in R^+$

$$NS_{r,d} \sim (1-C_d(r, r\rho))\,(X|X < r) + C_d(r, r\rho)\,R$$

where $P(R=r) = 1$ and X is a Poisson random variable of parameter $r\rho$, with $0 < \rho < 1$

Proof: By (1) and after straightforward calculations, the equilibrium probability function of $NS_{r,d}$ can be rewritten in terms of the 3rd Erlang formula as follows:

$$P(NS_{r,d} = i) = \begin{cases} C_d(r, r\rho)\, r! \,/\, (i!\,(r\rho)^{r-i} \sum_{j=0}^{d} \rho^j), & i = 0,1, \ldots, r-1 \\ C_d(r, r\rho) & , \; i = r \end{cases} \tag{6}$$

By (6), $P(NS_{r,d} = k \mid NS_{r,d} < r) = ((r\rho)^k / k!) / (\sum_{j=0}^{r-1} (r\rho)^j / j!)$ for $k = 0, 1, \ldots, r-1$ and by multiplying and dividing by $e^{-r\rho}$ we get the conditional probability function of the Poisson random variable, X, of parameter $r\rho$ given that $X < r$, from which the proposition follows. o

As a consequence of this proposition, for the ergodic M|M|r system (by taking the limits as d goes to $+\infty$ and with $0 < \rho < 1$), and $r \in N$

$$NS_r \sim (1 - C(r, r\rho))\,(X|X < r) + C(r, r\rho)\,R. \tag{7}$$

It is interesting to notice that, for the same parameter $r\rho$

$$(NS_{r,d} \mid NS_{r,d} < r) \sim (NS_r \mid NS_r < r) \sim (NS_{r,0} \mid NS_{r,0} < r) \sim (NS_{+\infty} \mid NS_{+\infty} < r) \tag{8}$$

where NS_∞ denotes the number of servers occupied in the M|M|∞ system and $NS_{r,0}$, denotes the number of servers occupied in the M|M|r|r system. Furthermore, for the ergodic M|M|r|r system and $r \in N$, $\rho \in R^+$, by taking $d = 0$ in the proposition

$$NS_{r,0} \sim (1- B(r, r\rho))\,(X|X \leq r) + B(r, r\rho)\,R. \tag{9}$$

Proposition 3: For the ergodic M|M|r|r+d system and $r \in N$, $d \in N_0$, $\rho \in R^+$

$$N_{r,d} \sim (1-C_d(r, r\rho))\,(X|X < r) + C_d(r, r\rho)\,(R+N_{1,d-1})$$

Proof: By (1) and after straightforward calculations, the equilibrium probability function of $N_{r,d}$ can be rewritten in terms of the 3rd Erlang formula as follows:

$$P(N_{r,d} = i) = p_i = \begin{cases} C_d(r, r\rho)\,(r!\,/\,i!)\,/\,((r\rho)^{r-i} \sum_{j=0}^{d} \rho^j), & i = 0, 1, \ldots, r-1 \\ C_d(r, r\rho)\,\rho^{i-r} \,/\, \sum_{j=0}^{d} \rho^j, & i = r, \ldots, r+d \end{cases} \tag{10}$$

We could proceed in the same fashion as before, but by noticing that $N_{r,d} = NS_{r,d} + N'_{r,d}$ the proposition follows. o

As a consequence, for the ergodic M|M|r system (by taking the limits as d goes to $+\infty$ and with $0 < \rho < 1$) and $r \in N$

$$N_r \sim (1 - C(r, r\rho))(X \mid X < r) + C(r, r\rho)(R + N_1). \quad (11)$$

Proposition 4: For the ergodic M|M|r|r+d system, and $r \in N$, $d \in N_0$, $\rho \in R^+$

$$T'_{r,d} \sim (1 - C_{d-1}(r, r\rho))\, 0 + C_{d-1}(r, r\rho)\, E_d$$

where E_d is the Erlang random variable whose two parameters are respectively, given by the random variable "G (d-1, 1-ρ) + 1" and the system's service rate, μ.

Proof. By (1) and after some more involving calculations the equilibrium density function of $T'_{r,d}$ can be rewritten in terms of the 3rd Erlang formula for $r \in N$, $d \in N_0$, $\rho \in R^+$ as follows:

$$\begin{cases} P(T'_r = 0) = 1 - C_{d-1}(r, r\rho) \\ f_{T'_{r,d}}(t) = \mu\, e^{-\mu(1-\rho)t}\, C_{d-1}(r, r\rho) \left(\sum_{j=0}^{d-1} \rho^j\right)^{-1} \left(\sum_{j=0}^{d-1} e^{-\lambda t}(\lambda t)^i / i!\right),\ t > 0 \end{cases} \quad (12)$$

From (12) it is calculated $(f_{T'_{r,d}}(t) \mid \bar{F}_{T'_{r,d}}(t))$, where $\bar{F}_{T_{r,d}}(t)) = P(T'_{r,d} > t)$, and the proposition follows. o

In the ergodic M|M|r system (by taking the limits in (12) as d goes to $+\infty$ and with $0 < \rho < 1$) for $r \in N$

$$P(T'_r = 0) = 1 - C(r, r\rho) \text{ and } f_{T'_r}(t) = C(r, r\rho)\, \mu(1-\rho)\, e^{-\mu(1-\rho)t},\quad t > 0$$

therefore with $E \sim \mathrm{Exp}(\mu-\lambda)$, which is the distribution of the total sojourn time in the M|M|1 system, with the same ρ and the same μ (λ is the arrival rate)

$$T'_r \sim (1-C)(r, r\rho))\, 0 + C(r, r\rho)\, E. \quad (13)$$

Proposition 5: For the ergodic M|M|r|r+d system and $r \in N$, $d \in N_0$, $\rho \in R^+$

$$T_{r,d} \sim (1-C_{d-1}(r, r\rho))\, S_r + C_{d-1}(r, r\rho)(E_d + S_r)$$

where S_r is the service time distribution of each server, ie. $S_r \sim \mathrm{Exp}(\mu/r)$

Proof: The result follows from proposition 4 and the fact that the total sojourn time of a customer in the system is given by its service time plus its waiting time in the queue. o

As a consequence, in the case of the ergodic M|M|r system, for $0 < \rho < 1$ and $r \in N$

$$T_r \sim (1-C(r, r\rho))\, S_r + C(r, r\rho)(E_1 + S_r). \quad (14)$$

It should be notice that S_r and E_d are independent random variables and that the proposition could also be rewritten as $T_{r,d} \sim S_r + C_{d-1}(r, r\rho)\, E_d$.

These propositions illustrate how the concept - 3rd Erlang formula - provides a more systematic way of studying the M|M|r|r+d system for $d = 0, \ldots, +\infty$ and $r = 1, \ldots, +\infty$.

Ramalhoto and Pacheco (1990 , 1991) used the same approach presented here to study the stochastic ordering properties, and the mean, variance, coeficient of variation and mode of the random variables considered in the above five propositions. It also should be noticed that, the various results, tables and computer programmes for the 1st Erlang formula can be used in our unified approach. Jagerman (1984) gives improved computations of the 1st Erlang formula and its derivatives, with practical computer programmes.

2. SECOND - ORDER PROPERTIES OF THE LOSS PROBABILITY

In the design of GI|G|r|r+d system the loss probability and its 1st and 2nd order properties in the basic parameters are important. The equilibrium loss probability of a M|M|r|r+d system is denoted by B_d (r, rρ) and can be rewritten in terms of the 3rd Erlang formula for $r \in N$, $d \in N_0$, $\rho \in R^+$, as follows:

$$B_d (r, r\rho) = P (N_{r,d} = r + d) = C_d (r, r\rho)\, \rho^d / \sum_{i=0}^{d} \rho^i \tag{15}$$

By applying (2) in (15)

$$B_d (r, r\rho) = ((1-\rho)\,(B^{-1} (r, r\rho)-1) + (1-\rho^{d+1}))^{-1}\, (\rho^d\, (1-\rho)). \tag{16}$$

In fact, B_d (r, rρ) can be seen as a direct generalization of B (r, rρ), clearly, B_0 (r, rρ) = B (r, rρ). It is interesting to mention here that, although B_0 (r, rρ) is the equilibrium loss probability of the M | G | r | r+d system when d = 0 , for d ≠ 0 its loss probability fails to have a simple and generally valid form in the non-exponential case. Another important performance measure is the equilibrium waiting-time probability (delay probability), which is denoted by D_d (r, rρ). In fact, for $r \in N$, $d \in N_0$, $\rho \in R^+$, C_d (r, rρ) = B_d (r, rρ) + D_d (r, rρ). It is also clear that D_d (r, rρ) can be seen as a direct generalization of C (r, rρ); the limit of D_d (r, rρ) as d goes to $+\infty$ is C (r, rρ).

The 1st Erlang formula can be extended into a transcendental function of the Kummer's function type, as follows:

$$B (r, a) = \left(\int_0^{+\infty} e^{-u}\, (1+u / a)^r\, d u\right)^{-1}. \tag{17}$$

See, for instance Jagerman (1974) and Jagers and Van Doorn (1986). The result (17) together with (2) allows an extension of C_d (r, rρ) to non-integral r and d, with "a" replaced by "rρ" (ρ is defined in the usual way, $\rho = \lambda\, (\mu\, r)^{-1}$, and μ now means the service rate of each server) and for $r \in R^+$, $d \in R^+$ and $\rho \in R^+$. In the same way, the general definition of B (r, rρ) given by (17) used in (16) gives the general definition of B_d (r, rρ) for $r \in R^+$, $d \in R^+$, $\rho \in R^+$. The first order properties of B_d (r, rρ) in terms of ρ, r, and d are presented in Ramalhoto (1993). Let us now consider its second order properties.

Proposition 6: For fixed $r \in N$, $\rho \in R^+$, $B_d(r, r\rho)$ is convex in d.

Proof: From (16)

$$\frac{\partial^2}{\partial d^2} B_d(r, r\rho) = \rho^d (\ln \rho)^2 (1-\rho) ((B^{-1}(r, r\rho) - 1)(1-\rho) + (1-\rho^{d+1}))^{-3} ((B^{-1}(r, r\rho) - 1)(1-\rho) + (1-\rho^{d+1}) + \rho^{d+1}) ((B^{-1}(r, r\rho) - 1)(1-\rho) + (1-\rho^{d+1}) + 2\rho^{d+1}). \quad (18)$$

For $\rho \neq 1$, this second derivative is > 0 because $((B^{-1}(r, r\rho) - 1)(1-\rho) + 1-\rho^{d+1}) = ((1-\rho) B^{-1}(r, r\rho) + \rho - \rho^{d+1}) > 0$ if $\rho < 1$ and < 0 if $\rho > 1$ (due to $B^{-1}(r,r\rho)-1 > 0$) and because $(1-\rho) B^{-1}(r, r\rho) + \rho > 0$ (due to $B(r, r\rho) > 1 - 1/\rho$). For $\rho = 1$, the inequation follows from L' Hôpital's rule.

The convexity properties in r for $B_d(r, r\rho)$, are the same as for the $C_d(r, r\rho)$ by (15) On the other hand by (2) and (16) these two functions depend on r just through $B^{-1}(r, r\rho)$. Jagers and Van Doorn (1986) showed that for $r \in R_0^+$, $B(r, r\rho)$ is convex in r and, $B^{-1}(r, r\rho)$ is log-convex in r, for fixed offered load.

Harel (1990) shows that the first Erlang formula, for $r \in N$ is a convex function in ρ if ρ is less than some ρ^*, and concave if ρ is greater than ρ^*. We report that, his results can be extended to $B_d(r, r\rho)$, for $r \in N$ and $d \in N_0$, at least if $r \leq 3$ or $(4 \leq r \leq 100, 0 \leq d \leq 2000)$. By denoting ρ^* by $\rho^*_{r,d}$, it can also be proved that: (a) $\rho^*_{r,d} = 0$ is equivalent to r = 1 and d = 0, i.e., the M|M|1|1 system; (b) $\rho^*_{1,d} < (=,>)\ 1$ is equivalent to $d < (=, >)\ 3$; (c) $\rho^*_{2,d} < (>)\ 1$ is equivalent to $d < (\geq)\ 3$. The calculations are not difficult although extremely long and tedious and full of finite sums to evaluate. The equilibrium loss probability of the M|M|1|1 system, $B_0(1, \rho) = C_0(1, \rho) = B(1, \rho) = \rho(1+\rho)^{-1}$ is obviously a concave function of ρ in all its range, i.e., $\rho^*_{1,0} = 0$. All the other proves are not presented here for obvious space reasons.

REFERENCES

Harel, A. (1990), Convexity Properties of the Erlang Loss Formulas, Operations Research vol. 38, nº3, May - June, pp. 499-505.

Jagerman, D.L. (1974), Some Properties of the Erlang Loss Function, Bell Sys. Techn. J. 53, pp. 525-551.

Jagerman, D.L. (1984), Methods in Traffic Calculations, AT & T Bell Labs Technical J. Vol. 63, No. 7, Sept., pp. 1283-1310.

Jagers, A.A. and Van Doorn, E.A. (1986), On the Continued Erlang Loss Function, Operations Research Letters, 5, 1, pp. 43-46.

Pacheco, A. and M.F. Ramalhoto (1990) Stochastic Order Relations in the M|M|k|n Systems, Proceedings of the Workshop - Project JNICT, 1990, pp. 43-93.

Ramalhoto, M.F. and Pacheco, A. (1991), Coefficient of Variation and Mode of Some Important Characteristics of Finite Capacity Systems, Proceedings of the 1st Conference in Statistics and Optimization, Tróia, Portugal, pp. 321-347.

Ramalhoto, M.F. (1993) Some Generalizations of the Two Classical Erlang Formulas, ISI -49th Session, Florence, August 25 - September 2.

An Efficient Approach for Down–and–out–Calls in a Binomial Model

Matthias Reimer and Klaus Sandmann
University of Bonn, Department of Statistics, Adenauerallee 24–42,
53113 Bonn, Federal Republic of Germany

The contract definition of a Down–and–out–Call[1] corresponds mainly to that of an ordinary european call. But in differnce to the later, the right to exercise the option vanishs as soon as the price of the underlying stock[2] S reaches respectively crosses a given barrier H during time to maturity. Thus, at time T, the payoff $h_D(.)$ of a D–Call with exercise price K depends on the past price path. This can be characterised in the following manner:

$$h_D\big(S(T)\big) = \begin{cases} \max\{0, S(T) - K\} & \text{if } S(t) > H \;\forall t \in [0,T] \\ 0 & \textit{otherwise} \end{cases} \tag{1}$$

The premium of a D–Call is bounded from above by that of an ordinary call option. One attracting feature of the option can be seen in this price discount. In this context, the barrier H represents a price one assumes unlikely to occur. Despite of the problem of path–dependency, Cox/Rubinstein (1985)[3] were able to present a closed–form solution for the arbitrage price within the "Black–Scholes–Enviroment":

$$\begin{aligned} C_D(t,S,T,K) &= S(t)N(x) - Ke^{-rs}N(x - \sigma\sqrt{s}) \qquad (2) \\ &\quad - S(t)\left(\frac{S(t)}{H}\right)^{-\frac{2r}{\sigma^2}-1} N(y) + Ke^{-rs}\left(\frac{S(t)}{H}\right)^{1-\frac{2r}{\sigma^2}} N(y - \sigma\sqrt{s}) \end{aligned}$$

with $N(\cdot)$ standard normal distribution, $s = T - t$, and

$$x = \frac{\ln S(t) - \ln K + (r + \sigma^2/2)s}{\sigma\sqrt{s}} \qquad y = \frac{2\ln H - \ln S(t) - \ln K + (r + \sigma^2/2)s}{\sigma\sqrt{s}}$$

The first part corresponds to the well–known Black–Scholes–Formula. The second part can be interpreted as an anti–option. We conceive the first derivative as the hedge ratio Δ and the second derivative as the gamma factor Γ:

$$\begin{aligned} \Delta\big(S(t)\big) &= N(x) - \alpha\left(\frac{S(t)}{H}\right)^{\alpha-1} N(y) \qquad (3) \\ &\quad + (1+\alpha)\frac{Ke^{-r(T-t)}}{H}\left(\frac{S(t)}{H}\right)^{\alpha} N(y - \sigma\sqrt{T-t}), \quad \forall S(t) > H \\ \Gamma\big(S(t)\big) &= \frac{1}{S(t)\sigma\sqrt{T-t}}\left[n(x) - \left(\frac{S(t)}{H}\right)^{\alpha-1} n(y)\right] - \frac{\alpha(\alpha-1)}{H}\left(\frac{S(t)}{H}\right)^{\alpha-2} N(y) \\ &\quad + \alpha(1+\alpha)\frac{Ke^{-r(T-t)}}{H^2}\left(\frac{S(t)}{H}\right)^{\alpha-1} N(y - \sigma\sqrt{T-t}), \quad \forall S(t) > H \end{aligned}$$

with x, y as above and $\alpha = \frac{-2r}{\sigma^2}$.

[1]in the following abbreviated with D–Call. The D–Call belongs to a whole class of "barrier options".
[2]We will assume a dividend–save stock. Here early exercise never occurs. This applies to the D–Call, too.
[3]Formula has been adjusted to the notation used here, the omission of the "rebate–term" doesn't impair the worthiness of the theoretical considerations; see also Rubinstein (1990).

One can see, that:

- the hedge ratio decreases in the near of H. This implies a negative gamma factor.
- the hedge ratio attains values bigger than one

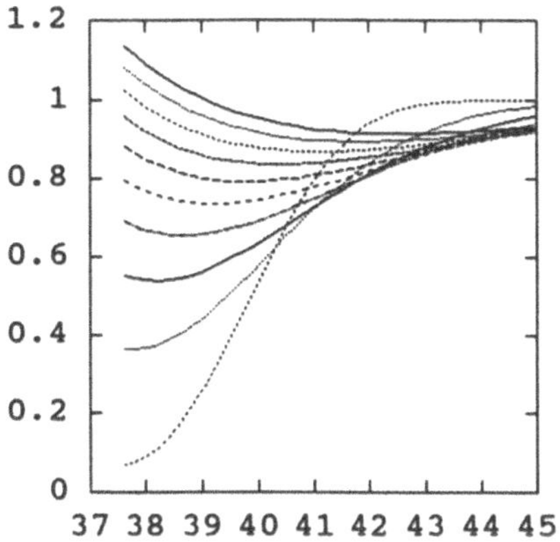

Fig. 1: Hedgeratio, different times to maturity

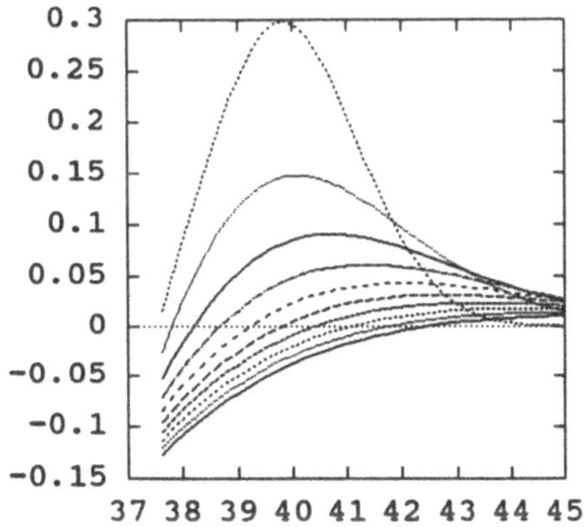

Fig. 2: Gammafactor, different times to maturity

Thus, in the environment of the barrier, the hedge ratio implied by the D–Call, doesn't increase with the price of the underlying. Consequently, there can be a stabilizing effect to the overall portfolio.
Cox/Rubinstein derive the formula (2) by means of the equivalent martingale measure, and thus not by using the argument of a self–finacing and duplicating portfolio strategy. So far, it isn't proved that one can take the first and second derivatives as hedge ratio and gamma factor. However, we show that this is admissable for the D–Call.

The Binomial Model

Although there exists already a closed–form solution one can achieve further insights to the problem by derivation of a binomial approach. Besides, this gives the opportunity to incorporate discrete dividends and early exercise, that means the valuation of an american–type option. Furthermore, this approach can be used for options without closed–form solution. In this context, the convergency behavior of this approach becomes important.
We start off the path independent binomial model for the stock[4] with constant relative price changes $u > 1 + r > d = u^{-1} > 0$, at which r is a constant interest rate per period.

$$S(n,i) = S(0,0)\, u^i\, d^{n-i} \quad \forall i = 0, ..., n \quad t_n \in \bar{T} = \{t_0 < ... < t_N = T\} \tag{4}$$

whereas $S(n,i)$ denotes the stock price at time[5] t_n in state i. If $C_D(n,i)$ denotes the price of a D–Call at time t_n and state i with maturity at time t_N, it follows from the usual duplication

[4]see Cox, Rubinstein(1979), respectively Rendleman and Bartter(1979)
[5]$\Delta t = t_{n+1} - t_n \quad \forall n = 0, ..., n-1$

argument[6]:

$$\begin{aligned} C_D\big(n,i\big) &= \begin{cases} 0 & S(0,0)u^i d^n - i \le H \\ \frac{1}{1+r}\big[pC_D(n+1,i+1) + (1-p)C_D(n+1,i)\big] & otherwise \end{cases} \quad (5) \\ C_D(n,i) &= \max\{0, S(0,0)u^i d^n - i - K\} \end{aligned}$$

and $p = \frac{1+r-d}{u-d} \in]0,1[$. From (5), one cannot recognize a binomial formula at once. However, let's imagine the D–Call as an ordinary Call minus a correction term. Thus, this term must include all those paths, which touch or cross barrier H during the time to maturity. Let H be a terminal knot of the tree structure, that means there $\exists j_H \in 0,...,N$ with $H = S(0,0)u^{N-j_H}d^{j_H}$. Now, by using the reflection principle[7](Feller 1968) one can derive the number of paths, which end with stock price $S(0,0)u^k d^{N-k}$ and have touched barrier H:

$$\binom{N}{2j_H + k - N} \; if \; N - j_H \le k \le 2(N-j_H); \quad \binom{N}{k} \; if \; k \le N - j_H; \quad 0 \quad otherwise \quad (6)$$

Now, the binomial formula for a D–Call evolves at once

$$\begin{aligned} C_D[t_0, S, T, K, H] &= S(t_0) \sum_{i=a\vee N-j_H}^{N} \binom{N}{i} (p')^i (1-p')^{N-i} \\ &\quad - \frac{K}{(1+r)^N} \sum_{i=a\vee N-j_H}^{N} \binom{N}{i} p^i (1-p)^{N-i} \\ &\quad - S(t_0) \sum_{k=a\vee N-j_H}^{2(N-j_H)} \binom{N}{2j_H + k - N} (p')^k (1-p')^{N-k} \\ &\quad + \frac{K}{(1+r)^N} \sum_{k=a\vee N-j_H}^{2(N-j_H)} \binom{N}{2j_H + k - N} p^k (1-p)^{N-k} \end{aligned} \quad (7)$$

with $p' = \frac{p\cdot u}{1+r}$, $a \vee N - 2j_H = \max\{a, N - 2j_H\}$, $a = \inf\{i \in \mathbb{N} | S_0 u^i d^{N-i} \ge K\}$. Thus, the value corresponds to the value of a portfolio consisting of stock and riskfree investment, whereas the proportions are given by the sum of the coefficients of $S(0,0)$ and the other terms respectively. Furthermore, the portfolio strategy constructed in this manner, is self–financing.

Convergence Properties of the Binomial Formula

Theorem: Let $\Delta t = \frac{T}{N}, u = \exp\{\sigma\sqrt{\Delta t}\}, d = u^{-1}$ and $1 + r = \exp\{\tilde{r}\Delta t\}$. The binomial formula (7) converges towards the solution of Cox/Rubinstein (2) for $\Delta t \to 0$. Especially, the discrete hedgeratio converges to the first derivative of equation (2).

Figure 3 shows the convergence behavior of the binomial formula. Here, you have to remember, that we assumed in equation (7) that barrier H resides at a terminal knot. For given H, this assumption isn't fullfilled for every refinement N of the tree. The binomial formula remains valid as long as $H \in [S_0 u^{N-j_H} d^{j_H}, S_0 u^{N-j_H} d^{j_H - 1}] for \; 0 \le j_H \le N$. With increasing refinement N, u,d and r change though. This explains the convergence behavior

[6] $H \le K$ otherwise the paths, which end between K and H, will not be considered as well.

[7] the applicability of the reflection principle to the given problem ows to the special structure of the tree and the assumption of a constant interest rate.

of the binomial formula. Let k be the minimum number of down-movements to reach the barrier, so you can determine the admissable degree of refinement [8] $N^*(k) \in \mathrm{N}$, which is compatible with the binomial formula depending on the choosen k.

$$H = S(0,0)exp\{-k\sqrt{\frac{T}{N(k)}}\sigma\} \quad \Rightarrow \quad N^*(k) := [N(k)] = \frac{k^2\sigma^2 T}{(log\frac{S(t_0)}{H})^2} - \epsilon \qquad (8)$$

But the convergence behavior of the formula can improved tremendously by considering a variation of the barrier H instead of the refinement. Let H_1 and H_2 be two barriers with $H_1 \leq H \leq H_2$, which represent terminal knots of a tree with refinement N. Let H_3 be another barrier close to the other two, but still below the initial stock price. The price of a D–Call can be computed by a quadratic approximation using the binomial formula (7) with barriers H_1, H_2, H_3. The following figures show an amazing improvement.

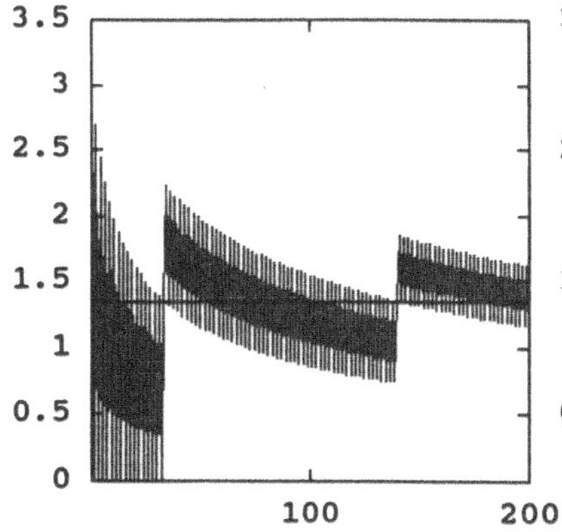

Fig. 3: Price of D–Call

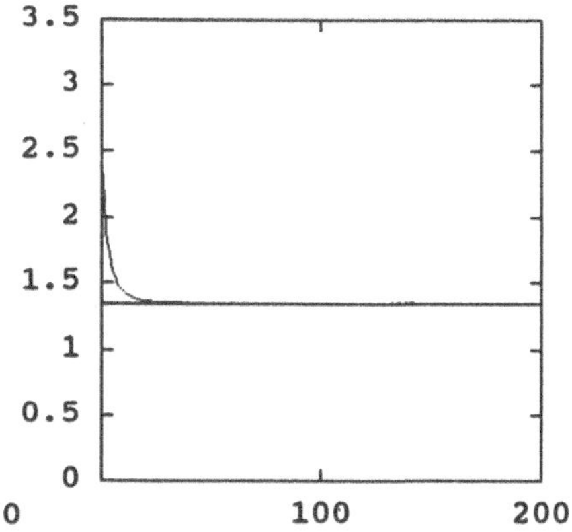

Fig. 4: Price of D–Call

References

Black, F; M. Scholes : "The Pricing of Options and Corporate Liabilities", Journal of Political Economy 81 (May–June 1973), S. 637-659.

Cox, J.; St. Ross; M. Rubinstein : "Option Pricing: A Simplified Approach," Journal of Financial Economics 7 (September 1979), S. 229-263

Cox, J.; M. Rubinstein : "Options Markets", 1985, Prentice–Hall, New Jersey.

Feller, W. : "An Introduction to Probability Theory and Its Applications", Wiley Series in Probability and Mathematical Statistics, Vol I+II, 1968, Wiley & Son, Inc. New York, London and Sidney.

Rendleman, R.; B. Bartter : "Two–State Option Pricing", Journal of Finance 34 (December 1979), S. 1093-1110

Rubinstein, M. : "Exotic Options", 1990, Working Paper University of California at Berkley.

[8] Example with $S(0,0) = 40, r = 5\%, \sigma = 15\%, T = 1year, H = 39$

$N(1) = 35.11$	$N(2) = 140.41$	$N(3) = 315.92$	$N(4) = 561.63$	$N(5) = 877.55$
$N^*(1) = 35$	$N^*(2) = 140$	$N^*(3) = 315$	$N^*(4) = 561$	$N^*(5) = 877$

Horizontal Stretching in the Mapping of Algorithms onto a Data-driven Array

Borut Robič
Jožef Stefan Institute, Laboratory for Computer Architectures
Jamova 39, Ljubljana, Slovenia

We analyze a well known parallel algorithm mapping scheme designed by Koren et al. (1988) and show that, in general, it results in a low area utilization. In particular, we show that algorithm mappings are horizontally overstretched across the target processor array. Ideally, two directly data-dependent operations u and v would be mapped onto two adjacent processors. In practice, however, this is rarely the case. In fact, we show that the distance between the two processors has an upper bound $\mathcal{O}(m+n)$, where m and n are the numbers of all data-dependent operations of u and v, respectively. We show that this bound is tight.

Introduction

A very broad application domain, including image/vision processing, seismic analysis, and medical signal processing, call for algorithms that posses properties such as regularity, recurrsiveness, and locality. Due to their deterministic nature in both time and space these algorithms can be efficiently exploited in systolic and wavefront processor design, as it was pointed out in Kung et al. (1987) and Kung (1988). However, many computationally demanding problems do not exhibit such a high regularity. For this sake, a data-driven processor array, capable of executing *any* given algorithm, was suggested by Koren and Peled (1987). The array consists of processors which are connected into a hexagonal pattern, i.e, each processor has exactly six neighbours. An arbitrary parallel algorithm is written in a high-level language and directly mapped onto the array using a mapping scheme which was described in Koren et al. (1988). Hence, the universality of the array was proved. However, one of the central problems of contemporary computer science is whether *efficient* universality can be found in the context of parallel computing. In what follows we show that the mapping scheme used by Koren et al. (1988) results in a low area utilization. As a consequence, such algorithm mappings exhibit two disadvantages. First of all, since time complexity of routing is not negligible, execution slow-down occurs due to remote communication between processors. Secondly, algorithm mappings may require a too large area. However, to evaluate the applicability of the proposed processor array, and to use it efficiently, one has to be able to map parallel algorithms onto it as optimally as possible.

Horizontal Stretching

Given a program in a high-level dataflow language the mapping scheme first translates the program into the corresponding data flow graph $G(V,A)$. An acyclic subgraph $G'(V,A')$ of G is then constructed using depth-search traversal. The set V of graph nodes can now be partitioned into layers $L_1, L_2, \ldots$, where the first one contains exactly the nodes having input degree 0 (i.e., input nodes) while L_i, $i>1$ consists of all the nodes with at least one input arc coming from L_{i-1} and none coming from $L_k, k \geq i$. Next, each layer is mapped onto its own row of processors in the array. The placement is performed according to associated labels, that is, L_i is placed onto i-th row. The nodes in each row are then permuted so that the paths (which still remain to be built) are expected to be as short as possible. Finally, the paths are build, i.e., it is determined how the arcs of G will be represented in the array.

Let us now examine some possible implications of the permutation of the nodes. After the initial placement of the layers the nodes in each row should be arranged so that the sum of the path lengths would be minimal. Since at this point the paths are not determined yet, each path length is approximated with column distance between the path's source and destination. Let $C(u,v)$ denote the column distance between two nodes u and v in the array, where $(u,v) \in A$, and let $\mathcal{N}_u = \{v | (u,v) \in A \vee (v,u) \in A\}$ denote the set of all neighbours of u in G. Ordering of nodes within the layers is an iterative process. During each iteration the array is traversed, row by row, at r-th row attempting to reduce the value of $\sigma_r = \sum_{u \in L_r} \sum_{v \in \mathcal{N}_u} C(u,v)$, until either no improvement is possible or a maximum number of iterations is exceeded. The reduction of σ_r is achieved by permuting nodes within a row according to a simple heuristic which places a node u in a column as close as possible to the center of mass for all the paths starting or ending in u. Formally, if $c(u)$ denotes the number of the column where u resides, then u is put in the column $c'(u) = \frac{1}{|\mathcal{N}_u|} \sum_{v \in \mathcal{N}_u} c(v)$ (or to the closest available one).

The permutation process is very fruitful since an average reduction of 46 % in the average path length and 52 % in the longest path length was reported in Koren et al. (1988). Nevertheless, permutation may have some undesired effects. In particular, we show that horizontal stretching of paths may occur. Let $(u,v) \in A$ be an arc in G and let $u \in L_s$ and $v \in L_t$, where $t > s$. Assume that $\mathcal{N}_u - \{v\} \subset L_i$ and $\mathcal{N}_v - \{u\} \subset L_i$; that is, all other neighbours of u and v reside in the same layer. Initial placement of layers may place subset $\mathcal{N}_u - \{v\}$ before $\mathcal{N}_v - \{u\}$, as indicated on Figure 1.

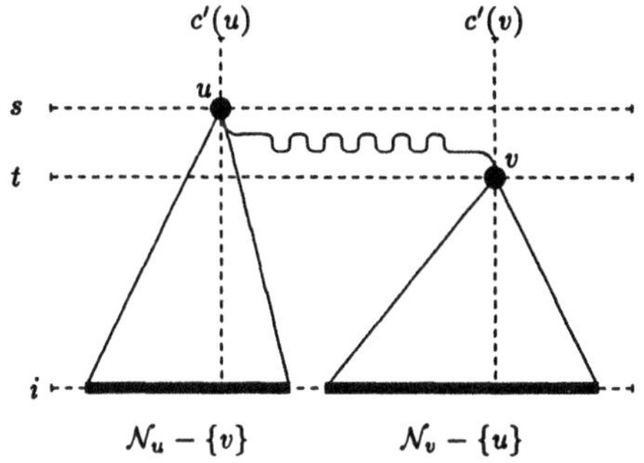

Figure 1: Horizontal stretching. Ideally, u and v would be mapped onto adjacent processors. The permutation process separates them.

Then, the permutation process puts nodes u and v into columns

$$c'(u) = \frac{1}{m}(c'(v) + \sum_{j=1}^{m-1} j) \quad \textit{and} \quad c'(v) = \frac{1}{n}(c'(u) + \sum_{j=m}^{m+n-2} j).$$

where $m = |\mathcal{N}_u|$ and $n = |\mathcal{N}_v|$. The solution of the system is

$$c'(u) = \frac{1}{mn-1}(\sum_{j=m}^{m+n-2} j + n \sum_{j=1}^{m-1} j) \quad \textit{and} \quad c'(v) = \frac{1}{mn-1}(\sum_{j=1}^{m-1} j + m \sum_{j=m}^{m+n-2} j).$$

Finally, the column distance between nodes u and v is

$$|c'(u) - c'(v)| = \frac{(m-1)(n-1)(m+n-2)}{2(mn-1)},$$

which is of order $\mathcal{O}(m+n)$. Note, that this bound is a tight one.

When $t = s + 1$, nodes u and v reside on neighbouring rows. Ideally, they would be put into two neighbouring processors. However, we have just seen that permutation process separates them and, at the same time, horizontally stretches the path between them.

A similar situation may occur on other layers, too. As a consequence, a path of length p (in G) may be mapped into a path (in the array) with the column distance of the source and destination to be $O(p(m+n))$. Note, that in this case the actual path is at least that long, since vertical distance between source and destination has been ignored.

These observations hold for processor arrays of any degree of connectivity. In particular, for the hexagonally connected arrays of Koren and al. we have $m, n \leq 6$ implying that u and v may be moved by the permutation process as much as 4 processors apart. Hence, a path of length p in G may be mapped into a path whose source and destination reside in columns which are $4p$ processors apart. Since the time needed to route data through intermediate processors is comparable to logical and additive arithmetical operations such a path stretching may imply considerable execution slow-down. Additional increase in path lengths may occur during the actual path construction since bottleneck situations are resolved simply by inserting new columns and/or rows, as described in Koren et al. (1988).

Solutions and Concluding Remarks

We have shown why the algorithm mappings produced by the scheme of Koren et al. (1988) are horizontally overstretched across the target data-driven array. Moreover, these algorithm mappings are also overstretched downwards across the array as it was demonstrated in Robič (1993). As a result, these mappings exhibit execution slow-down and require a too large area. Hence, the efficiency of such a universal processor array can be very low.

Based on the above analysis we designed an optimization process and added it to the mapping scheme. The process was inspired by dynamic physical systems and was described in Robič et al. (1991) and Robič et al. (1992). The results of the optimization show that the efficiency of the array can be considerably improved. In particular, we achieved more than 50 % saving in space and, at the same time, 30 % saving in time, on average. Such an efficiency improvement makes the universality of the data-driven array more attractive.

References

Koren I, Mendelson B, Peled I, Silberman G M (1988) A Data-Driven VLSI Array for Arbitrary Algorithms. *IEEE Computer* **21**(10):30-43.

Koren I, Peled I (1987) The Concept and Implementation of Data-Driven Array. *IEEE Computer* **20**(7):102-103.

Kung S Y (1988) VLSI Processor Arrays. *Prentice Hall.*

Kung S Y, Lo S C, Jean S N, Hwang J N (1987) Wavefront Array Processors – Concept to Implementation. *IEEE Computer* **20**(7):18-33.

Robič B (1993) Optimization of parallel algorithm mappings onto regular processor arrays. PhD Thesis, University of Ljubljana.

Robič B, Kolbezen P, Šilc J (1992) Area Optimization of Dataflow-Graph Mappings. *Parallel Computing* **13**(3):297–311.

Robič B, Šilc J, Blaznik P, Kolbezen P (1991) On Reducing the Dataflow-Graph Hosting Area. *Proc IEEE CompEuro '91*, pp. 138-142.

An optimal marketing strategy for heterogeneous groups of porkers

J. Roemen
Department of Econometrics
Tilburg University
P.O. Box 90153, NL 5000 LE, Tilburg

1 Introduction

In this paper the question is dealt with, how a profit maximizing farmer should distribute the sale of groups of porkers over time, taking into consideration that each group consists of subgroups differing in growth rate, that the meat price varies in time, and that the next fattening round can only start when all animals in the current round have been delivered for slaughter.

(Des)investment problems related to a stock of a living commodity have been considered by, among others, Chavas et al. [1], Feinerman [2], Paarsch [3] and Rausser et al. [4]. However, they restrict attention to the case where for one feeding schedule the same growth function holds for all the animals being fattened. Moreover, in this paper the decision rule for the situation where the market prices for meat are mutually dependent is worked out. No attention is paid to the choice of an optimal feeding schedule.

2 Problem

Nowadays, pork is mainly produced on specialized farms. For fattening, such a farm has a number of barns which are divided into compartments. Depending on its size a compartment contains a few tens to well over one hundred animals. Because of health considerations, usually the so called "all in all out" system is followed in production. That means that a compartment is occupied by young animals at one point in time and that all of these animals have to be delivered for slaughter, before the next fattening round in this compartment can start. After entering, the young porkers are fattened for some time, untill they are fit for slaughter. Here we assume that the farmer follows a feeding schedule as advised by an agricultural experimentation station, so the feeding regime is given and fixed.

During fattening, the animals in a compartment usually show variations in the weight gain per day. As a result, the length of the period that an animal needs to reach a certain weight, differs from animal to animal. In this study we assume that the animals in a compartment receive the same feed ration, so the weight variation has to be ascribed to differences in genetic qualities. For our purpose, it suffices to distinguish two subgroups in a compartment: fast en slow growers. Within these subgroups no substantial differences in growth qualities exist.

As soon as a porker has reached a certain minimal weight, the farmer can sell it to a slaughter house. The price which he receives, is not constant in time, but varies from week to week. Generally speaking, this week's price moves within a restricted interval around last week's price. Therefore, we assume that it is a stochastic variable which only depends on the price in the preceding week. The feed price and the interest rate show variability too, but their variability is much smaller, so we treat them as deterministic.

Because of the heterogeneity of the animals in one compartment, the "all in all out" system and the stochastic nature of the pork price, the farmer is confronted with the question how to distribute the delivery of fattened porkers over time.

3 Model and solution

The net financial result depends on the decisions taken by the farmer in each week of each fattening round. These rounds succeed each other uninterruptedly. Such a decision can be to sell this week a group of porkers or to postpone the sale and to continue fattening. These decisions are based on the weight of the animals, the price for pork, the expenses for feed and young pigs and the interest rate.

A porker can be sold as soon as it is fit for slaughter, i.e., when its weight is between a minimal and a maximal value. The fast growers reach this minimal weight at the age of $x_{1,min}$ weeks, while their latest delivery date is at the age of $x_{1,max}$ weeks. The sale of the slow growers can only start from $x_{2,min}(\geq x_{1,min})$ onward. The last possible week for this group to leave the farm is at the age of $x_{2,max}$ weeks. As long as the porkers have not yet reached their minimal weight or when they threaten to pass the maximum, the decision of the farmer is obvious. However, as soon as a group is fit for slaughter, the farmer has to choose between the two available decisions. By ending each fattening round at the suitable moment the farmer can realize a maximal financial result. For the determination of the suitable moment cut-off prices for pork are calculated for each week in which animals are fit for slaughter. At the cut-off level for a certain week the farmer is indifferent between selling in that week or selling in the future. If the market price for pork in a week exceeds the cut-off level for that week, the farmer should sell, in the opposed case he should postpone the sale and continue fatting.

For the calculation of the cut-off prices in the relevant period we formulate a Markov decision model. Here the system under study is the stochastic process $\{(\underline{z}_t, \underline{h}_t, \underline{p}_t), t = 0, 1, 2, ...\}$, where $\underline{z}_t$ stands for the age of an animal in week t, $\underline{h}_t$ for the composition of the compartment and $\underline{p}_t$ for the price of pork. Age ranges from 0 to $x_{2,max}$ weeks, while $\underline{h}_t$ takes on the value 1 if both subgroups are in the compartment and the value 0 if the slow growers are still being fattened and the fast growers have already been delivered. The price for pork takes on discrete values. We assume that it obeys a first order Markov scheme with stationary transition probabilities. The cut-off prices can be calculated from the optimality equations using standard methods given by Ross [5] or Tijms [6]. When a group consists of two subgroups, three vectors of cut-off prices are calculated, one for the fast growers, one for the group as a whole and one for the slow growers, given that the fast growers have been delivered.

4 Conclusion

In this paper a model is formulated which can be used to derive an optimal delivery strategy for heterogeneous groups of porkers. The feed schedule is assumed to be given. The central question is how the farmer should react on the variability of the pork price. The model provides a system of cut-off prices for pork during the weeks in which animals can be sold.

Literature

1. Chavas, J.P., J. Kliebenstein and Th. Crenshaw, Modeling Dynamic Agricultural Production Response: The Case of Swine Production, American Journal of Agricultural Economics, 1985, 636-646.
2. Feinerman, E., and P.B. Siegel, A dynamic farm-level planning model for beef feedlot production and marketing, Journal of Agricultural Economics, 1988, 413-425.
3. Paarsch, H.J., Micro-economic models of beef supply, Canadian Journal of Economics, 1985, 636-651.
4. Rausser, J.C., and E. Hochman, Dynamic Agricultural Systems: Economic Prediction and Control, North-Holland Publishing Company, New York, 1979.
5. Ross, S.M., Applied Probability Models with Optimization Applications, Holden-Bay, San Francisco, 1970.
6. Tijms, H.C., stochastic modelling and analysis: a computational approach, Wiley, New York, 1986.

A DISCRETE MIN-MAX ALGORITHM FOR INEQUALITY CONSTRAINTS

Berç Rustem
Department of Computing
Imperial College of Science, Technology & Medicine
180 Queen's Gate, London SW7 2BZ, UK

Forecasting with rival models is usually resolved by some form of forecast pooling. In policy optimization, a similar approach leads to the pooling of rival objective functions derived from the rival models (see Rustem, 1987; 1992). Thus, the optimal decision problem can be formulated as the optimization of the pooled objective functions subject to nonlinear constraints. Let α denote the pooling weights, with

$$\alpha \in \mathbf{E}_+^m = \left\{ \alpha \in \mathbf{R}^m \mid \alpha \geq 0 \, ; \, < \mathit{1}, \alpha > \, = 1 \right\},$$

where $\mathit{1} \in \mathbf{R}^m$ denotes the vector with every component unity. Consider the problem

$$\min_x \left\{ < \alpha, f(x) > \Big| \, h(x) \leq 0 \right\} \tag{1}$$

where, $\alpha \in \mathbf{E}_+^m$; $x \in \mathbf{R}^n$; $f : \mathbf{R}^n \to \mathbf{R}^m$; $h : \mathbf{R}^n \to \mathbf{R}^\ell$ and $f, h \in C^2$. In (1) each element of f, denoted by f^i, represents a rival objective function corresponding to a rival model. The restrictions $h(x) \leq 0$ are the inequality constraints imposed on the overall decision problem. In the above formulation, the vector α is fixed and defines the pooling weights. Also, generally, the number of models is much less than the number of decision variables, i.e. $n >> m$. One reason for this is that policy optimization is essentially dynamic in nature and the total number of decision variables is the product of the decision variables for one time period and the number of time periods.

Among possible choices of pooling weights, the robust pooling corresponds to the strategy that is invariant to whichever rival scenario, or model, actually turns out to represent the system. The pooling that corresponds to the robust policy is given by the solution of the min-max problem

$$\min_x \max_\alpha \left\{ < f(x), \alpha > \Big| \, h(x) \leq 0 \, , \alpha \in \mathbf{E}_+^m \right\} \tag{2}$$

where the worst case rival model scenario is computed *simultaneously* with the minimization over x. It is shown in Rustem (1987; Proposition 7.6) that the solution of (2) has a robust character. Whichever rival model turns out to represent the actual system, the optimal (min-max) strategy ensures that the objective function value will not deteriorate: it will be at least as good as the min-max value. The solution of (2) yields a value of α corresponding to the robust min-max strategy.

If the insurance provided by the robust, and cautious, policy has too high a cost in policy terms, then the decision maker could base the optimal policy on (1) with α chosen in the neighbourhood of the min-max value such that the policy can be made "acceptable" and at the same time as robust as possible. It must be said that *this strategy is only robust with respect to the known rival representations of the system.* If a further, possibly unknown, model of the economy exists and is not included in the set of rival models in (1), clearly the computed strategy cannot be expected to be robust with respect to this additional model. It can be shown that (2) is equivalent to

$$\min_{x} \max_{i \in \{1, 2, \dots, m\}} \left\{ f^i(x) \,\middle|\, h(x) \leq 0 \right\}. \tag{3}$$

In Rustem (1992) we discuss an algorithm for solving the equality constrained min-max problem. In this paper, we discuss an approach using an augmented Lagrangian formulation to directly solve the inequality constrained case given by (3). The algorithm involves an augmented Lagrangian formulation with a sequential quadratic programming subproblem, an adaptive penalty parameter selection rule; a stepsize strategy, convergent to unit steps, that ensures progress towards optimality and feasibility of the inequality constraints. The method used for handling inequalities is based on the nonlinear programming algorithm discussed in Rustem (1993).

The inequality constrained algorithm discussed in the paper, directly aims at measuring progress towards the min-max solution using a stepsize strategy. The algorithm defines the direction of progress as a quasi-Newton step obtained from a quadratic subproblem. An augmented Lagrangian function is defined and a procedure is formulated for determining the penalty parameter. The growth in the penalty parameter is required only to ensure a descent property. It is shown that this penalty parameter does not grow indefinitely. Convergence of the overall algorithm is established.

REFERENCES

Rustem, B., "Methods for the simultaneous use of multiple models in optimal policy design", in: C. Carraro and D. Sartore eds., *Developments in control theory for economic analysis* (Maritnus Nijhoff Kluwer Publishers, Dordrecht, 1987) pp. 157-186.

Rustem, B., "A superlineary convergent min-max algorithm for rival models of the same economic system", *Mathematical Programming* 53 (1992) 279-295.

Rustem, B., "Equality and inequality constrained optimization algorithms with convergent stepsizes", *J. Optim. Theory and Applic.* 76 (1993) 429-453.

ON TWO AND THREE PERSON EXCHANGE GAMES

Minoru Sakaguchi
Nagoya University of Commerce and Business Administration
Sagamine, Nisshin-cho, Aichi, 470-01, JAPAN

1.INTRODUCTION

Brams, Kilgour and Davis investigated the following non-zero-sum exchange game(abreviated by EG). Each of two players(I and II) draws a number (x and y, respectively) according to a uniform distribution on [0,1]. After observing his number each player can then choose either to keep(K) his number or to exchange(E) it for the other player's number. If only one player chooses E, an exchange of the numbers occurs with probability p. A player's payoff is the number he holds after the players have made their choices and a possible exchange has occured. The payoff matrix for this non-zero-sum two-person game is:

$$\begin{array}{c} \\ K \\ E \end{array} \begin{array}{c} \begin{array}{cc} K & E \end{array} \\ \begin{bmatrix} (x,y) & (py+\bar{p}x, px+\bar{p}y) \\ (py+\bar{p}x, px+\bar{p}y) & (y,x) \end{bmatrix} \end{array}$$

where $\bar{p}=1-p$. If p=0[1] then the game is an AND[OR] game in which both players[at least one player] must choose E in order for an exchange to occur. We consider the zero-sum game version in this paper. Denote by $\alpha(x)[\beta(y)]$ the probability that player I[II] chooses E if his hand is x[y]. Under this strategy-pair $\alpha(\cdot)$-$\beta(\cdot)$, the expected payoff to I is

$$(1.1) \qquad M(\alpha,\beta)\equiv\int_0^1\int_0^1 (\bar{\alpha}(x),\alpha(x))\begin{bmatrix} 1 & 1-2p \\ 1-2p & -1 \end{bmatrix}(x-y)\begin{bmatrix} \bar{\beta}(y) \\ \beta(y) \end{bmatrix}dxdy.$$

We shall also consider a bilateral-move variant of EG in which the players act not simultaneously but consecutively, namely: first acts player I and then player II. The procedure can be described in the following way:

Player	Hand	1st Move	2nd Move	payoff to I
I	x	K		
		E		
II	y	after K	K	$x-y$
			E	$(1-2p)(x-y)$
		after E	K	$(1-2p)(x-y)$
			E	$y-x$

When player II moves he knows which choice his opponent has chosen. Let $\alpha(x)$ denote the probability that player I chooses E at the 1st move. Also let $\beta(y)[\gamma(y)]$ denote the probability that player II chooses E at the 2nd move when his opponent has choosen K[E] at the 1st move. Then under his strategy-pair$(\alpha(\cdot);\beta(\cdot),\gamma(\cdot))$ the expected payoff to I is

$$(1.2)\qquad M(\alpha;\beta,\gamma)\equiv$$

$$\int_0^1\int_0^1[\bar{\alpha}(x)\bar{\beta}(y)+\{\bar{\alpha}(x)\beta(y)+\alpha(x)\bar{\gamma}(y)\}(1-2p)-\alpha(x)\gamma(y)](x-y)dxdy.$$

We call an exchange game simple if the payoff of player I is given by sgn $(x'-y')$, when the values of the numbers they finally get are x' for I, and y' for II. So in the simple exchange games we shall consider the payoff function are(1.1) and (1.2), with $x-y$ replaced by $\mathrm{sgn}(x-y)$. (Note that sgn t is defined by $1,0,-1$, if $t>0,=0,<0$, respectively).

2.SOLUTIONS OF TWO-PERSON EGS

We prove the following four theorems.

Theorem 1. For the EG with payoff function(1.1), the solution is as follows: The optimal strategies are common to both players and $\alpha^*(x)=\beta^*(x)=I_{[0,a]}(x)$, where $I_S(x)$ is the indicator function of the set S [0,1], and $a=(\sqrt{p\bar{p}}-p)/(1-2p)$. The value of the game is zero

Theorem 2. For the bilateral-move EG with payoff function (1.2), the solution is as follows: Let $a=(\sqrt{p\bar{p}}-p)/(1-2p)$, $b=(1/2)(1+a)$ and $c=a/2$. The optimal strategies of the players are

$$\alpha^*(x)=I_{[0,a]}(x),\quad \beta^*(y)=I_{[0,b]}(y),\quad \gamma^*(y)=I_{[0,c]}(y).$$

The value of the game is $-(1/4)p(1-a)^2$.

Theorem 3. For the SEG with payoff function(1.1) with x-y replaced by sgn (x-y), the solution is: The optimal strategies are common to both players and $\alpha^*(x)=\beta^*(x)=I_{[0,p]}(x)$. The value of the game is zero.

Theorem 4. For the SEG with payoff function(1.2) with x-y replaced by sgn (x-y), the solution is as follows: Let $b=(1/2)(1+p)$ and $c=p/2$. Then the optimal strategies of the players are

$$\alpha^*(x)=\begin{cases} 1, & \text{if } 0\leqq x<c, \\ \text{arbitrary in } [0,1], \text{ but satisfying } \int_c^b \alpha^*(x)dx=c, & \text{if } c<x<b, \\ 0, & \text{if } b<x\leqq 1. \end{cases}$$

$$\beta^*(y)= I_{[0,b]}(y), \text{ and } \gamma^*(y)=I_{[0,c]}(y).$$

The value of the game is $-(1/2)p(1-p)$.

3. THREE-PERSON SEG AND ITS SOLUTION

Finally we shall discuss the theree-person zero-sum simple exchange game (abreviated by SEG) as a natural extension of the two-person game model. The game proceeds as follows: At the biginning of a play three players I, II and III receive hands x,y,z, respectively, chosen at random and independently from a unit distribution in [0,1]. Then each player, looking at his hand privately, chooses either one of K and E. Choices by the players should be made simultaneously and independently.

If only one player chooses E, an exchange of his hand with each one of the players who chose K occurs with probability p/2, and no exchange among the three players occur with probability $\bar{p}$. If two players choose E and the other chooses K, an exchange of hands within the players who chose E occurs. If all players choose E then the two possible exchange among the all three players occur with probability 1/2 each. After choices are made and the corresponding "trade" occurs, the hands, they get finally, are compared and a player with highest hand wins.

Theorem 6. The solution to the three-person SEG is: Each chooses E if his hand is $a\equiv\sqrt{p}/(\sqrt{2}+\sqrt{p})$. The equilibrium values are 0, 0, 0.

4. REMARKS

Three remarks are given.

References

Brams,S.J., Kilgour,D.M., and Davis,M.D.: Unraveling in games of sharing and exchange, to appear.

Garnaev,A. Yu: On simple MIX game, Intern.J.Game Th.21(1992),237-247.

Sakaguchi,M.: Information structures and perfect information in simple exchange games, to appear in Math. Japonica, 38(1993).

Binomial Term Structure Models and the Forward Probability Measure: Algorithmic Model Specification and Simulation Results

Klaus Sandmann and Erik Schlögl
University of Bonn, Department of Statistics, Adenauerallee 24–42,
5300 Bonn, Federal Republic of Germany

Introduction

Following the seminal work by Ho and Lee (1986), many different approaches to modelling stochastic term structure movements have been proposed.[1] In this paper we take the algorithmic view, focusing on the calculation of state prices in binomial term structure models. This permits us to consider a large class of such models in one general framework.

It is the state prices, not the equivalent martingale measure, which determine the price of a contingent claim. Therefore, in our computer simulations, we concentrated on the interest rate distributions under the forward probability measure. We present the results of extensive simulations of the Ho/Lee and the Sandmann/Sondermann (1989/91) models as they pertain to these distributions and to the term structure movements these models imply.

Calculation of the state prices

Let us consider a path independent binomial spot rate model.[2] Let (j,i) denote the index for the i-th state in the j-th period. Given the initial term structure defined by today's bond prices $\{B_0(1); B_0(2); B_0(3); \ldots\}$, the no–arbitrage condition requires that the following relationships hold:

1. Under the local expectations hypothesis,[3] the state price $\pi_{1,\cdot}$ for each vertex in period 1 is equal to the discounted expected value of one dollar payable in the respective vertex, i.e.
$$\pi_{1,0} = \frac{1-p_0}{1+r_0} \quad , \quad \pi_{1,1} = \frac{p_0}{1+r_0} \tag{1}$$
where r_0 is the one–period interest rate (determined by $B_0(1)$) and p_0 is the probability of an upward movement of the term structure.

2. No arbitrage implies
$$B_0(2) = \frac{1}{1+r_{1,1}}\pi_{1,1} + \frac{1}{1+r_{1,0}}\pi_{1,0} \tag{2}$$

[1] Jensen and Nielsen (1992) survey a series of binomial term structure models; Heath, Jarrow and Morton (1992) extended the term structure literature to include models in continuous time.

[2] A generalization to include path dependent binomial models is self–evident. To do so would only complicate the notation unnecessarily, as the models discussed in this paper all assume path independency. Furthermore, path dependency can be introduced into the simulations discussed below only at considerable additional expense in computer time. This becomes necessary when one seeks to price path dependent contingent claims: Then the focus is on state prices $\pi_{j,\eta(j)}, \eta(j) \in \{0,1\}^j$, conditioned on the entire path $\eta(j)$.

[3] The local expectations hypothesis is the only expectations hypothesis compatible with the no–arbitrage condition. See Cox, Ingersoll and Ross (1981).

because both sides of the equation yield the same payoff: The right side can be interpreted as a contingent claim which pays $1/(1+r_{1,1})$ in $(1,1)$ and $1/(1+r_{1,0})$ in $(1,0)$. This allows the holder of the contingent claim to invest his period 1 payoff at the then prevailing spot rate just so he receives a payoff of 1 in period 2. Alternatively, he could have bought a two-period zero bond of face value 1 in period 0.

3. Analogously, we have for every period j :

$$B_0(j+1) = \sum_{i=0}^{j} \hat{\pi}_{j,i} \qquad \text{with} \qquad \hat{\pi}_{j,i} = \frac{\pi_{j,i}}{1+r_{j,i}} \tag{3}$$

4. The state prices in any period are determined by the state prices in the previous period and the local expectations hypothesis, i.e. setting values outside the binomial tree to zero.

$$\pi_{j,i} = p_{j-1,i-1} \cdot \hat{\pi}_{j-1,i-1} + (1 - p_{j-1,i}) \cdot \hat{\pi}_{j-1,i} \tag{4}$$

and must be such that their sum equals the price of the zero bond with the respective maturity.

These relationships permit the calculation of state prices by a forward substitution method, which was in its essence first published by Jamshidian (1991).

Model Specifications

Given the initial term structure, several degrees of freedom remain when calculating the state prices in accordance to the relationships described above. A binomial term structure model can be characterized by the way in which these degrees of freedom are eliminated through exogenous specifications. Three different approaches present themselves:

1. *Endogenous calculation of the spot rate process $\{r_j\}_j$ under exogenous specification of the transition probabilities $p_{j,i}$.*[4]

2. *Endogenous calculation of both the spot rate process $\{r_j\}_j$ and the transition probabilities $p_{j,i}$*, modelling the transition probabilities dependent on the spot rate realizations.[5]

3. *Exogenous specification of the spot rate process $\{r_j\}_j$ and endogenous calculation of the transition probabilities $p_{j,i}$.*

As an example, let us specify the Sandmann/Sondermann model in the forward substitution framework:

1. Exogenous transition probability (may be time and state dependent). For simplicity let us assume

$$p_{j,i} = \overline{p} \qquad \forall\, j, i$$

[4] Ho, Lee (1986) and Sandmann, Sondermann (1989/91) fall into this class.
[5] Ball (1989) proposes such a model.

2. Exogenous risk measure: the local standard deviation (volatility) $\sigma_{j,i}$ of the logarithmic spot rates

$$\sigma_{j,i}^2 = V_{p_{j,i}}[\log r_{j+1,\cdot}|r_{j,i}] = p_{j,i}\cdot(1-p_{j,i})\cdot\left(\log(\frac{r_{j+1,i+1}}{r_{j+1,i}})\right)^2$$
$$\Longleftrightarrow r_{j+1,i+1} = r_{j+1,i}\cdot\exp\left\{\frac{\sigma_{j,i}}{\sqrt{p_{j,i}\cdot(1-p_{j,i})}}\right\} > r_{j+1,i}$$

As a consequence of this functional relationship of the spot rate realizations in each period, equation (3) always has a unique solution, provided the initial forward rates were non-negative.

Simulation results

State prices and not the equivalent martingale measure determine option prices; consequently we consider the spot rate distributions not under the vertex probabilities, but under the *forward probabilities* $\pi_{j,i}^0$ instead, defined as follows:

$$\Pi^0 : \{(j,i) \in \mathbb{N}_0^2 \mid 0 \le j \le n; 0 \le i \le j\} \to [0;1]$$

for some time horizon n, with

$$\pi_{j,i}^0 = \frac{\pi_{j,i}}{B_0(j)} \quad \text{and} \quad \pi_{0,0}^0 = 1$$

Then the arbitrage price of a path independent contingent claim with payoffs $H_j : \Omega \to \mathbb{R}$ in the periods $0 < j \le n$ is given by

$$\sum_{j=1}^{n} B_0(j) E_{\pi_j^0}[H_j] \tag{5}$$

Limit results for spot rate distributions under the vertex probabilities have been derived explicitly elsewhere.[6] Our simulations show that while not identical with the distributions under the vertex probabilities, the distributions under the forward probabilities also very quickly stabilize when the (discrete) time line is divided into ever smaller units, suggesting that in the limit these distributions are stable and independent of the transition probabilities.

Consider figure 1. It shows the development of the spot rate distributions under the forward probabilities, in the Sandmann/Sondermann model. The initial term structure was 9, 8, 7, 6, 7, 8 (in discrete one-year forward rates, in percent), with constant forward rates within each of the six years. Note how the distributions are centered around the initial forward rates for the respective periods and how the distributions stabilize as the binomial tree fans out.

Perhaps the most important result of our simulation study concerns the term structure movements implied by the Sandmann/Sondermann model. The simulations show (and Sommer (1993) proves analytically) that the Ho/Lee model produces term structures that are (1) parallel in all states of any one period and (2) no matter what the form of the initial term structure, sooner or later there will only be rising term structures (in terms of yields or forward rates). In contrast, as can be seen in figure 2, the Sandmann/Sondermann model yields

[6] see Heath, Jarrow and Morton (1992) for Ho/Lee, Sandmann and Sondermann (1991) for their model.

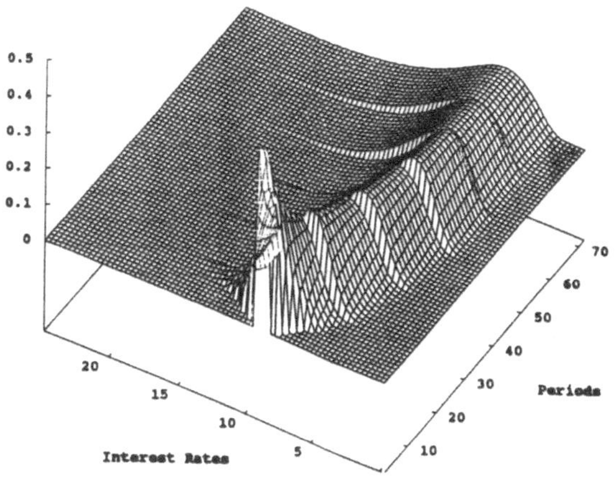

Figure 1: Distributions over time

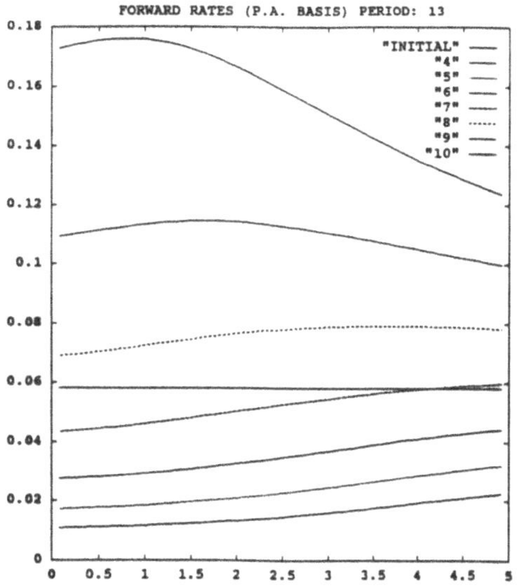

Figure 2: Possible term structures

a much wider class of possible term structures. Starting with a flat initial term structure and plotting the term structures in all states with a forward probability of 5% or more, we see that we get "normal" as well as "inverse" term structures with positive probability. Our simulations show that this is the case no matter what the slope of the initial term structure.

References

Ball, C.A. (1989): *A Branching Model of Bond Price Dynamics and Contingent Claim Pricing;* Working Paper, University of Michigan.

Cox, J.C.; Ingersoll, J.E.; Ross, S.A. (1981): *A Re-examination of Traditional Hypotheses about the Term Structure of Interest Rates;* Journal of Finance, 1067-1083.

Heath, D.; Jarrow, R.; Morton, A. (1992): *Bond Pricing and the Term Structure of Interest Rates: A New Methodology of Contingent Claim Valuation;* Econometrica, 77-105.

Ho, T.; Lee, S.-B. (1986): *Term Structure Movements and the Pricing of Interest Rate Contingent Claims;* Journal of Finance, 1011-1030.

Jamshidian, F. (1987): *Pricing of Contingent Claims in the One Factor Term Structure Model;* Working Paper, Merrill Lynch Capital Markets.

Jamshidian, F. (1991): *Forward Induction and Construction of Yield Curve Diffusion Models;* The Journal of Fixed Income, 62-74.

Jensen, B.A.; Nielsen, J.A. (1992): *The Structure of Binomial Lattice Models for Bonds;* Working Paper, Copenhagen Business Schools.

Sandmann, K.; Sondermann, D. (1989): *A Term Structure Model and the Pricing of Interest Rate Options;* Universität Bonn: Discussion Paper B-129.

Sandmann, K.; Sondermann, D. (1991): *A Term Structure Model and the Pricing of Interest Rate Derivatives;* Universität Bonn: Discussion Paper B-180.

Sommer, D. (1993): *Ho/Lee Revisited;* Universität Bonn: forthcoming.

MONTE CARLO SIMULATIONS AND THE PRICING OF OPTIONS IN THE DISCONTINUOUS CASE

Klaus Schäfer
Lehrstuhl für Kreditwirtschaft und Finanzierung
Johann Wolfgang Goethe–Universität Frankfurt
Mertonstr. 17–25, D — 60054 Frankfurt am Main

Based on the early work of *Black* and *Scholes* (1973) an enormous number of models to solve various option pricing problems has been derived. In these models besides the usual frictionless market conditions (e.g. no transaction costs, borrowing and lending at a known, constant short–term interest rate r, free short selling of securities) assumptions on the exercise characteristics of options (american, european), the dividend–behaviour in the case of stock options and the stochastic process of the underlying security have to be made. Exact valuation formulas or closed–form solutions are not available at all pricing problems. In such cases numerical procedures can be used to value derivative assets. Monte Carlo methods, first suggested by *Boyle* (1977), offer such procedures and give approximative solutions in many pricing situations.

Risk neutral valuation and Monte Carlo methods

The "fair" option value is usually found as the unique solution of a stochastic differential equation. If it is possible to derive the fundamental equation by hedging arguments, the option's value does not depend directly on the structure of investors' preferences. This characteristic of the so–called preference–free option pricing models was used by *Cox* and *Ross* (1976) in their risk neutral valuation approach. They showed that in such cases the option value could be derived by postulating some world where preferences are given and consistent with the specified parameter values. Then the preference–free solution of the pricing problem is, for example, equal to the equilibrium solution of the option's value in a world with risk neutral investors. Thus, the value of an european option on a non–dividend paying stock can be obtained by discounting the expected maturity option's value at the risk free rate r, e. g. in the case of an european call with exercise price K and maturity–date T_o the actual option price C is given by

$$C = r^{-T_o} \int \max\left(S(T_o) - K, 0\right)\, dF\left(S(T_o), T_o \middle| S\right), \tag{1}$$

where $F(S(T_o), T_o|S)$ is the distribution function of the stock price $S(T_o)$ at time T_o with respect to given S. For simplicity we assume that r and T_o are measured in periods and that the actual date is $t = 0$. Denoting the expectation operator by $E(.)$ we have

$$C = E(h(\vec{x})) = \int h(\vec{x})f(\vec{x})\, d\vec{x} \tag{2}$$

with density function $f(.)$ and $h(.)$ as the discounted maturity value of the option. For that reason, if the distribution of the terminal stock value is known, the value of the option can be obtained by the integration 1 and 2, respectively.

The formulation 2 of the pricing problem offers the opportunity to applicate the technique of Monte Carlo methods. To generate, for example, n possible stock price trajectories $S^i = S^i(0), S^i(1), \ldots, S^i(T_o)$ for $i = 1, \ldots, n$ with respect to the stochastic process, an estimate of the integral 1 or 2 is given by the crude Monte Carlo method, see e.g. *Hammersley* and *Handscomb* (1964),

$$C \approx r^{-T_o} \frac{1}{n} \sum_{i=1}^{n} \max\left(S^i(T_o) - K\,,\, 0\right). \tag{3}$$

Since the distribution of maturity–date stock prices is determined by the assumed stochastic process, it is obvious that the simulations of stock price paths can be prepared in algorithms to be implemented in a computer programme. This makes Monte Carlo methods not only easy to use but flexible because modifications with respect to different underlying stock return processes are easily realized.

The accuracy of the estimation is measured as the variance and results in a confidence interval. Besides this simple crude method there are more efficient procedures like the control variate and the antithetic variate method. It can be shown that the the crude Monte Carlo method is well applicable to discontinuous option pricing problems.

Option pricing and jump processes

In the standard *Black* and *Scholes* approach stock price movements are described by a continuous diffusion process. This model can't explain large price changes in short time. An alternative to that class of stochastic processes is the pure jump process of *Cox* and *Ross* (1976). The underlying price dynamics can be written as

$$\frac{dS}{S} = \mu dt + (Y - 1)dq \tag{4}$$

with time parameter t, drift term μ, jump amplitude $Y - 1$ and poisson process q with intensity λ. A closed–form solution can be derived only in the case of a very restrictive formulation of the jump behaviour. Applying a generalized version of Itô's Lemma to 4, see *Aase* (1988), we get the following recursive formula as the basis for the stock price simulation,

$$S(t+\Delta t) = S(t)\,\exp(\mu\Delta t)\prod_{j=n_t+1}^{n_{t+\Delta t}} Y_j, \tag{5}$$

where Y_j is the j-th jump amplitude and $n_t + 1$ and $n_{t+\Delta t}$ are the number of stock price jumps occured in the time interval $[0, n_t + 1]$ and $[0, n_{t+\Delta t}]$, respectively. By 5 and the fact that a riskless hedge can be constructed with a fixed Y, Monte Carlo methods are useful to give approximative option values in the pure jump situation.

Merton (1976) postulates a mixture of the continuous brownian motion process and the discontinuous poisson process for the stock price dynamics as

$$\frac{dS}{S} = (\alpha - \lambda k)dt + \sigma dw + dq, \tag{6}$$

where σ^2 is the variance of the stock's return, $k = E(Y-1)$ and dw is a standard Wiener process with drift α. Both the *Black* and *Scholes* ($\lambda = 0$ and therefore $dq = 0$) and the *Cox* and *Ross* ($dw = 0$) models are included in the jump–diffusion approach of *Merton*. Applying Itô's Lemma to 6 gives the generating function for the stock price trajectories by

$$S(t+\Delta t) = S(t)\,\exp\left((\alpha - \frac{\sigma^2}{2} - \lambda k)\Delta t + \sigma z_t\sqrt{\Delta t}\right)\prod_{j=n_t+1}^{n_{t+\Delta t}} Y_j, \tag{7}$$

where z_t is a normally distributed random variable with zero mean and unit variance. It can be seen by 6 and 7 that this approach allows discontinuous large price changes in short time in addition to the continuous stock price changes modelled by *Black* and *Scholes*. The jump component can be understood as the process to describe the arrival of very important, "abnormal" new information, while the continuous component models the arrival of the "usual" new information. Because this model allows such an intuitive economic interpretation, modelling stock price returns by mixed jump–diffusion processes has become very popular.

While *Merton* makes the additional assumption that the jump amplitudes are lognormally distributed to obtain a closed–form solution, Monte Carlo methods allow different distributions for the discontinuous part. For example, empirical stock price distributions could be used, too. Also a bernoulli process instead of the above poisson process can easily be included in this numerical approach. Such a bernoulli jump process is suggested by *Ball* and *Touros* (1985) to simplify empirical evidence on mixed stock distributions. For concrete results see *Schäfer* (1993). Furthermore, deterministic dividend payments can be considered without further analysis. One just has to include the dividend structure in the generating function 7. Thus, Monte Carlo methods can extend the applicability of the *Merton* approach in an important extent. Since it is possible to value american call options on dividend paying stocks in the pure diffusion case by simulation methods, the complex mixed jump–diffusion model needs other numerical procedures, like finite difference methods or quadratic approximations, which seem to be more efficient.

Further remarks

Monte Carlo methods provide a wide variety of applications to option pricing problems, see e.g. *Boyle* (1976), *Hull* and *White* (1987), *Hull* (1989) and *Schäfer* (1993). It was shown that especially the case of jump processes can be generalized in many aspects. Furthermore, Monte Carlo simulation is useful for the pricing of derivative securities with history dependent–payoff (exotic options) and in cases where the underlying stock returns are generated by complex mixtures of stochastic processes.

The empirical research of German's stock price behaviour is small. *Beinert* and *Trautmann* (1991) give some evidence upon jump–diffusion price processes. They contradict the CAPM–linked argument of *Merton* who assumed that the jump component represents unsystematic risk. If this assumption is not fulfilled, the hedge approach of *Merton* to derive a preference–free stochastic differential equation can't be applied any more. An alternative jump–diffusion model may be found in *Naik/Lee* (1990).

Literature references

Aase K K (1988) Contingent claims valuation when the security price is a combination of an Itô process and a random point process, Stoch Processes a t Applications 28: 185–220

Ball C A, Touros W N (1983) A simplified jump process for common stock returns, J o Financial a Quantitative Analysis 18: 53–65

Beinert M, Trautmann S (1991) Jump–diffusion models of German stock returns — A statistical investigation, Statistical Papers 32: 269–280

Black F, Scholes M (1973) The pricing of options and corporate liabilities, J o Political Economy 81: 637–654

Boyle P P (1977) Options: A Monte Carlo approach, J o Financial Economics 4: 323–338

Cox J C, Ross S A (1976) The valuation of options for alternative stochastic processes, J o Financial Economics 3: 145–166

Hammersley J M, Handscomb D C (1964) Monte Carlo methods. J Wiley. London

Hull J, White A (1987) The pricing of options on assets with stochastic volatilities, J o Finance 42: 281–300

Hull J (1989) Options, futures and other derivative securities. Prentice-Hall. Englewood Cliffs New Jersey

Merton, R C (1976) Option pricing when underlying stock returns are discontinuous, J o Financial Economics 3: 125–144

Naik V, Lee M (1990) General equilibrium pricing of options on the market portfolio with discontinuous returns, Review o Financial Studies 3: 493–521

Schäfer K (1993) Optionsbewertung und Monte–Carlo Methoden. forthcoming

NINE KINDS OF MONOTONE AND GENERALIZED MONOTONE MAPS

Siegfried Schaible
Graduate School of Management
University of California
Riverside, CA 92521

Monotonicity plays an important role in complementarity problems and variational inequality problems, like convexity in mathematical programming. Recently, seven kinds of monotone and generalized monotone maps were introduced; see Karamardian et al. (1990). In case of a gradient map, different types of (generalized) monotonicity of the gradient correspond to different types of (generalized) convexity of the underlying function. This gives rise to first-order characterizations of generalized convex functions, not known so far; see Avriel et al. (1988).

However in one case, namely strong pseudomonotonicity, only necessity, but not sufficiency of the gradient for the corresponding property of the underlying function could be shown. Subsequently, in Hadjisavvas et al. (1993) a counterexample has been given that proves that sufficiency does not hold in general. As a result, a weaker concept of strong pseudomonotonicity is introduced for maps in Hadjisavvas et al. (1993) such that strong pseudomonotonicity of the gradient is equivalent to strong pseudoconvexity of the underlying function; at least as long as the gradient is differentiable. In Hadjisavvas et al. (1993) we also define two new types of generalized monotonicity, namely semistrict and strict quasimonotonicity. In case of gradient maps they are equivalent to semistrict and strict quasiconvexity of the underlying function. This brings the total to nine kinds of monotone and generalized monotone maps, in complete analogy to corresponding convex and generalized convex functions; see Avriel et al. (1988).

For generalized convex functions several second-order characterizations are known; see Avriel et al. (1988). The earliest one, involving the gradient and the Hessian, was derived by Arrow et al. (1961). From the point of view of the related gradient map, it can be interpreted as a first-order characterization in terms of the gradient map and its Jacobian. In Karamardian et al. (1993) first-order characterizations of generalized monotonicity are derived for maps which are not necessarily gradient maps. Using a geometric approach, we obtain conditions which are both necessary and sufficient for pseudomonotone and quasimonotone maps, involving the map and its Jacobian. These conditions reduce to much simpler characterizations in the special case of an affine map $F(x) = M x + q$ where M is an nxn matrix and q, like the variable x, an n-vector. Such a map is a gradient map if and only if M is symmetric, in which case the underlying function is the quadratic $f(x) = 1/2\ x'M\ x + q'x$. Generalized convexity of quadratic functions has been extensively studied before; see Schaible (1981), Avriel et al. (1988). In Karamardian et al. (1993) we characterize generalized monotone affine maps where M is no longer assumed to be symmetric.

Finally, in Pini et al. (1993) we have studied generalized monotone maps under variable transformations. The results enable us to generate generalized monotone matrices of any size. Various necessary conditions and sufficient conditions are derived for generalized monotone maps and matrices. Furthermore, admissible translations of generalized monotone homogeneous linear maps are studied. Also, the maximal domain of generalized monotone affine maps is characterized, extending earlier results in Schaible (1981) to nonsymmetric matrices.

For other very recent developments on generalized monotonicity see Komlosi et al. (1993).

REFERENCES

Arrow K J, Enthoven A C (1961) Quasi-concave programming. Econometrica 29: 779-800
Avriel M, Diewert W E, Schaible S, Zang I (1988) Generalized concavity. Plenum Publishing Corporation. New York
Hadjisavvas N. Schaible S (1993) On strong pseudomonotonicity and (semi) strict quasimonotonicity. Journal of Optimization Theory and Applications 79, No 1. To appear
Karamardian S, Schaible S (1990) Seven kinds of monotone maps. Journal of Optimization Theory and Applications 66: 37-46
Karamardian S, Schaible S, Crouzeix J-P (1993) Characterizations of generalized monotone maps. Journal of Optimization Theory and Applications 76: 399-413
Komlosi S, Rapcsak T, Schaible S (eds.) (1993) Generalized convexity, Proceedings of the Fourth International Workshop in Pecs, Hungary, August 31-September 2, 1992. Springer-Verlag. Berlin Heidelberg New York
Pini R, Schaible S (1992) Invariance properties of generalized monotonicity. Working-Paper 93-04, Graduate School of Management, University of California, Riverside, October 1992. To appear in Optimization
Schaible S (1981) Quasiconvex, pseudoconvex and strictly pseudoconvex quadratic functions. Journal of Optimization Theory and Applications 35: 303-338

Equivalence of Cutting Stock Problems

Guntram Scheithauer
Department of Mathematics
Technical University Dresden
01062 Dresden, Mommsenstr. 13 - Germany

The cutting stock problem

In this paper the following one-dimensional cutting stock problem is considered:

> Let be given one-dimensional stock material which is sufficiently available. From the large lengths desired pieces of given (smaller) lengths are to cut in such a way that order quantities will be fulfilled and the number of stock lengths needed is a minimum.

This cutting stock problem can be viewed as a fundamental problem within the field of cutting and packing optimization since several generalizations are possible.

The following structure investigations and equivalence considerations are a bases for theoretical investigations of cutting stock problems, e.g. with respect to the modified integer round-up property (MIRUP) and the problem of determining the maximum difference over all cutting stock problems between the optimal value of the (integer) cutting stock problem and the optimal value of the corresponding LP relaxation problem (MAXGAP).

An instance of the one-dimensional cutting stock problem is characterized by the following Input-data: m number of pieces, $l = (l_1, \ldots, l_m)^T$ vector of piece lengths, $b = (b_1, \ldots, b_m)^T$ vector of order demands, L length of the stock material.

Without loss of generality it is assumed in the following that (A1) all data are integer, (A2) $l_1 > l_2 > \ldots > l_m \geq 1$, (A3) $L \geq l_1$ and (A4) $b_i \geq 1$, $i = 1, \ldots, m$.

The set

$$\Omega_m := \{(m, l, b, L) \ : \ \text{(A1) - (A4) are fulfilled}\}$$

is called **one-dimensional cutting stock problem with m pieces** ($m \in N_+$). Hence, the (general) **one-dimensional cutting stock problem** is the set

$$\Omega := \bigcup_{m=1}^{\infty} \Omega_m.$$

An element $(m, l, b, L) \in \Omega$ determined by its Input data is called **instance** of the one-dimensional cutting stock problem.

Modeling

Let $m \in N_+$, fixed. In the following the modeling of the cutting stock problem with m pieces is considered. Let $P = (m, l, b, L)$ be a given instance.

A vector $a = (a_1, \ldots, a_m)^T \in Z_+^m$ is called **cutting pattern**. A cutting pattern a is said to be **feasible with respect to** P if $l^T a \leq L$ holds.

A cutting pattern a is an **elementary** cutting pattern if a is a positive multiple of a unit vector.

A cutting pattern a is called **maximal with respect to** P if a is feasible but $a + e^m$ is not feasible with respect to P. Hence, in the one-dimensional case we have

$$a \text{ maximal with respect to } P \quad \Leftrightarrow \quad L - l_m < l^T a \leq L. \tag{1}$$

Let (M1) and (M2) denote the linear integer optimization models for the one-dimensional cutting stock problem which contain all feasible resp. all maximal cutting patterns.

Definition 1 *Two models (M) and (M') are* **model-equivalent** *(m-equivalent) if for any solution of (M) there exists a solution of (M') having the same objective function value and reversely.*

Statement 1 *(M1) and (M2) are m-equivalent.*

For that reason it is sufficient to consider only the maximal cutting patterns.

A maximal cutting pattern a of the instance $P = (m, l, b, L)$ is called **extremal with respect to** P if a is a corner point of the convex closure of $a^0 = 0$ and all maximal cutting patterns of P.

Statement 2 *Let $a \in Z_+^m$ be an extremal cutting pattern of P. Then always one of the three statements is true:*
a) $a = 0$, or
b) a is maximal and elementary, or
c)

$$\kappa^T a = \sum_{i=1}^{m} \frac{a_i}{k_i} > 1.$$

where $k_i := \lfloor \frac{L}{l_i} \rfloor$ and $\kappa = (\kappa_1, \ldots, \kappa_m)^T := (\frac{1}{k_1}, \ldots, \frac{1}{k_m})^T$.

Let (M3) denote the model of the LP relaxation of the one-dimensional cutting stock problem which contains all extremal cutting patterns.

Statement 3 *Let (M1') and (M2') denote the LP relaxation models to (M1) resp. (M2). Then (M3) is m-equivalent to (M1') and (M2').*

For the cutting stock problem $P = \Omega_m(l, L)$ (resp. for the instance $P = (m, l, b, L)$) let $A = A(P) = (a_{ij})_{m,n}$ with $a_{ij} = a_i^j$, $i = 1, \ldots, m$, $j = 1, \ldots, n$, denote the **pattern matrix** to P which contains all maximal cutting patterns.

Equivalence of instances and cutting stock problems

In the following, equivalence relations are investigated for instances and subproblems of Ω_m with fixed m.

Solution equivalence

Let be given two instances $P = (m, l, b, L)$ and $\bar{P} = (m, \bar{l}, \bar{b}, \bar{L})$ and let $a^1, \ldots, a^n$, resp. $\bar{a}^1, \ldots, \bar{a}^n$ denote their maximal cutting patterns. Furthermore, let $a^j = \bar{a}^j$ for $j = 1, \ldots, n$. The set $X(P) := \{x \in Z_+^n \, : \, e^T x = z^*(P)\}$ denotes the set of all optimal solutions of P where $z^*(P)$ is the optimal objective function value of P.

Definition 2 *The instances P and $\bar{P}$ are said to be* **solution-equivalent** *(s-equivalent) if $X(P) = X(\bar{P})$ holds.*

Statement 4 *Let $P = (m, l, b, L)$ be given. If $b_m \geq z^*(P)$ and $L - \sum_{i=1}^{m-1} l_i a_{ij} \leq l_m$ for $j = 1, \ldots, n$, then $\bar{P} = (m, l, b_1, \ldots, b_{m-1}, b_m - z^*(P), L - l_m)$ is s-equivalent to P.*

Statement 5 *Let $P = (m, l, b, L)$ with $b_m \geq 2$ and $P_1 = (m, l, b1, \ldots, b_{m-1}, 1, L)$ be given. If $z^*(P) = z^*(P_1)$ then P is s-equivalent to $\bar{P} = (m, l, b_1, \ldots, b_{m-1}, \bar{b}_m, L)$ for $\bar{b}_m \leq b_m$.*

Remarks: - Solution equivalence occurs if not all order constraints are active. More precisely, P has s-equivalent instances $\bar{P}$ with smaller stock length L when an index $i \in I$ exists such that the i-th order constraint does not be active for any optimal solution of P.
- A suitable representative of the class of s-equivalent instances could be an instance with either a "maximal" b or a "minimal" L.

Pattern equivalence

Let the subproblems $P = \Omega_m(l, L)$ and $\bar{P} = \Omega_m(\bar{l}, \bar{L})$ be given and let $a^1, \ldots, a^n$ resp. $\bar{a}^1, \ldots, \bar{a}^{\bar{n}}$ denote their maximal cutting patterns. Without loss of generality the cutting patterns can be assumed to be lexicographically decreasing.

Definition 3 *P and $\bar{P}$ are called* **pattern-equivalent** *(p-equivalent) if $n = \bar{n}$ and $a^j = \bar{a}^j$ for $j = 1, \ldots, n$.*

Statement 6 *P and $\bar{P}$ are p-equivalent if and only if the extremal cutting patterns $a^1, \ldots, a^{\bar{n}}$ and $\bar{a}^1, \ldots, \bar{a}^{\bar{n}}$ are identical.*

Structure equivalence

Let be given two subproblems $P = \Omega_m(l, L)$ and $\bar{P} = \Omega_m(\bar{l}, \bar{L})$.

Definition 4 *P and $\bar{P}$ are called* **structure-equivalent** *(st-equivalent) if for all $b \in Z_+^m$ holds: $X(l, b, L) = X(\bar{l}, b, \bar{L})$.*

Statement 7 *P, $\bar{P}$ p-equivalent $\Longleftrightarrow$ P, $\bar{P}$ st-equivalent.*

Characterization of equivalence classes

Statement 8 *$P = \Omega_m(l, L)$ is p-equivalent to $\bar{P} = \Omega_m(\bar{l}, \bar{L})$ if and only if $(l, L) \in Z^{m+1}$ is feasible for*

$$l^T \bar{a}^j \leq L, \quad j = 1, \ldots, n, \tag{2}$$

$$l^T(\bar{a}^j + e^m) \geq L + 1, \quad j = 1, \ldots, n, \tag{3}$$

$$l_i \geq l_{i+1} + 1, \quad i = 1, \ldots, m-1, \quad l_m \geq 1, \tag{4}$$

where $\bar{a}^j$, $j = 1, \ldots, n$, denote the maximal cutting patterns of $\bar{P}$.

It can be shown that for any class of p-equivalent cutting stock problems in Ω_m with $e^T a^j \leq m - 2 \; \forall j$ there exists at least one instance with $L \leq m^{m+1}$.

Dominance

Definition 5 *The cutting pattern a* **dominates** *the cutting pattern* $\bar{a}$ *if* $l^T a \geq l^T \bar{a}$ *for all* $l \in Z_+^m$ *fulfilling (A2). (for abbreviation:* $a >_d \bar{a}$*).*

Statement 9 *Let* a, $\bar{a}$ *be given cutting patterns. Furthermore, let* $s_i(a) := \sum_{j=1}^{i} a_j$, $i = 1, \ldots, m$. *Then it holds:*

$$a >_d \bar{a} \quad \Longleftrightarrow \quad s_i(a) \geq s_i(\bar{a}), \quad i = 1, \ldots, m.$$

Let $\tilde{a}^1, \ldots, \tilde{a}^{\tilde{n}}$ denote the cutting patterns in a given pattern matrix A which are not dominated. Then:

Statement 10 $(l, L) \in Z_+^{m+1}$ *fulfilles (2) if and only if* (l, L) *is feasible for*

$$l^T \tilde{a}^j \leq L \quad \text{for } j = 1, \ldots, \tilde{n}.$$

Furthermore, let $\hat{a}^1, \ldots, \hat{a}^{\hat{n}}$ be the (maximal) cutting patterns in A which dominate no other cutting pattern. Then it holds:

Statement 11 $(l, L) \in Z_+^{m+1}$ *fulfilles (3) if and only if* (l, L) *is feasible for*

$$l^T(\hat{a}^j + e^m) \geq L + 1 \quad \text{for } j = 1, \ldots, \hat{n}.$$

References

[1] S.Baum and L.E.Trotter, Jr., Integer rounding for polymatroid and branching optimization problems, SIAM J. Alg. Disc. Meth. 2 (1981) 4, 416-425.

[2] H.Dyckhoff, and U.Finke, Cutting and packing in production and distribution, Physica Verlag, Heidelberg, 1992.

[3] R. E. Johnston, Rounding algorithms for cutting stock problems, Asia-Pacific J. of OR 3 (1986) 166-171.

[4] O.Marcotte, The cutting stock problem and integer rounding, Mathematical Programming 33 (1985) 82-92.

[5] G.Scheithauer and J.Terno, About the gap between the optimal values of the integer and continuous relaxation one-dimensional cutting stock problem, Operations Research Proceedings 1991, Springer-Verlag, Berlin, Heidelberg, 1992.

[6] G.Scheithauer and J. Terno, Investigations on the MIRUP (modified integer round-up property) for the one-dimensional cutting stock problem, Working Paper, TU Dresden, 1993.

[7] J.Terno, R.Lindemann und G.Scheithauer, Zuschnittprobleme und ihre praktische Lösung, Verlag Harry Deutsch, Thun und Frankfurt/Main, und Fachbuchverlag Leipzig 1987.

Numerical Experiments to the Modified Integer Round-Up Property of the One-dimensional Cutting Stock Problem

Guntram Scheithauer and Johannes Terno
Department of Mathematics
Technical University Dresden
01062 Dresden, Mommsenstr. 13 - Germany

Introduction

A linear integer optimization problem (IP) has the modified integer round-up property (MIRUP) if the optimal value of any instance of IP is not greater than the optimal value of the corresponding LP relaxation problem rounded up plus one.

The aim of this paper is to investigate numerically whether the one-dimensional cutting stock problem has MIRUP.

The computational experiments with a lot of randomly generated instances of the one-dimensional cutting stock problem show that for all instances an integer solution was found which fulfills the MIRUP. Moreover, in the most cases the optimal value equals the optimal value of the corresponding LP relaxation rounded up.

In this paper, the following cutting stock problem is investigated:

> One-dimensional material objects (e.g. paper reels, iron slabs, wooden lengths) of a given length L are divided into smaller pieces of desired lengths $l_1, \ldots, l_m$ in order to fulfill the order demands $b_1, \ldots, b_m$. The goal is to minimize the total amount of stock material or, equivalently, to minimize the total waste.

In the following standard model the integer m-vector $a^j = (a_{1j}, \ldots, a_{mj})^T$ with $\sum_{i=1}^m l_i a_{ij} \leq L$ represents a cutting pattern and the integer variable x_j gives the number of times how often the cutting pattern a^j is cut.

$$z = \sum_{j=1}^{n} x_j \rightarrow \min$$

$$\text{s.t.} \quad \sum_{j=1}^{n} a_{ij} x_j \geq b_i, \quad i = 1, \ldots, m, \tag{1}$$

$$x_j \geq 0, \text{ integer}, \ j = 1, \ldots, n,$$

where n denotes the number of cutting patterns.

The model (1) is a special case of the model of the general linear integer optimization problem:

$$\begin{aligned} z = c^T x &\rightarrow \min \\ \text{s.t.} \quad Ax &\geq b, \\ x \geq 0&, \text{ integer.} \end{aligned} \tag{2}$$

Here, an instance $E = (m, n, A, c, b)$ is given by the following Input-data: the number of variables n, the number of restrictions m (without non-negativity conditions), the matrix A of coefficients, the objective function c and the right hand side b. Without loss of generality, all Input-data are assumed to be integer, and to ensure solvability, we assume $\max_{i=1,\ldots,m} l_i \leq L$.

Let $z^*(E)$ denote the optimal value of the integer problem and $z_c(E)$ the optimal value of the corresponding LP relaxation. Then we give the following definition:

Definition 1 *A linear integer optimization problem P has the* **modified integer round-up property (MIRUP)** *if*

$$z^*(E) \leq \lceil z_c(E) \rceil + 1 \quad \textit{for all instances } E \in P.$$

Computational results

Let $E = (m, n, A, c, b)$ be an instance of the one-dimensional cutting stock problem and let x^c denote an optimal solution of the corresponding LP relaxation. Rounding down of x^c yields an integer vector $\underline{x}$ with $\underline{x}_j = \lfloor x_j^c \rfloor$, $j = 1, \ldots, n$. If $\underline{x} \neq x^c$ then a residual problem can be defined with right hand side $\bar{b} := b - A\underline{x}$.

If the residual problem has the MIRUP then the initial problem has this property too. Hence, only the residual problems have to be investigated with respect to MIRUP. Based on the concept of residual problems and other theoretical results (see e.g. [10], [11]) a solution concept is developed.

For the numerical investigation of the one-dimensional cutting stock problem with respect to MIRUP we solved series of randomly generated instances. Thereby the Input-data are choosen from a uniform distribution on some ranges given below. For a given material length L and a choosen $m \in [\underline{m}, \overline{m}]$ the piece lengths l_i are in $[\lceil L/(m-2) \rceil, L/2]$ and the order quantities b_i are in $[2\underline{m}, 10\overline{m}]$. For each range $[\underline{m}, \overline{m}]$ 20 instances were generated.

The following table summarizes the results of one series with $L = 3000$.

m		termination			value		$\bar{E}$		aver.
$\underline{m}$	$\overline{m}$	op	it	ep	ex	MI	lb	h1	time
11	20	20	0	0	20	0	1	19	.3
21	30	20	0	0	17	3	0	20	2.3
31	40	19	0	1	12	8	0	20	8.4
41	50	11	0	9	15	5	0	20	21.7
51	60	10	0	10	17	3	0	20	41.6
61	70	11	0	9	14	6	0	20	75.9
71	80	11	0	9	18	2	4	16	116.7
81	90	14	1	5	16	4	2	18	168.0
91	100	12	0	8	18	2	1	19	250.5
101	110	16	4	0	11	9	0	20	336.8

The LP relaxation problems are solved using column generation technique. This process is terminated if the optimality condition is fulfilled (column **op**) or a solution with value $z(E)$ is found where $\lceil z(E) \rceil = \lceil z_c(E) \rceil$ (columns **it** and **ep**). **ex** gives the number of instances which are exactly solved since the integer round-up property (IRUP), i.e $z^*(E) = \lceil z_c(E) \rceil$, is fulfilled and, hence, MIRUP holds. **MI** gives the number of instances where a solution with MIRUP is found but optimality is not proved. The average times are in seconds on a PC 486 DX/ 50 MHz.

References

[1] S.Baum and L.E.Trotter, Jr., Integer rounding for polymatroid and branching optimization problems, SIAM J. Alg. Disc. Meth. 2 (1981) 4, 416-425.

[2] A.Diegel, Integer LP solution for large trim problem, Working Paper 1988 University of Natal, South Africa.

[3] H.Dyckhoff, and U.Finke, Cutting and packing in production and distribution, Physica Verlag, Heidelberg, 1992.

[4] M.Fieldhouse, The duality gap in trim problems, SICUP-Bulletin No. 5, 1990.

[5] P.C.Gilmore and R.E.Gomory, A linear programming approach to the cutting stock problem, Operations Res. 9 (1961) 849-859.

[6] R. E. Johnston, Rounding algorithms for cutting stock problems, Asia-Pacific J. of OR 3 (1986) 166-171.

[7] O.Marcotte, The cutting stock problem and integer rounding, Mathematical Programming 33 (1985) 82-92.

[8] O.Marcotte, An instance of the cutting stock problem for which the rounding property does not hold, Oper. Res. Lett. 4 (1986) 5, 239-243.

[9] G.Scheithauer and J.Terno, About the gap between the optimal values of the integer and continuous relaxation one-dimensional cutting stock problem, Operations Research Proceedings 1991, Springer-Verlag, Berlin, Heidelberg, 1992.

[10] G.Scheithauer and J. Terno, Investigations on the MIRUP (modified integer round-up property) for the one-dimensional cutting stock problem, Working Paper, TU Dresden, 1993.

[11] J.Terno, R.Lindemann und G.Scheithauer, Zuschnittprobleme und ihre praktische Lösung, Verlag Harry Deutsch, Thun und Frankfurt/Main, und Fachbuchverlag Leipzig 1987.

Optimality for a generalized Stackelberg problem

Heidrun Schmidt
Technical University Chemnitz-Zwickau
Department of Mathematics
PSF964
09009 Chemnitz
Germany

Nowadays the demand for the solution of bilevel programming problems is growing to a large extent for instance in economics by means of the principal-agency theory. In this field of application the inclusion of certain restrictions for the principal and considerations under non-uniqueness of the follower's reactions are necessary. Therefore a generalized Stackelberg problem of the following type will be considered:

$$\begin{aligned} F(x,y) &\to \text{“}\min_y\text{”} \\ G(x,y) &\leq 0 \\ \text{and } x &\text{ solves} \\ f(x,y) &\to \min_x \\ g(x,y) &\leq 0, \end{aligned}$$

where F, G, f, g : $\mathbb{R}^{n+m} \to \mathbb{R}$ are convex. Let G be divided in the largest possible part G_1 depending only on y and a part G_2 depending on x and y.

In according to the possible behaviour of the leader which is described in detail for the principal-agency theory in [5] the optimistic (i.e. [3]) and the pessimistic case ([4]) are only the extreme points. Therefore the following definition seems to be much better suitable for practical problems:

Definition 1 *The optimal solution of the above bilevel programming problem is defined by*

$$\Psi^o = \{(y,x) : \varphi^o_{\min} \leq F(x,y) \leq \varphi^o_{\inf\max},\ y \in \Gamma := \{y : G_1(y) \leq 0\}, x \in \Psi \cap \Gamma_x(y)\}$$

where

$$\begin{aligned} \Gamma_x(y) &:= \{x : G_2(x,y) \leq 0\}, \\ \Psi(y) &:= \operatorname{Arg}\min_x\{f(x,y) : g(x,y) \leq 0\}, \\ \varphi^o_{\min} &:= \min_y \min_{(\Psi\cap\Gamma_x)(y)} F(x,y) \text{ is the optimal value function in the optimistic case and} \\ \varphi^o_{\inf\max} &:= \min_y \inf_{y^n \to \bar{y},\, y^n \neq \bar{y}} \max_{(\Psi\cap\Gamma_x)(y^n)} F(x,y^n) \text{ in the pessimistic case.} \end{aligned}$$

Here the place of the upper level constraints $G(x,y)$ depends on the practical background, but let be added that the other possibility (the inclusion in the outer minimization over y) causes more mathematical problems (e.g. the nonuniqueness of $\operatorname{Argmin}_{\Psi} F(x,y)$ and $\operatorname{Argmax}_{\Psi} F(x,y)$, resp., is difficult to handle).

Furthermore, the optimal value function in the pessimistic case

$$\varphi^o_{\max} = \min_y \max_{(\Psi\cap\Gamma_x)(y)} F(x,y)$$

was replaced by $\varphi^o_{\inf\max}$ since $\varphi^o_{\max}$ does not exist in general because of the lack of the lower semicontinuity of $\varphi_{\max} = \max_{\Psi\cap\Gamma_x} F(x,y)$. The function

$$\varphi_{\inf\max}(\overline{y}) := \inf_{y^n\to\overline{y},\, y^n\neq\overline{y}} \max_{(\Psi\cap\Gamma_x)(y^n)} F(x,y^n)$$

is lower semicontinous in $\overline{y}$ and equals $\varphi_{\max}$ if $\varphi_{\max}$ is lower semicontinuous.

Theorem 1 *If $\{(x,y) : y \in \Gamma, x \in (\Psi\cap\Gamma_x)(y)\}$ is not empty and compact and a regularity condition for the problem of the lower level is satisfied, then the optimal solution set Ψ^o is nonempty.*

Proof:
The function $\varphi^o_{\min}$ exists as a result of [2] (Theorem 1) and the upper semicontinuity of $\Psi \cap \Gamma_x$ ([1], Theorem 4.2.2. (a) and Theorem 3.1.2.(2)). It yields $\varphi_{\inf\max} < \infty$ because of [4] (Proposition 2.3.1.). □

But the term $\varphi^o_{\inf\max}$ is not practical for the computation. Therefore, upper and lower bounds are necessary.

Last but not least let the optimality concept be explained by means of these very simple but nevertheless convincing examples.

Example 1:

$$(x-1)^2 + y^2 \to \text{“}\min_y\text{”}$$
$$x - y \leq 0$$
and x solves
$$y \to \min_x$$
$$0 \leq x \leq 2$$

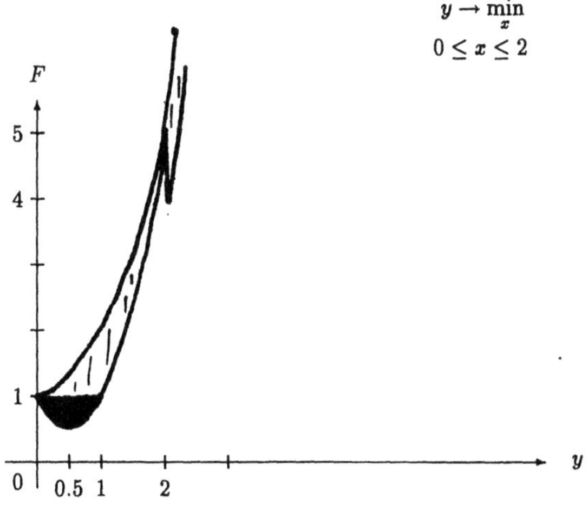

Its solution corresponds to the marked domain and the black area represents the values of the point-to-set mapping $F(x,y)$ $(x \in \Psi(y))$. We have

$$\begin{aligned} \varphi^o_{\min} &= 0.5 \\ \varphi^o_{\max} &= 1 \end{aligned}$$

and the nonuniqueness of $\operatorname{Argmin}_{\Psi} F(x,y) = \{0,2\}$ can be seen.

Example 2:

$$\begin{aligned} x + y^2 &\rightarrow \text{“}\min_y\text{”} \\ &\text{and } x \text{ solves} \\ &\quad yx \rightarrow \min_x \\ &\quad 1 \le x \le 2 \end{aligned}$$

Easily we can calculate that

$$\varphi_{\max}(y) = \begin{cases} y^2 + 2 & \text{if} \quad y \le 0 \\ y^2 + 1 & \text{if} \quad y > 0 \end{cases}$$

Therefore the optimum in the sense of Morgan [4] does not exist. But the optimal solution set Ψ^o is not empty.

References

[1] B. Bank, D. Klatte, B. Kummer, and K. Tammer. *Non-Linear Parametric Optimization.* Akademie-Verlag, Berlin, 1982.

[2] P.T. Harker and J.-S. Pang. Existence of optimal solutions to mathematical programs with equilibrium constraints. *Oper. Res. Lett.*, 7(2):61–64, 1988.

[3] Y. Ishizuka and E. Aiyoshi. Double penalty method for bilevel optimization problems. *Annals of Operations Research*, 34:73–88, 1992.

[4] M.B. Lignola and J. Morgan. Existence and approximation results for min sup problems. Report 36-90, Universita' degli studi Napoli, 1990.

[5] W. Zimmermann. *Operations Research.* R. Oldenbourg Verlag, München Wien, 1992.

Non-simple Polymatroids and Corresponding Submodular Functions

Gabriele Schneidereit
Fakultät für Mathematik, Technische Universität
PSF 4120, 39016 Magdeburg, Germany
Alexander Zaporoshetc
Department of Applied Mathematics and Informatics
Belarus State University
Minsk 220050, Belarus

In discrete optimization polymatroids are an interesting class of feasible solution sets [3, 4]. A polymatroid is given by

$$P(r) = \{x \in \mathbb{R}^n_+ : x(I) := \sum_{i \in I} x_i \leq r(I),\ I \subseteq N := \{1, 2, \ldots, n\}\},$$

where $r(I)$ is a rank function ($r : 2^N \rightarrow \mathbb{R}_+$), which is
1. submodular : $r(I_1) + r(I_2) \geq r(I_1 \cup I_2) + r(I_1 \cap I_2)$ for all $I_1, I_2 \subseteq N$,
2. isotone : $r(I) \leq r(I')$ for all $I, I' \subseteq N$ with $I \subset I'$,
3. normalized : $r(\emptyset) = 0$.

Due to the non-simplicity of a polymatroid, the verification of feasibility of the actual solution of a greedy algorithm is not efficient. For that reason, it is important to find conditions for the non-simplicity of polymatroids. We consider two approaches: the investigation of the facet-poset of a polymatroid and the investigation of a certain poset, which is generated by a vertex.

1 First approach

One approach to find conditions for non-simplicity is the investigation of the facet-poset of a polymatroid. Therefore, we need the vertex construction algorithm (VCA) of Edmonds [2]. Let $p = (p_1, p_2, \ldots, p_n)$ be a permutation of the natural numbers $1, 2, \ldots, n$ and s an integer, $0 \leq s \leq n$. Then $x(p, s)$ is a vertex of $P(r)$, where

$$x_{p_i} = \begin{cases} r(\{p_1, \ldots, p_i\}) - r(\{p_1, \ldots, p_{i-1}\}) & \text{for } 1 \leq i \leq s \\ 0 & \text{for } s < i \leq n. \end{cases}$$

An n-dimensional polymatroid $P(r)$ is called non-simple, if it includes a vertex, which is on more than n facets. We define a set I is r-closed, if for all I' with $I \subset I' \subseteq N$ the function $r(I)$ is strictly isotone. A set I is r-inseparable, if each partition of I into two sets ($I_1 \cup I_2 = I$, $I_1 \cap I_2 = \emptyset$) satisfies $r(I_1) + r(I_2) > r(I)$, that means, $r(I)$ is strictly submodular. The set of non-empty r-closed and r-inseparable sets we denote by $R(r)$.

A minimal representation for polymatroids was given by Edmonds [2]. Let the empty set be r-closed, which guarantees the n-dimensionality of the polymatroid. The minimal representation of any n-dimensional polymatroid $P(r)$ is given by the facets

$$F_i = \{x \in P(r) : x_i = 0\}, \qquad i = 1, 2, \ldots, n,$$
$$F_I = \{x \in P(r) : x(I) = r(I)\}, \qquad I \in R(r).$$

The set $R(r)$ is called facet-poset.

A family $\{I_1, I_2, I_1 \cup I_2, I_1 \cap I_2\}$ of four non-empty subsets of N is called r-diamond, if it satisfies $r(I_1) + r(I_2) = r(I_1 \cup I_2) + r(I_1 \cap I_2)$. An r-star is a family $\{I_1, I_2, \ldots, I_m; B\}$ $(2 \leq m < |B|)$ of non-empty subsets of N, where the sets I_j $(j = 1, 2, \ldots, m)$ are pairwise disjoint, $\bigcup_{j=1}^{m} I_j \subset B$ and $r(B) = r(\bigcup_{j=1}^{m} I_j) = \sum_{j=1}^{m} r(I_j)$.

When constructing a vertex x by using Edmond's VCA, exactly n facets including x occur. To obtain non-simplicity, an additional facet containing x is necessary. Therefore, an equation is needed, that includes exactly one set I which did not appear during VCA. Only now, this equation can lead to non-simplicity. From the three general properties of the function $r(I)$ two such equations follow: r-diamonds and r-stars.

Theorem 1 *Let $P(r)$ be an n-dimensional polymatroid. It is non-simple, if the facet-poset $R(r)$ contains an r-diamond $\{I_1, I_2, I_1 \cup I_2, I_1 \cap I_2\}$ or an r-star $\{I_1, I_2, \ldots, I_m; B\}$ $(m \geq 2)$.*

The idea of the proof is, to construct a special vertex x of $P(r)$ according to VCA and to determine $n + 1$ facets containing x by using the properties of r-diamonds or r-stars.

These conditions are the base for some other, more generalized, sufficient conditions for the non-simplicity of polymatroids.

Theorem 2 *Let $P(r)$ be an n-dimensional polymatroid. It is non-simple, if there is an r-diamond $\{I_1, I_2, I_1 \cup I_2, I_1 \cap I_2\}$ with I_1, $I_2 \in R(r)$ or if there is an r-star $\{I_1, I_2, \ldots, I_m; B\}$ $(m \geq 2)$, such that B is r-inseparable.*

The proof of this theorem consists of two parts: one part considers the case of the existance of an r-diamond and the other part investigates the case of the existance of an r-star. In the first case, the idea of the proof is the same as used for proving theorem 1. The second part shows, that from the existance of an r-star with the property mentioned in theorem 2 follows the existance of an r-star in the facet-poset $R(r)$, which is one of the conditions of theorem 1.

2 Second approach

Another approach to get conditions for non-simplicity is based on the theory of convex polytopes and graphs. For any vertex we can construct a poset by using the $O(n^2)$ algorithm of Bixby, Cunningham and Topkis [1], such that all linear extensions compatible with the partial order of this poset present all orderings, generating the given extreme point by VCA. This poset is defined as follows.

Let x be a vertex of an n-dimensional polymatroid $P(r)$ and let $\mathcal{L}$ be the family of all sets I with $x(I) = r(I)$. A partial order $\preceq$ on $cl(x) := \bigcup_{I \in \mathcal{L}} I$ is defined by:

$$i \preceq j \Leftrightarrow i \in \cap\{I \in \mathcal{L} : j \in I\}.$$

By $D_x = (V, E_x)$ let us denote the digraph of the poset $(cl(x), \preceq)$, where $V = cl(x)$, $E_x = \{(i,j) \,|\, i,j \in V, j \preceq i, \nexists k : j \preceq k \preceq i)\}$. The digraph $D_x = (V, E_x)$ contains a merging (i,j,k), if there exist two edges (i,j), $(k,j) \in E_x$ with $k \neq i$, $x_i > 0$ and $x_k > 0$. D_x contains a branching (i,j,k), if there exist two edges (j,i), $(j,k) \in E_x$, $i \neq k$, such that $x_j = 0$.

From the theory of convex polytopes it is also known, that an n-dimensional polymatroid is non-simple, if and only if there exists a vertex x, which has more than n adjacent vertices. By using this fact Girlich and Kovalev could find a sufficient and necessary condition for non-simplicity [5].

Theorem 3 *An n-dimensional polymatroid $P(r)$ is non-simple, if and only if there exists a vertex $x \in P(r)$, such that D_x contains a branching or a merging.*

By help of the theorems above we could show, that the conditions of theorem 2 are equivalent to the conditions of theorem 3.

Theorem 4 *Let $P(r)$ be an n-dimensional polymatroid. Then there exists a vertex x such that the digraph D_x contains a branching or a merging, if and only if there is an r-diamond $\{I_1, I_2, I_1 \cup I_2, I_1 \cap I_2\}$ with I_1, $I_2 \in R(r)$ or there is an r-star $\{I_1, I_2, \ldots, I_m; B\}$ $(m \geq 2)$, such that B is r-inseparable.*

References

[1] Bixby R.E., Cunningham W.H., Topkis D.M. (1985) The Partial Order of a Polymatroid Extreme Point. Mathematics of Operations Research 10:367-378

[2] Edmonds J. (1970) Submodular Functions, Matroids and Certain Polyhedra. Proceeding of the Calgary International Conference on Combinatorial Structures and Their Applications. Gordon and Breach, New York, pp.69-87

[3] Emelicev V.A., Kovalev M.M., Kravzov M.K. (1984) Polytopes, Graphs and Optimization. Cambridge University Press

[4] Fujishige S. (1991) Submodular Functions and Optimization. Annals of Discrete Mathematics 47, North-Holland

[5] Girlich E., Kovalev M.M. (1993) Classification of Polyhedral Matroids. To appear in ZOR

Evaluation Techniques for Disjunctive Logic Programs

Dietmar Seipel, Hans Argenton
University of Tübingen
Sand 13, D - 72076 Tübingen, Germany

Abstract

Non-Horn programs containing disjunctive rules allow for more advanced applications of deductive databases. But the inference process dealing with rapidly increasing amounts of disjunctive facts becomes much more intricate, because of the problem of finding resolvable atoms in the facts.

We present an efficient implementation of the disjunctive consequence operator T_P^S based on a compact data structure for disjunctive facts that speeds up the combinatorial search in a T_P^S-hyperresolution step.

1 Introduction

Deductive databases use logic programming as a powerful, declarative language for specifying queries to relational databases. A disjunctive logic program P is given by a set of rules of the form

$$p_1(X_1) \vee \ldots \vee p_m(X_m) :- q_1(Y_1) \wedge \ldots \wedge q_n(Y_n) \wedge \neg r_1(Z_1) \wedge \ldots \wedge \neg r_k(Z_k).$$

where $p_i(X_i)$, $q_i(Y_i)$ and $r_i(Z_i)$ are (positive) atoms with argument vectors X_i, Y_i and Z_i, respectively. There has been a lot of research on processing definite horn clauses (i.e. $m = 1$, $k = 0$), cf. [BaRa 86], [Ul 88/89], [CeGoTa 90], where the desired result is the minimal Herbrand model $\mathcal{M}_P$, cf. [Llo 87]. The possibly recursive program is evaluated iteratively in a set-oriented fashion based on the primitive operations of relational algebra, which can be executed efficiently on databases.

General disjunctive logic programs containing indefinite rules (i.e. $m > 1$) allow for more advanced applications. Rules without negated body literals (i.e. $k = 0$) specify the set of logically implied disjunctive facts (i.e. positive ground clauses), the so-called minimal model state $\mathcal{MS}_P$, cf. [LoMiRa 92]. Efficient techniques for computing $\mathcal{MS}_P$ iteratively as the least fixpoint of the consequence operator T_P^S are currently investigated. Indefinite rules with negation (i.e. $m > 1$, $k > 0$) can be evaluated by repeated computation of minimal model states w.r.t. certain disjunctive transformations of P, cf. well-founded semantics [VaGeRoSchli 91], generalized well-founded semantics [LoMiRa 92] and stationary semantics [Prz 90].

We will review some of the notations and theoretical foundations for disjunctive logic programming of [LoMiRa 92]. Following we will describe a bottom-up procedure that iteratively derives the disjunctive facts of $\mathcal{MS}_P$ and organizes them in a tree structure that is used for a fast hyperresolution of further disjunctive facts by T_P^S. For simplicity, we will use an example with definite rules and disjunctive facts. The presented ideas however are applicable to disjunctive rules as well.

2 Foundations of Disjunctive Logic Programs

Syntactically, a **deductive database** $DDB = (DB, P)$ is given by a set DB of facts, which resemble a relational database, and a logic program P, which consists of a set of rules for deriving new facts from DB.

(i) Given some atoms $p_i(X_i)$, where $1 \leq i \leq m$, $m \in \mathbb{N}_+$, and some literals $L_j(U_j)$, where $1 \leq j \leq n$, $n \in \mathbb{N}_0$. A disjunctive **fact** is given by

$$p_1(X_1) \vee \ldots \vee p_m(X_m).$$

A disjunctive normal **rule** r is given by

$$r: \underbrace{p_1(X_1) \vee \ldots \vee p_m(X_m)}_{\text{head}} \; :- \; \underbrace{L_1(U_1) \wedge \ldots \wedge L_n(U_n)}_{\text{body}}.$$

where the atoms $p_1(X_1), \ldots, p_m(X_m)$ form its head and the literals $L_1(U_1), \ldots, L_n(U_n)$ form its body. r is disjunctive, iff all its body literals L_i are positive. r is normal, iff $m = 1$. The head atoms are called **dependent** on the body literals. A disjunctive logic program is called **recursive**, iff there is a rule such that a body literal transitively depends on a head atom.

The **semantics** of a deductive database $DDB = (DB, P)$ is defined according to the bottom–up or naive evaluation algorithms, cf. [LoMiRa 92], as the least fixpoint of a closure operator T_P^S.

(ii) The **disjunctive Herbrand base** DHB_P of a disjunctive logic program P is given by the set of positive ground clauses

$$\text{DHB}_P = \{ A_1 \vee \ldots \vee A_k \mid k \geq 1, \; A_i \in HB_P, \; 1 \leq i \leq k \}.$$

A **Herbrand state** S of P is a subset $S \subseteq \text{DHB}_P$. The canonical form and the expansion of S are given by

$$can(S) = \{ C \in S \mid \text{there is no proper subclause } C' \text{ of } C \text{ in } S \}.$$
$$exp(S) = \{ C \in \text{DHB}_P \mid \text{there is a subclause } C' \text{ of } C \text{ in } S \}.$$

respectively, i.e. $can(S) \subseteq S \subseteq exp(S)$. S is called expanded, iff $exp(S) = S$.

(iii) The **disjunctive consequence operator** $T_P^S : 2^{\text{DHB}_P} \longrightarrow 2^{\text{DHB}_P}$ of a disjunctive logic program P maps Herbrand states to Herbrand states:

$$T_P^S(D) = \{ C \in \text{DHB}_P \mid C' \; :- \; B_1, \ldots, B_n. \text{ is a ground instance of a rule in } P,$$
$$B_1 \vee C_1, \; \ldots, \; B_n \vee C_n \text{ are in } D, \; C \text{ is the smallest factor of } C' \vee C_1 \vee \ldots \vee C_n \}.$$

A **model state** S of a disjunctive logic program P is an expanded Herbrand state of P such that every minimal Herbrand model of S is a Herbrand model of P.

Example 2.1 ([LoMiRa 92]) *Given the disjunctive logic program*

$$P = \{ \; getto(X,Y) \vee getto(X,Z) \; :- \; path(X,Y,via(Z)), at(X).;$$
$$at(X) \; :- \; getto(Y,X).;$$
$$path(was,ny,via(phil)) \vee at(ny) \; \}.$$

For the state $S_1 = \{ \; path(was,ny,via(phil)) \vee at(ny) \; \}$ *we have*

$$T_P^S(S_1) = \{ \; path(was,ny,via(phil)) \vee at(ny),$$
$$getto(was,ny) \vee getto(was,phil) \vee path(was,ny,via(phil)) \vee at(ny) \; \}$$

and for the state $S_2 = T_P^S(S_1)$ *we have*

$$T_P^S(S_2) = T_P^S(S_1) \cup \{ \; at(ny) \vee getto(was,phil) \vee path(was,ny,via(phil)),$$
$$at(phil) \vee at(ny) \vee getto(was,ny) \vee path(was,ny,via(phil)) \; \}.$$

For every **definite** logic program P the following sets are equal, cf. [Llo 87]: the logical consequences $\{ A \in HB_P \mid P \models A \}$ of P, the minimal Herbrand model $\mathcal{M}_P$ of P, the least fixpoint $lfp(T_P)$ of the definite consequence operator T_P, and $T_P \uparrow \omega$.

In general a **disjunctive** logic program P does not have a unique minimal model, but a set $\mathcal{MM}_P$ of minimal models. The following theorem relates model states to the disjunctive consequence operator and shows that – as for Herbrand models of definite logic programs – every intersection of model states again is a model state.

Theorem 2.2 (Model States) *Given a disjunctive logic program P.*

- *Characterization: An expanded Herbrand state D of P is a model state of P, iff $T_P^S(D) \subseteq D$.*
- *Intersection Property: The intersection $\cap_{i \in J} MS_i$ of every non-empty set $\{MS_i\}_{i \in J}$ of model states of P is a model state of P too.*

Thus, there is a unique **minimal model state** $\mathcal{MS}_P$ of a disjunctive logic program P, namely the intersection $\cap_{i \in J} MS_i$ of the set $\{MS_i\}_{i \in J}$ of all model states of P.

The following sets are equal, cf. [LoMiRa 92]: the logical (disjunctive) consequences $\{ C \in \mathrm{DHB}_P \mid P \models C \}$, the minimal model state $\mathcal{MS}_P$ of P, the expanded least fixpoint $exp(lfp(T_P^S))$ of T_P^S, the expansion $exp(T_P^S \uparrow \omega)$ of $T_P^S \uparrow \omega$, and the set $\{ C \in \mathrm{DHB}_P \mid \forall M \in \mathcal{MM}_P : M \models C \}$ of clauses implied by all minimal models of P. For a definite logic program $\mathcal{M}_P$ equals $can(\mathcal{MS}_P)$.

3 Optimization of the Consequence Operator

The disjunctive closure operator T_P^S applied to a Herbrand state S searches for all disjunctive facts $B_1 \vee C_1, \ldots, B_n \vee C_n$ in S that can be hyperresolved with a ground instance $C' \; :- \; B_1, \ldots, B_n.$ of a rule $r \in P$, deriving the smallest factor of $C' \vee C_1 \vee \ldots \vee C_n$.

Example 3.1 *Given the disjunctive logic program P with the transitive closure rule*

$$p(X,Y) \; :- \; p(X,Z), p(Z,Y).$$

and the Herbrand state

$$\begin{aligned} S = \{ \quad & p(a,b) \vee p(f,g), \; p(a,b) \vee p(f,h), \\ & p(a,b) \vee p(a,d) \vee p(a,c) \vee p(a,1), \; \ldots \;, \; p(a,b) \vee p(a,d) \vee p(a,c) \vee p(a,\mathsf{m}), \\ & p(b,c) \vee p(b,e), \\ & p(b,c) \vee p(g,1), \; \ldots \;, \; p(b,c) \vee p(g,\mathsf{n}) \quad \} \end{aligned}$$

From each of the facts $p(a,b) \vee p(a,d) \vee p(a,c) \vee p(a,\mathsf{i})$, $1 \le \mathsf{i} \le \mathsf{m}$, *and each of the facts* $p(b,c) \vee p(g,\mathsf{j})$, $1 \le \mathsf{j} \le \mathsf{n}$, *the T_P^S-operator derives a new fact*

$$p(a,d) \vee p(a,c) \vee p(a,\mathsf{i}) \vee p(g,\mathsf{j})$$

using the ground instance of the transitive closure rule $p(a,c) \; :- \; p(a,b), p(b,c)$.

In the following disjunctive facts will be considered as sets of atoms.
Assume for each body atom B_i, $1 \le i \le n$, facts $F_i^j \in S$, $1 \le j \le n_i$, with common intersection F_i such that $B_i \in F_i$. We will try to store F_i just once with pointers to the n_i difference sets $F_i^j \setminus F_i$.
Thus, once we have found that $B_i \in F_i$, we know that each F_i^j has the form $B_i \vee C_i^j$. Therefore the F_i^j can be used for $\prod_{i=1}^n n_i$ hyperresolutions producing facts that all have the common subclause $F_1' \vee \ldots \vee F_n'$, where $F_i = F_i' \vee B_i$.
As suggested, repeated application of the T_P^S-operator tends to rapidly increase the amount of intersections between derived disjunctive facts.

The **hasse diagramm** $\mathcal{H}_{S'}$ for the superset $S' = \{C_1 \cap \ldots \cap C_k | k \in \mathbb{N}_+, C_i \in S, 1 \leq i \leq k\}$ of a finite Herbrand state S contains all the mentioned intersection information. Because the cardinality $|S'|$ can be of exponential size $2^{|S|}$ we are looking for a suitable small subset S'' of S' ($S \subseteq S'' \subseteq S'$) that captures as much as possible common intersections of clauses in S. For every resolution step the whole data structure has to be searched for occurences of B_i. This suggests to reduce the number of edges as well as the number of nodes.

A **tree representation** of Herbrand states will turn out to be a reasonable choice.

Definition 3.2 *Given a Herbrand state S. Let $\mathcal{A}_S$ denote all the atoms occurring in the clauses of S. A tree $\mathcal{T} = (V, E)$ with a node labelling $l : V \longrightarrow 2^{\mathcal{A}_S}$* **represents** *$S$, iff*

(i) *each node $v \in V$ represents a clause $clause(v)$ as follows: $clause(v)$ is the union of the sets $l(v)$ for the nodes v on the path from the root to v,*

(ii) *the clauses $clause(v)$ of the leaves $v \in V$ are in S, and every clause $C \in S$ is represented by exactly one leaf of the tree.*

Example 3.3 *The following tree represents the Herbrand state of the previous example. The node identifiers are omitted, only the labels are displayed.*

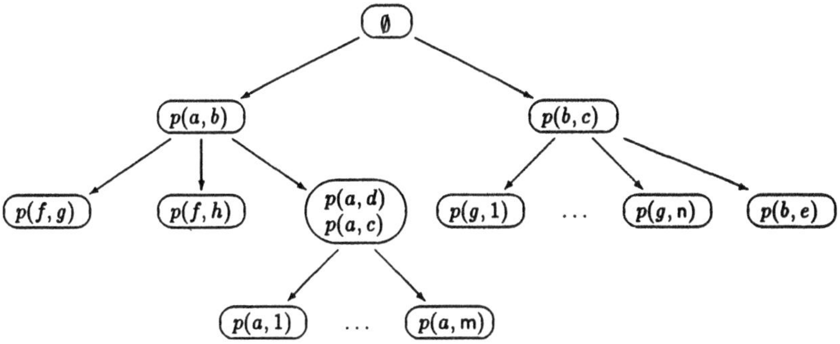

Based on tree representations $\mathcal{T}$ the T_P^S–operator is evaluated as follows:

initialization
let S be the set of disjunctive facts in the program P

while new facts derived

tree construction
determine a tree representation $\mathcal{T}$ with a labelling l for the actual set S of disjunctive facts

tree search
search for all disjunctive facts $B_1 \vee C_1, \ldots, B_n \vee C_n$ in the labelled tree $\mathcal{T}$, such that there is a ground instance $C' :- B_1, \ldots, B_n.$ of a rule $r \in P$

tree resolution
for each successful search derive a new disjunctive fact C as the smallest factor of $C' \vee C_1 \vee \ldots \vee C_n$ and add it to S (prune S by removing subsumed elements)

end

For tree construction of $\mathcal{T} = (V, E)$ we use as heuristic the minimizing of the sum of the arc lengths:

$$weight(\mathcal{T}) = \sum_{e \in E} length(e)$$

where $length(e) = \mid clause(v_2) \setminus clause(v_1) \mid$, for $(v_1, v_2) \in E$, i.e. we are looking for a minimal Steiner tree T, cf. [Vo 90], of the hasse diagram $\mathcal{H}_{S'}$. The price for this compact data structure is of course a lack of symmetry in the treatment of intersections compared to $\mathcal{H}_{S'}$.

We compared an implementation of the well–knwon Δ–iteration, cf. [GüKiBa 87], extended to disjunctive programs (method **M1**) for the fixpoint computation of T_P^S with an implementation of the tree–based resolution (method **M2**). We achieved very encouraging results for the path example, even without incorporating all possible optimization techniques, i.e. Δ–computation was done without trees, and tree update was done by appending a representing tree for the new facts to the old tree, instead of merging the trees, which might yield a tree with a much smaller weight.

Example 3.4 *The following table shows the ratio of the evaluation times for the fixpoint computations with the methods M1 (t_1) and M2 (t_2) for several values of* n, m *in the running example.*

n	m	t_1/t_2
2	2	*0.86*
3	3	*1.17*
4	4	*1.44*
5	5	*1.75*
6	6	*1.87*

n	m	t_1/t_2
2	1	*0.60*
2	2	*0.88*
2	3	*1.26*
2	4	*1.68*
2	5	*1.86*

4 Conclusion

For Herbrand states S with many overlapping facts the tree–based method outperforms pure Δ–iteration. Incorporating aspects of other data structures like hash tables and inverted lists is currently investigated.

An extension for computing the generalized well–founded semantics for disjunctive normal logic programs, i.e. rules involving negated body literals as well, is intended.

References

[BaRa 86] *F. Bancilhon, R. Ramakrishnan:* An Amateur's Introduction to Recursive Query Processing Strategies, Proc. ACM SIGMOD 1986, pp. 16-52.

[CeGoTa 90] *S. Ceri, G. Gottlob, L. Tanca:* Logic Programming and Databases, Springer, 1990.

[Da 92] *S.K. Das:* Deductive Databases and Logic Programming, Addison–Wesley, 1992.

[GüKiBa 87] *U. Güntzer, W. Kießling, R. Bayer:* On the Evaluation of Recursion in (Deductive) Database Systems by Efficient Differential Fixpoint Iteration, Proc. Intl. Conf. on Data Engineering 1987, pp. 120-129.

[Llo 87] *J.W. Lloyd:* Foundations of Logic Programming, Springer, second edition, 1987.

[LoMiRa 92] *J. Lobo, J. Minker, A. Rajasekar:* Foundations of Disjunctive Logic Programming, MIT Press, 1992.

[Prz 90] *T.C. Przymusinski:* Stationary Semantics for Disjunctive Logic Programs and Deductive Databases, Proc. North–American Conf. of Logic Programming, MIT Press, 1990, pp. 42-59.

[Ul 88/89] *J.D. Ullman:* Principles of Database and Knowledge-Base Systems, Volume I/II, Computer Science Press, 1988/89.

[VaGeRoSchli 91] *A. Van Gelder, K.A. Ross, J.S. Schlipf:* The Well–Founded Semantics for General Logic Programs, JACM, vol. 38(3), 1991, pp. 620-650.

[Vo 90] *S. Voß:* Steiner–Probleme in Graphen, Anton Hain, 1990.

AN ALGORITHM FOR FINDING THE GLOBAL MINIMUM OF MULTIEXTREMAL LIPSCHITZ FUNCTIONS

Yaroslav D. Sergeyev
Software Department
Nizhni Novgorod State University
603000 Nizhni Novgorod, Russia

In this paper we consider the one-dimensional unconstrained global minimization problem

$$\min\{ \varphi(x) : x \in [a, b] \}, \tag{1}$$

where the objective function $\varphi(x)$ in general case may be nonsmooth, but satisfies the Lipschitz condition

$$| \varphi(x) - \varphi(y) | \leq L | x - y |, \qquad x, y \in [a, b], \tag{2}$$

with a constant L, $0 < L < \infty$. Many numerical methods using the a priori known constant L have been proposed to solve the problem (1), (2) (see Evtushenko (1971), Galperin (1985), Hansen, Jamuard and Lu (1992a), Horst and Tuy (1990), Pijavskii (1972), Rinnooy Kan and Timmer (1989), etc.). But to have the exact value of L in general case it is necessary to evaluate $\varphi(x)$ in all points of [a, b]. Since this is impossible, some estimates of L are performed before the process of minimization. Another approach is presented by the methods (see Kushner (1964), Pinter (1992), Sergeyev and Grishagin (1993), Strongin (1973)) where behaviour of the objective function is estimated not before, but in the course of optimization. The method proposed here belongs to this group of the algorithms.

As Lipschitz constant L may provide a quite poor estimate of the actual slope of the objective function over an interval $[x, y] \subset [a, b]$ we calculate an estimate $\Lambda(x, y)$ of the local Lipschitz constant $L(x, y) \leq L$ of this interval. At every iteration k we construct an auxiliary piece-wise linear function $\Psi^k(x)$ tuning it according with the information (value of the function calculated at the k-th point produced by the method) obtaining during the process of minimizing. Slope of linear pieces of $\Psi^k(x)$ is not constant over the interval [a, b] in contrast with the methods proposed in Pijavskii (1972), Sergeyev and Grishagin (1993) and is changed in dependence on the subintervals of [a, b]. In the method proposed by Pijavskii the auxiliary piece-wise linear function has the slop equal to L for all iterations and this one is a low bound for $\varphi(x)$ at all iterations. The method of Sergeyev and Grishagin tries to construct a low bound over the whole interval [a, b] also. $\Psi^k(x)$ constructed by the method proposed may not be the low bound over the *whole* interval [a, b]. Nevertheless it is possible to prove convergence of the algorithm to the global minimizers of $\varphi(x)$.

ALGORITHM AND CONVERGENCE CONDITIONS

Two first trials (evaluations of the objective function) are executed at the points $x^0 = a$ and $x^1 = b$ of the interval [a, b]. To choose the (k+1)-th trial point, $k \ge 1$, we renumber the points $x^0, x^1, \dots, x^k$ of previous iterations by subscripts in increasing order as it follows

$$a = x_0 < x_1 < \dots < x_{k-1} < x_k = b.$$

Then we construct an auxiliary piece-wise linear function $\Psi^k(x)$ determined as follows :

$$\Psi^k(x) = \bigcup_{j=1}^{k} \psi_j(x),$$

$$\psi_j(x) = \max \{ \varphi(x_{j-1}) - r\Lambda_j (x - x_{j-1}),$$
$$\varphi(x_j) - r\Lambda_j (x_j - x) \},\ x \in [x_{j-1}, x_j],$$

here $r > 1$ is a parameter of the method and Λ_j is an estimate of the Lipschitz constant $L(x_{j-1}, x_j)$. We execute the (k+1)-th trial at the point

$$x^{k+1} = 0.5 (x_t + x_{t-1} - (z_t - z_{t-1}) / (r\Lambda_t)),$$

$$t = \arg\min \{ M(i) : 1 \le i \le k \},$$

where $z_i = \varphi(x_i)$, $0 \le i \le k$, and

$$M(i) = 0.5 (z_i + z_{i-1} - r\Lambda_i (x_i - x_{i-1})), 1 \le i \le k,$$

i.e. at the point corresponding to the most deep minimum of the function $\Psi^k(x)$. One of the possible ways to calculate Λ_j is the following one:

Step 1. Calculate the local estimate of $L(x_{j-1}, x_j), 1 \le j \le k$, as

$$\lambda_j = \max \{ | z_i - z_{i-1} | / (x_i - x_{i-1}) : j - p \le i \le j+p;\ 1 \le i \le k \},$$

where $p=p(j)\ge 0$ is a function determining a neighbourhood of $[x_{j-1}, x_j]$ in which local information about $L(x_{j-1}, x_j)$ is reliable.

Step 2. Calculate the global estimate of $L(x_{j-1}, x_j), 1 \le j \le k$, as

$$\gamma_j = \gamma^Q (x_j - x_{j-1}) / X^Q,$$

where

$$\gamma^Q = \max \{ | z_i - z_{i-1} | / (x_i - x_{i-1}) : j-Q \le i \le j+Q;\ 1 \le i \le k \},$$

$$X^Q = \max \{ x_i - x_{i-1} : j-Q \le i \le j+Q;\ 1 \le i \le k\},$$

where $Q=Q(j)\ge p(j)$ is a function determining a zone belonging to [a, b] in the way that all points outside of this one have no influence over $L(x_{j-1}, x_j)$.

Step 3. Calculate the resulting estimate Λ_j of $L(x_{j-1}, x_j), 1 \le j \le k$, as

$$\Lambda_j = \max \{ \lambda_j, \gamma_j, \zeta \},\ 1 \le j \le k,$$

where $\zeta > 0$ is a small number (parameter of the method).

Theorem (*sufficient conditions of global convergence*). Let x^* be a global minimizer of $\varphi(x)$. If there exists an iteration number k^* such that for all $k > k^*$ the inequality $r\Lambda_{j(k)} \ge L_{j(k)}$ holds, where $L_{j(k)}$ is the Lipschitz constant for the interval $[x_{j(k)-1}, x_{j(k)}]$ such that $x^* \in [x_{j(k)-1}, x_{j(k)}]$ then, x^* is a limit point of the sequence of trial points generated by the algorithm.

NUMERICAL EXPERIMENTS

We consider now the simplest realization of the method setting p=p(j)=1, Q=Q(j)=k for all j and k. In Table 1 we present results of numerical comparison of the algorithm (choosing r=1.1, $\zeta=10^{-6}$) with the methods proposed in Galperin (1985), Pijavskii (1972) and Strongin (1973) (with the parameter r=2) using test functions 1 - 10 from Hansen, Jamuard and Lu (1992b) with the search accuracy equal to 10^{-4}(b-a). For the methods of Galperin and Pijavskii the exact values of the Lipschitz constant have been used. In all methods the bound points of [a, b] have been taken as starting points.

Table 1

Function / Method	1	2	3	4	5	6	7	8	9	10	Average
Galperin	377	308	581	923	326	263	383	530	314	416	442.1
Pijavskii	149	155	195	413	151	129	153	185	119	203	185.2
Strongin	127	135	224	379	125	112	115	188	125	157	168.7
New	37	36	145	45	46	84	41	126	44	43	64.7

REFERENCES

Evtushenko Yu.G. (1971) Numerical Methods for Finding Global Extrema of a Nonuniform Mesh, *U.S.S.R. Comput. Math. and Math. Physics* 11: 1370-1403.

Galperin E.A. (1985) The cubic algorithm, *Journal of Math. Analyses and Applications* 112: 635-640.

Hansen P., Jamuard B. and Lu S.-H. (1992a) Global optimization of univariate Lipschitz functions: 1. Survey and properties", *Math. Programming* 55: 251-272.

Hansen P., Jamuard B. and Lu S.-H. (1992b) Global optimization of univariate Lipschitz functions: 2. New algorithms and computational comparison, *Math. Programming* 55: 273-293.

Horst R. and Tuy H. (1990) *Global Optimization-Deterministic Approaches*, Springer-Verlag, Berlin.

Kushner H. (1964) A new method for locating the maximum point of an arbitrary multipeak curve in presence of noise, *Journal of Basic Engineering* 86 (1): 97-106.

Pijavskii S.A. (1972) An Algorithm for Finding the Absolute Extremum of a Function, *U.S.S.R. Comput. Math. and Math. Physics* 12: 57-67.

Pinter J. (1992) Convergence Qualification of Adaptive Partition Algorithms in Global Optimization, *Math. Programming* 56: 343-360.

Rinnooy Kan A.H.G. and Timmer G.H. (1989) Global Optimization, *Optimization*, Ed. by G.L. Nemhauser, A.H.G. Rinnooy Kan and M.J. Todd, North-Holland, Amsterdam.

Sergeyev Ya.D. and Grishagin V.A. (1993) A Parallel Method for Finding the Global Minimum of Univariate Functions, *Journal of Optimization Theory and Applications*, (to appear).

Strongin R.G. (1973) On the convergence of an algorithm for finding a global extremum, *Engineering Cybernetics*, 11: 549-555.

Comparison of some classifiers based on parametric or nonparametric learning algorithms

Shaghaghi,F and Sadeghi,H
Institut für Statistik und
mathematische Wirtschaftstheorie
Universität Karlsruhe
Rechenzentrum Zirkel 2
76128 Karlsruhe Germany

1.Introduction

This Paper is concerned with comparison of different statistical and machine learning algorithms through application of these Methods in Credit-Scoring. Some Classical statistical Methods for classification can be considered as Methods of"learning from examples" or "supervised learning". Traditionally such statistical classifition Methods have been divided into two main groups of algorithms : parametric and non-parametric, depending on using the assumptions about the distribution of Attributes within each class.

In section two the classification of some classifiers will be discussed. Section three is devoted to application and evaluation of underlined Classification algorithms in Credit-Scoring.

2. Classification of Classifiers (learning algorithms)

Linear-Discriminant analyses is an example for statistical parametric learning algorithm, while Kernel and K-nearest-neighbour are known as statistical non-parametric learning algorithms.

On the other hand machine learning which is a subarea of Artificial Intelligence, covers widely different algorithmes in inductive concept learning (learning from example), such as ID3, CN2, NewID,..., which can be considerd as non-parametric learning methods, because there is no assumption about the distribution of attributes within each class necessary. Much of the research has been devoted to theoretical aspect or defining paradigms. Much less effort has been done to apply machine learning to the real world problem. Our attempt is to bear them on real-world application and compare them with known classical methods.

Here we discuss briefly the classifiers which we have used in our application in Credit-Scoring.

2.1 Prametric learning algorithms

Linear-Discriminant analysis is one of the classical statistical learning algorithms, which refers to classifying observations into two or more known classes depending on one or more quantitative variables through building the polynomial function. Different discriminant functions have been developed according to assumptions about the distributions of attributes and their covariance matrix.

2.2 Non-parametric Learning Algorithms

2.2.1 Statistical Algorithms

Kernel method is based on estimation of the density of attributes within each class using training set of the dataset. At each data point of a class is a "Kernel funktion" assumed. Depending on the choice of scaling parameter the shape of the Kernel function changes. The choice of scaling parameter is more important than the choice of kernel function.

k-nearest-neighbour procedure is based on density estimation. The nearest k point in training dataset will be observed to classify a new data point. The class of this new point is the most frequent class among them.

Classification procedure will be done through the Bayes classification method.

2.2.2 Machine Leaning Algorithms

Machine Learning reseach is now almost four decades old and covers different techniques such as Inductive learning methods, clustering system, neural networks, genetic algorithms, and so on. Although they look very different from each other but they are common in one asspect which is their adequacy to change systemperformance based on experience. In this paper we are concerned with Inductive learning or supervised learning (learning from example), which can be regarded as a very useful alternative to the classical statistical classification methods. These algorithms are divided in several ways. The most important is the language for expressing the result of classification task. Some Algorithms such ID3, C4.5, NewID use decision trees. Others such as the AQ-Family use logical formulations (if-then ruls) and so on. In following we discuss briefly some of the algorithms we used in our application in Credit-Scoring. One can find the theoretical issues of following algorithms in [2] [9] [10].

ID3-Algorithm uses instances whose classes are predefined through a fixed amount of properties. Then generates a decision tree over all these properties, such that all instances can be correctly classified. ID3 is developed by Ross Quinlan.

C4.5-Algorithm is based on ID3 but it generates decision trees and productions rules. It can handle the large scale dataset, the noisy data and missing values. [1]

NewID has been developed by Robin Boswell at Turing Institute. It generates decision trees and production rules. It can handle the continuous-valued classes which is not possible by C4.5.

CN2 is a rule structured algorithm and developed by Tim Niblett and Peter Clark at Turing Institue. It is able to handle the noisy data.

2.2.3 Neural Networks

Neural computing is a simplified manner of functionality of the human recognition[2]. It covers a variety of applications. They are appropriate to solve classification tasks, especially when the datasets are noisy or incomplete a neural network is able to give a resonable result. There are many different topologies of the networks. We have used Back-Propagation, Adaline and Madaline Networks.

---

[1] C4.5 is also developed by Quinlan

[2] For theoretical issues see [8]

3. Credit-Scoring as a Classification Task

3.1 General Remarks

Creditgranting institutes must decide whether or not to grant a credit to a customer on the basis of unsufficient a-priori information. The core of Credit-Scoring is to estimate and predict the applicant's ability of repayment of credit, in order to classify them as eligible (good risk) or not eligible (bad risk). Therefore credit-Scoring is an empirical issue and a classification task, based on learning from the past experiences and exampels. Traditionally, Credits were aworded by human judgment. Recently Credit-Scoring systems, based on statistical learning algorithms such as discriminant analysis, have become widely used. Applying machine learning algorithms to Credit-Scoring is not very known and is in ist infancy stage.

3.2 Empirical evaluation

We have used 3 datasets from the Credit-Scoring area, which is a real-world problem. The summary of the information about the datasets is in table 1.

datasets Information	Dataset I	Dataset II	Dataset III
Sources	large bank in Germany	large bank in England	Credit institute in Australian
# of example	1000	8900	690
# of attributes	20	39	14
# of numerical att.	7	16	6
# of categorical att.	13	23	8
# of classes	2	2	2
# of training dataset	656	5921	480
# of testing dataset	344	2978	210
spliting between two classes	30% to 70%	50% to 50%	44% to 56%

Table 1 : Characteristics of used datasets

To interpret the performance of different algorithms described in section 2, we have listed the achieved accuracy rates by each algorithms in table 2.

used different learning algorithms	Dataset I default accuracy-rate 70 %	Dataset II default accuracy-rate 50 %	Dataset III default accuracy-rate 56 %
Linear discriminant	72.3	64.3	82.7
Kernel (uninform) with	72 k=6	61 k=100	85.7 k=5
k-Nearest-Neighbour with	70 k=25	63 k=1	86.7 k=10
ID3	72	-	-
C4.5	75	90.6	84.9
NewID	68	86	85
CN2	74.4	86.1	84.3
Adaline-Network	73.5	-	83.5
Madaline-Network	71.2	-	81.1
Back-Propagation-Network	70.1	-	82.3

Table 2. Accuracy rates of different learning algorithms / dataset pairs in percent

Conclusion

In this paper we discussed sôme parametric and non-parametric learning (classification) algorithms and used 3 datasets from the real-world problem (Credit-Scoring) to compare and to evaluate their performances. Considering the accuracy rates achieved from above discussed algorithms/data set pairs, one can see that the machine learning and neural-networks algorithms have performed the same good results on these 3 datasets as classical statistical algorithms. Some results are even better. By Linear-Discriminant analysis only the attributes with numerical values were accepted. Neural networks are not handy for large datasets. The expression form of the result by machine learning (Decision trees or induced rules) are closer to human understanding than the matematical equations. To our respect machine learning algorithms and neural-networks can be regarded as reasonable alternative for development of the Credit-Scoring system.

References

[1] Carter, Ch. and Catlett, J. (1987). Assessing credit card applications using machine learning. *IEEE Expert*, 71-79.

[2] Clark, P. and Niblett, T. (1988). The CN2 induction algorithm. *Machine Learning3,4*, 261-283

[3] Fahrmeier, L. Häußler, W. und Tutz, G. (1984). Diskriminanzanalyse. In: Fahrmeier, L. und Hamerle, A. (Eds.) (1984). *Multivariate statistische Verfahren.* Verlag de Gruyter, Berlin.

[4] Hand, D. J. (1981). *Discrimination and Classification.* Jonhn Wiley & Sons, New York.

[5] Hand, D. J. (1982). *Kernel Discriminant Analysis.* Research stadies Pres, adivision of John Wiley & Sons, New York.

[6] Lachenbruch, P. A.(1975). *Discriminant Analysis.* Hafner Press.

[7] Nakhaeizadeh, G. and Graf, J. (1993). *Recent Development in Solving the Credit-Scoring Problem.* In print.

[8] Neural Ware inc. (1990).*Neural Computing. Neural Works Professionl II/Plus and Neural Works Explorer* Pittsburg.

[9] Quinlan, J. R. (1986). Induction of decision trees. *Machine Learning*, vol 1, 81-106.

[10] Quinlan, J. R. (1993). *C4.5 Programs for Machine Learning*, Morgan Kaufman, San Matheo.

GENERAL STRUCTURES OF PRIMAL SCALING INTERIOR POINT METHODS

Dong Xiao Shaw

School of Industrial Engineering
Purdue University
West Lafayette, Indiana 47907-1287

In this paper, we explore the general structure of primal scaling interior point methods. Specifically, we are able to analyze the primal scaling path-following method, potential reduction method and low-complexity affine scaling method under one simple framework. We believe that this approach provides a simple but inside analysis to understand interior point methods. We consider the linear programming problem in the following form:

$$(P) \qquad \begin{aligned} \min\ & c^T x \\ & Ax = b \\ & x \geq 0,\ x \in R^n . \end{aligned}$$

Here, primal scaling means we use affine scale $X = \text{diag}(x^0)$ to transform both primal and dual slack variables, and the projections P used in the algorithm is the orthogonal projection from R^n to null space

$$\{ y \mid AXy = 0 \} .$$

Given $x^0 > 0$ primal feasible, we define

$$d(z) = P\left(-\frac{n+\gamma}{f^0 - z} Xc + e\right)$$

for $-\infty < z < f^0$, where $f^0 = c^T x^0$ and e is a vector of all ones. Clearly, when $\gamma = \sqrt{n}$, $d(z^k)$ is the direction defined in Ye's (1991) potential reduction algorithm, where z^k is a lower bound at iteration k. While

$$-\frac{c_p}{\|c_p\|} = \lim_{z \to f^0} \frac{d(z)}{\|d(z)\|}$$

is the affine scaling direction analyzed by Dikin (1974). With a proper choice of the parameter

γ, $d(z)$ also includes Gonzaga's (1988) path-following method and Shaw and Goldfarb's (1990) projective path-following method. It can be shown that the constant-objective centering direction used by Barnes *etal* (1988) and Todd (1990) is also a member of $\{ d(z) \}$.

We present a unified approach to analyze all algorithms which take $d(z)$ as a step direction for some z. In this sense, we basically cover all the primal scaling algorithms. Specifically, we are able to analyze Gonzaga's path-following algorithm, Ye's potential reduction algorithm and Todd's low-complexity affine scaling algorithm in same framework. We believe that this approach is very simple and easy to understand. Except for the quadratic equation, all the tools used in analyzing the algorithms, such as affine transformation, orthogonal projection, and primal-dual potential functions, are common and conventional in interior point method literature.

We define and analyze the following equation of z for a given constant β,

$$\|d(z)\| = \beta$$

which is essentially the quadratic equation. This quadratic equation is related to the quadratic equation defined in projective space (see Shaw and Goldfarb (1990)), which is corresponding to a ball relaxation of the linear program in projective space. A variant of this equation was proposed by Freund (1988) without analysis and implicitly used by Todd (1990). We believe that this simple quadratic equation is very important in both theoretical analysis and computational practice. First, it is a powerful tool to analyze a very general class of algorithms. Second, it is a useful measurement to lift the lower bound in computation.

A necessary and sufficient condition of measuring the closeness to the central trajectory regarding $\|d(z)\|$ is also provided in the paper. The sufficient condition part has been widely used in many other papers (see, for example, Ye (1991)). We believe that this is a very general, important and crucial result regarding to the central path, so we formalize and restate it in our paper.

We first analyze the primal scaling path-following algorithms. We present a new path-following method in affine scaled space, which essentially shares some idea as the path-following projective method of Shaw and Goldfarb (1990). Instead of naively mapping the direction between two different spaces, we construct the new algorithm in the affine transformed space by applying the idea from the projective space. The key factor which leads the algorithm to converge is quite different than the existing primal scaling path-following methods. We also extend our path algorithm by allowing the line-search on the primal-dual potential function, and present a monotonic version algorithm. We rigorously show that Gonzaga's path-following algorithm is a special case of the path-following algorithm we proposed, where the procedure of solving the quadratic equation is skipped. Under our framework, Gonzaga's method can be analyzed in a very simple way.

Then, we study the general structure of a class of primal scaling potential reduction algorithms, which include Ye's (1991) and Freund's (1991) potential reduction algorithms, and Todd's low-complexity affine scaling algorithm, and modified Gonzaga's (1990) affine potential reduction algorithm are also included as the special cases. This generic algorithm can be regarded as the primal scaling version of Goldfarb and Shaw's (1991) projective generic algorithm. We refer all these algorithms as potential reduction methods because the complexity analysis of all these algorithms are all based on the reduction of the primal-dual potential function.

The dual update procedure of our potential reduction algorithm is based on solving a quadratic equation. It can be shown that our dual procedure is more aggressive than Ye's and Freund's one. However, if the dual update does occur in all three of them and the line-search is incorporated, all three methods produce the same lower-bound.

One of our main results is a generic algorithm which includes monotonic versions of all potential reduction algorithms mentioned above, Todd's low-complexity algorithm and modified version of Gonzaga's (1990) affine potential reduction algorithm as special cases. This generic algorithm has a worst case iteration bound of $O(\sqrt{n}\, L)$. Its dual update procedure is identical to our potential reduction algorithm, while the primal steps are taken along either a regular direction that can be picked arbitrarily from a cone, or a constant-objective centering direction.

Moreover, it can be shown that, with a proper choice of the step-length, no consecutive centering steps are required. In other words, one centering step is able to bring the current iteration point close enough to the central path to take the regular primal step. This result generalizes the one obtained by Todd and Vial (1992), where they showed that no more than three consecutive centering steps are required, for the low-complexity affine scaling algorithm, to bring the current iteration point close to the central path. (It is just a matter of choice of the parameters to decide exactly how many consecutive centering-steps are needed.) Hence, our generic algorithm fits the predictor-corrector path-following framework in the primal scaling space.

Reference

Barnes, E. R., Chopra, S. and Jensen, D. L. (1988). A polynomial time version of affine scaling algorithm, *Manuscript*, IBM T. J. Watson Research Center, Yorktown Heights, NY.

Dikin, I. I. (1974). On the convergence of an iterative process, *Upravivaemve Sistem* 12, 54-60.

Freund, R. M. (1988). Polynomial-time algorithm for linear programming based only on primal scaling projected gradients of potential function, *Mathematical Programming* 51, 203-222.

Goldfarb, D. and Xiao(Shaw), D. (1991). A primal projective interior point method for linear programming, *Mathematical Programming*, V.51, pp.17-43.

Goldfarb, D. and Shaw, D. (1991). On the complexity of a class of Projective Interior Point Methods, *Mathematics of Operations Research*, to appear.

Gonzaga, C. (1988). An algorithm for solving linear programming in $O(n^3 L)$ operations, in *Progress in Mathematical Programming: Interior Point and Related Methods*, N. Megiddo ed., Springer Verlag, NY.

Gonzaga, C. (1990). Polynomial affine algorithm for linear programming, *Mathematical Programming* 49, 7-21..

Karmarkar, N. (1984). A new polynomial time algorithm for linear programming, *Combinatorica* 4, 373-395.

Kojima, M., Mizuno, S. and Yoshise, A. (1988). A primal-dual interior point method for linear programming, in *Progress in Mathematical Programming: Interior Point and Related Methods*, N. Megiddo ed., Springer Verlag, NY.

Megiddo, N. (1988). Pathways to the optimal set in linear programming, in *Progress in Mathematical Programming: Interior Point and Related Methods*, N. Megiddo ed., Springer Verlag, NY.

Roos, C. and Vial, J.P. (1992). A polynomial method of approximate centers for linear programming, *Mathematical Programming*, 54, 295-305.

Shaw, D. and Goldfarb, D. (1990). A path-following projective interior point method for linear programming, *Journal of SIAM on Optimization*, to appear.

Todd, M. J. (1990). A low complexity interior point algorithm for linear programming, *Manuscript*, School of Operations Research and Industrial Engineering, Cornell University, Ithaca, NY.

Todd, M.J. and J.-P. Vial (1992). Todd's low-complicity algorithm is a predictor-corrector path-following method, *Operations Research Letters*, 11, 199-207.

Ye, Y. (1991). An $O(n^3 L)$ potential reduction algorithm for linear programming, *Mathematical Programming* 50, 239-258.

Scheduling and Allocation in High-Level Synthesis*

Jurij Šilc

Jožef Stefan Institute, Laboratory for Computer Architectures
Jamova 39, Ljubljana, Slovenia

The high-level synthesis task is to take a specification of the behavior required of a system and a set of constraints and goals to be satisfied, and to find a structure that implements the behavior while satisfying the goals and constraints. This paper is concentrates on scheduling and allocatin which seems to be the most important tasks during the synthesis. In particular, some of the basic scheduling/allocation techniques are discussed and a new scheduling/allocation approach is presented.

Introduction

The main step of the high-level synthesis, which is the core of transforming behavior into structure, includes operation *scheduling* and hardware *allocation*. Since these two tasks are essential in high-level synthesis they have been studied extensively and a variety of algorithms have been published. An excellent overwiev of the different schools of thought has been given by McFarland (1990). The scheduling and allocation are closely interrelated. In order to have an optimal design, both tasks should be performed simultaneously. However, due to the time complexity, many systems perform them separately or introduce iteration loops between the two subtasks. Scheduling involves assigning the operation to so-called *control steps*. A control step is the fundamental sequencing unit in synchronous systems; it corresponds to a *clock cycle*. Roughly speaking, operation scheduling determines the cost-speed tradeoffs of the design. Allocation involves assigning the operations and values to hardware, i.e., providing storage, function units, and communication paths, and specifying their usage. To minimize them together is usually too complex, so in many high-level synthesis systems they are minimized separately. Therefore, allocation is usually further divided into three subtasks – *variable binding*, *operation assignment*, and *data transfer binding*.

Scheduling/Allocation Algorithms

In what follows we will first describe two transformational scheduling algorithms. *Integer linear programming* algorithm implicitly uses branch-and-bound techniques for selection of transformations. An example of a heuristic based transformational scheduling algorithm is *Simulated annealing* based algorithm. Next we describe two iterative/constructive scheduling algorithms which belong to the list scheduling algorithms. The first one is the *Force directed* algorithm; it uses force as a priority function. The second one, named *Global arc minimization* algorithm, uses a complex priority function based on critical paths and operation's neighborhood.

Before proceeding we give some common definitions. Let $G(V, A)$ be a *flow graph*, where V is the set of operations and A is the set of dependencies (arcs), which is to be scheduled into s control steps. Let $n = |V|$ and $a = |A|$. Each of the operations is labeled as o_i, $1 \leq i \leq n$. A precedence relation between operations o_i and o_j is denoted by $o_i \rightarrow o_j$, where o_i is immediate predecessor of o_j. The *earliest* possible start time and the *latest* possible start time of o_i are S_i and L_i, respectively. There are m types of function units available. A function unit of type t is denoted by F_t. A relation between operation o_i and a function unit F_t is denoted by $o_i \in F_t$, if F_t can perform o_i.

*This research is supported by the Ministry of Science and Technology of the Republic of Slovenia under grant P2-1133-106/93.

Integer Linear Programming. In Hwang et al. (1991) integer linear programming is used to formulate the feasible scheduling problem. Let the cost of a function unit of type t be c_t and M_t be integer variables denoting the number of function units of type t needed. Finally, let $x_{i\tau}$ be $0-1$ integer variables where $x_{i\tau}=1$ if o_i is scheduled into control step τ; otherwise, $x_{i\tau}=0$. Assuming a one-cycle propagation delay for each operation and a nonpipelined execution, the feasible scheduling problem can finally be stated as follows:

$$\sum_{o_i \in F_t} x_{i\tau} \le M_t, \quad 1 \le \tau \le s, 1 \le t \le m;$$

$$\sum_{\tau=S_i}^{L_i} x_{i\tau} = 1, \quad 1 \le i \le n;$$

$$\sum_{\tau=S_i}^{L_i} \tau * x_{i\tau} - \sum_{\tau=S_k}^{L_k} \tau * x_{k\tau} \le -1, \quad o_i \to o_k \in A.$$

The first constraint states that no schedule should have a control step containing more than M_t function units of type t. It is clear that o_i can only be scheduled into a step between S_i and L_i, which is reflected in the second constraint. The third constraint ensures that precedence relations of the flow graph will be preserved. The objective function is a combination of time-constraint objective function $\min \sum_{t=1}^{m} c_t * M_t$ and resource-constraint objective function $\min C_{step}$, where C_{step} is total number of control steps required. This approach allows the user to control the resource-time tradeoff. More explicit resource-time tuning is the advantage of the next algorithm to be presented.

Simulated Annealing. Another type of transformational feasible scheduler based on the simulated annealing idea is given in Badia et al. (1992). The simulated annealing algorithm can be used for combinatorial optimization problems specified by a finite set of configurations and a cost function defined on all the configurations. The algorithm randomly generates a new configuration which is then accepted or rejected according to a random acceptance rule governed by the parameter analogous to temperature in the physical annealing process. The scheduling algorithm proceeds as follows:

```
T = T_initial;
X = Initial_schedule;
while "stop criteria" do
   for "n times" do
      Y = New_configuration(X);
      ΔC = Cost(Y) − Cost(X);
      if ΔC < 0 then X = Y
      else if random(0,1) < e^(−ΔC/T) then X = Y
   endfor;
   T = update(T)
endwhile
```

Algorithm starts on an initial configuration which is the schedule obtained by applying *as soon as possible* strategy, i.e. the start time of o_i is S_i, for each $o_i \in V$. The function *Cost* evaluates how good a configuration is. It is defined as $Cost(X) = \alpha Area(X) + \beta Time(X)$, where $Area(X)$ is the estimated total area of the resources used and $Time(X)$ is the total execution time corresponding to the given configuration X. The tuning of the algorithm is performed by taking different values for α and β. For example, if $\alpha \ll \beta$ the algorithm is closer to resource-constrained scheduler (since solutions efficient in speed become more important) while $\alpha \gg \beta$ makes the algorithm more time-constrained. Initially, a high temperature $T_{initial}$ is given in order to accept most new configurations even if they increase the cost. As temperature decreases, less configurations are accepted unless they have improved cost. Given a configuration X, a new configuration Y is generated either by insertion or removal of a register, scheduling an operation to next or previous control step, or by shrinking/expanding a control step (function *New_configuration*).

A similar algorithm appears in Devadas and Newton (1989) where it is also reported that the algorithm achieves excellent results. However, it performs scheduling and allocation symultaneously. This is also the characteristics of the approach which is to be presented next.

Force Directed Algorithm. Let us next describe a force-directed scheduling algorithm which is based on list scheduling with a force as a priority function. The first step consists of determining the time frames $[S_i, L_i]$ of each operation $o_i \in V$. Let $p_{i\tau}$ denote the probability that o_i will be scheduled into control step $\tau \in [S_i, L_i]$. A useful heuristic is to assume a uniform probability, i.e. $p_{i\tau} = \frac{1}{1+L_i-S_i}$. The next step is to take the summation of the probabilities of each type t of operation for each control step τ: $P(t,\tau) = \sum_{o_i \in F_t} p_{i\tau}$. The final step is to calculate the force $\mathcal{F}$ associated with each operation o_i and bounded to a temporarily reduced time frame $[S_i', L_i']$:

$$\mathcal{F}(S_i', L_i') = \sum_{\tau=S_i'}^{L_i'} \frac{P(t,\tau)}{1+L_i'-S_i'} - \sum_{\tau=S_i}^{L_i} \frac{P(t,\tau)}{1+L_i-S_i},$$

where t is the type of the operation o_i. Once all the forces are calculated, the operation-control step pair with largest negative force (or least positive force) is scheduled. Then P and $\mathcal{F}$ values are updated. The process is repeated untill all operations are scheduled.

The scheduling process described above is a part of the HAL system by Paulin et al. (1986). In particular the scheduling/allocation is performed symultaneously by stepwise refinement in an iterative loop consisting of four phases. The first phase (default allocation) allocates single-function processor to each type of operation. The second phase (preliminary schedule) balances the distribution of similar of operations using force-directed scheduling. The third phase (refined allocation) allocates single and multi-function processors. The last, fourth phase (final schedule) balances the distribution of operations requiring similar processor types.

Global Arc Minimization Algorithm. The last scheduling algorithm to be presented was developed by Šilc and Robič (1993) where both time and resource constrained scheduling algorithms were described. In this paper, however, we will concentrate only on the time constrained scheduling. We consider situation with $m = 1$, i.e., all function units are of the same type (as it is the case in preliminary scheduling in HAL system). The first step consists of determining the time frames $[S_i, L_i]$ of each operation $o_i \in V$ using *as soon as possible* and *as late as possible* schedules. Next, the minimum number f_{min} of function units needed is evaluated. To do this, a method based on the *extended critical parallelism* of flow graph was introduced in Šilc et al. (1990). During the execution of the scheduling algorithm the following sets of operations are maintained at each control step $\tau = 1, 2, \ldots, s$: $O_{ready}(\tau) := \{o_i | S_i \leq \tau \leq L_i\}$, $O_{urgent}(\tau) := \{o_i | S_i = \tau = L_i\}$, $O_{deferrable}(\tau) = O_{ready}(\tau) - O_{urgent}(\tau)$, and $O_{finished}(\tau) := \{o_i \in V | o_i$ has finished at $\tau\}$. Let $f(\tau)$ denote the number of occupied function units at some control step τ. Hence, there are $f_{min} - f(\tau)$ free function units at τ. Since urgent operations are always taken care off, in case of $f(\tau) < f_{min}$ some additional operations can be started. Note, that these operations are selected among deferrable ones. Selection was performed according to three priority functions: random selection, increasing execution time selection, and decreasing execution time selection. However, none of these criteria proved to be superior. Therefore, the algorithm is of a list-scheduling type and is given below:

$\tau = 0$
$f(\tau) = 0$
repeat
    if $f(\tau) > 0$ **then** $f(\tau) = f(\tau) - |O_{finished}(\tau)|$ **endif**
    $f(\tau) = f(\tau) + |O_{urgent}(\tau)|$
    if $f(\tau) < f_{min}$ **then**
        Let $O_{additional}(\tau) \subset O_{deferrable}(\tau)$,
        where $|O_{additional}(\tau)| \leq f_{min} - f(\tau)$.
        $f(\tau) = f(\tau) + |O_{additional}(\tau)|$
    endif
    $\tau = \tau + 1$
until $\tau = s$

After scheduling has been completed the allocation is performed, i.e., the index $\varphi(o_i)$, $1 \leq \varphi(o_i) \leq f$, $f = \max_{1 \leq \tau \leq s} f(\tau)$ of a function unit is computed for each operation $o_i \in V$. Since the communication between operations allocated to different function units is a time consuming operation, the goal is to allocate operations so that the communication time is minimized. Let us call an arc $o_i \rightarrow o_j$ a *global arc* if $\varphi(o_i) \neq \varphi(o_j)$, i.e., if operations o_i and o_j are allocated different function units. In order to minimize communication time an allocation criterion which keeps the number of global arcs as low as possible was successfully applied. The algorithm based on *weighted bipartite matching* and is described in Šilc and Robič (1993).

As we already mentioned, we have designed both time and resource constrained scheduling algorithms. Together these algorithms can be used to solve the feasible scheduling problem. In particular, the total cost of scheduling/allocation can be defined as a function $Cost(s, f, c)$ of the number of control steps s, the number of function units f, and the communication time c. Now, given some default number of control steps s (determined by the critical path of the flow graph), the time constrained scheduling/allocation (as described above) results in f function units and the total communication time c. Next, we iterativelly apply the resource constrained scheduling/allocation with $f - k$, $k = 1, 2, \ldots$ function units. Finally, we chose the most appropriate k, i.e. the scheduling with the lowest $Cost$. One can also iterativelly repeat the whole process starting at higher values of s. (Note, that the process may stop when s equals the sequential execution time of the flow graph.) Hence, our algorithm iterates the scheduling/allocation process changing the resource limits until a satisfactory design has been found.

Concluding remarks

The problem of translating behavioral description of a system into structural a one has been divided into a number of subtasks among which the operation scheduling and hardware allocation are the most important.

The scheduling problem has been researched quite extensively in the past. However, most of the solutions concentrate on systems with homogeneous function units. Moreover, neither of the efforts includes communication overhead. In order to be more realistic the communication delay has to be considered in high-level synthesis. Since allocation involves assigning the operations to hardware, it also determines the communication overhead. Thus, in high-level synthesis the scheduling and allocation are closely interrelated In order to have an optimal design, both should be performed simultaneously. Due to the time complexity, however, many systems perform them separately, or introduce iteration loops between the two tasks, as it was the case in our *Global arc minimization* scheduling/allocation approach.

References

Badia R M, Cortadella J, Ayguadé E (1992) Computed-Aided Synthesis of Data-Path by Using a Simulated-Annealing-Based Approach. *Proc. 9th IASTED Int'l Symp. Applied Informatics*, p. 326-329.

Devadas S, Newton A R (1989) Algorithm for Hardware Allocation in Data Path Synthesis. *IEEE Trans. CAD* 8(7):768-781.

Hwang C T, Lee J H, Hsu Y C (1991) A Formal Approach to the Scheduling Problem in High Level Synthesis. *IEEE Trans. CAD* 10(4):464-475.

McFarland M C, Parker A C, Camposano R (1990) The High-Level Synthesis of Digital Systems. *Proc. of the IEEE* 78(2):301-318.

Paulin P G, Knight J P, Girczyc E F (1986) HAL: A Multi-Paradigm Approach to Automatic Data Path Synthesis. *Proc 23rd ACM/IEEE DAC*, p. 263-270.

Šilc J, Robič B, Patnaik L M (1990) Performance Evaluation of an Extended Static Dataflow Architecture. *Computers and Artificial Intelligence* 9(1):43-60.

Šilc J, Robič B (1993) Program Partitioning for a Control/Data Driven Computer. *Journal of Computing and Information Technology* 1(1):47-55.

A MODELLING OF ENERGY-ECONOMY INTERACTION UNDER UNCERTAINTY

Nickolay.V. Simakov
Central Laboratory of Social & Economic Measurements
of the RUSSIAN Academy of Sciences, Krasikova str. 32
117418 Moscow, RUSSIA

The paper addresses problems of energy-economy interaction under uncertainty. One of the important problems of this research is to estimate the structure of energy demand in varios scenarios of development of economy. The impact of energy consumption on the rate of economic growth is also considered. The nonlinear adaptive econometric model is used to solve these problems. The system is functioning under uncertainty, parameters being determined by intervals.

This approach did not try to determine optinal trajectory of economic growth. We assume that this trajectory is predetermined. Our model is intented to calculate the equalibrium dynamics of economic sectors, when the total economic growth trajectory is given. These strategies are characterized by important indicators such as national income, investment, consumption ets.

Economical dynamics in matrix notations is given by

$$X_{t+1} = B_t X_t + \Gamma_t V_t \quad , \tag{1}$$

where X_t - output vector; V_t - vector of random errors; B_t , Γ_t - matrices depending on the technological matrix and matrix of fixed capital intensities. Estimation method is used for treatment of adaptation problem (see Simakov (1988)). We assume that vector Π_t - vector of exogeniously specified characteristics of economic growth is predetermined. The equations for observations are as follows

$$\Pi_t = H_t X_t + \omega_t \quad , \tag{2}$$

where ω_t - is a random vector modelling errors in the determination of Π_t .

It is required to determine optimal value of vector X_t with the restrictions in (1) imposed. The matrix H_t is determined by vector Π_t , which is the objectives of adaptation.

The problem is to construct such a trajectory of national economy indices X_t so that the values of $H_t X_t$ calculated on it will not differ very much in the mean squared sense from the specified characteristics of economy growth Π_t ; this is to be done through the use of permissible deviations of the vector V_t from the given vector $\bar{V}_t$.

The problem of adaptation of the system (1)-(2) to the given Π_t with quadratic criteria of quality is solved by Kalman filtering. The coefficients of matrices B_t and Γ_t in this problem are constant.

Let us consider case, when the coefficients in these matrices are variables. It is nonlinear optimal filtering problem. The algorithm for solving this problem was developed in the model (see Simakov (1992)). This approach allows to include an important economic information concerning possible dynamics of coefficients of matrices B_t and Γ_t .

Another important feature of problem (1)-(2) is difficulties in estimating random vectors V_t and ω_t . It is more natural to determine this vectors by intervals. The bounds of the intervals are to be given by experts.

The method of garanteed estimates suggested by A.B. Kurzhanski (1988) is used in the model . Algorithms of this method can admit disturbances of any type under apriori restrictions. I will report computational results for different algorithms.

The model was implemented on IBM PC AT in the form of interactive system. The interactive regime is effective in the multipal variants analysis of sector output dynamics corresponding to the given trajectory of economic growth.

REFERENCES

Simakov, N.V. (1990),"Adaptive Intersectoral Model for the Analysis and Forecast of Energy Consumption", Abstracts Int. Conf. on Operations Research , Vienna, Austria, 1990.

Simakov, N.V. (1992), "Econometric Approach for Modelling of Energy-Economy Interaction", Proceedings IFAC/IFORS/IIASA Int. Conf. on Modelling and Control of National Economies, Beijing, 1992, pp. 109-113.

Kurzhanski, A.B. (1988), "Identification - a Theory of Guaranteed Estimates", WP-88-55, IIASA, Laxenburg, Austria.

VALUE CONVERGENCE IN GENERALIZED MARKOV DECISION CHAINS

Karel Sladký
Institute of Information Theory and Automation
Academy of Sciences of the Czech Republic
P. O. Box 18, CZ–182 08 Prague 8

We consider a generalized Markov decision chain with state space $S = \{1, \dots, m\}$, action set Δ_i in $i \in S$ (Δ_i is finite, nonempty) and the set of policies $\Delta = \mathsf{X}_{i \in S} \Delta_i$. To each $\delta \in \Delta$, there exists an $m \times m$ "transition matrix" P_δ and an m by one real vector c_δ. We only suppose that P_δ is nonnegative, row sums can be greater than one. Hence the spectral radius of P_δ can also exceed unity. The set of all matrices P_δ is denoted by $\mathcal{P}$. Observe that the set $\mathcal{P}$ possesses some "dynamic programming conditions", i.e. denoting by $[P]_i$ the i-th row of the matrix P, then for any $i, j \in S$ and $P_{\delta_1}, P_{\delta_2} \in \mathcal{P}$ there exists $P_\delta \in \mathcal{P}$ such that $[P_{\delta_1}]_i = [P_\delta]_i$, $[P_{\delta_2}]_j = [P_\delta]_j$.

We will define affine function $\mathcal{L}_\delta(v)$ and $\mathcal{L}(v)$ from $\mathbb{R}^m \to \mathbb{R}^m$ by

$$\mathcal{L}_\delta(v) = P_\delta v + c_\delta, \qquad \mathcal{L}(v) = \max_{\delta \in \Delta} (P_\delta v + c_\delta),$$

hence the value iteration is given by

$$v^{n+1} = \mathcal{L}(v^n), \quad \text{for} \quad n = 0, 1, \dots, \quad \text{where } v^0 \text{ is the starting vector.}$$

Observe that in virtue of the "dynamic programming conditions" the componentwise maxima always exists.

Considering the matrix P_δ, let $\rho(\delta)$, resp. $\rho_i(\delta)$, be the spectral radius of P_δ, resp. of its diagonal submatrix P_{ii}^δ, and (cf. the Perron–Frobenius theorem) let us denote by $u(\delta)$, resp. $u_i(\delta)$, the nonnegative right eigenvector of P_δ, resp. P_{ii}^δ, corresponding to $\rho(\delta)$, resp. $\rho_i(\delta)$. Similar decomposition is also considered for (column) vectors c_δ, v^n.

Supposing that P_{ii}^δ's are the "largest" submatrices of P_δ having spectral radius $\rho_i(\delta)$ and strictly positive right eigenvectors $u_i(\delta)$'s, let $\nu_i(\delta)$ denote the number of diagonal submatrices of P_δ having spectral radius $\rho_i(\delta)$ that are "accessible" from the submatrix P_{ii}^δ. "Accessibility" is considered in the same way as in Markov chain theory.

Now we are in a position to formulate the following important fact on "uniform block-triangular decomposition" of any $P_\delta, \delta \in \Delta$ (see also Sladký (1980), Rothblum and Whittle (1982), Zijm (1982) and Whittle (1983) for details; observe that part (iii) of the following Proposition is included only for an easier formulation of the next Theorem).

Proposition. There exists a (fixed) permutation of rows and corresponding columns and an (independent of $\delta \in \Delta$ and obtainable by a policy iteration method) block-triangular decomposition of any $P_\delta, \delta \in \Delta$ with the following properties:

(i) P_δ with $\delta \in \Delta$ is upper block-triangular, i.e.

$$P_\delta = \begin{bmatrix} P^\delta_{11} & \cdots & P^\delta_{1h} & \cdots & P^\delta_{1r} & \cdots & P^\delta_{1q} \\ \vdots & \ddots & \vdots & & \vdots & & \vdots \\ 0 & \cdots & P^\delta_{hh} & \cdots & P^\delta_{hr} & \cdots & P^\delta_{hq} \\ \vdots & & \vdots & \ddots & \vdots & & \vdots \\ 0 & \cdots & 0 & \cdots & P^\delta_{rr} & \cdots & P^\delta_{rq} \\ \vdots & & \vdots & & \vdots & \ddots & \vdots \\ 0 & \cdots & 0 & \cdots & 0 & \cdots & P^\delta_{qq} \end{bmatrix}$$

(ii) There exists $\hat{\delta} \in \Delta$ such that for all $i = 1, \ldots, q$ for any $\delta \in \Delta$

$$\begin{aligned} &\rho_i(\hat{\delta}) \geq \rho_i(\delta), \quad \rho_i(\hat{\delta}) \geq \rho_{i+1}(\delta) \quad \text{with} \\ &\rho_i(\hat{\delta}) = \rho_{i+1}(\hat{\delta}) \Rightarrow \nu_i(\hat{\delta}) = \nu_{i+1}(\hat{\delta}) + 1, \quad \text{and} \\ &\rho_i(\hat{\delta}) u_i(\hat{\delta}) = P^{\hat{\delta}}_{ii} u_i(\hat{\delta}) \geq P^\delta_{ii} u_i(\hat{\delta}) \quad \text{where } u_i(\hat{\delta}) > 0, \quad \text{i.e. strictly positive.} \end{aligned}$$

(iii) We assume that

$$\begin{aligned} \rho_i(\hat{\delta}) &> 1 \quad \text{for} \quad i = 1, \ldots, h-1 \\ \rho_i(\hat{\delta}) &= 1 \quad \text{for} \quad i = h, \ldots, r-1 \\ \rho_i(\hat{\delta}) &< 1 \quad \text{for} \quad i = r, \ldots, q. \end{aligned}$$

However, some of the submatrices P^δ_{ii} may be vacuous; so it may happen that e.g. $P_\delta < 1$ for any $\delta \in \Delta$.

Using the "uniform block-triangular decomposition" of the set $\mathcal{P}$ of nonnegative matrices fulfilling the "dynamic programming conditions," we establish conditions under which the set of the fixed points of $\mathcal{L}$ is nonempty and the value iteration converges irrespective of the starting vector v^0. Similar results were also obtained in Koehler (1979), (1990) using different methods. In particular, our approach also enables to give the same characteristics to appropriate submatrices from the set $\mathcal{P}$.

Theorem. Let $\rho(P_\delta) < 1$ for at least one $\delta \in \Delta$. Then employing the uniform block-triangular decomposition of P_δ it holds:

(a) For $i = r, \ldots, q$ $\lim_{n\to\infty} v^n_i = v^\star_i$ exists irrespective of the starting vector v^0, and $v^\star_i$ is a unique solution of $v_i = \max_{\delta\in\Delta}(c^\delta_i + P^\delta_{ii} v_i + \sum_{j=i+1}^{q} P^\delta_{ij} v^\star_j)$.

(b) Let for $k = i+1, \ldots, r-1$ with $k > h$ $\lim_{n\to\infty} v^n_k = v^\star_k < \infty$ exist. Then a finite $\lim_{n\to\infty} v^n_i = v^\star_i$ exists if and only if for any P^δ_{ii} with $\rho(P^\delta_{ii}) = 1$ there exists no w_i such that

$$w_i \leq c^\delta_i + P^\delta_{ii} w_i + \sum_{j=i+1}^{q} P^\delta_{ij} v^\star_j. \tag{1}$$

Furthermore, $v^\star_i$ does not depend on the starting vector v^0.

(c) For $i = 1, \ldots, h-1$ existence of $\lim_{n\to\infty} v_i^n$ depends not only on P_δ's, c_δ's, but also on all v_k^0's with $k \geq i$. In particular, there always exists $v^0 > 0$ such that for $i = 1, \ldots, h-1$ $\lim_{n\to\infty} v_i^n = \infty$. Moreover, if we suppose that condition (1) is satisfied for $i = h, \ldots, r-1$, and that for $k = i+1, \ldots, h-1$ there exist nonempty sets $\mathcal{V}_k^0$ of (columns) vectors v_k^0 such that $\lim_{n\to\infty} v_k^n = v_k^\star$ (with $v_k^\star < \infty$) exists, then $\lim_{n\to\infty} v_i^n = v_i^\star < \infty$ if the following conditions are satisfied:

(i) There exists a solution, denoted $(\hat{w}_i, \hat{\delta}_i)$, of

$$w_i = \max_{\delta\in\Delta} \left(c_i^\delta + P_{ii}^\delta w_i + \sum_{j=i+1}^{q} P_{ij}^\delta v_j^\star \right) \tag{2}$$

such that $\rho(P_{ii}^{\hat{\delta}}) < 1$.

(ii) The starting vector v^0 is selected such that

$$v_k^0 \in \mathcal{V}_k^0 \quad \text{for} \quad k = i+1, \ldots, h-1, \text{ and}$$
$$v_i^0 \leq \hat{w}_i.$$

Corollary. Suppose that in Theorem condition (1) is fulfilled for $i = h, \ldots, r-1$ and condition (2) is satisfied for $i = k, \ldots, h-1$. Then if the starting vector v^0 is selected such that $v_i^0 \leq \hat{w}_i$ for $i = k, \ldots, h-1$, then

$$\lim_{n\to\infty} v_i^n = v_i^\star = \hat{w}_i \quad \text{for all} \quad i = k, \ldots, q.$$

References

Koehler G J (1979) Value convergence in a generalized Markov decision processes. SIAM J Control Optim 17: 180–186

Koehler G J (1990) Relationships between various Markovian decision problem classes. SIAM J Control Optim 28: 1452–1460

Rothblum U G, Whittle P (1982) Growth optimality for branching Markov decision chains. Mathem Oper Res 7: 582–601

Sladký K (1980) Bounds on discrete dynamic programming recursions I, models with non-negative matrices. Kybernetika 16: 526–547

Whittle P (1983) Optimization over Time – Dynamic Programming and Stochastic Control, Vol. II. Wiley, Interscience. London New York

Zijm W. H. M. (1982) Nonnegative Matrices in Dynamic Programming. Mathematical Centre Tract. Amsterdam.

Managerial Attitudes Toward the Valuation of Information Technology

Charles A. Snyder
Marc D. Miller
Department of Management
College of Business
Auburn University, Alabama, USA 36849-5122

As Tom Peters points out, "information is everything" to business organizations in their pursuit of competitive advantage and profitability [Peters, 1992 p. 109]. The intangible aspect of information, however, gives managerial personnel the vague task of placing value on the systems which create, collect, compile, and translate information into a source of profitability. The information systems (IS) literature has dealt with this issue from a quantitative standpoint with varying results [cf Matlin, 1979, West & Courtney, 1993]. However, when senior executives are asked to indicate how information technology expenditures are quantified, they cannot point to a hard measurable quantity that can express the value of the IS [Katz, 1993].

This points to the primary problem in measuring the IT justification behaviors of managers. The way IT investments are quantified is a function of the attitudes of managers who make the investment decisions. Fishbein and Azjen (1980) propose that behavior is a function of the attitudes toward a particular object and the subjective assessment of the attitudes of relevant others in the organization (subjective norm). Hence, a model of attitudes toward the uses of IT in the organization would be a predictor of justification behaviors.

Katz (1993) found that two major shortcomings of devising metrics for IT are that 1) IS management does not often recognize the strategic potential of IT and only focuses on cost savings within the operational realm, and 2) the measures derived to value IT expenses are usually representative of narrow interests within the organization. Dos Santos (1991) found that new technology projects that provide the opportunity for the organization to invest in other riskier projects have more overall value to the organization. Therefore, to fully value the potential and existing worth of IT investment, broad reaching consequences need to be factored into the manager's viewpoint of IT uses.

If managers have a broad strategic vision of the organizational uses of IT, then their behavior of assessing IT investment should encompass a broader, more comprehensive, and hence a more accurate, stance on IT value. The basis for this attitude is that some individuals perceive investments in IT as purely operational, i.e. IT has no competitive value and is purely a method of cost reduction. Others view IT investments as strategic weapons which can further the goals and objectives of the organization. Therefore, this perception could be placed on a continuum which rates the attitude toward IT investment from low strategic value to high strategic value.

Various factors explain the IT valuation attitudes. We hypothesize that four factors are important for explaining one's overall attitude toward the strategic uses of IT; 1) potential for strategic use, 2) potential for overall organizational infrastructure, 3) potential for long term use, and 4) perceptions of control over the investment. The sum of these attitudes are the factors which determine a manager's potential for assessing a broad strategic view of the investment and mark the placement on the continuum.

The attitude that IT has a potential for strategic uses of the investment is important to the alignment of IS efforts to the overall corporate focus and thus to proper valuation of the investment. Jeffery (1989) proposes that organizations that excel at the effective uses of IT focus on three core strategies related to the strategic function: base management, growth management and development management. These three areas represent a broad view of the potential the IT investment and thus must be considered when placing value on the justification of the investment.

The attitude that the IT investment has the potential for an overall enhancement of the infrastructure of the organization is also important to the attitudes toward IT value. Cash, McFarlan, and McKenney (1992) point out that today's business environment indicates the need to form information partnerships with not only your customers and suppliers, but also your competition and the industry as a whole. This points to the need for managers to have a broad view of the impact of IT investment to include not just the effects on the operational value but rather the alliances that IT can help forge. Cash et al. (1992) suggest that managers should ask the question "Is your company vulnerable to new information partnering, and are there ways to forge alliances of your own to preempt them? [page 105]." This question must be considered when determining the overall value of the IT investment.

The third contributing variable to a manager's attitude toward strategic valuation of an IT investment is the perception of potential for long-term use of the investment. Dos Santos (1991) indicates that many IT investments vary a great deal in terms of flexibility in determining how the project proceeds over time. Hence, IT investments are unlike many others which have the bulk of the initial outlay up front. This indicates that it is important for managers to realize the long term potential of both the cost and the benefits. Justifications of IT expenditures must take this into account in order to maximize the strategic benefits. This should result in behaviors which view the IT investment as long term with strategic potential.

Finally, managers must be able to perceive strategic control over the investment. If managers do not perceive that the IT project must be controlled to ensure compliance with the strategic focus of the organization, then justification of the IT expense will not be accurate. Identification of key trends, events, and changes in the firms environment that might influence how the firm functions is vital. Managers making justification decisions must feel confident in their own ability to understand what trends and events are taking place (Milliken, 1990). In addition, Lederer and Sethi (1991) found that if overall business planning is strategic versus tactical, implementation problems are less severe. This indicates that managers who have a strategic control perception of the IT investment and factor that into the justification process should have a more accurate assessment of the return on the expense.

Overall, manager's attitudes toward the expense of IT projects weigh heavily on their ability to exhibit behaviors which result in a strategic quantification of the expected return. Strategic expenses are cost justified on a regular basis in most organizations. They are however justified on the basis of a long-term orientation. This must be the orientation of IT investments and a manager's attitudes toward these investments will determine whether they are being treated as such.

This model of IT valuation provides a different perspective on assessing the means to which IT projects are justified. In the social science tradition, this model needs to be empirically tested with rigorous research methodology. This includes the development of scales which can accurately measure a manager's attitude toward IT investments. As social science research indicates, attitudes are keen predictors of behavioral intentions and further the actual behaviors themselves. The justification of IT investments is a behavior that has a means to be measured through the attitude of the IT expenditure having strategic value.

References will be made available at the conference

CONVERGENCES FOR SEQUENCES OF SETS AND LINEAR MAPPINGS

YVES SONNTAG
Université de Provence, Case X, URA 225-CNRS,
3, Place Victor Hugo, 13331 Marseille Cedex 3, France

CONSTANTIN ZĂLINESCU
University of Iaşi, Faculty of Mathematics,
6600 Iaşi, România

1. Introduction

Let E and F be nontrivial real normed vector spaces and $\mathcal{L}(E,F)$ be the class of continuous linear operators from E into F. Let $\{A;\ A_n,\ n\in \mathbb{N}\}\subset \mathcal{L}(E,F)$. We shall suppose that $A=\lim A_n$ in a certain sense: strong convergence, uniform convergence ...

Let also $\{X;\ X_n,\ n\in \mathbb{N}\}\subset \mathcal{F}(E)$ —the class of nonempty closed subsets of E— and $\{Y;\ Y_n,\ n\in \mathbb{N}\}\subset \mathcal{F}(F)$. We are interested by the following problem: if $X=$ C-$\lim X_n$ [$Y=$ C-$\lim Y_n$] for a given set convergence C (more exactly C = K –Kuratowski convergence, C = M –Mosco convergence or C = AW –Attouch-Wets convergence), do we have $A(X)=$ C-$\lim A_n(X_n)$ [$A^{-1}(Y)=$ C-$\lim A_n^{-1}(Y_n)$]?

Easy examples show that the above problem has not an affirmative answer in general. It will be necessary to impose supplementary conditions on E, F (to be complete or reflexive ...), on A, A_n (to be injective or surjective ...), on X, X_n [Y, Y_n] (to be convex or bounded ...).

We establish general results which are interesting, in our opinion, in stability problems in optimization and variational inequalities.

Of interest is also the particular case $Y=\{v\}$, $Y_n=\{v_n\}$ with $\|v_n-v\|\to 0$. G. Beer (1989) obtained interesting results in the case $F=\mathbb{R}$, but the problem is different when $\dim F\geq 2$. For F of arbitrary dimension we know only the results of I. Schochetman & R. Smith (1992). We remind the main results of this paper.

Theorem (Lemma 4.1 and Theorem 4.2 of [2]). *Let E, F be Hilbert spaces, $\{A;\ A_n, n\in \mathbb{N}\}\subset \mathcal{L}(E,F)$ be such that $(AA^*)^{-1}$ exists and is continuous (A^* is the adjoint of A), $\|A_n-A\|\to 0$ and $v, v_n\in F$, $\|v_n-v\|\to 0$. Then*

i) *$S:=A^{-1}(v)$ is nonempty; there exists n_0 such that, for $n\geq n_0$, $(A_nA_n^*)^{-1}$ exists and is continuous and $S_n:=A_n^{-1}(v_n)$ is nonempty.*

ii) *$S=K$-$\lim S_n$.*

iii) *$s:=A^*(AA^*)^{-1}(v)\in S$, and for $n\geq n_0$, $s_n:=A_n^*(A_nA_n^*)^{-1}(v_n)\in S_n$ and $\|s_n-s\|\to 0$.*

iv) *If $\operatorname{Im} A$ and $\operatorname{Im} A_n$ are closed, s [s_n] is the best approximation of 0 by elements of S [S_n].*

Our aim is to improve this theorem, without adding supplementary hypotheses, in several directions:

1) taking E and F general normed vector spaces,

2) replacing the singletons $\{v\}$, $\{v_n\}$ by arbitrary sets,

3) changing the convergence K in ii) by a much finer convergence – the convergence AW of Attouch-Wets,

4) obtaining similar results for the convergences M and $\dot{\mathrm{K}}$,

5) obtaining partial converses for some results, which show that the hypotheses are minimal.

In the sequel we mention some notations and definitions used later on. The fact that the sequence $(x_n) \subset E$ converges for the norm–topology to $x \in E$ is denoted by $x_n \to x$; if (x_n) converges to x for the weak–topology, we write $x_n \rightharpoonup x$. We remind that for $X,\ X_n \subset E\ (n \in \mathbf{N})$,

$$\liminf X_n = \{x \in E \mid \exists (x_n) \subset (X_n),\ x_n \to x\},$$
$$\limsup X_n = \{x \in E \mid \exists (n_k)\ \exists (x_{n_k}) \subset (X_{n_k}),\ x_{n_k} \to x\},$$
$$w\text{–}\limsup X_n = \{x \in E \mid \exists (n_k)\ \exists (x_{n_k}) \subset (X_{n_k}),\ x_{n_k} \rightharpoonup x\}.$$

Definitions 1.1. Let $X,\ X_n \subset E$.

a) We say that $X = \mathrm{K}\text{–}\lim X_n$ (*Kuratowski convergence*) if

$$(\mathrm{K}_-)\ \ X \subset \liminf X_n \ \text{ and } \ (\mathrm{K}_+)\ \ \limsup X_n \subset X.$$

b) We say that $X = \mathrm{M}\text{–}\lim X_n$ (*Mosco convergence*) if

$$(\mathrm{M}_-)\ \ X \subset \liminf X_n \ \text{ and } \ (\mathrm{M}_+)\ \ w\text{–}\limsup X_n \subset X.$$

Definitions 1.2. Let $X,\ X_n \in \mathcal{F}(E)\ (n \in \mathbf{N})$.

a) We say that $X = \mathrm{W}\text{–}\lim X_n$ (*Wijsman convergence*) if $d(u, X_n) \to d(u, X)\ \forall u \in E$,

b) We say that $X = \mathrm{AW}\text{–}\lim X_n$ (*Attouch–Wets convergence*) if

$$\sup_{u \in B} |d(u, X_n) - d(u, X)| \to 0 \quad \forall B \subset E,\ B \text{ nonempty and bounded.}$$

It is easy to see that AW $\Rightarrow$ W $\Rightarrow$ K $\Leftarrow$ M. The convergence AW is much finer than W, K and M on $\mathcal{C}(E) := \{A \in \mathcal{F}(E) \mid A \text{is convex}\}$.

In the sequel we shall use several hypotheses on $\{A; A_n, n \in \mathbf{N}\} \subset \mathcal{L}(E, F)$ (A' being the transpose of A):

(H1) $A_n x \to Ax\ \forall x \in E$ (strong convergence of (A_n) to A),

(H2) $x_n \to x \ \Rightarrow\ A_n x_n \to Ax$ (continuous convergence of (A_n) to A),

(H3) $x_n \rightharpoonup x \ \Rightarrow\ A_n x_n \rightharpoonup Ax$ (w–continuous convergence of (A_n) to A),

(H4) $A'_n \psi \to A' \psi\ \forall \psi \in F'$ (strong convergence of (A'_n) to A').

(H5) $\exists \alpha > 0\ \exists n_0 \in \mathbf{N}\ \forall n \ge n_0\ \forall x \in E : \ \|A_n x\| \ \ge \alpha \|x\|$,

(H6) $\exists \alpha > 0\ \exists n_0 \in \mathbf{N}\ \forall n \ge n_0 : \ A_n(U_E) \supset \alpha U_F$,

unde $U_E := \{x \in E \mid \|x\| = 1\}$. The condition (H5) is a kind of uniform injectivity of (A_n), while (H6) is a kind of uniform surjectivity of (A_n).

Definition 1.3. Let $\{A; A_n,\ n \in \mathbf{N}\} \subset \mathcal{L}(E, F)$. We say that $A = \mathrm{gr}\text{–}\lim A_n$, ***graphical convergence***, if (H1) and (H4) hold.

2. Results concerning Kuratowski and Mosco convergences

Consider the families $\{A; A_n, n \in \mathbb{N}\} \subset \mathcal{L}(E,F)$, $\{X; X_n, n \in \mathbb{N}\} \subset \mathcal{F}(E)$ and $\{Y; Y_n, n \in \mathbb{N}\} \subset \mathcal{F}(F)$. In this section we are interested to obtain the convergence of $(A(X_n))$ to $A(X)$ and of $(A^{-1}(Y_n))$ to $A^{-1}(Y)$ in the sense of Kuratowski or Mosco when (X_n) converges to X and (Y_n) converges to Y in the same sense. Of course we impose additional conditions on the sequence of operators and, sometimes, on the sequence of sets. Generally we have converse theorems, which means that our conditions are minimal.

The first result refers to Mosco convergence.

Theorem 2.1. *Suppose that $A = \text{gr-lim}\, A_n$, $X_n \subset X$ for every n and X is convex and bounded. If $X = \text{M-}\lim X_n$ then $\overline{A(X)} = \text{M-}\lim A_n(X_n)$.*

The result of Theorem 2.1 may be strengthened if we know that E is reflexive.

Theorem 2.2. *Suppose that E is a reflexive Banach space, $A = \text{gr-}\lim A_n$ and (X_n) is uniformly bounded (i.e. there exists a ball containing all X_n). If $X = \text{M-}\lim X_n$ then $A(X) = \text{M-}\lim A_n(X_n)$.*

We have a partial converse of Theorem 2.2.

Proposition 2.1. *Assume that F is reflexive and $\overline{A(X)} = \text{M-}\lim A_n(X_n)$ whenever $X = \text{M-}\lim X_n$ and (X_n) is uniformly bounded. Then $\{A; A_n, n \in \mathbb{N}\}$ satisfies (H2) and (H3). Moreover, if E is reflexive then $A = \text{gr-lim}\, A_n$.*

Now we want to establish results for Mosco and Kuratowski convergences of direct images and inverse images without imposing boundedness conditions on the sets of the sequences. So one can apply these results for sequences of cones, linear subspaces, etc. We shall need to use the hypotheses (H5) or (H6).

Theorem 2.3. *Suppose that $\{A; A_n, n \in \mathbb{N}\}$ satisfies (H2), (H5) and $\limsup A_n(E) \subset A(E)$. If $X = \text{K-}\lim X_n$ then $A(X) = \text{K-}\lim A_n(X_n)$.*

We have the following converse of Theorem 2.3.

Proposition 2.2. *Suppose that $\overline{A(X)} = \text{K-}\lim A_n(X_n)$ whenever $X = \text{K-}\lim X_n$. Then $\{A; A_n, n \in \mathbb{N}\}$ satisfies (H2) and $\limsup A_n(E) \subset \overline{A(E)}$. Moreover, if $A \neq 0$ then (H5) holds, too.*

For Mosco convergence we have the following result.

Theorem 2.4. *Suppose that E is reflexive, $\{A; A_n, n \in \mathbb{N}\}$ satisfies (H5) and $A = \text{gr-}\lim A_n$. If $X = \text{M-}\lim X_n$ then $A(X) = \text{M-}\lim A_n(X_n)$.*

We have the following partial converse of Theorem 2.4.

Proposition 2.3. *Suppose that $\overline{A(X)} = \text{M-}\lim A_n(X_n)$ whenever $X = \text{M-}\lim X_n$, and F is reflexive. Then $\{A; A_n, n \in \mathbb{N}\}$ satisfies (H2) and (H3). Moreover, if $A \neq 0$ then (H5) holds, too.*

We consider now inverse images.

Theorem 2.6. *Suppose that $\{A; A_n, n \in \mathbb{N}\}$ satisfies (H2) and (H6). If $Y = \text{K-}\lim Y_n$ then $A^{-1}(Y) = \text{K-}\lim A_n^{-1}(Y_n)$.*

The conditions on $\{A; A_n, n \in \mathbb{N}\}$ in Theorem 2.6 are minimal, as the next result shows.

Proposition 2.4. *Suppose that* $A^{-1}(Y) = \text{K-}\lim A_n^{-1}(Y_n)$ *whenever* $Y = \text{K-}\lim Y_n$. *Then* $\{A; A_n, n \in \mathbf{N}\}$ *satisfies (H2) and (H6).*

Let us give now similar results for Mosco convergence.

Theorem 2.7. *Suppose that* $\{A; A_n, n \in \mathbf{N}\}$ *satisfies (H1), (H3) and (H6). If* $Y = \text{M-}\lim Y_n$ *then* $A^{-1}(Y) = \text{M-}\lim A_n^{-1}(Y_n)$.

A partial converse of Theorem 2.7 is

Proposition 2.5. *Suppose that* $A^{-1}(Y) = \text{M-}\lim A_n^{-1}(Y_n)$ *whenever* $Y = \text{M-}\lim Y_n$. *Then* $\{A; A_n, n \in \mathbf{N}\}$ *satisfies (H3) and (H6).*

3. Results concerning Attouch–Wets convergence

The first result deals with images of sets, while the second one with inverse images.

Theorem 3.1. *Suppose that* $\|A_n - A\| \to 0$ *and there exists* $\alpha > 0$ *such that* $\|Ax\| \geq \alpha\|x\|$ *for every* $x \in E$. *If* $X = \text{AW-}\lim X_n$ *then* $\overline{A(X)} = \text{AW-}\lim \overline{A_n(X_n)}$.

Theorem 3.2. *Suppose that* $\|A_n - A\| \to 0$, (A_n) *satisfies (H6) and there exists* $\alpha > 0$ *such that* $A(U_E) \supset \alpha U_F$. *If* $Y = \text{AW-}\lim Y_n$ *then* $A^{-1}(Y) = \text{AW-}\lim A_n^{-1}(Y_n)$.

In the proof of the above two theorems we used the following characterization of AW–convergence given by Shunmugaraj (1990) (see also Y Sonntag & C. Zălinescu (1992)):

$$X = \text{AW-}\lim X_n \quad \Leftrightarrow \quad \begin{cases} \forall (x_n) \subset (X_n),\ (x_n) \text{ bounded} : d(x_n, X) \to 0, \\ \forall (x_n) \subset X,\ (x_n) \text{ bounded} : d(x_n, X_n) \to 0. \end{cases}$$

Corollary 3.3 (Beer (1989). *Let* $\{\varphi; \varphi_n, n \in \mathbf{N}\} \subset E'$, $\varphi \neq 0$ *and* $\alpha \in \mathbf{R}$.

i) *If* $\varphi = w^*\text{-}\lim \varphi_n$ *and* $(\|\varphi_n\|)$ *is bounded then* $\{x \mid \varphi(x) = \alpha\} = \text{K-}\lim\{x \mid \varphi_n(x) = \alpha\}$.

ii) *If* $\varphi = \lim \varphi_n$ *then* $\{x \mid \varphi(x) = \alpha\} = \text{M-}\lim\{x \mid \varphi_n(x) = \alpha\}$.

iii) *If* $\varphi = \lim \varphi_n$ *then* $\{x \mid \varphi(x) = \alpha\} = \text{AW-}\lim\{x \mid \varphi_n(x) = \alpha\}$.

The above results are then applied for establishing some stability results in optimization.

References

[1] Beer G (1989) Convergence of continuous linear functionals and their level sets. Arch. Math. 52: 482–489

[2] Schochetman I, Smith R (1992) Convergence of best approximations from unbounded sets. J. Math. Anal. Appl. 166: 112–128

[3] Shunmugaraj P (1990) "On stability aspects in optimization." Thesis, Indian Insitute of Technology Bombay, India

[4] Sonntag Y, Zălinescu C (1992) Set convergences: a survey and a classification. presented to Colloq. Int. Anal. Multivoque et Unilatérale, CIRM (submitted)

Solving the "Business System Planning"-Problem Using Specialized Branch & Bound Algorithms

Dieter M. Spahni
Institut für Wirtschaftsinformatik
Universität Bern
Hallerstrasse 6, CH-3012 Bern

The "Business System Planning"-Problem

IBM's Business Systems Planning (BSP) (cf. IBM (1980)) is the best known method for strategic IS planning which is proposed as a first step in the information engineering concept. It primarily uses matrices which show associations between processes and data classes. The elements of the BSP-matrix show the symbol C for processes creating and U for those using data classes (Fig. 1a).

The objective of BSP is determining independent subsystems in such a way that almost all symbols are positioned within the submatrices at the main diagonal of a rearranged BSP-matrix. All C-entries must reside within those submatrices in order to guarantee the assignment of a data class to the process that is creating it.

	D1	D2	D3	D4	D5	D6	D7	D8	D9	D10
P1				U	C					
P2					U			U	U	U
P3		U	U	U						
P4	C			C						
P5					U	C	C			
P6		C	C	C						
P7				C		U	U			
P8				C						
P9					U	C	C			
P10		C	C	C						
P11				C		U	U			
P12								C		
P13										U
P14								U	U	U
P15					U				U	
P16									U	C
P17									C	

Fig. 1a: Original BSP-Matrix (cf. Martin (1982))

	D9	D10	D8	D6	D7	D5	D1	D4	D2	D3
P17	C									
P16	U	C								
P13		U								
P12			C							
P2	U	U	U			U				
P14	U	U	U							
P9				C	C	U				
P5				C	C	U				
P1						C		U		
P15	U					U				
P4							C	C		
P6								C	C	C
P10								C	C	C
P7				U	U			C		
P8							C	C		
P11				U	U			C		
P3								U	U	U

Fig. 1b: Rearranged BSP-Matrix

Solving the BSP-problem with mixed integer programming

As a first approach, the problem can be modelled as a (modified) quadratic assignment problem, in which each row and each column has to be assigned to a subsystem. One of the techniques for solving this type of problem is to linearize it and then to apply mixed-integer programming. With this approach one has to fix the number of subsystems; the user is allowed to specify upper or lower bounds on the size of the subsystems (cf. Knolmayer 1993).

Solving the BSP-problem with boolean linear programming

The application of the Cluster Identification Algorithm (cf. Kusiak (1987)) allows to identify the set of submatrices fulfilling the constraint that all C-entries must reside within the created subsystems. These submatrices are called *baseblocks* because they represent the first solution to the original problem with the most and smallest subsystems possible. All other possible solutions must be unions of these baseblocks. Thus, the BSP problem can be modelled as a boolean linear model with $\frac{N(N-1)}{2}$ variables and $\frac{N(N-1)(N-2)}{2}$ constraints:

$$\forall i,j,k \in \{1,\dots,N\}: i<j<k$$

max $\quad \sum c_{ij}x_{ij}$

subject to
$$\left.\begin{array}{l} x_{ij}+x_{ik}-2x_{jk}\le 1 \\ x_{ij}+x_{jk}-2x_{ik}\le 1 \\ x_{ik}+x_{jk}-2x_{ij}\le 1 \end{array}\right. \quad \text{for all} \left\{\begin{array}{l} i=1,\dots,N-2 \\ j=i+1,\dots,N-1 \\ k=j+1,\dots,N \end{array}\right.$$

$$x_{ij}\in\{0,1\}$$

where
$$x_{ij}=\begin{cases}1 & \text{if baseblock i is united with baseblock j}\\ 0 & \text{else}\end{cases}$$

$c_{ij}=u_{ij}-p\cdot e_{ij}$ where

- u_{ij} number of U-entries between baseblocks i and j
- e_{ij} number of empty entries between baseblocks i and j
- p weighting factor, e.g. p=0.3

Boolean linear programs may be solved by applying standard software. However, several authors proposed specialized algorithms for their solution (cf. Balas (1965))

Solving the BSP-problem with a specialized Branch-and-Bound Algorithm

There may appear invalid solutions with respect to constraints as well as permutations of unique solutions within a set. Hence it is of importance to design an enumeration technique producing the smallest set of all possible solutions. The proposed algorithm creates the set of all valid solutions *without any duplicates* as shown by the enumeration tree in Fig. 2.

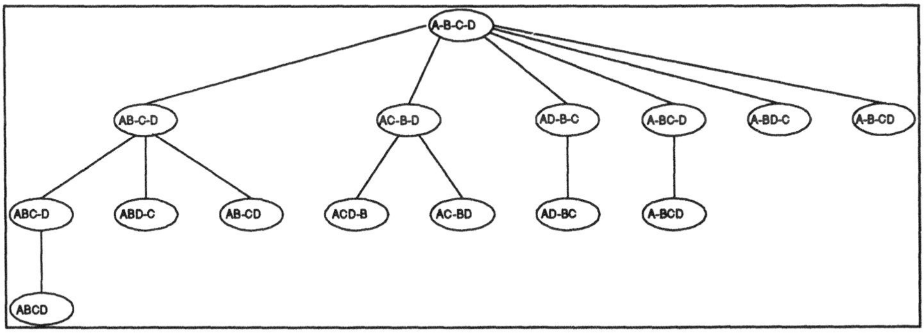

Fig. 2: All possible unions of 4 baseblocks A, B, C and D shown as enumeration tree

The number of nodes S_N within a tree for N baseblocks is

$$S_N = \sum_{r=2}^{N+1} f(N, r)$$

$$f(N,r) = \begin{cases} 1 & r=2 \\ 0 & r>N+1 \\ (r-1)\cdot f(N-1,r)+f(N-1,r-1) & else \end{cases}$$

N	S_N
1	1
2	2
3	5
4	15
5	52
6	203
7	877
8	4 140
9	21 147
10	115 975
11	678 570

Considering the properties of the enumeration tree, the computational resources needed can be significantly reduced by eliminating superfluous node evaluations. The most important property allows a permanent lowering of the objective function value of node X while evaluating its successors from left to right because *a union of two baseblocks along one arc from node X to node Y does no more appear on any subtree on the right-hand side of node X.*

Computational experiences

Depending on the chosen branch strategy, e.g. *Newest Bound First* (NBF) or *Best Bound First* (BBF), time and storage requirements differ vastly. For each number of baseblocks N, 100 problems were randomly generated. Solving these problems with the implemented prototype showed that BBF always required the least node evaluations but much storage; in comparison NBF used more node evaluations but minimal storage. The also implemented *Next Best Bound* (NBB) strategy resulted in an only moderate increase in both storage requirements and number of nodes evaluated. The results obtained are presented in Table 1.

The prototype was written in QBASIC; it evaluates about 2 500 nodes per minute running on a 486/DX2 PC and thus solves problems with 10 baseblocks in less than 5 seconds. First experiences with an appropriate implementation in C show a speed-up factor of up to 10.

		Number of evaluated nodes			Maximum number of nodes on stack (maximum storage used)		
Number of baseblocks N	Number of possible solutions S_N	Best Bound First BBF	Next Best Bound NBB	NBB compared to BBF	Newest Bound First NBF	Nest Best Bound NBB	NBB compared to NBF
6	203	11.47	12.68	11%	3.54	3.81	8%
7	877	18.15	21.81	20%	4.33	5.09	18%
8	4 140	39.32	45.87	17%	5.15	6.34	23%
9	21 147	75.76	90.79	20%	6.33	7.90	25%
10	115 975	159.54	188.72	18%	7.09	9.39	32%
11	678 570	269.26	316.11	17%	7.96	10.79	35%

Table 1: Prototype performance for 100 randomly generated problems for each number of baseblocks N

References

Balas E (1965) An Additive Algorithm for Solving Linear Programs with Zero-One Variables. Operations Research 13: 517-546

IBM (1980) Business Systems Planning: Handbuch zur Planung von Informationssystemen, IBM-Form GE 12-1400-1, IBM Germany

Knolmayer G (1993) The Application of Mixed Integer Programming to the "Business Systems Planning"-Problem, Paper presented at the DGOR/NSOR Conference, Amsterdam.

Kusiak A, Chow W.S (1987) An Efficient Cluster Identification Algorithms. IEEE Transactions on Systems, Man, and Cybernetics 17: 696-699

Martin J (1982) Strategic Data-Planning Methodologies. Englewood Cliffs. Prentice-Hall

A KNOWLEDGE-BASED ENVIRONMENT FOR DECISION SUPPORT

Zorka Strezova
MICROTEL - BULGARIA FOUNDATION
16 A, Al.Batenberg st., 1000 Sofia, Bulgaria

Introduction

A broad spectrum of ideas, approaches and tools for computer-support in complex problem solving has been proposed over the last decade and widely used in the design and implementation of decision support systems (DSS). The recent developments in the decision support (DS) technology are related to integrated use of methods and tools of modelling, simulation and artificial intelligence aiming at the design of intelligent DS environments.

In the paper are summarized the results of the design and implementation of an intelligent modelling and simulation environment for complex, ill-defined problem solving support. The architecture of an integrated software system comprising data, model, knowledge bases and a knowledge-based model management system has been designed. A problem-dependent software system SIMOS PAM has been implemented in a number of policy analysis applications.

Decision Support Cycle: Phases and Procedures

Following concepts and frameworks for DSS design launched in the 80's (Sprague and Carlson (1982), Sol (1983), etc., an extended definition of DS environment has been suggested: *intelligent modelling and simulation environment in complex, ill-defined problem solving support* (Strezova (1986).

A framework comprising a set of procedures supporting the problem solving process has been developed. The general phases of the DS cycle according to this framework are as follows: A. Problem Statement. B. Model Development. C. Model Assessment and Selection. D. Decision Support.

The first stage of the phase B concerns the design of a general model of the problem stated and identification of sets of model variables. It is next supposed that a set of conditions, representing problem states, defines a set of modelled alternatives of the problem stated; more than one parametrization is required to describe this set of alternatives.

The phase C consists in multimeasure cross-validation, assessment and selection of the set of modelled alternatives. The stages of this phase are as follows:

a) simulation of the set of modelled alternatives
b) 1st validation: screening procedure (Walker (1986)
c) 2nd validation: sensitivity analysis I
d) 3rd validation: sensitivity analysis II (metamodelling via regression analysis)

The phase D consists in analysis of the set of feasible alternatives via hypothesing future decision states of the problem modelled and a choice of the "best feasible" alternative for implementation.

Integrated Software Environment: Architecture and Functions

A generalized software system (GSS) intended for supporting the phases and the stages of the DS cycle has been designed. The GSS architecture consists of general purpose modules as is shown in Fig.1.

The Model Base (MB) is built as a pool of models comprising:

a) generative models (MS/OR models) intended to generate decision alternatives;

b) evaluative models (simulation, statistical and models of values) intended to validation and assessment of modelled alternatives. A Model Management System (MMS) provides set of functions such as model formulation, model analysis, model interpretation.

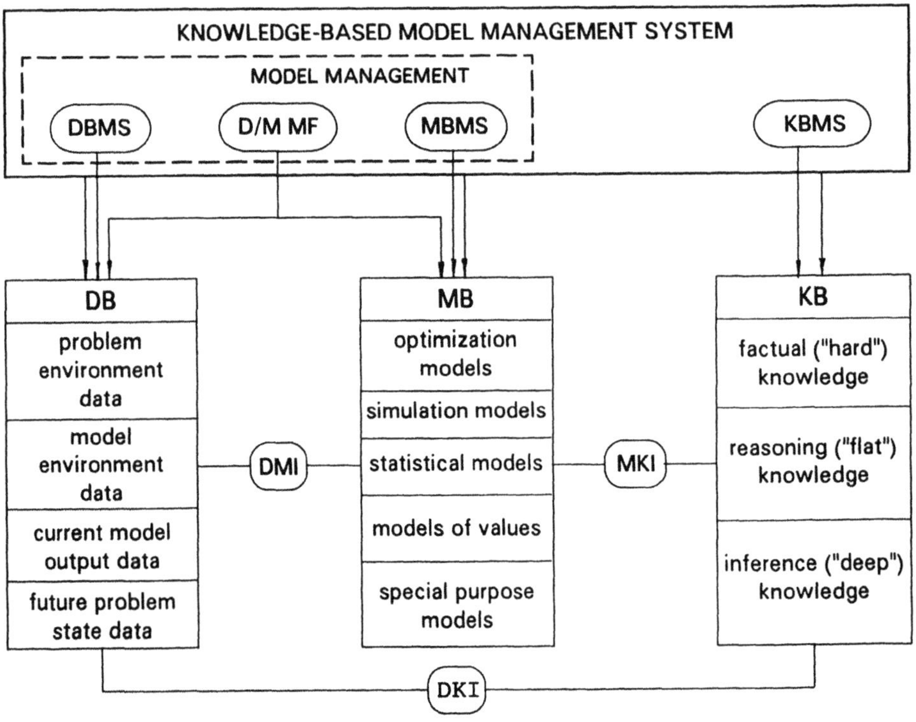

FIG. 1 Generalized Software System Structure

The Knowledge Base (KB) design process consists of phases and stages as follows:

A. Design (or choice) of knowledge shell.

B. Knowledge acquisition phase comprising two stages:

B.1. Knowledge shell parameterizing;
B.2. Parameter estimation stage.
C. Inference knowledge generation.

Designed in such a way the KB is intended to support the modelling stages of the problem solving cycle. The KB provides *metaknowledge* used for model building, model assessment, validation, comparison and selection of feasible alternatives. The integrated software system for management of the pool of DB, MB, KB (this pool represents an extended KB), is considered as a *Knowledge-Based Model Management System*.

Application

Following the GSS architecture a problem dependent software system SIMOS PAM has been developed. The model shell of SIMOS PAM comprises program packages such as Discriminant Analysis, Mixed Integer Programming, GPSS, CSMP, LRA and a number of special purpose models. The knowledge shell embodies sets of deductive, numerical and testing rules, and sets of hypotheses concerning possible future states of a class of applications.

The concepts, procedures and systems developed have been implemented in policy analysis applications concerning the transition to new political and economic structures in Bulgaria.

Conclusion and Research Directions

A knowledge-based approach to the design of DS environment has been suggested and implemented. The notion "knowledge" is considered in a larger sense: data, models, algorithms, solution procedures, operators, rules, options, heuristics, etc.

A number of problems related to the design of intelligent DS environments represents a challenge for further research: model management topics (Chang, Holsapple, Whinston (1993), KB validation & verification, design of distributed intelligent DSS, techniques for combined use of methods and tools of information and AI technologies, etc.

References

Chang, A-M., C.W. Holsapple, A.B. Whinston (1993). Model management issues and directions. Decision Support Systems, 9, 1.

Sol, H.G. (1983). Process and Tools for Decision Support Inferences for Future Developments, North-Holland.

Sprague, R.H., E.D. Carlson (1982). Building Effective Decision Support Systems, Prentice Hall, Englewood Cliffs.

Strezova, Z. (1986). Validation in ill-defined policy analysis. Proceedings of the 5th IFAC/IFORS Dynamic Modelling Conference, Budapest, 1986, Pergamon Press.

Walker, W.E. (1986). The use of screening in policy analysis. Management Science, 32, 4.

Optimal on-line detection of multiple parameter changes

Krzysztof Szajowski
Institute of Mathematics
Technical University of Wrocław
Wybrzeże Wyspiańskiego 27
PL-50-370 Wrocław, Poland

Suppose a random sequence $X = \{X_n, n \in \mathbb{N}\}$ appears consecutively. There are two random moments of time θ_1 and θ_2, independent of X. A probability characteristics of the observable random variables X change for the first time at instant θ_1 and for the second time at instant θ_2. We assume that the sequence X is Markov process given θ_1 and θ_2. Our objective is to find the strategy which immediately detects the distribution changes with maximal probability. The relevant problem of the double optimal stopping is constructed. The optimal strategy is found and the corresponding maximal probability is calculated.

Preliminaries

Suppose a random sequence $X = \{X_n, n \in \mathbb{N}\}$, $\mathbb{N} = \{0, 1, 2, \ldots\}$, is observed sequentially. There are Markov processes $X^i = \{(X_n^i, \mathcal{F}_n, \mu_x^i), x \in \mathbb{E}, n \in \mathbb{N}\}$, $i = 1, 2, 3$, and two random moments of time, θ_1 and θ_2, independent of the process. The random sequence is the result of switching between X^1 and X^2 in moment θ_1 and from X^2 to X^3 in θ_2. Our objective is to detect immediately this moments.

Such question arises in the quality control. The automat which produces some details changes his parameters. It makes that the details change their quality. Production can be divided to three sorts. Assuming that at the beginning of production process the quality is highest, from some moment θ_1 the products should be classified to lower sort and beginning with θ_2 the details should be categorized as at lowest quality. We want to detect the moments of these changes.

Shiryaev (1978) considered the disorder problem with one disorder when the observed random variables were independent given the disorder moment and when the mean distance between disorder time and the moment of its detection was minimized. The probability maximizing approach to the problem was used by Bojdecki (1979) and the stopping time which is in a given neighbourhood of the moment of disorder with maximal probability was found. The problem with two disorders was considered by Yoshida (1983) and Szajowski (1992). Yoshida (1983) solved the problem of optimal stopping the observation of the process X so as to maximize the probability that the distance between θ_i, $i = 1, 2$, and the moment of disorder will not exceed a given number (for each disorder independently) under assumption that X is Markov process given θ_1 and θ_2. The author construct the strategy which stops the process between the first and the second disorder with maximal probability. The reference to other papers treated variations of the disorder problem can be found in Szajowski (1992). The general approach to the disorder problem with one disorder moment was considered by Pelkowitz (1987).

In the present paper the probability maximizing approach to the optimal stopping developed by Bojdecki (1979) is extended to solve the double stopping problem (see Haggstrom (1967), Nikolaev (1979)) arising in the quickest detection of double disorders. In the next section the problem is formulated in a rigorous manner. The problem is reduced to the optimal stopping problem for the doubly indexed stochastic sequence and the solution of the double stopping problem is given.

The double "disorder problem"

Let $X = \{X_n, \in \mathbb{N}\}$, $\mathbb{N} = \{0,1,2,\ldots\}$, defined on $(\Omega, \mathcal{F}, \mathbf{P})$, be a potentially observable sequence of r.v.'s with values in $(\mathbb{E}, \mathcal{B})$, where $\mathbb{E}$ is a subset of the real line. Assume that the epochs of distributional changes are $\mathbb{N}$ valued $\mathcal{F}$ measurable r.v. θ_1 and θ_2, independent of X having the distribution

$$\mathbf{P}(\theta_1 = j) = p_1^{j-1} q_1, \ \mathbf{P}(\theta_2 = k | \theta_1 = j) = p_2^{k-j-1} q_2, \tag{1}$$

where $j = 1, 2, \ldots$, $k = j+1, j+2, \ldots$ and $p_i + q_i = 1$, $i = 1, 2$.

Suppose that on $(\Omega, \mathcal{F}, \mathbf{P})$ Markov processes $X^i = \{(X_n^i, \mathcal{F}_n, \mu_x^i)\}$, $i = 1, 2, 3$, are defined and we have

$$X_n = \begin{cases} X_n^1 & \text{if } n < \theta_1, \\ X_n^2 & \text{if } \theta_1 \le n < \theta_2, \\ X_n^3 & \text{if } n \ge \theta_2. \end{cases} \tag{2}$$

The measures μ_x^i, $i = 1,2,3$, are absolutely continuous with respect to some fixed measure μ_x and satisfy the following relations: $\mu_x^i(dy) = f_x^i(y)\mu_x(dy)$, where $f_x^i(\cdot) \ne f_x^j(\cdot)$, $i \ne j$ and $f_x^{i+1}(y)/f_x^i(y) < \infty$, $i = 1, 2$ for every $x, y \in \mathbb{E}$. The distribution of θ_i, $i = 1, 2$, is given by (1) and the measures μ_x^i, $i = 1, 2, 3$, $x \in \mathbb{E}$ are known. On the basis of the distribution of θ_1, θ_2 and measures μ_x^i, $i = 1, 2, 3$, $x \in \mathbb{E}$, we calculate the finite dimensional distributions of the observed process given $X_0 = x$ and we construct the probability measure $\mathbf{P}_x$ on $\mathcal{F} = \sigma(\bigcup_{n=0}^{\infty} \mathcal{F}_n)$, where $\mathcal{F}_n = \sigma(X_0, X_1, \ldots, X_n)$, $n = 0, 1, \ldots$.

Let $\mathcal{S}$ denote the set of all stopping times with respect to the filtration $(\mathcal{F}_n)$, $n = 0, 1, \ldots$ and $\mathcal{T} = \{(\tau, \sigma) : \tau < \sigma, \ \tau, \sigma \in \mathcal{S}\}$. Let us formulate $D_{d_1 d_2}$ problem. We want to determine a pair of stopping times $(\tau^*, \sigma^*) \in \mathcal{T}$ such that for every $x \in \mathbb{E}$

$$\begin{aligned} &\mathbf{P}_x(\tau^* < \sigma^* < \infty, \ |\theta_1 - \tau^*| \le d_1, \ |\theta_2 - \sigma^*| \le d_2) \\ &\qquad = \sup_{(\tau,\sigma) \in \mathcal{T}} \mathbf{P}_x(\tau < \sigma < \infty, |\theta_1 - \tau| \le d_1, |\theta_2 - \sigma| \le d_2). \end{aligned} \tag{3}$$

The double "disorder problem" vs. the double optimal stopping of Markov process

Denote $\mathcal{T}_m = \{(\tau, \sigma) \in \mathcal{T} : \tau \ge m\}$, $\mathcal{T}_{mn} = \{(\tau, \sigma) \in \mathcal{T} : \tau = m, \sigma \ge n\}$ and $\mathcal{S}_m = \{\tau \in \mathcal{S} : \tau \ge m\}$. Let us denote $\mathcal{F}_{mn} = \mathcal{F}_n$, $m, n \in \mathbb{N}$, $m \le n$. We define for $m, n \in \mathbb{N}$, $m < n$ and $x \in \mathbb{E}$ the two-parameter stochastic sequence $\xi_{mn}(x) = \mathbf{P}_x(|\theta_1 - m| \le d_1, |\theta_2 - n| \le d_2 | \mathcal{F}_{mn})$. We can consider the optimal stopping problem of $\{\xi_{mn}(x)\}$ on $\mathcal{T}_{mn}$ for $m < n$, $m, n \in \mathbb{N}$. A compound stopping variable (τ^*, σ^*) is said to be optimal in $\mathcal{T}_m$ (or $\mathcal{T}_{mn}$) if $\mathbf{E}_x \xi_{\tau^* \sigma^*} = \sup_{(\tau,\sigma) \in \mathcal{T}_m} \mathbf{E}_x \xi_{\tau\sigma}$ (or $\mathbf{E}_x \xi_{\tau^* \sigma^*} = \sup_{(\tau,\sigma) \in \mathcal{T}_{mn}} \mathbf{E}_x \xi_{\tau\sigma}$). Let us define $\eta_{mn}(x) = \operatorname*{esssup}_{(\tau,\sigma) \in \mathcal{T}_{mn}} \mathbf{E}(\xi_{\tau\sigma} | \mathcal{F}_{mn})$ and $\eta_m = \mathbf{E}_x(\eta_{mm+1} | \mathcal{F}_m)$. If we put $\xi_{m\infty} = 0$, then

$$\eta_{mn} = \operatorname*{esssup}_{(\tau,\sigma) \in \mathcal{T}_{mn}} \mathbf{P}_x(|\theta_1 - m| \le d_1, |\theta_2 - n| \le d_2 | \mathcal{F}_{mn}).$$

From the theory of optimal stopping for double indexed processes (cf. Haggstrom (1967), Nikolaev (1981)) the sequence η_{mn} satisfies $\eta_{mn} = \max\{\xi_{mn}, \mathbf{E}(\eta_{mn+1} | \mathcal{F}_{mn})\}$. Moreover, if $\sigma_m^* = \inf\{n > m : \eta_{mn} = \xi_{mn}\}$, then (m, σ_m^*) is optimal in $\mathcal{T}_{mn}$ and $\eta_{mn} = \mathbf{E}_x(\xi_{m\sigma_m^*} | \mathcal{F}_{mn})$ a.e..

Let us define

$$V_m = \operatorname*{esssup}_{\tau \in \mathcal{S}_m} \mathbf{E}_x(\eta_\tau | \mathcal{F}_m). \tag{4}$$

Then $V_m = \max\{\eta_m, \mathbf{E}_x(V_{m+1}|\mathcal{F}_m)\}$ a.e. and we define $\tau_n^* = \inf\{k \geq n : V_k = \eta_k\}$. The strategy τ_0^* is the optimal strategy of the first stop.

This construction describe the method of solving the considered "disorder problem".

Immediate detection of the first and the second disorder

For the sake of simplicity we shall confine ourselves to the case $d_1 = d_2 = 0$. It will be easily seen how to generalize the solution of the problem to solve $D_{d_1 d_2}$ for $d_1 > 0$ or $d_2 > 0$. First of all we construct multidimensional Markov chains such that ξ_{mn} and η_m will be the functions of their states. Let us introduce notation needed in the sequel (cf. Yoshida (1983), Szajowski (1992)). $\Pi_n^1(x) = \mathbf{P}_x(\theta_1 > n|\mathcal{F}_n)$, $\Pi_n^2(x) = \mathbf{P}_x(\theta_2 > n|\mathcal{F}_n)$, $\Pi_{mn}(x) = \mathbf{P}_x(\theta_1 = m, \theta_n > n|\mathcal{F}_{mn})$, for $m, n = 1, 2, \ldots$, $m < n$ and

$$\begin{aligned}
H(t,u,\alpha,\beta) &= \alpha p_1 f_t^1(u) + [p_2(\beta-\alpha) + q_1\alpha] f_t^2(u) + [1-\beta+q_2(\beta-\alpha)] f_t^3(u) \\
\Pi^1(t,u,\alpha,\beta) &= p_1 \alpha f_t^1(u)(H(t,u,\alpha,\beta))^{-1} \\
\Pi^2(t,u,\alpha,\beta) &= \{p_1\alpha f_t^1(u) + [\alpha q_1 + (\beta-\alpha)p_2] f_t^2(u)\}(H(t,u,\alpha,\beta))^{-1} \\
\Pi(t,u,\alpha,\beta,\gamma) &= p_2 \gamma f_t^2(u)(H(t,u,\alpha,\beta))^{-1}.
\end{aligned}$$

The basic formulae used in the proof of the theorem are given in

Lemma 1. *For each $x \in \mathbb{E}$, $m, n = 1, 2, \ldots$, $m < n$, and each Borel function $u : \Re \to \Re$ the following formulae hold*

$$\Pi_{n+1}^1(x) = \Pi^1(X_n, X_{n+1}, \Pi_n^1(x), \Pi_n^2(x)) \tag{5}$$

$$\Pi_{n+1}^2(x) = \Pi^2(X_n, X_{n+1}, \Pi_n^1(x), \Pi_n^2(x)) \tag{6}$$

$$\Pi_{m\,n+1}(x) = \Pi(X_n, X_{n+1}, \Pi_n^1(x), \Pi_n^2(x), \Pi_{m\,n}(x)) \tag{7}$$

with boundary condition $\Pi_0^1(x) = \Pi_0^2(x) = 0$, $\Pi_{m\,m}(x) = \frac{q_1 f_{X_{m-1}}^2(X_m)}{p_1 f_{X_{m-1}}^1(X_m)} \Pi_n^1(x)$ *and*

$$\mathbf{E}_x(u(X_{n+1})|\mathcal{F}_n) = \int_{\mathbb{E}} u(y) H(X_n, y, \Pi_n^1(x), \Pi_n^2(x)) \mu_{X_n}(dy). \tag{8}$$

By the above we have

$$\xi_{m\,n}(x) = \mathbf{P}_x(\theta_1 = m, \theta_2 = n|\mathcal{F}_{m\,n}) = \frac{q_2}{p_2} \Pi_{m\,n}(x) \frac{f_{X_{n-1}}^3(X_n)}{f_{X_{n-1}}^2(X_n)}.$$

We can observe that $(X_n, X_{n+1}, \Pi_n^1(x), \Pi_n^2(x), \Pi_{m\,n}(x))$ for $n = m+1, m+2, \ldots$ form a homogeneous Markov process. This allows us to reduce the problem of optimal stopping η_{mn} for each m to the optimal stopping problem of the Markov process $Z_m(x) = \{(X_{n-1}, X_n, \Pi_{n-1}^1(x), \Pi_{n-1}^2(x), \Pi_{m\,n-1}(x)),\ m, n \in \mathbb{N},\ m < n,\ x \in \mathbb{E}\}$ with the reward function $h(t,u,\alpha,\beta,\gamma) = \frac{q_2}{p_2}\Pi(t,u,\alpha,\beta,\gamma)\frac{f_t^3(u)}{f_t^2(u)}$.

Lemma 2. *A solution of the optimal stopping problem for $\{Z_m(x)\}$, $m = 1, 2, \ldots$ has a form*

$$\sigma_m^* = \inf\{n > m : \frac{f_{X_{n-1}}^3(X_n)}{f_{X_{n-1}}^2(X_n)} \geq R^*(X_n)\} \tag{9}$$

where $R^*(t) = p_2 \int_{\mathbb{E}} r^*(t,s) f_t^2(s) \mu_t(ds)$. The function $r^* = \lim_{n\to\infty} r_n$, where $r_0(t,u) = \frac{f_t^3(u)}{f_t^2(u)}$,

$$r_{n+1}(t,u) = \max\{\frac{f_t^3(u)}{f_t^2(u)}, p_2 \int_{\mathbb{E}} r_n(u,s) f_u^2(s) \mu_u(ds)\}. \tag{10}$$

The value of the problem $\eta_m = \mathbf{E}_x(\eta_{m\,m+1}|\mathcal{F}_m) = \frac{q_2}{p_2}\frac{q_1}{p_1}\Pi_n^1(x)R^*(X_m)$.

By lemmas 2 and 1 the optimal stopping problem (4) has been transformed to the optimal stopping problem for the homogeneous Markov process $W = \{(X_{m-1}, X_m, \Pi_{m-1}^1(x), \Pi_{m-1}^2(x)),\ m \in \mathbb{N},\ x \in \mathbb{E}\}$ with the reward function $f(t,u,\alpha,\beta) = \frac{q_1 q_2}{p_1 p_2}\frac{f_t^2(u)}{f_t^1(u)}\Pi^1(t,u,\alpha,\beta)R^*(u)$.

Lemma 3. *A solution of the optimal stopping problem (4) for* $n = 1, 2, \ldots$ *has a form*

$$\tau_n^* = \inf\{k \geq n : (X_{k-1}, X_k, \Pi_k^1(x), \Pi_k^2(x)) \in B^*\} \tag{11}$$

where $B^* = \{(t,u,\alpha,\beta) : \frac{f_t^2(u)}{f_t^1(u)} \geq p_1 \int_{\mathbb{E}} v^*(u,s)\mu_u(ds)\}$. *The function* $v^*(t,u) = \lim_{n\to\infty} v_n(t,u)$, *where* $v_0(t,u) = R^*(u)$,

$$v_{n+1}(t,u) = \max\{\frac{f_t^2(u)}{f_t^1(u)}, p_1 \int_{\mathbb{E}} v_n(u,s) f_u^1(s)\mu_u(ds)\}. \tag{12}$$

The value of the problem $V_n = v^*(X_{n-1}, X_n)$.

Based on Lemmas 2 and 3 the solution of the problem D_{00} can be formulated as follows.

Theorem 1. *A compound stopping time* $(\tau^*, \sigma_{\tau^*}^*)$, *where* σ_m^* *is given by (9) and* $\tau^* = \tau_0^*$ *is given by (11) is a solution of the problem* D_{00}. *The value of the problem* $\mathbf{P}_x(\tau^* < \sigma^* < \infty, \theta_1 = \tau^*, \theta_2 = \sigma_{\tau^*}^*) = \frac{q_1 q_2}{p_2}\int_{\mathbb{E}} v^*(x,s) f_x^1(s)\mu_x(ds)$.

The problem can be extended to optimal detection of more than two successive disorders. The distribution of θ_1, θ_2 may be more general. The general *a priori* distributions of disorder moments leads to more complicated formulae, since the corresponding Markov chains are not homogeneous.

References

T. Bojdecki (1979) *Probability maximizing approach to optimal stopping and its application to a disorder problem*, Stochastics, 3, pp. 61–71.

G. Haggstrom (1967) *Optimal sequential procedures when more then one stop is required*, Ann. Math. Statist., 38, pp. 1618–1626.

M. Nikolaev (1979) *Obobshchennye posledovatel'nye procedury*, Litovskiĭ Matematicheskiĭ Sbornik, 19, pp. 35–44.

M. Nikolaev (1981) *O kriterii optimal'nosti obobshchennoĭ posledovatel'noĭ procedury*, Litovskiĭ Matematicheskiĭ Sbornik, 21, pp. 75–82.

L. Pelkowitz (1987) *The general discrete time disorder problem*, Stochastics, 20, pp. 89–110.

A. Shiryaev (1978) *Optimal Stopping Rules*, Springer-Verlag, New York, Heidelberg, Berlin.

K. Szajowski (1992) *Optimal on-line detection of outside observations*, J. Stat. Planning and Inference, 30, pp. 413–422.

M. Yoshida, *Probability maximizing approach for a quickest detection problem with complicated Markov chain*, J. Inform. Optimization Sci., 4 (1983), pp. 127–145.

USING UNCERTAIN INFORMATION FROM A TELECOMMUNICATION NETWORK

Eulalia Szmidt
Systems Research Institute, Polish Academy of Sciences,
ul. Newelska 6, 01-447 Warsaw, Poland

The purpose of a real telecommunication network is to keep services on the best obtainable level. In order to do this, a network with overflows is often proposed. The idea boils down to collecting unserved parts of traffic from several lines (primary lines) and putting them together to another line which is not so busy (secondary line). A model of such network is presented which let us :

- examine general losses in a primary line,
- describe a distribution function of busy links and losses in a secondary line,
- fix a necessary number of links in a secondary line for chosen grade of service,
- compare various strategies of control (e.g. different connection of streams).

But in some situations it is also important to decompose the general losses in a secondary line again into individual streams. The oryginal method (based on probability theory) enabling such a decomposition is proposed. The results are presented and compared to other methods. Although the method was proposed for a telecommunication network, it may be used for other networks with overflows when uncertain information is obtainable.

METHODS

It is worth pointing out that the presented models are based on the measurements of a mean and a variance in an overload primary line. So parameters of a secondary line are calculated under uncertain circumstances. The model starts from an assumption of Normal distribution function of busy links in a line without losses. It is justified by the principle of maximum entropy - the most safe criterion in determining a distribution function under uncertain circumstances. The assumption was also verified by measurements in the real network.

Having a distribution function of busy links in a secondary line and knowing the parameters of each overflow we can evaluate losses of a separete overflow. First a distribution function of all the remaining overflows must be calculated. We obtain in effect only two distribution functions. Then probabilities of all possible losses from examined stream must be calculated and for each possibility of losses the event with the highest probability is accepted.

The method let us divide common losses in the most probable way. We obtain distribution function of losses (not only parameters). It is important when the losses "become overflows".

A lot of calculation were made to compare the presented method with other ones, Kuczura (1977), Manfield (1979) . The quantity results are available from the author. As far as the real network was examined, the quality results were also obtained.

Conclusions for a line without own calls :

- a stream with greater peakedness Z (Z is the ratio: a variance to a mean of a stream) has greater losses,
- as a number of links in a line increases, participation of a stream with greater Z in general losses :
- increases when the peakednesses Z_i of examined streams are of the same order,
- decreases when the peakednesses Z_i of examined streams are different.

Conclusions for a line with own calls :

- own calls are serviced better than overflowed calls,
- as the number of links in a line increases, percentage participation in general losses :
  - of own calls - decreases,
  - of overflowed calls - increases.

FINAL REMARKS

1. The proposed method deals with uncertainty in a telecommunication network.
2. The proposed method let us decompose total losses and distribute them into individual streams.
3. As a result we obtain the random variable distribution of losses from the chosen stream instead of the "pure" probability of losses.
4. Assumptions made for the model let us use it for different networks (not only a telecommunication network).
5. Computation times are comparable with other methods, Manfield (1979), Szmidt (1984).

LITERATURE

Kuczura A (1977) A Method of Moments for the Analysis of a Switched Communication Network Performance. IEEE trans. on Comm.No.2.

Manfield D, Downs T (1979) Decomposition of Traffic in Loss Systems with Renewal Input. IEEE Trans. on Comm. No.1.

Szmidt E (1984) Modelling of Chosen Phenomena in a Queueing System on the Basis of a Telecommunication Network. Ph.D.Dissert. Warsaw Technical University. (in Polish).

CHARACTERIZATIONS OF QUALITATIVE DATA

Ulrich Tüshaus
Institut für Unternehmensforschung
der Hochschule St. Gallen
Bodanstrasse 6, CH-9000 St. Gallen

Introduction

Within the interpretation step of a data analysis process—as one example—it would be helpful to rank the different variables according to their similarity to the solution. But then it is first necessary to define the "similarity to the solution" and how this can be measured appropriately.

One possible approach is the definition of a measure which describes the strength of "similarity" (or "concordance") numerically. With values varying between 0 and 1, such measure is usually called *index*.

It is obvious that the definition of such an index is based explicitly or implicitly on a specific data model. This fact clearly influences its applicability for a certain problem.

Typical application areas of indices can, however, be characterized as follows.

Properties of the data Having collected the data, it is useful to check whether the data actually have some common structure (as assumed) which then can be extracted by the application of a data analysis technique.

Properties of the solution Many data analysis techniques will determine a solution even if the specific data set does not fit the underlying model. An index can be used to examine how strong the solution supports the structure of the model.

Comparison of solutions As a result of the application of different analysis techniques to a single data set, a comparison of the solutions is often desirable. Because each objective function usually stresses a certain aspect of the data, an index measure can introduce an additional independent criterion.

Significance of variables In order to describe the significance of a certain variable, the structure of this variable is compared with the structure of the solution: here, it is assumed that its significance is higher if the variable is closer to the solution. This distance can be measured by an appropriate index.

These applications have also been the basis of two well-known indices (for the comparison of partitions resp. orders) which will be described in the following. It will be shown that these concepts fit into the framework of a more general index based on the *symmetric difference distance.*

Extended for the characterization of several binary relations, this index can be used, for example, to describe general properties of the data or the relative importance of certain variables with respect to a the solution.

Comparison of partitions

The underlying concept of the *Rand Index* had already been proposed earlier in different forms (and was several times rediscovered again; see, for example, (Hubert and Arabie, 1985) for the historical background). But Rand (Rand, 1971) was the first to formulate it for the comparison of two partitions by means of the entries of a contingency table.

The comparison is based on the observation which classes of the two partitions a pair of objects is assigned to. If the two objects are in the same class in both partitions, or in different classes in both partitions, this is considered as "similar", the other case (in the same class in one partition, in different classes in the other) as "dissimilar". Dividing the number of all unordered pairs of objects with similar classifications by $n(n-1)/2$, the total number of different (unordered) pairs of n objects, a measure of similarity is defined. This index is 0, if there is no similarity (one partition consists of a single class (with all objects), the other of n classes with one element); it is 1 if both partitions are identical.

Originally, Sokal and Michener (Sokal and Michener, 1958) have proposed their *simple matching coefficient* as a similarity measure for binary variables. Being interpreted as a measure for the comparison of two classifications, it corresponds to the Rand index.

Mirkin and Chernyi (Mirkin and Chernyi, 1970) have defined several axioms which should be satisfied by a measure of distance between two partitions. They show that the *symmetric difference distance* has these properties. In this context, they define the ratio

$$\frac{\text{distance between two specific partitions}}{\text{maximal distance between two arbitrary partitions}}$$

as the relative distance between the two partitions; this measure is complementary to the Rand index.

Comparison of orders

The origins of *Kendall's* τ go back as far as Fechner (1897) (see (Kruskal, 1958) for a historical review); Kendall (Kendall, 1938) not only rediscovered it, but introduced this coefficient in its modern nonparametric form.

For the comparison of two rank orders (complete orders), the coefficient τ is based on a notion of "disarray". The ranking of the objects in one order is compared to the ranking in the other: an intuitive measure of concordance is the number of inversions which are necessary to transform one order into the other. With n objects, the number of inversions, that is the number of pairs of objects with inverted rankings in the two orders, lies between 0 and $n(n-1)/2$. Thus, the coefficient τ (a symmetric coefficient of correlation) can be defined as

$$\tau = 1 - 2\frac{\text{number of inversions}}{(n(n-1))/2} \; .$$

The value -1 indicates perfect negative correlation (the two orders are completely inverse) while the value 1 is attained for perfect positive correlation (the two orders are identical). (With ordinal data—as in this case—the coefficient is used to describe not only the strength of a relationship but also its form. This leads to the concept of correlation.)

For characterizing the concordance of several orders, Ehrenberg (1952) and Monjardet (see (Monjardet, 1985)) both have developed coefficients which essentially are a form of "average τ".

Comparison of qualitative data

The indices discussed so far have been proposed for nominal resp. ordinal data.

To analyze different forms of qualitative data, one approach (Schader, 1978) represents qualitative data by the corresponding binary relations on I, the set of n objects. Using the ***symmetric difference***, a natural way to compare two relations R_k and R_l (i.e., two qualitative variables) is the following: $|R_k \triangle R_l| := |\{(i,j) \mid (i,j) \in R_k \text{ and } (i,j) \notin R_l, \text{ or } (i,j) \notin R_k \text{ and } (i,j) \in R_l\}|$, where the number of disagreements between R_k and R_l are counted. With $r_{ij} = 1$ if and only if iRj and $r_{ij} = 0$ otherwise, $|R_k \triangle R_l|$ can be rewritten as

$$|R_k \triangle R_l| = \sum_{i,j\in I} \left(r_{kij}(1 - r_{lij}) + (1 - r_{kij})r_{lij}\right) = \sum_{i,j\in I} (r_{kij} + r_{lij} - 2r_{kij}r_{lij})$$

With n^2 as the maximal distance between two arbitrary relations on a set of n objects, the index

$$\iota = 1 - \frac{|R_k \triangle R_l|}{n^2} \tag{1}$$

is a suitable measure of association. This index is 1, if both relations are identical ($|R_k \triangle R_l| = 0$), and is 0, if both are completely different ($|R_k \triangle R_l| = n^2$). As the symmetric difference distance is defined for arbitrary binary relations, this index can be used for all forms of qualitative data which can be represented by binary relations.

Common properties

When comparing *nominal data* (equivalence relations, i.e. reflexive, symmetric and transitive relations), the index ι corresponds to Rand's index c except for a simple transformation.

With $\sum_{i,j\in I,\, i<j} r_{kij}r_{lij}$ as the number of pairs of objects which are assigned to the same class for two specific variables k und l, and $\sum_{i,j\in I,\, i<j}(1 - r_{kij})(1 - r_{lij})$ as the number of pairs of objects which are assigned to different classes for these variables k und l, the index c for these two variables can be written in relational notation as follows:

$$c = \frac{\sum_{i,j\in I,\, i<j} r_{kij}r_{lij} + \sum_{i,j\in I,\, i<j}(1 - r_{kij})(1 - r_{lij})}{\binom{n}{2}}\,. \tag{2}$$

Using the symmetry and the reflexivity property of the equivalence relations, the expression for c can be transformed into

$$c = \frac{\frac{n(n-1)}{2} - \frac{1}{2}\sum_{i,j\in I}\left(r_{kij} + r_{lij} - 2r_{kij}r_{lij}\right)}{\frac{n(n-1)}{2}} = 1 - \frac{\sum_{i,j\in I}\left(r_{kij} + r_{lij} - 2r_{kij}r_{lij}\right)}{n(n-1)}$$

or

$$c = 1 - \frac{|R_k \triangle R_l|}{n(n-1)}\,. \tag{3}$$

Thus, for comparing equivalence relations, the following relationship between ι and c holds:

$$\iota = \frac{1 + c(n-1)}{n} \tag{4}$$

When comparing *ordinal data* (complete order relations, i.e. reflexive, antisymmetric, complete and transitive relations), the index ι corresponds to Kendall's τ except for a simple transformation. With

$$\sum_{i,j\in I, i<j} \left(r_{kij}(1-r_{lij}) + (1-r_{kij})r_{lij}\right)$$

as the number of pairs of objects which are in reverse order for two specific variables k and l, the index τ for these two variables can be written in relational notation as follows:

$$\tau = 1 - \frac{2\sum_{i,j\in I,\, i<j}\left(r_{kij}(1-r_{lij}) + (1-r_{kij})r_{lij}\right)}{n(n-1)/2} \tag{5}$$

Using the reflexivity, the completeness and the antisymmetry property of the complete order relations, τ can be written as

$$\tau = 1 - \frac{2|R_k \Delta R_l|}{n(n-1)} . \tag{6}$$

Thus, for comparing complete order relations, the following relationship between ι and τ holds:

$$\iota = \frac{(1-\tau)(n-1)}{2n} . \tag{7}$$

Remark

Analogous to the concept of the coefficient K (Monjardet, 1985) and with some similar properties, this index can be generalized to describe the concordance of several qualitiative variables of possibly different (nominal, ordinal, ...) type. When analyzing qualitative data, this index can be used, for example, to describe general concordance properties of the data or the relative importance of certain variables with respect to a solution.

References

Hubert, L. and Arabie, P. (1985). Comparing partitions. *Journal of Classification*, 2:193–218.

Kendall, M. G. (1938). A new measure of rank correlation. *Biometrika*, 30:81–93.

Kruskal, W. H. (1958). Ordinal measures of association. *Journal of the American Statistical Association*, 53:814–861.

Mirkin, B. G. and Chernyi, L. B. (1970). Measurement of the distance between distinct partitions of a finite set. *Automation and Remote Control*, 31(5):786–792. Translated from *Avtomatika i Telemekhanika*, No. 5, pp. 120–127, May, 1970.

Monjardet, B. (1985). Concordance et consensus d'ordres totaux: les coefficients K et W. *Revue de Statistique Appliquée*, 33(2):55–85.

Rand, W. M. (1971). Objective criteria for the evaluation of clustering methods. *Journal of the American Statistical Association*, 66(336):846–850.

Schader, M. (1978). *Anordnung und Klassifikation*, volume 9 of *Quantitative Methoden der Unternehmensplanung*. Verlag Anton Hain, Meisenheim/Glan.

Sokal, R. R. and Michener, C. D. (1958). A statistical method for evaluating systematic relationships. *The University of Kansas Science Bulletin*, 38:1409–1438.

HIGH ORDER ITERATIVE METHODS FOR NONLINEAR EGVATIONS

Otu Vaarmann
Institute of Cybernetics
Estonian Academy of Sciences
Akadeemia tee 21, EE0026 Tallinn

Approximate variants of classical iterative methods (Newton's, Gauss-Newton's, tangent hyperbolas, tangent parabolas etc.) having a large order of convergence are studied. Certain conditions are presented under which the approximate variants preserve the convergence rate intrinsic to these methods and some their computational aspects are discussed.

Many problems of scientific computation can be reduced to the numerical solution of a nonlinear equation

$$F(x) = 0 \tag{1}$$

where F is a sufficiently often differentiable operator from an abstract space X into another Y. In the general case the equation (1) may not have any solution in the classical sense or may have several solutions. This report aims at presenting a study of computing an approximate solution of the equation (1), if it exists, otherwise, a solution of (1) in the least squares sense, i.e. of minimizing the functional

$$\varphi(x) = \frac{1}{2} \|F(x)\|^2 \tag{2}$$

In the latter case it is assumed that F is a mapping between Hilbert spaces H_1 and H_2. A necessary condition for x^* to be a local minimum point is

$$[F'(x)]^* F(x) = 0 \tag{3}$$

where $[\cdot]^*$ denotes the dual mapping.

METHODS

This report discuss the use of approximate variants of methods with the high order convergence $p \geq 2$ of the type

$$x_{k+1} = x_k - Q(x_k, A_k^i), \ i \in I, \ I = \{1, \ldots, r\} \tag{4}$$

where $Q(x, A_k^i)$ is an operator from a Banach space E_1 into itself when a solution is seeked in the classical sense and from a that of the Newton method is that it and its variants could break down when F′ is singular or ill-conditioned at the solution point x^*. Methods of order $p \geq 3$ are taking advantage, at least, of a quadratic model and they can in this case perform successfully provided a sufficiently good starting point is available. On of the most popular ways to guarantee the global convergence is the "continuation strategy". All homotic methods suffers from the disadvantage the Jacobian at some points could become singular. In the latter case the implementation of methods with the convergence order $p \geq 3$ in conjunction with the "continuation strategy" might be successful. A more thorough discussion of computational aspects of these methods can be found in Meressoo, Vaarmann (1993) and Vaarmann (1992).

Burmeister W (1972) Inversionfreie Verfahren zur Lösung nicht linearer Operatorgleichungen. ZAMM 52: 101-110

Hald H (1975) On a Newton-Moser type method. Numer Math 23:411-426

Helfrich H.P (1969) Ein modifiziertes Newtonsches Verfahren Int. Schriftenz. z.Num Math 12. Birkh. Verlag. Basel

Meressoo T, Vaarmann O (1993) Numerical solution of certain decomposition-coordination problems in nonlinear programming. Symposium on Applied Mathematical Programming (ed. Istvan Maros). Budapest, Hungary, January 6-8, 1993: 422-429

Ulm S (1967) On iterative methods with successive approximation of the inverse operator. Eesti NSV Tead. Akad. Toimetised. Füüs.-Mat. 16: 403-411 (in Russ.)

Vaarmann O (1968) On some iterative methods with successive approximation of the inverse operator. Eesti NSV Tead. Akad. Toimetised. Füüs.-Mat. 17:379-390 (in Russ.)

Vaarmann O (1991) A theorem for methods with high order convergence. Eesti TA Toimetised. Füüs.-Mat. 40:99-104

Vaarmann O (1992)Some numerical methods of parameter identification in nonlinear models. Ill-Posed Problems in Natural Sciences (ed. A.N. Tikhonov) - Utrecht: VSP/Moscow: TVP Sci. Publ. 1992, 191-201.

Werzhbicki V (1969) On problem of iteration methods with successive approximation inverse operator. Mathematical Analysis 2: 31-38 (in Russ.)

COMPUTER SIMULATION OF OBSERVATION SYSTEMS UNDER ATTAINMENT OF SUPERSOLVABILITY BY MATHEMATICAL REDUCTION METHOD

Anatoliy Verlan
Institute of Simulation Problems in
Power Engineering
15 General Naumov St.
USS 252680 Kiev-164
Ukraine

Conception of construction for observation systems with the most reachable degree of resolution is based on application of special methods, algorithms and computer means for processing of observation results which form data interpretation system of measuring experiment. Organization of observation systems inclusive interpretation system is possible only on the base of computer modeling that provide passing of constructive decisions. In connection of this it is considered modeling method reproducing observation results and also realizing computer processes for interpretation of experimental data. As the base model of observation system it is accepted integral operator of Fredholm, so interpretation problem reduces to solving of one-dimentional intagral equation of first sort that is required attraction and optimal choice of regularization methods. Considered modeling system solves such problems: making equation precise and gathering of regularization information; preliminary selection of regularization methods and solving of integral equation; application of methods taking into account the specific of solving applied problem; elaboration of computer processes and structure for interpretation and its modeling on large computer complex; optimization and efficacy evaluation of regularization algorithms and structures, and also using of modeling system for interpretation of experimantal dependence; simplificity and specilization of modeling system; its realization on the basis of small digital and analog-digital computer complexes and so on.

Risk based equity cost calculation in banking

Mark Wahrenburg
University of Cologne, Staatwissenschaftliches Seminar
50923 Köln, Germany

Rajeev De Mello
McKinsey and Company
8703 Erlenbach/Zürich, Switzerland

In the Modigliani-Miller world of perfect capital markets there is no need to manage the idiosyncratic risk of corporations. However, bankruptcy costs, the tax system and agency costs deriving from information asymmetries create a rationale to control the total risk of a bank. The objective of bank risk management thus is to optimize the risk/return position of the bank. Since a bank consists of a portfolio of different and often interdependent risks, this objective can only be achieved by incorporating risk interrelations into the analysis. We propose a practical method how the total risk of a bank including risk interrelations can be determined and how the risk/return situation of individual business units can be evaluated from the total bank perspective. For our analysis we choose a continuous time portfolio model, in which a set of random risk factors drives the bank profit. This specification allows the inclusion of many different bank risks such as interest rate risks, foreign exchange risks, credit risks and risks from derivative products into one unifying framework. The bank profit is modeled using a first order Taylor series approximation of the pricing functions of bank assets and liablities. The total bank risk is expressed in terms of the standard deviation of profits over short periods of time. We then demonstrate how banks with decentralized decision making authority nevertheless can optimize their overall risk/return trade off by using the risk contribution of their business units to the total bank risk as the relevant measure of risk. The optimization of the toal risk position can be easily incorporated into the bank's accounting system by employing business unit equity costs that are based on their contribution to the total bank risk. The proposed concept provides senior management with a simple tool to allocate the bank's capital such that the bank's risk/return trade off is optimized and to provide business unit managers with incentives to optimize the total bank risk exposure.

Besides the optimization of the bank's risk/return trade off, the outlined framework has further promising applications in the field of risk measurement and risk management. We discuss how the concept can be used to visualize risk through scenario analysis, to monitor the bank's risk exposure, to evaluate the adequacy of the bank's equity capitalization and finally to set prices based on the bank's current risk situation. We further discuss the appropiateness of our equity cost concept to evaluate the risk adjusted performance of business unit managers or traders. It is shown that the concept provides a fair benchmark profit for performance evaluation only if the bank's total equity cost rate is the actually expected market risk premium on its assets and liabilities and if the bank portfolio is mean variance efficient. This implies that if the bank for some strategic reasons chooses an inefficient portfolio, calculatory profits or losses do not automatically indicate good or poor performance of business unit managers. While currently accounting profits are used both to guide risk taking decisions and to evaluate manager performance, sophisticated future risk management systems should use separate systems for the risk taking function and for risk adjusted performance evaluation. Since bank management wants to reward business units for both beating the market and for improving the total bank risk position, it needs two distinct incentive systems to pursue both goals.

An alternative approach to robust design problems

Johannes Wallacher
Institut für Statistik und Math. Wirtschaftstheorie
Universität Karlsruhe (TH)
D-76128 Karlsruhe, Germany

Robust design is a quality improvement technique based on experimental design. It is intended as a cost effective approach to reduce variation in products and processes and has been introduced by G. Taguchi, see e.g. Kacker (1985). The quality engineering ideas have been widely approved, whereas the proposed statistical procedures are still discussed controversially (e.g. Box (1985)).

This paper introduces an alternative approach which combines the principles of robust design with traditional response surface methodologies.

Let $x = (x_1, ..., x_k) \in \Omega_x$ be the vector of continuous controllable factors with a bounded region of operability $\Omega_x = \{(x_1, ..., x_k) | -b_i \leq x_i \leq u_i,\ b_i, u_i \in \mathbf{R}^+,\ \forall\, i = 1, ..., k\}$.

The noise factors Z_j, $j = 1, ..., l$, which are fixed during parameter-design experiments, are random variables with mean $E(Z_j) = 0$ and variance $Var(Z_j) = 1$.

Controllable and uncontrollable factors are combined in a single two-level factorial design matrix and the response Y is modelled empirically as a function $Y(x) = f(x, Z)$ depending on both kinds of factors. A first order model for the response is

$$Y(x) = \beta_0 + \sum_{i=1}^{k} \beta_i x_i + \sum_{i=1}^{k-1} \sum_{j=i+1}^{k} \beta_{ij} x_i x_j + \sum_{j=1}^{l} \gamma_j Z_j + \sum_{j=1}^{l} \sum_{i=1}^{k} \gamma_{ij} x_i Z_j + \varepsilon_Y. \qquad (1)$$

The $\delta = \frac{k(k+2l+1)}{2} + (l+1)$ unknown coefficients are estimated through the ordinary least squares method with the usual assumption that the random errors are independent and identically distributed with $E(\varepsilon_Y) = 0$ and $Var(\varepsilon_Y) = \sigma_Y^2 I$. Assuming that the noise factors Z_j are mutually independent, the mean and the variance of model (1) is

$$E(Y(x)) = \beta_0 + \sum_{i=1}^{k} \beta_i x_i + \sum_{i=1}^{k} \sum_{j=i+1}^{k} \beta_{ij} x_i x_j,$$

$$\begin{aligned} Var(Y(x)) &= (\gamma_1 + \sum_{i=1}^{k} \gamma_{i1} x_i)^2 + ... + (\gamma_l + \sum_{i=1}^{k} \gamma_{il} x_i)^2 + \sigma_Y^2 \\ &= b_0 + b^T x + x^T B x \end{aligned}$$

with $b_0 = \sum_{j=1}^{l} \gamma_j^2 + \sigma_Y^2, \quad b = 2(\sum_{j=1}^{l} \gamma_j \gamma_{1j}, ..., \sum_{j=1}^{l} \gamma_j \gamma_{kj})^T \in \mathbf{R}^k,$

and the symmetrical $k \times k$-matrix

$$B = \begin{pmatrix} \sum_{j=1}^{l} \gamma_{1j}^2 & \sum_{j=1}^{l} \gamma_{1j}\gamma_{2j} & \cdots & \sum_{j=1}^{l} \gamma_{1j}\gamma_{kj} \\ \sum_{j=1}^{l} \gamma_{1j}\gamma_{2j} & \sum_{j=1}^{l} \gamma_{2j}^2 & \cdots & \cdot \\ \cdot & & \cdot & \cdot \\ \cdot & & \cdot & \cdot \\ \cdot & & \cdot & \cdot \\ \sum_{j=1}^{l} \gamma_{1j}\gamma_{kj} & \cdot & \cdots & \sum_{j=1}^{l} \gamma_{kj}^2 \end{pmatrix}.$$

Operating conditions which minimize the variability subject to a given target τ are determined by the solution of the problem

$$\min Var(Y(x)) = b_0 + b^T x + x^T B x$$
$$E(Y(x)) = \beta_0 + \sum_{i=1}^{k} \beta_i x_i + \sum_{i=1}^{k} \sum_{j=i+1}^{k} \beta_{ij} x_i x_j = \tau,$$
$$x \in \Omega_x \,.$$

To check the influence of non-linear effects of the controllable factors a second-order design and model is employed.

The central composite design (CCD), Box & Wilson (1951), is an efficient experimental-plan, which consists of three parts:

(1) The two-level factorial of the first-order model as nucleus.

(2) A set of "star" points at a distance α from the design center.

(3) n_0 center runs.

The second-order model is

$$Y(x) \;=\; \beta_0 + \sum_{i=1}^{k} \beta_i x_i + \sum_{i=1}^{k} \beta_{ii} x_i^2 + \sum_{i=1}^{k-1} \sum_{j=i+1}^{k} \beta_{ij} x_i x_j + \sum_{j=1}^{l} \gamma_j Z_j + \sum_{j=1}^{l} \sum_{i=1}^{k} \gamma_{ij} x_i Z_j + \varepsilon_Y . \quad (2)$$

The variance $Var(Y(x))$ is unchanged, whereas the mean changes to

$$E(Y(x)) = \beta_0 + \sum_{i=1}^{k} \beta_i x_i + \sum_{i=1}^{k} \beta_{ii} x_i^2 + \sum_{i=1}^{k-1} \sum_{j=i+1}^{k} \beta_{ij} x_i x_j,$$

if the coefficients β_{ii}, $i = 1, ..., k$, are significant.

The adjusted optimization problem for robust design is

$$\begin{aligned} \min Var(Y(x)) &= b_0 + b^T x + x^T B x \\ E(Y(x)) &= c_0 + c^T x + x^T C x = \tau, \\ x &\in \Omega_x . \end{aligned}$$

with $c_0 = \beta_0$, $c = (\beta_1, ..., \beta_k)^T \in \mathbf{R}^k$ and

$$C = \begin{pmatrix} \beta_{11} & \beta_{12} & \cdot & \cdot & \cdot & \beta_{1k} \\ \beta_{12} & \beta_{22} & \cdot & \cdot & \cdot & \cdot \\ \cdot & & \cdot & & & \cdot \\ \cdot & & & \cdot & & \cdot \\ \cdot & & & & \cdot & \cdot \\ \beta_{1k} & \cdot & \cdot & \cdot & \cdot & \beta_{kk} \end{pmatrix} .$$

REFERENCES

Box (1985)	Discussion to Off-Line Quality Control, Parameter Design, and the Taguchi Method, in Journal of Quality Technology, Vol. 17, No.4, 1985, pp.189-190.
Box & Wilson (1951)	On the Experimental Attainment of Optimal Conditions, in Journal of the Royal Statistical Society, Ser. B13, Nr.1, 1951, pp.1-38.
Kacker (1985)	Off-Line Quality Control, Parameter Design, and the Taguchi Method, in Journal of Quality Technology, Vol. 17, No.4, 1985, pp.176-188

Workflow Model Verification of Cooperating Agents in Cardiological Intensive Care Units

Guido von der Weiden[1], Peter Szczurko[1], Bernhard Thull[2]
[1] Lehrstuhl Informatik V, RWTH Aachen, Ahornstr. 55, 52056 Aachen, Germany

[2] Helmholtz-Institut für Biomedizinische Technik an der RWTH Aachen, Pauwelsstr. 30, 52074 Aachen, Germany

I. Introduction

Critical care medicine makes high demands on personnel and the organization of work- and information-flow, as numerous patients have to be cared for simultaneously with the assistance of complex diagnostic and therapeutic measures 24 hours a day. This working environment is especially sensitive in terms of safety, caution and possible harmful consequences for the patient's life. The aquisition, analysis and documentation of the patient's vital parameters and therapy measures is becoming more precise and more complex today.

Consequently, in intensive care settings more people are involved in each individual case. At this point the management of information flow becomes a problem as communication occurs between the nurses and doctors of the same shift, and communication between staff from consecutive shifts.

Given the requirements of tight task coordination and team-based decision making, extensive synchronous and asynchronous exchange of information between different sites and people is needed (as shown in Fig. 1).

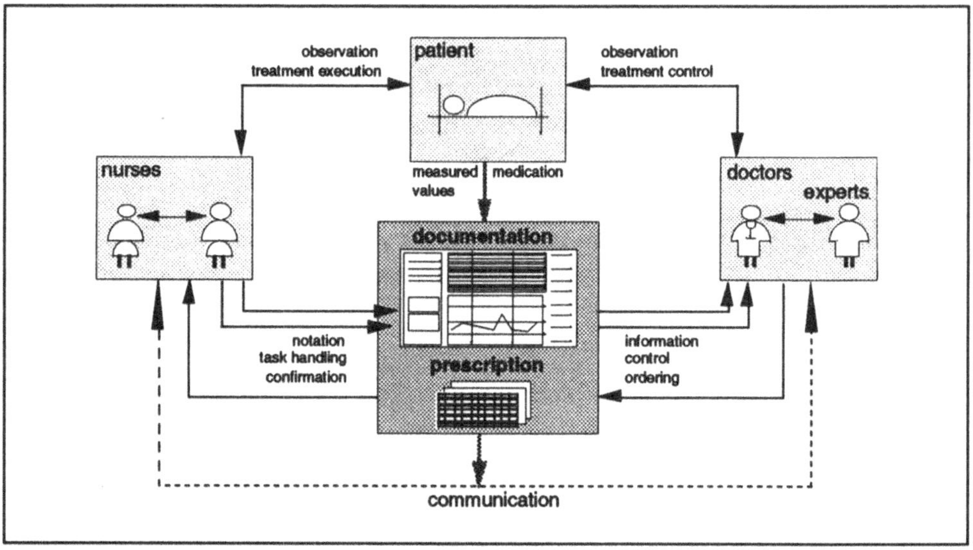

Figure 1: Information flow in the intensive care unit

Intensive care units include numerous man-machine and man-man-interfaces, therefore commonly used methods of work analysis can only cover specific aspects of the situation.

According to analyses, which focused on working environment (for example in [DONC90], [FRIES90]), the workflow in intensive care units has been found to be coordinated in a sometimes unstructered manner, often not completed and to an extent even poorly defined.

In real situations, deviations from the defined workflow appear. For example, the execution of treatments is defined in four main steps. Firstly, the doctor prescribes a treatment to the nurse (delegate). In the second step, the nurse registers the above (accept). Thirdly, after administering the medicine, s/he notes it in the patient's documentation (report). Finally, the doctor confirms that the task was fullfilled (confirm). This workflow especially includes the transition of responsibility.

In such a context, the handwritten documentation of the patient's vital state can lead to several critical situations. Typical situations here are changes in planned treatments, where the doctor changes treatments and this is not realised by the nurses. Additionally, is is critical for the doctor to judge the patient's state accurately if the documentation is not up-to-date for some reason (for instance, medicine may have been given by one nurse, but not yet documented by him/her).

The approach presented in this article provides a possible solution to this workflow coordination problem, which employs the example of the administration and documentation of medication in a cardiological intensive care unit. The detailed problem described below can be found in practically every medical context with two or more people involved as staff members.

Workflow coordination is also one of the main problems in many office and manufacturing processes (described in [KRKI88]), therefore the presented solution can be applied to a whole class of problems.

II. Workflow Modelling in Intensive Care Units

In the last decade, computer programs were regarded as information processing systems, the main point of their use being the processing of a large amount of data for loading, calculating and saving. This perspective changed to cooperative, task-oriented systems, when Winograd and Flores presented their new approach to software design in 1986 [WIFL86]. They developed protocols for action based on speech-theory and distinguished up to eight so-called speech-acts. The protocols were represented as state-transition diagrams, where each speech-act has two agents and a well-defined set of possible states, final states and transitions (action-flow presented in [MWFF92]).

Demeester (published in [DEME90]) adapted this concept to a medical context, refined and used its model to identify breakdowns in the analysis of an intensive care unit. These model descriptions were found to be insufficient in practise to cover all aspects of real situations. However, since then, he has developed a more refined model.

The goal of our research in this area was to find a way of modelling this description, which is able to suit these special requirements. So it is necessary to describe the workflow of several agents in one model, as the various workflows are independent from each other. Additionally, time constraints had to be considered. In modelling, the agent-driven workflow had to be combined with event-driven components.

At this point, state charts (described in [HARE87]) seem to be a suitable possibility for the workflow modelling process. They extend conventional state-transition diagrams with three elements, dealing, respectively, with the notations of hierarchy, concurrency and communication. On the other hand, their graphical representation is so compact, that it can be explained to our medical partners, for example, within minutes. For this reason, state charts are a promising instrument for cooperative design approaches.

III. Verification Approach

The verification process takes place in a triangular relationship between the real situation in medical care units, the workflow model aquisition and information system development, as shown in Fig. 2.

System design is seen as the mapping of reality to a computer program. It is divided into two single processes, a modelling process and a prototyping process, both making use of a workflow model.

The model process itself is divided into model acquisition and model verification. Model acquisition covers interviews, investigation and analysis. Model language and environment has proven itself to be difficult, since it had to be done with pencil and paper. Additionally, the model itself was becoming more and more complex.

Model verifcation is done in extensive group settings where the actual model is discussed and evaluated by the medical personnel.

Since this is all done theoretically on paper, it is fairly abstract and insufficient, but the only feasible way.

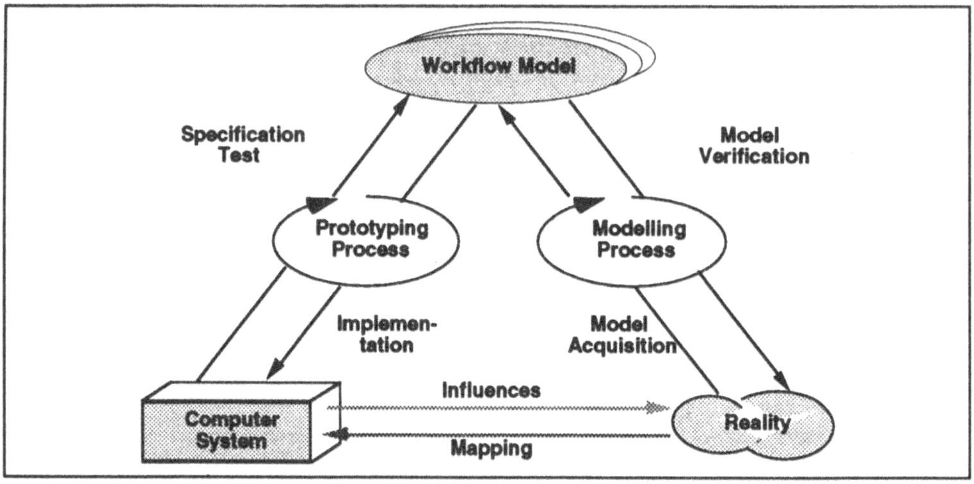

Figure 2: Workflow modelling steps

Implementation takes place as part of the prototyping process, where the workflow model is mapped to a computer program. This is a incremental process, where the user can evaluate prototypes of graphical user interfaces in terms of layout, handling and functionality. This leads to further developed specifications in the prototyping phase, which influences the verification of the workflow model, whether the model still correctly maps reality or not. This results in variations in the model, which also need to be regarded in the modelling process.

The use of a computer system alters organisation structures in reality, whilst parts of the new work organisation are adapted to the workflow. In this sense, real workflow is permanently changed in cycles, as new or altered requirements are given for the system.

The solution to this complex problem would be the verification of the separate transitions in a concurrent process.

Computer-supported coordination systems exert an influence on the world, such that the facts change. The work- and information flow in reality is being critically revised. This makes constant remodelling necessary, as an adapting process. It is in this manner that new problems may be thrown to light.

In the final phase of this process, a field test of the developed program is being planned.

IV. System Implementation

After the implementation of the current workflow-model had been completed, a prototype graphical user-interface was constructed (considering concepts presented in [TPRA93]). This interface was designed for the administration and documentation of medication in a cardiological intensive care unit. It is based on a UNIX-operating system using OSF/Motif, and is being used as the basis for further research.

The system uses touch-screen input to ease it's handling. Different views and functionalities are available, depending on whether the user is a doctor or a nurse.

Interaction with the system is primarily single task-orientated. The program guides the user through the workflow, and gives the user detailed warnings, when for example there is a time delay. History of changes in treatments are also available to avoid any doubt.

To realize optimal screen layout, a tool for interface construction has been used (UIM/X, HP Interface Architect). This enables the immediate testing and refinement of layout changes which we obtain in direct discussion with our medical partners. The research involves the medical personnel at every level of the design process. To achieve the best outcome, continued discussion and simulation is necessary.

Part of the resulting screen layout is shown in Fig. 3.

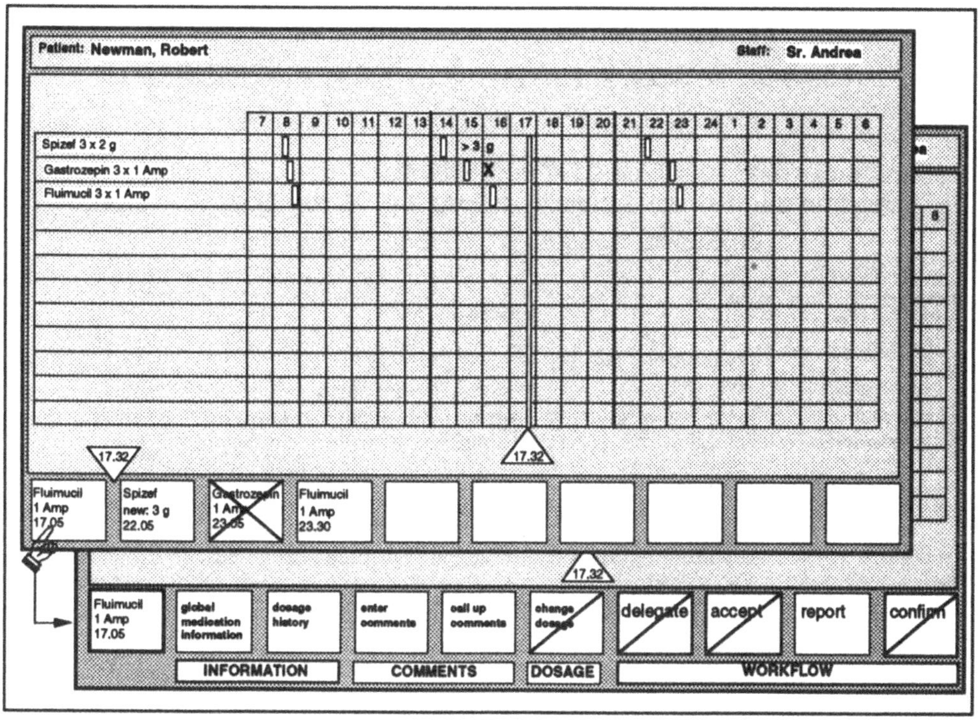

Figure 3: Schematic screen layout of program prototype

In the next step a field-test of the system is being planned. The medical partners are looking forward to the system having been evaluated. This evaluation will occur in an intensive care unit under real-time conditions, to allow a direct comparison with the paper documentation system which is currently being used.

Literature

[DEME90] Demeester, M., "Integrated Communication System for Intensive Care", in: AIM 90, Sevilla, Spain 1990, pp. 103 - 110

[DONC90] Donchin, Y., "The Nature and Causes of Human Errors in the Intensive Care Unit", Report HEIS-90-2, Department of Anesthesiology and Critical Care, Jerusalem, Israel, Hadassah-Hebrew University Medical Center, 1990

[FRIES90] Friesdorf, W., "Überwachung am Intensivbett - Informationsrepräsentation", in: W. Friesdorf, B. Schwilk, J. Hähnel (ed.), Ergonomie in der Intensivmedizin, Bibliomed, 1990

[HARE87] Harel, D., "Statecharts: A Visual Formalism for Complex Systems", Science of Computer Programming 8, North Holland, 1987, pp. 231 - 274

[KRKI88] Kraemer, K.L., King, J.L.,"Computer-based Systems for Cooperative Work and Group Decision Making", ACM Computing Surveys, 20(2), June 1988, pp. 115-146

[MWFF92] Medina-Mora, R., Winograd, T., Flores, R., Flores, F., "The Action Workflow Approach to Workflow Management Technology", Proceedings CSCW 92, 11/1992

[TPRA93] Thull, B., Popp, H.J., Rau, G., "Man Machine Interaction in Critical Care Settings", in: Special Issue of the IEEE/EMBS Magazine on "Intelligent Patient Monitoring and Management Systems", to be published 12/1993

[WIFL86] Winograd, T., Flores F., "Understanding Computers and Cognition: A New Foundation for Design", Ablex, 1986

Dually-Weighted Cross Decomposition for the Capacitated Facility Location Problem*

Paul Wentges
Institut für Unternehmensforschung der Hochschule St. Gallen
Bodanstr. 6, 9000 St. Gallen, Switzerland

Abstract

The cross decomposition algorithm of [van Roy 1986] is generally considered to be one of the most efficient procedures for solving the capacitated facility location problem. A modified version of this algorithm, called dually-weighted cross decomposition, is presented. In contrast to the cross decomposition algorithm, this approach does not use the optimal dual solutions of the primal subproblems or the optimal solutions of the dual master problem as Lagrangean multipliers for the dual subproblems. A specially weighted average of the previously constructed multipliers is used instead. Finite convergence of this approach is proven and first promising results are discussed.

1 Introduction

The capacitated facility location problem (CFLP) can be formulated as the following mixed-integer programming problem (see e.g. [Cornuejols et al. 1991] for a more detailed description of the problem) :

$$(CFLP)\left\{\begin{array}{ll} \min \sum_{j=1}^{n} f_j y_j + \sum_{i=1}^{m}\sum_{j=1}^{n} c_{ij} x_{ij}, & \\ \sum_{j=1}^{n} x_{ij} = d_i \ \forall\, i, & (1) \\ x_{ij} \leq d_i y_j \ \forall\, i,j, & (2) \\ \sum_{i=1}^{m} x_{ij} \leq s_j y_j \ \forall\, j, & (3) \\ x_{ij} \geq 0,\ y_j \in \{0,1\} \ \forall\, i,j, & (4) \end{array}\right.$$

where m represents the number of customers, n the number of potential facility locations, d_i the demand of customer i, and s_j the capacity of facility j. c_{ij} are the costs to transport one unit from facility j to customer i and f_j the fixed costs to maintain/build facility j. The variable y_j indicates whether facility j is opened ($y_j = 1$) or not, and x_{ij} represents the amount shipped from facility j to customer i.

*This paper was partly supported by "Schweizerischer Nationalfond zur Förderung der wissenschaftlichen Forschung (Grant 12-30140.90)".

The cross decomposition algorithm of [van Roy 1986] simultaneously exploits both the primal structure (temporarily fixing the variables y yields a normal transportation problem) and the dual structure (with relaxing the capacity constraints (3) in lagrangean fashion) of the (CFLP), i. e. combines Benders' decomposition and Dantzig-Wolfe decomposition in one single framework. The approach is motivated by the fact, that the primal subproblem can be viewed as a relaxed dual (Dantzig-Wolfe) master problem and the dual subproblem as a relaxed primal (Benders) master problem (see e.g. [van Roy 1983]).
The main steps of the algorithm can be described as follows (let (SD_μ) be the Lagrangean relaxation of $(CFLP)$ with respect to the capacity constraints (3) and the Lagrangean multipliers μ, (MD_k) the relaxed Dantzig-Wolfe master problem: $\max\{\delta : \sum_{j=1}^n f_j y_j^t + \sum_{i=1}^m \sum_{j=1}^n c_{ij} x_{ij}^t - \sum_{j=1}^n (s_j y_j^t - \sum_{i=1}^m x_{ij}^t)\mu_j \geq \delta \; \forall \, t \in T_k;\; \mu \geq 0, \delta \in \mathbb{R}\}$, (SP_y) the transportation problem obtained when y is fixed, and (MP_k) a relaxed Benders master problem; for a more detailed and explicit description of the problems see [van Roy 1986]):

Step 1: Initialize and get a dual solution μ^1 (by solving the primal subproblem (SP_{y^0}) with $y^0 \equiv 1$).

Step 2: Solve the dual subproblem (SD_{μ^k}): Let (x^k, y^k) be an optimal solution. Perform a convergence test; if the test is not fulfilled, go to step 5.

Step 3: Solve the primal subproblem (SP_{y^k}): Let $(\lambda^{k+1}, \nu^{k+1}, \mu^{k+1})$ be an optimal dual solution. Perform a convergence test; if the test is not fulfilled, go to step 5 (or step 4, see below), otherwise go to step 2 and set $k := k + 1$.

Step 4: Solve the primal master problem (MP_k): Let y^{k+1} be an optimal solution. Go to step 3 and set $k := k + 1$.

Step 5: Solve the dual master problem (MD_k): Let μ^{k+1} be an optimal solution. Go to step 2 and set $k := k + 1$.

In steps 2 and 3, cuts corresponding to the optimal solutions have to be added to the respective master problems; in each step, optimality has to be checked. If the Lagrangean dual is solved within a specified tolerance level τ (e.g. 0.5%), one switches to Benders' decomposition (only usage of steps 3 and 4).
The cross decomposition algorithm solves the (CFLP) in a finite number of steps, since the convergence tests prevent the algorithm from cycling and therefore, after finitely many steps, the method amounts to Benders' decomposition, which is known to be finite (see e.g. [van Roy 1983] and [Holmberg 1990], respectively).

2 Dually-weighted cross decomposition

[Holmberg 1992] proposed a modification of the cross decomposition algorithm (*mean value cross decomposition*) to solve linear programming problems, where, in contrast to the cross decomposition algorithm, not the last optimal solution of one subproblem is used as input to the other and vice versa, but the arithmetic mean of *all* previously obtained optimal solutions of the respective subproblem. No master problems are used anymore and asymptotic convergence towards the optimum can be proven.

A somewhat similar approach is suggested here for the (CFLP). Instead of using the optimal dual solutions of the primal subproblems or the optimal solutions of the dual master problem as Lagrangean multipliers for the dual subproblems (like in cross decomposition) or taking the arithmetic mean of all these multipliers (like in mean value cross decomposition), a specially weighted average of the previously constructed multipliers is used.
More precisely, let $\tilde{\mu}^k$ be either the optimal dual solution of the current transportation problem (SP_{y^k}) or the optimal solution of the dual master problem (MD_k), and $\mu^{\text{best},k}$ the Lagrangean multipliers corresponding to the best lower bound $(= v(SD_{\mu^{\text{best},k}}))$ after k iterations. Then, the new Lagrangean multipliers used in the next iteration for the dual subproblem are defined as

$$\mu^{k+1} = (\mu_j^{k+1})_{j=1}^n \quad \text{with} \quad \mu_j^{k+1} := (w \cdot \mu_j^{\text{best},k} + \tilde{\mu}_j^k)/(w+1),$$

where the weight w is defined as

$$w := \min\{9, (\text{number of iterations} + \text{number of improvements of the lower bound})/2\}.$$

If the lower bound can be improved in the next iteration step, then $\mu^{\text{best},k+1} := \mu^{k+1}$, otherwise $\mu^{\text{best},k+1} := \mu^{\text{best},k}$.
Thus, only a small move into the direction of the new multiplier $\tilde{\mu}^k$, which would be used in the normal cross decomposition algorithm, is performed. Furthermore, only those multipliers are considered in the next steps that led to an increase in the lower bound.
The minimum share of $\tilde{\mu}^k$ in the newly constructed multiplier μ^{k+1} (here: 1/10) may be altered in the course of the algorithm, for instance in case the value of the dual master problem does not decrease in a specified number of iterations.
The procedure leaves all the other steps of the cross decomposition algorithm unchanged and is called *dually-weighted cross decomposition.*
It can be (directly) shown that the following assertion holds (the cut belonging to (x^k, y^k) in (MD_k) is defined as $\sum_{j=1}^n f_j y_j^k + \sum_{i=1}^m \sum_{j=1}^n c_{ij} x_{ij}^k - \sum_{j=1}^n (s_j y_j^k - \sum_{i=1}^m x_{ij}^k)\mu_j \geq \delta$):
Lemma 1: Let $\tilde{\mu}^k$ be an optimal solution of (MD_k), $\mu^{\text{best},k}$ and μ^{k+1} defined as above, and (x^{k+1}, y^{k+1}) an optimal solution of $(SD_{\mu^{k+1}})$. Then the following holds:
If the cut belonging to (x^{k+1}, y^{k+1}) is already contained in (MD_k), then

$$v(SD_{\mu^{k+1}}) \geq v(SD_{\mu^{\text{best},k}}) + (v(MD_k) - v(SD_{\mu^{\text{best},k}}))/w.$$

That is, the lower bound always strictly increases, if a dual cut belonging to a solution of the dual subproblem already exists in (MD_k). Therefore, in combination with the convergence tests in steps 2 and 3 no cycling is possible without narrowing the duality gap $v(MD_k) - v(SD_{\mu^{\text{best},k}})$ in the course of the algorithm. This leads to the following theorem:

Theorem 1: The dually-weighted cross decomposition algorithm solves the (CFLP) in a finite number of steps.

The following two lemmas give more insight into the behaviour and characteristics of the procedure. Lemma 2 gives an upper bound on the possible improvement of the lower bound in the next iteration step, if a dual cut is generated a second time:

Lemma 2: (Same notation as in Lemma 1) If the cut belonging to (x^{k+1}, y^{k+1}) is already contained in (MD_k), then the increase of the lower bound in the next iteration step is limited to

$$(v(SD_{\mu^{\text{best},k+1}}) - v(SD_{\mu^{\text{best},k}})) \cdot (w-1)\,/\,w.$$

Lemma 3: (Same notation as in Lemma 1)

$$v(SD_{\tilde{\mu}^k}) \geq v(SD_{\mu^{\text{best},k}}) \Rightarrow v(SD_{\mu^{k+1}}) \geq v(SD_{\mu^{\text{best},k}}).$$

In other words, lemma 3 states that every time a normal cross decomposition step gives an improvement of the lower bound, the same is true for dually-weighted cross decomposition. It is important to note that the opposite does not hold, although a normal cross decomposition step possibly yields a higher improvement of the lower bound.

3 Results

The cross decomposition and the dually-weighted cross decomposition algorithms were tested on 27 examples with 19-108 potential facilities and 65-174 customers on the road network of Switzerland. In these examples, a tolerance level τ of 0.5% for the duality gap $v(MD_k) - v(SD_{\mu^{\text{best},k}})$ was used, in step 3 the dual solution $(\lambda^{k+1}, \nu^{k+1}, \mu^{k+1})$ was altered as described in [Wentges 1993], and at most thirty iterations were carried out.

With the new dually-weighted cross decomposition algorithm better results could be achieved in almost all examples compared to ordinary cross decomposition. The Lagrangean dual could now be solved within the tolerance level τ in 19 instead of 11 examples (where only in three of these 11 examples, the tolerance level was reached earlier by ordinary cross decomposition, and in two cases, the same number of iterations was needed). In all other examples the duality gap $v(MD_k) - v(SD_{\mu^{\text{best},k}})$ could be decreased substantially.

Remark: Weighting the Lagrangean multipliers as described above, may also be useful in other applications of Dantzig-Wolfe decomposition.

References

Cornuejols, G., Sridharan, R. and Thizy, J. M. (1991). A Comparison of Heuristics and Relaxations for the Capacitated Plant Location Problem. *European Journal of Operational Research*, 50:280–297.

Holmberg, K. (1990). On the Convergence of Cross Decomposition. *Mathematical Programming*, 47:269–296.

Holmberg, K. (1992). Linear Mean Value Cross Decomposition: A Generalization of the Kornai-Liptak Method. *European Journal of Operational Research*, 62:55–73.

van Roy, T. J. (1983). Cross Decomposition for Mixed Integer Programming. *Mathematical Programming*, 25:46–63.

van Roy, T. J. (1986). A Cross Decomposition Algorithm for Capacitated Facility Location. *Operations Research*, 34(1):145–163.

Wentges, P. (1993). On Benders' Decomposition for the Capacitated Facility Location Problem. In: Karmann, A., Mosler, K., Schader, M. and Uebe, G., editors, *Operations Research '92*, pages 155–158. Physica Verlag, Heidelberg.

PREASSIGNMENTS IN CHROMATIC SCHEDULING

D. de Werra
Department of Mathematics
Swiss Federal Institute of Technology
MA-Ecublens, CH-1015 Lausanne, Switzerland

Some types of scheduling problems can be solved as edge coloring models in bipartite multigraphs. It is in particular the case for preemptive open shop scheduling. The presence of additional constraints generally transforms this polynomially solvable type of problem into a difficult one. The study of polynomially solvable special cases is therefore interesting for guiding the development of general heuristic procedures.

Among these additional constraints, the so called preassignment constraints play an important role. They can be handled by saying that in the graph model some edges have been precolored and this precoloring must be extended to the whole graph (with a given number of colors available).

In general this problem is NP-complete; however we will consider special cases where the precolored edges are simply a bicolored path or cycle. This will lead us to study several classes of (multi-)graphs for which the extension of coloring can be done easily whatever cycle or path is precolored.

A <u>mouth</u> in a graph consists of three elementary chains of some parity having the same end nodes (the intermediate nodes are all distinct). A mouth is <u>even</u>(resp. <u>odd</u>) if the three chains are even (resp. odd). It is a <u>cone</u> if at least one of the three chains has length two.

A <u>cpi k-coloring</u> of the edges of a multigraph G is an assignment to each edge of one color chosen in the cyclically ordered set {1,...,k} such that:

a) all edges in a family of p parallel edges receive p cyclically consecutive colors (notice that if $p > k$ the same color can occur several times)
b) in every bundle of adjacent edges the colors form a cyclic interval.

A simple graph G is cpi-perfect if all multigraphs G* obtained by multiplying edges of G in an arbitrary way has a cpi k-coloring for any k.

Such colorings are needed in some types of cyclic scheduling.

Proposition 1

For a connected bipartite graph G the following statements are equivalent:

a) G is cpi-perfect
b) G is outerplanar
c) G does not contain a mouth as a partial graph.

Such graphs can be recognized and colored in polynomial time (Mahadev, Solot, de Werra, 1992). A handle is a chain of positive length attached to a cycle C at its endpoints x,y and such that at least one chain of C between x and y has all degrees two in G, $\Delta(G)$ is the maximum degree in G.

Proposition 2

For a graph G, the following statements are equivalent:

a) G is bipartite and does not contain an even mouth as a partial subgraph

b) Every non-trivial block of G can be reduced to a cycle by repeatedly removing the intermediate nodes and all the edges of an odd handle in the remaining graph

c) In all partials subgraphs H any bicolored cycle C can be extended to an edge $\Delta(H)$-coloring of H.

The graphs in proposition 2 can be recognized in polynomial time and their coloring can be extended in polynomial time (de Werra, Mahadev, Peled, 1992).

Proposition 3

For a simple bipartite graph G, the following statements are equivalent:

1) G contains no cone as a partial subgraph
2) For any partial subgraph H of G and for any cycle C in H, a bicoloring of C can be extended to an edge $\Delta(H)$-coloring of H.

Again these graphs can be recognized in polynomial time and the same holds for their coloring (extension) (Mahadev, Peled, de Werra, 1993). It is easy to see that the three classes of graphs (restricted to simple graphs) described in the propositions satisfy inclusion relations (due to the absence of mouths of various types).

REFERENCES

Mahadev N.V.R., Solot Ph., de Werra D. (1992) The cyclic compact open shop scheduling problem (to appear)

de Werra D., Mahadev N.V.R., Peled U.N. (1992) Edge-chromatic scheduling with simultaneity constraints (to appear)

Mahadev N.V.R., Peled U.N., de Werra D. (1993) Preassignments in preemptive open shop scheduling (submitted for publication)

RECONSTRUCTION OF PUBLIC FINANCE IN A STOCHASTIC DIFFERENTIAL GAME FRAMEWORK

David W.K. Yeung
School of Economics and Finance
and
Centre of Urban Planning & Environmental Management
University of Hong Kong
Hong Kong

In the past decade, there is an emerging trend for the use of game theoretical framework in studying government tax plicies. The game theoretical approach allows the possibility of simultaneous interactions between government policy and decentralized private decisions. This paper develops a stochastic differential game between the government and the public. The public chooses an investment strategy to maximize the present value of income net of tax and investment expenditures. The government controls the tax system and aims at maximizing a weighted sum of tax collected, the level of bonds outstanding and income net of investment expenditures. Two dynamic processes — one for the capital formation and the other for bonds accumulation — are present in the model. The dynamic processes are subject to stochastic shocks. A feedback Nash equilibrium solution of the game is obtained. The parabolic partial differential equations characterizing the value functions of the game equilibrium is solved explicitly. Closed-from solutions of the equilibrium investment strategy and tax policy are provided. The stationary (longrun equilibrium) joint density function of capital stock and bonds is also obtained.

THE GAME MODEL

Consider the following modified Futagami's (1989) type of macroeconomic system

$$dK(t) = \left[I(t)^{\frac{1}{2}} - \delta K(t)\right] dt + \Omega K(t) dz_1(t) \tag{1}$$

$$S(t) = I(t) \tag{2}$$

$$S(t) = u(t) \equiv \text{the control strategy of the public} \tag{3}$$

$$Y(t) = aK(t) - \pi K(t)^2 \tag{4}$$

$$C(t) = Y(t) + rB(t) - S(t) - T(t) \tag{5}$$

$$T(t) = \tau(t) \equiv \text{the control strategy of the government} \tag{6}$$

$$dB(t) = \left[rB(t) - T(t)\right] dt + \sigma B(t) dz_2(t) \tag{7}$$

where $K(t)$ is the volume of capital stock at time t, $I(t)$ is the level of real investment, $S(t)$ is real savings for investment purposes, $Y(t)$ is the level of output, $C(t)$ is real income net of savings and tax, $B(t)$ is the stock of government bonds, $T(t)$ is the amount of tax in real terms, δ is the rate of depreciation of the capital stock, r

is the discount rate, a and π are production function parameters. $z_1(t)$ and $z_2(t)$ are independent Wiener processes with $[dz_1(t)] = 0$, $E[dz_2(t)] = 0$, $\text{var}[dz_1(t)] = dt$, $\text{var}[dz_2(t)] = dt$.

The public's objective is to maximize expected real income net of savings for investment purposes and tax; that is,

$$\max_{u(t)} E_0 \left\{ \int_0^\infty C(s) e^{-rs} ds \right\}$$

$$= \max_{u(t)} E_0 \left\{ \int_0^\infty \left[aK(s) - \pi K(s)^2 + rB(s) - u(s) - \tau(s) \right] e^{-rs} ds \right\} \tag{8}$$

On the other hand, the government maximizies its popularity which is positively related to before tax income net of savings for investment purposes, and negatively to tax imposed and bonds outstanding. Specifically, its objective is:

$$\max_{\tau(t)} E_0 \left\{ \int_0^\infty \left\{ \gamma[aK(s) - \pi K(s)^2 + rB(s) - u(s)] - b\tau(s)^2 - \omega B(s)^2 \right\} e^{-rs} ds \right\} \tag{9}$$

where γ, b, and ω are the government's welfare weights.

FEEDBACK NASH EQUILIBRIUM SOLUTION

A pair of feedback strategies $\{u^*(s) = \phi^*(K, B, s),\ \tau^*(s) = \varphi^*(K, B, s)\}$ providing a Nash equilibrium solution for the stochastic game (1)–(9) is obtained vis-a-vis solving the parabolic partial differential equations (see Basar and Olsder (1982)):

$$\begin{aligned} -V_t = \max_u \Big\{ & \left[aK - \pi K^2 + rB - u - \tau \right] e^{-rt} + V_K \left(u^{\frac{1}{2}} - \delta K \right) \\ & + V_B(rB - \tau) + \frac{1}{2} \Omega^2 K^2 V_{KK} + \frac{1}{2} \sigma^2 B^2 V_{BB} \Big\} \\ -U_t = \max_u \Big\{ & \left[\gamma(aK - \pi K^2 + rB - u) e^{-rt} - b\tau^2 - \omega B^2 \right] e^{-rt} \\ & + U_K \left(u^{\frac{1}{2}} - \delta K \right) + U_B(rB - \tau) + \frac{1}{2} \Omega^2 K^2 U_{KK} + \frac{1}{2} \sigma^2 B^2 U_{BB} \Big\} \end{aligned} \tag{10}$$

In particular, they are:

$$\phi^*(K, B, t) = e^{2rt} \frac{1}{4} V_K^2 \quad \text{and} \quad \varphi^*(K, B, t) = -e^{rt} \frac{U_B}{2b} \tag{11}$$

where

$$V(K, B, t) = e^{-rt} \left[A_1 K^2 + C_1 K + F_1 B + G_1 \right]$$

$$U(K, B, t) = e^{-rt} \left[A_2 K^2 + C_2 K + D_2 B^2 + F_2 B + G_2 \right]$$

with

$$A_1 = \frac{1}{2}\left[(r + 2\delta - \Omega^2) - \sqrt{(r + 2\delta - \Omega^2)^2 + 4\pi}\right]$$

$$C_1 = \frac{2a}{r + \Omega^2 + \sqrt{(r + 2\delta - \Omega^2)^2 + 4\pi}}$$

$$F_1 = \frac{r - \sigma^2 - \sqrt{(r + \sigma^2)^2 + 4\omega/b}}{r + \sigma^2 + \sqrt{(r + \sigma^2)^2 + 4\omega/b}}$$

$$G_1 = \frac{a^2}{r\left[r + \Omega^2 + \sqrt{(r + 2\delta - \Omega^2)^2 + 4\pi}\right]^2} + \frac{2\gamma r}{b\left[(r + \sigma^2) + \sqrt{(r + \sigma^2)^2 + 4\omega/b}\right]^2}$$

$$A_2 = \frac{\gamma}{2}\left[(r + 2\delta - \Omega^2) - \sqrt{(r + 2\delta - \Omega^2)^2 + 4\pi}\right]$$

$$C_2 = \frac{2\gamma a}{r + \Omega^2 + \sqrt{(r + 2\delta - \Omega^2)^2 + 4\pi}}$$

$$D_2 = -\frac{b}{2}\left[r + \sigma^2 + \sqrt{(r + \sigma^2)^2 + 4\omega/b}\right]$$

$$F_2 = \frac{2\gamma r}{\left[r + \sigma^2 + \sqrt{(r + \sigma^2)^2 + 4\omega/b}\right]}$$

$$G_2 = \frac{\gamma a^2}{r\left[r + \Omega^2 + \sqrt{(r + 2\delta - \Omega^2)^2 + 4\pi}\right]^2} + \frac{\gamma^2 r}{b\left[(r + \sigma^2) + \sqrt{(r + \sigma^2)^2 + 4\omega/b}\right]^2}$$

One can readily obtain:

P1. The higher the current level of government bonds, the higher the amount of tax imposed.

P2. The larger the current capital stock the lower (higher) the level of investment if the current capital stock is smaller (greater) than $-C_1/2A_1$.

CAPITAL AND BONDS ACCUMULATION IN GAME EQUILIBRIUM

Capital and bonds accumulation in game equilibrium can be readily obtained by substituting (11) into (1) and (7):

$$dK(s) = \left\{\frac{1}{2}C_1 + (A_1 - \delta)K(s)\right\} ds + \Omega K dz_1(s)$$

$$= \left\{\frac{a}{r + \Omega^2 + \sqrt{(r + 2\delta - \Omega^2)^2 + 4\pi}}\right.$$

$$-\frac{1}{2}\left[\sqrt{(r+2\delta-\Omega^2)^2+4\pi}-(r-\Omega^2)\right]K(s)\Bigg\}ds+\Omega K(s)dz_1(s) \tag{12}$$

$$dB(s)=\left\{\frac{1}{2b}F_2+(\frac{1}{b}D_2+r)B(s)\right\}ds+\sigma B(s)dz_2(s)$$

$$=\Bigg\{\frac{\gamma r}{b[(r+\sigma^2)+\sqrt{(r+\sigma^2)^2+4\omega/b}}$$

$$-\frac{1}{2}\left[\sigma^2+\sqrt{(r+\sigma^2)^2+4\omega/b}-r\right]B(s)\Bigg\}ds+\sigma B(s)dz_2(s).$$

The stationary joint density function of K and B can be obtained as:

$$\xi^{ss}(k,b)=\eta^{ss}(K)\xi^{ss}(B)$$

$$=\frac{m}{\Omega^2}K^{2[A_1-\delta-\Omega^2]/\Omega^2}\exp\left[\frac{-C_1}{\Omega^2 K}\right]\frac{n}{\sigma^2}B^{2[\frac{1}{b}D_2+r-\sigma^2]/\sigma^2}\exp\left[\frac{-F_2}{b\sigma^2 B}\right] \tag{13}$$

Observe that for any given value of B, ξ^{ss} will reach a maximum at $K=\frac{-C_1}{2(A_1-\delta-\Omega^2)}$. Similarly, for any given value of K, ξ^{ss} will reach a maximum at $B=\frac{-F_2}{2b\left(\frac{1}{b}D_2+r-\sigma^2\right)}$. Two results follow directly.

P3. The higher the degree of uncertainty in the capital accumulation process — Ω^2, the lower the most likely realizable level of capital stock in the stationary state.

P4. The higher the degree of uncertainty in the bonds accumulation process — σ^2, the lower the most likely realizable level of bonds outstanding in the stationary state.

REFERENCES

Bazar, T. and G.J. Olsder (1982). *Dynamic noncooperative game theory.* Academic Press, New York.

Futagmi, K. (1989). A game theoretical approach to reconstruction of public finance. *Journal of Public Economics* **40:** 135–150.

STOCHASTIC FOREST MANAGEMENT BASED ON AN INTERACTIVE TECHNIQUE

Lidija Zadnik Stirn
University of Ljubljana
Biotechnical Faculty, Department of Forestry
Večna pot 83, 61000 Ljubljana, Slovenia

AREA DESCRIPTION

In the forest the silvicultural and utilization process is carried out by performing a sequence of decisions, like the felling and the planting of the trees. Within these practices the forest product is yielded. The amount of the yield should stay at an approximately fixed annual level. This could be realized by so-called "normal forest". Moreover, living and growing of the trees are affected by unpredictable natural circumstances. Therefore, the forest as a system contains both, the decision making and the probabilistic features. Stochastic dynamic models are very appropriate for providing the optimal forest management decisions maximizing the sustained timber production and net revenues to the society (Hool (1966), Lembersky et al. (1975), Binkley (1980), Kao (1982), Kaya et al. (1987), Hassler et al. (1988)).

A general stochastic dynamic model used for optimal forest management is described by Zadnik (1992). The forest process is treated as a discrete multistage process since the decisions are carried out only at discrete time points t $(t=0,1,\ldots,i,i+1,\ldots)$. These time points divide the time into time intervals. We say, that in the time point $t=i$ a forest as a system occupies a state $s^*(i)$ when it is described by the values of variables that define the state. The system makes a transition to a new state $s^*(i+1)$ in the lapse of time interval under the influence of the decision $d(s^*(i),h)$, where $h=1,\ldots,H$ and H is the number of all the possible decisions at the forest state $s^*(i)$: $s^*(i+1) = f(s^*(i),d(s^*(i),h))$. The forest process has a stochastic character. There exists the probability $p(s^*(i),s^*(i+1),d(s^*(i),h))$ of a transition to the state $s^*(i+1)$ during the next time interval, given that the system occupies the state $s^*(i)$ and that the decision $d(s^*(i),h)$ is undertaken. Each transition of the system generates the reward $r(s^*(i),s^*(i+1),d(s^*(i),h))$ associated with a net revenue from timber harvest and other revenues to the society. An optimal sequence of decisions and rewards are usually determined by the use of discrete stochastic dynamic programming (Vadnal (1976)).

Let us suppose that there are N states $s^*(i)$ in the forest system at each time point t $(t=0,1,\ldots,i,i+1,\ldots)$, numbered from 1 to N, and that the probability of the transition from the state $s^*(i)$ to the state $s^*(i+1)$ is a function only of these two states and not of any history of the system before its arrival in $s^*(i)$. This probability is constant over time (homogeneous stationary Markov model). Under these suppositions a discrete-time Markov process (Kouba (1977), Suzuki (1984), Zadnik (1987)) can be involved in the above described forest management model. In such a model, the state of the forest $s^*(i)$ is modelled using only the ratio of the various age classes of the forest. This means, that all the trees are distributed over a finite number of classes and that the trees move from one class to another independently of each other, i. e. there is no interaction among the individual trees taken into account. The last assumption is an extremely limiting one. That is why the focus of this paper is on the interaction among the individual trees, on the so-called interactive Markov model. It was proposed by Conlisk (1976), used in the studies of dynamics of social systems (Kulkarni et al. (1989), Omladič (1991), (1992)), but it has not yet been introduced to forestry.

INTERACTIVE MARKOV MODEL USED IN FOREST MANAGEMENT

All the trees (a large number of trees is assumed) of a managed forest are distributed within n mutually exclusive classes, assigned by $1,2,\ldots,k,j,\ldots,n$. In this case, it is possible to describe the state of the forest at each time point t ($t=0,1,\ldots,i,i+1,\ldots$) in a form of a vector $s(i) = (s_{1i},s_{2i},\ldots, s_{ki},s_{ji},\ldots,s_{ni})$. The probabilities p_{kj} for an individual tree to move from class k to class j in the next time interval form a stochastic matrix P in a homogeneous stationary Markov case. Universally, the matrix $P = [p_{kj}]$ is assumed not to depend on s(i), that is, not to depend on the interactive behaviour of the trees: $s(i+1) = Ps(i)$.

It is the interactive Markov model which includes the fact that individual trees follow not only their own development but are also influenced by the others. This model is derived from a general Markov model and concerns that the elements of P are functions of s(i). P is written as $P[s(i)]$. The model takes the interactive form:

$$s(i+1) = P[s(i)]\,s(i) \qquad (1)$$

For the sake of simplicity a linear dependence is assumed. The interactive transition probabilities being sensitive to s(i) are in the time interval from $t=i$ to $t=i+1$ given as:

$$p_{kj}(s) = a_{kj} + b_{kj}s_{ki} \qquad (2)$$

where: $k=1,\ldots,n$; $j=1,\ldots,n$; s_{ki} denotes the proportion of the trees being in the class k at the time point $t=i$; $s_{ki} \geq 0$ for $k=1,\ldots,n$ and $\Sigma_k\, s_{ki} = 1$; $a_{kj} \geq 0$; a_{kj} and b_{kj} have to be small enough, so that $0 \leq p_{kj}(s) \leq 1$.

Since each column of $P[s(i)] = [p_{kj}(s)]$ must sum to one, the normalization of $p_{kj}(s)$ is needed. A suggestion of Conlisk (1976) is accepted and $p_{kj}(s)$ is expressed as:

$$p_{kj}(s) = (a_{kj} + b_{kj}s_{ki})/A_j(s) \quad (3)$$

where $A_j(s) = \Sigma_k (a_{kj} + b_{kj}s_{ki})$; min $A_j(s) > 0$ for all (k,j).
The interactive Markov model defined with the equation (3) is a general Markov model if $B = [b_{kj}] = 0$. From such a point of view the matrix $A = [a_{kj}]$ presents the transition probabilities which are independent on s(i). The matrix A is easy to define in the application of the equation (3) in the above described stochastic dynamic model for forest management as A = P. Some numerical examples (Kouba (1977), Suzuki (1984)) have already been given for P. Further, the coefficients of matrix B expressing the interaction among the trees should be determined empirically. b_{kj} should be positive in the case of attracting influence, otherwise they should be negative. Given the values for the matrices $A = [a_{kj}]$ and $B = [b_{kj}]$, we have a complete dynamic model. The evolution of s(i) from any initial value s(0) is determined by the equation (1). The question on equilibria for the equation (1) follows. The equilibrium is such a vector s* that s(i) = s(i+1) = s(i+2) = ... = s*. Its components are positive; their sum equals to one. The equilibrium s* is the solution of the equation:

$$s^* = P[s(i)]s^* \quad (4)$$

At least one such s* exists because of the Brouwers fixed point theorem. As shown by Conlisk (1976), the matrix P[s(i)] satisfies the conditions of the Perron-Frobenius theorem. Therefore, there exists only one fixed point s* of the equation (4). Applying this fact to the problem of forestry, s* should be regarded as a "normal forest" state which ensures the demanded, approximately equal, annual yield from the forest.

By applying the interactive Markov model, in the forestry, another question appears: Under what conditions the state s* becomes stable as soon as the forest finds itself in a close neighbourhood of this state? As discussed by Omladič (1992), the state s* is stable if $B - B^T$ is small enough, i. e. if the matrix B is very near to a symmetric matrix. The statement needs some further investigation.

CONCLUSIONS

To describe the changes of the forest state the application of the interactive Markov model should normally take place in the case where the trees are stratified according to some biological or/and economic attributes (the simplest attribute is the volume of the tree). The choice of such attributes and the stratification may be very sensitive and may have a great influence on the results of the model. A great attention has to be paid also to the fact that in forestry an upward class mobility is prevailed (a tree passes to a lower class - the class 1 only in the case when the tree is cut and afforestation takes place). Because of this fact the model should be modified in the sense of new results presented by Kulkarni et al. (1989). Different growth rates of various classes interesting in forest modelling as well, are also discussed by Kulkarni et al. (1989). Because of large number of trees treated in the model, the trees with nearly equal properties should be grouped with the aim to make the problem controllable, without loss of the generality.

The presented interactive Markov model should not be taken for granted. How well it will fit in the above presented stochastic dynamic model, is also a matter of a serious empirical and statistical testing.

In general Markov process, the question of homogeneities is often in the limelight. We have to point out that the elements of P[s(i)] in the equation (2) are indirectly time dependent. Further, the influence of d(s*(i),h) on the state transition can be considered with an additional linear entry at the right side of equation (2). This idea goes beyond the scope of this paper and will be given elsewhere.

REFERENCES

Binkley C S (1980) Is Succession in Hardwood Forests a Stationary Markov Process. For Sci 26: 566-570
Conlisk J (1976) Interactive Markov Chains. Journal of Mathematical Sociology 4:157-185
Hassler C C, Disney R L, Sinclair S A (1988) A Discrete State, Continuous Parameter Markov Process Approach to Timber Harvesting Systems Analysis. For Sci 34: 276-291
Hool J N (1966) A Dynamic Programming Markov Chain Approach to Forest Production Control. For Sci Mon 12
Kaya I, Buongiorno J (1987) Economic Harvesting of Uneven-Aged Northern Hardwood Stands Under Risk. For Sci 33: 889-907
Kao C (1982) Optimal Stocking Levels Under Risk. For Sci 28: 711-719
Kouba J (1977) Markov Chain and Modelling in the Long-term Development of the Age Structure and Production of Forests. Scienta Agriculturae Bohemoslovaca 26: 179-193
Kulkarni M S, Kumar A (1989) Interactive Markovian Models of Progressive Trends. Journal of Mathematical Sociology 14: 45-65
Lembersky M R, Johnson K N (1975) Optimal Policies for Managed Stands: An Infinite Markov Decision Process Approach. For Sci 75: 109-122
Omladič V (1991) Nekateri modeli zaposlovanja in promocije. Blejsko met. srečanje, Metodološki zv. 8, Ljubljana: 123-135
Omladič V (1992) Applications of Interactive Markov Models in the Dynamics of Social Systems. Proceedings, 2nd Conference on Operational Research, Rovinj, Croatia, Oct. 5-7, editor Bahovec et al., HDOI: 185-193
Suzuki T (1984) The Gentan Probability, a Model for the Improvement of the Normal Forest Concept and of Forest Planning. Proceedings of IUFRO Symposium on Forest Management, Tokyo
Vadnal A (1976) Diskretno dinamično programiranje. Državna založba Slovenije, Ljubljana
Zadnik L (1987) A Stochastic Process in Forestry. Proceedings of SYM-OP-IS 87, Herceg Novi, Oct. 6 - 9: 1033-1039
Zadnik L (1992) Combinatorial Optimization in a Long-term Forest Management Process. Mathematical Modelling of Forest Ecosystems, edited by Franke et al., Sauerl. Verlag, Frankfurt: 168-174.

SOLVING DIAL-A-RIDE PROBLEMS IN PRACTICE

Doris Zepf
Universität Passau
Innstr. 29, D-94032 Passau

We want to represent the results of a joint work with a public transportation company. In the last years, the public transportation services were looking for alternatives for scheduled busses. As a result of decreasing demand for public transportation in the off-peak-hours, the aim was to provide more efficient means of transportation. One result of these considerations is the dial-a-ride system.

The dial-a-ride taxis have a fixed time-table, but they run only if required. The customer has to book them before. Moreover, there are fixed stops for departure, but the people are transported where they want, e.g. to their home.

The dial-a-ride system has the advantage of increasing rentability. Further it is more comfortable because of more security, decreasing travel time and easy transport etc.

Our goal is now to realize the automatic disposition of the taxis. We have to determine how many vehicles are necessary and to fix the routes the taxis have to drive, such that certain conditions are fulfilled and a given objective (cost) function is as low as possible.

From the transportation company we were given time restrictions. Because of the organizational structure it was necesseary to produce good solutions within 5 minutes such that a re-optimization can be called if belatet orders arrive or the side conditions change (e.g. if not enough taxis are ready to carry out the bookings).

Therefore we managed the problem with vehicle routing. We implemented fast heuristics that computed feasible solutions and improving procedures to improve the objective function. Moreover, to examine the quality of the solutions, we modelled the problem as a set partitioning problem. Based on this integer programming model, we compute lower bounds with cutting plane techniques.

METHODS

For the vehicle routing approach we constructed the graph in the following way. The region which is served is partitioned into a number of sections. The nodes of the underlying graph are in a one-to-one correspondence to the sections. Two nodes are connected by an edge if there is a street connecting the two corresponding sections without passing throughhh a third zone. The edge weights represent the time/distance between its endpoints.

In our special case the side constraints were the following. The maximal duration of a tour totals 15 minutes. The taxis have a maximal capacity of 4 persons. Further the comfort of the customer shall be increased, so there is a maximal delay (of 5 minutes) for him to be picked up. Because of the different departure times outward and inward demands are treated separately.

The current vehicle routing problem now has precedence constraints because every customer has to be picked up before he is delivered. On the other hand we are confronted with time windows because the customers must be picked up within a given time.

We implemented several constructing heuristics, similar to the greedy or insertion heuristics of the TSP or to the savings [1] heuristic. As improving methods we used 2-exchange and 2-Or-exchange methods inside a tour and between different tours.

In the set partitioning attempt we generate in a heuristic way feasible tours one vehicle can carry out following the time and capacity restrictions. The columns of the resulting matrix indicate which appointments each of the generated tours executes. We now have to solve the set partitioning problem

$$(IP) \qquad \begin{aligned} \min\ & c^T x \\ \text{s.t. } & Ax = \mathbf{1} \\ & x \in \{0,1\}^n \end{aligned}$$

where A is a 0-1-matrix with m rows and n columns and $\mathbf{1} = (1, \ldots, 1)$.

We start with the solution of the LP-relaxation $\min\{c^T x \mid Ax = \mathbf{1},\ x \geq 0\}$ and step by step add cutting planes to improve the lower bounds. The set partitioning polytope is a subset of both the set packing polytope and the set covering polytope. For this reason valid inequalities for the set covering or the set packing polytope are also valid for the set partitioning polytope.

We use the odd cycle and clique inequalities [2] of the set packing polytope as cutting planes. Further we have found new facet inducing graphs for the set packing problem that we also separate in a heuristic way.

If the cutting plane procedure doesn't find an integer optimum, we start a heuristic which successively tries to fix some of the non-integer components to 0 or 1 until an integer solution is found or no further fixings are possible. The heuristic not necessarily provides an integer feasible solution, but a lower bound that is compared with the upper bound provided by the vehicle routing heuristics.

RESULTS

For the given test problems our heuristics constructed optimal or near-optimal solutions. With our cutting plane procedures we could prove the optimality of our vehicle routing heuristics in many cases.

REFERENCES

[1] Clarke, G., Wright, J.: Scheduling of vehicles from a central depot to a number of delivery points. Operations Research 12 (1964), pp. 568 – 581.

[2] Padberg, M.W.: On the Facial Structure of Set Packing Polyhedra. Mathematical Programming 5 (1973), pp. 199 – 215.

Robust Mappings and Optimization

Deming Zhuang
Department of Mathematics and Computer Studies
Mount Saint Vincent University
Halifax, Nova Scotia, Canada B3M 2J6

The concept of robust sets and mappings was proposed in [4]-[5] to enlarge the classes of objectives and constraints of global optimization problems.

Definition 1 *Let X be a topological space and A be a subset of X. A is said to be* **robust** *iff*

$$\text{cl}\, A = \text{cl int}\, A, \tag{1}$$

where cl A *is the closure of* A *and* int A *is the interior of* A. $x \in A$ *is said to be a* **robust point** *of* A *iff* $x \in \text{cl int}\, A$. *If* x *is a robust point of* A, *then* A *is said to be a* **semi-neighbourhood** *of* x.

The concepts of robust sets, robust points and semi-neighbourhoods are extensions of those of open sets, interior points and neighbourhoods, respectively. Any open set of X, including the empty set, is robust. Any interior point of A is a robust point of A. Any neighbourhood of x is a semi-neighbourhood of x.

Definition 2 *Let X and Y be two topological spaces and $f : X \to Y$ be a mapping. f is said to be* **robust at** $x \in X$ *iff for any neighbourhood $U_Y(y)$ of $y = f(x)$, $f^{-1}(U_Y(y))$ is a semi-neighbourhood of x or x is a robust point* *of $f^{-1}(U_Y(y))$. f is said to be* **robust** *iff f is robust at every $x \in X$ or for any open set U_Y of Y, $f^{-1}(U_Y)$ is robust in X.*

The concept of robustness for a mapping is an extension of that of continuity. Any continuous mapping is robust, but a robust mapping may be discontinuous.

An approximatable mapping is a generically continuous mapping with "approximatable" discontinuous points of the graph:

Definition 3 *Let X and Y be two topological spaces and $f : X \to Y$ be a mapping. Suppose that S is the set of points of continuity of f. Then f is said to be* **approximatable** *iff*

1. *S is dense in X;*

2. *for any $\bar{x} \in X$, there exists a net $\{x_\alpha\} \subset S$ such that*

$$\lim_\alpha x_\alpha = \bar{x} \quad \text{and} \quad \lim_\alpha f(x_\alpha) = f(\bar{x}).$$

In the optimization theory and practice, the continuity of the mappings involved are not always guaranteed. Fortunately, the continuity of the mappings are also not indispensable. What we really need, in designing an algorithm to solve an optimization problem is the approximatability. Thus, the following theorem, assert the equivelance of approximatability and robustness of mappings in most useful cases, justifies the concept of robustness.

Theorem 1 [*2*] *Any approximatable mapping is robust. If X is a Baire space and Y satisfies the second axiom of countability. Then a mapping $f : X \to Y$ is robust iff it is approximatable. In this case, the set D of points of discontinuity of a robust mapping is always of the first category.*

The above theorem can be generalized to set-valued mappings, see [3].

Applications of robust mappings to global optimization and other areas can also be found in [9], [1], [4], [5], [6], [7], [8].

References

[1] Chew, S and Zheng, Q, *Integral Global Optimization: Theory, Implementation and Applications,* Lecture Notes in Econ. & Math. Sys., **298**, Springer-Verlag, 1988.

[2] Shi, S. Zheng, Q. and Zhuang, D. Discontinuous robust mappings are approximatable, to appear.

[3] Shi, S. Zheng, Q. and Zhuang, D. Set-valued robust mappings and approximatable mappings, to appear.

[4] Zheng, Q. Robust analysis and global minimization of a class of discontinuous functions (I), *Acta Mathematicae Applicatae Sinica* (English Series), **6** (1990), 205-223.

[5] Zheng, Quan, Robust analysis and global minimization of a class of discontinuous functions (II), *Acta Mathematicae Applicatae Sinica* (English Series), **6** (1990), 317-337.

[6] Zheng, Q. and Zhuang, D. Integral global optimization of constrained problems in functional space with discontinuous penalty functions, in *Recent Advances in Global Optimization,* C. A. Floudas and P. M. Pardalos eds., Princeton University Press, 1991.

[7] Zheng, Q. and Zhuang, D. Approximation of fixed points of robust mappings, to appear.

[8] Zheng, Q. and Zhuang, D. Finite Dimensional Approximation to solutions of minimization problems in functional spaces, *Optimization* **26** (1992) p. 33-50.

[9] Zheng, Q. Jiang, B. C. and Zhuang, S. L., A method for finding global extrema, *Acta Mathematicae Applicatae Sinica,* **1** (1978), 161-174 (in Chinese).

THE PROFITABILITY OF INSURANCE

Hans-Joachim Zwiesler
Abteilung Mathematik V
Universität Ulm
D - 89069 Ulm, Germany

What is profitability?

In our context profitability is a measure of the future financial outcome of an insurance contract from the point of view of the insurance company. It determines how profitable it is for the company to sell a certain type of insurance product. (In the following we concentrate on life insurance as an example.)

How do we measure profitability?

Since profitability is a future-oriented view of the profit or loss of an insurance contract, it is based on the yearly *expected cash-flow* of an individual contract *under realistic assumptions.* This contrasts the current practice in Germany where the calculation of premiums (for private insurance) makes use of idealized actuarial bases which contain substantial safety loadings.

The computation of the expected cash-flow must take into account all effects for the company (required reserves, taxation, solvency margin etc.). For the valuation of the expected cash-flow several methods can be used:

The *internal rate of return* is the interest rate that leads to zero as discounted cash-value of the expected cash-flow. It emphasizes the point of view that losses are investments of the company whereas profits are refunds together with interest.

The *year of break-even* is the first year in which the accumulated expected cash-flow is non-negative. It indicates how long it takes until the company's investment is paid back, i.e. when the product really starts to gain money for the company.

Both of these methods use only the company's perspective. They do not take into account the two other main factors, the *customer* and the *agent*. Their needs must be balanced against the company's need. For that purpose, one compares the premium and the initial commission to the cash-value of the expected cash-flow (using the risk discount rate, i.e. the minimal interest rate sought by the company). In relation to the premium, the cash-value should not exceed a certain limit (mainly determined by competition).
On the other hand, cash-value and initial commission should be proportional (where the constant of proportionality is again mainly determined by competition).

Which of these methods is used, depends on the specific circumstances.

The use of profitability in product-design

The investigation of profitability is a main tool in the design of a new insurance product. The underlying iterative process is described in the following diagram:

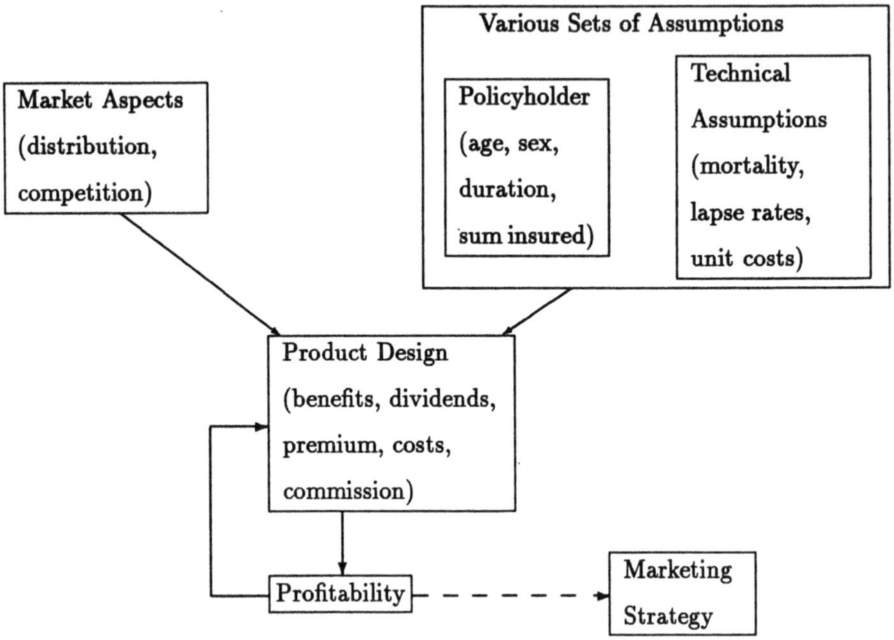

One has to take into account that the same product is sold to different policy holders and that assumptions are not accurately predictable. Therefore, it is indispendable that various sets of assumptions are considered which reflect the distinct possible future scenarios. The results of that analysis can be changings in the design of the product as well as further insight into which key factors mainly influence the profitability. These have to be given particular attention, e.g. in the context of marketing strategies.

The profitability of a company

Our definition of profitability can also be applied to evaluate whether the start-up of a new company will be a profitable investment or not. Here commercial assumptions (interest, inflation, costs etc.) and expected new business are used to calculate the excepted future cash-flow of the whole company and determine its profitability.

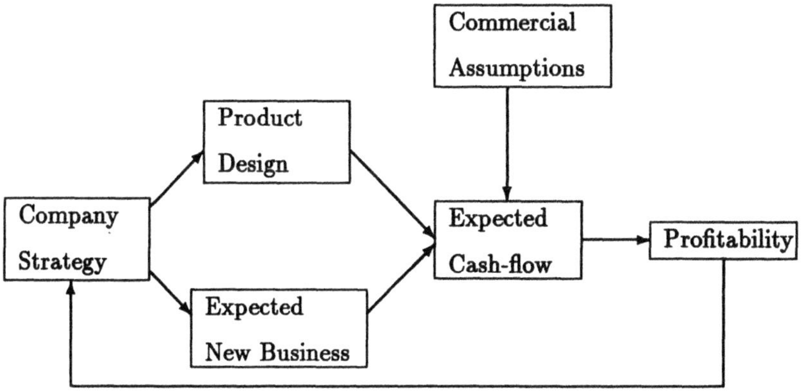

Product profitability and company profitability are not only useful as "a priori evaluation tools", but can serve for controlling purposes as well. In this case, the actual cash-flow is compared to the previously predicted cash-flow. The analysis of the deviation allows conclusions on the accuracy of the assumptions. The updated assumptions give rise to a new expected cash-flow whose profitability may give rise to modifications in the product-design or the company's strategy.

Bibliography

Forfar, D. and Gupta, A. (1986) The Mathematics of Profit Testing for Conventional and Unit-linked Business, o.O.

Goford, J. (1984) The Control Cycle-Financial Control of Life Assurance Company, Journal of the Student Society (of the Institute of Actuaries), Vol. 29, o.O.

Hare, D.J.P. and McCutcheon, J.J. (1991) An Introduction to Profit Testing, Special Note of the Institute of Actuaries

Lee, R. (1984) A Prophet of Profits - An introduction of the theory and application of profit tests, Journal of the Student Society (of the Institute of Actuaries), Vol. 29, o.O.

Smart, C. (1977) Pricing and Profitability in a Life Office, Journal of the Institute of Actuaries, Vol. 104, o.O.

Author Index

Achatz, H. 1
Altman, A. 5
Arakelian, T. A. 8
Argenton, H. 458
Arih, L. 288
Aust, E. 12
Bachem, A. 16
Barbucha, D. 20
Barneva, R. 64
Barth, P. 24
Becker, P. 28
Behnke, H. 32
Bendisch, J. 36
Błażewicz, J. 40
Bocanete, P. P. 43
Bockmayr, A. 47
Böhm, M. 50
Brachinger, H. W. 52
Braun, T. 56
Breitner, M. H. 60
Brimkov, V. E. 64,68
Brucker, P. 72
Buhl, H. U. 76
Caixeta Filho, J. V. 80
Casas, E. 84
Cepar, D. 88,92
Crama, Y. 97
Curiel, I. 216
Danchev, S. 68
Danielian, I. E. 8
Derigs, U. 36
Derks, J. 100
Devjak, S. 103
van Dijk, N.M. 108
Djellab, K. 115
Domanski, C. 119
Douven, R. 122
Drexl, A. 212,286
Driessen, T. 126
Dudek-Dyduch, E. 130
Dyduch, T. 134
Egle, K. 138
Ehrgott, M. 142
El-Banna, A.-Z. H. 145
Engwerda, J. 122,149

Fabian, C. 362
Faigle, U. 153,157
Farmer, K. 161
Fekete, S. 153
Fenyi, S. 138
Filipowicz, W. 20
Fischer, A. 165
Fleury, G. 115
Fortin, D. 169
Frauendorfer, K. 172
Fuchs-Seliger, S. 176
Funaki, Y. 126
Galbiati, G. 180
Garbe, R. 157
Gaul, W. 12
Gerhards, T. 190
Gernert, D. 194
Girlich, E. 198
Goessens, W. 200
Gourgand, M. 115
Greistorfer, P. 203
Gries, T. 207
Gubareny, N. 211
Haase, K. 212
Hamers, H. 216
Hammond, P. J. 219
Heerink, K. 157
Helbing, D. 251
Hellwig, K. 255
Hochstättler, W. 153,259,263
Höding, M. 198
Holmberg, K. 266
Indihar, S. 270
Ioannidis, C. 339
Isac, G. 272
Jacobs, S. 276
Jahn, J. 280
Jedrezejowicz, P. 20
De Jongh, A. 284
Jordan, C. 286
Jurisch, B. 72
Kaczmarek, J. 40
Katkov, A. F. 287
Kavkler, I. 288
Kern, W. 153
van de Klundert, J. 97
Knüppel, L. 292

König, H.-J. 296
Köpp, G. 300
Kolonko, M. 304
Konarzewska-Gubala, E. 306
Kormos, Z. 362
Koslik, B. 60
Krämer, A. 72
Kromberg, S. 263
Krysiak, A. 310
Ku, A. 313
Kubale, M. 317
Küfer, K.-H. 321
Lasch, R. 324
List, G. 331
Loebl, M. 259
Maffioli, F. 180
Magiera, R. 335
Malich, M. 16
Matthews, K. 339
De Mello, R. 513
Merzelj, F. 103
Mesko, I. 343
Mesko, T. 343
Metz, A. 36
Miller, M. D. 483
Moll, C. 259,263
Motnikar, B. 347
Mulec, F. 88
Nachtigall, K. 351
Neamtu, L. 43
Neumann, P. 355
Neumayer, P. 359
Nica, V. 362
Nickel, S. 366
Nußbaumer, A. 331
Oguz, O. 370
Oliveira, J. C. V. 80
Overbeck-Larisch, M. 373
Owsinski, J. W. 377
Pacheco, A. 412
Páles, Z. 385
Parys, D. 119
Pesch, E. 389
Pesch, H. J. 60
Peters, H. 100
Petriczek, G. 393
Pisanski, T. 347

Plachky, D. 397
Pola, C. 84
Porosinski, Z. 355
Potters, J. 216
Queryranne, M. 401
Quilliot, A. 115
Rabinovitch, M. 405
Radzik, T. 408
Ramalhoto, M. F. 412
Reimer, M. 418
Robic, B. 422
Roemen, J. 425
Rustem, B. 428
Sadeghi, H. 466
Sakaguchi, M. 430
Sandbiller, K. 76
Sandmann, K. 418,434
Schäfer, K. 438
Schaible, S. 442
Scheithauer, G. 445,449
Schlögl, E. 434
Schmidt, H. 452
Schneidereit, G. 455
Seipel, D. 458
Seredynski, F. 310
Sergeyev, Y. D. 463
Shaghaghi, J. 466
Shaw, D. X. 470
Silc, J. 474
Simakov, N. V. 478
Sladky, K. 480
Snyder, C. A. 483
Sonntag, Y. 487
Spahni, D. M. 491
Speckenmeyer, E. 50
Spieker, B. 157
Spieksma, F. C. R. 401
Strezova, Z. 495
von Stryk, O. 60
Szajowski, K. 355,498
Szczurko, P. 518
Szmidt, E. 502
Terno, J. 449
Thull, B. 518
Tijs, S. 216
Tratnik, M. 103
Tüshaus, U. 506

Tusera, A. 169
Tuy, H. 266
Uebe, G. 300
Uhrynowski, Z. 393
Uršič, E. 92
Vaarmann, O. 510
Verlan, A. F. 512
Wahrenburg, M. 513
Walkowiak, R. 40
Wallacher, J. 515
von der Weiden, G. 518
Wentges, P. 522
de Werra, D. 526
Wiesemann, T. 255
Will, A. 76
Yeung, D. W. K. 529
Zadnik Stirn, L. 533
Zalinescu, C. 487
Založnik, R. 92
Zaporoshetc, A. 455
Zepf, D. 537
Zhuang, D. 539
Zwiesler, H.-J. 542

GPSR Compliance

The European Union's (EU) General Product Safety Regulation (GPSR) is a set of rules that requires consumer products to be safe and our obligations to ensure this.

If you have any concerns about our products, you can contact us on ProductSafety@springernature.com

In case Publisher is established outside the EU, the EU authorized representative is:

Springer Nature Customer Service Center GmbH
Europaplatz 3
69115 Heidelberg, Germany

Batch number: 10726298

Printed by Printforce, the Netherlands